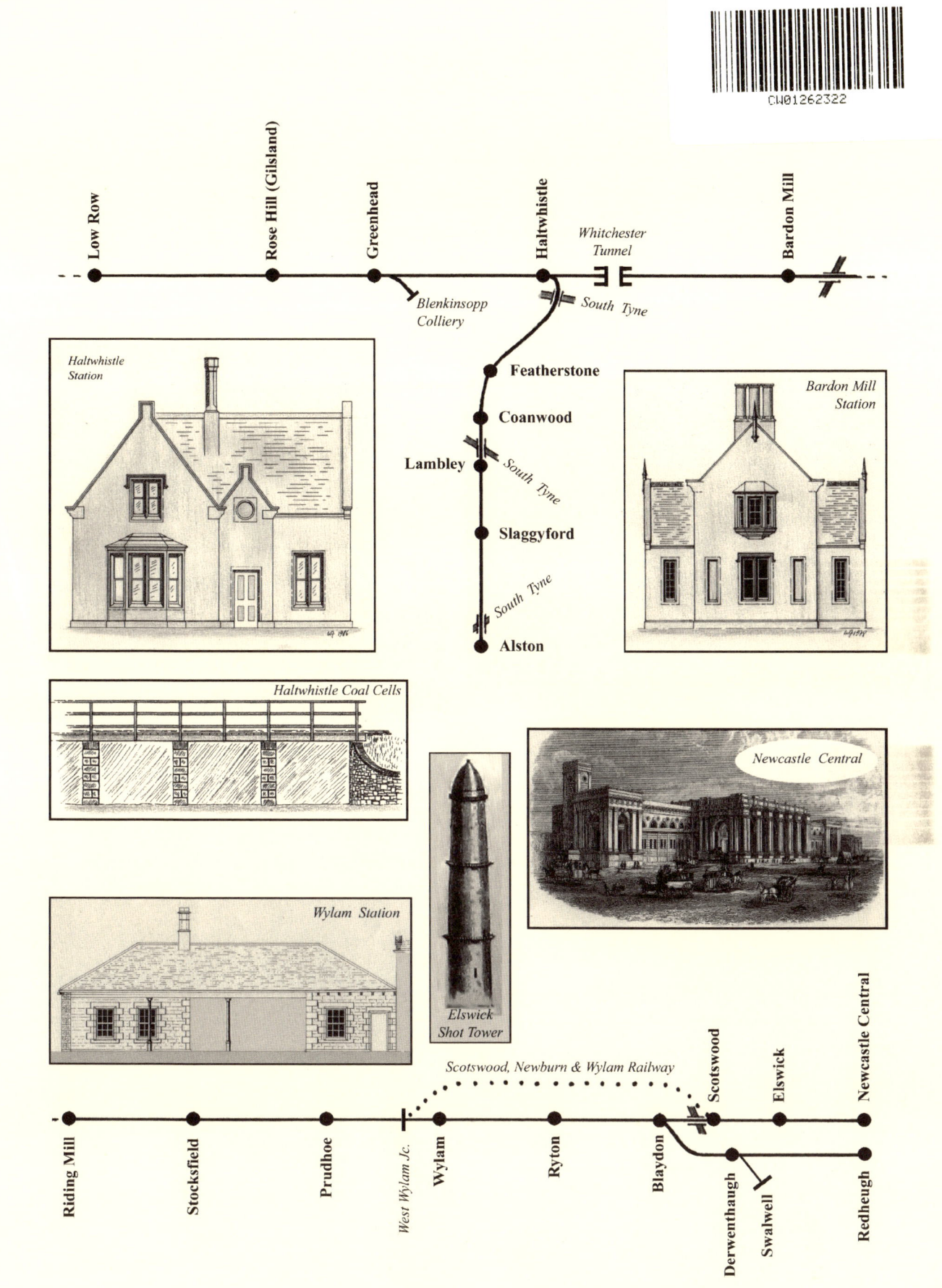

Title Page: An impression of Venus standing in Hexham station. The locomotive was supplied by Thompson Brothers, of Wylam, in January 1841 and this view represents the station as it then stood, bereft of any platform but with this distinctive trainshed, also seen in a view on page 4. The track comprises wrought-iron fish-bellied rails on sandstone blocks. (Bill Fawcett)

A History of the Newcastle & Carlisle Railway

1824 to 1870

Bill Fawcett

NORTH EASTERN RAILWAY ASSOCIATION

Copyright © Bill Fawcett

All rights reserved

No part of this publication may be reproduced, stored in a retrieval system, or transmitted, in any form or by any means, electronic, mechanical, photocopying, recording or otherwise, without the prior written permission of the publisher.

Published by the North Eastern Railway Association, August 2008

ISBN 978 1 873513 69 9

Layout by Bill Fawcett

Printed in Great Britain by Potts

THE NORTH EASTERN RAILWAY ASSOCIATION

Formed in 1961, the NERA caters for all interested in the railways of north-east England, in particular the North Eastern Railway and Hull & Barnsley Railway from their early history down to the present day. This extends also to the many industrial and smaller railways that operated alongside them. Interests range over all aspects of the development, operation and infrastructure of the railway, including such diverse activities as ports, shipping and road services, both for the general enthusiast and the model-maker.

With over 700 members, regular meetings are held in York, Darlington, Hull, Leeds and London. A programme of outdoor visits, tours and walks is also arranged. There is also an extensive library of books, documents, photographs and drawings.

Members receive a quarterly illustrated journal, the *North Eastern Express*, together with a newsletter covering membership topics, forthcoming meetings and events in the region together with book reviews and a bibliography of recent articles of interest. Over 190 issues of the *Express* have been published to date.

The Association also markets an extensive range of facsimiles of NER documents, including diagram books and timetables, while it is developing an expanding range of original publications, available to members at discounted prices.

A membership prospectus can be obtained from the Membership Secretary: Mr. T. Morrell,
8, Prunus Avenue, Kingston Road, Willerby, Hull, HU10 6PH.

A sales list of other NERA publications can be obtained from the Sales Officer:
Mrs. C.E. Williamson, 31 Moreton Avenue, Stretford, Manchester, M32 8BP.
Please enclose a stamped, addressed 9 inch by 4 inch envelope with your enquiries.

NERA Website: http://www.ner.org.uk

The Railway employed this handsome heraldic device on the door panels of its first-class carriages. This example comes from the former British Railways collection, and is reproduced by courtesy of the National Railway Museum.
It has been painted on a plain panel of varnished wood, but the background has been altered here to give an impression of the 'claret' coaching-stock livery which had been adopted by 1843.

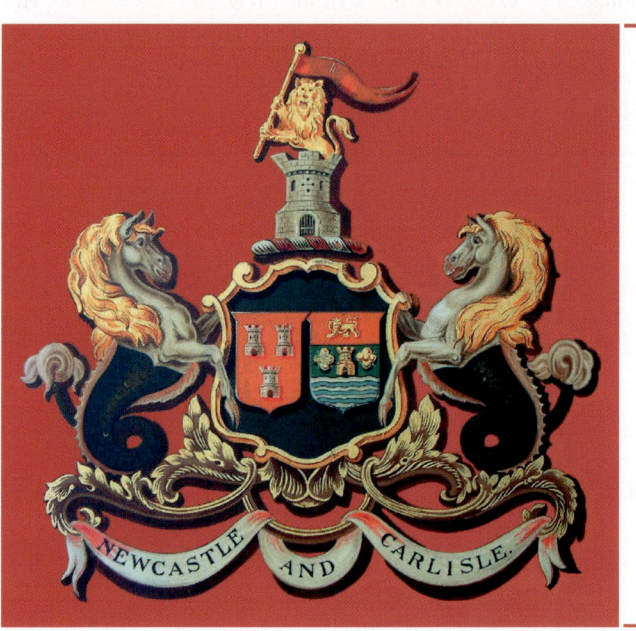

The Railway purloined the arms of Newcastle (3 castellated towers) and Carlisle, placing them side by side on this ornate shield. Newcastle's coat of arms also supplied the crest (the tower and lion at the top) and the supporting seahorses.

Contents

Introduction   *page*
Chapter 1   *Romans, roads and canals*   6
Chapter 2   *The Railway Promoters*   16
Chapter 3   *1825 - 1829: Finding a Route*   24
Chapter 4   *An Act and an Engineer*   30
Chapter 5   *Underway at Last*   38
Chapter 6   *Building the Railway*   50
Chapter 7   *Engineering Works between Carlisle and Blaydon*   70
Chapter 8   *East from Blaydon*   94
Chapter 9   *Consolidation and Expansion: 1839-1852*   110
Chapter 10   *The Alston Branch*   122
Chapter 11   *The Final Lap: 1852-1870*   138
Chapter 12   *Train Services and Traffic*   148
Chapter 13   *Locomotives and Rolling Stock*   160
Chapter 14   *Permanent Way and Signalling*   181
Chapter 15   *Buildings*   187
Chapter 16   *Organisation and People*   214
Chapter 17   *Accidents and Incidents*   224
Epilogue   231
Endnotes   235
Index   247

Acknowledgements

The principal archival sources are the railway company records held by the National Archives, at Kew. However, much original material relating to early schemes is held by the local studies section of Newcastle Central Library and the library of Newcastle Literary & Philosophical Society, an institution in which some of the leading promoters of the railway would have routinely encountered one another. Tyne and Wear Archives, in Newcastle; Northumberland Archives, at Woodhorn; the Mining Institute, in Newcastle; Carlisle Library and the Cumbria Records Office at Carlisle Castle are also important sources of material. I am grateful to the staff at all these institutions for their helpfulness. Thanks are also due to Gateshead, Hexham and Haydon Bridge libraries, the National Library of Scotland, the British Library, the Institution of Civil Engineers Library and the Guildhall Library in London. I owe a particular debt to Tullie House Museum and Art Gallery, in Carlisle, and Tyne & Wear Museums for allowing me to reproduce material in their collections, notably John Wilson Carmichael's sketches showing the railway under construction. The staff of Network Rail York Record Centre also kindly hunted out bridge drawings for the line.

This book has been a long time in gestation, and I am indebted to many people who have contributed ideas or material over that time. It is impractical to record everyone, but I should like to express my thanks to Mike Chrimes and Carol Morgan at the Civils, Christopher Dean, Alison Gunning of the Lit & Phil, the late Ken Hoole, Geoff Horsman, Stafford Linsley, the late John Mallon, Stuart Rankin, Neville Stead, George Tinkler and the late Ann Wilson; David Williamson also deserves my thanks for encouraging the North Eastern Railway Association in its publications programme.

I owe a particular debt to a number of people. John Fleming made his collection freely available and had intended to contribute the chapter on locomotives and rolling stock, but died before he could do so; I am grateful to Margaret and Charles for helping me to subsequently locate material. Angus MacLean has kindly allowed me to reproduce drawings made by his father, John S. MacLean, who published the first history of the railway in 1948; this remains a very attractive account, though MacLean was unable to obtain access to the minute books of the railway. Mike Jackson kindly made available his transcripts of early newspaper reports and notices. Denis Perriam has an exhaustive knowledge of Carlisle history and has shared this with me in an unstinting fashion and also done much to secure illustrations. Bob Rennison has long been interested in the early years of the railway and we have had some very useful discussions about this, while he has fleshed out my knowledge of the early engineers and other Tyneside characters to a considerable degree. He also undertook the daunting task of reading a draft of the text. John Addyman has also performed his customary service in reading the text and bringing to bear not only his own extensive knowledge of the period but a practical perspective as a former railwayman. Any errors of fact or interpretation remain my own responsibility.

Bill Fawcett   June   2008

1838

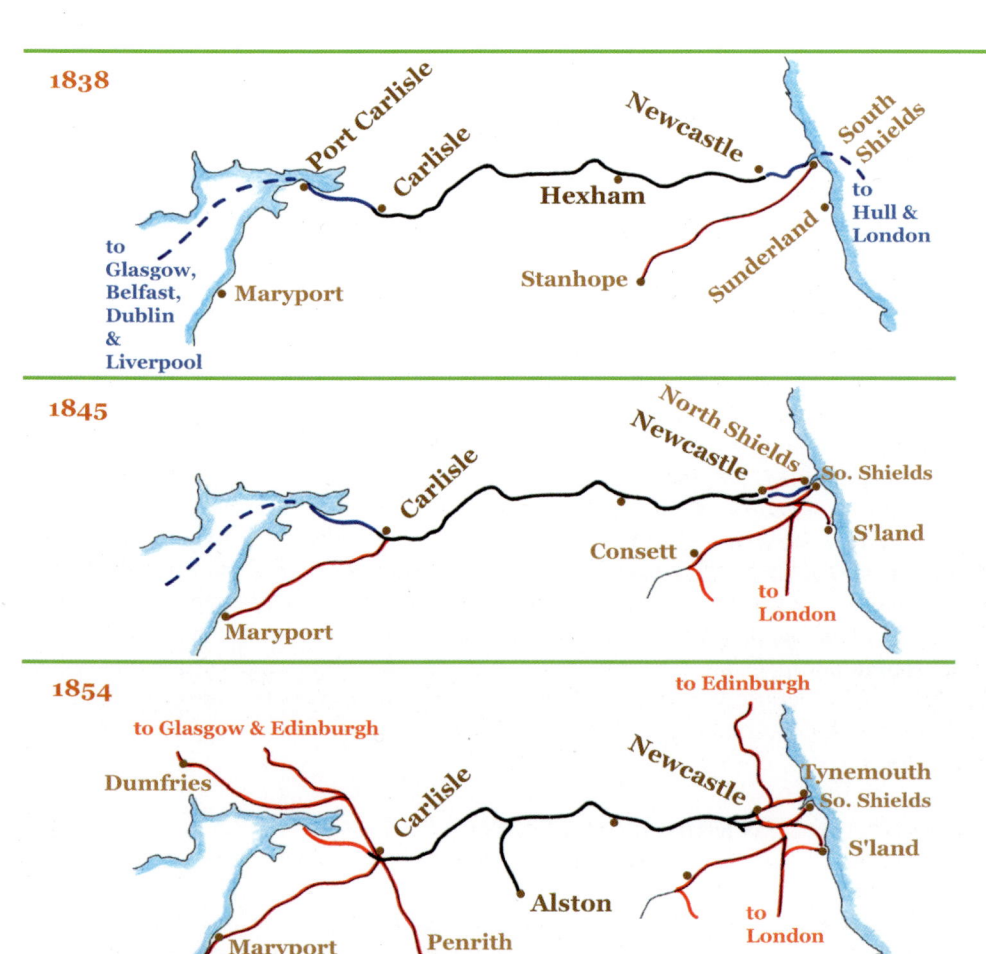

1845

1854

Three Snapshots, illustrating the evolution of the public railway network in the vicinity of the Newcastle & Carlisle Railway.

It is shown in black. Other railways are depicted in red and shipping routes in blue.

A classic view of Hexham, looking over the station and the 'Nurseries' beyond towards the town centre, crowned by the Abbey. This postcard view was probably drawn in the late 1850's and gives a fairly accurate representation of the station buildings, then recently enlarged, and the distinctive trainshed. The engine, however, is more freely drawn, though it does capture the contemporary atmosphere. Unlike other railways, N&C trains ran on the right, and the track between the train and the station building was a siding, serving the goods shed which just creeps into the view at bottom left. The low passenger platform was not so generous as depicted here; it was squeezed between the running lines and barely 3 feet wide. Today, both station buildings and goods shed survive but the view beyond contains much less greenery. (courtesy of Hilary Kristensen)

Introduction

170 years ago, on 18 June 1838, a cavalcade of some thirteen trains celebrated the formal completion of the first railway to cross the island of Great Britain, from the Carlisle Canal in the west to Gateshead in the east, just across the River Tyne from Newcastle. It would be a further three years before the next coast-to-coast link was finished, albeit a much longer one, from Liverpool to Hull.

The Newcastle & Carlisle Railway had been some time in the making. Its promoters first got together in 1824 and planned to get an Act of Parliament, giving them powers to take land and build the line, in the session 1825-6. However, problems arose, they withdrew their Bill and took three years to get back to Parliament, obtaining their first Act in May 1829. It took a further year for construction to begin and it tended to proceed in a rather stop/go fashion, chiefly because of the difficulties of raising capital in the early eighteen-thirties. The enterprise was largely funded by local investors, principally from Tyneside.

Lead traffic began using part of the line in the latter part of 1834, under a private arrangement, but public traffic only began in March 1835, with the opening of the section from Blaydon to Hexham. Further stages opened during the next few years, culminating in the celebrations of June 1838. At that time the N&C was virtually the sole public railway on Tyneside, the only other rival for that title being the Stanhope & Tyne, which had opened in 1834 but was essentially a mineral line. In 1839 that all changed. The N&C opened a line into Newcastle itself, while other railways began services from Newcastle and Gateshead to North and South Shields, at the mouth of the Tyne, and to Sunderland's northerly neighbour: Monkwearmouth. At Carlisle, the N&C remained the only railway for somewhat longer, though it did not operate in isolation. Instead it formed part of a comprehensive transport network, embracing steamer services to Liverpool, Ireland and the West of Scotland.

The Newcastle & Carlisle is therefore very much an early railway in character, engineering and operation. Much of its interest derives from the fact that we can see how the directors, their engineers and officers were still learning the ropes and making up the rules as they went along. What gives added piquancy to their story is the contrast between the experience which some directors brought to the project and the background of their first engineer, Francis Giles. Three Board members: Nicholas Wood, Benjamin Thompson and George Johnson had considerable experience in the design and operation of colliery waggonways, while Wood was the author of a *Practical Treatise on Railroads* and a judge at the Rainhill Trials. Giles was a very capable engineer, as his works continue to demonstrate, but he had no practical experience of railways prior to taking on the project.

Many of the trunk routes of the eighteen-thirties have been radically altered to cope with increased traffic or later forms of traction, the London & Birmingham being the sadly classic example. The Newcastle & Carlisle is unusual in that it still fulfills a strategic role in the modern railway network, handling a significant volume of coal traffic as well as passengers, yet it retains much of its original infrastructure in a largely unaltered state. Giles's assistant and successor John Blackmore, who oversaw construction and contributed some innovative timber bridge designs, could come back today and recognise most of his creations. This means that we can travel the line and savour something of the flavour of the eighteen-thirties, without having to take three hours over the journey and endure the doubtful delights of a stuffy first or open-sided second-class carriage. The pleasure is enhanced by the delightful scenery encountered most of the way, crossing Pennine streams on high bridges in the west and occupying a grandstand seat on the brink of the Tyne in the east.

Apart from a flirtation with George Hudson, the first Railway King, who leased the line for eighteen months, the Newcastle & Carlisle Railway maintained a robustly profitable independence until 1862, when it merged with its mighty neighbour, the North Eastern Railway. Even then, the NER kept a fairly loose rein. Engineering activities, including locomotives, were integrated into the NER hierarchy but the line retained its own manager, reporting directly to the NER general manager, until February 1871. That is taken as the end date of this history, enabling us to see how the 'Carlisle Section' bedded down within the North Eastern system. Subsequent events will be covered in a companion *Survey of the Newcastle & Carlisle Railway*, to be published in the next few years. This will take the reader on an exploration of the line, looking at the way in which all significant locations have developed down to the present day.

As I am dealing with a period in which the railway and its works were conceived in 'imperial' units: miles, yards, feet and inches, I have used these whenever quoting original dimensions, so as to avoid misleading approximations. In general, however, measured drawings of bridges and buildings are accompanied by a scale in both feet and metres. Costs and wages are also expressed in their original units: pounds, shillings and pence, expressed in the following format: £4 6s 8d.

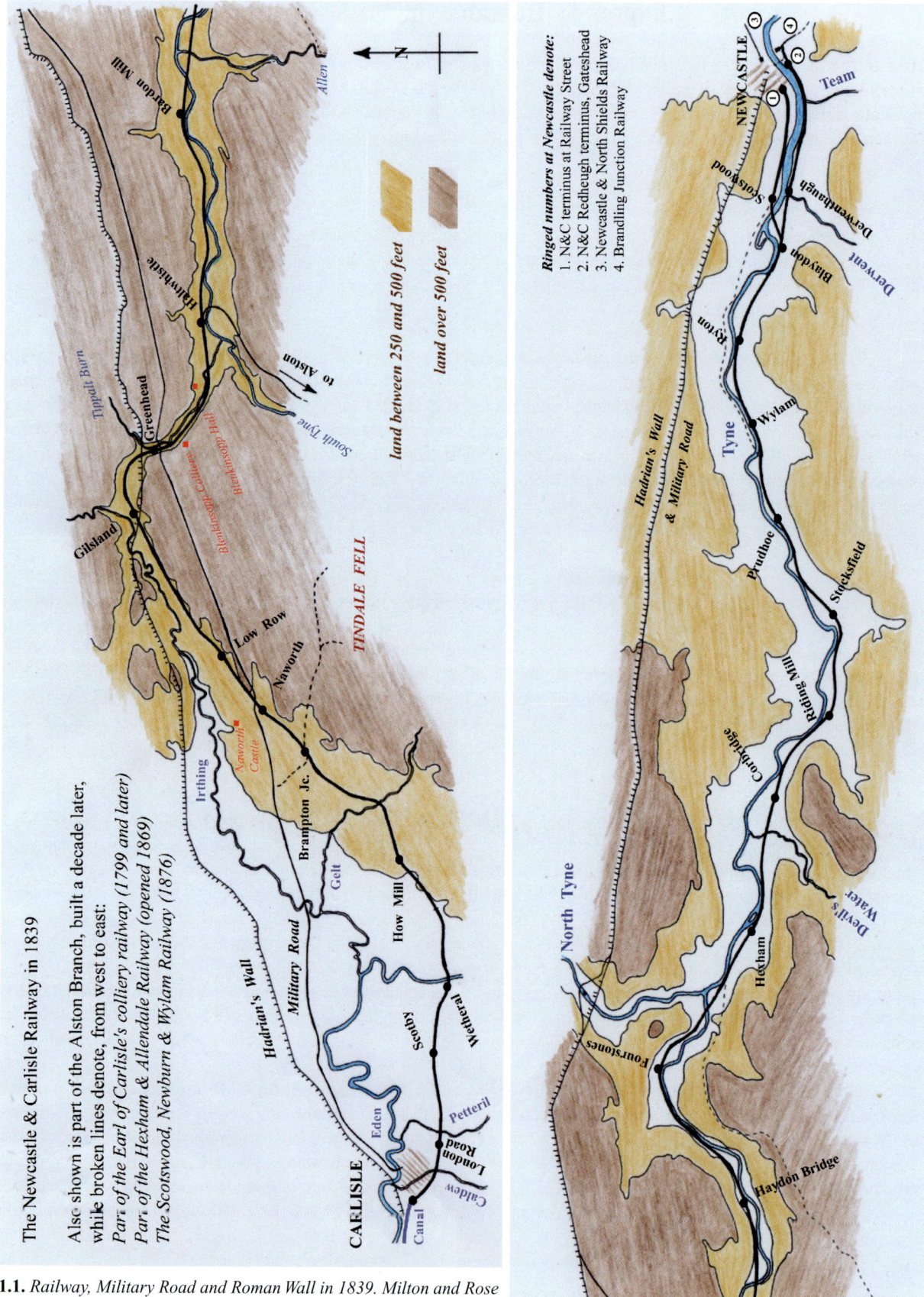

1.1. *Railway, Military Road and Roman Wall in 1839. Milton and Rose Hill stations are shown with their later names of Brampton Junction and Gilsland.*

Chapter 1: Romans, roads and canals

The route between Newcastle and Carlisle has an impressive pedigree. For most of the three centuries from AD 100, it was Rome's 'North West Frontier', taking a strategic course through the Tyne-Eden Gap between the Pennines and the hills of the Scottish Border. Thanks to the Solway Firth, this provides one of the shortest crossings of the island of Great Britain. An even shorter one occurs a hundred miles further north, between the Firths of Forth and Clyde, and was adopted by the Romans for their frontier for about twenty years from AD 142, before falling back on the Tyne-Solway line.

The Forth-Clyde frontier was marked by an earthwork, the Antonine Wall, of which significant traces remain, but these cannot compare with Hadrian's Wall - arguably the finest military monument of the Roman Empire. In the late first century, a road - Stanegate - had been built to link the forts at Corbridge and Carlisle, which were already served by military roads from the south, such as Dere Street which ran from York. On a visit to Britain in 122, the Emperor Hadrian conceived the frontier work which bears his name and runs from Wallsend on Tyne, about three miles east of Newcastle, to Bowness on Solway, about twelve miles west of Carlisle.

The Roman Wall keeps as far as possible to the high ground on the northern rim of the Tyne Valley, most dramatically where it snakes along the edge of the whinstone crags between Sewing Shields and Cawfields. Two miles south of Cawfields is Haltwhistle, where the Tyne valley swings south into the hills and the low-level route west is continued by the Tippalt Burn, before crossing a watershed almost five hundred feet above sea level and then proceeding down the Irthing and Eden valleys. The Wall itself takes to the edge of the high ground on the north side of the Irthing before eventually dropping down to Carlisle.

1.2. *(right) View east along Hadrian's Wall from Steel Rigg, north-west of Bardon Mill. (Bill Fawcett)*

1.3. *A westbound train crossing the Wall behind the milecastle on the west bank of the Poltross Burn at Gilsland. (Bill Fawcett, 2007)*

Imperial rule ended in 407, and the Wall lost its purpose, although Stanegate survived in part within the later network of tracks and roads, for example at Newbrough. The Saxon period saw the development of Corbridge and Hexham, down in the Tyne Valley, while later ages brought towns at Haydon Bridge and Haltwhistle, on the Tyne, and Brampton, above the Irthing. Rome's east-west communications legacy was irrelevant to their needs, but the tracks which evolved instead were barely adequate. The situation was highlighted by the Jacobite Rising of 1745, when the London government was endeavouring to move troops west to Carlisle. Marshall Wade found that neither the high-level track which followed the Roman Military Way, alongside the Wall, nor the valley roads were fit to handle his artillery. This convinced his masters of the need for a new route and thus was born the 'Military Road' whose central section (B6318) still provides a memorably scenic journey today.

The Military Road was a turnpike, built under an Act of Parliament passed in May 1751. Like other turnpikes it drew its revenue from tolls on the users, but it was unusual in that its construction was totally funded by the government on account of its strategic function. This also determined the route, which followed that of Hadrian's Wall from Newcastle as far as Greenhead, near the watershed, but then took the high ground on the opposite (south) bank of the River Irthing. For much of the way the new road ran uncomfortably close to the Wall, sometimes stealing its site. The road passed through Brampton, but was of limited value to the townships along the Tyne, being - for instance - three hundred feet higher than Haltwhistle although little more than a mile distant; Hexham and Corbridge were passed at distances of three to four miles. To meet their needs, a number of other turnpike trusts were established - sometimes to improve existing roads, sometimes to build completely new ones. The Military Road cost some £22,450 to build and the work progressed gradually, with completion in 1758, a comparable timescale to that of the Newcastle & Carlisle Railway though at under three percent of its cost. Thereafter, the maintenance of the road was funded from tolls.[1]

Turnpike Roads in the Tyne Valley in 1804

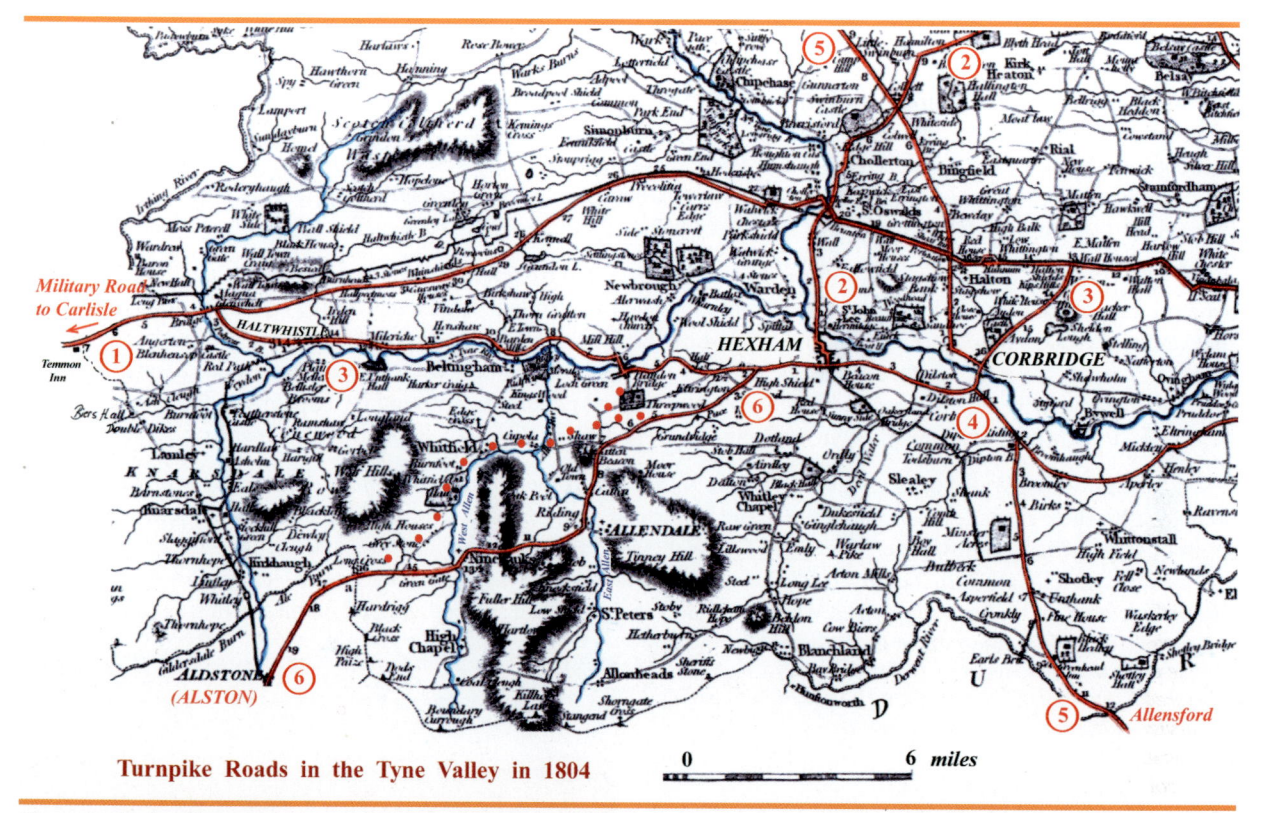

The principal valley road was turnpiked under an Act of 1752 and left the Military Road at Shibdon Bar, rejoining it at Greenhead after passing through Corbridge, Hexham, Haydon Bridge and Haltwhistle. It was augmented by a direct route from Gateshead to Dilston Bar, just west of Corbridge, under a turnpike act of 1777. Thus the dawn of the nineteenth century saw the route between Newcastle and Carlisle equipped with a reasonable network of valley roads, along which a public coach was able to complete the journey in twelve hours.

Despite these improvements, there was a perception that the route required an additional transport link, better suited to the efficient movement of bulk and heavy loads and less susceptible to damage from them. In the eighteenth century, this usually meant a canal. The Tyne was navigable, in its tidal stretch, as far as Newburn (two miles above Blaydon), though bedevilled by islands and sandbanks. Further upstream it was ill-suited to being adapted for navigation, through a combination of shallows, a rocky bed, and floods which were sometimes very severe. Despite this, a serious proposal was made at the start of 1710 to make the Tyne navigable from Newburn to Hexham. [2] John Errington, a landowner, offered to do this at his own expense in return for the sole right to the resulting income. His proposal was endorsed by the county justices, meeting at the Northumberland Quarter Sessions in January 1710, and on 28 February a Bill granting powers to form the navigation had its first reading in the House of Commons. Fortunately, perhaps, for Errington's pocket, nothing further was done.

At Carlisle, the Eden is a broad and handsome river, but again wholly unsuited to navigation: it suffers from shallows on its short course to the Solway, where its estuary is further bedevilled by extensive sandbanks. Carlisle therefore sought improved access to the sea, and the canal idea was revived in the late eighteenth century, this time as a through route from the Solway to the Tyne. By then, Britain had already been crossed by a small-ship canal: the Forth & Clyde Canal, which had got from Grangemouth (on the Forth) as far as Glasgow in 1775 and was opened through to a harbour at Bowling, on the Clyde, in 1790. This has a summit three hundred feet lower than would have been required on a Tyne-Solway canal. [3]

William Chapman and the Tyne-Solway Canal

The Tyne-Solway canal became a serious proposition largely thanks to the efforts of the engineer William Chapman (1749-1832).[4] Chapman was born in Whitby, the eldest son of Captain William Chapman - who moved first to Wearside and then to the Tyne, where he established the Willington ropeworks in 1789. Young William began his career as a mariner, but then became a merchant and coal fitter (i.e. a factor for the collieries). With his brother John he leased two Tyneside collieries: St. Anthony's and Wallsend, but they were made bankrupt in 1782, and William then moved into engineering, of which his colliery enterprise had already given him useful experience. He spent a decade in Ireland, where he became engaged on several successful canal and dock schemes, but returned to Newcastle in 1794, following his father's death.

Date of First Act for Each Road:

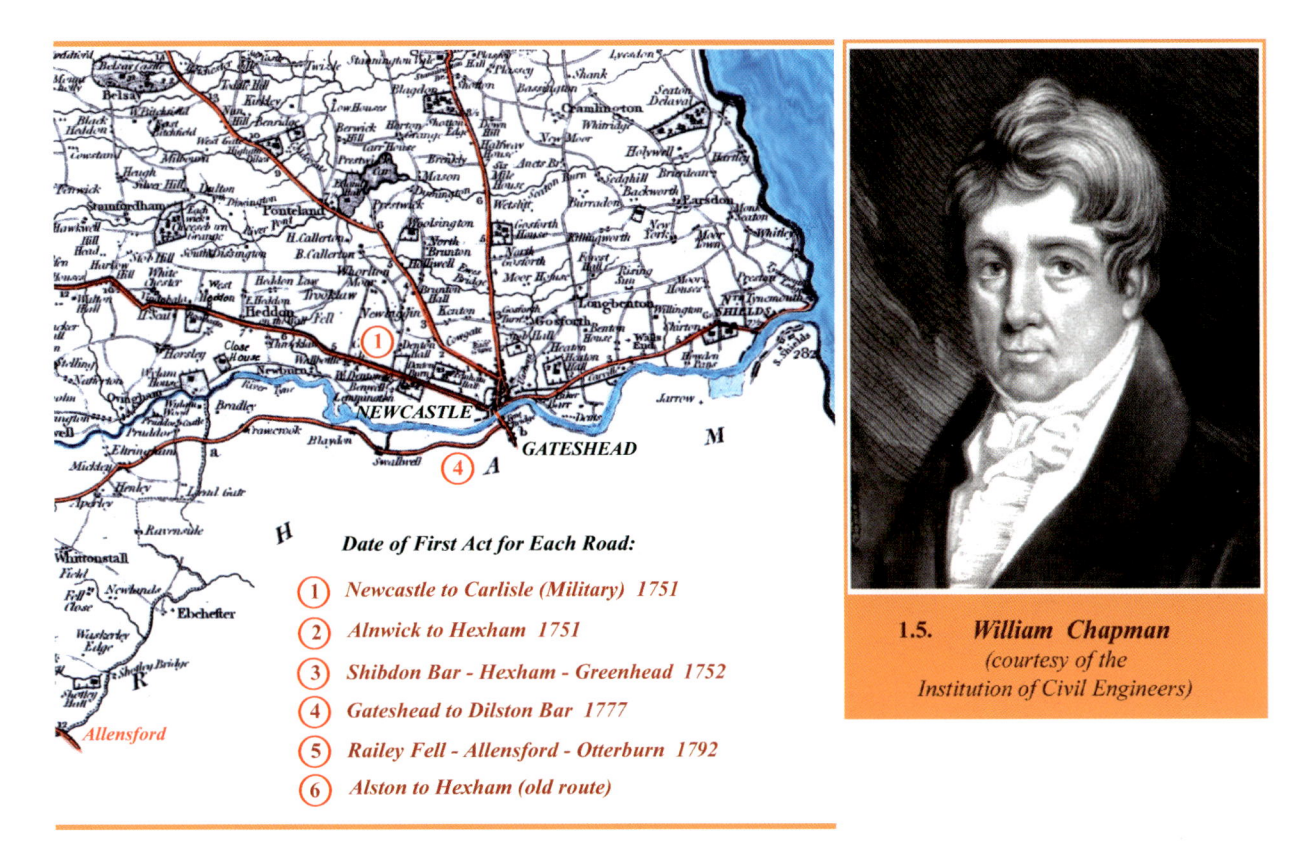

① Newcastle to Carlisle (Military) 1751
② Alnwick to Hexham 1751
③ Shibdon Bar - Hexham - Greenhead 1752
④ Gateshead to Dilston Bar 1777
⑤ Railey Fell - Allensford - Otterburn 1792
⑥ Alston to Hexham (old route)

1.5. *William Chapman (courtesy of the Institution of Civil Engineers)*

1.4. *Part of Smith's 1804 map of Northumberland, with the turnpike roads serving the Tyne Valley picked out in red. The later route of the Alston turnpike is shown by red dots, continuing down Allendale via Whitfield and crossing the river at Cupola Bridge.*

Though the ropeworks absorbed some of his energies, Chapman continued to develop his career as an engineer, and one of the first things he turned his attention to was the Tyne-Solway canal, writing that it 'has long been a favourite object with me' A number of people subscribed towards the costs of a survey, and on 5 January 1795 he published his first report, detailing a route.[5]

Chapman's scheme was ambitious. At the west end he recognised that a canal would have to reach down the Solway virtually to Bowness, in order to avoid the sands, and suggested that they might as well continue it by way of Wigton to Maryport, instead. This would add about 22 miles, but no extra locks, and attract significant local traffic. At the east end, he discarded the idea of opening into the Tyne near Newburn and instead proposed keeping the canal two hundred feet above the river and having a basin on the north side of Newcastle, near the Town Moor. This would provide good access to the town centre, with the option of later building an extension (with a numerous flight of locks) down to a dock at the Ouseburn, near its entry into the Tyne.

In this first scheme, Chapman maximised the length of the summit level, so as to facilitate the construction of two branches: to Penrith and up the North Tyne valley. The latter was a somewhat speculative suggestion, for the indefinite future, but the Penrith branch was a serious proposition - intended to be carried through to Ullswater, so as to give access to the Lake District slate industry.[6] Another proposal was for a branch from the summit level down the west side of the South Tyne valley, upstream of Haltwhistle, to serve the coal and lead mines of Tindale Fell and Alston Moor. This was to be much narrower and shallower than the main line of canal, with the possibility of road crossings being provided by paved fords, with overflows to keep the water level down, instead of bridges.[7]

Chapman's main line bypassed Hexham and Corbridge, in the interests of maintaining height, and drew a counter proposal for a canal on the south side of the Tyne, from Stella to Hexham.[8] The outcome was a war of pamphlets and letters, with another engineer, John Sutcliffe of Halifax, being engaged by the 'South-siders'.[9] Sutcliffe had far less practical experience of canals than Chapman; his one venture - the Somersetshire Coal Canal - was in the early stages of construction, and his reports did not adequately address the problems of continuing the line through to Carlisle. Chapman responded with a detailed report, published in three parts from 26 June to 10 August 1795, and this was endorsed by his friend William Jessop, who had been called in for a second opinion.[10] Jessop (1745-1814) had very wide experience and was regarded as the leading engineer of his generation, so his support of Chapman and their joint estimate of the costs cleared the way for the promoters to raise money and prepare a Bill for Parliament.

William Chapman's 1795 proposal for a Canal from Maryport to Newcastle upon Tyne

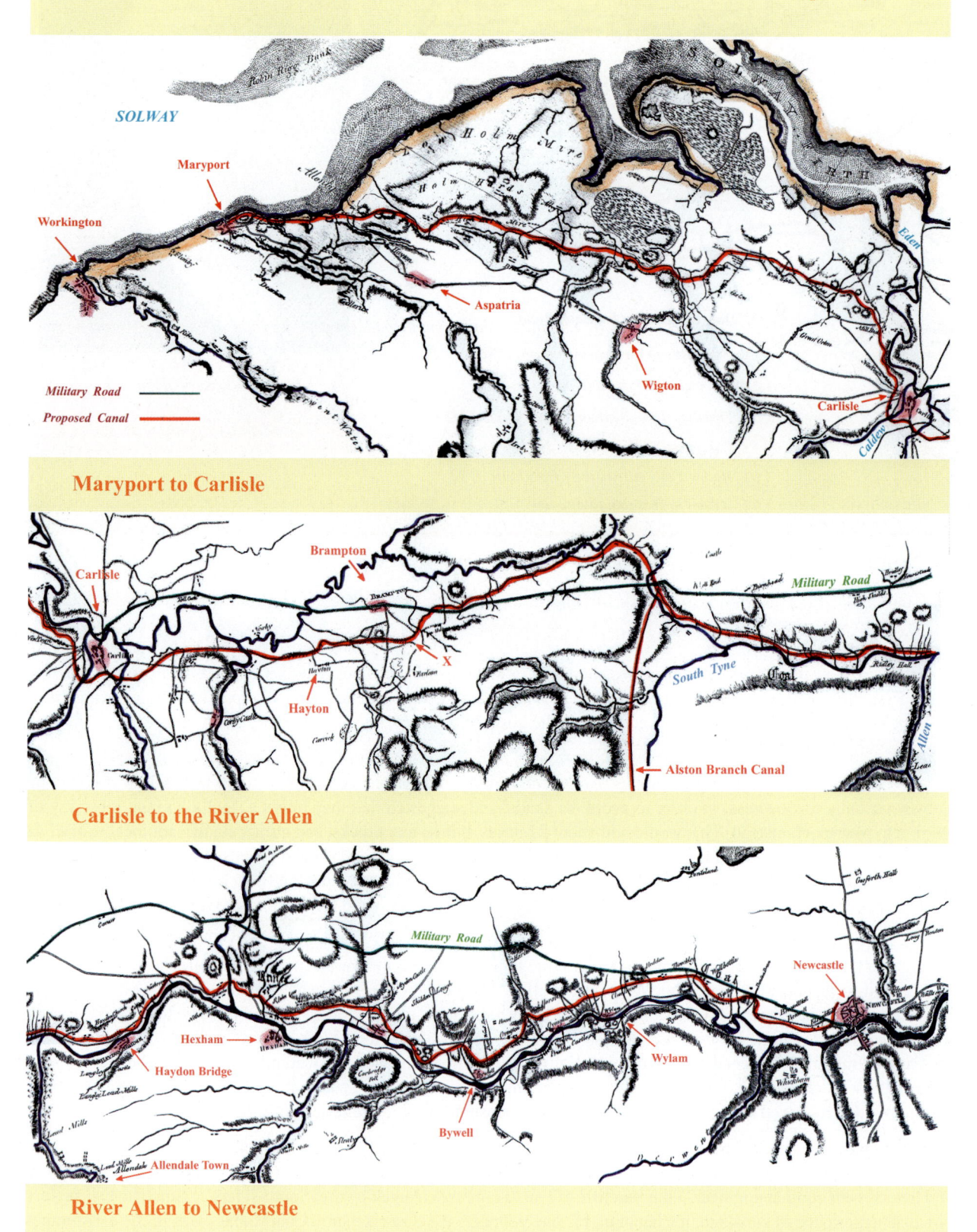

Maryport to Carlisle

Carlisle to the River Allen

River Allen to Newcastle

1.6. William Chapman's 1795 plan for a canal from Maryport to Newcastle. The original is a conventional map, but, for convenience, it has been reproduced here as three strip plans confined to the immediate vicinity of the route. It has also been coloured up to distinguish the canal (red) and Military Road (green). The 'Alston' branch canal is not labelled as such on the original, though referred to in his report, and just appears to be a sketch for a tentative route. The Penrith branch is not shown. The 1829 Parliamentary line of the Newcastle & Carlisle Railway, heading west from Hexham, joins the canal route at Haydon Bridge and follows it as far as the point marked X (near Brampton). The canal then proceeds north of Hayton while the railway goes well to the south.

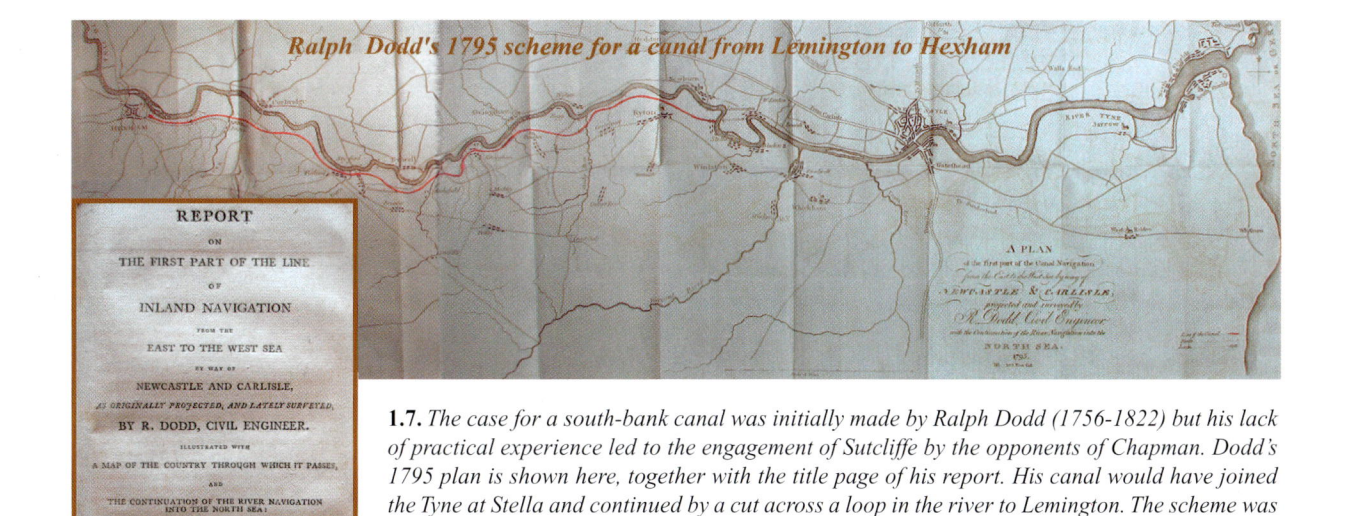

1.7. *The case for a south-bank canal was initially made by Ralph Dodd (1756-1822) but his lack of practical experience led to the engagement of Sutcliffe by the opponents of Chapman. Dodd's 1795 plan is shown here, together with the title page of his report. His canal would have joined the Tyne at Stella and continued by a cut across a loop in the river to Lemington. The scheme was revived in 1810 by his son Barodall Robert Dodd. On both occasions it was put forward as the first stage in a navigation linking the two seas, but in neither case was the western continuation of the canal seriously thought out.*

Chapman's detailed route, of June 1795, is reproduced here and reveals some changes from January's report, brought about by more detailed surveys and the needs of the lead industry. Lead had been a British export since Roman times, and the two mining areas of the north Pennines which could benefit from a Tyne-Solway canal were Alston Moor, owned by Greenwich Hospital and partly worked by the London Lead Company, and Allendale, owned by the Blackett/Beaumont family and largely worked by them. In both cases ore was smelted in the vicinity of the mines and the lead was then transported, initially by packhorse, down to Tyneside for refining. Although there was an established route by the 'Lead Road' and its successor turnpike from Alston to Hexham, it would require only a short, downhill journey from this route, near Langley, to reach a canal basin at Haydon Bridge. Chapman had therefore revised the scheme so as to shorten the summit stretch and then lock down to river level at Haydon Bridge. The canal was then to continue, lock-free, at that height through to Newcastle, ending up 205 feet above the Tyne.

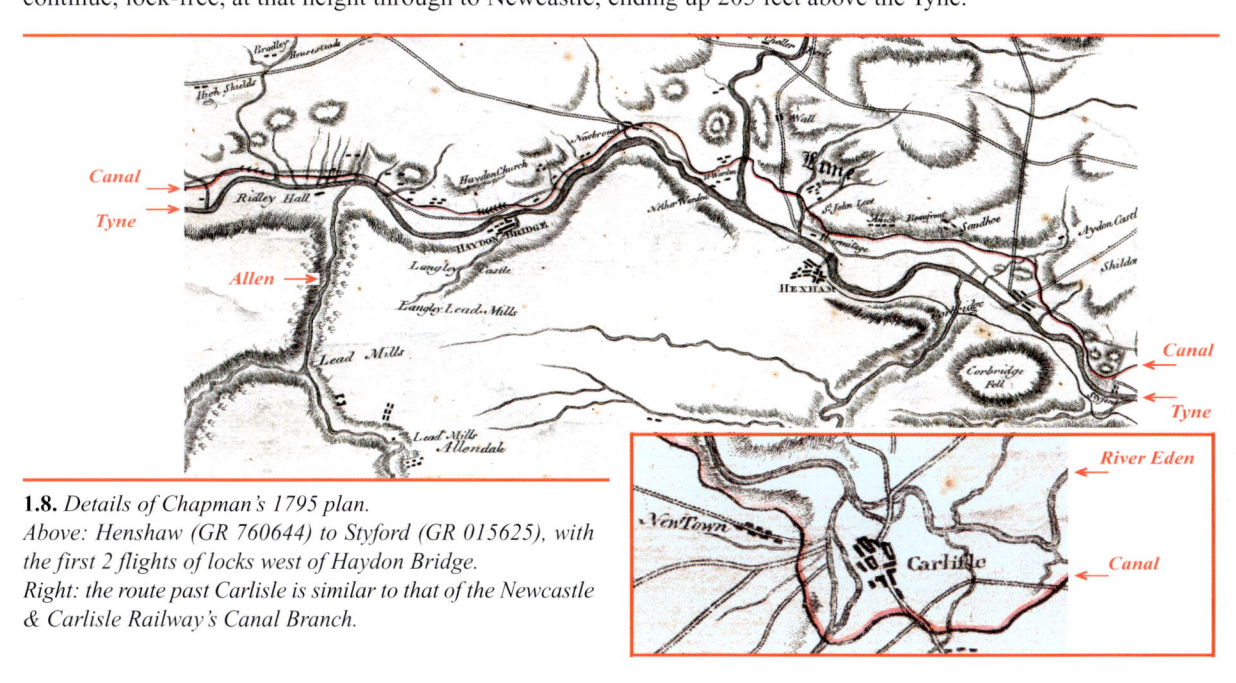

1.8. *Details of Chapman's 1795 plan.*
Above: Henshaw (GR 760644) to Styford (GR 015625), with the first 2 flights of locks west of Haydon Bridge.
Right: the route past Carlisle is similar to that of the Newcastle & Carlisle Railway's Canal Branch.

West of Haydon Bridge, the canal would have climbed 240 feet up the vales of Tyne and Tippalt to a summit level starting near Greenhead. He envisaged a summit cutting through 'a drained or consolidated bog, which may be easily excavated' and the line of the present railway would have been followed to the site of the later Brampton Junction station. There, the main line of canal would have swung west, to begin the descent to Carlisle - one entailing a flight of presumably twenty locks in order to manage the initial 196 feet drop down to Low Gelt Bridge. The Penrith branch kept to the present railway alignment as far as its splendid Gelt Bridge, and would have required a comparable canal aqueduct. The railway then swings west to Carlisle, but the canal would have headed south for the high ground on the east side of the Eden valley.

Chapman and Jessop estimated the cost of the main line from Newcastle to Maryport as £355,067, for 93 miles of canal and the link between the canal and river at Newcastle - conceived in the first instance as an inclined plane in the vicinity of Elswick. Subscriptions were invited, but after more than a year the amounts pledged still fell well short of this estimate, so the promoters went to Parliament with just the stretch from Newcastle to Haydon Bridge, as a first instalment.

Plans were formally deposited on 26 September 1796, allowing affected parties plenty of time to assess its impact before the committee stage.[11] The petitioners in favour included Greenwich Hospital and the Mayor and Burgesses of Newcastle.[12] The principal opposition came from four landowners, who felt that the amenity of their country estates would be spoiled by the canal. Of these, John Hodgson, of Elswick Hall, and John Errington, of Beaufront (near Hexham), had a plausible argument in that a canal running close to the 200 feet contour would be a conspicuous feature of the parkland in front of their mansions. Similar objections, though with a slighter foundation, were to be raised to the much lower-lying Newcastle & Carlisle Railway. In addition, of course, Chapman's canal could not expect to find many friends in Hexham, while its opponents found the money to employ not just Sutcliffe but the distinguished civil engineer John Rennie (1761-1821) as expert witnesses. The 'South-siders' had also commissioned a further report from Sutcliffe, published on 3 January 1797 and showing how his Stella - Hexham canal could be extended to Haydon Bridge.[13] The committee stage took place in April 1797, with a fairly lightweight contribution from Rennie, who had not even been to see the route, and six days detailed examination of Sutcliffe. Chapman recorded that the bill was rejected on its third reading.

A Carlisle Canal

William Chapman had plenty of other work to occupy him, but he never lost interest in the canal project. The end of the Napoleonic Wars in 1815 heralded a more promising climate for investment, and two years later a subscription was begun for a survey for a canal from Lemington, on the Tyne, to Carlisle.[14] Owing to opposition that survey was not pursued but a committee was formed to promote a direct canal from Carlisle to the Solway. Chapman's report was adopted in 1818, and on 6 April 1819 the royal assent was given to an Act for a canal almost 12 miles long, entering the Solway near Fishers Cross, about a mile upstream from Bowness and soon to be aggrandised as Port Carlisle. Although this was much less ambitious than Chapman's earlier schemes, it was designed for larger vessels; a depth of 8 feet 6 inches allowed it to take boats up to one hundred tons: twice the size envisaged in 1795. [15]

Leading landowners gave their support, with Cumberland's chief magnate, the Earl of Lonsdale, venturing £5,000, the largest individual subscription. Carlisle businesses were well represented, including large investments by two families who were to be prominent also in the Newcastle & Carlisle Railway. These were the cotton spinners, Peter Dixon & Sons, who staked £4,000, and the Forster banking family, with £2,000. The first section of the canal came into use in May 1822 but completion took a further year, with a formal opening on 12 March 1823, when the Newcastle barrister James Losh, soon to become chairman of the railway promoters, noted that it 'Cannot fail of being highly useful to the public though possibly it may not greatly repay the adventurers'. [16] This was a prescient judgment. The canal's utility was to be enhanced by the opening of the Newcastle & Carlisle Railway, which reached Carlisle in 1836 and the canal basin in 1837. Completion of the railway's central section, in 1838, made the canal a vital link in a rail and sea communication between the Tyne (then Britain's second-busiest port) and Glasgow, Ireland and Liverpool. The rapid growth of the railway network meant, however, that this role would not be sustained for long.

Canal or Railway?

The possibility of building a railway from Newcastle to Carlisle instead of a canal was raised in 1805 by William Thomas, who drew up a report and estimates for a line from Newcastle as far as Hexham, largely following Chapman's canal alignment.[17] Thomas had in mind a cast-iron plateway, whose L-shaped rails would permit the passage of common road vehicles, and he envisaged a horse being able to draw a train of three wagons. The route was to have a double track: one line for each direction, with passing loops at half-mile intervals to enable light carriages to overtake the heavier vehicles.

At this time Chapman was still intending a canal, but he kept an open mind about the potential of railways. In 1806 he took a share in the East Kenton and Coxlodge collieries, near Newcastle, and this led to his involvement in the construction of a railway, four miles long, to serve them. This employed iron rails and had a gauge of almost 4 feet 8 inches. He went on to become involved in the design of steam locomotives, beginning with a pioneering bogie engine, built in 1813 and used on the Heaton colliery line. Thus in 1817, when a Newcastle and Carlisle canal survey was again being contemplated, the idea was also to examine the alternative of a railway. When Chapman came to consider the question of linking Newcastle and Carlisle yet again, in 1824, he judged that it was now opportune and more economic to build a railway rather than a canal.

1.9. *John Wilson Carmichael's 1835 sketch of the Carlisle Canal Basin. View looking south east, with the canal warehouse extreme right and Carlisle Castle extreme left. (Tullie House Museum & Art Gallery)*

1.10. *The canal warehouse, seen from the low viaduct which carried the Newcastle & Carlisle Railway to its terminus at the canal basin. This end of the basin was built up above ground level, hence the stone basement to the warehouse. This was built in 1821 and demolished in 1974. The building behind is a goods warehouse built by the North British Railway. The canal was converted into a railway during 1853-4 and leased to the North British from 1862. Clearance and redevelopment have removed all evidence of railway and canal at this point, other than the gatehouse, just off this view to the right.*
(J.M. Fleming, 1966)

1.11. *Bridge over the former canal near Drumburgh. The original canal bridges had a pair of opening leaves seated on low stone abutments. In converting the canal to a railway, the abutments were raised to carry these iron spans. In this case the new masonry has been corbelled out above the rounded corners of the original. The surface of the present track lies close to the original water level. Additional support has been provided to cope with modern road traffic.* *(Bill Fawcett, 2007)*

Chapman's views were published as an open letter, dated 8 June 1824 and addressed notionally to Sir James Graham (1792-1861), a Cumbrian landowner and noted agricultural improver, whose father had been a promoter of the Carlisle Canal.[18] Sir James went on to a political career which encompassed First Lord of the Admiralty and Home Secretary, and was to prove quietly helpful to the Newcastle & Carlisle Railway project.[19]

Chapman now claimed his 1795 canal alignment to be equally suitable for a railway, with modest deviations to substitute inclined planes for flights of locks. He regarded the long summit level as a particularly attractive feature and suggested that a mixture of self-acting inclines and ones worked by stationary steam engines could handle the gradients elsewhere. This was by then standard practice in the railways of the Durham coalfield, exemplified by George Stephenson's Hetton Railway, which had opened in November 1822. Chapman left open the question of how to haul trains on the level, though he did not envisage using horses at this stage, allowing only that they 'ought to be admitted under certain regulations'. He argued that horses were not needed and 'experience in the vicinity of the Tyne and Wear has proved that by due arrangement, unnecessary to discuss at present, trains of heavy loaden waggons, each containing 53 hundredweight [one Newcastle chaldron], are moved at the rate of 6 or 7 miles an hour.'

Somewhat blithely, Chapman estimated the cost of a double-track railway, plus overtaking loops, at £3,000 per mile, inclusive of Parliamentary expenses, land purchases (presumably) and any machinery. With a length of 64½ miles this gave a cost of £193,500, compared with a 1797 figure of £279,141 for the comparable stretch of canal. Fully converted to the merits of the railway, he went on to argue that the passage through the canal locks would occupy ten hours (not allowing for any queuing), in which time 'by the railway, such articles of conveyance as require quickness of passage would proceed from one extreme to the other'. Allowing a canal speed of just over three miles per hour, Chapman argued that the total boat transit time would be thirty hours, which meant in practice allowing two days for the passage.

A railway along the canal alignment was open to all the criticisms previously made by country landowners and the proponents of a south Tyneside route, so on 20 July 1824 he explored an alternative low-level route from Newcastle to Lemington, extrapolating from prior knowledge how it then could be continued to the west.[20] This gave a railway starting at The Close, a riverside street in Newcastle, and proceeding along the edge of the Tyne to a river crossing near Newburn. It would then continue along the south side of the Tyne, gaining sufficient height to pass on the south side of Hexham and eventually crossing the South Tyne to the south-west of Haltwhistle. Approaching the west, Chapman still held out the prospect of a branch line up the Eden Valley and then across to Penrith, and argued for the summit level to be prolonged so as to facilitate this. This implied a route fairly close to that now followed by the railway between Naworth and Corby.

With the national economy in a healthy state and the coal trade ever growing, the time was right to proceed, and twenty-one respected local figures addressed a requisition to the High Sheriff of Northumberland, calling for a county meeting to discuss the issue. They hoped to use this to launch a subscription for the railway, but were thwarted by the canal party. At the meeting, on 21 August 1824, Colonel Coulson (see chapter 2) led for the railway, but the opposition was forcefully expressed by the Newcastle solicitor William Armstrong. Somewhat ironically, he was the father of the future Lord Armstrong, innovative engineer and arms manufacturer. Sir Matthew White Ridley cut the knot by proposing a committee of enquiry, which was appointed at the meeting, held its first session immediately, and commissioned Chapman to produce a further, detailed report on the canal and railway options. The barrister James Losh was an active member of this committee and noted of a later meeting, on 6 October, that it 'was by no means numerously attended nor did there seem to be much zeal ... I think however that the measure will finally succeed, as a canal seems to be unattainable and some communication between Newcastle and Carlisle for the purpose of transporting heavy goods is evidently a matter of great importance.'[21]

Chapman reported on 27 October 1824.[22] By now aged 75, he was already committed to several major schemes, including the Marquess of Londonderry's proposed new harbour at Seaham, on the Durham coast. So he relied largely on the surveys conducted thirty years before, and concentrated on the technical details of the proposed railway. The canal was quickly dispensed with. His earlier scheme had envisaged fifty ton barges, drawing a maximum of four feet. To conform with the Carlisle Canal he doubled their capacity, increasing the draught to eight or nine feet. As a result he came out with an estimate of £888,000, more than three times his former figure, to build a canal requiring 117 locks in 64½ miles. The railway was costed at £252,488, including land purchase and 15% for supervision and contingencies. This seems remarkably low, especially since - in order to allow for sidings - Chapman based the costs on a four-track line. On the subject of traction he remained equivocal, citing the experience of locomotives on the Hetton Railway and Benjamin Thompson's system of rope haulage by stationary steam engines on the Fawdon Colliery line. He left open the option of using horses on the levels or gentle gradients.

Reviewing Chapman's latest report, the *Tyne Mercury* asked what sane person would pay to be conveyed from Hexham to Newcastle in something like a coal wagon and to be drawn for the greater part of that distance by a roaring steam engine.[23] The prospect was not particularly attractive, given the unreliable locomotives and uneven track of the day. Indeed, when George Stephenson's Stockton & Darlington Railway opened the following year, well-heeled passengers were conveyed in well-sprung, horse-drawn carriages.

1.12. The Tyne at Corbridge is an impressively broad, but deceptively shallow river. Completed in 1674, the seven arches of this bridge make up a total span of almost 500 feet. This was the only Tyne bridge to survive the Great Flood of 1771, though the southernmost arch (off the picture to the left) was rebuilt a half century later. The bold corbels below the parapet were inserted to carry a widened roadway in 1881. (Bill Fawcett, 2007)

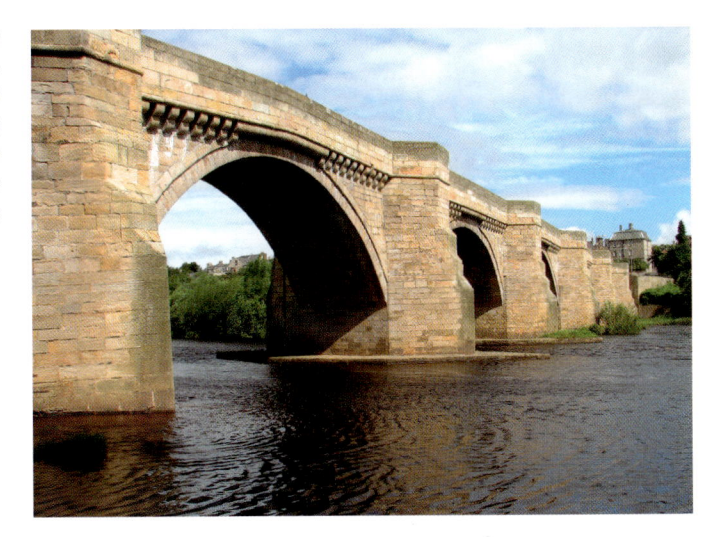

To reassure the doubters and confirm the actual sum needed to build the railway, a second opinion was sought from Josias Jessop (1781-1826), the second son of Chapman's old friend and colleague, William Jessop. Josias was, no doubt, selected on Chapman's recommendation but was in any case well qualified for the task, having recently completed the survey for the Cromford & High Peak Railway - a remarkable line destined to cross the limestone heights of Derbyshire by a mixture of inclines and levels. Jessop's report, of 4 March 1825, was phrased very tactfully but made it clear that Chapman's costs were inadequate.[24] He added £40,000 to the railway estimate, but concluded that its cost would only be one third that of the canal and it would be far more effective in opening out local trade because of the ease with which branches might be made. While deferring notionally to Chapman's judgment, Jessop made it clear that he preferred a lower alignment at the west end, preferably dropping down into the Irthing Valley as soon as possible and serving Brampton by a short branch line.

The committee reported to a county meeting at the Moot Hall in Newcastle on 26 March 1825, where a unanimous resolution was passed in favour of making a railway, followed by the opening of a subscription list. The lead was taken by James Losh, who recorded the proceedings in his diary. Despite the meeting being 'thinly attended', he felt that 'its approbation will have a good effect in forwarding what I consider a pressing speculation, both with a view to public utility and the profit of the individual subscribers. After the county meeting was over a meeting of the persons intending to support the railroad was held. I there moved a set of resolutions for opening a subscription etc and a prospectus was read and approved. About £20,000 was immediately subscribed [i.e. pledged]. At first every person seemed to hold back, as if unwilling that their names should stand first. I therefore thought it necessary to make a beginning and put my name down for 20 shares [£2,000] and then most of those present followed my example.'

The next stage was a meeting of the subscribers, by now denoted the 'Shareholders of the Newcastle upon Tyne and Carlisle Rail-Road Company' at Newcastle's Assembly Rooms on 9 April. This elected twelve directors, one of them being James Losh, who duly became chairman. It also appointed solicitors and bankers and called for a deposit of £2 on each share. Thus, after thirty years debate, the railway was born. No doubt, those present anticipated its completion within about five years; in fact another decade was to pass before the formal opening of any part.

1.13. Newcastle's Assembly Rooms were the venue for general meetings of the N&C shareholders until 1852, when these were transferred to the spacious but much smaller boardroom in the newly-completed offices at Central Station. This view was published in 1827 but the building, constructed in 1774-6 and situated in Fenkle Street, looks much the same today. (from MacKenzie's History of Newcastle)

Chapter 2: The Railway Promoters

Introduction

To understand the railway, we need to know something of the people promoting it. First, however, we must anticipate the progress of the scheme from 1825 to 1829. The Newcastle meeting on 9 April 1825 had elected twelve directors, raised to 24 on May 21, and their priority was to secure subscriptions so that a detailed survey could be commissioned in readiness for submitting a private bill to Parliament, whose standing orders required that plans be deposited with the clerks of the peace for each locality before the end of November. Chapman's estimate, increased by Jessop, was rounded up to give £300,000 as the capital required by the company. One sixth of this was reserved for investment by landowners along the route, in the largely unrealised hope that they would take shares in part payment for land. The remainder, £250,000, was made available for public subscriptions.

Arrangements were made to receive applications at specified banks and lawyers' offices in Newcastle, London and Carlisle, and the response was very encouraging, with the *Tyne Mercury* of 10 May 1825 reporting that the subscription list was full and shares were standing at a premium.[1] A list of May 25 reveals that £251,000 had been subscribed, in shares of £100, although the actual amount that shareholders needed to find at this stage was only £2 per share - enough to fund the survey and initial parliamentary expenses.[2]

The survey went ahead and a bill was taken to Parliament, with widespread support, but determined opposition from a couple of landowners along the route. This would have been no real problem by itself, but the directors became aware of errors in the deposited plans which might enable their opponents to have the bill thrown out. At the same time, they were running into difficulties accommodating the Earl of Carlisle, who had extensive colliery interests near Brampton. On 12 February 1826, chairman James Losh recorded a meeting at which - after much discussion - the directors decided to withdraw their bill until the next session of Parliament. He noted that this delay would give them an opportunity to modify the route so as to perhaps save money and conciliate opponents. Another factor was the fear that Parliament might be forced to dissolve while the bill was in progress, while an unspoken consideration may have been a tightening of credit which had followed a succession of private bank failures in late 1825.[3]

In the event, there was to be a delay of three years before the bill returned to Parliament. During this time there were extensive revisions to the west end of the route, between Denton and Carlisle, while a successful effort was made to secure more participation by investors from the Carlisle area. The Newcastle & Carlisle Railway's first Act of Parliament received the royal assent on 22 May 1829, and the first directors of the incorporated company were elected on 16 October.

The pattern of investors

The evolving pattern of investment in seen from three lists of subscribers. One shows all those at 25 May 1825; another shows the situation about the time the renewed application was made to Parliament, while the third lists all people holding ten or more shares in August 1829.[4] In May 1825, the £251,000 was made up of just £7,000 on the Carlisle list, £82,000 on the London one, and the remainder in Newcastle. Allowing that some London investors subscribed on the Newcastle list, because of family or business ties, and two Liverpool ones bolstered the meagre Carlisle subscription, these sums are broadly indicative of where the money came from.

Of the 1825 Carlisle list, only £5,500 came from Cumberland and while John Forster, the Carlisle banker, made a good showing there was no trace of the city's leading industrialists - the Dixon cotton-spinning dynasty. They had already committed themselves heavily to the city's canal, which met its most urgent transport needs, and probably wished to see how the railway project developed. However, by 1828/9 the Dixons were prepared to back it handsomely, with a total subscription of £2,000, while the Forsters had upped their investment from £500 to £2,000. Overall, the Cumbrian share had risen to something like £12,000 - though still only about 4% of the total capital.

The three year pause brought a drastic decline in London's share. In 1825 the London list attracted the majority of big investors: fifteen subscribed for more than £2,500 each, five of these for £5,000. Most of this was speculative money, which drifted elsewhere. The London list fell to a quarter of its 1825 total, the majority of those remaining being the smaller investors - of five hundred or a thousand pounds - who had other reasons than the purely financial to engage in the venture. Of the fifteen top 1825 subscribers, thirteen dropped out altogether though one - Arthur MacNamara - apparently unconnected with the region - actually increased his stake, from £2,500 to £5,000.

Thus the burden of the project fell largely on Tyneside and Northumberland. There, the vast majority of the big investors of 1825 kept faith with the scheme; some indeed raised their stake, and the chief losses - still not seriously numerous, were among the small fry. The final 1829 investors were overwhelmingly people from the region or with a stake in it, who saw the railway as a vital contribution to the future health of their own businesses and estates, while also viewing it as a potentially good long-term investment in its own right.

The size of individual shareholdings was to some extent conditioned by the rules relating to the Board of Directors. From 1829 until May 1852, when their number was reduced to ten, the company had thirty directors, ten of whom retired in rotation each year but were normally re-elected without opposition. Table 2.1 shows the chronological succession of directors, of whom there were sixty-six during the railway's thirty-three year life. Three (one after 1852) were nominated by the Earl of Carlisle, under the terms of the company's 1829 Act; the remainder were elected at the shareholders' main annual meeting, held in March. To be eligible to vote one had to own a minimum of five shares (£500), receiving an extra vote for every further five shares up to a maximum of four votes. To stand for the Board one had to hold a minimum of ten shares. Thus £500, £1,000 and £2,000 could be seen as preferred values of shareholding, a view which is borne out by the 1828/9 lists.

Prominent Investors

To get some picture of the people who promoted the railway, we shall travel along the route from west to east and look at some of the prominent figures involved and the businesses whose needs justified the scheme.

Carlisle: the Forsters and Dixons

The Forster and Dixon families provided about a third of the Cumbrian investment in 1829 and four of the thirty directors, while the Forsters were also bankers to the Carlisle sub-committee of directors, which was to handle the payments to west-end contractors during the construction of the line. John Forster I had established the Carlisle Bank with his sons in 1792 and by the late eighteen-twenties it was in the hands of his son John II and grandson John III, who both subscribed handsomely to the railway and became directors.[5] By 1831 John III had raised his stake to 32 shares, while his brother William had acquired ten and succeeded their father as a director in 1832. During construction their bank advanced modest sums of working capital when the railway's finances proved tight, but they became over-extended by advances to a couple of Carlisle builders, William Gate and William Smith Denton. Denton constructed the railway's two great viaducts at Wetheral, but fate rewarded him unkindly: both he and the Forsters were declared bankrupt towards the end of November 1836.[6]

The Dixons were paragons of prosperity. Their cotton-spinning dynasty originated with Peter Dixon of Whitehaven, who in 1783 married Mary Ferguson of a prosperous Carlisle textile family. Their sons John (1785-1857), Peter (1789-1866) and George (1793-1860) came into the business and in 1809 they and their father took a lease of the Fergusons' cotton mill at Warwick Bridge, two miles downstream from the railway's majestic Eden Viaduct. From this nucleus they grew into the main employers of nineteenth-century Carlisle. By 1847 they employed eight thousand people at four mills, including Warwick Bridge but dominated by a new mill completed in the west of Carlisle in 1836; its three hundred feet chimney still dramatically punctuates the skyline.[7] The canal was very important for shipping in raw material and despatching their products, and they were its second-largest investors, with £4,000. The railway held out the prospect of cheaper coal, their fuel, and so despite holding back in 1825 they invested substantially in 1828. By 1831 Peter (junior) and George had raised their holdings to fifteen shares each and John to sixteen.

Peter and John were directors from 1829 and played an active part during the difficult years when money was scarce and the railway's construction proved rather protracted. The works at the west end of the line were under the supervision of the Carlisle committee, who often seemed more eager to get on with building the line than their counterparts in Newcastle. The latter, however, represented the bulk of investors and so retained something of a whip hand. After all his efforts, Peter Dixon left the Board in March 1846 on a very sour note, having fallen out with his colleagues over the level of charges for coal traffic, something which concerned him both as a major industrial consumer and as a colliery proprietor. John Dixon stayed on for a further three years, having also become a director of the Lancaster & Carlisle Railway. Having disposed of his shares in the N&C, he was succeeded on the Board in March 1849 by brother George, who later served as vice chairman and representative of the Carlisle interest.

2.1. *Dixons' Mill, built in justified anticipation of the fall in coal prices which would result from the opening of the west end of the Newcastle & Carlisle Railway. Now converted to housing. The great chimney lies off to the left.   (Bill Fawcett)*

Colonel Coulson and the Blenkinsopp Colliery

An energetic early promoter was John Blenkinsopp Coulson (1779-1863), of Blenkinsopp Hall, near Greenhead, and Jesmond, near Newcastle. Despite disposing of the Jesmond estate in 1809, he remained one of a small group whose interests spanned both ends of the route. Of particular interest to him was the coal on the Blenkinsopp estate, which would be made far more competitive in the Carlisle and Irish markets by the building of the railway. The Blenkinsopp royalty was leased by the Earl of Carlisle, whose Tindale Fell collieries were the main suppliers of the city, but the Earl's lease fell in 1835 and around 1827 he was made aware that it would not be renewed. Instead, a Benkinsopp Coal & Lime Company was set up to take on the lease. The partners were all promoters of the railway, and this soured relations with the Earl, thereby causing several years delay to the railway project, as we shall see in chapter 3.

Colonel Coulson (he was in the Northumberland militia) was not a partner in the colliery company but could expect about the same return, through rent, as its promoters. Prominent among these were John and Peter Dixon and John and William Forster. Others were Thomas Crawhall, the railway's first Secretary, his brother William, and the lead magnate Thomas Wilson, together with John Studholme, the railway's west-end surveyor.[8] All but Studholme were directors of the railway. The Irish market was an important target, since Ireland's natural coal deposits are slight and of poor quality, and the Blenkinsopp company not only opened an agency in Dublin but built up a small fleet of ships to carry coal down the Carlisle Canal and across to the Irish capital.[9] The first was probably *Blenkinsopp*, built by William Bell of Carlisle and launched at the canal basin on New Year's Day, 1838. Coulson served on the N&C Board until its 1852 slimming, while his eldest son - also John Blenkinsopp (1799-1868) - was a director from March 1848 until the merger with the North Eastern.

2.2. *John Wilson Carmichael's engraving of Blenkinsopp. The N&C had to divert both the Tippalt Burn and the turnpike road, whose iron bridge is seen just in front of the wooden railway bridge. Behind is Blenkinsopp Hall, for which the railway provided a diverted drive, new lodges and an ornamental bridge.*

The Lead Industry: 1: Greenwich & Brandling

Two great centres of the lead industry in the north Pennines were Alston Moor and Allendale, both served by the railway - albeit at a distance. Alston Moor formed part of the enormous 'Northern Estates' of Greenwich Hospital, formerly the property of the Earls of Derwentwater but sequestrated after the third earl chose the losing side in the 1715 Jacobite Rising. In 1735 the revenues from the Derwentwater Estates were allocated to the Royal Naval Hospital, and in 1749 they were granted the properties outright. Up to 1832, the Northern Estates were managed by a pair of Receivers, based in Newcastle, and at the time we are considering these were Thomas Wailes and Robert William Brandling (1775-1849), the latter being a considerable coalowner in his own right and for a time chairman of the Tyne & Wear coalowners' cartel - the Limitation of the Vend.

The Hospital took a progressive view of the development of its estates and their transport needs. From 1778 they made substantial loans to turnpike trusts in connection with the Northumbrian roads; in 1797 they supported Chapman's Canal Bill, and in 1823 they commissioned a report on roads from John Loudon MacAdam, acting on his suggestions to assist the merger of several existing turnpikes into a new Alston Moor Turnpike Trust, one of the largest in Britain at the time.[10] Accompanying this were several new works, including a link from Langley down to Haydon Bridge which would in due course prove vital in getting lead down to the railway. On the Receivers' recommendation they endorsed the Newcastle & Carlisle Railway project, and though the Hospital did not take up shares, they made land available on very favourable terms. The railway passed through Greenwich properties alongside the Tyne at Dilston, near Corbridge; Allerwash and Fourstones, west of Hexham; and also west of Haydon Bridge. The company was sold the land at its agricultural value, payment of the capital being deferred until such time as the investors should receive a dividend of 5%; meanwhile the railway paid a fair rent while enjoying the perquisites of ownership.[11]

Newcastle & Carlisle Railway Board of Directors:

There were originally thirty directors, three of them nominated by the Earl of Carlisle (nos. 1 to 3). Their numbers were reduced to ten in May 1852.

#	Director	Term
1.	(EoC) Earl of Carlisle	to March 1835	John Ramshay March 1835 until Merger
2.	(EoC) James Loch, MP	to March 1833	Andrew Robert Fenwick March 1833 to March 1835	George Gill Mounsey March 1835 to 1849	William Carrick December 1849 to May 1852 Reorg.
3.	(EoC) George Gill Mounsey	to March 1832	James Thompson March 1832 to July 1851 (death); seat abolished May 1852
4.	William Woods	only director to serve throughout until Merger
5.	Lord William Powlett	Served until May 1852 Reorg.
6.	Mayor of Newcastle	to March 1833	James Graham Clarke March 1833 to 1836	Mayor of Newcastle March 1836 to May 1852 Reorg.
7.	George Anderson	to 1831 (death)	Nicholas Wood 28 October 1831 to May 1852 Reorg.
8.	Thomas Richard Batson	to March 1842	Richard Shortridge March 1842 to ? March 1852	John Fogg Elliott March 1852 to Merger
9.	Thomas Wentworth Beaumont	to December 1844	John Garnett Atkinson December 1844 to May 1852 Reorg.
10.	Matthew Bell	Served until May 1852 Reorg.
11.	John Brandling	to March 1845	George Clayton Atkinson March 1845 until Merger
12.	Job James Bulman	to May 1834	John Lionel Hood May 1834 to March 1839	James Losh (junior) March 1839 to June 1853	William Dunn June 1853 to Merger
13.	Nathaniel Clayton	to March 1832 (death)	Rev. Ralph Henry Brandling March 1832 to March 1838	Matthew Anderson March 1838 to Merger
14.	Christopher Cookson	to May 1832 (death)	George Johnson March 1833 to January 1852 (death)	Henry Liddell March 1852 to Merger
15.	John Blenkinsopp Coulson	Served until May 1852 Reorg.
16.	Joseph Crawhall	to April 1853 (death)	Isaac Crawhall May 1853 to Merger
17.	Thomas Crawhall	to September 1833 (death)	Mayor of Newcastle October 1833 to March 1835	John Diston Powles March 1835 to March 1848	Peter Dickson March 1848 to May 1852 Reorg.
18.	John Dixon	to early 1849	George Dixon March 1849 to March 1856	Philip Henry Howard March 1856 to Merger
19.	Peter Dixon	to March 1846	William Isaac Cookson March 1846 to May 1852 Reorg.
20.	Thomas Fenwick	Served until May 1852 Reorg.
21.	John Forster	to April 1832	William Forster April 1832 to March 1837	Thomas Anderson March 1837 to March 1842	Joseph Hawks March 1842 to January 1845	Alfred Ward Powles January 1845 to March 1848 … (still No. 21) … John Blenkinsopp Coulson (junior) March 1848 to Merger
22.	John Forster (junior)	to March 1837	William Crawhall March 1837 to March 1849	Isaac Crawhall March 1849 to May 1852 Reorg.
23.	Alfred Hall	Served until May 1852 Reorg.
24.	Henry Howard	to March 1835	Philip Henry Howard March 1835 to May 1852 Reorg.
25.	James Losh	to September 1833 (death)	Mayor of Carlisle October 1833 to March 1845	William Malcolm March 1845 to March 1847	Theodore Walrond March 1847 to early 1852	Robert Cowan March to May 1852 Reorg.
26.	William Losh	Served until May 1852 Reorg.
27.	Matthew Plummer	Served until May 1852 Reorg.
28.	Benjamin Thompson	to May 1842	John Bulman March 1843 to May 1852 Reorg.
29.	Thomas Wilson	Served until May 1852 Reorg.
30.	J. G. Lambton, Earl of Durham	to March 1837	Marquess of Blandford/Duke of Marlborough March 1837 to July 1845	William Balleny July 1845 to May 1852 Reorg.

Table 2.1. *Newcastle & Carlisle Railway Directors from 1829 to 1862.*

Robert William Brandling did not invest in the railway, but his two brothers were large shareholders, with 25 shares each. John Brandling (1773-1847) was an original director, while the Reverend Ralph Henry (1771-1853) served from March 1832 to March 1838, much of the time as vice chairman. Both were closely involved in the tortuous manoeuvres to extend the railway along the south bank of the Tyne towards Gateshead, discussed in Chapter 8. These involved the creation of a short-lived Blaydon, Gateshead & Hebburn Railway, with John as chairman, only to be superseded by Robert William's vision of 'Brandlings' Railway', later known as the Brandling Junction. Despite their substantial land holdings and collieries, the Brandlings ran into financial problems during the eighteen-forties and their connection with the N&C ceased when John, having sold all his shares, stepped down as a director prior to the March 1845 meeting.[12]

The Lead Industry 2: Beaumont and Crawhalls

The biggest concentration of investment in the railway, at the outset, came from a major landowning family, the Beaumonts, and the Crawhall brothers, who were variously their agents and also energetic entrepreneurs in their own right. Of six brothers, four served as directors, and until the 1852 re-organisation of the Board it was usually blessed with a pair of Crawhalls. The Beaumonts were extremely wealthy, deriving much of their substance from the marriage of Diana Blackett to Thomas Richard Beaumont (1758-1829). They enjoyed income from collieries as well as the WB (Wentworth/Blackett) lead mines in an ore field straddling the upper reaches of Allendale and Weardale. Most of the Allendale ore was smelted in the dale and the metal was then transported down to the Beaumont refinery at Blaydon. From there it could be despatched down the Tyne to any destination. Most of Greenwich Hospital's Alston Moor lead, worked either by the London Lead Company or by smaller partnerships, also found its way down to the Tyne, where there were several major lead works, most conspicuously that of Ward, Walker, Parker & Co. in Elswick, with its tall shot tower.

T.R. Beaumont subscribed £5,000 to the railway in 1825 and his eldest son, Thomas Wentworth Beaumont (TWB), invested a further £1,000. TWB had purchased the Bywell estate on the Tyne and preferred this to the family's Yorkshire seat at Bretton. He took a keen interest in their Northumbrian properties and became the largest single investor in the railway, as well as the 'richest commoner in England', following the deaths of his father, in July 1829, and his mother, in 1831. As an MP he could assist the railway in Parliament, and served as a director until December 1844, although he hardly ever attended Board meetings. He was on good terms with James Losh, who audited the lead business and ran his electoral campaigns in Northumberland. Beaumont could, however, be erratic and there was an awkward moment at the start of 1834 when it seemed that he might sell his shares in the railway. That would have been a blow to public confidence in the venture, and his Chief Lead Agent, Benjamin Johnson, argued strongly and successfully against the move, pointing out that the lead business stood to gain between £1,000 and £1,500 a year through reduced transport costs once the railway reached Haydon Bridge.[13]

T. W. Beaumont (1792 – 1848)

The Crawhall brothers form a fascinating group among the N&C promoters, and an influential one - with a total of a hundred shares (£10,000) in 1831. They were an Allendale family: sons of Thomas Crawhall (c1748-1812), latterly T.R. Beaumont's agent at Allenheads. Thomas and his wife Anne Bownas had six sons who reached manhood, and almost as many daughters. John (1774-1832) became Beaumont land agent at Allenheads. Thomas (c1779-1833) was first Secretary of the railway. George (1780-1852) became WB lead agent in upper Weardale - responsible for all the mines and works there, and William (1784-1849) held the corresponding post at Allenheads. Joseph (1793-1853) is best known as the grandfather of the eponymous Tyneside artist and was a prosperous ropemaker, but - as we shall see - his interests extended much further. Finally, Isaac (1795-1877) began by helping brother George in Weardale and ended up as Lord of the Manor at Nun Monkton in Yorkshire. Thomas, Joseph, William and Isaac all served as directors of the railway.

Thomas Crawhall moved to Newcastle to take up a post in the Beaumont Lead office, while also, like his brothers, developing extensive business interests on his own account. These prospered, while in November 1827 he took charge of the lead office as Head Cashier or Chief Agent, following the death of its former head, Mr. Morrison.[14] Thomas held the post, with its £400 salary, for little more than four years. After Diana Beaumont's death, TWB came in as a new broom, regarding the Crawhalls as somewhat old fashioned, and at the end of 1831 he confided to James Losh his wish to dispense with them.[15] In the end Thomas was the only one to be immediately affected, resigning at the end of June 1832 in favour of Benjamin Johnson. William and George carried on until 1845, when William began to suffer attacks of 'paralysis' and Beaumont took the opportunity to bring in Thomas Sopwith to take charge of both the Allendale and Weardale mines, though retaining Isaac Crawhall for a time as sub-agent in charge of the latter.[16] Thomas Crawhall's departure from WB Lead was no financial hardship since by then he had become a well-paid Secretary to the Newcastle & Carlisle Railway, while other ventures included the Blenkinsopp company, Rotherhope Fell lead mine, and Callerton colliery. By his early death, in 1833, his properties included farms in Weardale and Allendale and a London house close to fashionable Cavendish Square, as well as his country villa just outside Newcastle: Benwell Tower.[17]

Thomas Crawhall was not solely concerned with making money. He was an early member of Newcastle's Society of Antiquaries and a founder of its Natural History Society.[18] His involvement in the railway is likely therefore to have been prompted by a sense of the common good as well as loyalty to the Beaumont/Crawhall interest and a shrewd perception that it would eventually earn good money. In May 1825 he put his name down for 25 shares and later, perhaps urged by his friend James Losh, became unpaid Secretary to the promoters. This will have consumed a lot of time, particularly while the company's Bill was passing through Parliament. He was confirmed as Secretary on 19 August 1829, at the first meeting of shareholders after gaining their Act, and also became a director. He was also the formal Clerk to the Company, and his labours were recognised on 5 March 1830, when the Board agreed to grant him the considerable salary of £500 a year, with effect from the previous October.[19] It is worth noting that, prior to 1852, directors received no fees, the only exception being the three 'managing directors' appointed in 1833. Thomas attended most Board and committee meetings held in Newcastle up to his death on 14 September 1833, aged only 54. This seems to have been quite unexpected, and James Losh noted that he 'will be a great loss in many respects', adding after warm praise of Thomas that he was 'conscientious and orderly in all he undertook' but 'could want flexibility and be a bit obstinate.'

A candidate to succeed Thomas Crawhall as Secretary was brother Joseph, who served as a director from 1829. However, someone conveniently discovered that the Act did not permit anyone to serve as both a director and Secretary, at which point he withdrew and the Newcastle solicitor John Adamson was appointed instead, at a much reduced salary of £200.[20] This was perhaps the desired outcome since Joseph, though a valuable member of the Board, was also obstinate and could occasionally go off at an awkward tangent. He survived the 1852 reorganisation and served until his death on 27 April 1853. He was succeeded by brother Isaac, who continued until the merger with the North Eastern.

2.4. *Joseph Crawhall's painting of merchants on Newcastle Exchange c1826. The only N&C promoters identified are Nathaniel Clayton, who had just clocked up 40 years as town clerk (7th from left, leaning on his stick – see p. 23) and (next to him, facing our left) Thomas Cookson, with ten shares. (courtesy of the Literary & Philosophical Society of Newcastle upon Tyne)*

Joseph was a convivial character and a fair artist. The Crawhall brothers remained close and Joseph chronicled their sporting and social activities in a humorously illustrated account of the 'Park House' club. Our concern, however, is with his business activities, which give an insight into the nature and networks of the Tyneside 'merchants' who dominated the railway's shareholders and directorate.[21] Joseph held only ten shares, just enough to qualify as a director, and his main business interest was the St. Ann's ropeworks, in the east end of Newcastle, which he established in 1812. In addition, however, he shared with brother Thomas an interest in Rotherhope Fell mine and acted as an agent for lead sales, notably on behalf of the Hudgill Burn mine, in Nentdale. This was one of those rare, fabulously profitable mines, worked by John Wilson and Company of Nent Hall. Some of their profit was ploughed into the railway, with John and Thomas Wilson each taking ten shares, and the latter serving as a director until 1852.

Joseph Crawhall was also engaged, with his brothers, in a prosperous candlemaking venture - tallow candles being used in lead mines. Most intriguing is his involvement in shipping. Many Tyneside merchants and landowners ventured money as shares in ships - predominantly colliers engaged in the London and overseas coal trade, which were on the lookout for return cargoes - such as Baltic timber - for which they could quote attractively low rates. Joseph's accounts for 1822-27 reveal investments in more than a dozen ships, in shares ranging from a sixteenth to a quarter, sometimes in partnership with people who were to become fellow railway directors. One ship was the whaler *Lady Jane*, in which he held a quarter share alongside Matthew Plummer, the second and longest-serving chairman of the N&C, and Thomas Richard Batson (1783-1845), a merchant and banker, who was an N&C director until March 1842.[22] Another of Joseph's ventures into transport was as treasurer of a turnpike trust formed to build a new road up Allendale and over into Weardale (the present B6295). Set up by an Act of 5 May 1826, its main purpose was to improve access to the Beaumont mines, and the Crawhall brothers featured prominently among the many trustees.[23]

The final chain in the lead business was the refinery, of which there were several on Tyneside. These were represented on the Board by Alfred Hall (1778-1853), a leading refiner with a factory at Bill Quay. He was a major investor, subscribing for thirty shares at the outset, and remained on the Board until 1852. His and the Crawhalls' interlocking business interests are typical of Tyneside merchants and landowners at the time, and provided a firm foundation for a venture like the railway. Some investments, particularly mining, required a long-term view - a readiness to wait patiently for returns, which proved particularly valuable in the case of the Newcastle & Carlisle Railway.

James and William Losh

We are now at the east end of the route, and ready to look at James Losh, the N&C's first chairman, before moving to his successor - Matthew Plummer. Losh was a well-known figure on Tyneside: a barrister and a reforming Whig, much involved with the Beaumont family. While promoting the Newcastle & Carlisle Railway, he was also campaigning against slavery and for electoral reform. His long-standing acquaintances included Earl Grey, who ultimately carried the Reform Bill, and Lord Chancellor Brougham - people to be valued when carrying the railway measure through Parliament.

It was helpful that Losh straddled both ends of the railway: Cumberland and Tyneside. He was born on 10 June 1763, the second of four sons of John Losh of Woodside, a small country estate about four miles south of Carlisle. After studying at Cambridge, he entered Lincolns Inn before settling permanently on Tyneside in 1799. He already had business interests there; indeed there was a family link with Tyneside industry from the previous generation, while his eldest brother John, who inherited Woodside, had established an alkali factory at Walker, downstream of Newcastle.

2.5. James Losh, carved in classical garb by local sculptor J.G. Lough, commands the stairhall of Newcastle's Lit & Phil., placed there as a mark of the great respect which contemporaries felt for him. (courtesy of the Literary & Philosophical Soc. of Newcastle)

James Losh drew a substantial income from two colliery ventures in Gateshead: Tyne Main and Saltwellside. The former was a new winning, which caused some anxiety but was earning him £2,400 a year (as a 40% share) by 1824.[24] Thus he could afford to launch the 1825 railway subscription with his £2,000, confident that it would be some years before the whole sum was called up. More importantly, he understood the needs of industrialists yet also moved widely in social and political circles, which he could tap to support the scheme. He was therefore a very suitable choice as first chairman, and his death on 23 September 1833, while travelling in Yorkshire, must have come as a great shock, particularly happening only nine days after the loss of Thomas Crawhall. Fortunately, the deputy chairman, Matthew Plummer, had been very active in the affairs of the railway and smoothly took over the reins.

While James Losh's role was to be significant but short, his brother William (1770/1 - 1861) lasted on the Board from 1829 until May 1852. William is best known as a founding partner of the firm of Losh, Wilson & Bell, whose Walker Iron Foundry lay next door to brother John's alkali works.[25] William was a pioneer in various aspects of early railway engineering. In 1816 he and George Stephenson took out a joint patent for various improvements relating to locomotives and rails, and it seems simplistic to suggest, as Samuel Smiles did, that Losh - with his practical understanding of foundry techniques allied to an extensive knowledge of chemistry - contributed no more than the money. Later, he patented a rail, which was adopted for the N&C's early permanent way, Losh granting them a free licence. His most useful railway invention was a composite wheel, which reduced the risk of fracture and was specified for N&C rolling stock for much of the company's existence; many of the wheelsets were indeed ordered by the N&C from Losh, Wilson & Bell and then supplied to their carriage and wagon builders. Losh built up a holding of twenty-six shares in the railway, while his partner, Thomas Bell, supported the venture to the extent of ten.

Matthew Plummer

On 20 July 1848 a dinner was held in Newcastle's Assembly Rooms in honour of Matthew Plummer, who had completed almost two decades as successively deputy chairman and chairman of the railway.[26] Matthew Bell, of Woolsington, a Northumberland MP and original director, had the pleasure of handing over a service of silver plate on behalf of the shareholders and making a speech. This was a familiar exercise, since Bell - though he almost never attended a Board meeting - habitually gave the vote of thanks at the close of the shareholders' March assembly. On this occasion we may trust the substance behind the purple prose, namely that Plummer had put in a great deal of work on behalf of the company, despite his many other business interests, and that he had never drawn a penny in the way of fees. The occasion was intended as a valedictory celebration, the railway having been leased to George Hudson, the Railway King.

Plummer's connection with the project went back far beyond the railway, having been a supporter of Chapman's 1797 canal scheme. Plummer was then in his twenties, born in 1772 at Thormanby in Yorkshire. His father, Benjamin, had two farms, one tenanted from James Graham Clarke, of Fenham, a Newcastle merchant who recruited young Matthew to a mercantile career on Tyneside. William Fordyce, in his *History of Durham*, published the year after Plummer's death, charts Matthew's career as a merchant, a shipbroker and insurance broker, a partner in the Northumberland flax mills - down by Newcastle's Ouseburn, partner in a bottle works and - latterly - as a partner in the Haswell Coal Company.[27]

These were not casual engagements, but sustained enterprises. As we have seen he was also a ship owner, and Fordyce records his engagement 'in most of the undertakings and questions which affected the port of Tyne'. In his spare time he was vice-consul for the United States of America and also found an opportunity to run the railway with 'energy, economy and skilful management'. The diaries of one of the railway officers, Richard Lowry, reveal that Plummer was quite an approachable man, ready to take time to listen seriously to suggestions.

Plummer subscribed for ten shares in the railway, and evidently joined the provisional Board when it was enlarged in May 1825. He was more involved with the detail of the scheme than James Losh. Thus in April 1827 he was appointed to a five-man committee to audit the bills and examine the question of errors in the survey of the route.[28] His fellow members were Thomas Crawhall, William Losh, William Woods (a banker and the company's final chairman) and Alfred Hall. In January 1827 the same committee was reappointed to conduct the routine business of the enterprise, which was a great relief to James Losh since it meant the main board need only meet once a month. Elected the first vice-chairman of the incorporated company in 1829, Plummer already bore much of the managerial burden by the time he succeeded Losh in September 1833.

By 1848, Plummer was seventy-six and foresaw an end to his active involvement with Hudson's lease of the line from 1 July that year. In the event, Hudson fell from power and the N&C resumed control of their line from 1 January 1850, keeping a reluctant Matthew in bondage as chairman until 4 June 1851. Even then, his work was not over and he produced a report on the reorganisation of the company's office establishment, which was duly implemented. He finally stepped down as a director at the May 1852 reorganisation, and died at his home in Sheriff Hill, high above Gateshead, on Christmas Day, 1856. The railway connection was renewed by one of his grandsons, Sir Walter Richard Plummer (born 1858), who was elected to the North Eastern Railway Board on 2 June 1905.[29]

Plummer was succeeded as chairman by James Losh, junior, (1803-58), the eldest son of the first chairman. Like his father, Losh practised as a barrister, but never showed the same degree of interest in political and social questions. He had been a director since March 1839 but did only two years in the chair, stepping down from the Board on 6 June 1853, following his appointment as a County Court judge. He was succeeded in turn by a Newcastle banker William Woods (1787-1864), who had the distinction not only of being the last chairman of the railway but of being the only director to serve throughout from 1829 to 1862. Woods served briefly on the North Eastern Railway board, joining it on 13 February 1863, and dying on 12 June 1864. (Woods is considered further on page 139)

John Clayton

John Clayton never graced the Board, but as Newcastle's town clerk and chief legal adviser to the railway he wielded more power than most directors. He was described as having 'all the craft and subtlety of the devil; great talents, indefatigable industry, immense wealth and wonderful tact.'[30] All this was at the service of the N&C, which he helped steer round various obstacles. Born in 1792, he was a younger son of Nathaniel Clayton, who had been town clerk from 1785. Nathaniel stepped down in December 1822 and John succeeded him, remaining town clerk until 1867. John's legal practice was carried on in partnership with brother Matthew, while brother Michael ran the London branch of the firm and therefore handled the railway's legal business there. Between them the Claytons held sixty-five shares in the railway in 1829, and Nathaniel served on its Board until his death in 1832.

John Clayton was something of a visionary. A keen antiquary, he inherited Chesters Roman fort as part of his father's country estate, and went on to purchase, excavate and restore much of the central section of Hadrian's Wall. Yet he was active in the rebirth of Newcastle, supporting and advising the enlightened entrepreneur Richard Grainger in his plans for a new town centre. Clayton was a keen supporter of railways. He encouraged Newcastle Corporation to invest in the N&C (100 shares) and later in the Durham Junction, of which he was one of the main promoters. His negotiating skills brought the Tanfield coal onto the Carlisle line, in the face of competition from the Stanhope & Tyne Railway, though the main beneficiary from this proved to be the Brandling Junction Railway. Clayton was much impressed by George Hudson, the Railway King, and played a key role in negotiations between Hudson and parties on Tyneside, including the N&C. Clayton's own investments proved extremely profitable, and he left a considerable fortune at his death in 1890. Yet he was a frugal man, whose exercise in bad weather was to walk up and down the alleys of the Grainger Market or the platforms of Newcastle Central Station, both of them buildings which he had helped to bring about.

John Clayton (1792 - 1890)

Chapter 3: 1825 - 1829: Finding a Route

Introduction

The Newcastle upon Tyne and Carlisle Rail-Road Company was formally born at the subscribers' meeting on 9 April 1825, and in the space of a month it had enough subscriptions pledged to proceed with the next phase - which was a detailed survey of the route, by then somewhat altered from the only detailed plans then existing, namely those for William Chapman's 1797 canal. Enough was already known of the likely route to enable the promoters to approach the agents of the leading landowners along the way, as a result of which they duly secured the endorsement of the Duke of Northumberland, who held properties in the vicinity of Prudhoe and Farnley, and Greenwich Hospital, together with a cautiously favourable response from the Earl of Carlisle. The survey itself posed something of a problem in that the seventy-six year old Chapman was already heavily committed to works at the East London Dock and Seaham Harbour. In the event, a cheap alternative surfaced in the form of Benjamin Thompson, one of the promoters, who undertook to assist Chapman free of charge and increasingly took over the role of engineer.[1]

Benjamin Thompson (1779-1867)

Thompson was not an engineer in the conventional sense, but he had considerable experience of colliery railways, as well as management of collieries and ironworks.[2] Born on 11 April 1779 at Whiteley Wood Hall, Ecclesall, near Sheffield, he attended Sheffield Grammar School before heading to South Wales, where he established ironworks with his brother John. He was also involved in mines and ironworks in Shropshire, which he left for Tyneside in 1811, making the area his home for the rest of his life. Thompson was persuaded north by the assignees of the bankrupt partnership of Harrison, Cooke & Co., in order to sort out their collieries in readiness for sale.[3] He took up residence at Eighton Cottage, near to Harrison & Cooke's Urpeth Colliery, and became managing partner in a group which bought that pit from the assignees. Thompson expanded the colliery and extended and partially rebuilt its waggonway, which ran to shipping staiths on the Tyne at Bill Quay. On that line the former owner, Samuel Cooke, had introduced to the North East the use of stationary steam engines to haul wagons up inclines. Thompson became a staunch advocate of rope haulage - eventually developing a 'reciprocating' system of stationary engines to haul wagons on the level as well, in preference to using either horses or the admittedly primitive and unreliable early steam locomotives.

He patented this idea in 1821 and tried it out first on the Urpeth system at the mile-long Birtley Fell 'level', sandwiched between Blackhouse and Eighton Banks inclines.[4] These were worked by stationary engines, to which he coupled extra winding drums and ropes to haul the wagons on the level. This gave a valuable saving, compared with horse power, and next year he introduced it on the waggonway which he had built in 1818 to link Fawdon colliery (north-west of Newcastle and another enterprise rescued from the Harrison & Cooke failure) with shipping staiths at Scotswood. The best demonstration came with a new railway, the Brunton & Shields, designed from the outset to exploit reciprocating haulage. This originated as a joint venture by Thompson and William Harrison, who had been a partner in Harrison & Cooke and later promoted the Stanhope & Tyne Railway. The Brunton & Shields was being planned while Thompson was engaged in his early work for the N&C. Built during 1826, it came into 'full operation' at the start of 1827.[5] Nearly ten miles long, it linked Fawdon and Wideopen collieries with deep-water staiths at Whitehill Point, barely three miles short of the Tyne's mouth. Wagons travelled at a speed of 6 mph, and this performance much impressed two leading engineers, James Walker and John Urpeth Rastrick, when they looked at it in January 1829 on behalf of the Liverpool & Manchester Railway. As a result, they cautiously recommended using the 'reciprocating system' on the L&M, but the Rainhill Trials fortunately led to the adoption of locomotives instead.

Benjamin Thompson therefore came to the N&C project with a respectable pedigree as a railway designer, though none of his schemes had involved any appreciable civil engineering works. Chapman had the early ventures into the 'reciprocating system' in mind when he wrote his 1825 report, and was presumably quite happy to have Thompson take on the bulk of the work.

1825: The route evolves

Despite the demands of his other business ventures, Thompson got down to work quickly, and on 14 June 1825 reported that he had been with Chapman over the route from Newcastle as far as Brampton. As a result, he suggested various changes to Chapman's scheme. The most significant of these was his abandonment of the high-level route at the west end in favour of the one proposed by Jessop, dropping down the Irthing Valley to Carlisle. He also suggested a riverside route past Corbridge and Hexham instead of Chapman's higher and more southerly one. Following William Thomas's 1805 proposal, he advocated a double track line with overtaking loops.

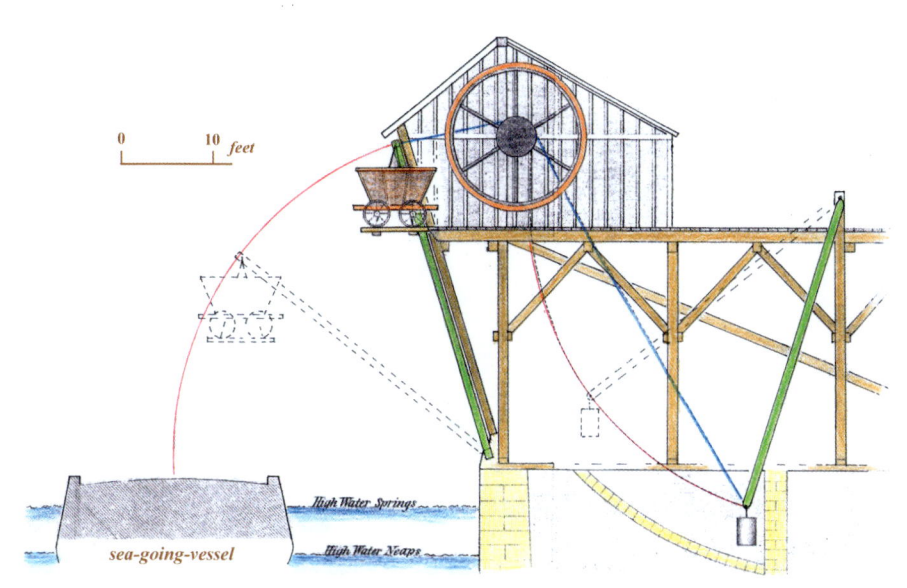

3.2. *Benjamin Thompson's second design of coal drop, brought into use at his Bewicke Main staith in August 1813. The red arcs show the trajectories of the pairs of swinging arms (shown green) from which are suspended the wagon and counterweights. These arms are linked by ropes (blue) to the brake wheel, which is shielded from the weather by a small cabin. (modified version of the drawing published in 1847 in 'Inventions, Improvements & Practice of Benjamin Thompson', a valedictory essay of his later years)*

William Chapman and Benjamin Thompson had a number of overlapping interests, including colliery railways and improved means for shipping coal from chaldron wagons into ships' holds. Traditionally, coal was discharged down chutes from staith to ship, breaking up some of the mineral into small coal which was of less value. In 1807 Chapman patented a 'coal drop', which allowed wagons to be lowered vertically down to the hold and then discharged, but this was evidently used only for a limited time at one staith. Thompson then devised his own coal drop, which lowered the wagon in an arc out across the ship. This came into use in August 1812 at the staith served by his Urpeth colliery railway. (Bewicke Main) 1813 brought a simplified design, illustrated here, which formed the basis for the coal drops widely used on the Tyne and Wear during the following decades.

3.3. *In revising Chapman's route, Benjamin Thompson endowed the Newcastle & Carlisle Railway with some notable riverside stretches, where it runs poised on a wall, high above the Tyne, though the means of engineering this had to be sorted out by Francis Giles, his successor. This is one of the celebrated series of engravings published in parts from 1836 to 1838 after drawings by the Tyneside artist John Wilson Carmichael (1800-68). It shows the railway following the south bank of the Tyne at Wylam, with the colliery (left) and ironworks on the far side. The ironworks was founded in 1836 by Benjamin Thompson and his sons George Annesley (c1808-1881) and Benjamin James (c1815-1900) to take advantage of the newly-opened railway, to which it was linked by rails laid on the Tyne bridge, seen in the distance, which was built at the same time. Thompson lived at Wylam Hall but the works was managed by his sons, as Thompson Brothers, and went on to build several locomotives for the N&C (see chapter 13). A recession at the start of the eighteen-forties led to the failure of the business, and the sons were declared bankrupt in February 1842, Benjamin following in May. George left the North East, but his father and brother found managerial posts in the industry. Indeed, for a time, Benjamin James was manager of the Walker Iron Foundry.*

Carmichael's depiction of the train owes something to imagination. Thus the N&C was not a pioneer of six-wheeled carriages, and its trains ran on the right-hand track, not the left.

By now it seems that the committee were beginning to lose patience with poor old Chapman. James Losh noted on 29 July 1825 that 'our engineer, W. Chapman (though I believe well acquainted with his profession) is by no means an effective person'. Chapman became increasingly sidelined, and when the Parliamentary plans for the railway were formally deposited on 30 November they bore Thompson's signature only.[6] The detailed surveys for these were carried out under his direction by an experienced pair of land surveyors: William Fryer (1788-1864), of Newcastle, and John Studholme (1787-1847), of Carlisle. Fryer conducted the survey from Newcastle to the summit, near Gilsland, and Studholme did the west end. The work was done in haste - though such surveys usually were - and, unfortunately, some of Fryer's levels proved to be wrong.[7]

3.4. *Part of the 1825 Deposited Plan, showing the main line's riverside route into Newcastle, together with the branch to Thornton Street, serving the upper town.*

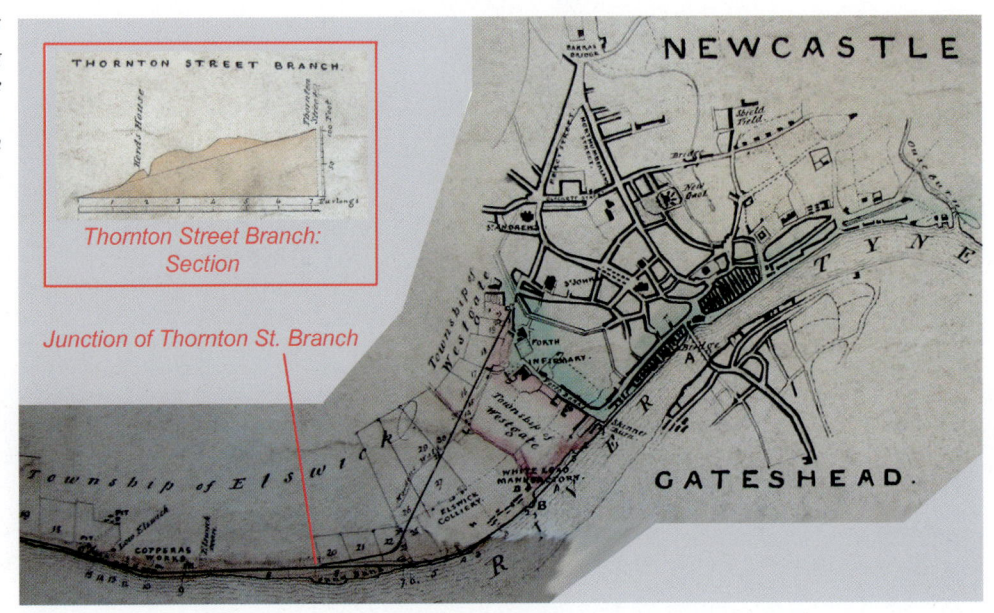

The deposited plans represent a further evolution from the route described by Thompson back in June, and substantial stretches correspond to the line as finally built. A major change was in the first Tyne crossing heading out of Newcastle, which had been moved east to Scotswood. This enabled the railway to serve the Beaumont lead refinery at Blaydon. The eastern terminus of the railway is significant: it was to begin on Newcastle Quay, immediately downstream of the 1781 Tyne Bridge, whose low arches were a barrier to sea-going shipping - though so indeed were the sandbanks of the undredged river itself. After passing under the bridge approach, the line was to be carried on a timber jetty in front of the Close, a major riverside street, west of which the company intended to build a lengthy stone quay to accommodate the railway and serve the river.[8] From here a steeply-graded branch was planned up to Thornton Street, to serve the upper part of town. This would require a stationary engine, but the gradients throughout the main line were such as to permit that to be worked by horses, the promoters having now decided against both 'reciprocating inclines' and locomotives.

3.5. *In June 1825 Thompson had been considering a Tyne crossing near Riding Mill, but the deposited plan moved it much further downstream to Scotswood. To accommodate the ironworks at Lemington, a branch line was proposed along the north bank from Scotswood. A Swalwell Branch was also planned, though shown as proceeding no further than the Derwent Bridge on the turnpike from Gateshead. Beaumont's lead refinery is shown on the river bank at the east end of Blaydon, which was then just a modest village.*

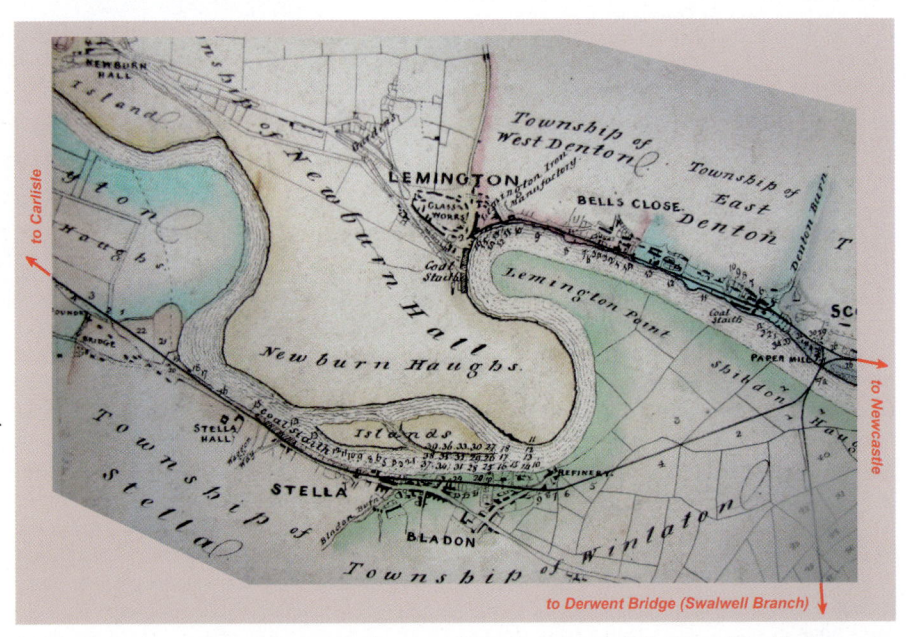

Other branches envisaged included a short one to convey goods to and from the centre of Hexham. Finally, there was a Brampton branch, which led the promoters into trouble with the Earl of Carlisle and must now be considered more closely.

26

3.6. *Shipping below the Tyne Bridge at Newcastle. Passing through the second arch, with its mast lowered, is one of the famous keels, which loaded coal at staiths upriver and trans-shipped it to seagoing vessels downstream. The railway would have finished just below the bridge, next to the Guildhall, which is facing us directly across the river. This was to give access to Newcastle Quay, but terminal facilities, such as warehouses, would have been sited upstream, where there was more (and cheaper) land available.*

3.7. *(below) Part of the deposited plan was drawn to a larger scale to show the railway in relation to the riverside. This reveals the land which would have been made up between the railway and the river bank. The stone quay would have stretched west from the foot of Forth Banks, with the wooden jetty to the east.*

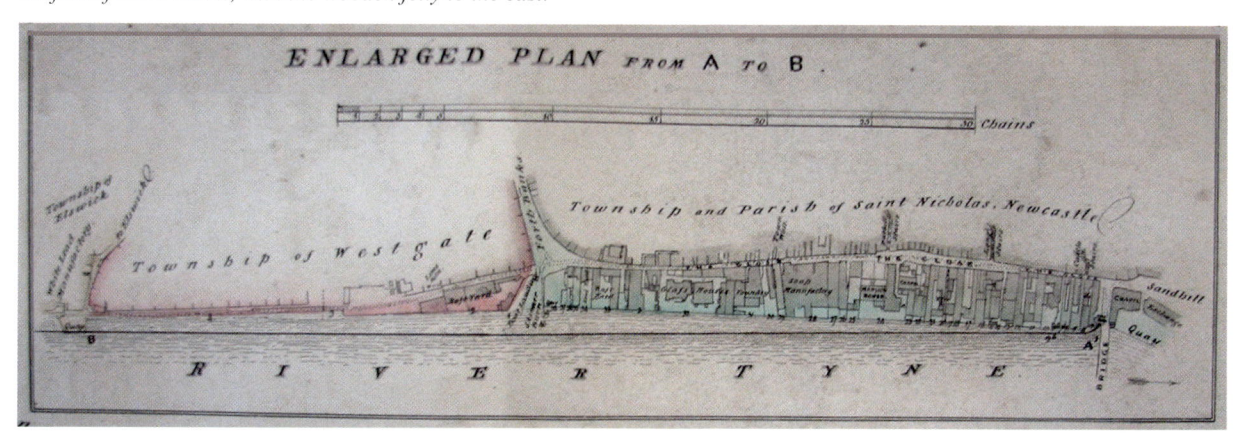

James Thompson and the Brampton Problem

The first railway to serve Brampton was not the Newcastle & Carlisle but the waggonway opened in 1799 from the Earl of Carlisle's collieries on Tindale Fell, about four miles south-east of the town.[9] In referring collectively to these pits it is convenient to adopt the North Eastern Railway's terminology of 'Kirkhouse colliery', Kirkhouse being the operational centre of the waggonway. From Brampton, coal could be conveyed along a fairly easy road to Carlisle. By contrast, coal from Blenkinsopp colliery (leased by the Earl of Carlisle) faced a longer journey over the watershed to reach the city. The Newcastle & Carlisle Railway would change all that, offering a much cheaper route from Blenkinsopp and removing the price advantage of Kirkhouse. This induced Colonel Coulson not to renew the Earl's lease of the Blenkinsopp mine, which ran until 1835, and to encourage the rival Blenkinsopp Coal & Lime Company, discussed in chapter 2. Coulson's intentions became public about 1827, and caused particular annoyance to James Thompson, the Earl's agent at Kirkhouse.

James Thompson (1794-1851) was a local man, who began work at Kirkhouse in 1808, succeeding as agent in 1819. He took great pride in the waggonway and its improvement, and as an engineer he was able and progressive, sharing George Stephenson's faith in the ultimate triumph of the steam locomotive. This would have made him impatient with Benjamin Thompson (no relation), who had no confidence in locomotives at this stage, and helps to explain his reluctance to seek an accommodation with the railway promoters.

One of James Thompson's early objectives was the extension of the Kirkhouse waggonway to Carlisle, something which he found hard to sell to successive Earls: Frederick (1748 - 4 September 1825, 5th Earl) and George (1773-1848, 6th Earl), and their chief adviser, the noted barrister-auditor James Loch.[10] Chapman's 1824 proposals brought the matter to a head, and Thompson prepared an ambitious plan, aimed at giving his employer a monopoly of rail transport west of the watershed. His idea was that the Earl should build a line from Carlisle via Brampton to Greenhead (near Blenkinsopp), where it could meet the proposed railway from Newcastle. Loch warmed to the idea but the Earl was very reluctant to take on the capital expenditure involved, and George Stephenson was invited to give a second opinion. George relished the opportunity, and sent his capable assistant, Joseph Locke, to survey the area.[11] Stephenson's 23 August 1824 report fully endorsed Thompson's scheme and pointed out that the stretch west from the summit, near Gilsland, to Carlisle could readily be worked by locomotives. He also stressed the threat to the Earl's coal monopoly posed by Chapman's proposal.

The Earl was not persuaded, and simply authorised a reconstruction and extension of his Kirkhouse waggonway. He was happy to let other promoters have the risk and expense of building a railway from Newcastle to Carlisle, so long as his interests were safeguarded. One of those interests was his country seat at Naworth Castle, about two miles east of Brampton. Any railway had to avoid encroaching on the Naworth parkland, which effectively blocked access to the town of Brampton. (Figure 3.8) Chapman's route skirted the south side of Naworth, which entailed keeping about five hundred feet above sea level and passing a mile and a half south-east of the town. Benjamin Thompson's route ran to the north of Naworth, following the River Irthing past Lanercost Priory at about 150 feet above sea level. This took the line a mile and a half north of Brampton and about 250 feet below the town.

The southerly route was preferable to James Thompson, as it would cross the Kirkhouse waggonway and provide the shortest route for coal to Carlisle. The northerly route was longer, with an incline 1.6 miles long at a gradient of 1 in 36 on the N&C Brampton branch. The Earl and Loch were not terribly perturbed by that prospect, but eventually allowed Thompson to call in George Stephenson for a second opinion. Reporting on 18 November 1825 he echoed Thompson's concerns and this helped to push the sixth Earl, who had succeeded to the title in September, into a state of less than benign neutrality towards the N&C project. Thus, when the N&C ran into difficulties with one of the landowners along the route of the Brampton branch, the Earl was persuaded to ignore their appeals for assistance in resolving the problem.

Meanwhile, trouble was brewing at the east end of the N&C route, where George Stephenson had made another unwelcome appearance. His assistant, Joseph Locke, had surveyed an alternative route for the main line east of Corbridge. It was later claimed that this had been done at the request of Greenwich Hospital, but this appears to be an instance of George being devious. Greenwich had already endorsed the N&C scheme; there is no record of any such survey in their minutes, and that stretch of the route did not involve any of their property.[12]

The only obvious beneficiaries from George Stephenson's east-end survey were two dissenting landowners - John Hodgson, of Elswick Hall, and Charles Bacon, of Styford, who objected to the line passing anywhere near their properties. Stephenson solved this by the same means as the Grand Old Duke of York: marching his men up the hill only to march them down again. His line climbed about two hundred feet up the north side of the Tyne Valley at Corbridge, with the aid of one stationary engine, only to climb back down again near Newcastle, accompanied by another.[13] The alleged benefit of this was that it gave access to the higher part of Newcastle. George also got Locke to check parts of the N&C survey, thereby revealing the errors in Fryer's levels, which prompted the well-known remark from Michael Longridge to Robert Stephenson: 'Your father has been employed by the persons who oppose this Railway and on examining the line has found greater errors in the levels than were made by his assistants in the Liverpool & Manchester road. Robert, my faith in engineers is wonderfully shaken!'[14] These defects might have enabled Hodgson and Bacon to have the Bill thrown out. Coupled with the problem at Brampton, this persuaded James Losh and his colleagues into a tactical withdrawal.

1826-8: Getting it Right

The Bill was withdrawn in February 1826, just as the Liverpool & Manchester was about to begin its successful passage through Parliament, which had to wait another three years for an opportunity of considering the N&C scheme. The big achievement of these apparently fallow years was to completely recast the route at the west end of the line so as to meet the demands of the Earl of Carlisle without antagonising other landowners in the process. The result was to bring the route back to a high-level alignment, in part that originally advocated by Chapman, and in the process to endow the railway with some of its most impressive, and costly, engineering features - notably the viaduct crossing the River Eden at Wetheral, the tall skew bridge over the River Gelt, and the very deep Cowran Cutting.

The revision of the west end route was not achieved without difficulty, and one feels that James Thompson was less than helpful. His ideas about railway alignments and making them suitable for locomotives, rather than horses, were entirely sound. The problem is that he often seems to have been more concerned to expand his own empire and frustrate the N&C project than to engage in a constructive dialogue. Had the promoters been able to get him on board and benefit from his undoubted expertise, the scheme might have got back to Parliament a year or two sooner. However, their condescending attitude towards him made this impractical.

The key to the Brampton impasse was the adoption of a line south of Naworth, though even this required several iterations before the alignment was finally resolved. With some relief, James Losh and his committee first approved a southern route in February 1827. This would have followed the present railway as far as Brampton Fell but then swung a little to its north in order to begin a gradual descent towards Carlisle. This took the line towards the village of Hayton and incurred the wrath of the local laird, Sir Hew Ross, whom it was going to be very expensive to placate. Benjamin Thompson then tinkered with an unsatisfactory compromise which cut west from Brampton Fell to rejoin the northerly alignment near the junction of the rivers Gelt and Irthing. The problem with this scheme was that it entailed a stationary engine to haul traffic over an intermediate summit. Naturally, Benjamin Thompson felt this to be no hardship and persuaded the promoters accordingly.

This took things to February 1828. James Thompson stood out against the compromise route with its incline and, fortunately, received full backing from James Loch and hence the Earl. He had prepared detailed proposals for a more southerly route, keeping further up towards the fells, and once again George Stephenson was turned to for a second opinion, which proved a full endorsement.[15] Having got nowhere with Sir Hew Ross, the N&C promoters finally adopted the idea on 8 April and John Studholme was despatched on a detailed survey.[16]

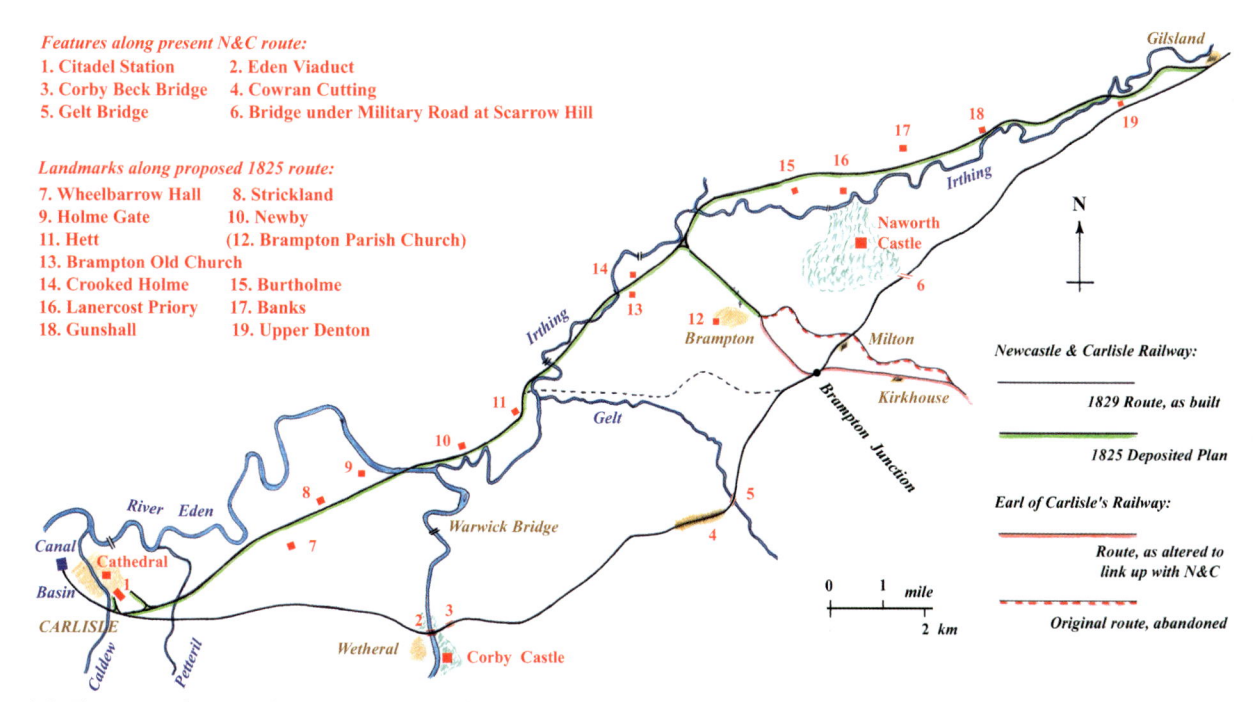

Features along present N&C route:
1. Citadel Station   2. Eden Viaduct
3. Corby Beck Bridge   4. Cowran Cutting
5. Gelt Bridge   6. Bridge under Military Road at Scarrow Hill

Landmarks along proposed 1825 route:
7. Wheelbarrow Hall   8. Strickland
9. Holme Gate   10. Newby
11. Hett   (12. Brampton Parish Church)
13. Brampton Old Church
14. Crooked Holme   15. Burtholme
16. Lanercost Priory   17. Banks
18. Gunshall   19. Upper Denton

3.8. *The west end routes of November 1825 and November 1828; the latter was approved by Parliament in 1829 and duly built. The 1825 route had an incline descending for 8 miles at 1/108 from Gilsland to the junction with the Brampton branch. The longest sustained gradient on the 1829 route is 4 miles at 1/107 west from Cowran Cutting. The broken line west from Brampton Junction is Benjamin Thompson's compromise route. (Bill Fawcett)*

Crucial to the successful adoption of this route was the attitude of Henry Howard of Corby Castle, since the line would now skirt the edge of his picturesque and locally-renowned gardens. Howard (1757 - 1842) was a distant kinsman of the Earl, both being descended from the late sixteenth-century Thomas Howard, Duke of Norfolk. Their attitudes were very different, however. Henry Howard belonged to the school of patriarchal but very public-spirited landowners, and was prepared to make some compromise of his own amenity for the public good. He therefore not only accepted the intrusion of the railway into his property, subject to certain safeguards, but on 17 April 1828 accepted the chair of the Carlisle promoters of the scheme and worked assiduously to secure the support of his fellow landowners.[17]

3.9. *Corby Castle gardens, tumbling down to the Eden. The Howards held open days, when the railway enabled people to make excursions from Carlisle to the gardens.*

A particular coup for Howard was to secure their former opponent Sir Hew Ross as a subscriber, his example then being used to encourage others.[18] One person with whom he made no early headway was the Earl, who, despite having the route tailored to meet his needs, continued to maintain a very frosty stance, bolstered by the prospect of maintaining his local coal monopoly should the project fail. Howard wrote in July 1828 that the Earl's objections 'will be the astonishment of the Whole County' and 'it would not be a very creditable thing in the eyes of the public that ... a disruption with Colonel Coulson ... should appear to be the motive of the rejection of this great undertaking'.[19] A *modus vivendi* was finally agreed at a meeting of Howard and the Earl on 19 August.[20]

The Parliamentary plans deposited in 1828 show only minor changes along the remainder of the route, compared with the 1825 scheme.[21] Objections were still raised by the lairds of Elswick and Styford, but otherwise the scheme enjoyed widespread support and stood little chance of failing in Parliament unless there were technical defects to be exploited. In fact there were, but these failed to frustrate the Bill.

Henry Howard, of Corby

Chapter 4: An Act and an Engineer

Passing through Parliament

The railway envisaged at the end of 1828 followed a route between Carlisle and Blaydon which, with minor deviations, is that of the present-day line. Its intended mode of operation, however, belongs to a quite different world. All along the promoters had envisaged it as a sort of turnpike road with rails, open to anyone whose vehicle met the company's standards. As a result, they decided to restrict its operation to horses, and clauses were voluntarily included in their Bill prohibiting the use of steam locomotives throughout the line and forbidding the construction of stationary steam engines in the vicinity of specific country houses, including Henry Howard's Corby Castle and T. W. Beaumont's Bywell Hall.

The locomotive clause has frequently been scoffed at as evidence of backwardness, yet it was a pragmatic response to their situation. William Chapman, with several locomotive designs to his credit, had originally proposed that either they or Benjamin Thompson's 'reciprocating' inclines be employed. However, neither option was terribly satisfactory for use on a route intended to be open to all comers, while horses posed no problem. It is instructive to recall that George Stephenson's Stockton & Darlington Railway originally used locomotives solely to haul the heavy coal and mineral trains. Goods and passenger traffic were handled by private contractors, using horses, and it was only in 1833 that the S&D took this business in hand and introduced steam traction throughout its main line.

At the beginning of 1829 the steam locomotive was still a somewhat awkward and unreliable machine, a situation which was to be transformed within two years, with Robert Stephenson's *Planet* of 1830 becoming the first engine to form the basis of a large and successful 'class' of locomotives. In the meantime the N&C's locomotive clause avoided one bone of contention with landowners at a time when the committee were still sore from their west-end struggle. Some members no doubt reasoned that a line built for horsepower would prove serviceable for locomotives, and if these improved and became widely accepted it would not be difficult to secure consent for their use. This is broadly what happened.

The N&C promoters and their opponents made extensive preparations for the Parliamentary contest. Both sought the assistance of George Harrison, who had done a notable job as counsel for the opponents of the Liverpool & Manchester Railway, and Messrs. Hodgson and Bacon got there first. They must have been put to considerable expense, having also engaged George Stephenson as their adviser. As a result evidence against the Bill was provided by the formidable trio of Robert Stephenson, Joseph Locke and John Dixon, who had been one of George's two resident engineers on the S&D and was now, like Locke, engaged on the Liverpool & Manchester.

Benjamin Thompson was at a tactical disadvantage in that his own railway ventures, including the Rainton & Seaham line then under construction for the Marquess of Londonderry, had not entailed any Parliamentary ordeals, being on land either owned by the railway proprietors or rented by them under wayleaves. Most of the preparation for the N&C was delegated to others, acting on his instructions. The plans and sections were prepared by John Studholme and Thomas Oswald Blackett (1790 - 1847), who had replaced the unfortunate William Fryer and had the recommendation of having surveyed part of the Liverpool & Manchester Railway. They calculated the earthworks, and estimated their cost, while Studholme also prepared traffic estimates. Test borings were carried out at some locations, notably by Blackett at the site of the Tyne bridges at Scotswood and Warden to find out how far down they would need to pile in order to reach rock.[1] The cost of all the bridges was then calculated by Studholme's father-in-law, the very experienced Carlisle contractor and architect Paul Nixson, who had built Sir Robert Smirke's bridge over the Eden there (1817).

Despite these generally thorough preparations, Thompson seems not to have appreciated that he would be faced with opponents hunting keenly for every possible weakness. Thus he took a remarkably *blasé* attitude towards the very real flood problem, choosing levels which presumably minimised the earthworks involved but put large stretches of the route at risk. He also seems not to have fully thought out the issue of bridge heights in relation to the railway levels, something which emerged all too painfully in relation to the Tyne crossing at Scotswood. There the ensuing error was conveniently attributed in Parliament to a misunderstanding with Blackett, who organised the copying of the deposited plans. However, these came back from the London lithographers on 10 November 1828, leaving plenty of time for Thompson to pick up any errors. In evidence, Blackett commented that Thompson was not 'so acquainted with the plans' as to be able to identify the error.[2] The truth seems to be that Thompson was very busy with other projects, was giving his services for nothing, and complacently assumed that James Losh and Henry Howard had done enough to ensure an easy passage through Parliament.

Losh and Howard had certainly done a lot. As early as April 1828 Howard had secured a commitment by Viscount Lowther, one of the Westmorland MP's and heir to the region's chief magnate - the Earl of Lonsdale - to 'take charge' of the Bill in the Commons.[3] Lowther was also a director of Greenwich Hospital. As the committee stage drew near, Losh marshalled his influential friends, writing on 6 February 1829, for instance, to Earl Grey.[4]

4.1. *The February 1829 estimates. Left: Benjamin Thompson's summary figures. Below: Paul Nixson's estimates for timber bridges over the Tyne, Tippalt, Petteril and Caldew.*

Outstanding issues with the Earl of Carlisle were resolved during March, resulting in clauses which gave him the nomination of three directors and an embargo on the railway providing coal depots within the Barony of Gilsland, from Low Row to just east of Corby; this protected his monopoly of coal sales in that area. The Bill was then examined by a House of Commons Committee, chaired by Lowther and sitting from 20 March to 1 April 1829. Local representatives on the committee included William Ord (1781-1855), of Whitfield Hall in Allendale, a cousin of the Brandling Brothers and MP for Morpeth. People like him were not slow to intervene in the questioning and, in Ord's case, even to supply some additional testimony. It can be presumed that several had already made up their minds in favour of the scheme.

Charles Bacon (1760 - 1830) and his son Charles Bacon Grey (1796 – 1855; he added the name Grey in compliance with an inheritance) were the railway's most implacable opponents. Bacon's house, Styford Hall, lay back from the north bank of the Tyne, but, in order to improve the view across the river, he had purchased a property on the south bank at The Riding, paying well over the odds to its previous owner, Anthony Surtees. Bacon was in the process of landscaping this site, through which the railway wished to pass, and he was in no way appeased by their offers to screen the line by forming a tree-clad mound between it and the river.[5] The Commons committee were not disposed to give him a veto over the project, but a clause was added stipulating that the railway had to be built exactly along the Parliamentary line, removing the 100 yards limit of permitted deviation either side of that line which otherwise applied. Another clause required the company to make the wooded mound already offered.

4.2. *Styford Hall, from the south bank of the Tyne. (Bill Fawcett)*

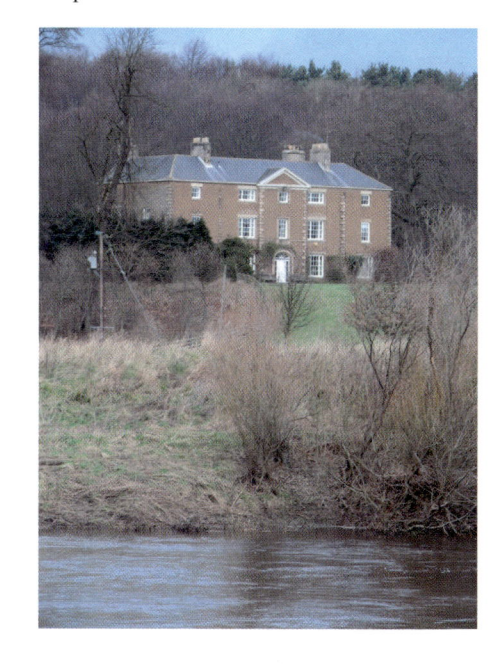

4.3. *Elswick Hall, designed by John Stokoe, was completed in 1803 for Hodgson's father. It was the heart of a large estate on the western edge of Newcastle. Hodgson sold the Elswick Estate to Richard Grainger, creator of a splendid new neo-classical town centre. Grainger developed parts of the estate but kept the Hall and its immediate grounds for his residence. This portion later became a public park but Newcastle Corporation allowed the Hall to become derelict, and it was demolished in 1977.*
(engraving published 1827 in Eneas Mackenzie's history of Newcastle.)

John Hodgson's objections were more commercial. His home, Elswick Hall, was a fine neo-classical villa standing just west of Newcastle, with grounds sweeping down to the Tyne. The railway would be completely out of site from the Hall and its lawns, and his objection was rooted in a wish to develop the riverside property for middle-class housing. This would have been a plausible claim were it not that his riverside tenants already included a colliery, a lead works and a bleach factory.[6] The committee therefore gave no weight to that but did accept his concerns about the Thornton Street branch, most of which ran through his land in an area eminently suitable for villa development. A clause was therefore added making the construction of that branch conditional on his consent.

The main points made by the opposition counsel, Harrison, against the Bill were the vulnerability of the line to flooding and problems relating to Scotswood Bridge. He fielded Stephenson's team, who readily established that between ten and fifteen miles of the route might be awash during serious floods. However, the committee evidently felt that this could be addressed by altering the levels and alignment within the Parliamentary limits of deviation, so no change was made other than the insertion of a clause specifying that the South Tyne bridge near Warden (west of Hexham) should have a clearance of twenty-two feet above 'Summer Water Level'.

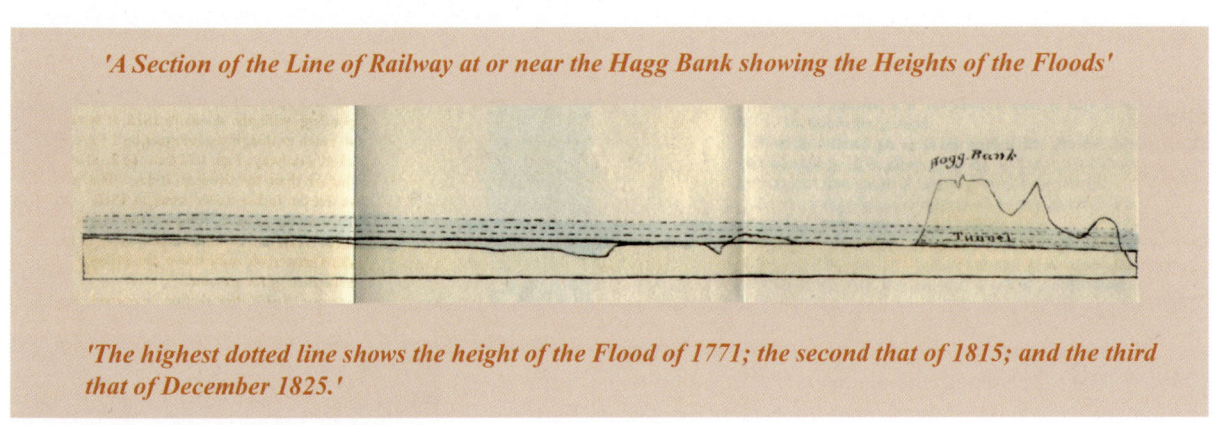

'A Section of the Line of Railway at or near the Hagg Bank showing the Heights of the Floods'

'The highest dotted line shows the height of the Flood of 1771; the second that of 1815; and the third that of December 1825.'

4.4. *Evidence by Joshua Richardson showing the flood levels in relation to the railway between Prudhoe Haugh (left: GR103642) and the proposed tunnel at Hagg Bank (right: GR110643). The 1815 flood would have covered the railway to a depth of almost nine feet at the proposed tunnel. (from William Boag: volume of Commons Evidence, pub. Newcastle, 1829)*

Scotswood Bridge was an altogether more tricky issue, raising questions as to Thompson's competence and his veracity as a witness. Two bridges were currently proposed there: one for the railway and another for the new road being promoted from Newcastle to Blaydon, later known as Scotswood Road. The road party planned a suspension bridge, designed by the Newcastle architect John Green on the principles established by Sir Samuel Brown. Discussions had taken place between both sets of promoters and between Green and Thompson as to whether they might combine in a single bridge, but the two schemes proved incompatible, partly because Thompson allegedly claimed that the level of Green's bridge - 17 feet 6 inches above high water - was too high.[7] Thompson apparently said that the railway would have to cross the Tyne at an elevation of only 6 feet 6 inches above high tide, in order to maintain satisfactory levels. Green pointed out that this would not provide adequate clearance for the keels: the sailing vessels which took coal downriver to the deepwater shipping berths. Thompson responded by saying that they could sail at half tide, but as the creator of Fawdon colliery's coal-shipping staith at Scotswood he must have known this was nonsense, since keels had to set off within a couple of hours of high tide to be sure of clearing sandbanks further down river.[8]

4.5. *John Hodgson (1806-1869) became master of Elswick at 21 and soon became the leading promoter of a new road from Newcastle to Blaydon, linking with the turnpike to Dilston Bar and Hexham. As well as improving access to the west, the road would open up the lower part of his estate for lucrative development. Hence, in part, Hodgson's opposition to the railway. Only a few years later, because of interests downriver, he was heavily involved in promoting the Newcastle & North Shields Railway and became its deputy chairman. Of his two brothers, Richard (born 1812) became a notorious chairman of the North British Railway and the staunchest opponent of the merger between the Newcastle & Carlisle and North Eastern Railways. In 1836 John Hodgson became Hodgson-Hinde, in compliance with the terms of an inheritance. Brother Richard, in 1870, disguised himself with his mother's name, becoming Hodgson-Huntley.*

This difference became public at a meeting of the two sets of promoters on 15 November 1828, and John Clayton, Newcastle's town clerk and the N&C's chief legal adviser, had immediately recognised the harm this could inflict on the railway scheme, if it was seen as an obstacle to navigation.[9] On 19 November Clayton wrote a letter to the road-bridge party saying that Green had been misinformed and Thompson intended to cross the river at a height of nineteen feet. A comparable figure was subsequently used in a sketch provided to enable Paul Nixson to estimate the cost of the railway bridge, yet the sections placed before Parliament showed a railway level of only 6 feet 6 inches, the claim being made that a pencil line which showed the greater bridge height had been inadvertently rubbed off before the plans were despatched for lithographing.[10]

This gave rise to the following exchange in the Commons committee as Thompson was questioned by Harrison:[11]

Do you mean to state, that the level of your railroad, as you approach the river, is consistent with the height you have given of the bridge ? - *The bridge will be higher than the line of the railroad.*

Shall you have an inclined plane over it ? - *Yes.*

Is the inclined plane laid down ? [i.e. on the section] - *No.*

Do you mean to say that you have laid a correct section of the line, if you are obliged to interpose an inclined plane, inclined both ways, which is not in the section ? - *I laid it down in the original plan and section, but it is not in the present plan.*

How comes it not to be in the present plan ? - *I am scarcely able to say.*

Thompson in fact intended to keep the line from Newcastle at the level of the quayside until nearing Scotswood, and then approach the bridge on a gradient of 1 in 144. To minimise the rise, the bridge was conceived as a shallow timber 'platform', stiffened by deep trussed parapets and borne on stone piers. To his credit, Thompson had realised, and pointed out to Green, that a suspension bridge was unsuitable for railway use - on account of the 'undulation that would take place, by the waggons passing over it'.[12] This was something which the Stockton & Darlington, then building a similar suspension bridge to carry its Middlesbrough branch over the Tees, had yet to realise - the hard way.

4.6. *John Green's 'Chain Bridge' at Scotswood.*
The promoters were in Parliament at the same time as the N&C, and obtained their Act on 13 April 1829. The first stone of the south abutment was laid on 21 July 1829, and the bridge was opened with great ceremony on 12 April 1831. A clause was included in the first N&C Act to protect the interests of the Scotswood company by preventing pedestrians and road vehicles from using the railway bridge planned there. Scotswood Bridge had a span of 370 feet, and latterly carried heavy traffic such as John Green could never have dreamed of. In 1967 the present bridge was opened and the old one, which could easily have been retained for pedestrians, was swiftly and thoughtlessly demolished.

(sketch from Smiths Dock Journal, *No. 74, 1929)*

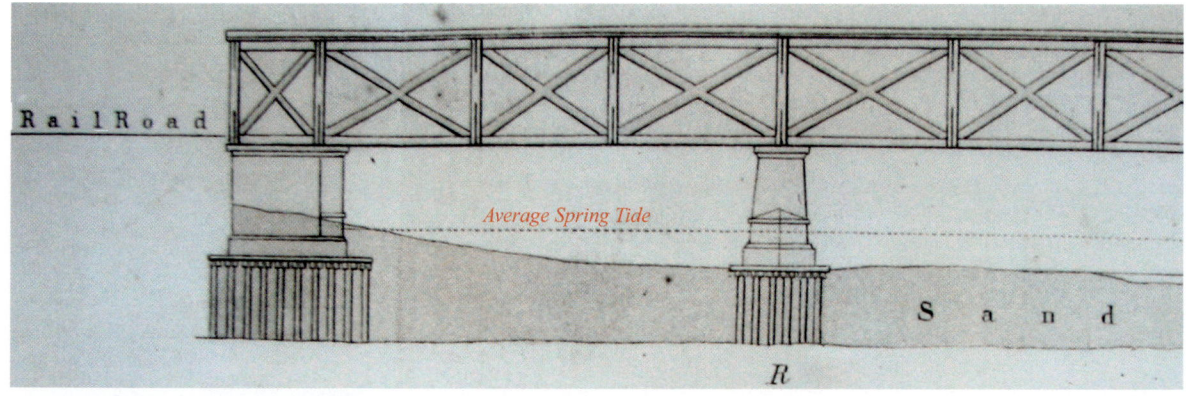

4.7. Benjamin Thompson's design for the railway bridge at Scotswood.

After questioning many witnesses about Scotswood Bridge, the committee were content with an additional clause stipulating that it must have a 'clear height of nineteen feet above flood in ordinary Spring tides'. George Stephenson must have enjoyed this episode. He had no time for Thompson, and his aversion to steam locomotives. Indeed, he seems to have held a grudge against the N&C directors for overlooking his own talents when it came to building a railway so near to his own birthplace at Wylam. They had a laugh in store, however, when Joseph Locke was called on to give evidence in support of George's up and down-hill alternative route east of Corbridge, with its two stationary engines. Locke was a very able witness, but he was called on to defend the indefensible and, surprisingly, it was the committee members who really tore into him, administering the *coup de grace* with the exchange:

Committee: Which would be the greater inconvenience to encounter, two inclined planes every day or to have the railroad flooded twice a year ?

Locke (after some prevarication): *I think the inconvenience, altogether, would be greater upon an inclined plane.*

So, despite shortcomings in Benjamin Thompson's plan and performance, the Newcastle & Carlisle Railway Bill passed its Commons committee stage by a majority of 16 to 2. William Chapman was there to see it, but evidently played no part. The opposition made a last bid by securing a further report by another well-respected engineer, George Leather, which attacked Thompson's costings and ridiculed the practicality of some of his riverside route.[13] This proved a waste of money, and the Bill got its Commons third reading on 1 May, passing smoothly through the Lords to receive the royal assent on 22 May 1829. Now the real work had to begin.

Acquiring an Engineer

The promoters left Parliament victorious but somewhat bruised, and realising that they needed to reassure investors as to the scheme's practicability and cost. To achieve this they had already sought a report from another civil engineer, Francis Giles (1787 - 1847), who was particularly noted for the quality of his surveys. Giles had a detailed look at the east end of the route during 4 - 7 May 1829 in the company of Thompson and some of the committee.[14] He then returned to London while his assistants examined the remainder of the line. The outcome was a report, dated 29 May, which met the promoters' needs perfectly, confirming both route and costs. The committee had already decided to aim first for the completion of the stages at either end: Haydon Bridge to Newcastle and Blenkinsopp to Carlisle, and Giles suggested that if a start was made in the present summer these portions might be 'fully formed and rendered quite fit to receive the railway' by the end of 1831. Giles was then asked to prepare a more detailed report and estimates for the first general meeting of proprietors of the incorporated company on 19 August 1829. He arrived in Carlisle a week beforehand, and walked the route, paying particular attention to the scale and nature of the bridges required. The ensuing report continued to endorse Thompson's judgment, with some modest amendments to the alignment, principally to alleviate the flood problem. Its detailed estimates conveniently gave a total, inclusive of land purchase, of just under £300,000 (the share capital authorised by Parliament). Giles gave a timetable for construction, which forecast completion in 1832.[15] In this he differed wildly from Thompson, whose estimate of eight years to finish the work was to prove just about right, though for financial rather than engineering reasons.

Meanwhile, James Losh and his colleagues were tackling the subscription list. Parliamentary rules specified that the £300,000 authorised capital had to be fully subscribed (though only the deposit actually paid up) before the powers of the Act came into force. At the time of the royal assent subscriptions totalled only £241,700, but the deficiency was met for the time being by Losh, the Crawhalls and other directors at the meeting on 19 August, where Giles put his name down for twenty shares and they increased their holdings.[16] This hurdle cleared, the shareholders adjourned until 16 October, when they elected the 'House list' of directors - i.e. those proposed by and largely comprising the outgoing committee.[17] Afterwards, the bulk of the Board enjoyed a well-earned celebration dinner.

The search continued for further investors and also for an engineer to supervise construction. Francis Giles had only been drawn in as adviser, and, despite his twenty shares, the options remained open. James Loch, nominated to the N&C Board by the Earl of Carlisle, was a director of the Liverpool & Manchester Railway, and he advocated engaging George Stephenson as N&C engineer.[18] Loch offered to act as intermediary and argued that Stephenson's name would attract Liverpool investors to the scheme. This did not appeal to the bulk of his fellow directors, who decided to seek a 'Working Engineer' who could be relied upon to give his full time to the company. On the face of it, this should have ruled out the already busy Giles; in practice it did not. On 8 December an advertisement was approved seeking such a person and inviting candidates to submit a statement of 'their pretensions and terms' by the 26th. Three days later, on the 29th, the directors considered a list of eight candidates, which included Giles, Thomas Storey, Peter Nicholson, and a comparatively unknown young man of 23 called Isambard Kingdom Brunel.[19]

A choice was finally made on 8 January 1830. The directors noted that Storey, who offered his services at £600 a year, was precluded from working more than three days a week by his engagement with the Stockton & Darlington, for whom he served as Engineer in Chief. This ruled him out, which was fortunate, since his talents were rather limited and did not extend to handling capably the major bridges and river walls along the proposed line. Brunel came with the recommendation of the Earl of Lonsdale and a readiness to devote his whole time to the venture for £500 a year plus up to £200 expenses. He met the directors and caught the imagination of several, including James Losh, however caution prevailed and Giles was selected. Losh noted 'Of Giles individually I have a good opinion and I really hope that if we have a good active working Committee, he may answer our purpose very well. I cannot help thinking, however, that his election was secured by a species of manoeuvring and that there is some danger of his being too much connected with a party amongst the directors. The rival candidate, Mr. Brunel [he was their second choice], appeared to me an intelligent and active young man and I preferred him because he would have given us his whole time and attention.' [20]

'Time and attention' were to prove a problem for Giles. His terms of appointment specified a salary of £700 to cover himself and his 'Principal Assistant', the latter to be 'constantly resident on the Work'. This sum covered all expenses, including plans and working drawings, while it was agreed that if he also chose to employ his pupils on the line (as he duly did) that must be at no expense to the company.[21] An area which was not clearly specified, and proved a bone of contention between Giles and the company, was the position of the surveyors - Blackett and Studholme - who went on to do further detailed survey and valuation work under his direction. He felt they should be paid by the company, while the directors took the opposite view.

Giles signified his acceptance in a letter of 11 January, which also said that he would 'devote as much time to them personally as will be satisfactory to the Directors.' Things did not work out quite like that, and he only served as their 'Operative' engineer for three years, after which he was retained as consultant, but rarely consulted. One should not underestimate his achievement, however. The works he initiated for the railway have proved extremely durable - more so than many later railway structures - and testify to the quality of both design and supervision. The latter was largely the responsibility of John Blackmore (1801 - 1844), sent up as Giles's principal assistant, employed as operative engineer after the breach in relations, and eventually serving as a very capable Engineer in Chief.

Francis Giles: A Biographical Sketch

At the time of his appointment, Giles was 42 and enjoyed a considerable reputation as a surveyor, but his experience as a 'constructive' engineer had been confined to much smaller enterprises than the N&C. He was born on 10 October 1787 at Walton on Thames, and was trained in surveying by his brother Netlam (1775-1816), whose partner he duly became.[22] The brothers were regularly engaged by the elder John Rennie (1761-1821) to conduct surveys in connection with canals, harbours and coastal works but after Rennie's death Francis Giles embarked on a more independent career as civil engineer and surveyor. Despite this he continued to do work occasionally for Rennie's second son, Sir John (1794-1874), who had been Giles's assistant, learning the ropes, during a notable survey of the Galloway and Antrim coasts in 1814 intended to identify harbour sites for the Irish traffic.[23]

Francis Giles's earliest independent engineering work is probably the River Ivel Navigation in Bedfordshire.[24] The river was canalised in 1757-8 from its junction with the Great Ouse, at Tempsford, as far as Biggleswade. In 1819 the navigation trust adopted Giles's plan for a six-mile extension from Biggleswade to Shefford, and construction began in Autumn 1822, opening to traffic in December 1823. This involved significant lengths of new cut to bypass the river meanders, while Giles also rebuilt the flash locks on the old navigation as modern pound locks. The clients were clearly satisfied, for in 1825 he was given the post of County Surveyor to Bedfordshire.

Other works of the eighteen-twenties included Bridport Harbour and two sea walls: the North Bull Wall on the approach to Dublin, in collaboration with the Dublin Port Engineer, George Halpin, and the Leasowe embankment at the north end of the Wirral, on the approach to Liverpool. These will have provided a sound background for the river walls encountered on the N&C.

Another canal of this period was the Hertford Union - a short but strategic East London link between the Regent's Canal and Lea Navigation, built in 1829-30. This gave canal traffic from the Midlands access to the Thames downstream of its big loop round the Isle of Dogs. Like the Ivel Navigation it was graced by neat cast-iron overbridges but its significance to us is that the work was apparently supervised by Giles's principal assistant - John Blackmore, soon to be despatched north to take care of the Newcastle & Carlisle. More canal and harbour works were to follow during the eighteen-thirties and forties.

4.8. *(right) Ivel Navigation: bridge and lock chamber on Giles's extension at Holme, a mile south of Biggleswade. Railway competition killed the navigation, which was abandoned in the 1870s. Holme has a weir in place of the upper lock gate, and the bridge has lost its decorative railings and gained extra brick support. Nonetheless, it is one of the best surviving sites. The roadway was built up on iron plates, resting on the bottom flanges of the cast-iron beams.* (Bill Fawcett, 2007)

4.9. *Hertford Union Canal: Bridge at Gun Lane, looking east.*
4.10. *(right) Detail of bridge at foot of lock near Parnell Road, with five arch ribs secured by a pair of tie rods.* (Bill Fawcett, 2007)

Giles's reputation as a surveyor led to his involvement with various railway schemes, sometimes for the promoters, sometimes for their opponents, as with the Liverpool & Manchester Railway. He has attracted unmerited scorn for his Parliamentary evidence in 1825 against George Stephenson's proposals to build the L & M across Chat Moss. What critics ignore is that this was not impartial advice. Giles was paid by the Bill's opponents to survey the route and to seek out and exaggerate any possible weakness in George's plan, just like any 'expert witness' at the present day. Stephenson, understandably, never forgave Giles's remark that 'no engineer in his senses would go through Chat Moss'. Giles himself was the target of George's equally dubious evidence when it came to the 1834 Bill for the London & Southampton Railway (L&S), for which Giles provided a good, economical and gently graded route. He oversaw the early stages of building the L&S, but problems which we shall explore later led to his withdrawal from both this and the N&C. However, the related scheme for the first Southampton Dock retained Giles as engineer, though it was largely completed by his son Alfred (1816-95), one of several children of his marriage on 14 April 1814 to Mary Anne Wyer.

The last railway to be started under Francis Giles's direction was the Reading, Guildford & Reigate Railway (RGRR).[25] He was appointed Engineer in Chief in September 1845 and shortly afterwards agreed to have Robert Stephenson associated with him as consultant. This was convenient as Stephenson was Engineer to the South Eastern Railway, with which the RGRR were already holding discussions as potential lessees. Unfortunately, just before he was due to give evidence on the RGRR Bill, at the end of April 1846, Giles was struck by a fit, from which he never fully recovered. The company got their Act in July and Alfred Giles stood in for his father at meetings until Francis' death on 4 March 1847 at his home in London's Adelphi Terrace. Robert Stephenson then took over as Engineer in Chief, with Alfred managing the works as before. At the start of 1848, however, Robert stepped down from the SER because of heavy commitments elsewhere. He strongly urged the Reigate directors to keep Giles in charge of the works, but Alfred was dispensed with as an economy and the new SER Engineer Peter William Barlow took them in hand. It is a credit to Francis that the Reigate line was built almost within his budget and that Alfred went on to a distinguished career, including a term as President of the Institution of Civil Engineers. Of all Francis Giles's works the Newcastle & Carlisle Railway remains his most distinctive achievement.

Francis Giles's early visits to the Newcastle & Carlisle route.

We have a word portrait of Giles's visits to Tyneside in May and August 1829 thanks to the journal kept by Joseph Hekekyan, a young Egyptian who had been sent to Britain to get a training in engineering and was attached to Giles during this period.[26] Coming from a Catholic family, Hekekyan completed his education at Stoneyhurst College in Lancashire and was therefore fluent in English language and customs. His journal conveys a vivid picture of the logistical problems involved in managing a number of works spread around the country during the pre-railway age, and may give us some sympathy for Giles when we encounter the N&C directors' later complaints about the infrequency of his visits.

The May trip was Giles's first look at the route, although he had some familiarity with the area, having done surveys of the lower Tyne and Wear for the elder Rennie. On the way several days were spent in Lincolnshire surveying the Ancholme Drainage and Navigation for (Sir) John Rennie. They went on to Gainsborough and posted during the early morning of 3 May to Bawtry. Having breakfasted there, they picked up the *Rockingham* coach to Wentbridge, where Giles had business with the quarry and its railway. After dining at Wentbridge, they took the coach to York, boarded the *Edinburgh Mail* and arrived at Newcastle at 3 a.m. on 4 May. After just a few hours sleep at the *Queen's Head* they met Benjamin Thompson and walked up the south bank of the Tyne along the proposed route as far as Prudhoe, then doubled back to Wylam where a post-chaise had been ordered to take them back to Newcastle.

Next day they further examined the stretch west of Wylam with Thompson and spent the night at Hexham, where they dined with Colonel Coulson, while the following day was again spent on the route east of Hexham. At issue were the flood risk and the tunnel at Hagg Bank, eventually dealt with by adopting Giles's suggestion of a higher alignment and a cutting in place of the tunnel. On 7 May Giles left by the *Mail* for Wentbridge and London, but Hekekyan and an un-named Giles assistant looked at a proposed north bank branch to Lemington ironworks and were then shown round Thompson's collieries and 'beautiful rail-roads'. After some local sightseeing, Hekekyan resumed work on 11 May, walking the route from Haydon Bridge to Glenwhelt (Greenhead) on 11 May and the remainder to Carlisle the following day. The upshot of all this was Giles's brief report of 29 May.

The August visit began with a *Mail* journey from London to Liverpool, starting at 8 p.m. on 8 August and arriving at 6 p.m. the following day, a rate of progress which the young Egyptian thought remarkably good. Ferry and coach took them to Leasowe Castle, which was their base for inspecting progress with Giles's Mersey embankment. On 11 August they took the 4.30 p.m. *Mail* from Liverpool to Preston, where they changed coaches and eventually arrived in Carlisle, 120 miles from Liverpool, in just twelve hours.

The idea was to walk the whole route to Newcastle and determine, in particular, the scale of the underbridges required for streams and rivers. Wind and rain delayed their departure, but on the 13th they set out, despite the weather, and got as far as Gilsland before doubling back to a Brampton inn for the night. There they dined well off 'cod's head and shoulder, roast leg of mutton, roast leg of pork, two boiled fowls, a brace of moor game, apple and jam pastry and a fine list of wines.' Thus fortified, they were able to cope with even heavier rain the following day, when walking to Hexham. In one sense the rain was a blessing since it gave them an opportunity to see the streams in spate, and on route 'we measured every burn and ascertained the heights of the different floods from the neighbouring inhabitants.' Hopefully Hekekyan gave little hint of his view that 'the women are very ugly and their families are filthy - pigs are allowed to live in the same room they live in.' Next day they continued in heavy rain and were unable to use the ford at Stocksfield, where T. W. Beaumont had yet to build the present Tyne bridge. Monday 17th was spent in their hotel at Newcastle calculating quantities and making a fair copy of their report, work which spilled over into the following morning, though the afternoon was spent in a trip down the Tyne followed by dinner at John Clayton's house.

Clayton prepared a 'faithful abstract' of Giles's report, which went down well at the shareholders' meeting on August 19. Afterwards there was no rest for the engineer and his assistants, who took the 9.30 p.m. *Mail* to York, arriving there in nine hours despite roads which were in places 'covered with water up to the horses' bellies.' With forty minutes to wash and breakfast, they continued to Wentbridge for a brief look at the quarries and to dine before taking a coach and four to Tempsford, at the foot of the Ivel Navigation. A boat took them to Biggleswade, from which they walked Giles's extension to Shefford and then a coach took them on to London, arriving at 10.30 p.m. on the 20th.

Chapter 5: Underway at Last

Getting Started

Looking at the early years of the N&C, one is struck by the sluggishness with which the directors proceeded. It took them four years, from 1825 to 1829, to obtain their Act; seven months then passed before appointing Francis Giles to supervise construction; even then 1830 was to drift by with little progress evident on the ground. By contrast, fifteen years later George Hudson was to have the 40-mile York - Scarborough line built within a year of its Act. The comparison is, of course, unfair. By 1844 railway building was a familiar activity; Hudson's York & North Midland was a highly profitable company which had no trouble raising money, and their Scarborough branch was very easy to build. Nonetheless it is a reminder of what could be achieved, given a strong enough will. A fairer comparison is with the Liverpool & Manchester Railway, which got its Act on 5 May 1826 and appointed George Stephenson engineer within two months. Construction began within weeks and the thirty-mile route was completed in a further four years.

Giles got his orders at a planning meeting on 19 March 1830, which asked him to review the whole line and the levels, report on any improvements he deemed expedient, and suggest where to start.[1] The directors had long ago agreed to start work simultaneously at both ends, and now clarified this by saying they wished to begin by building ten miles at each end and wanted Giles to consider which stretches were expedient and most productive. Commercial logic suggested they should proceed with the sections from Hexham to Blaydon, for the lead traffic, and Blenkinsopp to Carlisle, for the western coal traffic, but these also entailed many of the major engineering works, such as the great west-end bridges and the Eltringham and Wylam river walls. The same meeting authorised a modest call on shareholders, making a total of just five pounds per £100 share, inclusive of any deposit or call already paid.

Supervising Giles were two committees, one at either end. The Newcastle construction committee was set up on 29 January 1830 and initially comprised just five directors: Alfred Hall, William Losh, Thomas Richard Batson, Thomas Crawhall and William Woods, though their numbers were soon augmented.[2] They met weekly, and the boundary of responsibility with the Carlisle committee was set at Ridley Hall bridge, between Bardon Mill and Haydon Bridge. The Carlisle minutes were regularly considered by the Newcastle committee, which from time to time disbursed funds to their Carlisle colleagues from the company's account at Sir Matthew White Ridley's bank.

The Carlisle committee got going earlier and showed more determination to actually proceed with building the line. It met for the first time on 4 November 1829, with Henry Howard in the chair, and drew in such prominent local directors as the Dixons, the Forsters and Colonel Coulson, as well as a leading Carlisle solicitor, George Gill Mounsey, who was one of the Earl of Carlisle's three Board nominees.[3] Another lawyer, William Nanson, was appointed Secretary, and his £105 salary included the use of his office for their meetings, while his staff kept the committee's books. Nanson (c1792 - 1868) was an ideal choice. Town clerk of Carlisle from 1818 to 1847, when the post passed to his son John, he had already served as an energetic Secretary to the Carlisle Canal Company. One of his staff was a young man called Richard Lowry, who found himself looking after the Carlisle Committee's accounts and, with Nanson's blessing, joined the railway when its west end opened in 1836. Lowry served the railway for over half a century and kept a diary throughout, which we shall have recourse to quite often in subsequent pages.[4]

Since there was no uncertainty over the west end route, the Carlisle committee was able to make an early start, doing so formally on 25 March 1830, when Henry Howard laid the first stone of the Eden Viaduct - the most ambitious of the railway's engineering works and one built entirely on his property in Wetheral and Corby.[5] Nothing much happened then until 22 April, when Giles's assistant, the twenty-eight year old John Blackmore, made his first appearance in Carlisle.[6] Within a couple of days he was making a trial opening of a quarry at Wetheral, the directors having agreed that Giles could employ direct labour in building the west abutment of the viaduct to provide an opportunity for trying out the local sandstone.[7] Giles established a good relationship with the Carlisle committee, most of whom did not see themselves as experts in colliery waggonways and were therefore prepared to accept his professional advice more readily than their counterparts at the east end. Giles's actual appearances were few and far between, but Blackmore proved an experienced, able and hard-working deputy, who soon made himself at home and indeed married into the Nixson contracting family of Carlisle.

Things progressed more slowly at the east end, where Thomas Oswald Blackett was engaged in a resurvey at a fee of a guinea a day plus expenses. By mid April 1830 he had completed the stretch from Eltringham to Wylam, just over three miles, and was continuing east towards Blaydon.[8] With accurate data in hand Giles now proposed alterations in the line to reduce the flood risk. Thus from Blaydon to Crawcrook he suggested raising it to the level of the 1815 flood but met with a short-sighted and timid response from the Newcastle committee, who felt it would be better to adhere to the Parliamentary level, apparently to avoid trouble with landowners.[9] Eventually Giles won his point, but he had to go through similar trials in respect of an improved alignment at Prudhoe Haughs, where the landowners were Hugh, third Duke of Northumberland, and his brother Algernon, Lord Prudhoe (later fourth Duke). Though the Duke favoured the railway, his agents raised some problems over the changes and Giles had to argue the necessity for these with his directors.[10]

Giles also made a rod for his own back by proposing a change in the east-end route, which would have required a second Act. Two aspects of the Parliamentary line had been criticised by various parties. One was the route from Blaydon to Newcastle, with some people feeling that it would be better to continue along the south bank of the Tyne to a point downstream of Newcastle's Tyne Bridge; Giles did not take this up but it was to become a serious issue. The other was the

5.1. *The Eden Viaduct. On 16 July 1836, with the west end opening due in three days time, the 'Cumberland Pacquet' carried an advertisement for Matthew Nutter's view of the bridge, available as an uncoloured engraving for three shillings or the coloured version, seen here, for 4s 6d. The view is from the north, with Wetheral Mill in the foreground and the woodland of Corby Castle clothing the far bank. Built by William Smith Denton, the bridge was completed in August 1834, although delays with the remainder of the route delayed its opening to public trains for two years. Meanwhile it was used by another contractor, George Grahamsley, for the movement of spoil and materials along a temporary railway. With five arches of 80 feet span and 93 feet height, it was briefly one of the most impressive railway bridges anywhere. The Liverpool & Manchester Railway's Sankey Viaduct, opened in 1830, is about 100 feet longer, but with arches of only 50 feet span.* (J. M. Fleming collection)

Scotswood bridge, with various people arguing that the line should revert to Chapman's 1824 proposal and cross the river further upstream. Giles had first backed this idea in a report of 11 September 1829, when he was acting simply as consultant.[11] He suggested continuing the line from Newcastle along the north bank of the Tyne through Lemington and as far as Cat House, near Ryton, where it would cross the river to rejoin the Parliamentary route. He argued that the Lemington route would be cheaper and better than that through Blaydon, partly because a Tyne bridge upstream of the limit of navigation need not be so high as one at Scotswood.

Giles reported again on the comparative merits of the Blaydon and Lemington routes in June 1830, arguing that the latter would cost £10,000 less to build and be more satisfactory.[12] 'The obstruction to the navigation of the river, and the wear and tear of an expensive bridge at Scotswood, will be avoided by adopting the Lemington line. The effect of that wear and tear must be a continuing expense to the company; for in consequence of the badness of the foundation it will be necessary to construct the piers of Scotswood bridge of wood piles, and however they may be protected, they must unavoidably be injured by the bodies of ice carried up and down the river by each reflux and influx of the tide.' Such problems were avoided by John Green, whose Scotswood suspension bridge - opened on 12 April 1831 - employed towers founded at the river's edge.

Giles's arguments had some engineering validity, and the railway's Scotswood bridge was indeed to prove an annoyance to navigation though not an obstruction. However, he overlooked the commercial and political realities. Some directors backed him, John Clayton for instance, but T. W. Beaumont and the Crawhalls required the railway to serve the Beaumont lead refinery at Blaydon, and building them a branch line along the south bank of the river from Ryton would have eaten up the Lemington route savings and increased the operating costs. James Losh and Matthew Plummer can hardly have relished wasting money on a Parliamentary Bill for the Lemington route.

On 24 June 1830 the Board delegated Losh, Alfred Hall and Thomas Crawhall to walk the two alternative routes the following day. They set out, accompanied by Joseph Crawhall, Benjamin Thompson and John Clayton and escorted by Giles and Blackmore, but the day was wet and they only completed the northern route. Next morning at 8 a smaller party set out along the southern line and in the afternoon they adjourned to Clayton's chambers to discuss the matter. Despite Clayton and Giles's continued advocacy of the north bank, the majority opted for Blaydon and the south bank.[13] The issue was also debated at the shareholders' meeting, a month later, and the directors subsequently decided to invite John Buddle, the leading colliery viewer of the day, to assess the quantities of coal likely to be shipped on each route.[14]

The Blaydon route was adopted, but the dissensions among the Board are emphasised by James Losh's diary note of their 16 August meeting, which took the final decision. 'I presided as chairman and succeeded in carrying the measure which appeared to me essential to our success - that we should proceed with the Parliamentary line at the Newcastle end, as they have done at the Eden not very far from Carlisle. John Clayton opposed my views, but I had a large majority. Beaumont attended [very unusually] and took a prudent and proper part in the debate.' This hurdle cleared, the first east-end contracts were let at last on 18 October 1830, covering the riverside stretch from Stella, just west of Blaydon, to Prudhoe.[15] Others soon followed, and the Newcastle directors envisaged holding a formal 'start of work' celebration on 1 March 1831 at the laying of the first stone of the bridge over the Stocksfield Burn.[16] In the event this was deferred and there was to be no counterpart to Henry Howard's Eden Viaduct ceremony.

Getting the Land

Work was able to start early on Henry Howard's property because there was no problem about securing the land. Indeed, many of the major landowners proved helpful, with Greenwich Hospital even easing the railway's cash flow problem by deferring the payment of the purchase money, with only a modest rent being demanded in the interim. Where negotiations failed or were dragging on, the directors could call on their compulsory purchase powers and get a jury to fix the land price, but Losh was very reluctant to do so, since jury valuations could be quite arbitrary. In the March 1832 Annual Report he proudly announced that it had not been found necessary 'in any instance' to resort to a jury. As he spoke, work on their river wall at Eltringham was standing idle because they hadn't been able to persuade the landowner to co-operate and even Losh was having to threaten him with a jury.[17] As usual, things tended to go more smoothly at the west end, where land-agent, surveyor and shareholder John Studholme was valuing the land and negotiating its purchase, but even there juries were required in some cases.[18]

Agricultural land was obtained at prices ranging from 30 years rent, in the case of Greenwich Hospital, to 35 in the case of the Duke of Northumberland and Lord Prudhoe; 33 seems to have been a typical settlement.[19] Even their old enemy Charles Bacon Grey, who succeeded to Styford on his father's death in 1830, came to an amicable, if costly, settlement, graciously agreeing to accept £3,000 in return for the land required and releasing the company from their obligation to screen the line with a tree-clad mound.

Organising Construction

Giles first set out his views on construction in his report to the shareholders' meeting on 19 August 1829.[20] At that stage he advocated using the forthcoming winter to cut and form the easier parts of the line, make drains, and dig out foundations and quarry stone for the 'common bridges' and culverts. In those days it was unwise to attempt masonry work during the cold winters, since the mortar then in use set slowly and took up to two months to gain full strength, so the smaller bridges and the river walls were to be started the following spring. The foundations of the major bridges were to go in during the summer, while the deep cuttings and embankments were to follow the progress of the culverts and small bridges. Rather optimistically, Giles forecast completion throughout in the space of three years.

In the event, both the plan of campaign and the timetable turned out quite differently, but the directors did follow Giles's recommendations regarding the construction contracts: 'these operations may be carried on by the labourers and masons of the country, in such order as will gradually train them to a proper knowledge of their work, and afford the means of ascertaining the best and cheapest methods by which the roadway can be formed. The country will also be much benefited by thus employing the local workmen. I therefore recommend that the work should be progressively let in parcels to working contractors, and not in large contracts.'

This is broadly what happened, but it implied a close degree of supervision by Giles's staff and placed quite a lot of faith in the small contractors' abilities to organise their finances. Recognising this, Giles organised 'state of the art' technical support for them. Detailed specifications were provided for the works, and the major bridges were erected with the aid of elaborate temporary stagings and a variety of cranes. In addition, the N&C provided materials for a 'temporary way' of iron bars on wooden sleepers - to transport spoil in 'ballast' wagons, with swivelling and tipping bodies, also supplied by the company.[21] In October 1830 the directors advertised for models for these wagons, at 1/6 scale, offering first and second premiums of £5 and £2. They made their choice on 5 November, and the design finally adopted is shown in figure 13.21, a sketch by the invaluable Carmichael, who was clearly intrigued by their operation.

It is instructive to compare this approach with Giles's adversary, George Stephenson, on the Liverpool & Manchester Railway. There, Josias Jessop had advocated the employment of a single contractor, but this was not entirely practical given the scarcity of contractors experienced in works of that scale. Stephenson went to the opposite extreme and employed a mixture of direct labour and very small contractors for the earthworks, engaging more experienced contractors for the bridges and tunnels.[22] Thomas Telford, called in to report on progress, was highly critical of Stephenson's ill-organised approach, much of the work being conducted without formal contracts, but the saving grace was the supervision provided by Stephenson himself, who set up home in the vicinity, and - more significantly - that of his able assistant engineers. Joseph Locke, William Allcard and John Dixon were experienced men who supervised different stretches of the line, while another assistant, Thomas Longridge Gooch, prepared the working drawings.

5.2. *Gelt Bridge. A pencil sketch made by J. W. Carmichael in 1835. As well as the usual timber centering, on which the arches have been formed, it shows a travelling crane by which masonry could be taken to any point. The viewpoint is looking east, with stone for the completion of the bridge apparently stacked at the far end. Middle Gelt Bridge crouches low down to the left, carrying the road which passes through the far span of the railway bridge. (Tullie House Museum & Art Gallery, Carlisle)*

5.3. *Detail from Carmichael's 1836 sketch of the Caldew bridge (Canal Branch) being built by George Grahamsley. There were two cranes, one on each bank. Each was built up from timbers, with the main vertical post swivelling in a pair of collars, the upper one of these being stayed by four guy-lines attached to wooden stakes driven into the ground. Note the stone counterweight at the right-hand end, close to the two operators, working a windlass on a platform 27 feet above the ground.*

On 20 February 1836 the 'Cumberland Pacquet' reported an accident resulting from one of the guy-line stakes having pulled loose in the soft ground. The resulting shock pulled another stake loose and the crane toppled over, sending the two men flying from the platform. One escaped with surprisingly slight injuries but the other, John Hodgson, fell on his head and died immediately. The inquest jury found no blame in Grahamsley's arrangements and contented themselves with imposing a nominal deodand of a shilling. One imagines, however, that the guy-lines will have been double-staked thereafter.
(Tullie House Museum & Art Gallery)

Giles's approach was distinctly professional, rooted in the sort of practice he had encountered with the elder John Rennie, and all the N&C work was advertised by the directors and let by competitive tender. Unlike Stephenson, however, Giles was based in London, where he had other work to attend to, and only made periodic visits to the North. Giles was therefore heavily dependent on his Principal Assistant, John Blackmore, who was paid by him. Several pupils were also engaged on the work and during the course of 1831 two of Giles's staff were transferred to the railway's payroll as Inspectors or Assistant Engineers, along with one local recruit. The first was Thomas Dodd, who remained on the project until February 1836, after which he joined Giles's second railway venture: the London & Southampton Railway.[23] The second was George Larmer, of whom more shortly, and the local man was Wylam Walker, born at Hebburn on Tyne in 1794. Walker joined the N&C payroll in October 1831, receiving, like Dodd, a salary of thirty shillings a week.[24] He was employed until the completion of the through route, being given six months notice in August 1838, and then set up his own business, living thereafter in Hexham.[25]

George Larmer was Giles's nephew, born at Sunninghill, on the edge of Windsor Great Park, in 1807.[26] His parents, James Larmer and his wife Frances Giles, later moved to Reigate in Surrey. Larmer became a pupil of uncle Francis and was formally engaged by the railway on 28 December 1831, on a salary of £100, as 'Surveyor of Masonry' at the west end.[27] However, at the end of the year he received a half-year's salary, subsequently being paid quarterly. This implies that he had already been working for the company since July 1831, while a note by Henry Howard on a drawing of the Corby Beck Viaduct takes the story back further.[28] This states that Larmer designed the viaduct and the first stone was laid on 18 May 1831 by Howard's son and heir, Philip Henry. Howard also credited Giles as 'architect' of the bridge, implying, as one might expect, that Larmer did the detailed drawings from an outline specification by Giles.

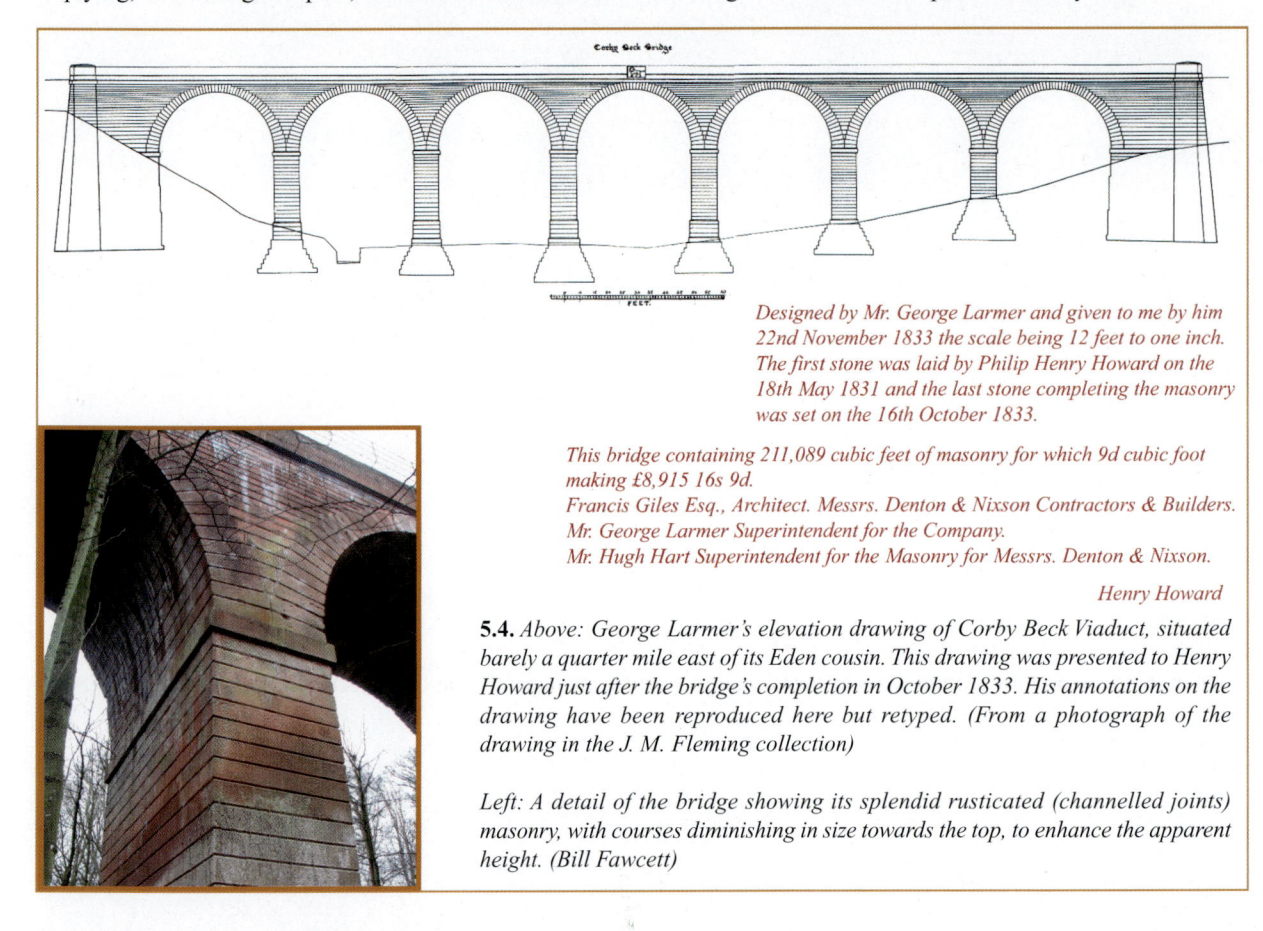

Designed by Mr. George Larmer and given to me by him 22nd November 1833 the scale being 12 feet to one inch. The first stone was laid by Philip Henry Howard on the 18th May 1831 and the last stone completing the masonry was set on the 16th October 1833.

This bridge containing 211,089 cubic feet of masonry for which 9d cubic foot making £8,915 16s 9d.
Francis Giles Esq., Architect. Messrs. Denton & Nixson Contractors & Builders.
Mr. George Larmer Superintendent for the Company.
Mr. Hugh Hart Superintendent for the Masonry for Messrs. Denton & Nixson.

Henry Howard

5.4. *Above: George Larmer's elevation drawing of Corby Beck Viaduct, situated barely a quarter mile east of its Eden cousin. This drawing was presented to Henry Howard just after the bridge's completion in October 1833. His annotations on the drawing have been reproduced here but retyped. (From a photograph of the drawing in the J. M. Fleming collection)*

Left: A detail of the bridge showing its splendid rusticated (channelled joints) masonry, with courses diminishing in size towards the top, to enhance the apparent height. (Bill Fawcett)

As well as supervising the major bridges, Larmer evidently acted as resident engineer for the stretch from Carlisle to Blenkinsopp (Greenhead), but the company's cash-flow problems led to him being laid off for almost six months in 1834, resuming his post in October of that year.[29] He finally left the railway in September 1836, two months after the opening of the west end of the line, and was succeeded by Peter Tate.[30] The occasion for Larmer's departure was his uncle's London & Southampton Railway. Giles's principal assistant engineer on that project, William Lindley, wished to leave and set up his own practice. However, Larmer never joined the L&S. Giles ceased to be its operative engineer at the start of 1837 and Larmer returned to Carlisle, where he set up his own practice.

With one principal assistant and three assistants, there were no more engineers supervising the N&C than on the Liverpool & Manchester, which was only half its length. However, we do not know how many other pupils of Giles may have become involved, while cash-flow problems ensured that the amount of line under construction at any one time was well within the compass of the staff available to scrutinise it. The impeccable quality of the masonry work throughout the Newcastle & Carlisle Railway suggests that Larmer and his fellow assistants did their job very thoroughly.

John Blackmore

John Blackmore was a key figure during the early years of the Newcastle & Carlisle Railway. He oversaw its construction, and effectively became Engineer in Chief from the opening of the first section in 1835. He later took on an increasing amount of outside consultancy, and succeeded George Stephenson as Engineer to the Maryport & Carlisle Railway, in which capacity he oversaw the building of most of their original route. The workload led to health problems, which indirectly resulted in his tragically early death in 1844.

John Blackmore was born in London on 19 May 1801. He was the youngest of eleven or more children of Edward Blackmore, a tailor of Henrietta Street, Covent Garden, and his wife Dorothy.[32] Edward was a local man, born in the area in the summer of 1755, and his business evidently prospered, since he retired to Lambeth, where he was described as 'gentleman' prior to his death during the summer of 1831. In the absence of other information, we must assume that young John trained as an engineer or surveyor with Francis Giles, and by 1828 he was described as Giles's 'principal assistant'.

During 1828-9 Blackmore appears to have been engaged on the Hertford Union Canal, and he did not accompany Giles on his 1829 surveys of the N&C route.[33] However, he may have worked on aspects of the scheme in Giles's office before being sent north to supervise the construction of the railway as Resident Engineer. His arrival is first recorded in Carlisle, on 22 April 1830, and the direction of the major bridges at that end of the line occupied much of his time at first, though he eventually set up home in Newcastle. The railway was a work on a vastly larger scale than anything Blackmore had previously been engaged in but he handled it very ably.

While at Carlisle, Blackmore became friendly with contractor and architect Paul Nixson (christened Nixon but changed to Nixson), whose partner William Smith Denton was building the major viaducts at Wetheral and Corby. Blackmore eventually married Paul's niece, Anne Nixon, born 1813 and daughter of Paul's deceased brother William Nixon (1760-1824), who had been bridgemaster for West Cumberland. The ceremony took place on 22 December 1835 at Dent, where the family had a marble works and which Paul had adopted as his retirement home. By then Blackmore had supplanted Giles as N&C Engineer, and was becoming well established in his profession.

Blackmore's career emerges in more detail in later chapters. It is sufficient to note here that by 1843 he was suffering from the effects of overwork and was undergoing medical treatment to alleviate this. Part of this involved the use of steam baths, scalding in which led to his tragic death on 15 March 1844. Anne was left with two young daughters: Dora, aged six, and Rosa, not quite four. Just prior to this Blackmore had taken on an experienced young engineer, John Addison (1820-1903), as his Principal Assistant. Blackmore's practice ceased with his death and Addison went on to work for the engineers Locke & Errington, initially on the Lancaster & Carlisle Railway. Eventually, by a happy coincidence, he became the Manager of the Maryport & Carlisle Railway.[34]

Wylam Walker

Walker was born at Hebburn in 1794 and worked for a long time as 'land agent and manager' for Thomas Wade of Hylton Castle, Sunderland, before joining the N&C. After leaving the railway he leased Greenwich Hospital's Prudham Quarry, near Fourstones, previously operated by the N&C, and ran two fireclay works making bricks, tiles, and field and sanitary drain pipes: the Dilston works and one at Corbridge. Richard Lowry supplemented his early railway income by acting as agent for Walker at Carlisle. Walker lived at Orchard House, Hexham, where he died in August 1890.

George Larmer

Larmer's further career is quite interesting. He set up his own practice as engineer and surveyor in Carlisle about the start of 1837 [35] and subsequently became involved in schemes for a railway from Lancaster to Carlisle. He made a survey and report for a local committee of an 'inland line' up the Lune Valley, earlier advocated by Joseph Locke, and this was one of several projects considered by Parliament's Smith-Barlow Commission, set up to inquire into Anglo-Scottish and Anglo-Irish railway routes.[36] The Commission suggested that Larmer adapt his route to serve Kendal, and this he did, producing a scheme which forms the basis for the present main line, engineered by Locke & Errington. Locke made one significant change: abandoning Larmer's summit tunnel at Orton in favour of the notorious climb over Shap at a gradient of 1/75. Larmer's steepest gradient had been 1/150.

Larmer was engaged as resident engineer for the construction of the northern end of the Lancaster & Carlisle Railway (L&C), of which John Dixon was an active director, but in June 1847 Larmer moved to one of Locke's Scottish lines, accompanied by the thanks of the L&C Board for his 'zeal and attention'. He did not remain long in Scotland, and by 1851 he was living in Reigate, where his parents and elder brother had been long established. He set up his own business there as civil engineer and surveyor, married, and seems to have settled down to a fairly uneventful life, concerned chiefly with surveying and modest forays into architecture. He died in 1887.[37]

What Giles meant in practice by letting the work to small contractors can be judged by looking at the first stretch to be completed - the seventeen miles from Blaydon to Hexham. Contracts were let for short stretches, at most three or four miles, and, as was then usual, earthworks and masonry bridges were let separately. As a result, there were about as many contracts as miles. Giles has been criticised for this, yet, as we shall see later, the construction costs of the N&C were relatively low and seem to justify a policy which also helped to build up a cadre of trained local workmen and experienced contractors and avoided the necessity to draw in 'navvies' from far afield. We shall consider engineering works and contractors in more detail in the next chapter, but it is helpful to look briefly at one of the early works, the Wylam River Wall, and the most energetic of the company's contractors, George Grahamsley, to get an idea of what was involved.

John Wilson Carmichael's engraving, The River Wall at Wylam Scars, is reproduced at the start of chapter 3. It shows a train curving along the south bank of the Tyne and depicts the noble sweep of the river and the Wylam colliery and ironworks on the far bank. What it does not show is the engineering involved in giving the railway passenger this ringside seat. The line actually encroaches in part on the river bed and is retained by an almost vertical wall of sandstone. Above the tracks rises the vegetated scarp of the Wylam Scars, which formerly swept right down to the river's edge.

The river wall at Wylam was one of the first east-end works to be let, on 18 October 1830, and went to Robert Wilson, William Greaves and George Grahamsley, of Newcastle, at prices per cubic yard of 3s 11d for the walls themselves, 5s 2d for the associated earthworks, and 9d for the ordinary and undemanding riverside embankment to the east of the retaining walls.[38] The partners seem to have coped ably with the work, and on 18 January 1831 they received the contracts for bridges on the sections either side of Wylam. Three months later they were given another contract for the river wall at Eltringham, west of Prudhoe.[39] The Wylam river wall was reported at the end of March 1832 as being complete save for the parapet, and it shows both Giles and his contractors to advantage.[40] Except where the formation has been widened, what we see now is the original structure, built in random dressed sandstone from the locality and retaining an earth and rock filling between it and the original hillside. Perfectly plain, it has no conspicuous batter or out-curving toe, as in the adjoining piece rebuilt further out into the river by the North Eastern Railway.

5.5. Detail of Wylam River Wall at the junction of NER work (left) and the original. (Bill Fawcett)

Contracting partnerships were often quite fluid. Grahamsley and Greaves seem to have parted company with Wilson, for new work at least, during 1831 and went on to secure more contracts from the N&C than anyone else, including two substantial stretches in which they were sole contractors, for masonry and earthworks: the Carlisle Canal Branch and the route from Scotswood to Newcastle. George Grahamsley also gave Parliamentary evidence on Giles's behalf in connection with the London & Southampton Railway.[41]

Accounts of early railway construction are usually accompanied by lurid newspaper reports of navvies out on the spree, but the Newcastle & Carlisle appears to be an exception. This may be a reflection of the small scale of the individual contractors and the fact that they were locally based. The total number of men engaged on construction at any one time was in any case surprisingly modest: James Losh estimated it as just 800 in October 1832, with the prospect of pushing the number up to two thousand if the company obtained additional finance.[42] Also the country was not yet involved in large-scale railway building, so one can credit Losh's occasional remarks that an increase in the N&C construction force would mop up sporadic unemployment among local lead-miners and colliers.[43] The engineering works themselves attracted surprisingly little attention, but the North East - awash with colliery lines - saw no particular novelty in railway construction, while the great viaducts and river walls already had their parallels in the extensive harbour works being pursued on both the east and west coasts to meet the demands of the coal trade.

Cash Fails to Flow

Given the brisk progress with the Wylam river wall - one of the more critical elements in the path of the east-end route - it is surprising that the first portion of the railway - from Blaydon to Hexham - did not formally open until March 1835. Much of the explanation lies in the severe problems experienced by the company in securing an adequate supply of capital. Like other railways, the N&C was to find that its construction estimates fell well short of the final cost. However, long before this became apparent, the scheme was running into trouble because of the failure

5.6. *Wylam River Wall. A modern coal train heading east along the western portion of the wall. The NER widened this part of the formation by cutting back the hillside. Further east they did so by rebuilding the river wall as seen in fig. 5.5. That picture also shows how stretches of wall have acquired a shallow protective skirt at the foot to reduce the risk of scour damage.*
(Bill Fawcett, 2007)

of a significant minority of shareholders to pay up when called upon. This in turn seems to have made the Newcastle group of directors over-cautious when making calls, thereby squeezing the cash flow even further and slowing down the progress of the work, which, of course, did nothing to foster confidence.

The 1829 Act contained a carrot and stick to encourage shareholders to pay up when called. The carrot was a power to pay interest out of capital on money invested: the directors duly paid 4% to people who had paid up at least £25 per £100 share. The stick was the ability to declare shares forfeit if people fell behind with their calls; this right was, however, vested in a general meeting of shareholders rather than just the Board. Three months notice had to be given of forfeiture, after which the process had to be confirmed by a shareholders' meeting. The value of this strategy was in any case dependent on the ability of the directors to sell the forfeited shares in order to raise capital.

The Board proceeded cautiously in the matter of calls. Subscribers had been required to make an initial deposit of £2 per £100 share. The first call, bringing the total paid to £5, was made in March 1830. By August 1832 the calls totalled £40 per share, which should have brought in £120,000 whereas the sum received was only £86,440.[44] This was serious stuff, a shortfall of 28%, and the directors decided to charge 5% interest on unpaid calls, but were probably unable to make this work. Consideration was also given to suing defaulting investors, with the Board deciding in June 1832 to proceed against James Price and a Mr. Featherstone, *pour encourager les autres*.[45] The first actual forfeitures seem to be those confirmed by the March 1834 AGM. 227 shares were declared forfeit - 7½ % of the total capital and including some embarrassingly prominent figures, for example 20 shares belonging to Alfred Hall, 10 to John Forster and 5 to William Forster; the largest block was 33 shares belonging to Job James Bulman.[46] Hall and the Forsters paid up – only parts of their shareholdings had unpaid calls, but Bulman's assets were in the hands of assignees.

The 1829 Act gave the N&C the usual power to borrow money up to one third of the authorised share capital, in their case to raise a further £100,000. Initially, the Board used it to obtain relatively small advances from its bankers to keep up payments to contractors. As their cash flow worsened, the directors looked for ways to make full use of their borrowing powers without incurring a punitive interest burden, and their thoughts turned to the Public Works Loans Board (PWLB), also known as the Exchequer Loan Commissioners. This body had been set up to assist with the financing of worthwhile public works, such as harbours, roads and bridges, through the provision of loans at a reasonable, but still commercial rate of interest. They had already helped out the Liverpool & Manchester Railway with an advance of £100,000 during 1827.[47]

The first approach to the PWLB was made informally by Francis Giles in November 1831.[48] He learned that no help would be forthcoming until the company had spent one third of its authorised capital, namely £100,000. A formal approach was made in February 1832, when the directors indicated that they would reach that level of spending later in the year. The response was encouraging but the PWLB pointed out that the wording of the 1829 Act implied that the whole of the £300,000 capital had to be expended before the borrowing power came into force. To remedy this, the N&C went immediately to Parliament for a second Act, including in their petition the argument that they were 'desirous, for the sake of employing the poor [one of the PWLB's objectives], to proceed rapidly in the execution of the' railway.[49] This is where Losh's Parliamentary contacts came in useful, for the petition went in almost three weeks after the time limit for private bills but was still accepted - the bill duly went ahead and received the Royal Assent on 23 June 1832. Noting this was about to happen, the PWLB formally registered the grant application on 20 June.

Details of the company's finances, progress and prospects were supplied to the PWLB and Giles briefed their consulting engineer, Thomas Telford, on the scheme while Giles and Thomas Crawhall also waited on the PWLB commissioners in September 1832 to answer outstanding questions.[50] At the beginning of October the PWLB's shrewd secretary, John Brickwood, arrived in Carlisle to inspect the route and met up with directors there and at Hexham. At his final meeting Brickwood told them that he had formed a much more favourable impression of the undertaking than he had previously held and he advised them on the further details required by the commissioners.[51] By then the company had notionally spent the requisite £100,000, although this included a 10% retainer on contractors' bills, which was held back until each contract had been completed.

Giles's estimates, confirmed by no less a person than Telford, indicated that a further expenditure of £224,189 would be required to complete the two end sections, from Carlisle to Haltwhistle and Newcastle to Hexham, with a further £73,986 to build the 17 mile central section. This brought the cost just under the £400,000 total of capital and borrowing powers, while the company felt that the position would in any case be eased once they were obtaining revenue from the two ends. Brickwood was less sanguine, advising his commissioners that the traffic forecasts indicated ample security for a loan but that the cost was likely to exceed £400,000. He also questioned under the terms of the 1829 Act, which 'contemplates an entire work from Newcastle to Carlisle ... whether a partial completion of the work at each end will justify the company in demanding tolls for the portion so completed.' This seems a very narrow legalistic interpretation, but the PWLB took his advice and on 15 November agreed to advance £100,000 only after the N&C had spent a total of £200,000, the sum being offered in instalments matching those spent by the N&C out of its final £100,000 capital.

This was very bad news. The directors had almost within their grasp a lifeline which would enable them to complete both ends of the line and get traffic flowing before finishing the rest. Now it had, effectively, been snatched away and this provoked a crisis in the company's finances. The response was to appoint a small group - the Buddle committee - to see what economies might be made in construction, but within six months Losh had made a further approach to the PWLB which led them to soften their terms, got the company out of trouble and enabled them to dispense with some of the more unfortunate and short-sighted of the economies proposed by the Buddle committee.

This time, Losh and several fellow directors went down to London to see the PWLB. Their first meeting was with Losh's fellow Cumbrian, Sir James Graham - then First Lord of the Admiralty, who offered his support, followed by a preliminary session with Brickwood, who proved 'friendly and accommodating'.[52] A little juggling had been done to raise the notional amount spent so far to £150,000 - 'availing themselves of the late low price of iron, the directors entered into a contract [for iron rails] for the whole quantity that will be necessary for completing the work, amounting to about £50,000'.[53] Losh, Benjamin Thompson, Thomas Crawhall and John Clayton met the commissioners on 9 May 1833, and the upshot was an agreement to advance the company £100,000 in four equal instalments, the first being paid on receiving proof of the existing expenditure, the second on proof that the N&C had spent both the first instalment and an equal amount of their own capital, and so on. Interest was due at 5% and the principal was to be repaid within twenty years by equal annual instalments commencing in year four. Naturally, no further interest was to be paid out of capital to the shareholders, and the loan was secured by a mortgage on the line and its future income.

This solved the immediate problem, and the company received its first £25,000 instalment in July 1833, a second in May 1834, the third in November 1834 and the final one in June 1835.[54] By then the section from Blaydon to Hexham had been open to public traffic for two months, but the company was running out of capital and was not in a position to complete the first stage at the west end.[55] The issue was addressed by the company's third Act, which received the royal assent on 17 June 1835 and included powers to increase their capital by £150,000. To hasten things on, however, the railway approached the PWLB for a further loan, and Brickwood made another visit to the line in mid September, looking over it with Giles and various directors. He was clearly impressed, and parts of his report are worth quoting for their sense of immediacy:[56]

'The bridge at Corby over the River Eden ... may be considered as a Stupendous Work, as well as the deep cutting at Cowran Hill. The Corby Beck and the Gelt Bridge are also fine structures. These works are all built of excellent stone, obtained on the spot, an inestimable advantage in the completion of this railway, and it gives to the structures thereon a solidity and elegance scarcely equalled in any similar undertaking. The expense has however been very great...'

'From Hexham, distant from Newcastle about 17 miles, the rail road has been opened, we travelled the principal part of the way thereon in a Car, to which was attached a locomotive engine, and proceeded sometimes at the rate of 30 miles an hour; and although this end now terminates at Blaydon, 4 miles from Newcastle, yet the amount of tolls received from passengers etc since the opening has exceeded what could have been anticipated, as will appear from the authenticated account of such receipts.'

Brickwood gave a ringing endorsement of the project and its prospects but was careful to secure further safeguards for the public purse and terms which would compel the company to complete the line throughout. So the PWLB agreed on 8 October 1835 to advance a further £60,000 on condition that no interest or dividend be paid to investors until the line had been completed from end to end. They also required the directors to provide a personal bond 'in the penalty of £150,000' for the due and proper application of the £60,000 loan, together with a personal commitment to provide such further funds as might be required to complete the line throughout. This bond was strong stuff, but Matthew Plummer (who had succeeded Losh) and his fellow directors were men of substance and the opening of the first section had clearly renewed their confidence. The bond was duly provided by Plummer, John Dixon and John Forster of Carlisle, Joseph Crawhall, William Woods, Thomas Fenwick and Thomas Richard Batson. The loan followed in December 1835, by which time the investment prospects of the railway were improving anyway.[57]

Giles: The Parting of the Ways

The cash crisis of late 1832 was accompanied by a loss of confidence by the directors in their engineer. We have seen that Losh had misgivings about Giles at the time of his appointment, and by July 1831 he was referring to this as a 'false step'.[58] The first serious issue to arise between Giles and the Board was that of surveyors. Studholme and Blackett had been retained to carry out detailed surveys under Giles, which the Board felt he should pay for. A strict interpretation of his terms of appointment would support that view, but Giles felt otherwise.

The situation was complicated by the fact that Studholme, in particular, was doing work which went well beyond Giles's contractual remit - having been engaged by the Carlisle committee to value land and negotiate its purchase. Giles himself argued that the surveyors' charges were wholly due from the directors and that where they appear to have been doing the duty of the engineer, this was in 'corroboration' of what Giles had previously done and 'to promote despatch in the undertaking'.[59] Matters came to a head in December 1830, when the Board agreed to 'continue' Studholme and Blackett until they had completed the particular surveys on which they were currently employed. Thereafter they were definitely to be regarded as Giles's assistants and paid by him. This did not end the dispute, for in February 1831 Blackmore reported that Blackett's survey was still incomplete but he declined to finish it, stating that he had no authority from Giles to do so - presumably he had not been paid and was putting pressure on the directors.[60] Studholme's position was clarified in September 1831, when Giles informed the Carlisle committee that he took responsibility for the surveyor's fees from 13 May 1830, except for the work related to land valuation and purchases.[61]

In 1832 the county magistrates accepted that the old bridge was unsafe. After dithering about its £9,000 cost, the new one's foundation stone was laid in April 1833. Built by the Eden Viaduct contractor, William Denton, it only came into use in January 1835. The design resembles the railway's Petteril bridge but with the added grace granted by a curving roadway as distinct from a flat top.

5.7. Francis Giles's road bridge across the River Eden at Warwick Bridge. (Bill Fawcett)

Giles got on much better with the Carlisle directors than the Newcastle ones, and indeed Henry Howard gave evidence on his behalf in connection with the London & Southampton Railway bill [62], while Peter Dixon was probably instrumental in his being commissioned by the county magistrates to design a road bridge across the Eden at Warwick Bridge.[63] Losh and his colleagues, however, became irritated by the infrequency of Giles's visits to the line and the extent of his other commitments, including the London & Southampton, to which he was appointed engineer in 1831.[64] Given Blackmore's experience and competence, Giles's absence will have had little impact on the supervision of the works but it made liaison with the directors rather difficult.

A source of friction was Giles's inexperience in relation to railways, compared with directors like Benjamin Thompson. This was made worse by the failure of people like Thompson to realise the limitations of their own skill and understanding when it came to civil engineering, and the monthly directorial inspections of the line, instituted in August 1831, could see supplementary and even contradictory instructions being handed out to Blackmore and the contractors. The Board's pool of expertise deepened considerably with the appointment of Nicholas Wood (1795 - 1865) as a director in October 1831. Wood was a distinguished colliery viewer - member of that brotherhood of mining engineers which gave the North East a rich resource of engineering expertise. He was also a prosperous colliery proprietor, an associate of George Stephenson and a recognised expert on railways. Having published the first edition of his *Practical Treatise on Railroads* in 1825, Wood had served in 1829 as one of the judges at the Rainhill trials.

5.8. *Nicholas Wood, enthroned in the Wood Memorial Hall of the North of England Institute of Mining & Mechanical Engineers, in Newcastle. (statue by A. Wyon, picture by Bill Fawcett, courtesy of the Mining Institute)*

Wood's expertise was very valuable to the N&C, while his reputation also helped bolster confidence in the venture. However, his arrival was bad news for Giles, insofar as Wood could be influenced by and act as a conduit for the prejudices of his friend George Stephenson. An example of this is provided by a letter written by George in November 1831. Wood had been asking his friend for an opinion of Giles's proposals for the tunnel through the Cowran Hills and its likely cost. George gave a reasoned reply but added 'If Giles were in as bitter repute in the North than he is here he would not long remain on the Newcastle & Carlisle Railway.' George then referred to a circular whose 'object was to expose the gross injustice of Mr. Giles's demands upon the Chester & Liverpool Railway' in respect of his charges for surveying a route.
(Skeat, 'George Stephenson: The Engineer and his Letters')

Poor Giles now had at least two experts to contend with on the Board, but the immediate trigger for the breach was the financial crisis the company found itself in towards the end of 1832 coupled with a loss of confidence in his ability to forecast construction costs. Losh was particularly aggrieved that these were exceeding the estimates and that Giles had not briefed them about this in good time. The last straw was his failure to provide a firm estimate of the cost of completing the section between Newcastle and Hexham. This had been promised for 14 December, and on the 28th the Board formally minuted their 'astonishment' at its non-appearance and the lack of any explanation.[65] Giles turned up in person on 4 January 1833, giving a verbal report but still no precise figures. A week later he attended the Newcastle Committee and gave verbal estimates for the completion of each section of line but expressed 'a desire that the particulars should be examined and revised by Mr. Thompson and Mr. Wood before being laid before the Board.' The directors assented to this, but his estimate 'so far exceeded his former one, without satisfactory answers for so great an increase' that on 18 January they appointed a committee to survey the works, report on the present conduct of them, and recommend which section to complete first. There may have been some dissent from this proposal, since Thomas Crawhall took the unusual step of recording that the motion for the committee was moved by Matthew Plummer and seconded by Ralph Henry Brandling.

   The Buddle committee, as it may conveniently be called, comprised the most respected colliery viewer of the age - John Buddle (1773-1843), together with Nicholas Wood, Benjamin Thompson, James Thompson of Kirkhouse, and George Johnson (1784-1852), another leading viewer, who went on to become a director in March 1833. They reported on 7 and 19 March and 6 April 1833 and suggested various economies.[66] The line was being built with a double track formation, and the Buddle committee's most drastic and shortsighted recommendation was to build the future bridges only to a single track width. This would have been a desperate expedient, entailing the rebuilding of the overbridges once they came to double the line, and Giles argued successfully against this. He also won his point against the directors when they tried to have the lofty Gelt bridge built as a single-track structure with a wooden 'platform' carried on stone piers, but was unable to change their view that the partially-completed Farnley tunnel, east of Corbridge, should be continued as a single-line bore; this later saddled them with widening the tunnel while maintaining traffic through it. A compromise was achieved over the river wall at Eltringham, which the committee considered doing away with; this would have left the line very vulnerable, and the wall proceeded instead at a reduced height, having to be raised in 1839 when the formation was widened for double track.[67]

Nicholas Wood's influence is evident in the Buddle report's criticism of the width of Giles's formation. For a double track Giles allowed 22 feet between the side walls of his overbridges whereas the committee suggested 24 feet. Later experience has proved them to be right.

Giles responded robustly and lucidly to the points raised but Losh remarked in his diary note of the railway's March 1833 AGM, that his 'conduct seems to be now generally denigrated.' On 16 April directors from both ends of the line met at Hexham to consider the implementation of the Buddle report, and minuted their regret at Giles's absence, noting that 'his personal attention is not adequate to protect the funds of the Company from expenditure which might have been avoided.' The crunch came a few weeks later, while Losh, Clayton, Thomas Crawhall and others were in London attending to the PWLB loan. Discussing Giles the day after meeting the commissioners they agreed that he should not continue in charge of the company's operations but be retained instead as consulting engineer, avoiding any public breach which would have caused a loss of confidence.[68] Their formal note is worth recording:

> 'It is admitted that considerable dissatisfaction with Mr. Giles exists - his errors seem to have arisen chiefly from the want of his personal presence in the North. The Deputation think that a general meeting of the Directors to be held at Hexham should determine whether or not the separation between Mr. Giles and the Company is desirable and if the decision should be in the affirmative then the Deputation recommend that it should be so arranged that the separation should be amicable and without hostility on either side.' A passage crossed out suggested that three months after deciding on the change Giles should 'become the consulting engineer of the Company - receiving payment when consulted - but that the operative Engineer should act under the direction of the company and be entirely independent of Mr. Giles.'

Despite the misgivings of Howard and others, the proposal was carried at a Board meeting on 28 May, and the following month saw the appointment of a Managing Committee, comprising Nicholas Wood, George Johnson and Benjamin Thompson, who were the only N&C Board members to be paid for their services prior to 1852.[69] Under their direction the works were carried forward by John Blackmore, and the Board took care not to consult Giles if they could possibly avoid it. His role after June 1833 was largely confined to liaison with and reports to the Public Works Loans Board, which brought him back to the line for a tour of inspection up to twice a year. After a few years the connection fizzled out.

The sidelining of Giles was handled with tact, and Matthew Plummer, who succeeded Losh as chairman, reported to the March 1834 AGM that the 'valuable assistance' of 'Mr. Giles, the able and eminent Engineer' was being retained as consultant. Two years later, reporting on the progress of the works, Plummer remarked that 'the foundation of this excellence of construction was laid by Mr. Giles' and has 'been followed up by his able assistant Mr. Blackmore, now the operative Engineer of the Company, under the direction of the Managing Committee.'

Partly on the strength of his early work for the N&C, Giles was engaged to survey a route for the London & Southampton Railway (L&S), and was the principal witness for their Parliamentary Bill in 1834, when George Stephenson appeared for the opposition. On 12 September 1834 the L&S appointed Giles 'Principal Engineer' in charge of construction, but the honeymoon was to be painfully short.[70] Two years later he revised his estimates up by 50% and the Lancashire investors, who held half the capital, forced an investigation into the progress of the works. In December 1836 the directors resolved to put the supervision into other hands and Giles tendered his resignation, though to 'spare his feelings and professional character' the resolution was not written up in the minutes and Giles was told his salary would continue for six months, without requiring anything other than his assistance in carrying a money Bill through Parliament.[71] Joseph Locke stepped in as his successor but Giles could not keep his mouth shut and made statements which jeopardised the progress of the Bill. As a result, the circumstances of his departure were made public.

A passage from the report of the Lancashire shareholders strongly criticised his contracting policy on the L&S: 'Giles's system of employing small contractors, supplying them with materials and trusting to superintendence as the check on the proceedings, was admitted by all but himself to be a failure, and it was evident to all but Mr. Giles that works executed in that manner, exclusive of uncertainty as to their completion, would in reality cost more than those for which an adequate price should be paid to responsible contractors.' Experience on the Newcastle & Carlisle suggests that this judgment is unduly harsh, though it has clouded perceptions of Giles ever since. Although the N&C ultimately cost about three times the original estimate, part of this excess is attributable to the directors themselves and includes the facilities and rolling stock required to enable the company to work its own traffic, something not envisaged originally. Costs are discussed in chapter 9; it is enough to note here that the degree of cost over-run on the N&C is not unusual for early railways. For example, the cost of earthworks and permanent way on the London & Birmingham Railway came to almost double the original estimate.[72] The most revealing comparison is with the Liverpool & Manchester Railway, where comparable elements of the construction cost were consistently higher than those on the N&C. Giles surely deserves more credit for this than he has hitherto been given.

Chapter 6: Building the Railway

Introduction

The first formal arrangements for directors to routinely scrutinise the progress of the works were made on 26 August 1831, when the Board set up a Visiting Committee to make monthly inspections. Its first outing came four days later, when Matthew Plummer and Thomas and Joseph Crawhall formed the party, but the membership was deliberately varied from month to month.[1] The visiting directors were mainly concerned with the east end, leaving the west to their Carlisle colleagues, and they normally met for breakfast before travelling along the route. The establishment of this regime was a symptom of the Board's growing concern at Giles's management of the works, and the 'visitors' were not slow to point out to Blackmore and the contractors things which required correction, so that even before Giles was sidelined the directors had already encroached to some extent on his responsibilities.

Having dispensed with Giles, in all but name, the Managing committee was set up by a Board meeting of 26 June 1833, and the Newcastle construction committee was then wound up although the Visiting committee continued to function for a further three years, making its last outing apparently on 5 April 1836. After that, the Board as a whole made inspection trips along the line but much less frequently. The Carlisle committee remained in being until 1846 to supervise contractors' payments at the west end and in order to protect west-end interests, which were sometimes in danger of being over-ridden by the directors in Newcastle.[2]

Benjamin Thompson, Nicholas Wood and George Johnson comprised the original Managing committee, and one senses that they relished their active engagement in the detail of the railway. They certainly devoted a lot of time to it - usually meeting at least weekly in the early days, though of course there was not a full house for every meeting. In return each received a fee of £100 a year, but this was no more than a notional acknowledgement of the time abstracted from their other enterprises. For all three were busy men. Wood was building up a colliery kingdom which would make him a very rich man, while Thompson was expanding his interests with the formation of ironworks in the area - first at Birtley and then at Wylam. Thompson over-reached himself financially, and in March 1841 he found it prudent to depart for an extended sojourn in Boulogne, leaving Wylam ironworks in the hands of his sons.[3] This only deferred his problems, for they became bankrupt in February 1842 and he followed in May. The flight to Boulogne had already ended his active involvement in the railway, and a new director took his place at the March 1843 AGM.[4]

In the circumstances, it is not surprising that no mention was made of Thompson by shareholders at the 1843 meeting, despite all that he had done for the company. Other directors had lost by his failure, notably the banker William Woods, who had become the principal proprietor of Thompson's Brunton & Shields Railway.[5] Despite this, Woods may well have found Thompson his next berth, as manager of the Hareshaw ironworks, near Bellingham, in which role he briefly re-enters our story in chapter 9. Wood and Johnson continued as the Managing committee until George Hudson took a lease of the railway in 1848, but their formal role was latterly much reduced; instead of general supervision it became more a matter of considering specific issues referred to them by the Board.

There has never been a railway management quite like the N&C Managing committee in its early days. The first task was to press on with construction and get as much of the line built as they could with the limited funds available. To further this, they made frequent site visits, during which they gave detailed instructions for the progress of the works. Although the Carlisle committee retained oversight of works at the west end, the managing directors made extended visits to the west when necessary, notably during the summer of 1834. They also guided the Board on issues such as whether to operate the traffic themselves and whether - contrary to the 1829 Act - to adopt steam locomotives. Wood's influence is evident in the experiments they conducted on different types of rail and in the detailed specifications which they negotiated for the early locomotives. Indeed, for years after appointing a Locomotive Superintendent, in 1835, the specification of new engines lay more in Wood's hands than his.

6.1. Advertisement seeking tenders for the transport to construction sites of materials being supplied by the N&C for use by its contractors:

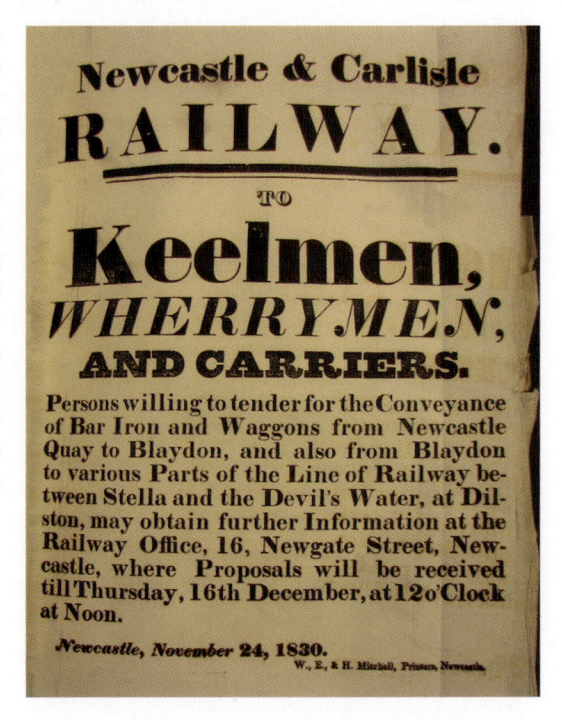

> *Bar iron, for the formation of the temporary way, and Ballast Wagons, for the conveyance of spoil along this way.*

> ### George Johnson
>
> George Johnson was born on 4 May 1784, his father then being viewer of Byker colliery, near Newcastle. George became a prominent member of the same profession and also built up substantial investments in the industry, including a share in the colliery at Willington, which became his home.[6] He put in a lot of work as a managing director of the N&C and continued to take a keen interest in its operation throughout the eighteen-forties, until the Hudson lease. Richard Lowry records frequent visits by Johnson to the Newcastle terminus, and it emerges that he was a very approachable man, who was happy to listen to suggestions, to discuss issues where his own views differed from those of the railway's officers, and to provide a conduit by which their ideas could be fed back to the Board.
>
> Johnson also became involved with the Newcastle & North Shields Railway, which served Willington. He and Nicholas Wood were members of its Provisional Committee, and in September 1835 Johnson, Benjamin Thompson and John Jobling reported on the proposals made by its consulting engineer, John Straker.[7] The Brandling Junction Railway saw Johnson again in harness with Nicholas Wood, and they were both signatories to the August 1844 agreement by which it passed to George Hudson. Johnson also found himself acting for Benjamin Thompson's Birtley Iron Company in a dispute with the Marquess of Londonderry over the valuation of the first railway to Seaham Harbour, which the Birtley company had built and Londonderry was attempting to obtain on the cheap. Johnson was also a promoter of the Whittle Dean Water Company, which provided a much improved water supply to Newcastle and Gateshead. He died at Willington House on 26 January 1852, leaving a respectable fortune, including shares valued at £16,000 in the N&C.

An Overview

Before looking in detail at progress under the Managing committee, it may be useful to summarise the stages in which the railway opened to the public. In general, the formal opening took place on the date given, with normal traffic commencing the following day.

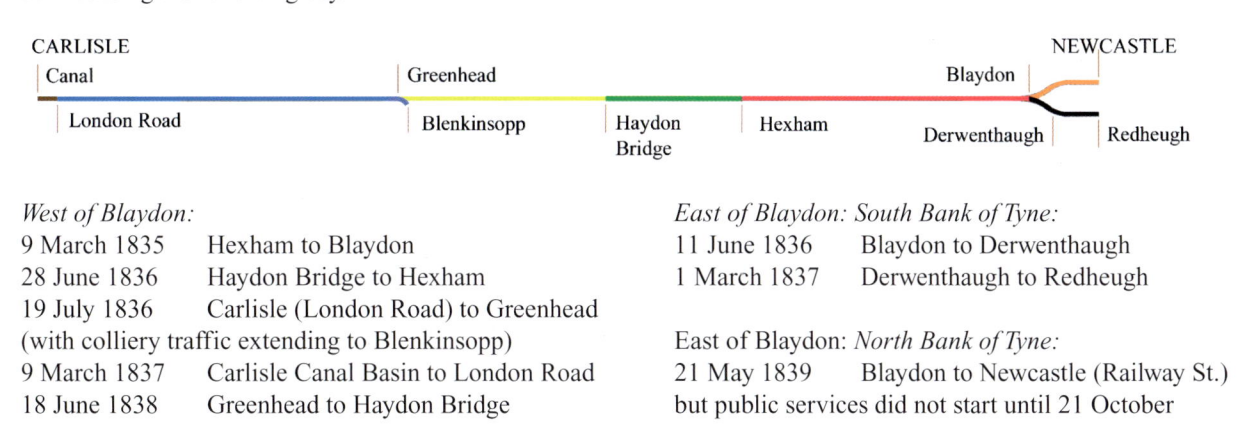

CARLISLE — Canal — London Road — Greenhead — Blenkinsopp — Haydon Bridge — Hexham — Blaydon — Derwenthaugh — Redheugh — NEWCASTLE

West of Blaydon:
9 March 1835   Hexham to Blaydon
28 June 1836   Haydon Bridge to Hexham
19 July 1836   Carlisle (London Road) to Greenhead
(with colliery traffic extending to Blenkinsopp)
9 March 1837   Carlisle Canal Basin to London Road
18 June 1838   Greenhead to Haydon Bridge

East of Blaydon: South Bank of Tyne:
11 June 1836   Blaydon to Derwenthaugh
1 March 1837   Derwenthaugh to Redheugh

East of Blaydon: North Bank of Tyne:
21 May 1839   Blaydon to Newcastle (Railway St.)
but public services did not start until 21 October

Blaydon was then a small village, whose significance lay in being home to Beamont's lead refinery and a convenient point for a temporary terminus with a quay on the River Tyne, passengers being conveyed to and from Newcastle either by boat or by horse omnibus along the Scotswood Road. It was an area with a railway pedigree extending back to the seventeenth-century, when waggonways had been built serving pits in the Chopwell and Ryton areas and leading to shipping staiths at Stella, barely a mile upstream from Blaydon.[8] The possibility of acquiring some of this traffic was a factor in the minds of those directors who favoured continuing the N&C east of Blaydon along the south bank of the Tyne to a deep-water shipping point downstream of Gateshead, rather than adopting the Parliamentary route, via a Scotswood bridge, to Newcastle.

The ensuing arguments occupied a lot of directorial time, and the issue was further complicated by the arrival on the scene of a Great North of England Railway company, which wished to build a line from Newcastle to Darlington and the South. As will be seen from the summary of opening dates, the N&C ended up building lines along both banks, and their complex evolution is deferred to chapter 8, which also examines the physical features of these routes. One important outcome of the east end deliberations is that the railway did not reach Newcastle until 1839, though the town had been served by a ferry from the Gateshead (Redheugh) terminus for two years previously.

The formal opening of the line into Newcastle on 21 May 1839, though it was not yet fit for public use, was a technical device to comply with Parliament's requirement that the railways authorised by the company's first two Acts be completed within ten years of the passing of the first Act, which had received the Royal Assent on 22 May 1829. Following the real opening, in September, the company applied to the county justices for a certificate of completion, which was granted at the October quarter sessions and stated that the railway had been completed before 21 May.[9] The directors naturally felt that their undertaking to the Public Works Loans Board was met by the completion of the through route during 1838, and a first dividend of 4% was declared to their patient shareholders at the March 1839 AGM. Though payment of interest on calls had been discontinued at the end of 1833, at the behest of the PWLB, it is a measure of Matthew Plummer's ingenuity that shareholders had since been receiving debentures in lieu of this and now had the opportunity to convert these into cash also.[10]

The Giles Legacy: Blaydon to Hexham

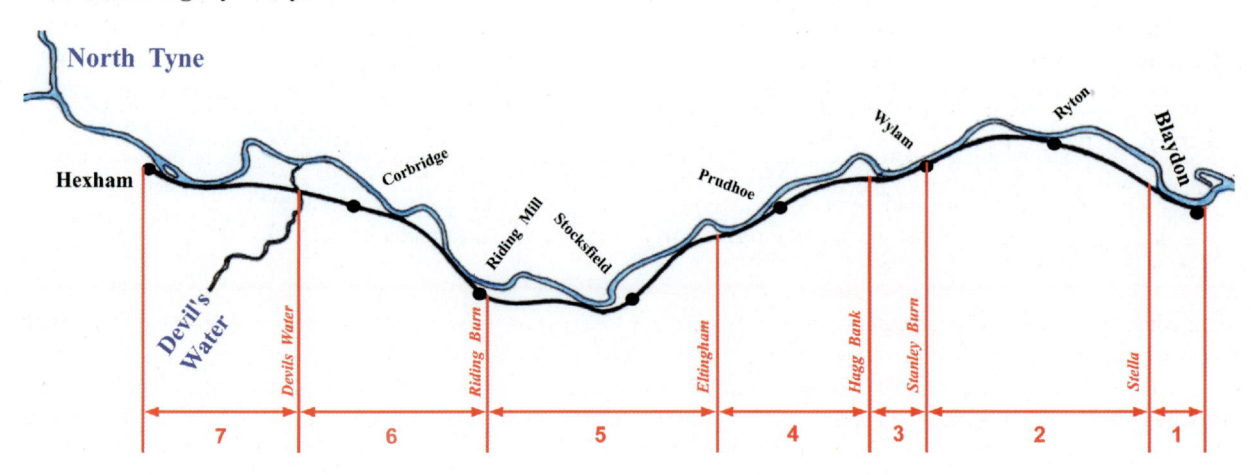

It is appropriate to begin with the first portion of line to be completed, namely from Blaydon to Hexham. For contracting purposes, Giles split this 16¾ miles stretch into seven sections, illustrated in Figure 6.3 (above) and ranging in length from two-thirds of a mile to four and a quarter. Separate contracts were let for the earthworks and the masonry work and their boundaries did not always coincide, so the diagram is something of a simplification. For example, section 6 is broken up by Farnley tunnel, half a mile east of Corbridge, while the earthworks on section 5 were split into two contracts after the original undertakers pulled out.

The first contracts at this end of the line, covering the earthworks on stages 2 to 6 and the Wylam river wall, were advertised with a closing date for tenders of 14 October 1830 and were let later that month.[11] The masonry bridges for the same stretch were divided into four contracts, with sections 4 and 5 being combined into one. These were advertised with a closing date of 16 December and let the following day. Two of the masonry contractors quickly backed out, and the bridges on sections 2, 4 & 5 were therefore relet to Wilson, Greaves & Grahamsley, who were already building the Wylam river wall in section 3. Two of the earthworks contractors also pulled out during the course of 1832, and had to be replaced. Most of them, however, coped quite well.

Two contracts were let on 22 April 1831: for the Eltringham river wall, at the west end of section 4, and for the Stella retaining walls and other works on section 1. Two more followed on 21 July, for the earthworks and bridges on the relatively straightforward section 7. This left only Farnley tunnel, where Giles had been revising the alignment, which was only approved in July 1831. At the end of October a contract was let for bricks to be made on site for the tunnel lining, using local clay, but the tunnel contract itself was deferred so that it could be considered at the same time as a major tunnel at Cowran, at the Carlisle end of the line.[12] Farnley tunnel was eventually let on 16 December to Jacob Ritson & Robert Perry. Ritson had already got the contract for the bridges on this section (No. 6), in partnership with Stokoe and Robinson, so this was a convenient arrangement. The contracts now averaged about one a mile. By comparison, Robert Stephenson was to organise the London & Birmingham Railway, three years later, with just thirty contracts in 112 miles, some of these being for individual major works such as Kilsby tunnel.

Good progress was made with most of the N&C east-end works, however Farnley tunnel held up the completion of the line and warrants close examination because of the light it sheds on the way the N&C functioned. The problem lay not with Ritson, a very capable contractor, but in the organisational abilities of the directors and their engineer. Farnley tunnel took the line through a low spur around which the Tyne makes a pronounced loop, and Giles originally envisaged making it about 280 yards long and using the spoil to form the low embankment carrying the line west to Corbridge. Ritson began in the customary way by driving a narrow drift from the west end. By late March 1832 he had completed 180 yards of this, and at the beginning of May the N&C contracted for a supply of coal to their brickyard at the west end.

> ### *Jacob & William Ritson*
>
> Jacob Ritson did a substantial amount of work as a masonry contractor for the N&C. Born at Allendale in 1795, he became a stonemason and was still based in Allendale Town when he won his first contract for the railway in December 1830, in partnership with Messrs. Stokoe and Robinson. This was for the masonry between the Riding Burn and Devils Water. (Figure 6.3: section 6) Farnley tunnel was taken on in partnership with Robert Perry, but Ritson was alone for his two subsequent masonry contracts: Hexham to Haydon Bridge (1834-6) and the continuation on to Melkridge (1837-8). He was a very dependable contractor, and the river wall at Capons Cleugh, downstream of Haydon Bridge, is a fine testament to his ability.
>
> The N&C launched Ritson on a contracting career, and he followed the N&C by taking on a stretch of the Great North of England Railway, near Northallerton, in partnership with his cousin, William Ritson. The eighteen-forties saw Jacob as a partner in the Ridsdale ironworks (see chapter 9) and he ended that decade building railways at New Cumnock, in Ayrshire. During the eighteen-fifties he retired to Hexham, and died in 1877. [13]
>
> The most successful of the contracting Ritsons was William, born at Muggleswick in August 1811. He evidently learned the ropes working with Jacob on the Haydon Bridge and Melkridge contracts and was his partner until 1849, when he went to Wales to build the Vale of Neath Railway. He spent a decade building railways in Wales and south west England before heading back to Scotland to build the Waverley Route's summit tunnel at Whitrope, a less happy experience. His last work was the Hexham & Allendale Railway (chapter 11) after which he retired to Hexham, where he died on 19 November 1893. [14]

Meanwhile, the company was negotiating with the Duke of Northumberland's agent with a view to securing a site to dump spoil at the east end of the tunnel, pending which there was some uncertainty as to where the east portal might be. In August, having obtained a site, the Board agreed to shorten the tunnel to 170 yards and have an extended cutting at the east end, which would generate much more spoil.[15] The east portal was now fixed but the next modification was to the profile. Giles had designed the tunnel with a width of 22 feet and a height of 18 feet to the crown, but on 21 September the Board decided that it should be 22 feet high. Possibly someone had a view to the problems of engine blast on the tunnel roof should they ever employ steam locomotives. Whatever the reasoning, the message was not conveyed to Jacob Ritson, and on a site visit on 23 October 1832 the directors found the side walls being built using a template designed for the lower height.[16] The directors were also upset by the quality of the bricks, which they considered much too weak and totally unfit for use, and the brickyard had in any case been damaged by recent floods. All this raises questions about supervision by and communication with Mr. Giles.

Ritson gave up the bricks in favour of a stone arch, and James Losh and Joseph Crawhall visited on 12 December 1832, when they found eighteen feet of tunnel fully arched and a further 12 feet equipped with side walls and invert. This was at the west end, but work had also begun on opening up the east end. Unfortunately, the visitors came away with the impression that the extra height the Board had ordered was not needed, but in any case all was overtaken by the Buddle Report, which recommended a much smaller single-line bore. Giles expressed an 'earnest wish' that no change be made, but was ignored, and on 2 April 1833 Joseph Crawhall and Benjamin Thompson visited the work and told Ritson of the Board's intention. By then 29 yards had been arched and a further ten were almost complete.

6.4. The east portal of Farnley tunnel (GR 003631) is original, though the bore beyond was widened to double track in 1844-5. The tunnel was abandoned in 1962, having been bypassed by a cutting. (D. Ibbotson)

Ritson was summoned to a Board meeting on 9 April to discuss terms for a reduced bore - fourteen feet wide and only sixteen feet high (from rails to crown). He offered to do this for £9 per yard length, compared with £12 on the current contract, but the directors thought this 'unreasonable'. Work then seems to have virtually stalled, since only about 40 yards had been completed by 19 August, when Ritson came to an agreement with the Managing Committee.[17] Under this he received £250 compensation and contracted to build the remaining 132 yards (with 2 yards overlap into the existing section) at £7 a yard, to a profile 14 feet wide and 18 feet high.

Months had been lost and the double-track route had been sacrificed to produce a saving of only £400, which hardly seems like a managerial triumph. To make matters worse, the reduced volume of spoil would not be sufficient to form the embankment further west, so the formation of the cutting at the east end of the tunnel was held up until such time as its spoil could be led through the tunnel to make up the deficiency.

To make up for lost time, Jacob Ritson pushed the work ahead on double shifts, stopping only from midnight Saturday to midnight Sunday. By November 1833 the tunnel was averaging 0.8 yards a day, and by 22 April 1834 there was felt to be only three weeks' work left, so the Managing committee advertised the east-end cutting contract, which went on 22 May to Joseph Ritson.[18] By July spoil was being led through the tunnel, and the cutting and embankment were almost the only obstacles to completing and opening the line. The other problem lay between Stella and Blaydon, where there was a stretch with the railway and turnpike road squeezed in beside the river, entailing a modest river wall and a high retaining wall above the railway, to bear the road. The contractor, Gibson Kyle, was accused of 'negligence and delay', though he must have had an awkward task advancing the work with minimal interference to the colliery waggonways and their staiths.[19] Elsewhere, good progress was being made with the laying of the permanent way, this work having been let in two contracts back in March.[20]

The directors show up badly in this account, yet in their other affairs we know that many of them were very capable and successful businessmen. In the mining industry, for example, they were ready to face considerable financial risks but they knew that the potential rewards could be huge. Railways as a part of the coal industry were familiar enough, but they normally entailed only modest engineering works, with predictable costs. Railways which had to stand on their own and make a living without guaranteed traffic were a different matter, especially when the costs seemed to be getting out of hand. The directors were not to know that they could build a line costing three times the original estimate and develop enough traffic to still earn dividends up to 6%. They were also fettered by a loss of public faith in the venture until the first part of the line had opened and earned traffic well in excess of all forecasts. Thus they were over-cautious, though certainly not wanting in energy and attention.

Opening - and Briefly Closing

While the N&C was building, the steam locomotive was undergoing a rapid evolution into a reliable and effective machine. The Stockton & Darlington Railway had confined their use to coal and mineral traffic, with private contractors using horses to handle passengers and goods, but in 1833 the company took all the haulage in hand on its main line and substituted locomotives. September 1834 brought the opening of the Leeds & Selby Railway, engineered to main-line standards by James Walker (1781-1862) and employing locomotives from the outset. As the first section of the N&C neared completion it was clearly time for the N&C to rethink its carrying policy.

The issue came to a head in May 1834, during discussions relating to the Blaydon, Gateshead & Hebburn Railway, intended to continue the N&C route along the south bank of the Tyne.[21] The Managing committee had recommended that a 'Carrying Company' be formed to operate the trains on both lines and were asked to prepare a report including details of the capital required to provide wagons, carriages and 'locomotive engines'. This was considered on 13 June, when the Board abandoned the principle of having a line open to all comers and resolved instead to either retain carriage in their own hands or else negotiate an exclusive right with another company.

The die was apparently cast but, as usual, the directors proceeded cautiously and only on 21 October did they formally commit themselves to the steam engine. Fortunately, the gradients - designed for horse traction - were also suitable for steam, with nothing worse than a short stretch at 1/250 east of the summit level although there were almost 4 miles at 1/107 further west. They were shackled by the clause in the 1829 Act expressly forbidding locomotives but decided to amend it in the next session of Parliament and meanwhile circulate landowners with a letter seeking their consent *pro tem*. This contained a persuasive testimony from Hardman Earle, who had originally opposed the Liverpool & Manchester project because of its interference with his family estate. He now found nothing offensive about locomotives and, indeed, had become an active director of the L&M, which he described as 'rather an object of interest' to local residents. So, the Managing committee was despatched to make arrangements for the supply of engines, carriages and wagons with a view to opening to the public early in 1835.

The first recorded directorial trip by train along the line came on 22 July 1834, when Matthew Plummer and Thomas Batson were functioning as the Visiting Committee and met up with Blackmore at Stella.[22] They travelled on various stretches of line in contractors' wagons and had the opportunity of trying out some of the newly-laid permanent way, which by then extended for about nine miles. Three weeks later, arrangements were made for the first commercial traffic to use the line: lead, conveyed from Hexham and Stocksfield to Blaydon on behalf of T. W. Beaumont and Joseph Crawhall.

For several months, Benjamin Johnson, Beaumont's chief lead agent, had been stockpiling lead at Hexham in anticipation of the railway opening and was anxious to have it shipped. The issue was raised at the next directors' visit, on 14 August, when Plummer and his colleagues made an agreement on the spot with the Farnley cutting contractor, Joseph Ritson, to carry lead down the railway in ballast wagons.[23] Although work on the Stella walls was still dragging on, Blackmore promised to have the track ready to begin the lead traffic on 25 August 1834. So Ritson's horse-drawn wagons had the unheralded distinction of opening the line, running over a mixture of permanent and temporary way. The arrangement was not reported formally to the Board until 26 November, when the directors resolved that Ritson might 'continue to lead the whole of the lead belonging to these gentlemen' or any others who might offer lead for shipment, his price being ¾d per ton-mile. The same meeting considered an application by the owners of the *Dr. Syntax* coach to be allowed to place that on the line. Their request was declined, however, on the grounds that it would be unsafe to run the coach over the 2¾ miles of temporary way which by then remained.[24]

Meanwhile, the approach to landowners regarding the use of steam engines had received a generally favourable response, with the company undertaking to use coke rather than coal so as to minimise the smoke nuisance. They were therefore emboldened to conduct the formal opening of the railway from Blaydon to Hexham on 9 March 1835 using the two locomotives, *Rapid* and *Comet*, recently supplied by the Tyneside firms of Robert Stephenson and Robert Hawthorn. The event aroused immense popular interest and won many column inches in the local press.[25]

6.5. *Part of J. W. Carmichael's action-packed engraving of Hexham station, showing 'Comet', the first locomotive to arrive on the railway, supplied by Robert Hawthorn in February 1835. It is a tolerably accurate depiction of the locomotive and of the original station house. The carriages are treated with much greater freedom, but the one behind 'Comet' appears to be an original 'close' carriage, for first-class passengers, with some open-sided second-class carriages on the extreme right. (see chapter 13) The carriage on the left appears to be a product of Carmichael's imagination: not entirely open but hardly closed either. The wagons convey the impression of the low-sided stock used for the transport of general goods. Hexham Abbey dominates the skyline, thrown into prominence by the artist's omission of the steep hillside which actually flanks the south side of the town. The view was taken from the level crossing at the east end of the station and engraved by J. Archer, from Carmichael's ink drawing, and published in 1836 by Currie & Bowman of Newcastle.*

The two inaugural trains were scheduled to leave Blaydon at 10 a.m. and were not restricted to directors and other dignitaries. Open wagons, with makeshift benches, were provided for a large number of ordinary people who made their way on foot from Newcastle and Gateshead, fortunately accompanied by fine weather. The company's new carriages were reserved for directors, leading shareholders and guests, such as the Mayor of Newcastle and his party who travelled upriver by the state barge from the Mansion House. A few people, such as Benjamin Thompson and his party, travelled in private carriages loaded onto flat wagons. A brass band on each train enlivened the festivities. Each train comprised 29 vehicles, weighing about 100 tons, rather more than a normal load for the locomotive, so the precaution was taken of placing a pumping engine on one of the wagons to replenish their water supplies.

The trains set off late, because of the delayed arrival of the Mayor's barge, but all went smoothly, though the pump had to be called on twice to draw water from the Tyne to top up *Comet's* tender. After celebrations at Hexham, the trains returned to Blaydon and the promoters and their friends adjourned to a celebratory dinner at Newcastle's Assembly Rooms, during which Matthew Plummer expressed their gratitude to the landowners for assenting to the use of locomotives. Normal services began the following day but were soon to be disrupted by the one dissenting landowner: Charles Bacon Grey of Styford.[26]

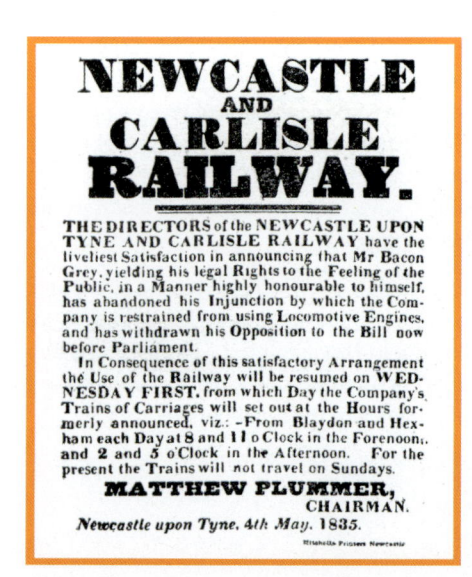

6.8 – 6.10. *(opposite) The Eden Viaduct at Wetheral. Originally, it was formally referred to as Corby Bridge.* (Bill Fawcett)

6.6. *(left) A poster announcing the resumption of train services after Charles Bacon Grey had 'in a manner highly honourable to himself, abandoned his injunction.' This conciliatory phrasing is typical of Matthew Plummer's tactics throughout the affair. By contrast, John Clayton employed sarcasm. Addressing a public meeting held in support of the railway, he reminded them how Bacon Grey had readily accepted cash in lieu of the screening mound provided for in the 1829 Act. 'Having the choice of the mound or the money ... he chose the solace of the cash in preference to the comfort of seclusion (laughter & applause) ... perhaps he had been influenced by a desire to give the public a view of his mansion, and the passengers an opportunity to decide whether Styford were an ornament to the railway, or the railway an ornament to Styford. (loud applause and laughter)' Clayton then went on to make the serious point that landowners like Henry Howard, who were at least as much affected, 'thought the public entitled to benefit by every improvement that science could devise' and had 'cordially acquiesced.'*
(Report of meeting on 30 March 1835, chaired by the Mayor of Newcastle)

Charles Bacon Grey and his father had been two of the most active opponents of the N&C Bill in 1829, but had quickly come to terms with reality once it passed the Commons. The arrival of locomotives rekindled his antagonism and also gave him a handy excuse to attack the railway, which he did by obtaining an injunction to restrain the company from their use. There was nothing the directors could do to prevent this, so they simply closed down the line and marshalled public opinion, including pressure from other landowners, to force Grey's acquiescence. Public services halted on 28 March, but the stoppage could only be temporary since the company's Bill, then being shepherded through Parliament by Philip Henry Howard MP, would repeal the original locomotive clause. Having made his point, Bacon Grey withdrew his opposition with effect from 5 May, securing an agreement that the company would not apply to Parliament for power to use 'Raw coal or any fuel equally offensive', and locomotive-hauled services resumed the following day.[27]

Progress in the West: Blenkinsopp to Carlisle.

6.7. *The west end: Carlisle to Scarrow Hill.*

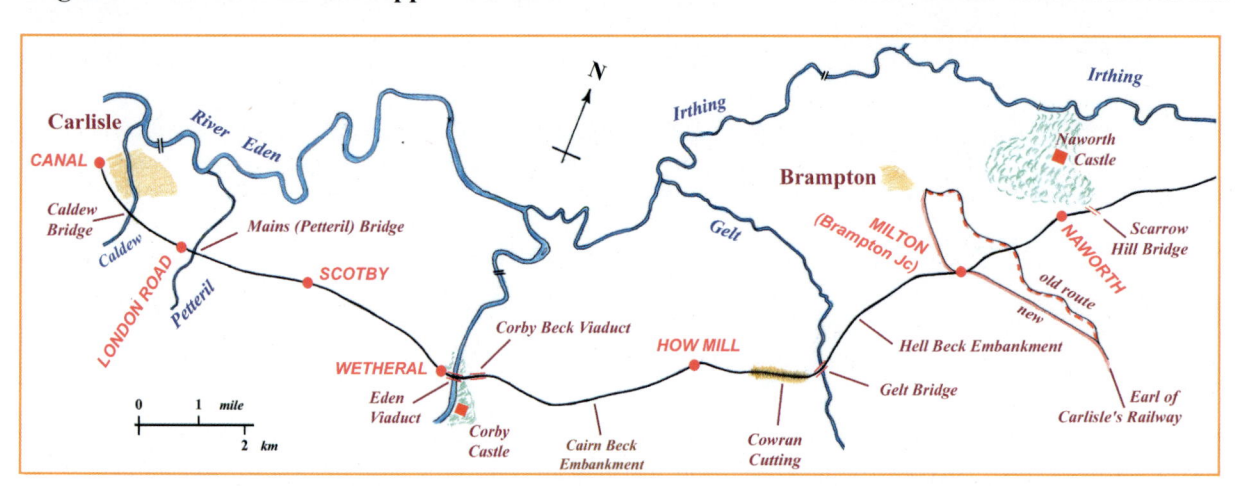

The west end of the route is very different from the east. There are no walled passages squeezed into a steep riverbank; instead the line cuts across the grain of the western valleys, with lofty bridges over the Gelt, Corby Beck and Eden. The most arduous section to build was the traverse of the sandy Cowran Hills, begun as a tunnel but eventually carried through as a very deep cutting. Giles clearly did not anticipate problems at Cowran, the contract for which was only let in December 1831, by which time work had been in progress at the Eden Viaduct for some eighteen months.

Blackmore had been carrying out preliminary trials with the local stone at Wetheral before the first contract for the Eden Viaduct was let, on 22 July 1830.[28] This was the first construction contract on the entire line, and it went to John Prudhoe Robson and Thomas Robson of Newcastle. Henry Howard, then in his mid-seventies, was clearly keen to get on with the work but the directors were perhaps too quick off the mark. This contract was for the foundations only, in order to minimise the initial outlay, but barely a week later Giles advised that a new contract should be advertised covering the whole of the bridge, together with the viaduct over Corby Beck, and all the other masonry works between the Eden and London Road in Carlisle. Robsons won the expanded contract, together with that for the next stretch of line - from Corby to Hell Beck - but then ran into difficulties with the Wetheral stone, which they used as an excuse for giving up both contracts in December.[29] Robsons later undertook the notable Willington Dene Viaduct, on the Newcastle & North Shields Railway, but went bankrupt in the course of the work.[30]

The N&C contract was immediately relet to Nixson & Denton of Carlisle, who were probably the most experienced of the local contractors.[31] In practice the contract comprised the bulk of the masonry bridges from Carlisle to the west end of the Hell Beck embankment (GR 534582), just east of the Gelt, but excluding the Gelt Bridge itself. William Smith Denton was the partner in charge of this contract and his memorial is the Eden Viaduct. With five semicircular arches of eighty feet span, this was arguably the most notable railway viaduct yet built - Sankey, on the Liverpool & Manchester, had only fifty feet spans - although it was to be outshone by the railways of the eighteen-forties. It did not, however, entail any engineering novelties: Telford, for one, had done comparable works (such as Lothianburn viaduct) for his roads and canals. Nor did it involve any foundation problems, since the bedrock was conveniently accessible.

The Eden Viaduct made good progress, with the foundations of the river piers getting above the 'summer water line' by late May 1831.[32] In June 1832 Denton was embarking on the arches but having difficulty quarrying large blocks of stone, so Giles amended the design to reduce the depth of the arch ring on this and the nearby Corby Beck Viaduct.[33] October 1833 saw the completion of the Corby Beck bridge, while December brought the closing of the last arch of the Eden bridge, leaving only the spandrels and parapet to be built.[34] These went very slowly. In December Denton had promised a completion date of mid March 1834, but that passed with work still outstanding, though by June only the parapets remained to be built. There followed a fortnight in which no work was carried out at all, to the exasperation of the Managing committee, who were making extended visits to Carlisle monthly at this time.[35] Their concern was that the delays were holding up the start of George Grahamsley's work on Wetheral cutting, spoil from which was to be led over the bridge to form various embankments beyond. The viaduct was eventually finished on 27 August, and Grahamsley began using it the following day. A month later the committee arranged with Grahamsley a scheme for forming the cutting more rapidly, though this entailed extra labour and additional outlay, which Wood and colleagues were strongly tempted to charge to Mr. Denton.[36]

Denton's behaviour comes over as being cavalier, even foolish, given that he was at the same time seeking to renegotiate his contract so as to get the railway to pay Henry Howard's royalty on stone quarried on his land, something which was explicitly the contractor's responsibility. He was also in trouble with Howard for refusing to fill the quarry and reinstate the site as originally specified; over that issue the railway held the whip hand, retaining a portion of Denton's payment and ordering Blackmore to have the work done by direct labour if need be. A further minor irritation arose when Denton placed inscriptions in the parapet, recording the engineer and contractor, despite specific instructions to the contrary. One cause of Denton's delay in completing the Eden Viaduct was his engagement at Giles's Warwick Bridge, to which all hands were diverted in an attempt to make rapid progress during the summer months. The Managing committee were not amused to see work pressing on there at a time when everything was at a standstill on the viaduct. They were not to realise that his finances were becoming badly strained and that he was striving to minimise his immediate outlay.

Nixson and Denton

The firm of Nixson and Denton built most of the bridges on the eleven mile stretch from Carlisle (London Road) to Scarrow Hill, and did so with impeccable workmanship. This was only to be expected, given their pedigree. The roots of the business lay in William Nixon (c1731-1802), stonemason, of Cumdivock, six miles south west of Carlisle.[37] He developed a substantial building business and trained his sons William (1760-1824) and Paul (1768-1850). Young William became a partner in his father's enterprise and continued to operate from Cumdivock. He also did some architectural design and in 1816 became one of two bridgemasters for Cumberland, responsible for 'Allerdale Wards above and below Derwent'. In 1789 he married Elizabeth Carr, and one of their daughters, Anne (born 1813), married John Blackmore in December 1835. William had died a decade before, on 2 March 1824.

Paul altered his surname to Nixson and moved to Carlisle, where he developed a thriving business as a building contractor, together with statuary works, and a marble works at Dent. He had an artistic bent and also practised locally as an architect, while on building a new marble works at Finkle Street in Carlisle, during 1823, he included an exhibition hall for the *Society for the Encouragement of Fine Art*, of which he was a founder. Works built by Nixson in Carlisle range from Thomas Rickman's Trinity Church (1828-30) to Sir Robert Smirke's Eden Bridge (1812-15). By the start of 1824 he had taken on a young partner, William Smith Denton, who married his daughter Sarah in January of that year.[38] Denton was a Yorkshireman, then aged 25, who took on an increasing share of the business. 1824 also saw the marriage of Paul's daughter Elizabeth to the surveyor John Studholme, whose activities on behalf of the railway led to Paul being engaged to estimate the costs of the bridges and give evidence during the passage of the 1829 Bill. He proved a good witness, giving firm, cogent evidence under cross examination. Five years later Francis Giles got Denton to do the same in respect of the first London & Southampton Railway Bill.[39]

Nixson and Denton won their first railway contract at the end of 1830 but Paul seems to have retired from the business by then, and the inscription on the Eden Viaduct gives sole credit to Denton. Indeed Nixson must at some point have relinquished his share in the partnership, though the name was kept, since Denton became bankrupt as a result of the failure of Forsters' Bank in November 1836, but Nixson was not dragged down by the affair.[40] Loans to the firm of Nixson & Denton contributed in large measure to the collapse of the bank, and it would appear that Denton actually lost by his N&C contracts, specifically in respect of the Eden Viaduct, even though the N&C directors had eventually provided a modest supplementary payment. As usual, Denton's personal property was all sold by his assignees, and he and Sarah emigrated to find a new life in America, probably assisted by Paul Nixson. Denton died in Chicago in 1854. Nixson lived in retirement at Dent, where he died in 1850.

John Studholme

Studholme crops up frequently in the early history of the N&C and as a promoter of the Blenkinsopp venture. He was born in Carlisle in 1787 to Joseph Studholme and his wife Mary Moor.[41] He developed a very successful career as a land surveyor, and prepared many tithe maps for Cumberland, but was also keenly interested in agriculture and by 1829 was farming some five hundred acres at Kingmoor, just outside Carlisle.[42] He later received a service of silver plate from the Agricultural Society of Cumberland for his pioneering work in the introduction of tile drains into the county.

Studholme was very well acquainted with the area through which the N&C proposed to run, and prepared the traffic forecasts for the 1829 Bill in addition to his surveys for the company. In the wake of William Denton's bankruptcy he acquired part of the Finkle Street marble works as his office, while the Forster bankruptcy led to his buying John Forster's villa at Morton Head, now part of western Carlisle but then a rural retreat where Studholme lived and farmed until his death in 1847. Studholme was related to John Blackmore by their marriages to Nixson cousins, and his will left the Blenkinsopp shares to Blackmore, however the engineer had died first.

6.12. *Carmichael's engraving of the bridge under the Military Road at Scarrow Hill, looking east. This appears on the title page of his 'Views on the Newcastle & Carlisle Railway'.*

6.13. *(below) Another Carmichael sketch of the Gelt Bridge under construction. This view is taken from the south. (Tullie House Museum & Art Gallery, Carlisle)*

Denton seems to have caused no problems further east, where he had won a contract in September 1833 for the bridges between Hell Beck and Scarrow Hill (GR 569619), where the line crosses the Military Road.[43] The earthworks on that stretch had been let long before in two contracts, of September 1830 and June 1832, to John McKay.[44] On the latter occasion McKay was also engaged to build the lofty Gelt Bridge, which nearly fell victim to the Buddle committee's economies. On 3 July 1833 the Managing committee saw McKay with a view to substituting a timber structure on the partially-completed stone piers. Blackmore was asked to prepare a design but McKay demanded a level of compensation which made the resulting saving not worth having, so Giles's original scheme was allowed to proceed.[45] By the end of the year the abutments and piers were up to twenty-five feet, but things then seem to have slowed down, perhaps influenced by delays at the nearby Cowran Hills. Carmichael's pencil sketches of the bridge were probably made about July 1835, with the arches recently completed and the spandrels being built up.

Just west of the Gelt Bridge is Cowran cutting - half a mile long and up to 110 feet deep. This was a huge excavation for the period, involving a land take - at its widest point - of 324 feet between boundary walls. The original plan was for a tunnel, 740 yards long, although as late as October 1831 discussions were taking place about the possibility of crossing the hill with a pair of inclines, something which Giles tried hard and successfully to persuade the directors against. Having despatched that potential folly, in December 1831 the Carlisle committee let a contract to Robert Wilson, in partnership with a Mr. Grimshaw, to drive an exploratory drift three hundred yards long at the west end.[46] The hill is basically sand, but Giles did not anticipate any significant problems. However, Wilson & Grimshaw made slow progress, and in May 1832 Giles placed a 'Working Contractor' - one Mr. Smith - there to supervise the men at the contractors' expense.[47]

On 15 June 1832 Wilson & Grimshaw attended the directors and made an optimistic forecast.[48] The actual outcome emerges from Robert Wilson's weekly progress reports to the directors, and was nothing like as good. Over the next thirteen working days, operating twenty-four hours a day, the drift only progressed 28 feet 4 inches. On 2 July they came into quicksand and the rate fell to just 32 inches in three days; a week later there was a landslip within the hill leaving a void ten feet wide in the surface above the drift, and Wilson reported that it was unsafe to proceed further. Work did carry on, slowly, but early August brought another 'run' in the sand.[49] This must have been not only gruelling work but immensely disheartening for the men labouring within the hill. Matters were made worse by the refusal of the Carlisle committee to advance any money to Wilson & Grimshaw, ostensibly because they had not yet signed the contract. That, however, was because the N&C had not finalised the document, and the Newcastle directors had the sense, and humanity, to advance £300 to the contractors.[50] That was perhaps the outcome desired by the Carlisle directors, who found difficulty prising money out of their east-end colleagues.

Giles and Benjamin Thompson had known there would be some water to contend with inside Cowran Hill but had no means of knowing the scale of the problem. The trouble was that the sand was interleaved with thin layers of impermeable clay which meant that there was effectively a series of reservoirs trapped within the hill and continually being replenished. The N&C formally gave up the tunnel on 23 August, agreeing to recompense Wilson & Grimshaw and to advertise a contract for an open cutting instead, somewhat to the chagrin of the landowner, Thomas Henry Graham, who was not consulted beforehand.[51] No time was lost, and the new contract was let on 12 September 1832 to Grahamsley, Greaves & Reid of Newcastle, who were already working at the east end of the line. All this added significantly to the company's costs: £508 was spent in total on Wilson's drift, which achieved nothing, while the huge cutting was going to cost far more than the tunnel would have done, plus a payment of £900 to Graham for the extra land taken.

6.14. *Carmichael's sketch of Cowran Cutting during construction, looking west. The road bridge at the west end can be seen, with tracks leading through it to convey spoil to embankments further west. This bridge was probably built by William Denton. Grahamsley built the one at the east end, whose abutments can be seen under construction beyond the timber staging.*
(Tullie House Museum & Art Gallery, Carlisle)

Giles reduced the land take a little by constraining the bottom of the cutting between fourteen-feet-high retaining walls, while draining the hill with a concealed masonry culvert. Grahamsley seems to have made reasonable progress with the excavation, but building the culvert and retaining walls proved a problem because of the wet sand. By the end of 1834 the cutting had probably been driven right through but progress with the culvert was 'very disheartening', only a hundred yards having been completed, out of 700.[52] J. W. Carmichael's pencil sketch shows the contractors' temporary way laid throughout and work progressing on the retaining walls, which Grahamsley expedited by having men work eight hour shifts, round the clock, illuminated at night by naphtha flares.

6.15. A diverted East Coast express heading through Cowran in April 1989, during electrification works between Newcastle and Edinburgh. (Bill Fawcett)

> ### *George Grahamsley*
>
> George Grahamsley (c1806-46) became the most trusted of the N&C's contractors. He entered the picture as the younger partner of Robert Wilson and William Greaves (born c1790) on the early masonry contracts at the east end of the line. Greaves and Grahamsley appear to have branched off by themselves in 1831, for new work, and soon after took on a new partner Edward Reid (also spelled Reed). Greaves dropped out about the end of the decade, and contemporary references make it clear that Grahamsley was, in any case, the dominant figure in the partnership.
>
> Cowran required the excavation of a million cubic yards of 'sand and gravel' and was the largest cutting attempted so far on a British railway or canal. Grahamsley provided some insight into the work in the course of evidence he gave in June 1834 for Giles's London & Southampton Railway Bill, for which he had prepared the earthworks estimates.[53] Much of the spoil was led west, to form embankments such as Cairn Beck, and the falling gradient in that direction meant that the wagons could be despatched by gravity, with a horse riding on the train before hauling the empty wagons back up to Cowran. To expedite the progress of the embankments, the ingenious and energetic Grahamsley devised a machine which allowed four wagons to be teamed (the spoil tipped out) in the time normally taken by one. He gave some interesting testimony as to the merits of different types of labourer. The directors had encouraged him to employ a number of unemployed colliers 'off the parish' but he did 'not consider them the best hands for the work'. By contrast, he found that farmworkers, though unused to physical labour on the scale achieved by a habitual navvy, became 'decidedly the best' after a short amount of practice.
>
> Grahamsley seems to have carried out most of the earthworks between Cowran and Carlisle, and he was also sole contractor for the continuation of the line to the canal basin.[54] He therefore set up a yard and workshops at Robert Street, Carlisle, and explored a few other business opportunities there, such as marketing Newcastle grindstones, brought in by the railway.[55] He gave up the Carlisle yard in the course of 1839, a year which saw the completion of the line from Scotswood to Newcastle, for which he was again sole contractor. That entailed a battle with the elements, since dismally wet weather led to successive landslips which tested even his 'well tried powers and energy'.[56] Grahamsley worked on a number of railways, for example forming part of the Hartlepool Railway at the same time as Cowran Cutting, but few can have involved anything so remarkable as his last work for the N&C: the enlargement of Farnley tunnel to take double track. This was carried out during 1844-5 without significant interruption to the trains, even though it entailed excavating to form a new arch well above the original.
>
> Grahamsley found time in 1838 to get married, and lived latterly with his wife Jane at Laverack Hall, three miles SSW of Jarrow.[57] Sad to relate, his health gave way during 1846. In September he went to Winchester, seeking an improvement, but died there at the end of the month.[58] The business was carried on, as Grahamsley & Reid, by Edward Reid, whose last works for the N&C were the Alston Branch viaduct at Haltwhistle and the reinstatement of bridges near Allerwash, destroyed by floods in 1852.

6.16. *Detail from Carmichael's engraving of Cowran Cut, looking west. It gives the atmosphere of the early trains, albeit shown on the wrong track. Until 1838, all passenger trains were mixed, with goods wagons marshalled between carriages and engine.*

The directors had intended both ends of the line to open simultaneously, but this was now out of the question. The delays at Cowran meant there was no point pressing on rapidly with the remainder of the west-end works, and in April 1833, in the wake of the Buddle Report, the Board halted operations between Milton (Brampton Junction) and Blenkinsopp in order to conserve funds, although contracts had been let on this stretch as early as December 1831 and some work must have been well underway.[59] They also held back from starting the final section of the west-end route between London Road, Carlisle, and the Canal Basin. Indeed, though this formed an integral part of the original main line, it was increasingly regarded by the Newcastle directors as the 'Canal Branch', which is how it will be referred to in future here. This naturally aroused the suspicions of the Carlisle committee. Their particular *bête-noire* was John Clayton, who was keen to concentrate resources on extending the east end through to Haydon Bridge at the expense of the west; this led to a degree of anguish during May 1834, with the Carlisle directors threatening to take the matter to the Exchequer Commissioners.[60]

Ultimately all was resolved more or less amicably; the Managing committee were keen to see progress in the west and the arrival of Exchequer funds enabled work to resume between Milton and Blenkinsopp. The first stage of the west-end route, from Carlisle London Road to Greenhead, had its public opening on 19 July 1836, though it had already come into use for coal traffic from the Earl of Carlisle's collieries. The reconstructed portion of the Earl's own railway, linking up with the N&C at what was later called Brampton Junction, had begun operation in early July, with its own formal opening on the 15th. Blenkinsopp colliery also now had access by rail though its production was hampered for some time by the need to develop new workings because James Thompson had done his best to exhaust the existing ones prior to the Earl surrendering the lease.[61]

The east end of the railway had been extended to Haydon Bridge in June, so 1836 brought the ultimate completion of the railway reassuringly into prospect. However, the year ended on a sad note with the bankruptcies of Denton and the Forsters. The other Carlisle directors must have sensed problems on 20 October when Forsters' Bank refused to make any further payments to contractors. The committee generally had a debt of five or six thousand pounds at the bank, but their credit was sound and this refusal must have come as a surprise. The immediate need was met by the despatch of £2,000 from the railway's main bankers, Sir Matthew White Ridley and partners, in Newcastle.[62] The crunch came on 19 November, when the Forsters filed for bankruptcy and William Forster appeared at the Carlisle committee to put them in the picture.[63] Underlying the bank's problems were their advances to William Denton and, coincidentally, another builder, William Gate. In examination, John Forster revealed that he 'had fears as to Denton for twelve months ... when he took the railway bridge his balance was much less.'[64] Assuming this refers to the Eden Viaduct, it appears that the Forsters were ultimately laid low by the railway which they had done so much to encourage. They had considerable private assets, in property, but these were sold up over the next few years and, after the declaration of a final dividend to their creditors in 1844, the *Carlisle Journal* reported that they had been left 'penniless.'[65] By then the railway was a flourishing business. The N&C had met its debts to the Forsters' assignees in large measure by the issue of debentures for £5,000, payable after five years and probably bearing 5% interest.

6.17. *Carmichael's sketch of the River Caldew bridge at Carlisle, just over 2 months into construction. Temporary bridges convey materials, and one river pier is taking shape just to the right of the left-hand crane. Blocks of stone for this pier and the east (right) abutment are being dressed on the bank. Carmichael does not show any shelter, but it is likely that an open-fronted shed would have been put up for the use of the masons. Stone blocks are also evident as counterweights for the two cranes. The Cathedral shows up towards the left.* (Tullie House Museum & Art Gallery, Carlisle)

Meanwhile, the Canal Branch had been proceeding in a stop/go fashion. In response to the urgings of the Carlisle directors and the Managing committee, a contract had been let to George Grahamsley at the start of July 1834, but work was halted the following April to cope with the latest cash-flow crisis.[66] An exception to this command was the bridge over the River Caldew, where the managing directors urged work to proceed immediately with putting in the piers and abutments, before the floods, which were commonly expected every August.[67] This was done, and by mid July 1835 the east abutment and one pier had been formed.[68] Carmichael's sketch shows the bridge as it then stood, and by the end of the year it was ready to receive its three arches. However, March 1836 did not see the line in quite the 'state of considerable forwardness' described by the managing directors in their report to the AGM. The first traffic on the branch evidently came on 25 February 1837, when Richard Lowry noted that they had sent some grain down the line to Dalston Road for the first time, while the formal opening took place on 9 March.[69] This saw a modest version of the customary celebrations, with flags fluttering from every bridge. The Newcastle directors came across and joined the opening train, hauled by *Hercules*, which was followed by a pair of gaily decorated coal trains. *Goliah* pulled twenty wagons of Lord Carlisle's coal and *Atlas* did the same for the Blenkinsopp company. These were duly discharged into the vessels *Eden* and *Swan* at the Canal Basin, and the wagons returned to London Road crammed as full as could be with poor folk who fancied the free ride, despite all the coal dust. The east end of the railway had been extended to Gateshead (Redheugh) eight days before, and the railway now began to carry through goods between the two seas, despite the two transhipments involved because of the break in the middle of the route.[70]

Filling in the Middle: Blenkinsopp to Hexham

The middle stretch of the route, between Blenkinsopp Colliery and Hexham, comprised two distinct sections. The portion from Blenkinsopp to Haydon Bridge would always have been the last to be completed, since it was not expected to generate much local traffic. Haydon Bridge to Hexham, however, was originally intended to open as part of the first phase at the east end and was only deferred because of the financial crisis at the end of 1832. Its completion was very important to those major investors: Beaumont and the Crawhalls, together with Greenwich Hospital, since it would cut out eight miles of the Lead Road between Langley and Hexham and substitute just three miles, downhill, to a railhead at Haydon Bridge. It was also important to Greenwich Hospital's tenants with quarries and lime kilns near Allerwash.

By the summer of 1834 light was becoming visible at the end of the tunnel, and on 12 August the directors felt confident enough to let the Hexham to Haydon Bridge section.[71] The masonry works were let to Jacob Ritson, and the earthworks to William Hutchinson. The line begins with an easy stretch along Tyne Green, west of Hexham station, then crosses the South Tyne at Warden, before another straightforward run as far as the bridge over the Settlingstones Burn (GR 876673). After that the railway keeps very close to the river for much of the way to Haydon Bridge, a mile being across the lower slopes of Haydon Fell, where it plunges into the Tyne. This entailed stretches of embankment originally protected from scour by a stone facing, or revetment, and an impressive length of river wall at Capons Cleugh. (GR 863661)

Building the line across the Capons Cleugh ravine entailed close collaboration between Ritson and Hutchinson, with Ritson building the wall directly up from the river and Hutchinson then filling behind and above it, rail level being about ten feet higher than the top of the wall, which is itself sixteen feet high. By May 1835 Ritson was piling for the wall's foundations and had run a temporary timber bridge across the river in order to fetch stone from a quarry on the far bank.[72] That was no mean exercise in itself, given the width of the Tyne at this point, even though it becomes very shallow in dry weather. By September Ritson had 250 yards of the wall raised to between five and eleven feet, with about another eighty feet still to be started. This brisk progress was fortunate since the winter brought heavy rains, resulting in 'wet, spongy ground' which 'baffled every endeavour' of Hutchinson to press his earthworks forward.[73] Even so, by March 1836 Hutchinson was backing up behind the river wall, having given the masonry time to set, and the line was formally opened on 28 June. With the opening of the west end of the railway the following month, it was clearly time to press on with the middle section, between Blenkinsopp and Haydon Bridge.

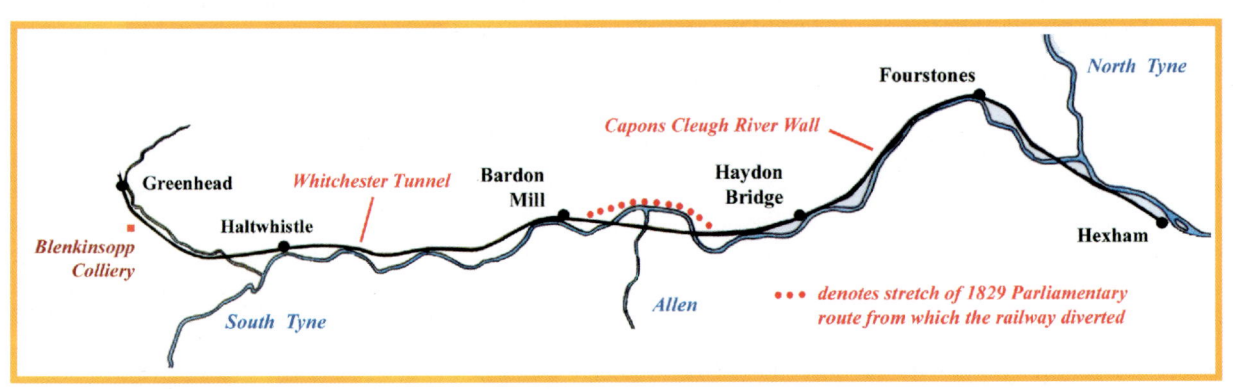

This final twelve-mile stretch is relatively undemanding in engineering terms, partly because of an alteration made to the 1829 Parliamentary route. This kept to the north bank of the Tyne west of Haydon Bridge and would have required substantial stretches of river wall in the vicinity of Ridley Hall Bridge. Instead, the line was diverted for two miles onto the south bank. This entailed two crossings of the South Tyne and one of the River Allen but these bridges are quite modest affairs and the remainder of the diversion is on a low embankment through the riverside meadows. The company were fortunate to obtain the co-operation of John Davidson of Ridley Hall, through whose lands the line was diverted, although it took some time to negotiate his price down to an acceptable level. Thus talks began in July 1836 and a final agreement was only settled in March 1837.[74]

64

6.20. *Carmichael's engraving of Whitchester Tunnel, viewed from the west. The diverted turnpike road is seen passing over the tunnel portal and then dipping down to the left, below a freshly-excavated rock face of friable sandstone, The former roadbed and part of the river bed have disappeared under the railway. A group of navvies provides foreground interest.*

6.18. *(left) The river wall at Capons Cleugh, looking east, with a GNER (Great North Eastern Railway) express diverted during engineering works between Newcastle and Edinburgh in the closing months of the GNER franchise. (Bill Fawcett, 2007)*

A modest departure from the Parliamentary route took the line through a short tunnel at Whitchester, a mile east of Haltwhistle station, and this formed the boundary between the two sections into which this stretch was divided for contract purposes. Anticipating that the tunnel might be the slowest work, it was included in the western section, let to George Grahamsley in September 1836. [75] Immediately west of the tunnel, the Tyne was diverted to a more southerly course and the railway embankment was formed on the old river bed. This involved a cut and fill operation, with the hillside being cut back to accommodate a diversion of the turnpike road. Contracts for the eastern section, to Haydon Bridge, were let in February 1837, anticipating by a few weeks the final agreement with Davidson. [76] Masonry went to our old friend Jacob Ritson and earthworks to William Hutchinson. Things evidently went smoothly, and the line opened to the public in June 1838, completing the last link between the Tyne and the Solway, even if the eastern terminus was still at Redheugh, on the Gateshead bank of the Tyne, rather than Newcastle.

Grand Opening

The formal opening of the final stretch, from Blenkinsopp to Haydon Bridge, was scheduled for 18 June 1838, the anniversary of Waterloo, and - with eight years of construction behind them - the directors chose to celebrate in style.[77] Five trains were scheduled to leave Carlisle about 6 a.m. for Newcastle, and at 9.30 the first of these arrived at Redheugh, carrying the Carlisle directors and that city's Mayor and Corporation. They were conveyed across the Tyne in the state barges belonging to Newcastle's Corporation and Trinity House and settled down to breakfast at the Assembly Rooms.

Thirteen trains made the return leg to Carlisle, employing all the company's locomotives except for its oldest, *Comet*. The idea was for the Newcastle party to accompany the Cumbrians to Carlisle and return to Newcastle during the early evening. Unfortunately, the N&C's organisation broke down, with eager crowds invading the reserved carriages as well as boarding the open carriages and adapted wagons on offer to them. The weather also played its part, mutating from fog to heavy rain and soaking many of the participants, while one train ran into another at the beginning of the return from Carlisle. It was a memorable day for the participants, especially those in the last train which wandered back into Redheugh station some time after 6 a.m

6.21. *The 'Gateshead Observer' advertised a special supplement describing the 'most remarkable features' of the country traversed by the N&C. This formed part of the issue of June 16, so that people could take it with them to the opening, 2 days later.*

Carlisle to Blaydon in 1838

Having watched the line under construction, we shall take a ride along it in the summer of 1838, starting with a lift on a goods train from the canal basin. The tracks run along its west quay, where we can see wagons from Blenkinsopp and the Earl of Carlisle's collieries discharging coal for shipment to Ireland. If we choose the right day we shall also encounter Irish cattle being herded reluctantly into a line of the company's distinctive cattle wagons with their drop-down ends.

The land falls a little from the basin, so the railway runs on a low sandstone viaduct, of six arches, up to the bridge across the Port Road, leading to Port Carlisle and Bowness. Wigton Road is also bridged but the Dalston Road is crossed on the level. Our journey is taking us through open country, skirting the city, but this will soon be built up and a harbinger of change is Dixons' Shaddon Mill. Its massive bulk rises on the left, and it and other industries are served by coal depots situated along the Canal branch. Almost a mile from the canal basin, we cross the River Caldew on a handsome stone bridge and enter an area which the next decade will see transformed by the arrival of the Lancaster & Carlisle and Maryport & Carlisle Railways. For the moment, however, it remains a rural scene as we approach the busy London Road and the railway's main depot.

6.22. Bridge conducting Lorne Crescent under the Canal Branch. This originally lay in open country. The bridge has gone, but the gate pier remains. (Bill Fawcett, 1973)

London Road yard is a busy place, though the warehouse is quite small and many goods are stored outdoors, under tarpaulins. The biggest feature is the coal depot, with tracks running on top of stone cross-walls which form a series of cells into which coal is discharged from the company's bottom-door chaldron wagons. Beyond that is the engineering department's province, with a complete range of workshops. We must look to our train, however, and we have several choices to make. We could take one of the newly-introduced expresses, which do the sixty miles to Redheugh (Gateshead), the current eastern terminus, in just three hours. For a shilling less, we can have a more leisurely journey, taking at least an hour longer, in one of the 'mixed' trains, with passenger carriages marshalled behind a string of goods wagons. This will be more interesting, but what class to travel? If it were raining we might opt for a fully-enclosed first-class carriage, costing ten shillings single fare to Redheugh, equivalent to three days wages for young Mr. Lowry, the goods clerk, whom we can see giving orders to one of the yard men. As it's a fine day, we'll choose the cheapest class and the best views, occupying one of the seats placed on top of the luggage vans, but we must avoid the fate of George Turnbull, who stood up at the wrong moment and bashed his brains out on a bridge. Time to board, and as there are no platforms we make use of the carriage steps and big brass grab handle.

Leaving Carlisle, we cross the River Petteril and soon hear the engine working hard as it tackles the start of the steady climb to the watershed. The first stop is Scotby, with one of the railway's neat station houses in the fashionable Tudor Revival style. We are in rising country now, and soon plunge into Wetheral cutting, with the station at the far end. This is a more elaborate building than most, in deference to the Howards of Corby Castle, and we get a good view of their wooded *demesne* and of the river far below as we head across the Eden Viaduct. All too soon we are at the other end and crossing the main street of Corby, but this is followed by another vista as we take to the viaduct across the Corby Beck. Almost a mile further on, a siding leads off left to serve Broadwath coal depot, a substantial and neat affair with a handsome lodge gracing its entrance. We then traverse a picturesque, hummocky sort of country on our way to the next station, How Mill.

6.23. Brampton Junction, looking east in 1964. It developed into a small railway community, with the station doubling as post office. All the houses went in the nineteen-seventies, leaving only the footbridge and waiting shed. (Bill Fawcett)

The view ahead is blocked by the wooded Cowran Hills, and just half a mile from How Mill we come to the bridge which straddles the western entrance to the famous cutting. We emerge from its depths through another arch and then curve left onto the lofty Gelt Bridge. Crossing the bridge we get a view of the Pennines, looming up on the right. The climb is nearly over and we come out into relatively bare country, almost four hundred feet above our starting point. Approaching Milton station (later renamed Brampton Junction), we see the Earl of Carlisle's line from Brampton curving in on the left. The station itself has no special facilities, but there is a water tank at which our locomotive may pause for refreshment. As we leave, we notice the Earl's railway heading in from Kirkhouse, with a coal train waiting for us to clear the line so it can proceed to Carlisle. A little further on we come to Milton crossing, where one may glimpse the original route of the Earl's railway.

6.24. *A contemporaneous painting of the Canal Basin, looking towards the castle and cathedral. To the right of the ships are chaldron wagons which have come down the railway. Behind the two middle ships can be seen the arms and platform of a coal drop, used to lower a wagon over the ship in order to discharge coal or coke. The principle is similar to that of the Thompson drop shown in figure 3.2, but operating at a very much lower height and in a simpler fashion.* (courtesy of George Tinkler)

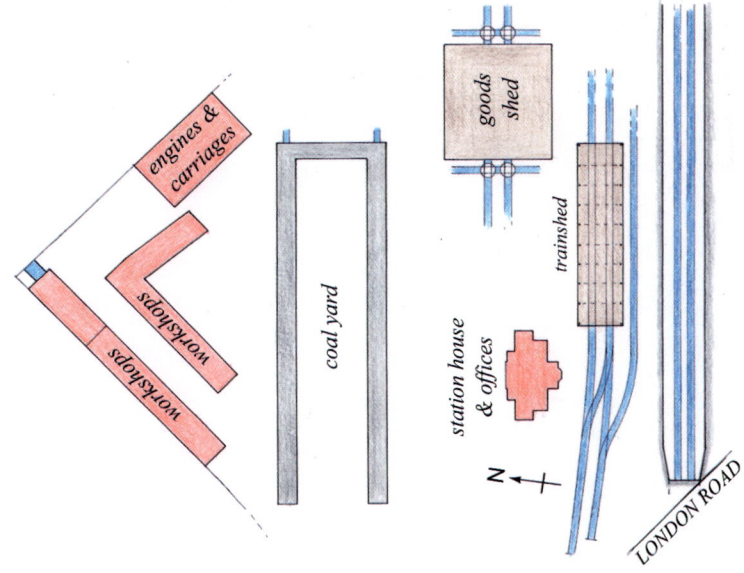

6.25. *Carmichael's sketch of London Road station, looking east. Its buildings are discussed in chapter 15. On the right is the Mains cotton mill with a prominent cupola; B&Q now occupy the site. In front of it runs the trackbed of the Canal Branch, still under construction when this view was taken in 1836. At the left is a crane of a typical canal and railway design, one of which can still be found in the coalyard at Greenhead. Behind it is the roof of the engine shed.* (Tullie House Museum & Art Gallery, Carlisle)

6.26. *Conjectural reconstruction of London Road in 1838, working back from 1/500 OS of 1863-4. Only a few representative tracks have been shown. The Canal Branch drops to a lower level than the station, so that Maryport or Lancaster trains using London Road in the 1840's had to run past the station and then set back into it.* (Bill Fawcett)

The line now passes through the woods of the Naworth Estate, and we cross the road leading to the castle. Trains stop here if the Earl requires, but it will be several years before anything is provided in the way of a station house. A shallow cutting takes us to the bridge under the Military Road at Scarrow Hill and soon after we get our first views over the Irthing Valley, with the Border hills in the background. The railway follows a contour high up the valley side, some 300 feet above the river, and soon comes to the isolated station at Low Row. This is little more than a well-plenished wayside, with the station serving as an agricultural railhead.

The Irthing is followed to Gilsland, where we cross the Roman Wall and the river strikes north; the celebrated spa is to be found in its wooded ravine a mile from the station, overlooked by the prominent bulk of Shaws Hotel. Confusingly, the station is called Rose Hill, taking its name from a spur whose top was cut off to make way for the railway. The arrival of the line has done much to promote the popularity of the spa. Leaving Gilsland, we enter the watershed, a somewhat desolate and boggy tract of land at the end of which there is a good view of Thirlwall Castle, with the Tippalt Burn tumbling down alongside. The burn has been straightened and runs beside the railway into Greenhead. Though the village is tiny, this is an important station for coal traffic originating at the Blenkinsopp colliery and, until a few months ago, it was a railhead for road coaches over the central section of the route. It has an engine shed and quite extensive workshops. Leaving Greenhead, we part from the Military Road, which heads off to follow the Roman Wall on its spectacular course past Housesteads. Passing the connection from Blenkinsopp colliery and lime works on the right, we continue down the valley towards Haltwhistle, with a brief glimpse of Colonel Coulson's Blenkinsopp Hall on the left.

At Haltwhistle station we get our first look at the Tyne (strictly the South Tyne), which we are to follow for the rest of our journey. Approaching Whitchester tunnel, our route has been formed partly within the riverbed and provides a foretaste of the views to be had later on. We run through riverside meadows, or haughs as they are known locally, on our way to the next station, Bardon Mill, and the line continues like this all the way to Haydon Bridge. On our way we catch a brief glimpse up the tight, wooded glen of the River Allen as we cross it on a bridge sandwiched between the two Tyne crossings. Haydon Bridge is the railhead for the lead business, and a busy place on that account. It also has a small workshop for wagon repairs. Heading on, the hills gradually close in, resulting in the spectacular riverside section at Capons Cleugh, already illustrated, and this is succeeded by a brief flurry of industry at Allerwash, where William Benson has lime kilns served by the railway. The valley widens out again on the approach to Fourstones, the next station, which also has limekilns, together with a small colliery and the Prudham stone quarry. All of these are set to expand as a consequence of the railway.

After Fourstones, the line skirts the foot of Warden Hill and then bridges the South Tyne for the last time. Soon after, we see its smaller fellow, the North Tyne, joining in and then follow the Tyne Green into Hexham. Its station is a bustling place, inconveniently sandwiched between a pair of level crossings and with the passenger amenities limited to an office and the roof which spans the tracks immediately in front of it, affording little shelter when rain and wind combine in an assault. One consolation is the view, with fields sweeping up to the picturesque old town, clustered around its abbey. We now continue along an open stretch of the valley to Corbridge, crossing on our way the Devils Water, with a glimpse of ruined Dilston Hall, one-time home of the Derwentwaters, whose ill fortune brought Greenwich Hospital into the locality. Corbridge station is divided awkwardly by a level crossing on the turnpike road at the foot of Tinkler Bank. From here, the line keeps to the rising ground at the back of the haugh until it is forced onto the riverbank at Farnley Scar, penetrated by the notorious single-track tunnel.

We emerge from the tunnel into a stretch of deep cutting and then cross more meadowland to reach Riding Mill station. There, we are very close to the Tyne but see nothing of it thanks to the measures taken to screen the railway from the windows of Styford Hall. The same happens on the approach to the next station, Stocksfield, which serves T.W. Beaumont's Bywell estate. It used to be a railhead for lead traffic, but that has declined recently with the running down of Beaumont's Dukesfield smelter. We now follow another easy stretch of line, over the level haugh, before coming to the second of the great river walls. This takes us across the face of Eltringham Scar to Prudhoe station, from which a ferry crosses the river to the ancient village of Ovingham. Prudhoe itself is a small village well up the hillside, but is set to grow with the expansion of coal mining locally, fostered by the railway. At present, however, the station is thought to warrant nothing more substantial than a wooden cabin; not even the customary agent's house.

Leaving Prudhoe we again follow an easy route over the haugh as far as Hagg Bank, pierced by a cutting rather than the tunnel originally contemplated by Benjamin Thompson. After that we arrive at another spectacular riverside stretch, running along the river wall to Wylam station. This used to be linked by ferry to the village on the north bank, but Mr. Thompson and his sons have developed an ironworks there and a bridge has been built across the Tyne by public subscription. Designed by Mr. Blackmore, it also carries a railway track to the works.

From Wylam we traverse the foot of the rising land alongside the haugh past Ryton, the next station, with views across the Tyne to coal trains operating on the historic Wylam waggonway. Finally, we cross the neck of a big loop made by the river to reach Stella, an ancient shipping point for the collieries of the Winlaton area but one which is likely to decline rapidly once this railway gains access to the Tyne downstream of Newcastle Bridge. The hills are closing in again on the south, forcing us onto the final stretch of river wall, with another retaining wall above the line to secure the turnpike road, which also has to be squeezed in. We are now coming to our destination, Blaydon station, a curiously makeshift sort of place, perched on the edge of the river in what used to be part of Mr. Beaumont's lead yard.

The route described here remains in use 170 years later, and substantially unaltered, except for the Canal Branch. That has been cut back to the junction with the Maryport line, barely a third of its former length, and the remainder destroyed.

6.27. *Looking east from Brampton Junction station footbridge in LNER days. On the right is the Earl of Carlisle's Railway heading into a cutting on its way to Kirkhouse. The N&C main line curves away to the left of the signalbox on its way to Naworth. To the left of that some LMS wagons are standing in the goods yard, where the North Eastern Railway built a large goods shed (just off the picture) in 1883. (courtesy of Denis Perriam)*

6.28. *The watershed, half a mile east of Gilsland station. At this point the railway is about 450 feet above sea level, and skirts what would have been quite a boggy tract when the line was under construction. Ahead are the crags of the Whin Sill, the great volcanic outcrop which bears the Roman Wall along its crest. Travellers have only a brief glimpse of this before the railway heads down the valley of the Tippalt Burn.*

(Bill Fawcett)

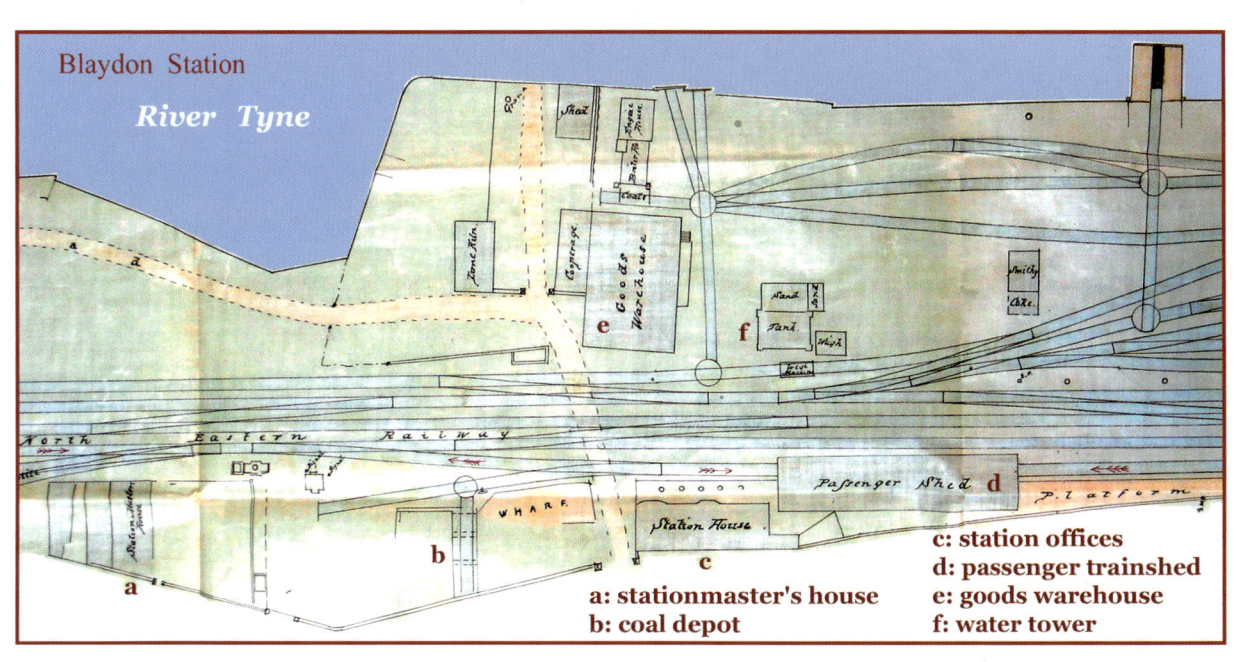

a: stationmaster's house
b: coal depot
c: station offices
d: passenger trainshed
e: goods warehouse
f: water tower

6.29. *Blaydon station's cramped layout lingered into NER days as this plan prepared for the Board of Trade indicates. The station building shown here was probably built in 1844 to replace the makeshift original. However, even with the arrival of a platform in the 1850's all passenger trains had to be dealt with on a single track forming a loop from the main running lines. Figure 12.9 is a photograph of this layout taken in N&C days from the stationmaster's house at 'a'.*

The Roman Bridge at Alcantara

7.2. *Benjamin Thompson's design for the Eden Viaduct, with three spans of 55 feet flanked by ones of 45 and 35 feet.*

7.3. *Francis Giles's signed elevation drawing for the Eden Viaduct, with 80 feet (24m) spans.*

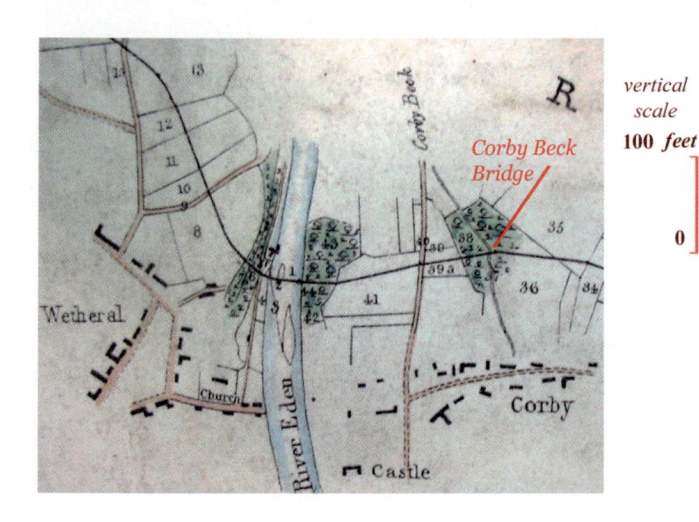

7.4. *Details of the Wetheral and Corby area from the Deposited Plan of November 1828.*

Chapter 7: Engineering Works between Carlisle and Blaydon

Introduction

The significant engineering works on the main line between Carlisle and Blaydon are largely confined to bridges, tunnels and river walls. The two most notable earthworks are Cowran Cutting, which involved a million cubic yards of excavation and was described by Blackmore as the largest in the country, and the seventy-feet high embankment across Hell Beck, about a mile further east.[1] The latter was an object of interest to contemporaries but forestry has since obscured its features. The aim of this chapter is to look at major and characteristic examples of the engineering works, not to catalogue all of them.

The engineering features between Carlisle and Blenkinsopp and between Blaydon and Hexham were begun during Giles's term as engineer. The remainder were conducted throughout under Blackmore and the Managing committee, but the only significant differences between these and the earlier works are the introduction of Blackmore's distinctive timber-trussed river bridges and a limited use of cast-iron bridge girders.

Other than modest amounts of timber and iron, the staple building material for N&C engineering structures was the local sandstone. In the Carlisle area this is a dark red stone, which weathers with a fairly uniform colour except where this is modified by the presence of lichens. This is used down the line as far as Scarrow Hill, just east of Naworth. Further east, one finds a honey-coloured freestone which is very easy to work when fresh from the quarry but hardens on subsequent exposure. It also darkens on weathering but often takes on hints of other colours due to traces of metals. The finest of the Northumbrian freestones is that from Prudham Quarry, near Fourstones, which the railway took on a 21 year lease from Greenwich Hospital. Acting on Blackmore's recommendation, arrangements for this were made in September 1835 by Wylam Walker, who was then the assistant engineer supervising works between Hexham and Haydon Bridge, and who subsequently took the quarry lease on his own account.[2] As well as being used on a variety of engineering works west of Hexham, the Prudham stone was used for many N&C buildings, culminating in its employment at Newcastle Central Station. In later years this stone was to be used in prestige buildings in many other parts of Britain.

The Major Masonry Bridges

The major masonry-arch bridges are concentrated at the west end of the line, between Brampton and Carlisle, and range in size from the Eden Viaduct down to the Mains Bridge over the River Petteril. The Eden Viaduct is the most spectacular but it has a small cousin just a quarter mile further east in the form of the viaduct crossing the valley of the Corby Beck.[3]

7.5. *The classic view of the Eden Viaduct, looking downstream (north) from the former ferry slip at Wetheral.*
(Bill Fawcett)

The Eden and Corby Beck Viaducts

The Eden Viaduct, officially known to contemporaries as 'Corby Bridge', is a traditional round-arched masonry structure of five eighty-feet spans, carrying the rails over ninety feet above the river. This is impressive enough, but the original intention was for something more elaborate in order to complement the view from Henry Howard's gardens at Corby Castle. Benjamin Thompson visited Corby on 7 May 1828 to discuss the bridge with Howard and, after leafing through various volumes in his library, they settled on the Roman bridge over the River Tagus at Alcantara in Spain.[4] This is one of the most famous bridges of antiquity, with six arches diminishing gradually in span from the central pair through the two outer ones. Thompson's version is shown in Figure 7.2, with three middle spans of 55 feet, flanked by ones of 45 and 35 feet. Giles soon put paid to this idea as being too costly, since it required two more piers than the eventual bridge, and even his first detailed report of August 1829, while acting simply as consultant, described the intended bridge as finally built. Thompson's bridge would have been a rather fussy affair, while Giles's viaduct is a design of noble simplicity.

The facing masonry throughout is rusticated ashlar, i.e. smooth faced, with two of the angles bevelled in order to emphasise the horizontal joints. This enhances the impression of strength, while the apparent height of the bridge is exaggerated by two strategies: one is a progressive reduction in the depth of the masonry courses facing the spandrels (the areas between the arches and parapet) as one proceeds up the wall; the other is a gradual reduction in the depth of the arch ring from springing to crown. The bridge was built largely from stone quarried in Howard's plantation on the west bank, the working being filled in and landscaped afterwards. The facing material, however, is from the Newbiggin quarries 'long tried and proved in the buildings about Carlisle'.[5]

7.6. *The cast-iron parapet of the footway cantilevered out from the north face of the Eden Viaduct. This was added by Peter Tate, John Blackmore's successor. (Bill Fawcett)*

While the railway was conceived as a horse-worked line, open to all comers, the intention was to lay a roadway between the rails over the bridge.[6] This would replace the long-established ferry between Wetheral and Corby, and the 1829 Act permitted the railway to charge tolls and to compensate Henry Howard, as owner of the ferry rights. However, the adoption of locomotives led to second thoughts and the directors decided not to proceed with the carriage road despite pressure from Howard to do so, in order to provide access from Corby to Wetheral station. Pedestrians were permitted to use the bridge, subject to a penny toll, and in 1851 they were provided with the present footway cantilevered out from the north face on cast-iron brackets.

7.7. *Corby Beck viaduct, looking west. Since this picture was taken the trees have taken over, and the carriage drive has almost vanished. (J.M. Fleming, May 1971)*

Corby Glen lies only a quarter of a mile to the east and also formed part of Henry Howard's *demesne*, with a carriage drive running down the middle. The railway is carried sixty feet above the Corby Beck and could have been borne on an embankment (a bone of contention with the economists of the Buddle committee), but Howard insisted on a viaduct, so as to preserve and indeed enhance the views. At one stage it was envisaged with a central 'triumphal arch' over the carriageway, but again Giles entered with a breath of common sense and substituted a simple design with seven arches of forty feet span. Howard's carriage drive, now long disused, is marked by a heraldic Howard lion in the parapet above. The stone was won from a quarry close to the site, and the detailing of the bridge conforms to that of the Eden Viaduct.

7.8.

Details of the Eden Viaduct and (bottom right) the Howard lion on Corby Beck viaduct.
Shown above it is the inscription to Henry Howard at the west end of the Eden Viaduct.

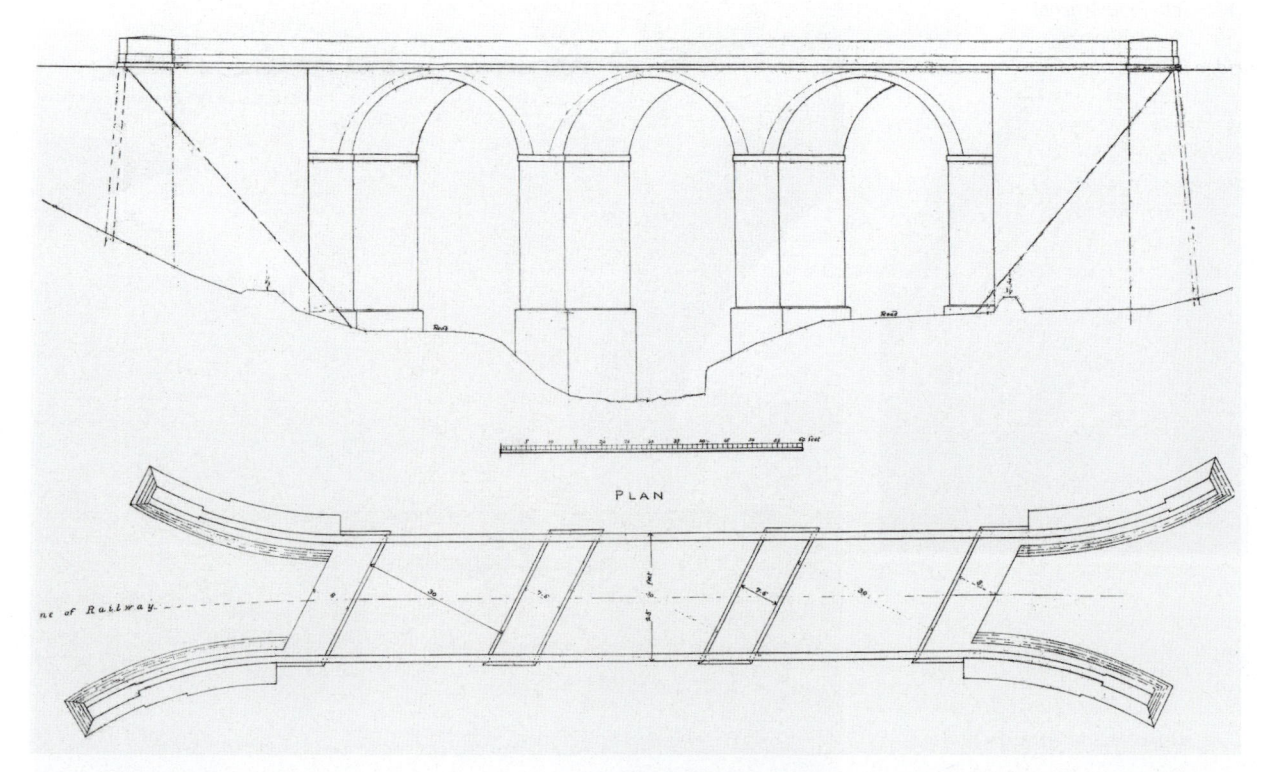

7.9. *John Blackmore's drawing for the Gelt Bridge, dated May 1832.*

The Gelt Bridge

The railway crosses the ravine of the River Gelt by a skew bridge of three spans carrying the line fifty-six feet above the modest Middle Gelt road bridge. The spans are only thirty feet, with a skew of 27 degrees, but the bridge has a very real presence. Although the design shares many similarities with the Eden and Corby Beck viaducts, the surface treatment of the stone differs. Thus the arch voussoirs are ashlar, but the piers and spandrels have rock-faced masonry, with dressed margins, giving a more rugged effect than the precise rustication of the two viaducts. The abutments appear far more conspicuous than in those bridges, and are strengthened, visually at least, by a subtle batter which starts some feet back from the end faces.

7.10. *Inscriptions are placed at the foot of each abutment, one English, the other Latin.*

7.11. *Arch detail, showing the winding courses. (both Bill Fawcett)*

Francis Giles and the contractor, John McKay, signed their handiwork with masonry plaques set into the abutments but credit should also be given to Thomas Slack, a stonemason from Langholm, who supervised the work on behalf of McKay. His role emerges from newspaper reports and a letter written to the *Newcastle Chronicle* in 1836 by Henry Welch, Bridge Surveyor to Northumberland. Evidently, none of the engineers: Giles, Blackmore or Larmer, gave instructions regarding the setting-out of the masonry courses of the Gelt's skew arches. Instead Slack sorted these out using the geometrical rules described by Peter Nicholson, a stonemason's son, in his 1827 *Treatise on Masonry and Stone Cutting*. Slack is reported to have carved a turnip to provide a three-dimensional image for his masons.[7] Welch's interest stemmed from a desire to put the record straight in respect of inflated claims being made by Charles Fox, then a resident engineer on the London & Birmingham Railway, to have developed the first rules for setting out a skew arch. Blackmore declined to comment. The credit for being a pioneer of masonry skew arches goes to our old friend William Chapman, who had employed them on his Kildare Canal half a century before, in the seventeen-eighties.

7.12. *Gelt Bridge from the north, with the road bridge just in front of it. An atmospheric view, taken by John Fleming in May 1971, from the same standpoint as the Carmichael view below.*

7.13. *J.W. Carmichael's engraving of the Gelt Bridge.*

7.14. *A view along the south face, showing the vigorously wrought masonry and the splay of the abutment wall.*
(Bill Fawcett)

7.15. *A diverted East Coast express heading east from the Gelt in April 1989, during electrification works between Edinburgh and Newcastle. (Bill Fawcett)*

75

The Petteril Bridge at Carlisle

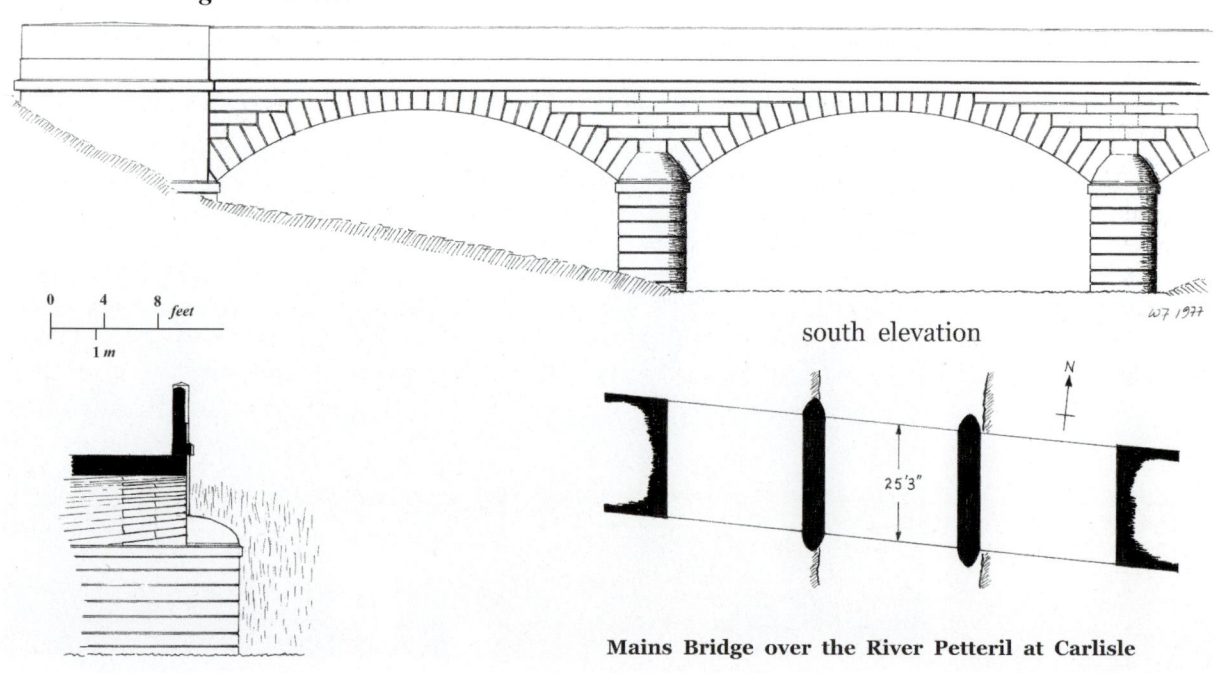

7.16. *Measured drawing of the bridge over the River Petteril. (Bill Fawcett, 1977)*

On its approach to Carlisle the railway crosses the River Petteril by the Mains Bridge, built by William Denton and completed in 1833. The arches were finished at the start of the year, with work on the spandrels being deferred until the warmer spring weather.[8] It is a low but elegant structure of three segmental arches of thirty feet span, with a slight skew of about 7 degrees. The masonry joints are boldly rusticated, as at the Eden, but for this purpose the voussoirs are grouped in pairs and triples to create a superficial illusion of greater size and strength. Giles's turnpike bridge at Warwick Bridge (Fig. 5.7) is developed from his Petteril design but benefits visually from the graceful curve of its road and parapets. The Petteril Bridge was widened on the north side in 1890 to carry additional tracks but the original south elevation remains visible. Unlike the major bridges, it has required life-support work, with a concrete shell being formed against the soffit of the easternmost arch.

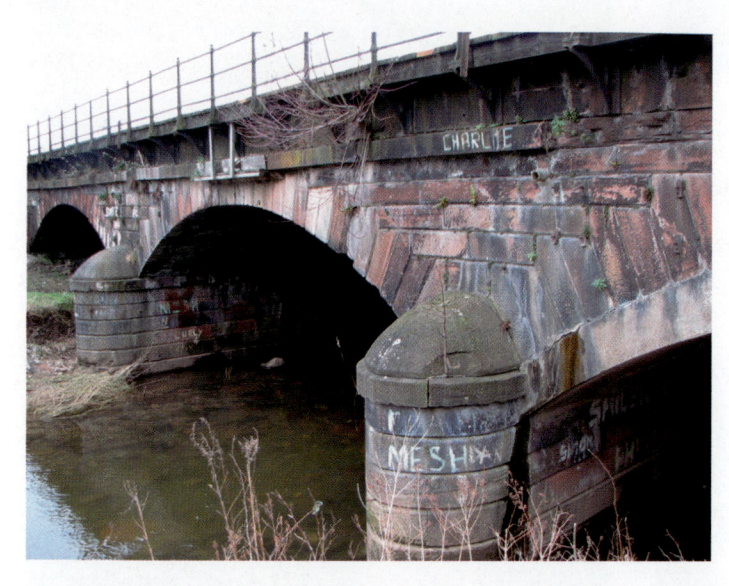

7.17. The Petteril Bridge looks rather sorry for itself nowadays. It carries traffic joining from the Settle & Carlisle line at Petteril Bridge Junction, as well as Newcastle trains. There used to be extensive sidings in this area, so the NER provided the walkway cantilevered out from this south face of the bridge, behind which the original parapet remains intact. The NER appear to have built a timber structure to carry extra tracks on the north side, prior to building the permanent extension in 1890. The north elevation of the extension is faced with rock-faced red sandstone but the N&C parapet has been reused on top.

(Bill Fawcett, 2007)

The River Caldew bridge on the Canal Branch was similar, though unskewed and with arches of 35 feet span. It had a very short life; having opened to traffic in 1837, it was demolished in August 1846 after serious subsidence.[9] When the bridge was about to be started, the managing directors noted that piles might have to be sunk to a considerable depth because of alluvial deposits in the area. Both Grahamsley and Blackmore must have been misled into thinking they had piled to a firm foundation, for some of the piles eventually punched through and in April 1846 one pier sank two feet. More piles were driven alongside to carry the railway on a temporary timber structure, which probably lasted until 1867, when a new bridge was built with two spans of cast-iron arches on stone abutments and a central pier.[10] That was later rebuilt with plate girders, to form the fourth bridge on this site, but has been demolished.

Masonry Overbridges

The masonry bridges spanning the railway fall into just two standard types: the basic overbridge and an extended version, referred to at the time as a 'tunnel' and used for a few turnpike road crossings. The latter is now represented only by the ones at London Road, Carlisle, at Scarrow Hill on the A69 stretch of the Military Road, and at Greenhead on the B6318 stretch of the Military Road.

The standard overbridge is a very distinctive design, which appears to have originated with Giles's work on the Newcastle & Carlisle and found little employment elsewhere. It was perpetuated by John Blackmore on the later stages of the N&C and, modified only in minor details, appeared in Blackmore's work for the Maryport & Carlisle Railway during 1839-42. A final flowering came in the late eighteen-forties, albeit further modified, with the work of Blackmore's successor, Peter Tate, on the northern end of the N&C's Alston Branch. The design has no exact predecessor in Giles's canal bridges, although it could have been conceived as a reworking into masonry of their segmental arch cast-iron overbridges. The detailed design was probably worked up by either Thomas Dodd or George Larmer.

7.18. *A typical N&C overbridge, carrying the road to Morralee Farm, a little way east of the River Allen crossing. (GR 80664) It was built by Jacob Ritson and completed in 1838.*
(Bill Fawcett)

7.19. *(right) Liverpool & Manchester Railway overbridge a few hundreds yards east of Lea Green station. (Bill Fawcett)*

The basic overbridge is a shallow, segmental arch clasped between a pair of abutments with wing walls running parallel to the railway. This gives it a distinctive, closed-in air. The arch voussoirs are rusticated and their prominent joints continue across the shallow spandrels, an effect also employed in the overbridges of the Liverpool & Manchester Railway. The N&C bridges look, and are, relatively narrow. Giles adopted a width of 22 feet between parapets for his underbridges and this is also the breadth of his tunnels and the minimum distance between abutment walls for the overbridges, measured above the plinth. In practice the overbridge openings vary according to local circumstances, and a few are as much as twenty-five feet broad. By comparison, the Liverpool & Manchester Railway adopted a minimum width of 25 feet 7 inches, while Robert Stephenson went for 28 feet on the London & Birmingham but dropped this to only 24 in the tunnels.[11] The logic of Giles's formation, or should we say Benjamin Thompson's, was to have five feet between the two tracks, on a double track line, with 3½ feet clearance on the outside to allow a refuge space for anyone who happened to be on the line while a train was passing. George Stephenson had also adopted a five feet separation between tracks on the L&M and it was Robert Stephenson, on the L&B, who introduced the dimension which earned this space its subsequent name: 'the six foot'.

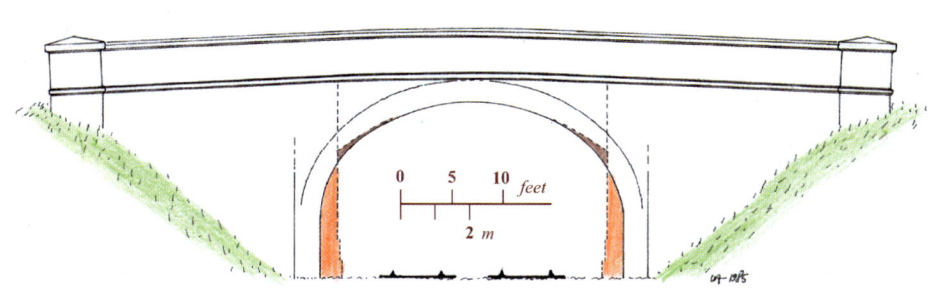

7.20. *Comparison of one of the wider N&C bridges (the 25 feet How Mill) with Robert Stephenson's standards, exemplified by a standard bridge on the NER Wellfield line, opened in 1878, two decades after his death. (from site surveys, Bill Fawcett)*

77

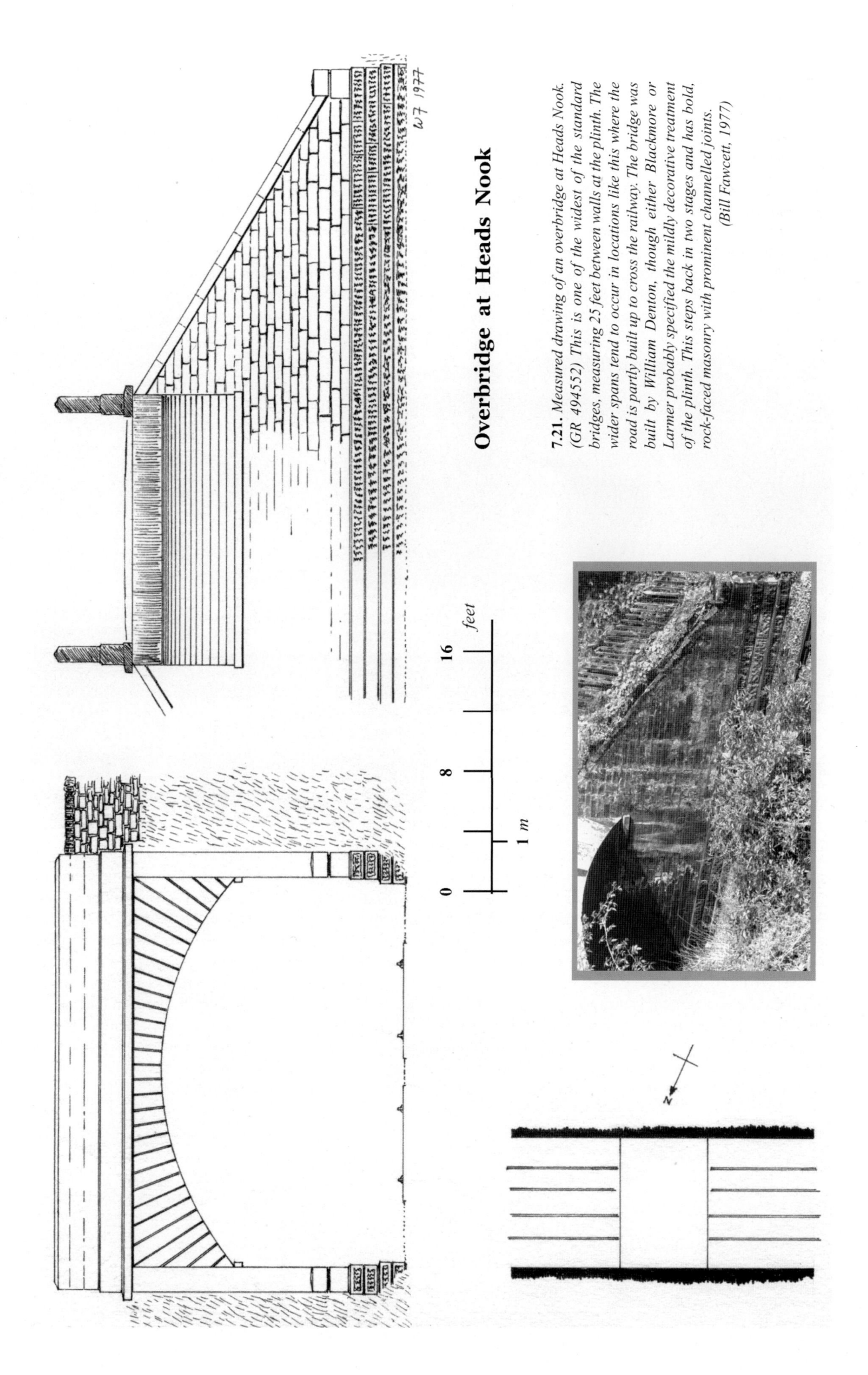

Overbridge at Heads Nook

7.21. *Measured drawing of an overbridge at Heads Nook. (GR 494552) This is one of the widest of the standard bridges, measuring 25 feet between walls at the plinth. The wider spans tend to occur in locations like this where the road is partly built up to cross the railway. The bridge was built by William Denton, though either Blackmore or Larmer probably specified the mildly decorative treatment of the plinth. This steps back in two stages and has bold, rock-faced masonry with prominent channelled joints.*

(Bill Fawcett, 1977)

7.22. *Bridge at the west end of Cowran Cutting. (GR 520568) Built by William Denton, it demonstrates another variant in surface treatment of the masonry. The horizontal joints are channelled to produce the rusticated effect seen already on the Eden Viaduct. The red sandstone of the arch and parapet appears to have become discoloured by generations of steam locomotives. (Bill Fawcett)*

The bridge built by George Grahamsley to carry an estate track at the east end of Cowran Cutting represents a departure from orthodoxy. The depth of the cutting leads to it having a deeper, almost semicircular arch, whose voussoirs are treated as a conventional arch ring, emphasised by a rock-faced treatment. The plinth displays yet another variant on surface treatment, with bold horizontal joints and rock facing creating an almost ribbed effect.

All this is in contrast with the suave handling of the Maryport & Carlisle Railway bridge shown at the foot of the page. That reverts to the original N&C concept, but with the neat drum ends to the parapet which Blackmore favoured in his Maryport work.

7.23. *A diverted East Coast express heading round the curve from the Gelt Bridge into Cowran Cutting. (GR 529571) (Bill Fawcett, April 1989)*

7.24. *An original Blackmore bridge carrying a farm road over the Maryport & Carlisle Railway just east of Wigton. (GR 267494). In the background is another fine bridge carrying the former A596 road to Carlisle. (Bill Fawcett)*

East Portal

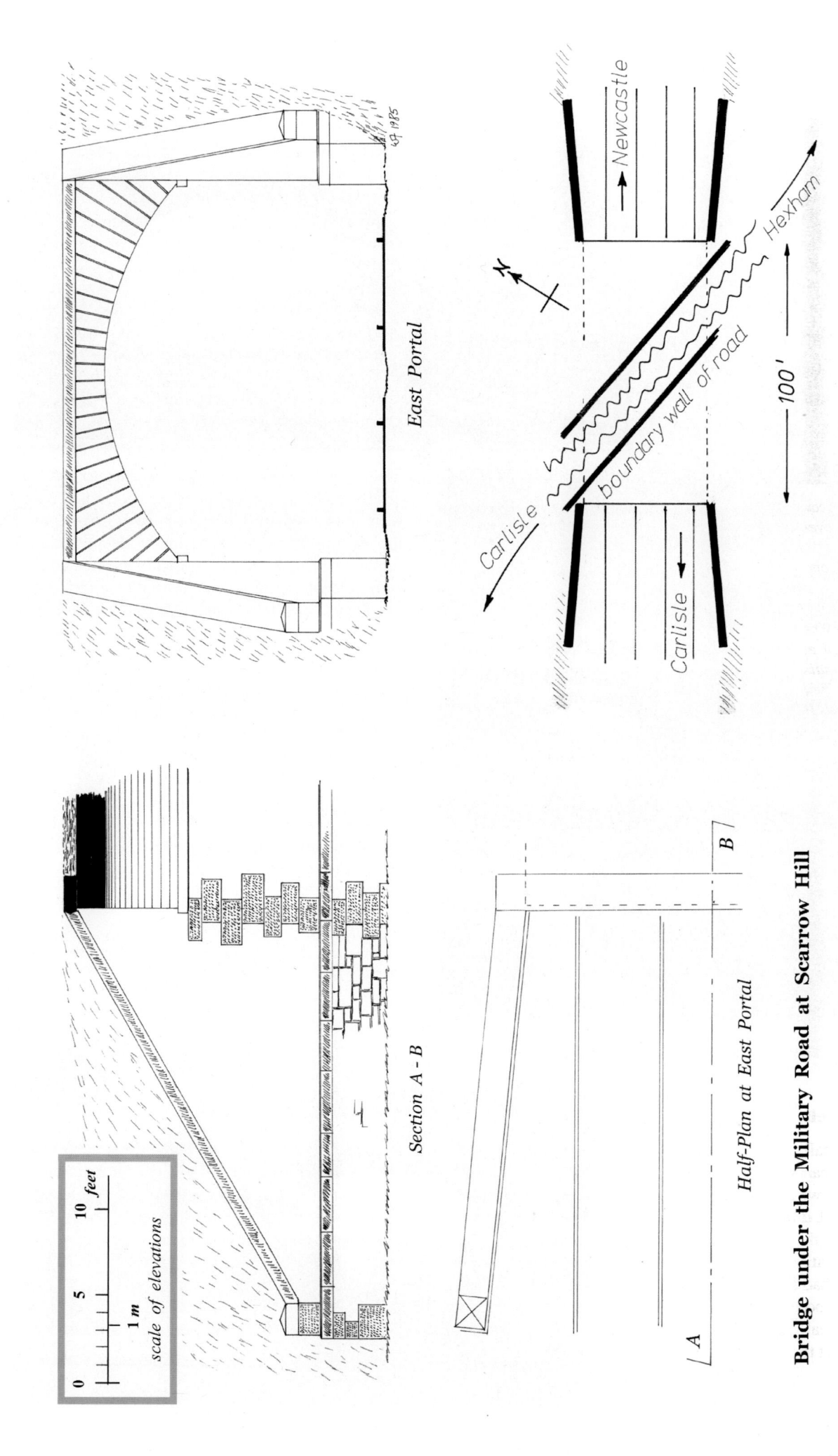

Section A - B

scale of elevations

Half-Plan at East Portal

Bridge under the Military Road at Scarrow Hill

The extended overbridges were generally used to provide a skew crossing by the turnpike road without actually building a skew arch. The classic example is Scarrow Hill (GR 568619), which formed the frontispiece to Carmichael's volume of engravings as a symbol of transport old and new. Its basic structure is like a standard overbridge, extended to a length of a hundred feet. The road runs diagonally across the top. Designed to cope with horses and carts, the bridge now bears a heavy traffic of up to forty-tonne lorries. As early as 1954 a concrete 'mattress' was inserted below the road to take some of the strain off the arch, while further works have been carried out in recent years. The only visible consequence of this has been the replacement of the stone walls, which formerly flanked the roadway, by concrete ones to protect the railway from flying cars and lorries.

7.26. *Scarrow Hill Bridge, looking east, with the railway telegraph taken over the top by the pole seen here. (J.M. Fleming, May 1977)*

7.25. *(opposite) Measured drawing of the bridge. (Bill Fawcett).*

7.27. *Whitchester Tunnel. East portal with the eighteenth-century house, later aggrandised, perched partly on top. (left) View from above the west portal towards Haltwhistle. (Bill Fawcett)*

Tunnels

Originally, there were two tunnels: Whitchester and Farnley. As already noted, the 200 yard Whitchester Tunnel did not form part of Giles's original scheme, and was designed entirely by Blackmore. However, it exemplifies how Farnley tunnel would have turned out had Giles's original intentions there been followed. Whitchester is cut through a small spur of land, dropping down to the Tyne, and the overburden is quite shallow: sixty feet at its deepest spot and barely eleven where the road crosses the tunnel at the west end. Despite this there have been significant problems with water penetration. The original lining comprised a single ring of sandstone, varying in thickness from one to two feet, but the NER had to carry out extensive repairs as early as 1870-1.[12] These evidently involved the insertion into some stretches of the bore of cast-iron arches bearing panels of brickwork. We shall come across this technique also at Farnley, which was dealt with at the same time. Outwardly, the tunnel appears as built, except for the massive steel bracing placed against the west portal to keep the land above in place.

Bridge under the railway at Durranhill

south elevation

22 ft 6 in
10 ft 9 in
25 ft
25 ft

elevations
plan
feet

7.29. *Measured drawing of a bridge providing farm access beneath the line at Durranhill, near Carlisle. (GR 427551)*
(Bill Fawcett, 1975)

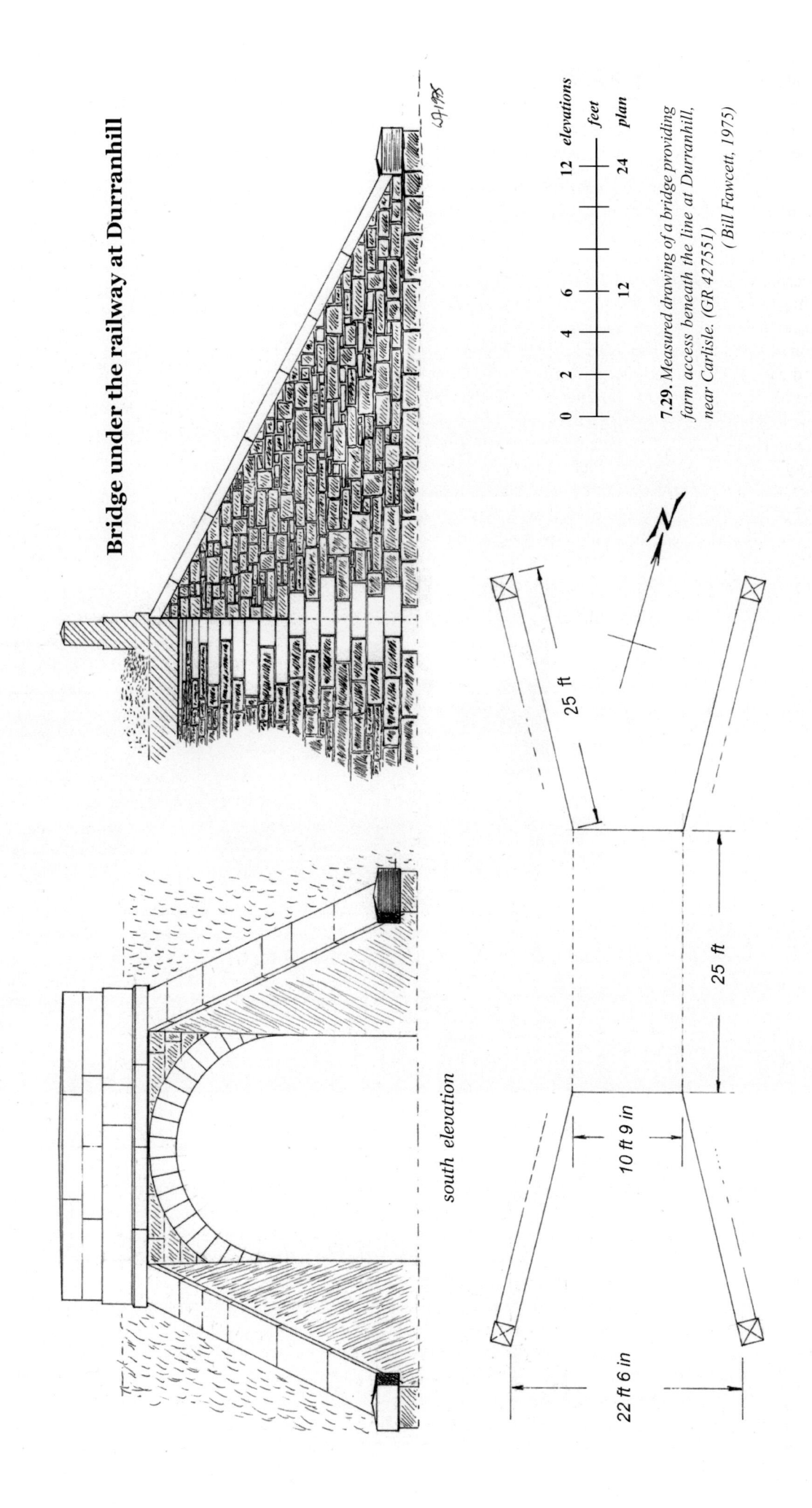

The construction of Farnley has been described in some detail, with a quarter of its length, at the west end, being 22 feet wide for double track, as Giles intended, and the rest only 14 feet wide. Within a few years of opening the directors were forced to double the single-track sections of their line in order to cope with the traffic. At Farnley they had either to drive another single-track bore or enlarge the existing tunnel without interrupting the traffic. They eventually opted for the latter course, and the work was carried out by George Grahamsley during 1844-5 to the designs of Blackmore's successor, Peter Tate.[13]

The enlargement is an amazing piece of work, which reflects great credit on both Tate and Grahamsley, a familiar figure from earlier works, who won the tunnel contract in July 1844.[14] He drove a drift above the existing arch and built a new arch above it, at the same time evidently replacing both of the side walls; the old masonry was then taken out from below, presumably in short sections during the middle of the night, when there were no trains.[15] This must have been painstaking work but only one incident is recorded, on 28 December 1844, when a portion of the old tunnel roof gave way while Grahamsley's machinery was being shifted above. This halted the trains briefly but did not significantly delay the reconstruction. The *Newcastle Journal* of 25 October 1845 reported the completion of 'the arching' the previous day and work presumably then pressed ahead on doubling the track. Extensive repairs were carried out by the NER in 1870-71 but the tunnel was still something of a liability because of inadequate clearances, so that in later years trains with certain types of rolling stock were not allowed to pass each other inside it.[16] Eventually, British Railways bypassed it with a deep cutting, the spoil from which was used in the construction of a new marshalling yard at Lamesley, near Gateshead. The tunnel bypass opened on 27 May 1962.[17]

7.28.
Farnley Tunnel View inside east portal showing cast-iron supporting arches. (Bill Fawcett)

In its final form Farnley Tunnel is something of a puzzle. The west end begins as Giles intended, with a sandstone ashlar arch and sidewalls extending some distance back from the entrance. He then planned to continue the arch in brick but, as we have seen, this was abandoned in favour of stone - for a time at least. The east end has similar masonry walls carrying a brick arch supported by a succession of sturdy cast-iron ribs, bearing on the side walls and leaving only five-feet long panels of brick exposed. Similarities to Whitchester imply that both arch and ribs date from a strengthening and partial relining during 1870-71.

The Smaller Masonry Underbridges

The smaller underbridges fall into two groups: masonry arch structures, which are considered here, and ones with timber decks carried on stone abutments - used where clearances were a problem. The standard masonry-arch underbridge provided for farm access is exemplified by one at Durran Hill, near Carlisle. This formed part of William Denton's first contract, and has a round arch spanning 10 feet 9 inches. The bridge itself is carried out in ashlar but the wing walls are of squared rubble. It is worth looking closely at the perfect proportions and careful finish of the parapet.

Just under a mile to the east, at Scotby, is an example of the sort of bridge required to cross a village road. This requires a wider span - about 21 feet - but there is not much height to play with, so Giles adopted a shallow segmental arch, with pronounced radiating joints, very much like one of the standard overbridges.

7.30.
Scotby Bridge, looking a little the worse for wear in 2007. (Bill Fawcett)

Bridge over the Stocksfield Burn

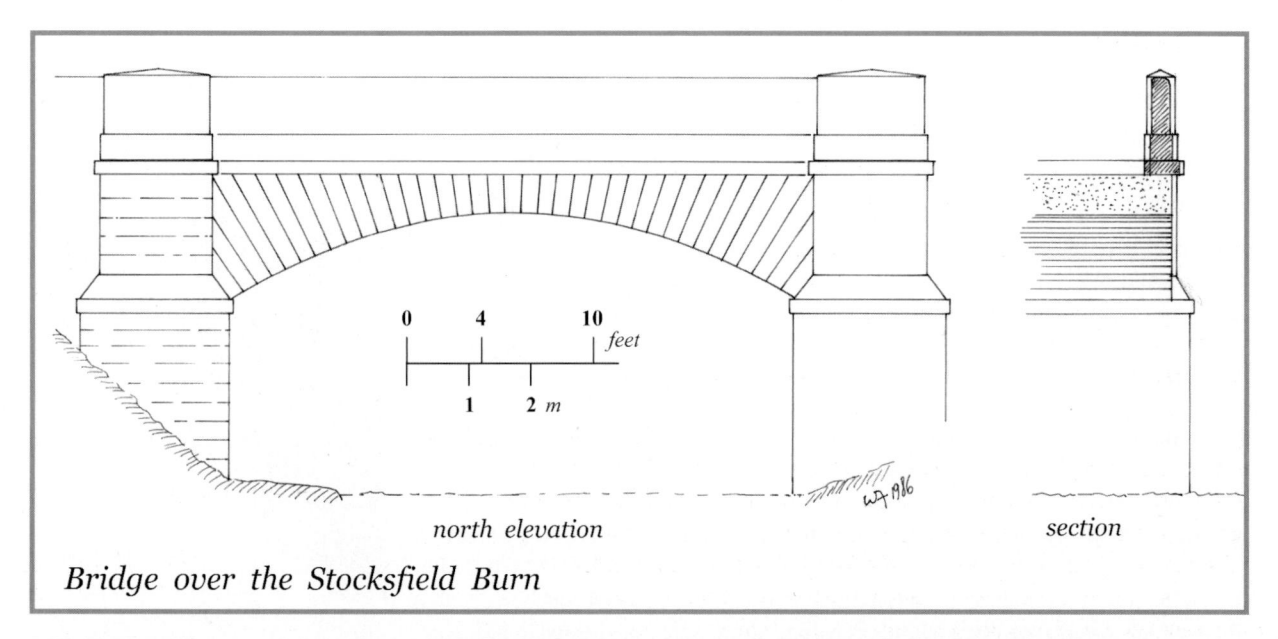

7.31. *Measured drawing of the bridge across the Stocksfield Burn, at the east end of Stocksfield station. The NER widened the structure on the opposite (south) side to take an additional track. Section taken through crown of arch.   (Bill Fawcett, 1986)*

Clearances similarly determined the arch form of the bridges over the numerous tributary streams crossed by the railway: round-arched where space permitted, as in the case of the Riding Burn at Riding Mill, and segmental at the Stocksfield Burn - both 30 feet spans. The Riding Burn arch settled during construction, though this was not felt to be serious at the time and the visiting directors simply told the contractor to rebuild the parapet walls so that it was not evident from above.[18] It has since been reinforced with a brick arch below the original. The most striking example of these bridges is that over the Poltross Burn, on the county boundary between Cumberland and Northumberland. Only 20 feet in span, it originally rose fifty feet from water level to the crown of the arch, with the abutments stepping back gracefully in two slight setbacks.[19] Blackmore left very little depth between the arch ring and trackbed, and this will have been a factor in the NER's decision to reconstruct the arch during the early nineteen-hundreds. At the time, there was concern about the effects of heavier locomotives and loads on the N&C bridges, particularly those with iron spans, but also extending to some of the masonry structures. The Poltross bridge had a replacement brick arch inserted eight feet below the original, which no doubt helped to brace the abutments better. The old arch was removed and the space above the new one was filled up with ballast. The arch bricks are frankly exposed on the face of the bridge, but the walls above were reconstructed in stone to match the abutments so that the alteration is not immediately obvious.

7.32. *Part of J.W. Carmichael's engraving of the railway at Rose Hill (Gilsland). The train has just left the station (right) and is heading towards the Poltross Burn bridge (left). Shaw's Hotel is the prominent building in the distance, overlooking the Spa, which lay in the wooded ravine of the Irthing, just to the right of it.*

Timber Bridges

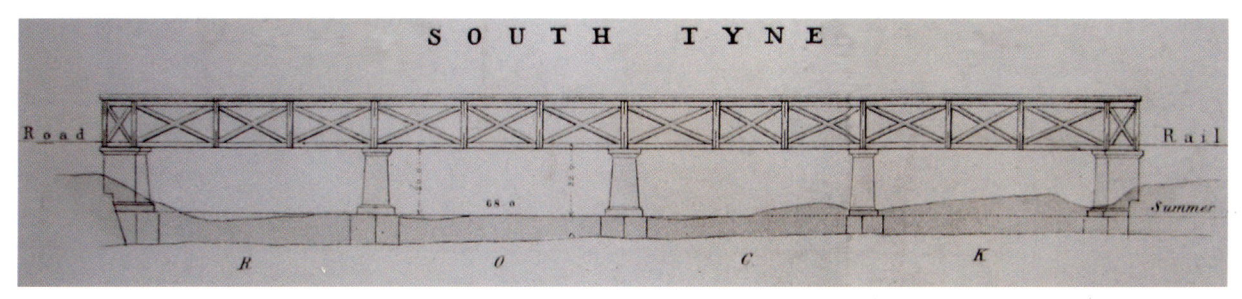

7.33. *Benjamin Thompson's design for the South Tyne bridge at Warden.*

In his plans for the line Benjamin Thompson envisaged the use of timber 'platforms', two feet deep, carried on stone piers, for a number of important river crossings. The idea was to reduce the earthworks by carrying the railway at a lower height than would be required for masonry-arch structures, and his drawings show the employment of heavy, braced timber trusses. In his August 1829 report Giles endorsed the principle for the South Tyne bridge at Warden, suggested a timber and iron structure for the Tyne at Scotswood, and generally opted for masonry-arch structures elsewhere. Quite what Giles had in mind for the timber bridges is unclear since no major ones were put in hand prior to his departure. Their design fell instead to Blackmore.

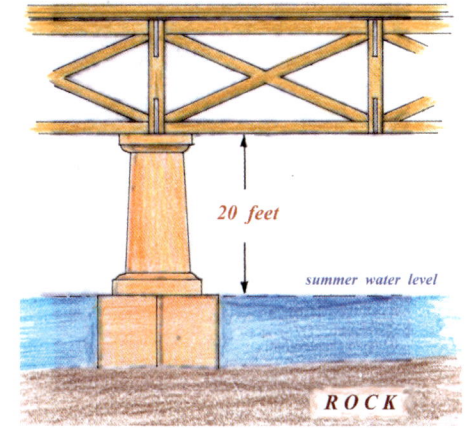

7.34. *John Blackmore's Warden Bridge, looking upstream with West Boat suspension bridge beyond. (J.W. Carmichael)*

The first of Blackmore's timber river crossings is Warden bridge, over the South Tyne. This had trussed timber platforms borne on stone piers and abutments. By December 1834 stones were being prepared on site for the bridge, which the directors originally envisaged having an 'iron top'.[20] Three months later they noted that Blackmore had designed a cheaper timber 'top'; another economy was to build it only twelve feet wide, to take a single line of railway.[21] Opened to traffic in 1836, it was widened to double track during 1839, which entailed enlarging all the piers and abutments.[22] Warden formed the model for three subsequent river crossings, over the South Tyne and Allen, between Haydon Bridge and Bardon Mill. Built for double track from the outset, these have piers of beautifully-finished sandstone ashlar, curving gracefully to a slightly pointed cutwater and now carrying their third superstructure.

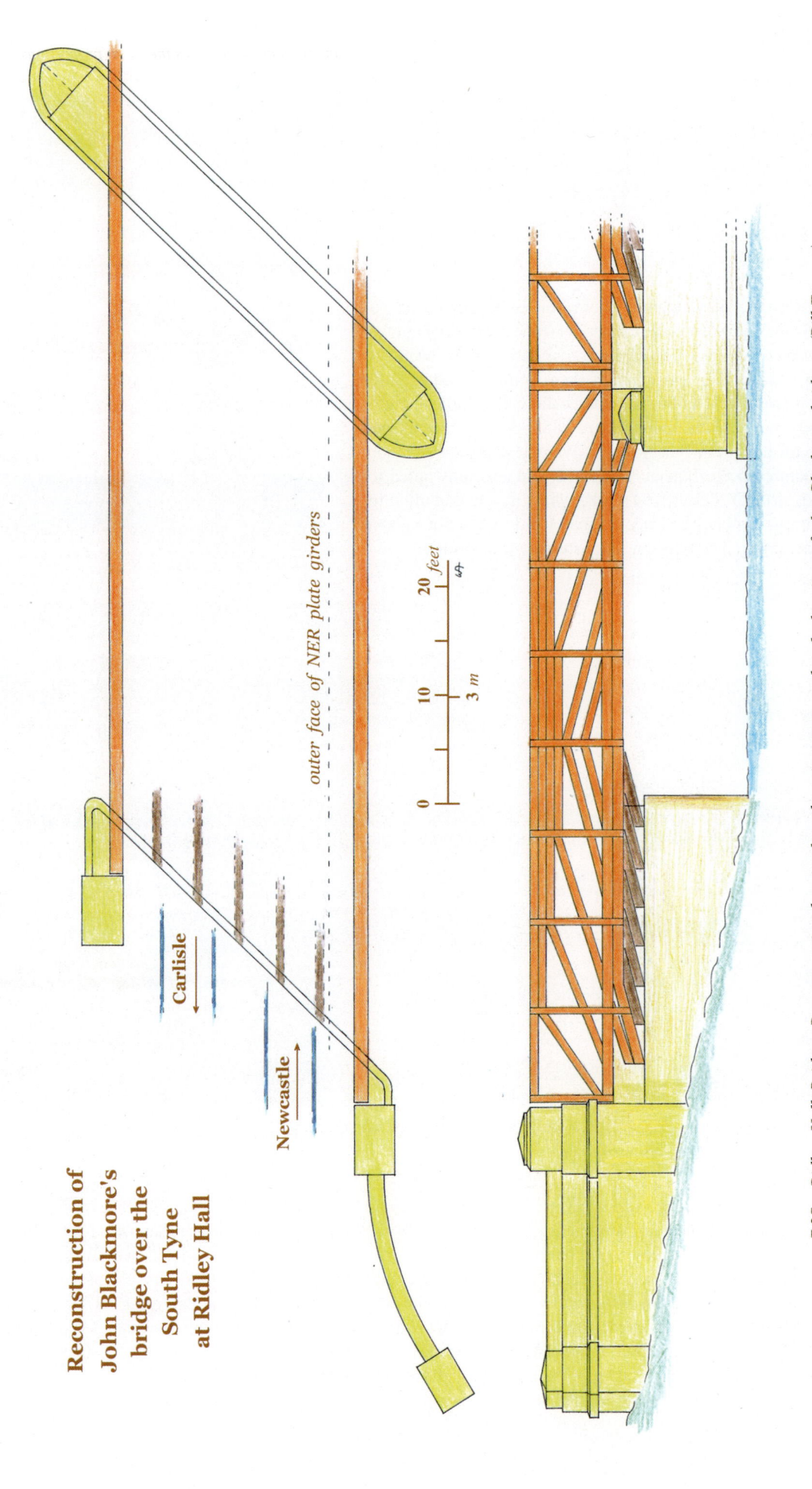

Reconstruction of John Blackmore's bridge over the South Tyne at Ridley Hall

Carlisle

Newcastle

outer face of NER plate girders

0   10   20 feet
0   3 m

7.35. *Ridley Hall Bridge: Reconstruction drawing based on site survey and early drawings of other Blackmore bridges. (Bill Fawcett) Partial south elevation and plan.*

86

7.36. *A modern coal train crossing the South Tyne at Ridley Hall. (GR 792643) The size of the wagons emphasises the squat proportions of the bridge, now onto its third deck – a steel plate girder structure of 1907 supplied by Sir William Arrol & Co. There are 4 girders, and the tracks were originally laid on longitudinal waybeams, one on each girder. The formation has since been ballasted up and is laid with transverse-sleepered track. The original masonry, constructed by Jacob Ritson, survives largely unaltered. (Bill Fawcett)*

Blackmore's original timber trusses are illustrated in Carmichael's engraving of Warden Bridge and the 1840 Smith-Barlow Report on Anglo-Scottish railway links, while there is also a contemporary scale drawing of the Scotswood bridge, which is discussed in chapter 8. Together with site measurements of the surviving masonry, these form the basis for the reconstruction of the South Tyne bridge at Ridley Hall presented opposite. The trusses are a much more thoughtful design than those proposed by Thompson, and were commended by Sir John Rennie, who said they represented 'a considerable success' on Blackmore's part.[23] The deck is supported on a line of raking shores, bearing on the piers and abutments, while its outer beams also form the bottom chord of the outer trusses. A second line of raking shores extends from the piers towards the top member of this truss, while further raking timbers make up the other main structural elements.

The origins of Blackmore's design appear to lie in the long-established and highly durable timber bridge-building traditions of Switzerland. Hans Ulrich Grubenmann's bridge over the Rhine at Schaffhausen was begun in 1755, and employed separate sets of raking struts from pier to deck and deck to upper beam.

Schaffhausen Bridge: spans 172 & 193 feet

That bridge was destroyed during Napoleon's invasion but the same principle was developed in a number of surviving bridges built by Blasius Balteschwiler (1752-1832).[24] His 1810 bridge over the River Limmat at Baden is illustrated here, showing the strong similarities to the N&C design. One difference is that of scale. The Swiss bridges tend be much greater in span, and the trusses, which carry roofs to keep the snow off, are deeper than Blackmore's and employ more substantial timbers. Blackmore's direct source is unknown, but he may have been inspired by the *Encyclopaedia Britannica*, whose third edition (1797) had addressed the issue.

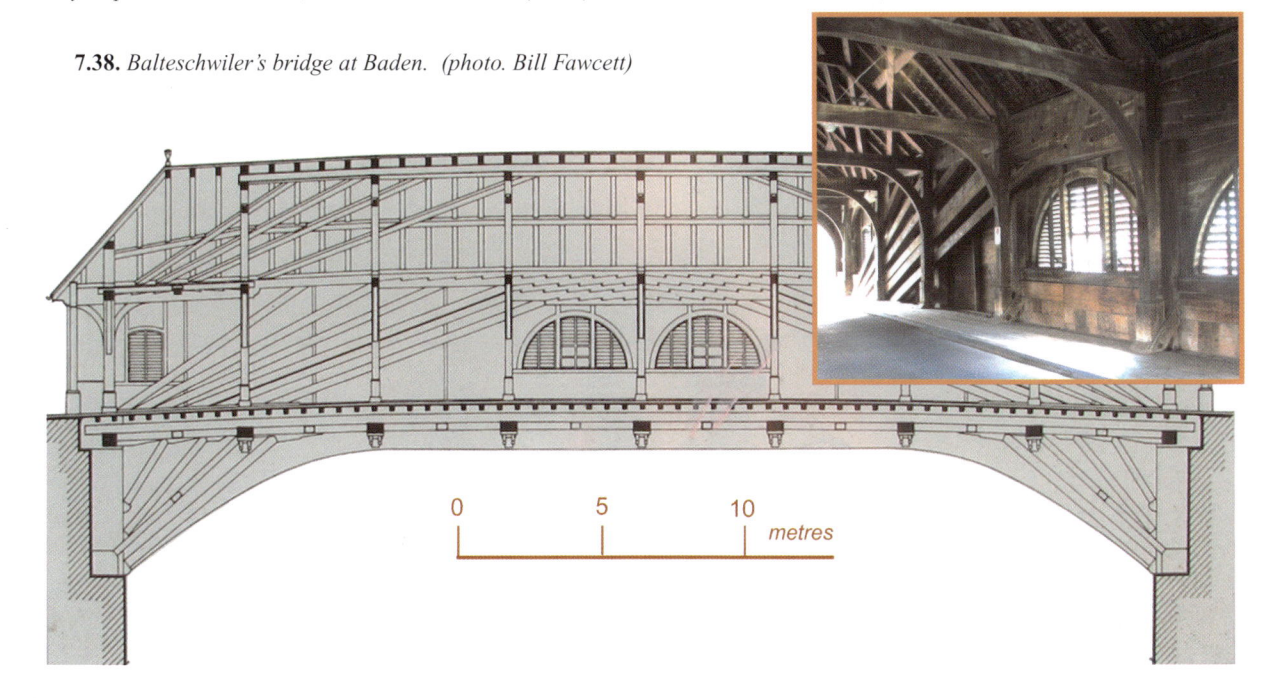

7.38. *Balteschwiler's bridge at Baden. (photo. Bill Fawcett)*

87

7.40. *(above) East abutment of the bridge over the South Tyne at Lipwood (GR 813641), two miles west of Haydon Bridge. (Bill Fawcett)*

7.39. *One of Jacob Ritson's carefully crafted piers rising from the limpid waters of the River Allen.(GR 801642)   (Bill Fawcett)*

Blackmore's trusses employed timber from Memel, in East Prussia, which was then a popular source. It was quite durable but the preservative techniques then available, such as Kyanising, were of limited value. The joints were heavily dependent on iron straps and fastenings; they tended to open up under the stress of railway traffic and the increasing weight of locomotives and rolling stock, and it must have required frequent attention to keep them tight. Thus Blackmore's bridge trusses were only good for about thirty years before replacement became necessary. In this respect they were no better or worse than most designs by his British contemporaries, which were all conceived as temporary expedients until growing traffic called for and paid for their successors.

Most of Blackmore's timber trusses were replaced during the eighteen-sixties by the North Eastern Railway, which simply substituted wrought-iron plate girders on the original masonry. The three river bridges between Bardon Mill and Haydon Bridge were rebuilt in this way during 1865-6.[25] In two notable cases - Scotswood and Warden - fate stepped in and carried them off by fire. Warden was burned in 1848, and Blackmore's successor, Peter Tate, rebuilt it with cast-iron arches on the old masonry. A further spate of rebuildings occurred during the bridge strengthening campaign of the early nineteen-hundreds. In most cases the N&C river bridges just had steel plate girders substituted for the forty-year-old ironwork, but at Warden the opportunity was taken to realign the route so as to ease the curves. During 1904 a new steel lattice bridge was built upstream of the old one, which was then demolished, leaving only the bases of the piers on view.[26]

Probably the smallest of Blackmore's trussed timber bridges was the 29 feet span over the Tippalt Burn adjacent to Colonel Coulson's Blenkinsopp Hall estate. There was no obvious clearance problem, so timber was presumably adopted for economy. It had stone abutments between which a replacement stone arch was eventually thrown; a third - invisible - reconstruction placed a concrete saddle above the arch to relieve the load.

Blackmore also adopted quite a lot of short timber spans on stone abutments for underbridges crossing farm tracks and minor roads; indeed these were his standard design on the Redheugh branch. They will have been replaced at various times using a variety of materials - cast-iron, wrought-iron and then steel, usually with little change to the overall appearance of the bridge. British Rail continued the renewal process with concrete slabs and beams, still with minimal visual impact until recent years, when a determination to improve lineside access and clearances has led to the imposition of some extremely ugly and top-heavy bridge decks.

A much happier outcome was obtained in the case of the bridge over the drive to Colonel Coulson's Blenkinsopp Hall, again a Blackmore design. This is the only bridge which strives to be ornamental, with a castellated parapet ending in octagonal turrets. Its stone arch is just a facade, an elegant veneer to a deck now made up of four reinforced-concrete slabs. An 1844 return describes it as a stone arch but in NER days, at any rate, it had the rails laid on waybeams sitting in cast-iron trough girders.[27] The construction of the railway past Blenkinsopp Hall involved the diversion and straightening of the Tippalt and the diversion of the turnpike road to run alongside the line. It also entailed replacing Colonel Coulson's drive with one on a new alignment, and it is quite likely that the elevation design for the bridge was supplied by Coulson's architect, John Dobson, who was working on extensions to the Hall at the time.

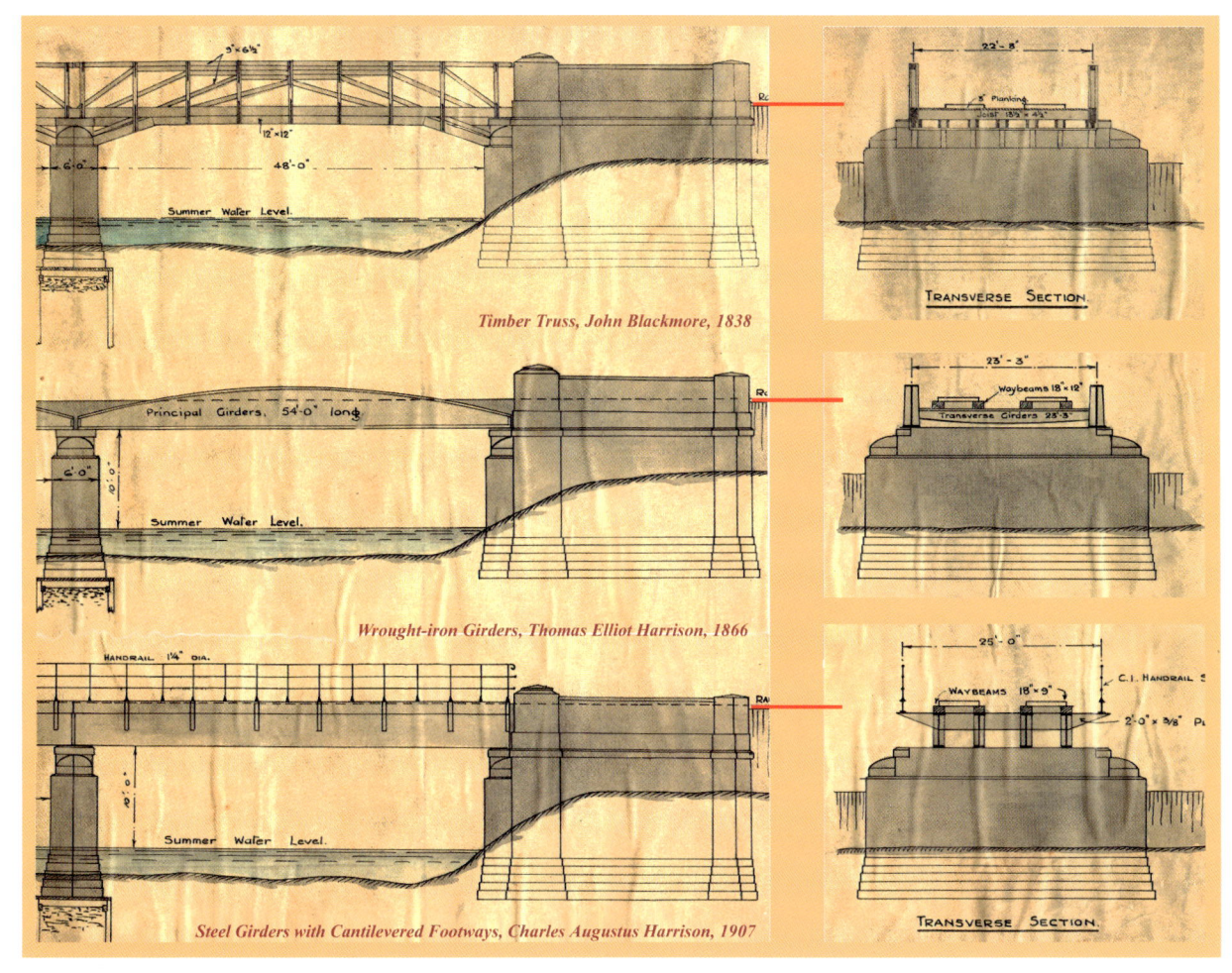

7.41. *Drawing by Thomas Appleyard, of the LNER, illustrating successive reconstructions of the bridge over the River Allen. The first rebuilding, in 1866, was with T.E. Harrison's characteristic hog-backed girders, which can still be seen at Scotswood Bridge. The red lines denote the rail level, which has been raised on each occasion.   (J.M. Fleming collection)*

7.42. *Bridge over Blenkinsopp Hall drive. (GR 689637). Inset is a view through it of the lodge which the N&C had to construct for Colonel Coulson in connection with the re-routing of his drive.   (Bill Fawcett)*

89

Blenkinsopp Hall Bridge

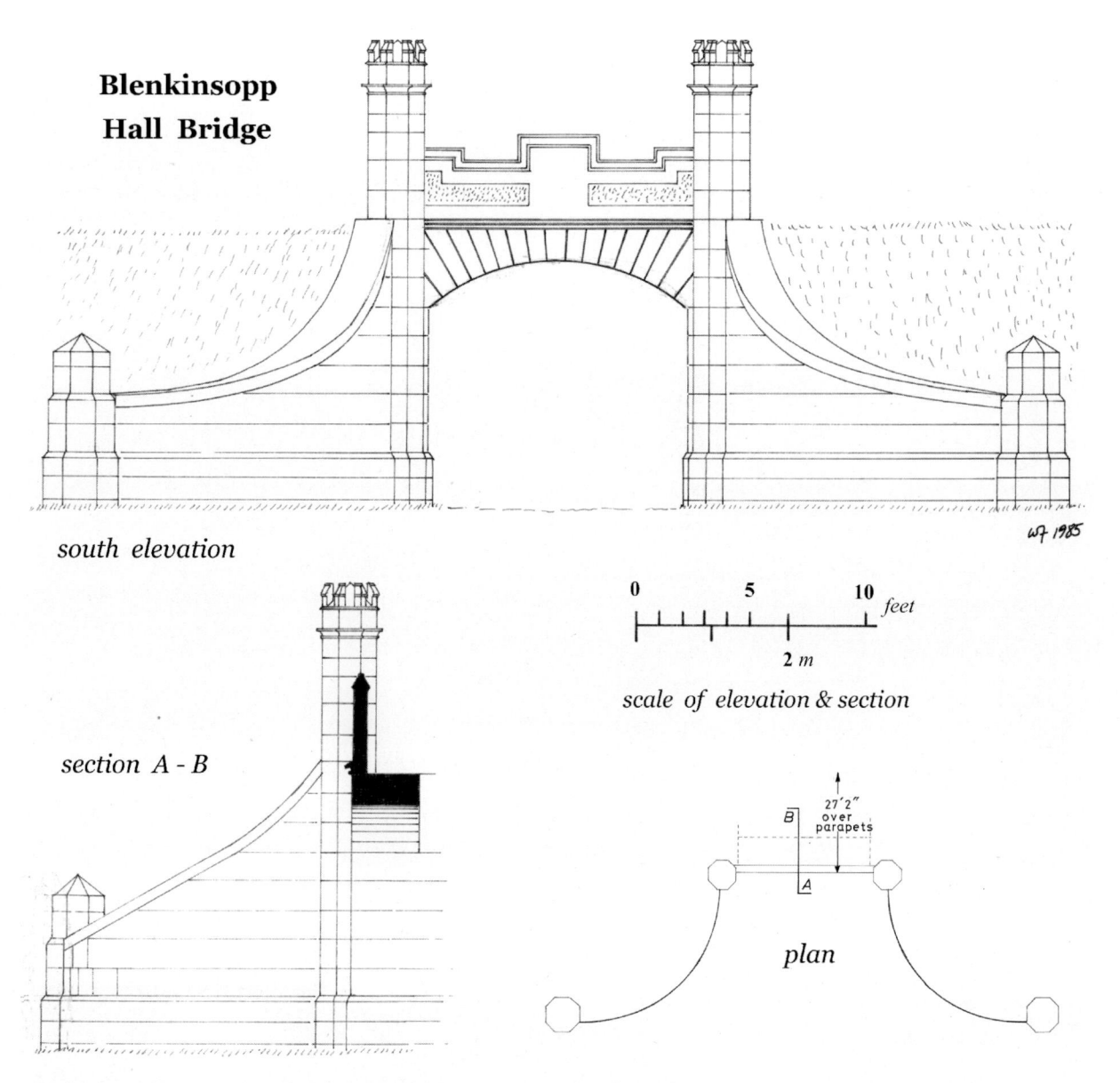

south elevation

section A - B

scale of elevation & section

plan

27′2″ over parapets

7.43. *Measured drawing of the bridge over Blenkinsopp Hall drive. (Bill Fawcett, 1985)*

7.44. *(right) Cast-iron skew overbridge of 22 feet span carrying the turnpike road (A69) just west of Haltwhistle station. The abutments have now been extended and carry a concrete deck. Half elevation taken from an LNER drawing.*

7.45. *(below) Detail from Carmichael's engraving of Blenkinsopp, showing 3 bridges over the Tippalt Burn: the cast-iron one carrying the diverted turnpike road; the timber one for the railway; and the original masonry-arch road bridge.*

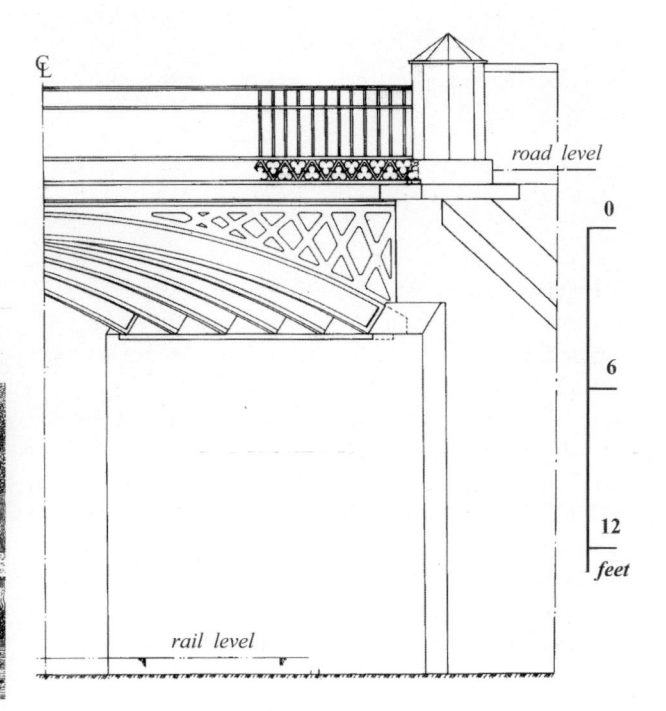

road level

rail level

90

Iron Bridges

Francis Giles used cast iron for his canal overbridges, probably in order to minimise the construction depth and so the height by which existing roads would have to be raised. On the N&C, however, he was committed to masonry bridges wherever possible. He built no iron bridges on the line, though he was happy to contemplate one in his first proposal for the Petteril Bridge (August 1829) as well as the Tyne crossing at Scotswood. Blackmore also avoided iron structures for some years, and his first essay was probably the 24 feet span of the Wigton Road underbridge on the Canal Branch.[28] Even that was rather forced on him, since the railway began building a masonry arch but the road trustees pointed out during construction that this would be lower than the height specified. So, in the course of 1836, a shallower cast-iron span was provided instead.

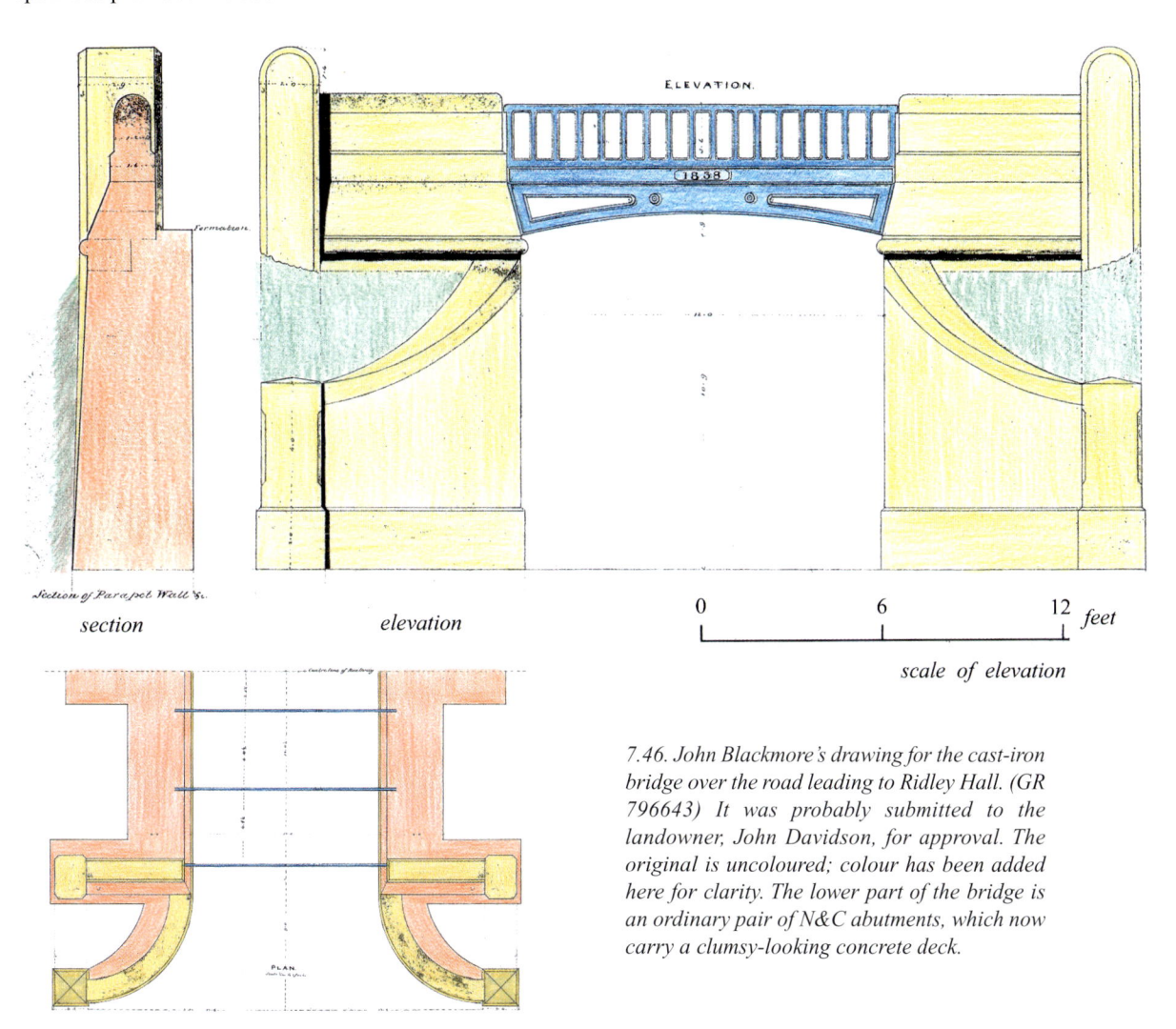

7.46. John Blackmore's drawing for the cast-iron bridge over the road leading to Ridley Hall. (GR 796643) It was probably submitted to the landowner, John Davidson, for approval. The original is uncoloured; colour has been added here for clarity. The lower part of the bridge is an ordinary pair of N&C abutments, which now carry a clumsy-looking concrete deck.

Shortly afterwards, Blackmore designed three cast-iron bridges for the central section of the railway: Greenhead to Haydon Bridge, which opened in 1838. One carried the line across the road leading to Ridley Hall, and was very similar in principle to the Ivel Navigation and Hertford Union Canal bridges. Six segmental-arched ribs, two for the parapets and four for the tracks, spanned the twelve-feet opening and were stayed by a pair of transverse rods, bolted through.[29] The bridge was treated as a formal gateway, to the extent that the flanking parapets ended in round-topped piers of a neo-classical character. The second bridge was at Haltwhistle, and carried the turnpike road across the railway on a slight skew. This entailed a wider span and deeper arch, with a pattern of diagonal bracing in the spandrels.[30] The third bridge was at Blenkinsopp, and carried the diverted turnpike across the diverted Tippalt; again there was a strong reference back to the canal designs. Blackmore went on to provide a number of cast-iron bridges on the extension into Newcastle, opened in 1839, where he was called on for long spans with minimum constructional depth. These are discussed in chapter 8. Further cast-iron bridges were designed by his successor, Peter Tate, including overbridges which the company was obliged to substitute for turnpike road crossings at Hexham and Corbridge. None of the cast-iron bridges survive, though in most cases their masonry abutments remain in use.

River Walls

The traveller from Newcastle as far as Haltwhistle is regaled with splendid views of the Tyne, often enjoying a grandstand seat on the very brink of the river. This was inherent in Benjamin Thompson's 1825 proposals for the route, but was not achieved without some effort. At times the railway follows a straightforward path along low embankments traversing the haughs, or riverside meadows. In other places it employs the cut and fill technology often adopted by the canal builders: material is excavated from the slopes above the railway and then dumped below it to create a shelf which is part cut and part fill. Sometimes this carries the line across the edge of the rising ground bordering the haugh, but in places it is built out into the river, traversing the face of a steep slope, or 'scar', as at Wylam and Eltringham. In these locations the formation is only held in place by a near-vertical retaining wall rising straight from the river. To build these, the contractors had to work with the Tyne, and be ready to down tools whenever it was unwilling to cooperate.

7.47. *The river wall stretching east from Capons Cleugh, designed by Blackmore and built by Jacob Ritson. (Bill Fawcett, 1993)*

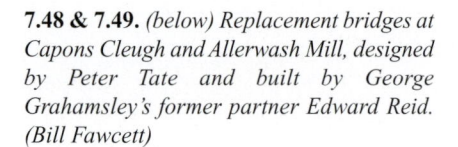

7.48 & 7.49. *(below) Replacement bridges at Capons Cleugh and Allerwash Mill, designed by Peter Tate and built by George Grahamsley's former partner Edward Reid. (Bill Fawcett)*

These river walls were major undertakings, yet tantalisingly little information has surfaced about how they were built, although we know that Jacob Ritson piled for the foundations of the one at Capons Cleugh. That was designed after Giles's departure, and modest changes can be seen from its predecessors, such as Wylam. It has a pronounced batter and employs larger stones, roughly squared and laid in courses. Ritson seems to have been fortunate with the river, enjoying generally placid conditions in which he could employ a low timber bridge to fetch stone from the south bank. The Tyne has many faces, however. In dry seasons it is a broad, rolling stream with a gravelly bottom exposed in a host of shallows. Come heavy rain and it is a threatening torrent which, in the Great Flood of 1771, managed to sweep away most of its bridges. The danger was amply demonstrated on 7 July 1852, when a heavy downpour swelled the local streams, which swept away the bridges over the Capons Cleugh and Settlingstones Burns. That incident is looked at in chapter 17; it is sufficient to note here that Peter Tate, who was then the company's engineer, had temporary timber structures in place within the course of the next day and a half and designed the permanent replacements.[31] Both were, naturally, on a larger scale, notably at Allerwash Mill, where he replaced a fifteen feet arch over the Settlingstones Burn with one of almost forty feet. The N&C had already taken precautions against scour by the Tyne itself by building some groins out into the river, which had the effect of pushing the flow towards the south bank, the property of Greenwich Hospital, somewhat to the chagrin of their Receiver, John Grey.[32]

7.48. *(left) Capons Cleugh bridge. (GR 863661)*
7.49. *Bridge over the Settlingstones Burn. (GR 871669)*

Peter Tate

Peter Tate was an engaging and resourceful character, who became Engineer to the N&C after Blackmore's death in March 1844, and continued in post under the NER until finally persuaded to retire in July 1872, in his 77th year. Peter was born in Newcastle on 24 August 1795, the son of John Tate and his wife Ann Black.[33] Peter's extensive obituary, evidently written by one of his brothers, says nothing of their father's occupation but another account written just a few years later states that John was 'a Stella man and a wherry builder of some note.' This fits in with the careers taken up by Peter and the three brothers who outlived him. John, born 1800, had become a railway engineer and moved to the Maryport area by the mid eighteen-forties; later he was in business at Harrington as a wagon maker.[34] William, born about 1803, became a timber merchant in Sunderland. George, born about 1809, became a carver and gilder, also settling in Sunderland and working initially on wooden ships but turning later to picture frames.

George was born in the Blaydon area, which fits in with the Tates having moved to somewhere in the vicinity of Stella, and Peter began his career as a carpenter at the nearby Towneley Colliery. During his time there Peter and his colleagues built a racing boat and he showed his ingenuity by devising an 'outrigger', enabling them to use longer oars, an invention later 'erroneously attributed' to Henry Clasper, a celebrated Tyneside oarsman. Peter's ability is said to have been noted by 'officials connected with the railway' when Gibson Kyle was building the retaining walls near Stella, so it may be that he had gone to work for the contractor. He clearly developed a knowledge of masonry construction since his name first appears in the N&C records in September 1836, having been appointed to succeed George Larmer in supervising the masonry and other works at the west end of the line.[35] Tate was based in Carlisle, and from 1838 succeeded Blackmore in making the regular engineering reports to the Carlisle Committee.

Blackmore had two assistants, the other being Benjamin Scott, based in Newcastle. Scott left the railway in 1841 to take up a post under Blackmore on the Maryport & Carlisle Railway and was not replaced; instead Tate moved to Newcastle as sole assistant in the early part of 1842. A vigorous economy drive was by then underway, and this led to a savage pruning of Blackmore's salary, on the basis that he was primarily engaged now as consultant with Tate doing the day-to-day management. Poor Blackmore became ill during 1843 and took little further part in the company's affairs up to his death on 15 March 1844. Four days later Tate was appointed his successor, with a modest pay rise from £140 to £155, backdated to the start of the year in recognition of his having acted as Engineer for some months already. He immediately showed his mettle by devising and overseeing the enlargement of Farnley tunnel, no doubt with some input from the resourceful contractor, George Grahamsley.

Unlike Blackmore, Tate was not involved in the surveys for new lines: he had neither the time nor the expertise for these. He was, however, engaged in designing bridges for them. The most ambitious are the Forth Banks viaduct and bridge, described in the next chapter, but his hand is also evident in the northern portion of the Alston branch. He evidently designed most of that line's bridges north of Shaft Hill (Coanwood) but it is unlikely that he contributed to the Tyne bridge (Alston Arches) at Haltwhistle, though he made an excellent job of its partial reconstruction after serious flood damage in 1852. Bridge fires also demonstrated his ability to improvise and get the trains running again. Warden Bridge burned on 27 July 1848, losing all but one span, but Tate had the line back in business three days later. The line had been leased by George Hudson a few weeks earlier, so Tate now came under Thomas Elliot Harrison, who became Engineer in Chief for the duration of the lease, which ceased at the end of 1849. It is possible that Harrison advised on the permanent replacement at Warden, using cast-iron arches on the old piers, carried out under Tate's direction during 1851-2. They were in harness again during 1860, when Scotswood Bridge burned down to the water line. Harrison was consultant and Tate built a new structure on the stumps of the old one within the space of three weeks. His temporary bridge lasted the best part of a decade.

Tate also designed buildings for the N&C, the most distinctive being the elegant waiting sheds put up during the eighteen-fifties, while he was proud enough to sign his name, in cast iron, to the water tower which survives at Haltwhistle. The merger with the North Eastern Railway, in 1862, saw him carry on as Engineer to the Carlisle Section, though now responsible to John Bourne, the NER Northern Division Engineer, who had years before, while in private practice, carried out the first surveys for the Alston branch. Peter Tate put in a further decade under the NER, retiring in July 1872 when the directors presented him with a gratuity of £500 'in consideration of his very long and faithful service.'[36]

Peter married quite late and had no children. He must have got to know Mary Hargreaves while working in Carlisle, and they wed there on 29 April 1845. She was about seven years younger but died after only a decade of marriage, on 19 April 1855. The following year, Peter married again, this time to a widow, Frances Simpson, who had two children, then in their late teens: Edward and Jane. Richard Lowry paints a happy picture of the Tates routinely taking a train up the Tyne on a summer evening and strolling near Bywell, though he was embarrassed when Jane had some fun flirting with him.[37] She went on to marry one of the N&C clerks, William Watson, and they lived with Peter at his final home: Rosewood House, Heaton Road, where he died on 20 February 1879. The chief beneficiaries from his will were 'Jenny' and his nephew George, son of brother William and, it appears, also in the service of the Newcastle & Carlisle Railway.[38]

Chapter 8: East from Blaydon

Introduction

The N&C reached Blaydon in 1835, but took a further four years to complete the line into Newcastle. Life was complicated by disagreements among the directors as to the best route and by the need to take account of other railways being promoted on Tyneside. In the event the company built two lines, one along each bank of the Tyne. The southern route reached its Redheugh terminus, on the riverside just west of Gateshead, at the beginning of March 1837. The north bank route, climbing well away from the river, opened to a provisional terminus half a mile west of Newcastle in 1839. 1847 brought an extension of passenger services to temporary premises at the west end of the building site which became Central Station, to which N&C travellers finally gained entry at the start of 1851. In the event, each route was of long-term value, with the south bank providing a useful channel for coal and mineral traffic even though for many years it was hampered by the steep Redheugh Incline, worked initially by a stationary engine and latterly with the aid of powerful banking locomotives.

The completion freed the company to begin paying dividends. Interest payments to shareholders had ceased at the end of 1833, at the behest of the Public Works Loans Board, but Matthew Plummer invented an ingenious stratagem by which investors received debentures in the following years in lieu of the promised interest.[1] The arrival of the railway at Newcastle, in 1839, fulfilled the directors' bond to the PWLB and enabled the N&C to redeem these debentures and distribute a first dividend of 4%, declared at the March 1839 AGM.

Indecision

The 1829 Act provided for the N&C to cross the Tyne at Scotswood and then follow the riverside to the Tyne Bridge at Newcastle. This would give access to what was then the commercial hub of the town, but the local topography actually splits the centre into two parts. Newcastle is sited at a point where hills close in on both banks of the river, and the land rises steeply behind the Quayside to an upper town, over a hundred feet above the Tyne. The lower town housed warehouses, many businesses and the Exchange, but the bulk of Newcastle was in the upper part, home to the churches and castle. This area was not well provided for in the 1829 Act, which allowed the company to build a branch from the riverside, near the 'Herd's House' to Thornton Street, on the west fringe of the upper town. This would climb 114 feet at a gradient of about 1/50 and Giles pointed out that it would be unsuitable for horse operation, and require a stationary engine.[2]

Despite Giles's misgivings, the company proceeded to negotiate with John Hodgson, of Elswick Hall, for the land needed. They were in an awkward position since they required land from him for both the main line and Thornton Street branch, but the Act provided that the latter could only be built with his consent. Hodgson in fact proved willing to sell but indicated that he wished to take the valuation to a jury, hoping thereby to get a better price. In September 1830 James Losh and his colleagues decided to play a waiting game, and informed Hodgson that his land was not needed 'at present'.[3] By then other railway schemes were entering the public arena and engaging the directors' attention. October 1830 brought the announcement of a proposal to apply to Parliament to build a line from Newcastle down the north bank of the Tyne to North Shields, followed in November by notice of a rival one along the south bank from Blaydon to South Shields and Monkwearmouth.[4]

The North Shields promoters intended to start from the Quayside and make a junction there with the Newcastle & Carlisle Railway. They opened subscriptions in February 1831 and engaged Robert Stephenson and Joshua Richardson to carry out a survey but the scheme ground to a halt amidst arguments about the route. It was eventually revived, with John Hodgson as vice-chairman, and the Newcastle & North Shields Railway opened on 22 June 1839, but the route had been revised and its terminus was in the upper town, with no link to the N&C.

The original North Shields scheme complemented the Carlisle line, and attracted the support of several N&C promoters.[5] The south bank proposal was a different matter. It too could be seen as an extension of the Carlisle line but part of its route involved territory which the N&C itself might wish to occupy. Its emergence seems to have focused the minds of Losh and his colleagues on the traffic potential of the south bank and encouraged a very cautious response on their part to the overtures made by the 'Blaydon & Gateshead Railway' promoters. Discussions continued throughout most of 1831-3 without getting very far, the N&C Board being divided as to the relative merits of their Parliamentary route and a south bank one. At issue was the fact that a south bank route had the potential to be extended to a deep-water shipping point downstream of the Tyne Bridge at Newcastle, which formed a barrier to seagoing shipping. This was an attractive feature for the colliery proprietors and one which could not be achieved so readily by a north bank route heading straight for the town centre. Despite this, it seemed at first as if the directors would press ahead with the Scotswood route, and they resumed contact with John Hodgson, eventually purchasing the land required on the river frontage of his Elswick estate.[6] However, a Board meeting on 10 September 1833 finally decided to take the plunge in favour of the south bank instead.

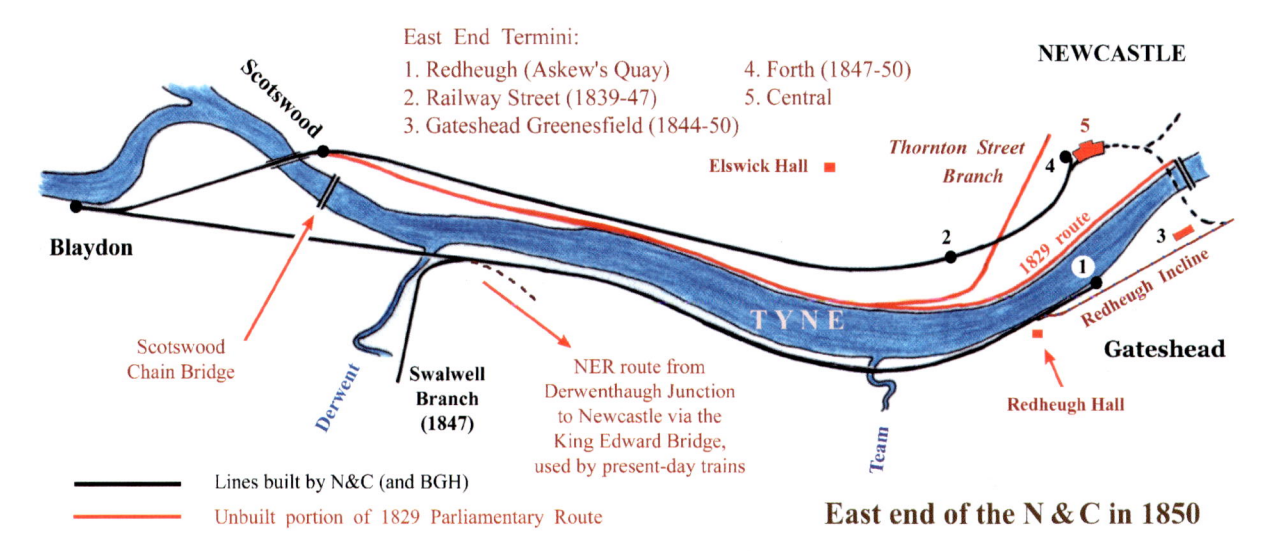

8.1. *The east end of the Newcastle & Carlisle Railway, showing the relationship between the 1829 Parliamentary route and the lines actually built, together with the successive east-end termini.*

This important meeting was the last conducted under the old regime of James Losh and Thomas Crawhall, who both died within a fortnight. John Price attended on behalf of the Blaydon & Gateshead promoters and reported an offer of land from an enthusiastic backer, Sir Thomas Clavering, who was keen to see the railway extended beyond Gateshead to a shipping point well downstream. A factor in everyone's thinking was the Stanhope & Tyne Railway, then under construction, which was going to offer a competitive advantage to the collieries it served by linking them to deep water at South Shields, close to the river mouth. The N&C Board therefore decided to move their Tyne crossing downstream from Scotswood to Derwenthaugh, at the mouth of the River Derwent, about a third of the way from Blaydon to Gateshead, and to endorse the idea of the line being made along the south bank by a separate company in which each N&C shareholder should have the option of holding a 'corresponding interest'. The exact route and the issue of proceeding beyond Gateshead were referred to the managing directors.

Blaydon, Gateshead & Hebburn

The upshot of all this was the formation of a Blaydon, Gateshead & Hebburn Railway (BGH), with John Blackmore as Engineer. It planned to build a line along the riverside as far as Gateshead and then pass the town by means of an incline and tunnel, eventually regaining the river by another incline down to a terminus at Hebburn Quay, about five miles downstream of Newcastle. The low-level route between Blaydon and Gateshead meant that the N&C could branch off at any point and form a bridge across to the north bank quays. Thomas Sopwith surveyed the route under Blackmore's direction and prepared the plans, which were deposited in November 1833 ready for a Parliamentary Bill.[7] Subscriptions were opened, and brought a rather disappointing response from existing N&C shareholders but the subscribers elected a provisional committee on 20 February 1834 which was entirely made up of N&C directors:[8]

Matthew Plummer, Ralph Henry Brandling, William Losh, William Woods, John & Peter Dixon, Colonel Coulson, Benjamin Thompson, George Johnson, Nicholas Wood, Henry Howard, Thomas Fenwick & John Forster.

Working behind the scenes, John Clayton and Nicholas Wood stole a march on the Stanhope & Tyne, which had hoped to attract the coal traffic of the Tanfield area, then being handled by a waggonway which reached the Tyne upstream of Gateshead. Clayton and Wood arranged that the BGH should rebuild the Tanfield Railway and link with it, thereby acquiring the business.[9]

The BGH Act got the royal assent on 22 May 1834, with a clause inserted during its passage to safeguard the interests of the PWLB by giving the N&C the option of making that portion of the route from Blaydon to their Tyne crossing, the exact location of which was still undecided despite the previous year's resolution in favour of Derwenthaugh.[10] If, within three months of the Act passing, the N&C were to 'enter into an engagement binding in law' by which they agreed to undertake 'any part of the line between Blaydon and Gateshead within two years of this agreement' then the BGH 'shall abandon in favour' of the N&C so much of the line as the N&C shall make.

The BGH shareholders held their first general meeting on 9 July and elected directors. These were still largely representative of N&C interests, with John Brandling as chairman, but his deputy, George Thomas Dunn, was one of the promoters of the Scotswood Chain Bridge and an independent character even though he was also a substantial N&C shareholder.[11] The new Board went on to appoint the managing directors of the N&C as a Managing committee for the BGH, with salaries of £100 each for Thompson, Wood and Johnson, and before long they were proceeding to let the first contracts.[12]

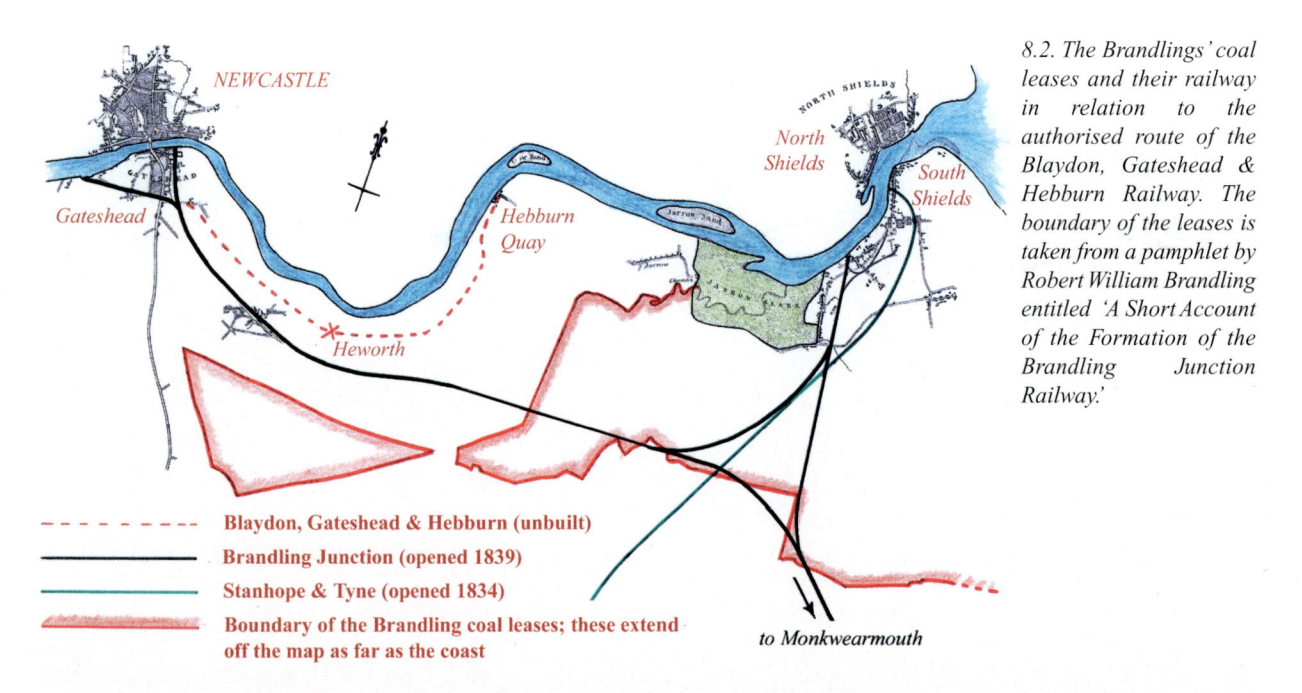

8.2. The Brandlings' coal leases and their railway in relation to the authorised route of the Blaydon, Gateshead & Hebburn Railway. The boundary of the leases is taken from a pamphlet by Robert William Brandling entitled 'A Short Account of the Formation of the Brandling Junction Railway.'

Meanwhile, the N&C Board were considering the wisdom of taking up the option in the BGH Act and making the first portion of the line from Blaydon as far as Redheugh Hall, at the west end of Gateshead, and forming their Tyne crossing there. This was debated for two months, with a decision in favour of Redheugh finally being taken on 21 August 1834.[13] There was one dissenter, Joseph Crawhall, who felt that it would prejudice the interests of Callerton colliery, in which he was a partner and which had intended to bring its coal onto the N&C at Scotswood. Powers to build the line to Redheugh and a Tyne bridge there were granted in the N&C's third Act, which received the royal assent on 17 June 1835. This also increased their capital by £150,000, made up of £90,000 in shares and the second PWLB loan of £60,000. The 1829 powers for the Scotswood bridge route to Newcastle were still retained.[14]

By then, trouble had broken out east of Gateshead, thanks to (Robert) William Brandling, brother to BGH chairman John and N&C deputy chairman Ralph. The Brandlings had colliery interests in Yorkshire and near their family seat at Gosforth, but in addition John and William had leased the rights to mine coal in a large tract of land lying between Gateshead and the coast.[15] William had the idea of building his own railway to open up this area, which ultimately took shape as a line from Gateshead to Hedworth, dividing there into two routes: one to South Shields, at the mouth of the Tyne, the other to Monkwearmouth, at the mouth of the River Wear. This was in direct competition with the BGH scheme and negotiations got underway in the autumn of 1834.[16] Attempts at a compromise, by which the Brandling Railway might start from a junction with the BGH at Heworth, fell through. William was determined and fairly unscrupulous, for example publishing details of their correspondence in the *Tyne Mercury* in an attempt to put pressure on brother John and his fellow directors.[17]

To reinforce his position William obtained an Act of Parliament on 30 July 1835 which gave him and John powers to acquire land for the Brandling Railway, though only with the landowners' consent.[18] They had already published a prospectus which led to the formation on 7 September of a public company, the Brandling Junction Railway, which was incorporated by another Act of 7 June 1836 and bought out the brothers' private interests in the form of rights held under leases and the previous Act.[19] William Losh was the only N&C director to join the Board of the Brandling Junction, but Nicholas Wood turned up as its supervising engineer, with George Stephenson as consultant. The 1836 Act contained a remarkable clause, enshrining the dictatorial Robert William as managing director for life, rather than leaving this to the discretion of the shareholders.

The BGH was thus caught in a pincer movement between its parent, the N&C, and William Brandling. By May 1835 Matthew Plummer had begun distancing himself from the BGH. He was not a man to indulge in needless confrontation, and probably felt that N&C interests could be met equally well by letting Brandling have his way at no cost to the Carlisle company. During December 1835 terms were discussed on which the N&C would take over the powers and responsibilities of the BGH and this handover was authorised by a BGH shareholders' meeting on 18 February 1836.[20] The N&C had meanwhile sorted out an arrangement by which the bulk of these rights and responsibilities would be handed over to the Brandling Junction, leaving the N&C with the task simply of completing the stretch from Blaydon to Redheugh.[21] The BGH had built just over a mile and the N&C finished the rest by the end of February 1837. The demise of the BGH seems to have gone unlamented by most people except its deputy chairman, George Thomas Dunn, who was also frustrated in his attempt to become a director of the N&C. A Newcastle alderman, he went on to become a troublesome critic of the N&C in the town council and inspired a vexatious lawsuit regarding land transactions between that body and the railway.[22]

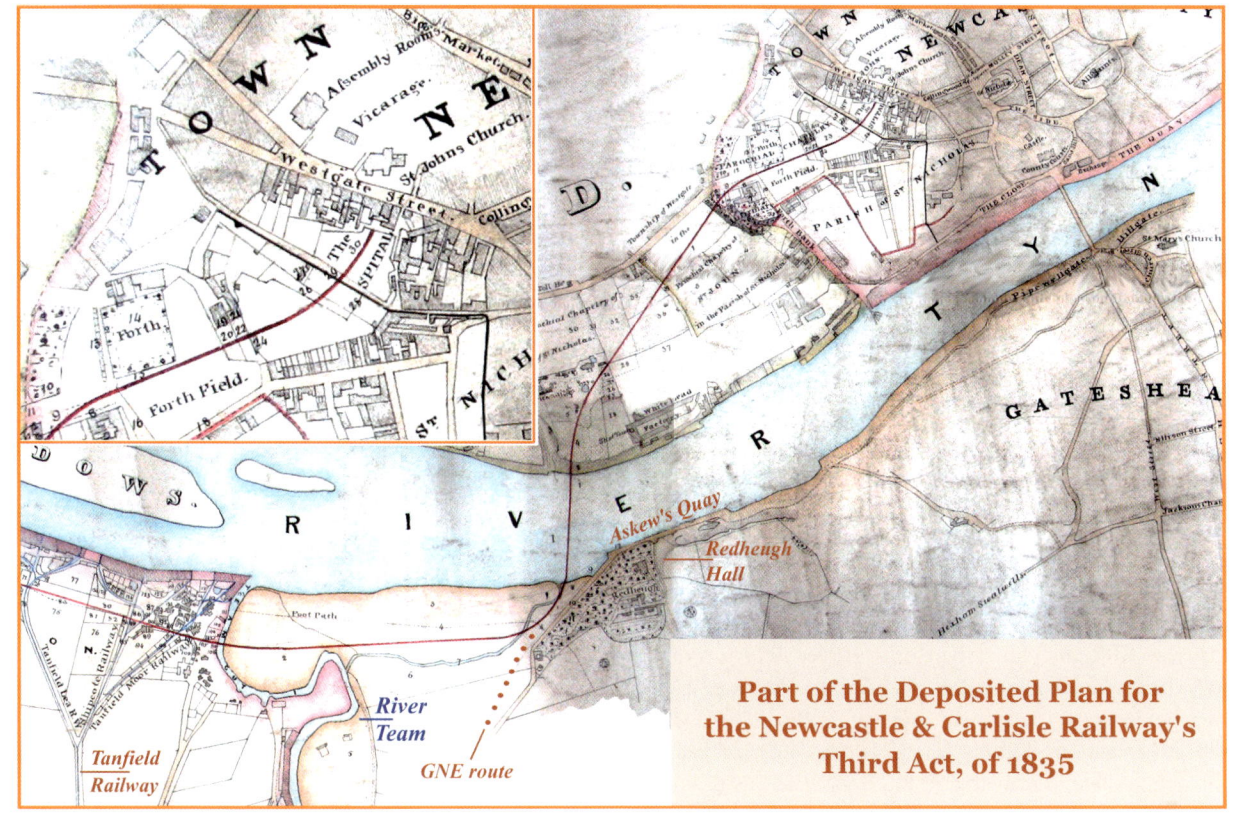

8.3. *A portion of the Deposited Plan for the N&C line from Blaydon to The Spital, authorised by their third Act, shown as a thin red line. The plan does not attempt to show the full extent of development east of Redheugh on the Gateshead bank, so the empty spaces are a little misleading. Inset is an enlargement of the final stage of the route up to the Spital. The vacant land shown there, in the form of the Forth Field and Spital, provided a convenient route for the railway.*

The Great North of England Railway and the Tyne Bridge

A complicating factor in events on the south bank was the Great North of England Railway. Fostered in Darlington, this obtained an Act on 4 July 1836 to build a line from Newcastle to Darlington followed by one on 30 June 1837 to continue on to York. In the event the company went ahead with the stretch south of Darlington first, completing this in 1841, but ran out of money before it could make a start on the northern bit. Nonetheless it figured prominently in the thoughts of N&C directors during the late eighteen-thirties.

The 1835 N&C Act authorised a Tyne bridge near Redheugh Hall at a height of only twenty feet above high water level, thus enabling the company to lay in tracks to the quays on the north bank, as promised under its original Act. From the north end of the bridge the main line was to climb 88 feet to a terminus at the Spital, open ground already purchased from Newcastle Corporation and corresponding today to the east end of Central Station and the adjoining part of Neville Street.[23] The ascent would have involved a long stretch at a gradient of 1/22, and trains would have been worked by a stationary engine. Plummer and his partners envisaged providing a road on their Tyne bridge alongside the railway tracks, which would have been a useful source of toll revenue, whereas their 1829 Act prohibited them from allowing vehicles or pedestrians across a Scotswood bridge so as to protect the monopoly of John Green's chain bridge.

The GNE originally planned to approach Tyneside via the Team Valley, like the present main line, but on a low alignment, making a junction with the N&C at the south end of their Redheugh bridge and using them to reach the Spital.[24] The N&C therefore delayed work on their bridge while discussions took place. However, the GNE engineer, Thomas Storey, began to doubt the wisdom of the low-level bridge and steep incline. A GNE deputation met with the N&C directors in Newcastle on 18 August 1836 and was offered a route on the N&C alignment 'at any higher level if required', the idea being for the railway to remain N&C property but the GNE would pay some share of the capital cost and a toll.[25] Afterwards, Storey advised his deputation that it was expedient to adopt the N&C plan but to cross the river at a height of 74 feet above high water mark. A consideration in this was William Brandling, who wanted a connection to Newcastle from his railway, planned to run at a high level through Gateshead. This effectively put the scheme out of court for the N&C. Unless they had a two-tier bridge, it would be necessary to climb up to the Tyne crossing on the south bank, by means of an incline or a lengthy deviation, and have another incline on the north bank to give access down to the Quayside.

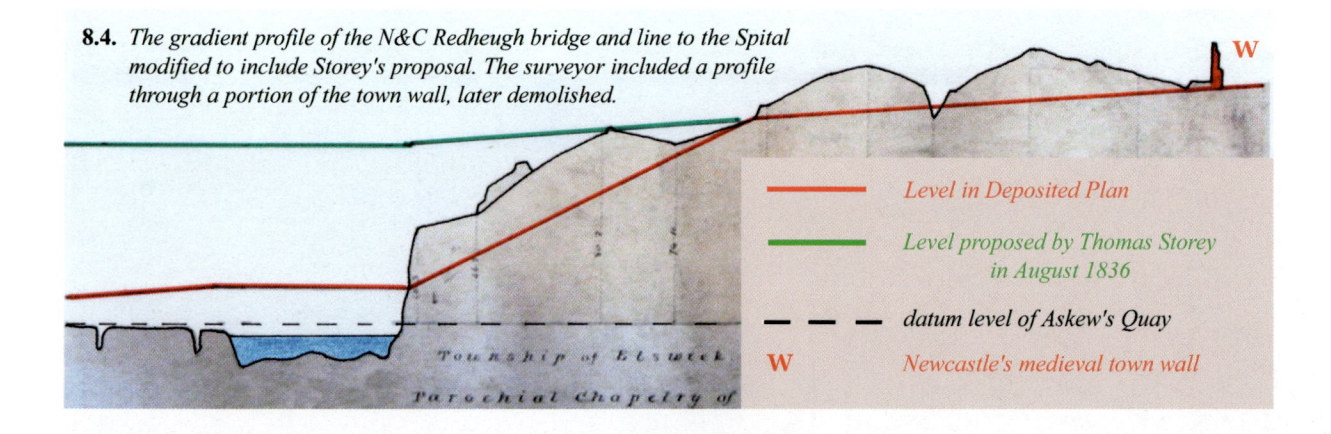

8.4. *The gradient profile of the N&C Redheugh bridge and line to the Spital modified to include Storey's proposal. The surveyor included a profile through a portion of the town wall, later demolished.*

― *Level in Deposited Plan*
― *Level proposed by Thomas Storey in August 1836*
- - - *datum level of Askew's Quay*
W *Newcastle's medieval town wall*

Another factor in the debate about the bridge was Richard Grainger (1797-1861), the inspired entrepreneur who was then providing Newcastle with an elegant neo-classical new heart. He had eyes on the development potential of the Elswick estate, which he was soon to purchase from John Hodgson, almost bankrupting himself in the process. Grainger envisaged building riverside quays, with industry behind and then a genteel residential suburb on the slopes above. To enhance the commercial prospects of this venture he published proposals during 1836 for a low-level railway bridge upstream of Redheugh at the Herd's House, with a riverside terminus for all the railways then planned.[26] Railway links could be provided by branches along the riverbank and up to the Spital, but Grainger envisaged the main link to the upper town being a new road, a mile long, from this Elswick terminus to the recently-completed New (Grainger) Markets.[27] This idea came to nothing. The GNE became increasingly keen to build their own high-level route into Newcastle, offering to make it available to the N&C, but this did not appeal to Plummer and his colleagues, who were determined to retain independent access.[28]

The issue was finally resolved in the early months of 1837. In February the N&C Board asked Blackmore to prepare plans and estimates for four different bridge sites, ranging from Scotswood to Gateshead, the latter at heights of 80 and 100 feet above the Redheugh terminus.[29] The matter was discussed at the March AGM which empowered the Board to proceed quickly with a line into Newcastle, leaving the route at their discretion. By now the south bank route had been completed through to Redheugh, and on 12 April the directors met at Scotswood and took a walk down the line with Blackmore who explained the various bridging options on the way. Four days later the Board chose the original Parliamentary alignment at Scotswood, confirming this at a meeting on 25 April where John Brandling, who naturally favoured a high-level bridge near Gateshead, was the only dissenter.[30] The following month the Scotswood bridge contract was advertised - eight years after the company had first obtained powers for it.[31]

Features of the Route from Blaydon to Redheugh

This 3¾ mile stretch of line was opened in three stages. On 11 June 1836 Blackmore and John Adamson, the company's Secretary, formally opened the section from Blaydon as far as the River Derwent with a train of passengers and goods, continuing by steamer to Newcastle.[32] Freight traffic was extended to the River Team in September, and the ceremonial opening through to Redheugh was held on 1 March 1837, accompanied by 'a procession and much rejoicing'.[33] Now the railway virtually served Newcastle, accessible by the company's ferry to a station in the Close or by a brisk walk down to the Tyne Bridge. The N&C had inherited from the BGH powers to build a mile-long branch from the mouth of the Derwent to Swalwell, but were in no hurry to proceed and it was shelved for a decade. In response to an approach from the proprietors of Swalwell colliery, the N&C apparently laid the branch with some old track, recovered from the main line during renewals, and it opened on 24 May 1847. Responsibility for improving the Tanfield line and linking it to the N&C near Redheugh was given to the Brandling Junction, as the main beneficiaries from its traffic: Tanfield coals only passed over some 250 yards of the N&C before heading off up the Redheugh Incline.

The Redheugh branch was undemanding in engineering terms. It ran along the flat riverside haughs, crossing the road from Blaydon to Scotswood Chain Bridge on the level, and the only overbridge was a low timber one carrying a colliery waggonway, which folded back to let the trains pass.[34] The original underbridges all had timber 'platforms' on stone abutments, the only significant ones being those over the Rivers Derwent and Team: the former with six 28 feet spans, including at least one over land, while the Team had three of 39 feet. Their woodwork was provided by Cuthbert Burnup, a Newcastle joiner and coachbuilder more familiar as the supplier of the company's early carriages. The line passed close to Redheugh Hall, belonging to Adam Askew, and continued along Askew's Quay to a temporary passenger station at the west end of Pipewellgate. This was known as Redheugh station and comprised a wooden carriage shed and office range, together with some goods storage and a crane. From there, the N&C conveyed goods and passengers by ferry across the Tyne to No. 66, the Close.

8.5. *Carmichael captured the atmosphere of the Redheugh branch in this view. The trees on the extreme right belong to the grounds of Redheugh Hall, alongside which the line begins its passage along Askew's Quay to the terminus. In the distance we can see the Tyne Bridge, with the tower of St. Mary's church to the right. Dominating the whole scene, on the opposite bank, is the shot tower of Walker's Lead Works, which survived into the nineteen-sixties before being needlessly destroyed. Left from this is the engine house of Elswick colliery. Standing in isolation on the north bank at far left is the Herd's House, which is where Grainger's 'central station' would have been situated.*

8.6. *Carmichael's view of Redheugh station. In the foreground, a train of coal wagons is being hauled up the Brandling Junction's Redheugh Incline by rope, and is about to pass over a wooden-trussed bridge, identical with those employed on the N&C Redheugh branch itself. A passenger train occupies the modest wooden station shed, while behind its locomotive is the funnel of the steam boat waiting to convey passengers to the N&C's rail-free station at Newcastle's Close. The Redheugh station crane, used to trans-ship goods to and from vessels, can be seen far right. On the opposite bank, the Infirmary shows up as the prominent white building towards the left. The site of Central Station lies immediately to the right of it.*

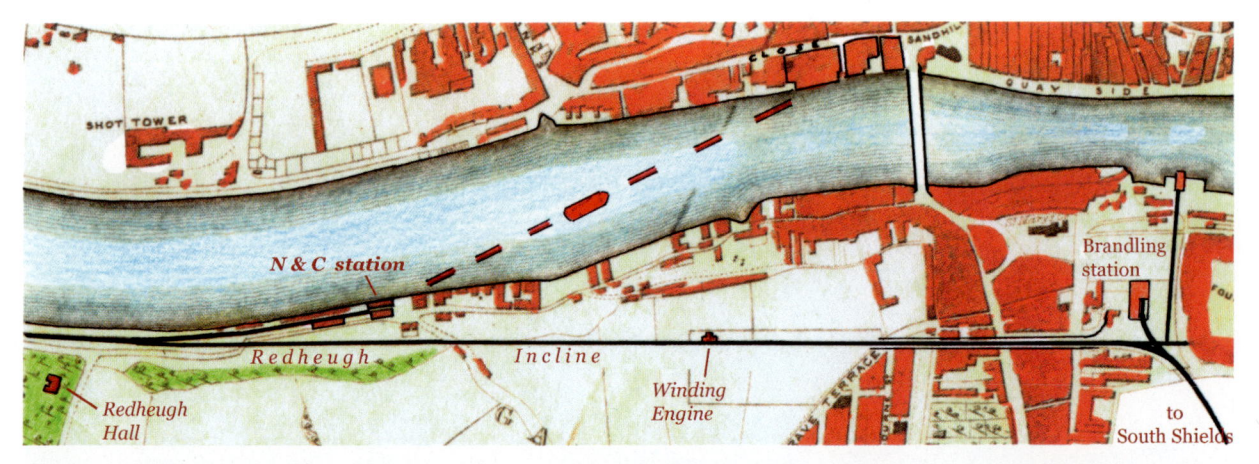

8.7. Map published by Collard in 1841, annotated to highlight the railways and show the ferry between Redheugh and the first Newcastle 'station' at No. 66, The Close. The link to the Tanfield Railway branched off the N&C just west of Redheugh Hall.

The continuation of the line through Gateshead fell to the Brandling Junction Railway, and was complicated by the way the land rises steeply from the Tyne. John Blackmore's BGH route would have addressed this with an incline at 1/15, worked by a stationary engine, followed by a tunnel under the town centre.[35] Advised by Nicholas Wood, Brandling lengthened the incline, easing the gradient to 1/23, and carried his line through the town on a viaduct instead of the tunnel. This Redheugh Incline and Gateshead viaduct formed the first part of the Brandling Junction to open, on 15 January 1839, along with another incline down to a riverside quay at the east end of town.[36] Together, these enabled coal from the Newcastle & Carlisle to be shipped downstream of the Tyne Bridge, though facilities were much improved by the opening of the lines to South Shields and Monkwearmouth, later that year.

The long-awaited opening of the N&C route into Newcastle took place in 1839, but the Redheugh terminus remained important since it was more convenient for Newcastle Quayside than the provisional terminus on the north bank. Indeed, the Redheugh branch gained in importance from 18 June 1844, when George Hudson's Newcastle & Darlington Junction Railway opened, superseding the abortive GNE scheme and completing the last link in railway communication between London (Euston) and Tyneside. Its trains utilised part of the Brandling Junction Railway but ran into a fine new passenger station in Greene's Field, at the head of the Redheugh Incline. N&C passenger services were thereupon diverted from the Redheugh terminus and ran instead up the incline into Greenesfield station, so as to connect with trains from the south. The Carlisle trains therefore ran in two sections, originating at Newcastle and Gateshead and uniting at Blaydon.

8.8. Redheugh c1906, with the depot on the riverbank and the incline heading up under the newly-completed King Edward Bridge.

8.9. There was a striking contrast between Redheugh and the grand Greenesfield Station, illustrated by the 'Gateshead Observer'. It was designed by George Hudson's friend George Townsend Andrews but only served as Tyneside's main-line railhead for six years and was then converted into locomotive workshops.

THE GATESHEAD STATION OF THE NEWCASTLE-UPON-TYNE AND DARLINGTON RAILWAY.

This arrangement lasted until the opening of the first phase of Newcastle Central Station in August 1850. Greenesfield station thereupon closed, and there was no point in continuing to run any Carlisle trains over the south bank route. However, the N&C did, for a time, provide a service of Saturday market trains over part of the Redheugh branch, running from Derwenthaugh to Newcastle via Blaydon and Scotswood bridge. The south bank came back into regular passenger use with British Rail's closure of Scotswood bridge in 1982. All services over the N&C now use the Redheugh branch from Blaydon to just east of the Derwent bridge and then branch off on a link built by the NER to their 1906 King Edward Bridge over the Tyne. The remainder of the Redheugh route has been abandoned.

The North Bank: Approaching Newcastle

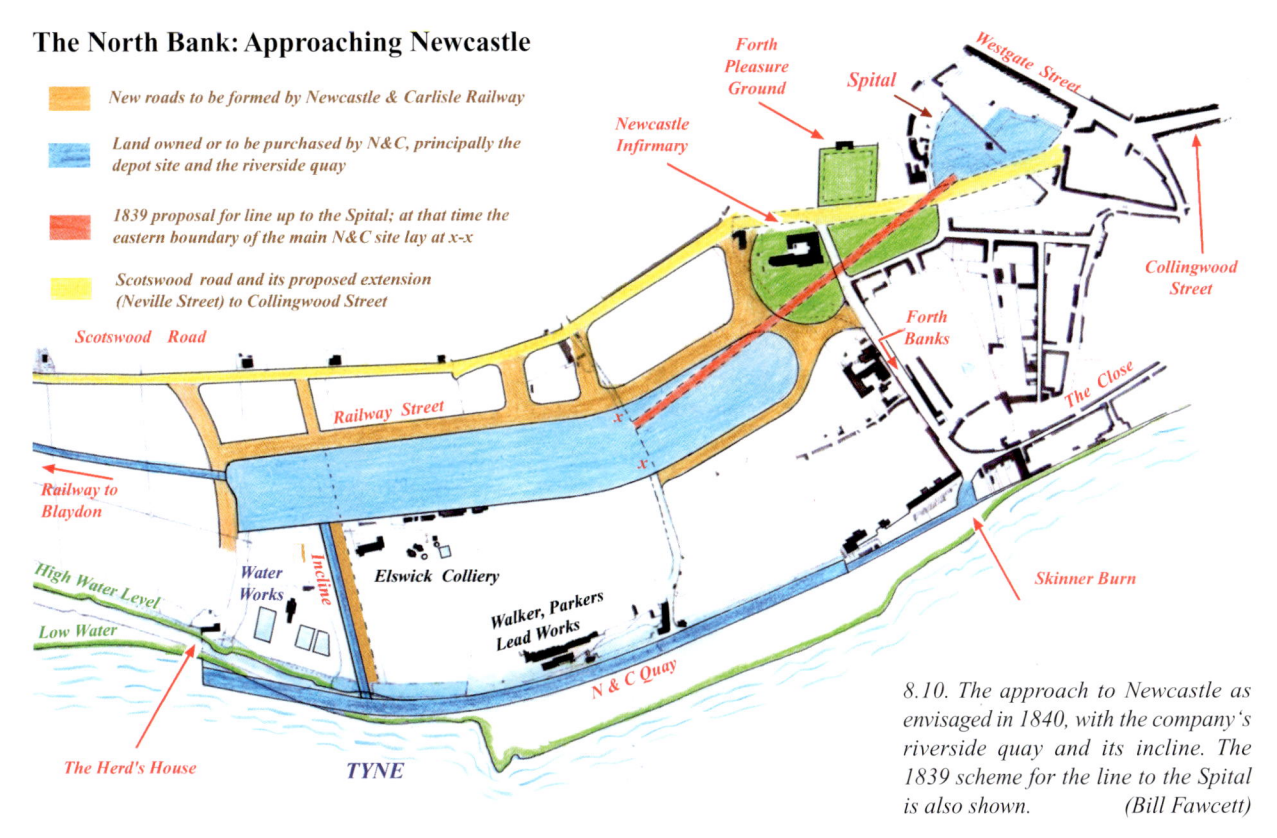

- New roads to be formed by Newcastle & Carlisle Railway
- Land owned or to be purchased by N&C, principally the depot site and the riverside quay
- 1839 proposal for line up to the Spital; at that time the eastern boundary of the main N&C site lay at x-x
- Scotswood road and its proposed extension (Neville Street) to Collingwood Street

8.10. The approach to Newcastle as envisaged in 1840, with the company's riverside quay and its incline. The 1839 scheme for the line to the Spital is also shown. (Bill Fawcett)

Under the terms of the directors' personal bond with the Public Works Loans Board, they were obliged to complete a route from Carlisle to Newcastle, and Redheugh was not an acceptable substitute. Thus the directors' decision in April 1837 to proceed with a route via Scotswood has to be seen as an expedient way of meeting this commitment. Their minds were also focused by the realisation that the construction powers granted by the 1829 Act ran out after ten years, and renewing them for the Scotswood bridge might involve a costly Parliamentary contest. However, once over the bridge the idea was to foresake the 1829 Parliamentary route along the riverside in favour of one which would climb gradually towards a terminus near the upper part of town. The exact location of this depot was a matter for further debate within the Board and various locations were favoured, including the Spital - which the company already owned; a site further west, offered by Grainger; and one near the Newcastle Infirmary. While his masters talked, Blackmore got on with engineering a line to a provisional terminus at what became Railway Street, half a mile west of the present Central Station.

Work proceeded rapidly with Scotswood bridge, but the company had no Parliamentary powers for the new route east from there, so that 'many months were lost in treating with the proprietors [of property] and combating the objections of the Scotswood [Chain] Bridge Company', stoked up by Alderman Dunn.[37] By February 1838, work on the bridge was well advanced, with the piers and the south abutment in place, but only then did construction begin on the remainder of the line, which was placed in the hands of our old friend George Grahamsley.[38] His 'well-tried powers and energy' could be relied on to secure rapid progress once the land had been obtained, but the weather then did its best to frustrate his efforts.

One problem posed by the change of route from the Parliamentary alignment was that of railway access to the riverside. Both Newcastle Corporation, who had invested £5,000 in the N&C, and the directors had always seen this as an important aspect of the venture and felt that it still had to be provided. The actual outcome was somewhat bizarre. The N&C had agreed with the Corporation that the railway should build a new quay stretching from the Herd's House to the mouth of the Skinner Burn, and this was eventually begun under a contract let to Richard Grainger in July 1838.[39] It was to be linked to the new main line by an incline at a gradient of 1/8½, worked by a stationary engine. Grainger purchased the Elswick estate in January 1839, and one outcome was an agreement that he would share the expense of building the western part of the quay, stretching almost half a mile from the Herd's House to Parker's lead works, which would be an asset to his Elswick development.[40] However, the bold developer had over-reached himself financially, and the N&C appear to have bought his share in the quay as part of the Grainger rescue operation mounted by John Clayton.[41] The incline had been built and the quay finished to a point about 800 feet short of the intended west end, when the directors began an economy drive in 1841.[42] Work on the quay was halted anyway because Grainger, still acting as contractor, was hiding from his creditors. In the event the temporary standstill became a permanent one. The N&C never laid the intended tracks on either the incline or quay. Part of the latter was eventually bought by the adjoining lead works, while the incline was taken over by the Elswick Gasworks, which laid tracks at the top end to provide their access from the N&C.[43]

Waybeams

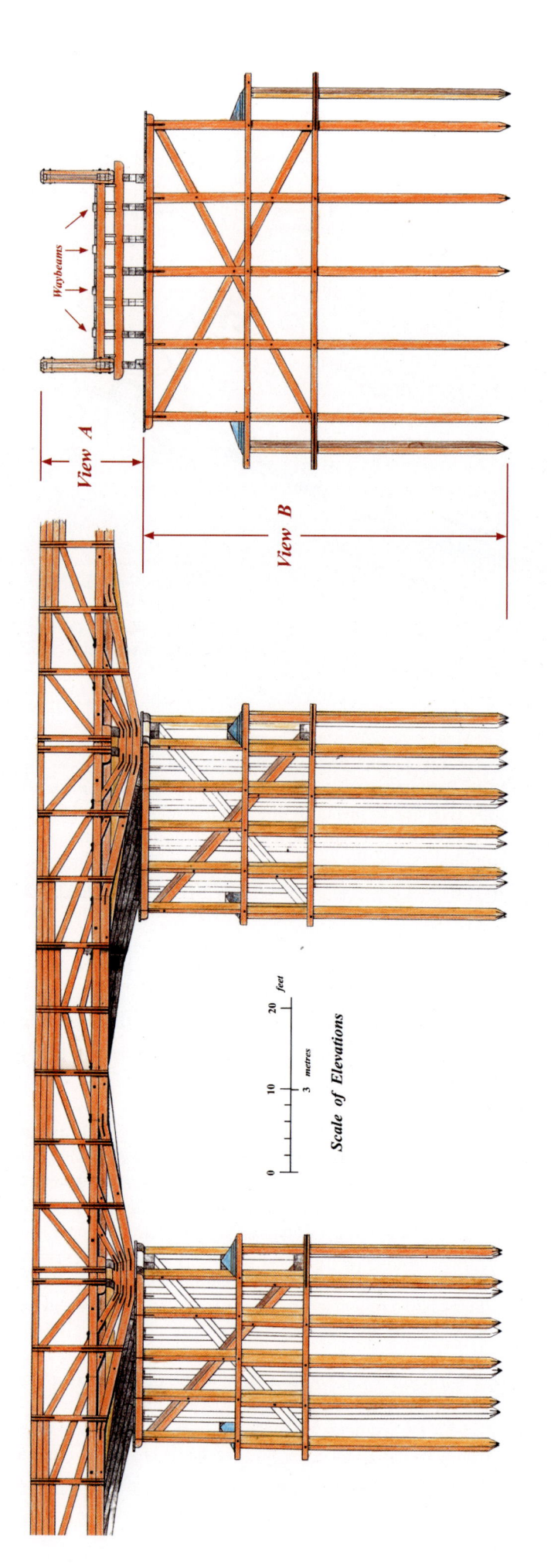

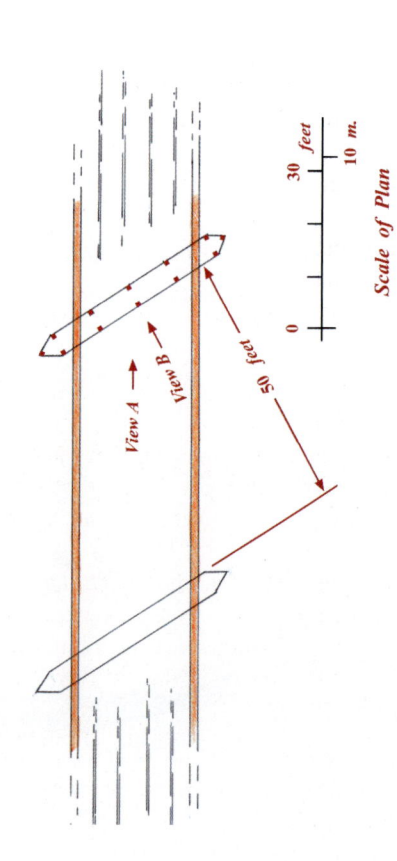

View A

View B

Scale of Elevations
0 — 10 — 20 feet
0 — 3 metres

Scale of Plan
0 — 30 feet
0 — 10 m.

50 feet

View A
View B

8.12. *Scotswood Bridge. A coloured version of the drawing published by John Weale in 1855, based on a drawing by Blackmore. This fails to show the obnoxious spikes. At either end, the superstructure was carried by a stone abutment, similar to those of the South Tyne bridges between Haydon Bridge and Bardon Mill. There were two spans continuing over Blaydon Haughs at the south end, with a pier placed on the edge of the riverbank. This obstructed the hauling path, which was required when hauling the keels in bad weather. Clayton recognised that the company had no right to do so and promised that they would reinstate the path.*

The line from Blaydon to the temporary terminus at Railway Street was formally opened on 21 May 1839, enabling the directors to claim that the railway had been completed; the justices of the peace subsequently signed a formal notice to this effect.[44] However, the parade of directors and local dignitaries, accompanied by a band, was pure theatre. The earthworks were still incomplete and the line was not finally opened to the public until 21 October, when three 'very elegant and commodious omnibuses' began conveying passengers between the station and Newcastle's principal coaching inns: the *Queen's Head, Turk's Head*, and *Turf*.[45] Shortly after, Nature struck again 'with a most unprecedented continuance of wet weather, which lasted almost without interruption for some months'.[46] New earthworks are always vulnerable to heavy rain, and for much of the winter the company had to abandon one track, of the double line route, in order to concentrate on the struggle to keep services going on the other.

The N&C had secured a huge piece of land, 300 feet wide and almost 1800 feet long, for their various depots in Newcastle, and they placed their coal depot in the north-west corner of this. The directors were vacillating, however, about the final locations for the passenger and goods stations, and provided temporary wooden premises for these on the northern boundary of the site, fronting Railway Street. A plan of February 1839 shows the Spital back in favour for the permanent station, reached by a line extending from the depot site in a mixture of cutting and tunnel.[47] That idea was abandoned, and the Board settled instead on extending the existing site towards the town and placing a passenger station at the east end, facing Newcastle Infirmary. This scheme was encapsulated in plans deposited in February 1840, while this 'Infirmary' station was actually shown as built on a map of Newcastle published the following year.[48] The map sought to be up to date, but proved premature.

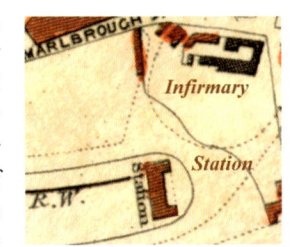

8.11. *Detail from Collard's map, showing the Infirmary terminus which was never built.*

Because the land slopes down to the south, extensive earthworks were required to build up a level site for the depots, retained by a stout stone wall along the southern boundary. By March 1841 the directors were able to report that this had been done, providing a site almost half a mile long.[49] Having gone to all this expense, however, the new passenger station was not built there, although an impressive goods station eventually was. The arrival on the scene of George Hudson to provide the main line between Darlington and Berwick led to further negotiations, discussed in the next chapter, which resulted in the construction of the present Central Station as a joint venture. In the interim, the N&C kept its goods business at Railway Street but moved the passengers to a second temporary station, Forth, at the west end of the Central Station site.

Engineering Works between Scotswood and the Infirmary

The major engineering feature is Scotswood bridge. Benjamin Thompson originally proposed this as the timber truss on stone piers illustrated in Figure 4.7. Test bores had been made through the gravelly riverbed by his surveyor Oswald Blackett, revealing that bedrock was attainable at reasonable depths.[50] Francis Giles, however, was unhappy about the riverbed and advocated lightening the structure by the adoption of timber piers. This was eventually done, but the design of the bridge went through several mutations on the way.

Giles himself suggested in August 1829 a bridge of five 100 feet spans, each comprising curved iron ribs from which a wooden platform would be suspended by means of iron rods.[51] This was very new technology, having just been pioneered by George Leather at Leeds, and was later to form the basis for the road deck of Robert Stephenson's High Level Bridge at Newcastle. Giles's idea was not taken up directly, and in September 1832 the directors advertised for bridge designs, offering premiums of £10 and £5.[52] Consideration of the entries was delayed until the end of July 1833, and both premiums went to the Green family.[53] The first premium went to the architect John Green (1787-1852), designer of the Scotswood Chain Bridge, for a deck suspended from a timber arch, while the second went to his nephew - also John Green (1807-1868) - for a variant design, employing cast-iron segments for the arch. The elder Green was an accomplished and experienced bridge designer, whose scheme would have provided five spans of 120 feet each. It was not implemented but he went on to adopt a similar principle for the West Durham Railway's Wear Bridge at Willington, begun four years later.[54]

The Scotswood bridge actually built during 1837-8 proved very different. It was one of Blackmore's trussed timber designs, basically similar to Warden but with piers formed from timber piles. It was a skew bridge, with eleven openings of only fifty feet span, measured on the square.[55] These were regarded as uncomfortably narrow by the keelmen, a further hazard being the iron 'spikes' attached to the piers to provide some protection from ice floes, which were more of a concern then than now.[56] The spikes tended to attract flotsam and pack ice and further impede the navigation, so in February 1838, with the piers completed but the superstructure only just begun, the keelmen and wherrymen presented a petition to Newcastle Town Council, the river authority, complaining of the hazard.[57] This did not get them very far since the 1829 Act only specified the height of the bridge not the width of the individual spans, which were no narrower than those of the Tyne Bridge at Newcastle. Familiarity in this case undoubtedly bred contempt, and many people were delighted when the bridge was consumed by fire on 9 May 1860.[58] A temporary replacement, on the original piles, was succeeded by the present structure of six hog-backed, wrought-iron girder spans on tubular cast-iron piers, begun in 1868.

8.13. *Part of Carmichael's engraving of Scotswood Bridge, looking east with the Chain Bridge in the distance.*

8.14. *T.E. Harrison's replacement bridge. The contract for the ironwork was let to Palmers of Jarrow on 18 August 1868 at £21,997 10s 7d. It was important to avoid any significant interference with traffic, so the work will have been somewhat protracted. The hog-backed girders are typical of Harrison's work at this period and are a larger version of those used in his replacement of timber spans in other N&C river bridges. The bridge is hardly elegant but a doubling in the size of the spans, compared with its predecessor, must have been a great boon to river traffic. (Bill Fawcett)*

Other than its Tyne bridge, the feature which distinguished this stretch of line from the remainder of the N&C thus far was Blackmore's adoption of cast iron for the road underbridges.[59] Chief among these was the skew bridge over the Scotswood Bridge Company's Newcastle to Scotswood road near Paradise. This had a 50 feet span (measured on the skew) employing three segmental girders, each formed in two sections, bolted together through flanges at mid span. All this was well-established technology. The beams sat in shoes fixed to a skewback of the stone abutments. The NER eventually widened the line on the north side, doubling it from two to four tracks, and replaced the cast-iron beams with a wrought-iron plate girder structure.

East of Paradise the line was carried on an 'embankment' formed by earth fill between massive stone retaining walls. This approach was adopted for two reasons: it minimised the amount of land required and it reduced the amount of earth fill needed, this being in short supply since there was only one significant cutting on the whole line.[60] The relatively low elevation of the railway east of Paradise meant Blackmore had to use cast-iron beams to minimise the construction depth in bridging the wide streets leading from Scotswood Road down to the river. The street widths were designed to facilitate future development of the area, and his bridges ended up with road spans of between 34 and 35 feet accompanied by pedestrian arches through the abutments on one or both sides. Some were enlarged by the NER to take more tracks and all had their girders replaced in wrought iron.

8.15. *Scotswood station (dem), with the line curving round onto the bridge. What we see is the upper half of a two-storey station house, whose occupants could also watch out for fire breaking out on the bridge. A watchman's cottage was provided on the opposite bank.   (J.M. Fleming)*

8.16. *The bridge at Paradise (dem), looking along the Scotswood Bridge Company's road towards Newcastle. Geordie Ridley immortalised it in 'Blaydon Races', as the spot where the bus wheel flew off, consigning its passengers: 'some to the Dispensary and some to Dr. Gibbs's and some to the Infirmary to mend their broken ribs's.'   (Bill Fawcett, c1966)*

8.17. *Dunn Street bridge, named after the vexatious alderman, lies at the west end of Railway Street. View down towards the Tyne, with the legacy of the Elswick Gas Company prominently in sight. The stone wall on the left formed the western boundary of the N&C depot site, while the brick wall above is a relic of Forth Junction signalbox. The inset view shows the original pedestrian arch, in channelled masonry, reinforced underneath by one in brick.   (Bill Fawcett, 2007)*

105

The Advance to Central Station

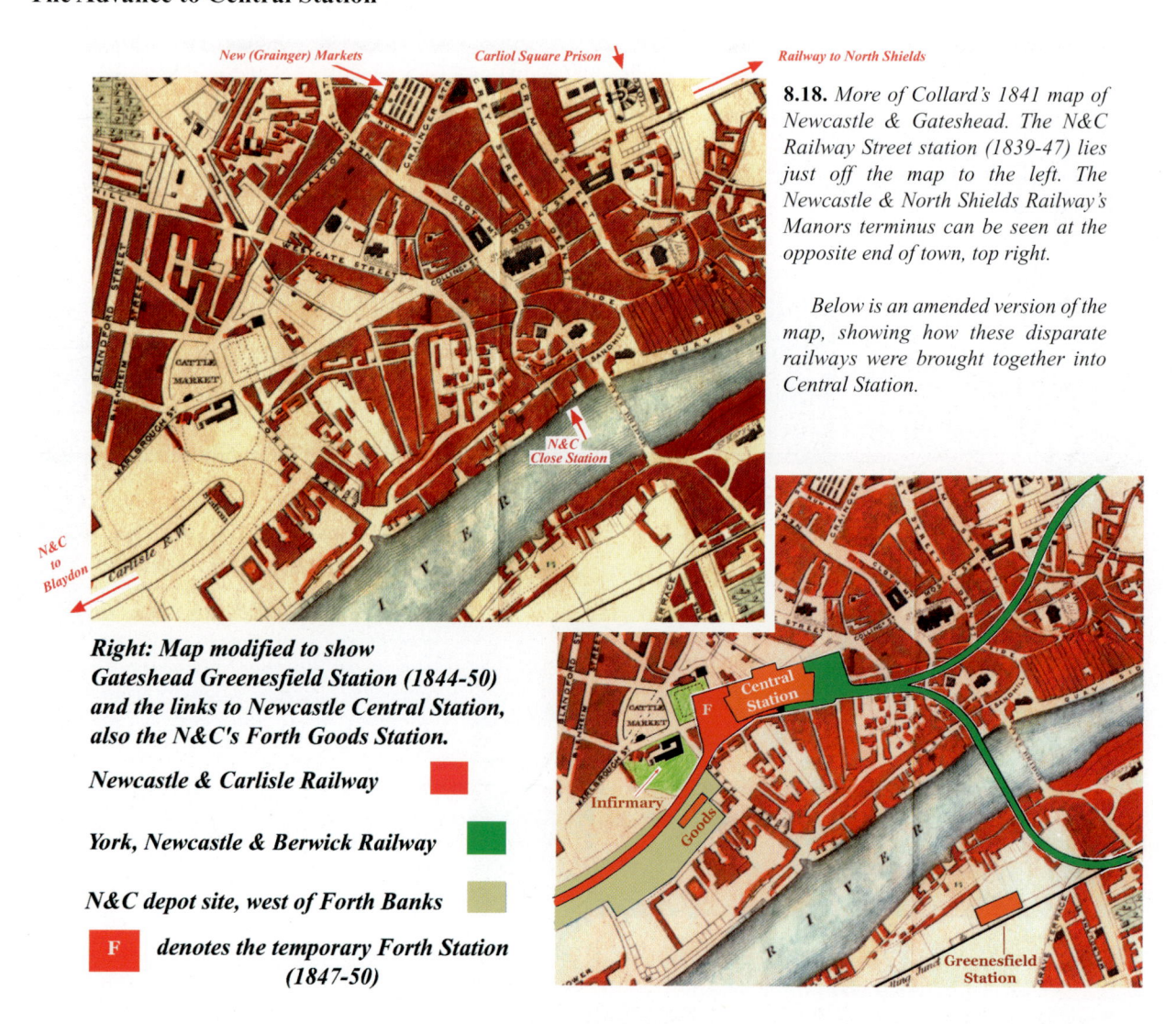

8.18. *More of Collard's 1841 map of Newcastle & Gateshead. The N&C Railway Street station (1839-47) lies just off the map to the left. The Newcastle & North Shields Railway's Manors terminus can be seen at the opposite end of town, top right.*

Below is an amended version of the map, showing how these disparate railways were brought together into Central Station.

Right: *Map modified to show Gateshead Greenesfield Station (1844-50) and the links to Newcastle Central Station, also the N&C's Forth Goods Station.*

Newcastle & Carlisle Railway

York, Newcastle & Berwick Railway

N&C depot site, west of Forth Banks

F denotes the temporary Forth Station (1847-50)

Although the moves leading to the N&C's sponsorship of Newcastle Central Station belong to the next chapter, this is a convenient point to describe the extension of the railway up to it. The line was authorised by the N&C's fifth Act, of 1846, but work began well in advance of this since land purchases had begun two years earlier, and the two main landowners, the Infirmary and the Corporation, had proved very helpful. Much of the route lay within the existing depot ground, after which it skirted the Infirmary gardens, taking a small strip from the bottom of these. It then bridged Forth Banks to reach a provisional terminus, partly on the site of the Forth pleasure ground.

John Blackmore had died in March 1844, so the survey for the line was carried out by a freelance engineer and surveyor John Bourne, while Peter Tate designed the engineering features and oversaw construction.[61] It involved a modest climb from the depot ground to the higher level of Central Station, so the line set off up a ramp, between stone retaining walls, before bridging Shot Factory Lane (now Redheugh Bridge Road) and continuing on a low sandstone viaduct of 39 segmental arches. This bore three tracks and finished up with a cast-iron skew bridge of 33 feet span across Forth Banks. The temporary 'Forth' station lay roughly on the site now occupied by the glazed area at the west end of Central Station.

8.19. *The approximate site of the temporary Forth station, seen in September 1964. The building on the left used to house the NER Accountant's Office on the upper floor, while St. Mary's cathedral climbs above the station roof on the right. (Bill Fawcett)*

8.20. *An engraving of Peter Tate's viaduct and bridge over Forth Banks, looking west from the site of the temporary station. The Infirmary gardens are on the right, and the bridge was intended to form an ornamental feature in the view from them. Just left of the tree can be seen that commanding feature of the Elswick skyline: the Shot Tower. (J.M. Fleming collection)*

This was the first new stretch of the N&C to come under the requirement, introduced in 1840, that passenger railways should be inspected by the Board of Trade before being permitted to open. The inspectors were seconded officers of the Royal Engineers, and Captain Coddington examined the extension on 15 February 1847, passing it as fit for purpose and complimenting various aspects of the construction.[62] He described the viaduct as a 'substantial and very handsome structure' but the original masonry has been almost entirely hidden from view by the NER's construction of the Forth Goods Station against its south face and widening from three to four tracks on the north side, while Peter Tate's Forth Banks bridge has been completely replaced.

The need for a Board of Trade inspection took the directors by surprise. It had not occurred to John Adamson, and plans had been made for an opening in January until Anthony Hall, the locomotive superintendent, pointed out the requirement.[63] Even then the directors took the matter rather lightly and dragged Peter Tate off to look at another part of the line, while Coddington conducted his inspection in the company of Richard Lowry, by then head of the Newcastle station, and John Challoner, the Chief Agent.[64] Neither was competent to speak on engineering matters but the Captain was fortunately satisfied by his subsequent conversation with Tate.

Passenger trains began using the new line on 1 March 1847, but it had already enjoyed two formal openings before Captain Coddington ever saw it. The official event, organised by the directors, took place on 6 November 1846 but, unknown to them, Peter Tate had carried out his own celebration the previous evening.[65] Accompanied by Anthony Hall, Richard Lowry and some platelayers, he took an engine and a few wagons over the line as far as Forth Banks, where they stopped in the middle of the bridge to enjoy a bottle of whisky and drink 'Prosperity to the Railway'. The officers then retired to Lowry's office to tuck into his brandy.

8.21. *The north face of the viaduct has been made somewhat ugly by its widening in brick to carry a fourth track. The arches were exploited to give access to the Forth Goods Station on the other side. (Bill Fawcett, 2007)*

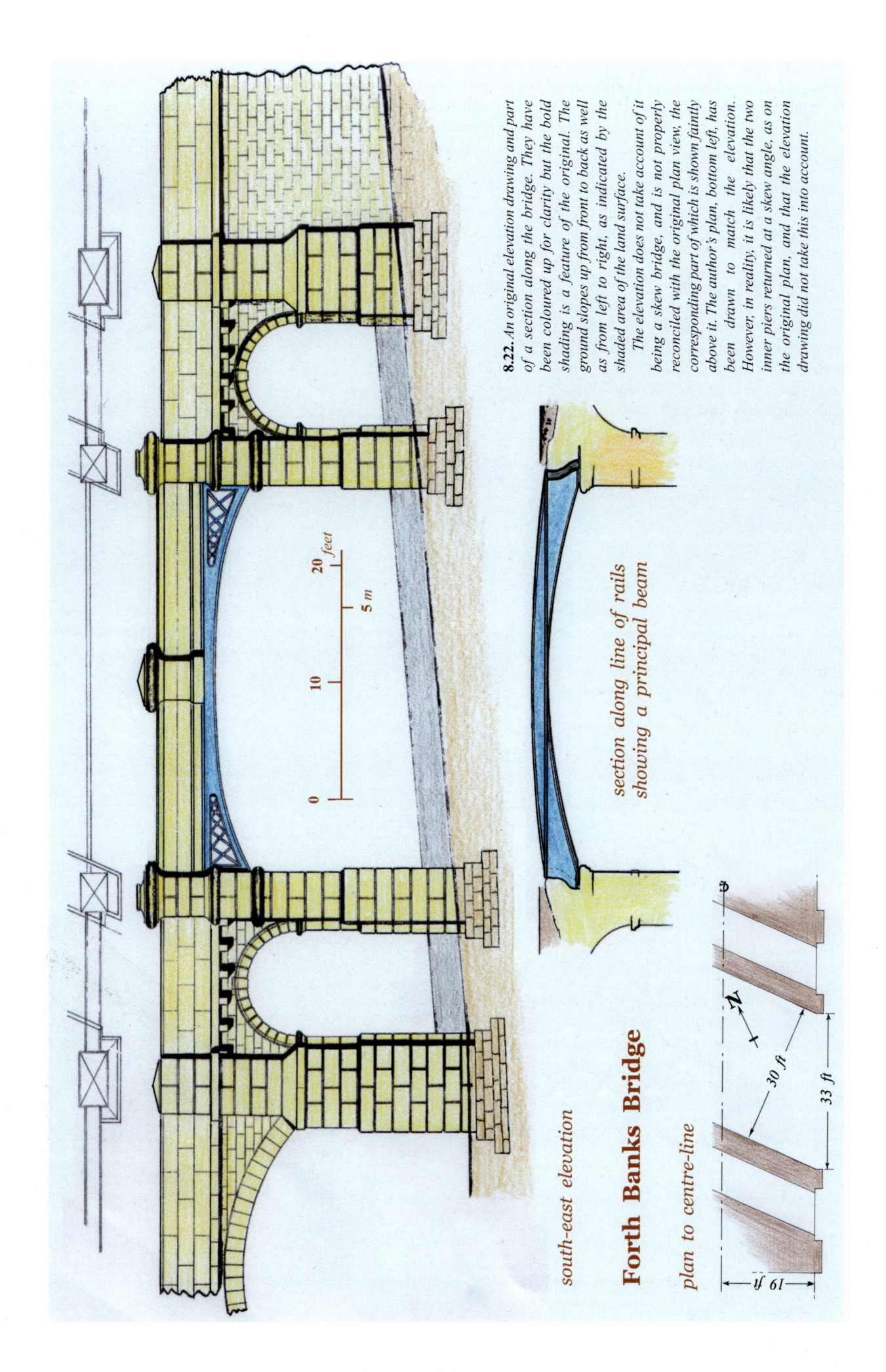

8.22. *An original elevation drawing and part of a section along the bridge. They have been coloured up for clarity but the bold shading is a feature of the original. The ground slopes up from front to back as well as from left to right, as indicated by the shaded area of the land surface.*

The elevation does not take account of it being a skew bridge, and is not properly reconciled with the original plan view, the corresponding part of which is shown faintly above it. The author's plan, bottom left, has been drawn to match the elevation. However, in reality, it is likely that the two inner piers returned at a skew angle, as on the original plan, and that the elevation drawing did not take this into account.

south-east elevation

section along line of rails showing a principal beam

Forth Banks Bridge

plan to centre-line

108

The engraving of the Forth viaduct (fig. 8.20) was based on a painting commissioned by the directors and illustrated opposite page 48 of MacLean's History.[67] Its depiction of the bridge over Forth Banks differs in minor decorative details from the elevation drawing, evidently by Peter Tate, which is reproduced here. An early section drawing suggests that the engraving is closer to the built design. In the manner of Robert Stephenson's bridges on the Euston extension, the cast-iron facing arches are treated ornamentally, and their structural role amounts to little more than bearing the parapets. The long section shows the beams which handle the live load, each carrying an individual rail secured to a timber waybeam set in a trough in the upper part of the girder. The depth of the upper curve of the girder corresponds to this trough. The parapet is somewhat ambiguous. It was obviously meant to look like stone but one would expect it to be cast iron, painted stone colour, which would also have been the original colour of the arch below. The section, however, shows a thick enough parapet to have been actually built of stone. The width of the viaduct between parapets was about 35 feet, to accommodate three tracks. This compares with 22 feet, for two tracks, on the original N&C bridges, and indicates that Tate had moved with the times and adopted a six-feet spacing between tracks.

The Forth viaduct is Tate's most extensive work, and draws on his earlier experiences as Blackmore's assistant. The masonry arches are a scaled-up version of the viaduct at the Carlisle Canal basin, whose construction Tate oversaw during his early time with the company, while the form of the cast-iron bridge girders may well be informed by Blackmore's design for the Paradise bridge. No drawings for that survive, but the dimensions of the beams are known and imply a similar shape to that shown here.

1847 saw the N&C equipped, at long last, with a station in the centre of Newcastle, and the temporary Forth premises served for almost four years, with services being transferred into Central Station on 1 January 1851.[66] The north bank route was the N&C main line and acquired additional importance with the establishment alongside of Sir William Armstrong's Elswick Works, one of the great Victorian industrial enterprises. However, the decline in rail-borne freight in the latter part of the twentieth century and the deteriorating condition of the 1868 Scotswood bridge led to a decision to concentrate all traffic on the south bank, making use of a link built by the NER from Derwenthaugh Junction to the King Edward Bridge. Somewhat ironically, this is a route the N&C might have embarked on themselves in 1837, had they not been committed to the ultimately abortive link to Newcastle Quayside. Scotswood bridge closed from 4 October 1982 and the north bank now has rails only on the 1847 extension and a short portion of the 1839 route, ending at Water Street bridge. This provides access from Central Station, via a reversal at Water Street, down to a civil engineer's depot on the site of the demolished Forth Goods Station. Portions of the 1839 route have been completely destroyed, notably at Paradise where the railway has vanished under road improvements, but Scotswood bridge survives to carry a water main.

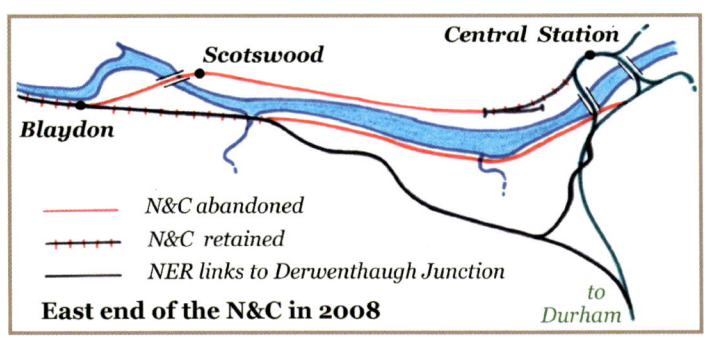

8.24.
This building is said to have begun life as the temporary passenger station at the Forth. (James Russell, 'The Newcastle & Carlisle Railway' in 'Railway Magazine', 1900, p.228). This seems entirely credible, although a later tradition claims it as the N&C Redheugh station. It was re-erected in Sunderland Road, Gateshead, at the corner with High Street, serving as a group of dwellings. E. Dodds photographed it on 26 June 1886, shortly after the introduction of the steam trams, whose tracks provide something of a railway atmosphere to the scene.
(Gateshead Central Library)

Chapter 9: Consolidation and Expansion: 1839 - 1852

Finances

Within months of the first section of line opening to the public, in 1835, it became evident that traffic on the railway was going to exceed all forecasts. This is just as well, since the final capital cost of the project turned out about three times the estimate. Large cost over-runs were not unusual in early railway construction, and in this case there were a number of changes in policy which partially explain the excess. By the end of 1839 the main line and Redheugh Branch had been completed, leaving only the extension up to Newcastle Central, and it is instructive to look at the costs incurred up to then and compare them with the estimates which accompanied the 1829 Bill. The following table does so, taking out the construction cost of the Redheugh Branch from the 1839 total though it has not been possible to separate the cost of the land taken for that branch. The construction cost of the Thornton Street Branch has also been removed from the 1829 total, though its land cost has not been separated. Otherwise the table provides a direct comparison between the schemes authorised and built. Figures are rounded to the nearest pound. [1]

	1839	**1829**
Legal Expenses, including Parliamentary & Conveyancing	13,413	17,000 *(Legal & Engineering)*
Surveying & Engineering Design & Supervision	19,791	
Land Purchase & Damages	122,340	36,004
Earthworks, Bridges, Tunnels etc	432,956	131,542
Permanent Way Materials and Laying	157,948	84,696
Carriage of Materials & Rails	5,171	
Locomotives, Rolling Stock & Boats	45,750	*not contemplated*
Depots, Stations & Machinery	17,947	*not contemplated*
Printing, Advertisements & Stationery	2,446	
Incidental Expenses	23,270	
Discounts, commissions etc	2,129	
Total	**846,122**	**269,242**

It is worth noting that Giles, in his detailed report of August 1829, revised the Bill estimates, given above, increasing them by a total of 8%. His figures were based on a double-track formation, laid initially with a single track with frequent passing places. Among other considerations, the 1839 figures are boosted by the company's decisions to employ locomotives and to be the sole carrier; the latter, of course, boosted their income as well since they were able to charge haulage dues and wagon rents as well as tolls. The increased capital expenditure for depots, locomotives and rolling stock was only £63,697 but there was to be a lot of further spending under this head in the future. Opting for locomotives had entailed laying sturdier rails than originally anticipated, and the rest of the discrepancy under the permanent-way heading is accounted for by the doubling programme: by the end of 1839 about two-thirds of the route mileage was double track.

Where the original estimates really fell down was under land purchase and construction. John Studholme's original estimate of land costs was based on a take of 551 acres for 63 route miles, equivalent to 8.7 acres per route mile, at a cost of £65.5 per acre. This, of course, made no provision for depots and the fairest comparison with the actual costs is obtained by looking at the seven route miles purchased from Greenwich Hospital. [2] These entailed a land take of just over 77 acres, or 11 acres per mile, which is not that far above the original estimate. Studholme was, however, much too optimistic about the price. Greenwich was a very reasonable vendor: its Receiver, John Grey, set a price of £90 per acre, based on 30 years of an agricultural rent of £3, giving a total cost of £6,999-3-9, equivalent to a thousand pounds per route mile instead of the estimated £570.

If we apply the Greenwich figure to the total route mileage built by 1839, some 64 miles, this gives a basic land cost of some £64,000, to which must be added damages such as those paid to Charles Bacon of Styford in lieu of his screening 'mound'. Land in urban areas such as Carlisle and Newcastle was, of course, going to cost a lot more than that out in the country. Elswick, with its obvious development potential, must have been quite expensive, and the enormous tracts taken for depot ground there and at the Spital probably account for the best part of fifty thousand pounds. Even so, the final average of £1,900 per route mile compares very well with other railways of the period. The Liverpool & Manchester had paid out £95,305, excluding the land for its Liverpool depots, for a line half the length: over £3,000 per mile.[3] The London & Birmingham, saddled admittedly with very high land costs on the Euston extension and the need to sweeten various landowners, paid out £706,152 for a route not quite twice the length of the N&C.[4] By these standards, the N&C was a real bargain.

The discrepancy between construction costs and estimates seems due largely to faulty or optimistic estimating. From the outset the line was envisaged with earthworks and bridges wide enough for double track, though we have seen that some parts of the formation and underbridges were built to single-track width for economy and later widened. The only significant unforeseen excess, therefore, was the excavation of Cowran Cutting, where a

9.1. *An impression of the Newcastle & Carlisle in the early forties, with 'Venus', supplied by Thompson Brothers in January 1841, hauling a mixed train through the bridge under the Military Road at Scarrow Hill. When the railway was being built there was no firm convention about which track to run on. Most companies chose to run on the left, but the N&C chose the right and stuck to it. The permanent way depicted is the original one of fish-bellied rail laid on stone sleeper blocks.   (Bill Fawcett)*

million cubic yards of sandy ground were removed at the exceptionally cheap rate of sixpence per yard compared with the eightpence which Francis Whishaw thought to be the norm.[5] Even taking the whole of this is as an extra it adds only £25,000. That said, the overall construction cost averaged about £7,100 per mile for earthworks, bridges, tunnels, river walls and fencing. By contrast the Liverpool & Manchester averaged about £6,700 per mile for earthworks alone, exclusive of bridges, tunnels and the formation over Chat Moss.[6] So again the N&C seems a rather good bargain, and a vindication of Messrs. Giles and Blackmore as well as the managing directors.

To sustain this outlay, Matthew Plummer and his colleagues used successive N&C Acts to increase the company's capital and borrowing powers.[7] Their 1829 Act had authorised £300,000 capital and given powers to borrow a further £100,000. By the end of 1839 the authorised capital had reached £690,000 in shares and £260,000 in loans, of which £150,000 had originally been borrowed from the Public Works Loans Board (PWLB). By then the company was making scheduled repayments of capital to the Exchequer, so that 1839 saw the N&C pay out £9,000 in principal and £6,310 interest to the PWLB; they also paid out a surprising £13,307 interest to other lenders. Since the same year saw a revenue of £86,491 and working expenses of only £37,235 the company's finances were still very healthy, as reflected in the dividends: 6% during 1839 and 1840. To pay these the company was also able to draw in part on the £124,639 profits earned during 1835-8 and ploughed back into construction at the behest of the PWLB.

Plummer was a very astute fellow in financial matters, as his handling of the Greenwich Hospital purchase reveals. The Hospital had agreed to defer payment of the purchase money until the N&C declared a 5% dividend, meanwhile accepting the £3 per acre rent, in return for which the directors enjoyed the full privileges of ownership, except for the mineral rights. By 1839 John Grey felt it was time to get the conveyance settled, and this was signed at the end of the year.[8] The railway, however, continued to pay rental and the purchase money was not handed over until 1862, in readiness for the merger with the NER. Thus the company effectively enjoyed a loan of some seven thousand pounds at a favourable interest rate of three and a third percent, contrasting with the 5% rate of their Exchequer Loan.

The company's success, in terms of serving the community, can be gauged partly from its revenue. Another indicator is the price of coal in Carlisle, which fell from seventeen to ten shillings a ton as a result of the N&C, while that city's canal saw its revenue double during 1836-40 largely as a result of the railway connection.[9] Another benefit to the local economy which would not have been foreseen at the outset is the extent of employment by the railway itself. James Losh had envisaged up to two thousand being engaged temporarily during construction, though the actual number probably peaked nearer fifteen hundred. However, the permanent workforce of the operational railway grew rapidly and had reached about 570 by 1841.

Financial Retrenchment: 1841-3

Having made a very good start in its first five years of operation, the N&C was then at the receiving end of one of the British economy's periodic upsets. Bad harvests were largely responsible for a deterioration in the country's external balance of trade, with knock-on effects for industry during 1840-3, including a decline in the output of iron. The N&C saw a 6 % increase in traffic during 1840 but the directors remarked on a general trade recession during the winter of 1840-1, exacerbated by severe weather, and forecast worse to come.[10] The actual outcome is summarised in the following table, which charts the railway's gross income, rounded to the nearest pound. It is notable that up to the end of 1841 this was recorded as 'revenue' in the accounts, but was thereafter divided into 'cash received' and 'outstanding debts for traffic'. This reflects the impact of the recession on the company's customers, some of whom were proving very slothful about paying up. It also means that the figures for 1840 and 1841 include a significant element of debt which was carried over into the 1842 figure. Because of this the actual fall in revenue from 1841 to 1842 is hard to quantify and is not as severe as may first appear.

	Revenue (£)	
1840	89,117	
1841	87,664	
	Cash Received for Traffic etc	**Cumulative Debts for Traffic**
1842	74,293	10,938
1843	73,948	10,994
1844	78,485	17,390
1845	87,822	16,781

Traffic had been declining for several months by February 1841, when the directors decided to appoint a Committee of Economy to examine staffing and wage levels, wages being the principal component in the operating costs. This comprised the Managing committee plus two Newcastle directors, William Woods and Joseph Crawhall, and two Carlisle ones, James Thompson and Peter Dixon, the latter being one of the most hawkish advocates of economy.[11] The idea was for them to start their investigations following the March AGM, by which time they had lost one of their members: Benjamin Thompson. He was an early casualty of the recession, fleeing to Boulogne to escape his creditors in the course of March. He played no further part in the direction of the railway but re-enters our story later as manager of an ironworks at Bellingham, on the North Tyne.

Having acted promptly to appoint the 'economists', the sense of urgency then waned and it required a prompting from the Newcastle Committee, in September 1841, to get the survey of the company's stations and other establishments underway.[12] Lowry noted that the committee was to 'examine the duties of each person upon the line in order that a reduction might be made ... both as regards wages and the number of their servants.' He added, perceptively, that the company would not benefit that much by the lowering of salaries and would have to 'direct their attention to the locomotive power and the maintenance of the works.'[13] The detailed investigation was carried out by the two men best suited, the managing directors: George Johnson and Nicholas Wood. On 15 October they descended on the Newcastle station to conduct a 'gentlemanly' interrogation into the duties of all the men and the handling of the accounts.[14] Having devoted all morning to that, they proceeded along the line, conducting similar enquiries at every station. This took two days, and included a detailed investigation of the activities of the locomotive and engineering departments.

The managing directors made further visits during the course of October and discussed their proposals for reorganising work with senior officers, showing a readiness to amend their ideas if persuaded.[15] Discussions continued at the Board throughout November, with the final decision to endorse their recommendations being made at the end of the month.[16] On 7 December, Adamson and Blackmore went along the line to convey formal notice of the changes to the agents and the engineering foremen: an unwelcome Christmas present for many. The investigation has left a very valuable record in the form of a staff audit, detailing the name, wage and occupation of every employee, together with the redundancies and wage cuts implemented at that stage.[17] Extensive use is made of this in later chapters.

The ensuing cuts bore most heavily on the locomotive department, which saw an initial seventeen redundancies in December 1841 with more to follow.[18] Anthony Hall's department was overmanned as a consequence of the piecemeal opening of the line, which had led to there being workshops at four locations: Blaydon, Haydon Bridge, Greenhead and Carlisle. Their fate is discussed in chapter 13; it is enough to note here that a considerable economy in running costs was achieved by shedding much of the Carlisle workforce during 1842 and building new workshops at Newcastle in place of those at Blaydon. In general, the wage cuts and redundancies were selective and carefully thought out. Thus platelayers and their labourers, the largest single group of workers on the line, were left largely untouched as were gatekeepers - virtually the lowest-paid at 12 shillings a week. Engine drivers saw their wage cut from 4s 8d a day (£72-16-0 a year) to 4s 6d. Firemen saw cuts of between two and four pence a day and it was a similar tale in the workshops.

Wage and job cuts were made among station staff, principally the manual workforce, resulting, for example, in a drop of almost 40% in the wage bill for yard and warehouse men at the Newcastle station.[19] The majority of the agents (station masters in later parlance) at the smaller stations received a salary cut in the course of February 1842, generally of the order of up to 10%, though William Lowry at How Mill, a rather quiet spot, saw his salary fall from £50 to £40. Benjamin Cail, of Haydon Bridge, was worst hit, with a drop from £100 to £60; his station had lost in importance with the completion of the line, but he had also got on the wrong side of the directors and this was seen as an invitation to resign, which he duly did.

The agents at the principal stations were not affected in this round of surgery, but some of the senior officers were. John Adamson had his Secretarial salary pruned from £400 to £300 but the most drastic cut was reserved for John Blackmore, down from £600 to £325. This reflected his reduced involvement with day-to-day operation, handled instead by Peter Tate, who received a modest pay rise. The economy drive also brought one station closure: the Close, whose business was transferred to Railway Street and Redheugh from the end of 1841.[20]

At the March 1842 AGM Plummer paid tribute to the way in which the workforce had accepted these cuts, though without actually indicating that they might be reversed when receipts improved. In fact, the continuing recession led to a further round of cuts. November 1842 saw the managing directors engaged on another inquisition, resulting in redundancies and pay cuts among the workmen the following February, while a Board meeting at the end of March 1843 decided on the medicine to be served up to the senior officers and agents. Adamson underwent a further cut, while his counterpart as Carlisle Secretary, William Nanson, was dispensed with altogether.[21] All the senior officers and principal agents had their pay reduced, but Blackmore got the harshest treatment, with his salary brought down to a mere retainer of £100 p.a. As a result of all this, the 1843 wage bill fell to 69% of the 1841 level.[22]

The best indicator of the success of the economy drive is the railway's Operating Ratio: working expenses as a percentage of receipts. This had peaked at 45% in 1840, but been cut to 39% in 1842 and 36% in the two succeeding years, a very impressive achievement, particularly on the part of the workforce. This enabled the company to make selective cuts in goods rates, to stimulate traffic, but the critical factor was the national economy, which was picking up again in the latter part of 1843. As a result, dividends, which had fallen to 4% in 1842-3, were up to 5% in 1844, eventually reaching 6% again in 1847. Interest rates fell, and with money available at a lesser cost than the PWLB loan Plummer arranged for this to be paid off prematurely, with final instalments of £42,000 in 1844 and £58,000 in 1845. Selective restorations of the wage cuts seem to have been made from December 1844 onwards, but the Board was careful to ensure that it kept a tight grip on costs in the future.

The recession in the early forties meant a weak share market. This posed a problem for the directors in respect of additional share capital which had been authorised in 1841. The strategy adopted confirms Plummer's reputation as a canny businessman. Rather than sell the new shares at a substantial discount, the directors held on to them and raised capital, as and when needed, by raising loans on their personal security instead.[23] In 1845, with an investment boom - the *Railway Mania* - getting underway, the company's stock was attracting a premium and they were able to begin selling these shares at up to 27½% more than their nominal value. The resulting profit, which went entirely to the company, more than covered the interest on the debenture loans which had been obtained in the interim, and the remainder was put towards the 5% dividend of 1845. The following year's 5½% was met entirely from operational revenue.

Main Lines to the North

Something which occupied the attention of N&C directors throughout the eighteen-thirties and early forties was the issue of the main line from London and its continuation into Scotland. The Great North of England Railway brought the main line from the south as far as Darlington in 1841, but had no money to continue further. Its extension to Newcastle was achieved by the York entrepreneur George Hudson (1800-71), later to become famous as the first *Railway King*, who in 1841 was simply chairman of a modest link in the main-line route, the 24-mile York & North Midland Railway. Despite the economic recession, Hudson was able to form a Newcastle & Darlington Junction Railway (NDJ), which obtained its Act in June 1842 and opened the line to Gateshead just two years later.

It had become evident by 1839 that the GNE would be unable to continue north of Darlington, so Nicholas Wood came up with an alternative proposal, the Northern Union Railway, in collaboration with the engineer Thomas Elliot Harrison (1808-88).[24] Wood was Engineer to the Brandling Junction and Harrison to the Stanhope & Tyne and its satellite, the Durham Junction Railway. They proposed to use these lines, together with part of the Clarence Railway in south Durham, to form the main-line extension with a minimum of new construction. The idea hung around for two years and was then taken up by Hudson, with Robert Stephenson as Engineer and Harrison serving as Stephenson's right-hand man; a role from which he graduated to become Engineer in Chief of the York Newcastle & Berwick Railway and its successor, the North Eastern.

Rechristened the Newcastle & Darlington Junction and bereft of the Clarence Railway element, Hudson launched the scheme at a meeting in York on 6 September 1841, to which he had invited representatives of other railways with a vested interest in securing the completion of the main line. [25] Thomas Fenwick and Nicholas Wood attended on behalf of the Newcastle & Carlisle while John Clayton was there nominally on behalf of the Durham Junction. Since the financial climate was not favourable to investment, Hudson asked the companies present to guarantee a dividend to NDJ shareholders, and it says much for his confident personality and the overtures he had made prior to the meeting that he succeeded. Seven railways were represented and they approved the proposed route, agreed to a capitalisation of half a million pounds and undertook to collectively lease the NDJ for ten years at a rent which would yield a 6% return. They also agreed to take shares in the undertaking. Clayton was won over by Hudson at this meeting, and subsequently seems to have been a keen supporter. Probably, as in his relationship with Richard Grainger, Clayton was impressed by a man of vision who got on with things, and he was determined to help.

In the event, the improving economy enabled Hudson to dispense with the guarantees to the NDJ, while the N&C realised a profit of £4,618 on its investment in the project, selling its NDJ shares during 1843.[26] The NDJ was opened formally on 18 June 1844 to Gateshead Greenesfield station - at the head of the Redheugh incline, and from then on the N&C diverted its south bank passenger trains over the incline and into the new station, so that they could connect with services to and from the south as well as local trains on the Brandling Junction.[27] Redheugh, however, continued to play a useful if modest role as a goods station.

From June 1844, the N&C formed the final link in a chain of railways from London to Carlisle, and continued to provide the main-line service for the Border City until the completion of the Lancaster & Carlisle Railway, in December 1846. By then, the issue of how to continue the trunk railways into Scotland had been resolved, but only after a lot of wrangling.

To us it seems natural that the west coast route should continue directly from Carlisle to Glasgow (and Edinburgh) and the east coast route from Newcastle to Edinburgh. In the eighteen-thirties there had been an influential body of opinion which felt that the available traffic would only justify a single railway being built across the Border. The N&C directors saw this as an opportunity, and made several efforts to make their line the springboard for an 'inland' route, reached from both Newcastle and Carlisle. [28]

9.2. N&C advertisement of April 1846 for the service between Carlisle and London, noting that private (road) carriages and horses would be carried through without change of vehicle.

Even among protagonists of an east coast line, the route itself proved contentious. Today, the line continues across the Tyne from Gateshead to a station in Newcastle, and then through coastal Northumberland to Berwick and hence Edinburgh. That seemed the natural thing to George Stephenson, who was an ardent advocate of a coastal railway. However, the direct route from Newcastle to Edinburgh runs via Carter Bar and the Border towns of Jedburgh and Galashiels, and this alignment attracted support, particularly north of the Border, though it entails crossing the main ridge of the Cheviot Hills. To understand the rivalries involved we have to jump back to 1836. That year saw two schemes being offered to the public for railways between Newcastle and Edinburgh. The Grand Eastern Union would have followed a fairly similar route to the present main line, while Stephen Reed's Tyne & Edinburgh Railway would have employed the N&C as far as Warden, before heading up the North Tyne and Redesdale. [29] It would have tunnelled under Carter Bar to reach Jedburgh and Galashiels, before splitting to serve both Edinburgh and Glasgow. Neither proposal was put to Parliament.

In 1836 Plummer and his colleagues were far too busy completing their own line to take much interest in the Scottish question. However, in September 1838 they instructed John Blackmore to survey a route to Edinburgh and Glasgow, again starting near Warden.[30] His report was approved by the Board in January 1839, when they decided to meet the coastal route protagonists, so as 'to convince them of the superiority of Blackmore's line.' [31] The rivals were not persuaded, but Blackmore's plan was launched at a public meeting in May 1839 and won endorsement from Newcastle Corporation, the Roxburgh Commissioners of Supply and a meeting of Midlothian landowners.[32] His route followed the North Tyne up to Kielder and crossed the hills at the Note o' the Gate, the summit of the present B6357 road. This brought it into the top of the Rule Water valley, and after swinging round Ruberslaw and passing Denholm it joined the alignment later adopted by the Waverley Route to Edinburgh. Little traffic could be expected to originate between Warden and Denholm (railhead for Hawick) unless optimistic forecasts for the North Tyne coalfield proved correct. Blackmore's was one of many schemes considered by Parliament's Smith-Barlow Commission, appointed to assess railway links from London to Edinburgh, Glasgow and Dublin, and they came down in favour of a west-coast route, basically having in mind access to Glasgow, while leaving the door ajar for an east-coast one.

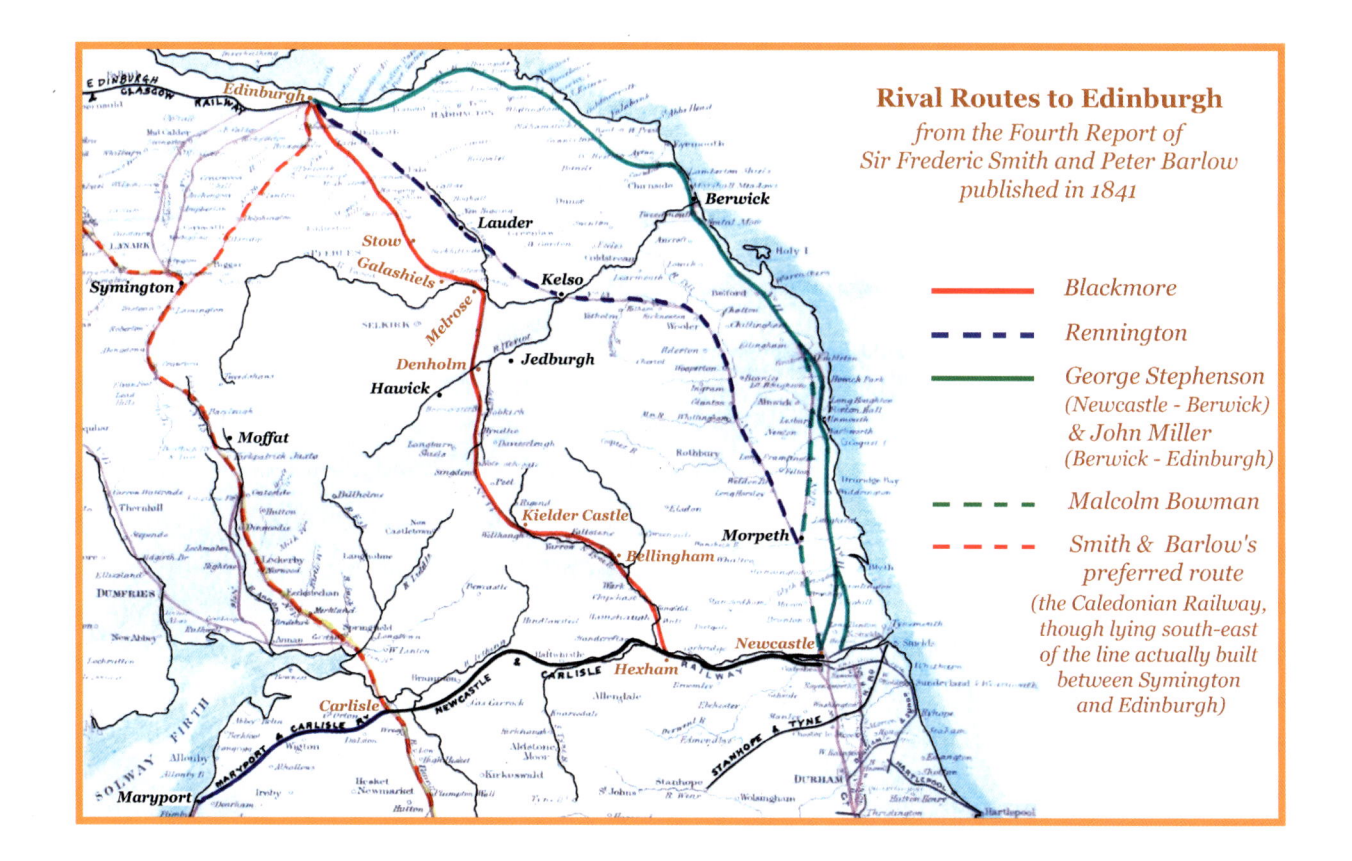

Rival Routes to Edinburgh
*from the Fourth Report of
Sir Frederic Smith and Peter Barlow
published in 1841*

― *Blackmore*

--- *Rennington*

― *George Stephenson
(Newcastle - Berwick)
& John Miller
(Berwick - Edinburgh)*

--- *Malcolm Bowman*

--- *Smith & Barlow's
preferred route
(the Caledonian Railway,
though lying south-east
of the line actually built
between Symington
and Edinburgh)*

In the light of the commission's report, the N&C Board asked their managing directors, Wood and Johnson, to review the position. They reported in November 1843 in favour of a different route, branching off much further west, near Gilsland, and curving into Liddesdale to follow something like the eventual Waverley Route through Hawick and Galashiels.[33] The Board then attempted to interest George Hudson and his engineers, George and Robert Stephenson, in the scheme. Hudson and the Stephensons went over the line with Wood and Johnson but, not surprisingly, remained firmly committed to the idea of an East-Coast route.[34] Undeterred, the N&C Board issued a prospectus for a Central Union Railway along the Wood-Johnson line, while Plummer attended a meeting of west-coast railway companies in February 1844 at the Liverpool & Manchester Railway office, where he advocated it as the continuation of the Lancaster & Carlisle Railway.[35] In the event this gap was filled instead by the Caledonian Railway, which got its Act in 1845 and opened from Carlisle as far as Beattock in September 1847. It was completed throughout to Glasgow and Edinburgh in February 1848. 1847 saw the Caley seeking powers for a branch to Langholm, with a further branch off it from Longtown to Brampton. This was endorsed by the N&C, with Nicholas Wood giving evidence in Parliament, but came to nothing.[36] Throughout all these proceedings it is evident that Plummer and his colleagues, while keen to foster a route which would develop traffic on their line, had no intention of committing any of their company's money towards building it.

Meanwhile things were happening in the east. Still hankering to become a vital link in the Anglo-Scottish chain, the N&C discussed with the architect John Dobson the practicability of providing a high-level railway bridge from the Brandling Junction line at Gateshead to the site which they had purchased for a station at Newcastle's Spital. In November 1843 Dobson was asked to finalise plans for Parliamentary deposit, and on 19 December the directors gave their attention to the three designs which he had come up with.[37] There had long been agitation for a high-level road bridge across the Tyne, and two of Dobson's proposals provided for both road and rail traffic: in one case a double-track railway with a 30 feet roadway alongside, in the other a railway deck stacked above a road. The latter design seems to have envisaged an iron railway structure superimposed on a masonry-arch bridge, so only the concept anticipates the present High Level Bridge.

The possibility of the N&C forming any part of the main line faded in July 1844, when the North British Railway obtained an Act to build a line from Edinburgh to Berwick. A railway between Berwick and Newcastle therefore became inevitable, and the Stephensons' coastal route was the obvious one. Hudson promoted a Newcastle & Berwick Railway along this line but opted, against George Stephenson's preference, to site the Tyne crossing downstream of Newcastle, at Bill Point.[38] This would enable him to continue using Greenesfield station, from which he promised to build a high-level road bridge to Newcastle, whose Corporation reluctantly went along with this idea, as being the best scheme on offer. The N&C directors were not happy, as it would leave them stuck with an isolated terminus of their own near the Infirmary.

Fortunately for Newcastle, Hudson did not have the field to himself, and Brunel's rival Northumberland Railway was also up for consideration in the 1844-5 session of Parliament. Hudson was anxious to secure the support of both the Corporation and the N&C, and at a meeting in January 1845 he gave in to the demands of Plummer and his directors for a central railway station on a site of their choosing, at or near the Spital.[39] To also meet his commitments to the council this entailed a railway bridge across the Tyne, incorporating a carriage road. Thus were born two of the grandest monuments of the early railway era: Robert Stephenson's High Level Bridge and John Dobson's Central Station. The former was paid for entirely by Hudson's companies; the latter was a joint venture with the N&C, which paid only a quarter of the cost, yet specified both site and architect.

John Blackmore and the Maryport & Carlisle Railway

For seven years, from 1836 to 1843, the N&C was the only railway serving Carlisle, where its main transport partners were the steamships to Liverpool, Ireland and Glasgow. Maryport, out on the open coast, had been developed by the Senhouse family as a coal-shipping port and in 1835 the first moves were made towards linking it by rail with Carlisle.[40] The initial reaction of the N&C's Carlisle directors was unfavourable.[41] They feared the effects of competition from West Cumberland coal on N&C revenues and several no doubt felt more personal concerns about the possible impact on Blenkinsopp colliery, the Earl of Carlisle's mines, and the Carlisle Canal. This attitude softened - the line was, after all, a completion of William Chapman's original vision - and in 1836 the directors had friendly discussions with the promoters and their engineer, George Stephenson.

The Maryport & Carlisle got its Act in 1837, but construction went slowly, and friction built up between the directors and Stephenson, who handed in his resignation at the end of October 1839.[42] Blackmore's commitments on the N&C were by then much reduced, and he was therefore able to develop other consultancies. He was well known in Carlisle, and was appointed Engineer to the M&C on 19 November.[43] His tasks were to complete the short stretch of line then in progress, from Maryport to coal mines at Arkleby, and to design and oversee the remainder. That first section opened in July 1840 and in February 1841 Blackmore was appointed Engineer in Chief on the same salary, £600, as he then enjoyed on the Newcastle & Carlisle.[44] He did a sound job but had problems with the Maryport company's Secretary, William Mitchell, an interfering character.[45] Blackmore resigned in May 1843, shortly after completing the stretch from Carlisle to Wigton, for whose opening the N&C provided the locomotives and rolling stock.[46] Mitchell then took over as Engineer, Secretary and Manager - rapidly driving the railway into a morass and leaving in disgrace in 1847. East of Arkleby, Blackmore's hand is evident in the bridges, while a family resemblance can also be seen between his Tudor-Revival buildings on the N&C and the station at Aspatria, opened in 1841.

Up to 1841, Blackmore had two assistants on the N&C: Peter Tate, at Carlisle, and Benjamin Scott, at Newcastle, who also managed his private office.[47] Under the economy drive, Scott went to supervise work on the Maryport & Carlisle, and Tate moved to Newcastle, with increased responsibilities and a modest pay rise. Blackmore, as we have seen, had his salary halved but he had developed other consultancy, apart from the Maryport line. He was Engineer to the Newcastle & Gateshead Union Water Company, which got an Act in 1840 but fizzled out after a few years.[48] That left no trace, but we still use the stone abutments and centre pier of Blackmore's timber bridge over the Tweed at Norham, opened in 1841 and accompanied by a toll house which looks like a refugee from the N&C.[49]

By 1842 Blackmore's relations with the N&C Board were becoming somewhat frayed. Lowry noted that he was frustrated by the company's spending on temporary buildings at Newcastle, rather than the permanent depot which he had been planning, and that he was fairly outspoken in his comments to the directors.[50] Things got worse the following year. Lowry had noted several times that Blackmore's 'studies' were taking a toll on his health, and on 25 February 1843 he recorded that 'I suspect he is gradually approaching to a most unenviable and lamentable state. I believe before long he will become imbecile - this I think is arising from his close study and from his deep reflection and bad temper but which latter ... is I think the result of the former. It will be a pity if such a man should fall into that state.'[51] Blackmore was evidently approaching a breakdown, something which can only have been hastened by the drastic second pay cut just a month later. In the circumstances it was unfortunate but perhaps unavoidable that he should have resigned from the Maryport company shortly afterwards. It is probably indicative of his mental state that the N&C got the managing directors, rather than their Engineer, to look into the western Anglo-Scottish route during the summer and asked Dobson to report on the Tyne bridge.

A contemporary account colourfully relates that Blackmore's brain 'yielded under the pressure of his duties and increasing anxiety.'[52] Early in 1844 he was taking treatment on medical advice, which included vapour (steam) baths, presumably in Alderman Dunn's Westgate Road premises. The outcome was ghastly. He had been recovering, but was badly scalded in one of these baths, and, after what must have been an agonising few days, died at home in Newcastle on 15 March 1844, aged 42.[53] The N&C held its AGM later that month but no mention was made in the directors' report of the engineer who had done so much for them. Peter Tate was given a pay rise, backdated to the start of 1844, and eventually acquired the title of Engineer in Chief.[54] The reality is that he ran the engineering department of the operational railway but played only a limited role in relation to schemes for new lines, such as the Alston Branch. For these the company drew on outside expertise.

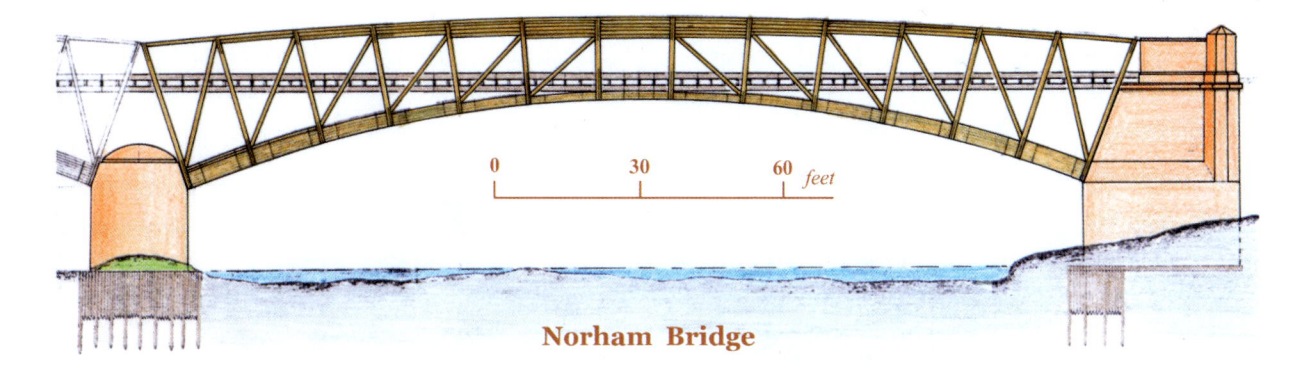

Norham Bridge

9.4. John Blackmore's design for the Tweed Bridge at Norham was published by John Weale in 1855. It had two timber spans of 190 feet, employing an ingenious variant on the trusses which he had used for the Newcastle & Carlisle Railway: in this case a combination of truss and laminated arch, with the roadway threaded between. One suspects that he had an eye on John Green's North Shields Railway viaducts but also read up Karl Wiebeking's treatise.

9.5. Blackmore's trusses had been replaced or strengthened before Norham bridge was reconstructed in 1885-7. Nonetheless, the new arches still rely on his abutments and central pier, the latter much heightened. View towards south bank. (Bill Fawcett)

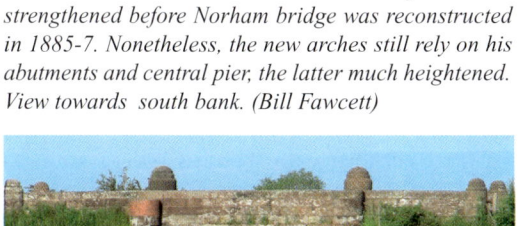

9.6. Blackmore's bridge taking the Maryport line under the turnpike road east of Wigton. (GR 267495)   (Bill Fawcett)

The North Tyne and Alston

It is hard now to visualise the North Tyne and Redesdale as industrial centres, but in the eighteen-forties some people had expectations of developing a significant iron industry there, based on local ore and coal. [55] Hareshaw ironworks, at Bellingham, opened in 1839 and made pig iron, which was transported by road to the proprietors' foundry in Hexham. One of the partners was Thomas Richard Batson, a Newcastle alderman and a director of the N&C until March 1842. Batson was killed in a road accident near his Redesmouth home in March 1845, not long after the enterprise had been taken over by its lenders, the Union Bank of Newcastle, which put in our old friend Benjamin Thompson to run the business. [56] The Bank invested heavily, but could not achieve commercial success and the works closed in 1849, never to reopen. Ridsdale ironworks, four miles away, was a totally separate venture but also lasted from just 1839 to 1849, though the site was bought in 1862 by William George Armstrong, pioneer of hydraulic machinery and modern ordnance, to provide iron-ore for his Elswick Works.

In 1845 the area seemed to hold out reasonable prospects, if only decent transport could be provided. Two of the Ridsdale partners were familiar figures from the early years of the N&C: Jacob Ritson, the contractor, and John Green, the architect.[57] Green was also a leading promoter of an 'inland' Anglo-Scottish railway through the area: the Newcastle, Edinburgh & Direct Glasgow Junction Railway. A Bill was put forward for the Parliamentary session 1845-6, at the height of the *Railway Mania*, with John Green and his son Benjamin named as its 'local engineers', and the distinguished Scottish railway engineer, John Miller, as Engineer in Chief.

The N&C had lost interest in the North Tyne as a route into Scotland, but the directors saw the Greens' line as a potential threat, and therefore engaged a Newcastle surveyor, John Bourne, to plan a line from Warden to Bellingham with a branch to Woodburn and Ridsdale. This was included in their Bill for the session 1845-6, along with plans for a branch up the South Tyne from Haltwhistle to Alston and Nent Head.[58]

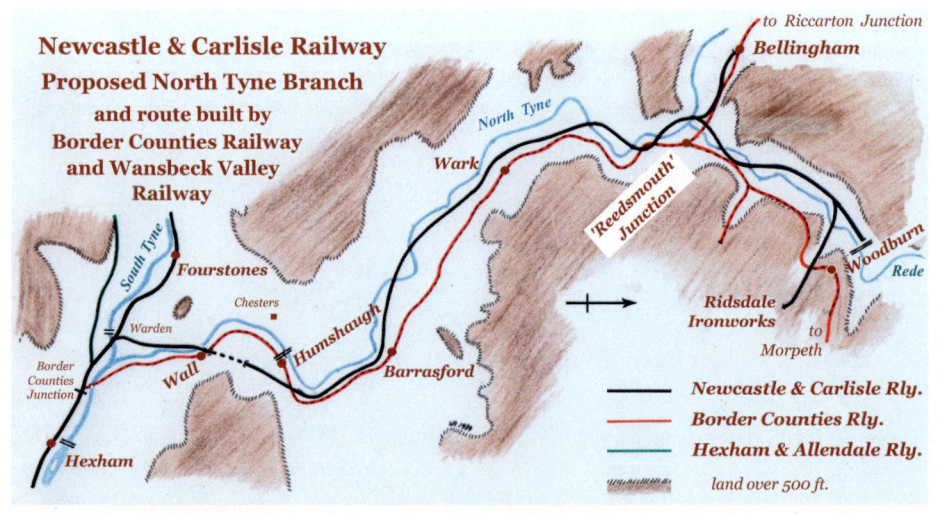

9.7. The North Tyne branch would have had a tunnel and numerous river crossings. The scheme was evidently not optimised for cost, and would have been modified a lot before execution. From Redesmouth, a branch was to serve West Woodburn, with a stationary engine hauling traffic up the hillside to the Ridsdale Ironworks, 400 feet above. The area was eventually served by the Border Counties Railway and the Wansbeck Valley line, branching off it at Redesmouth. Both are discussed in chapter 11.

The cost and traffic estimates for the two branches are revealing:

North Tyne Branch	capital cost: £260,000	annual income: £12,648	(4.9%)
Alston & Nenthead Branch	capital cost: £210,000	annual income: £18,835	(9%)

One can sympathise, in this case, with the N&C's perennial critic George Thomas Dunn, who argued that the investment would be a pointless dilution of capital. The company's capital account had reached almost £1,236,000 by the end of 1845, and these two branches would swell it by a further 38% without anything like a proportionate increase in revenue. The shareholders, however, gave their endorsement to the Bill, but the N&C lacked support for its North Tyne Branch locally, where people felt they would be better served by a through route to Scotland and rallied to the rival. Benjamin Thompson gave evidence in support of the N&C in June 1846 before the Commons committee, but they deleted the branch from the preamble of the Bill; meaning that the N&C had failed to establish their basic case.[59] The rival promoters were equally fortunate, with Parliament throwing out their entire scheme and thus saving the investors from their own folly. Parliament passed the rest of the N&C Bill but the turnpike trusts took the opportunity to have a clause inserted to bring the railway into line with current legislation by requiring bridges to replace level crossings on the main line at Hexham, Corbridge and Stocksfield.[60] The royal assent was granted on 28 August 1846, and the Alston Branch, designed to serve the N&C's important customers in the lead industry, is considered in chapter 10.

The Departure of Dixon

1846 brought the departure from the directorate of Peter Dixon, amidst accusations that Matthew Plummer had a dictatorial grip over company policy. It is an interesting paradox that all the directors had other business interests which were far more important to each of them individually than the railway, yet the Board maintained a very close scrutiny even over operational issues. Thus if Richard Lowry had an idea for a special train, in connection for example with the Carlisle Races, he did not take this to the Superintendent, John Chantler, or the Chief Agent, John Challoner. Instead he would tackle George Johnson, if that managing director was making one of his surprisingly frequent visits to the Newcastle station, or else beard Plummer in his office down on the Quayside. Plummer would indicate his approval, unless there was something contentious about the proposal, and place it before his fellow directors as a matter of form. Lowry would then draw up an advertisement, but even this had to be cleared by the chairman before appearing in the local papers.

Inevitably, the policy of the directors in such matters as rates and services was coloured by their private interests as well as those of their shareholders, but generally these were in harmony. Offering fair rates for traffic was good for both. Virtually all the Board held significant investments in the coal industry, and during 1844-6 these led to friction between the directors at the east and west ends. The focus was Blenkinsopp colliery, which was not proving as profitable as had been hoped. The arrival of the Maryport & Carlisle Railway in 1843 had opened up the Carlisle market to pits in West Cumberland, and the Blenkinsopp proprietors felt hampered by the discriminatory rates applied by the N&C: 2¼d per ton-mile for 'landsale' coal, such as that sold in Carlisle, and 1¼d for coal sent for shipping by sea. The Dixon brothers were major shareholders in the mine, and in December 1844 Peter Dixon brought the matter before the Board, which agreed to look into this as part of a general review of coal rates. He calculated that the railway would benefit from an increase in traffic, despite a reduction in rates, but the managing directors reported otherwise and coal rates stayed as they were.[61]

The Blenkinsopp company then delivered an ultimatum, declaring that the colliery would cease operation on 18 February 1845 unless their views were met.[62] Plummer and the other directors were not to be browbeaten, and the mine duly closed. The Haltwhistle Coal & Lime Company, which had begun delivering to the Carlisle market at the end of October 1843, also halted production. Coal rates continued to receive the Board's attention throughout the year, with John Dixon, Colonel Coulson and Joseph Crawhall rallying behind Peter Dixon but they were outnumbered by the Newcastle directors. The Earl of Carlisle's representative, James Thompson, sat on the fence. His collieries only employed the N&C for half the distance travelled by Blenkinsopp coals and he was probably amused by the distress of his commercial rivals. Meanwhile, the Carlisle newspapers rallied to the Blenkinsopp cause, but to no practical effect.

The east-west divide was exacerbated in January 1846, when the Mickley Coal Company, based near Prudhoe, began shipping coal over the railway to Carlisle, claiming that they could get a higher price there than at Newcastle. Meanwhile Peter Dixon had made the conflict into a personal issue with an anonymous, but readily identifiable, pamphlet entitled *Newcastle & Carlisle Railway Abuses*, written in the form of an open letter to Matthew Plummer, beginning with the statement that 'it is well known that they [the directors] are not a unanimous body, and that their proceedings are governed – chiefly, if not entirely – by the will of the Chairman ... it is for the shareholders to enquire why one individual has thus become invested with the entire direction of the concern.' He then went on to argue strongly, and not without some justice, the case for a general reduction in all rates, including passenger fares, though he took an over-optimistic view of the extent of the consequent traffic growth. Already, an experiment in lowering the goods rates from Ireland had produced little effect on the volume shipped, and simply reduced the railway's income.

In a second edition of the pamphlet, Dixon committed himself further, and suggested appointing a committee of investigation, in order to 'restore the concern to a healthful condition [as] its declining income ... and the reduced value of shares ... sufficiently testify.' In his frustration he also went on to cast doubt on the safety of passengers. This was irresponsible behaviour, calculated to shake public confidence in the company, and Dixon left the Board prior to the March 1846 AGM. Ironically, Blenkinsopp colliery, the original *causus belli*, resumed production at the same time.[63]

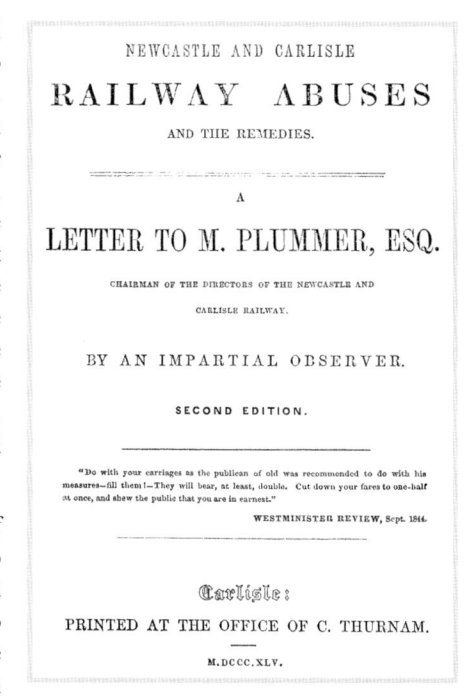

Peter Dixon had not quite finished, and a further 'anonymous' letter was not only published in the newspapers but posted up on hoardings.[64] His charges about the company's finances helped to inspire some scurrilous claims during the passage of the Alston Branch Bill, it being argued by opponents that the railway had borrowed sums far in excess of its powers. In fact what the directors had done was to secure loans for the company on their personal security rather than release new shares onto the market while these were standing at a discount. After all this the controversy died down, no doubt to the relief of John Dixon, who shared his brother's concerns but remained on the N&C Board to look after the family interest. Two years later, the management of the line changed hands anyway, demonstrating that Plummer was not that concerned with power for its own sake and in due course exposing the public to a much less benign regime than that of 'Old Matthew'.

Hudson Takes Over

On 2 June 1848 John Grey, the Greenwich Receiver, wrote to the Hospital's Secretary: 'The event has come to pass which I dreaded and the Carlisle Railway is transferred to Hudson's dominion - no mercy will be shown to us now in the way of charges and accommodation - his object being to throw all he can in the way of the York and Berwick line in opposition to the Caledonian and Lancaster [Lancaster & Carlisle Railway].'[65] Two days earlier the directors had agreed to lease their railway to George Hudson, who ended up in control for some eighteen months.

For the background to this we have to look first at the disparate fortunes of the N&C and the Maryport & Carlisle. The latter had good traffic potential but, thanks to William Mitchell's mismanagement and directorial *laisser-faire*, it drifted into a mess. A takeover by one of the neighbouring companies was seen as a way out, and in 1847 the shareholders appointed a committee to negotiate with the the N&C, the Lancaster & Carlisle, and the Whitehaven Junction Railway to see which would offer the best terms for a lease, purchase or merger.[66] Plummer and his colleagues were cautiously encouraging, but had to report in March 1848 that the Maryport directors had held out for terms 'such as could not be prudently entertained.' Shortly afterwards the newly-completed Caledonian Railway began negotiations to lease not just the Maryport company but also the Newcastle & Carlisle. This would have been quite a coup, but it was totally unacceptable to George Hudson, who thereupon entered the fray.[67]

The N&C directors felt no particular concern about remaining independent, and pursued discussions with both parties. The age profile of the Board is of some relevance. Matthew Plummer was 76, and looking forward to retirement, but he was quite a lot older than other active colleagues. Colonel Coulson was 69, but apparently keen to carry on, John Dixon and George Johnson were 63 and 64, while Nicholas Wood and Joseph Crawhall were youthful by N&C standards, at 53 and 55. Plummer explained the rationale of the lease to a shareholders' meeting on 16 May 1848, remarking that 'he was as favourable to the line as anyone, for he had been enthusiastically attached to it from the commencement, but ... he recommended all to act prudently and cautiously. (Applause) The increase of the revenue had not been effected without some expense ... He fully believed that the Carlisle Railway ought to be a 10% [dividend] line ... They must however bear in mind how far the late stagnation in trade operated upon them.'[68] The shareholders endorsed continued negotiations, and agreed to meet again on May 31 to consider the directors' final recommendation. On the morning of the 31st the directors decided in favour of Hudson, the Caledonian having withdrawn their offer.[69]

The Secretary, John Adamson, took the unusual step of recording that William Woods, the banker, moved the motion in favour of the lease, seconded by John Dixon of Carlisle. Colonel Coulson and Peter Dickson, a London shareholder, argued for the company to retain its independence but a united front was presented to the shareholders' meeting in the afternoon, which gave its consent. Hudson was granted a lease from 1 July 1848 at a rent equivalent to a 6% return on the N&C capital, rising to 7% after three years. Since the N&C was already paying 6%, this does not match the generosity of some of the Railway King's earlier leases, such as the 10% paid to the Great North of England Railway. However, the British economy had now tightened again and both parties preferred to take a realistic view of future prospects. Hudson leased the Maryport line at 4% from the start of October.[70]

The practical details of the lease had yet to be sorted out, and the agreement was only signed by Hudson and Plummer on 5 July.[71] Two days later the N&C Board formally ratified it and appointed as Manager James Allport, the general manager of the York Newcastle & Berwick Railway (YNB). The lease was a personal one, in Hudson's name, but this was for expediency. Everyone knew that the intention was to transfer it to the YNB once the shareholders and Parliament had given their consent. However, the potato famine of 1846 had been followed by a banking crisis in 1847 and the investment boom was over, while railway receipts were also on the decline. Hudson found it impossible to sustain his well-concealed strategy of raising capital for new lines and then milking this to boost dividends, so, with returns falling, there was widespread unrest among YNB shareholders about the leases of the two Carlisle companies. Despite this they gave their consent to a Bill being brought forward to sanction these, including provisions for a merger of the companies.[72]

Approval was given at the Berwick company's AGM on 20 February 1849, but the same meeting saw the appointment of a committee to enquire into share dealings, which was to lead to the disclosure of Hudson's financial misdemeanours. Amidst scandal, he resigned the YNB chair from 4 May and the Berwick shareholders, finding their finances a lot less healthy than they had been led to believe, repudiated the N&C and M&C leases.[73] For a while, the dethroned monarch retained hopes of re-establishing himself in the railway world, and Clayton acted as go-between in negotiations through which Hudson offered, as late as August 1849, to retain a personal lease of the N&C.[74] Clayton seemed to favour this, but Hudson's financial credibility was much weakened, though not yet shattered, and on 7 November 1849 a N&C shareholders' meeting unanimously approved the Board's recommendation that the company resume its freedom at the end of the year.[75]

For the duration of the lease, the Carlisle line came under James Allport, with the YNB's Thomas Elliot Harrison assuming the role of Engineer in Chief.[76] Separate accounts were maintained for the N&C and the existing organisation was largely retained, although the Chief Agent, John Challoner, was rather sidelined, with the goods and mineral traffic being brought under Charles Henry Smith, the YNB Goods Manager.[77] With the decline in traffic during 1848, Hudson admitted to a shortfall of £1,024 between the profits of the N&C, for the first six months of the lease, and the rental, despite a variety of economies.[78] These included the dismissal of some staff, including two of the longest-serving agents: John Scott of Blaydon and William Greene, who had run the show at Carlisle ever since the opening. A very petty move was the withdrawal of night-time lighting (oil lamps) from second and third-class carriages: the *Carlisle Journal* of 27 October 1848 commented that 'drunken men carrying guns and accompanied by dogs' are not infrequently their inmates to the 'terror of more timid passengers.' Little criticism seems to have been voiced by N&C shareholders, secure in their 6%, but an exception was Dr. William Cowan, a Cumbrian investor. He pointed out that traffic between Newcastle and Liverpool was being diverted away from the N&C to run via York, and, after the company regained control, he raised the case of staff dismissed by Hudson, with a view to their reinstatement.[79]

It is easy to regard the Hudson interlude as of no real importance in the long term, but it did bring some lasting benefits, not the least being that Harrison made a start on the renewal of the line's old-fashioned and somewhat inadequate permanent way. In the final settlement between the Carlisle company and Hudson works like this had to be charged against the company, as did expenditure on building Central Station and the Alston branch.

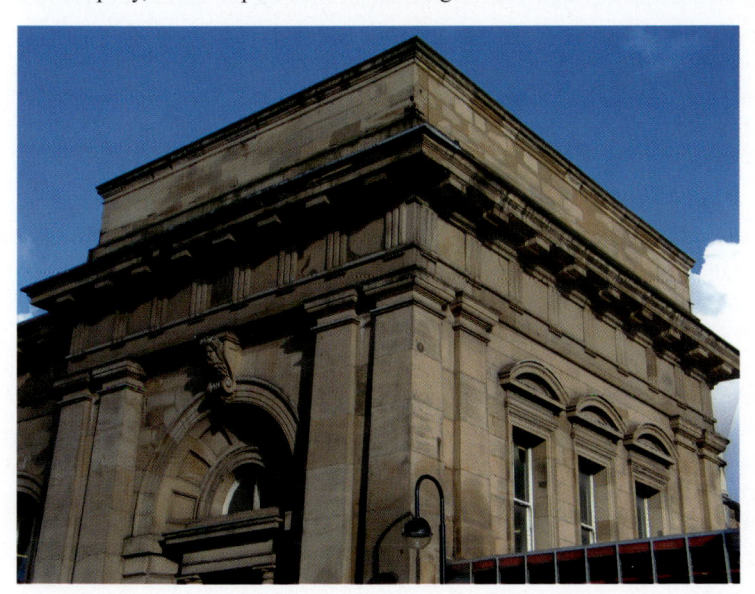

9.9. *The west end of Newcastle Central Station, with the Newcastle & Carlisle Railway boardroom located behind the three prominent first-floor windows on the right-hand wall. During Hudson's lease, progress on the N&C portion of the station was delayed, apparently to expedite work on the YNB's east end. Thus the formal opening of the station by Queen Victoria and Prince Albert, on 29 August 1850 only ushered into use the YNB section. Carlisle trains did not enter the station until 1 January 1851. The N&C offices occupied almost a third of the entire building.*

(Bill Fawcett)

Recovery and a New Board: 1850-53

With the economy recovering but confidence battered by the Hudson debacle, railway revenues and share values took some time to improve. The N&C fared better than many. In 1847 it had enjoyed a revenue of £115,825, with expenses running at an operating ratio of only 40%, a very healthy situation. On this basis it had paid a dividend of 6%, holding this for the following year as well thanks to the Hudson lease. In 1849 the dividend fell to 4½%, then to just 4% - the lowest dividend ever declared by the company - for 1850-3, after which it rose again. Of the major companies, the Great Western bottomed at 4% at this time, while the London & North Western managed to hold 5.

On 20 July 1848 Matthew Plummer's impending retirement had been celebrated at a valedictory ceremony, where the shareholders presented him with a service of plate.[80] Now, in the aftermath of the Hudson lease, he was reluctantly obliged to stay on while the directors sorted out their accounts with Hudson and the YNB. During the course of 1851 the company offices moved home from the Forth across Neville Street to spacious premises in the west end of Central Station, which their trains had been using from the beginning of the year. Plummer finally retired from the chair after eighteen years in the post, and was succeeded on 4 June 1851 by James Losh, junior, son of the first chairman.

An even bigger break with the past was to come the following year. As Dr. Cowan pointed out on several occasions, the N&C Board, thirty strong, was needlessly large for a mature railway.[81] Powers to reduce its size had been taken in the company's 1849 Act, and these were put into effect during May 1852. The new Board comprised just ten directors, one being a nominee of the Earl of Carlisle. Among those departing were many prominent figures from the early days, including Plummer himself, Colonel Coulson and Nicholas Wood. Of the 1829 directors only William Woods and Joseph Crawhall remained.

The annual elections of directors, a third retiring each year but generally standing again, were normally a formality in which the shareholders approved a list put forward by the Board, who usually took the precaution of co-opting any new directors a few weeks in advance of the March AGM.[82] The drastic slimming down in May 1852 meant that the elections would, for once, be contested.

9.10 James Losh, junior, was born in 1803 at the family home, Jesmond Grove, and followed his father into a career as a barrister. He never became a public figure to anything like the same extent but did serve for many years on Newcastle Corporation. He joined the N&C Board in March 1839 but resigned from 6 June 1853, having become a County Court judge. He died on 1 October 1858.

To avoid a free-for-all, the shareholders met on 3 May and appointed a committee to prepare a list of 12 candidates whom 'they deemed most eligible'.[83] Only a third of the nominating committee was drawn from the existing Board. The committee canvassed other opinions and on 10 May produced a shortlist divided into nine 'top' candidates and three others. A shareholders' meeting on 31 May made its selection from these, choosing all three of the 'second-rank' names. The latter included Joseph Crawhall and John Blenkinsopp Coulson, junior, eldest son of Colonel Coulson. Among those favoured by the committee but discarded by the meeting were Dr. Cowan, who earned the lowest share of votes, and Coulson's younger brother, Captain Gustavus (RN).[84] In doing so, the shareholders seem to have fallen in with the preferences of the outgoing Board, and may well have been influenced by an impassioned speech by William Woods, who disagreed with some of the committee's recommendations, notably their advocacy of the younger of the Coulson brothers.

In the course of his speech, Woods recalled how none of the existing directors were paid for their services, the Managing committee having been disbanded at the time of the Hudson lease, and how they had often been put to personal expense in connection with the railway, and 'had trudged miles and miles, wet and dry, to see after the construction of the works'. The new Board, meeting for the first time on 7 June 1852, set new rules, which included fees, but only for directors who turned up to meetings - fixed for 11 a.m. alternate Mondays - no more than a quarter hour late and left no more than half an hour before the end, 'such time to be according to the station clock.' They also elected to continue with James Losh as chairman, maintaining the east-west balance by having George Dixon, of Carlisle, as his deputy.

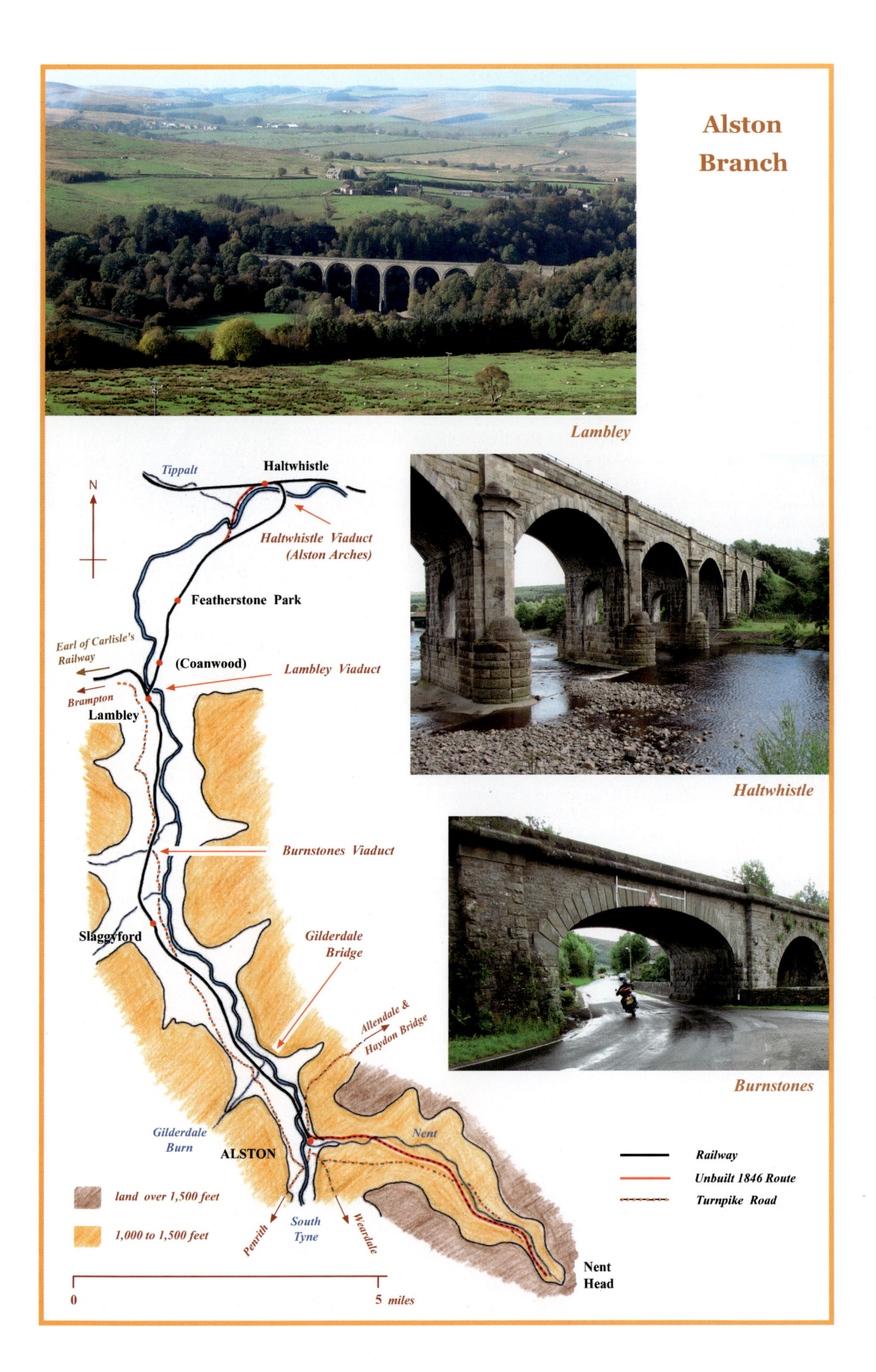

Alston Branch

Lambley

Haltwhistle

Burnstones

Map labels:
- Tippalt
- Haltwhistle
- Haltwhistle Viaduct (Alston Arches)
- Featherstone Park
- Earl of Carlisle's Railway
- Brampton
- (Coanwood)
- Lambley Viaduct
- Lambley
- Burnstones Viaduct
- Slaggyford
- Gilderdale Bridge
- Allendale & Haydon Bridge
- Gilderdale Burn
- ALSTON
- Nent
- Penrith
- South Tyne
- Weardale
- Nent Head

Legend:
- land over 1,500 feet
- 1,000 to 1,500 feet
- Railway
- Unbuilt 1846 Route
- Turnpike Road

0 — 5 miles

Chapter 10: The Alston Branch

Origins

Prior to its closure in 1976 the Alston Branch offered one of the most scenically rewarding railway journeys in the North of England. Fortunately, almost the entire trackbed and bridges remain intact and available for use by walkers and cyclists and, for a few miles, by travellers on the narrow-gauge South Tynedale Railway.

The logic of the line was simple enough. It was provided primarily to serve the lead industry of Alston Moor, although it was also linked by a short branch at Lambley to the Earl of Carlisle's colliery system. Allendale was also an obvious target for a branch, to serve the Beaumont lead interests, but its topography made this more difficult to provide and it was already quite well served by the road down to the railhead at Haydon Bridge. The town of Alston and nearby Nent Head, the centre of the London Lead Company's operations, also enjoyed road links to Haydon Bridge but these entailed significant initial climbs up onto the moor, before dropping down into Allendale. By contrast, the valleys of the South Tyne and River Nent offered a downhill route all the way to Haltwhistle on the N&C main line.

It is unlikely that Matthew Plummer and his colleagues would have embarked on the Alston Branch without the spur provided by rival schemes. They were aware that it would be quite costly to build and that it would not attract much additional traffic to the company. However, they were not prepared to have other railways nibbling away at their business and in 1845 there seemed a real risk of that with the promotion of a Wear Valley Extension Railway (WVE).[1] This was a scheme dreamed up by the Stockton & Darlington Railway, whose Wear Valley Railway was then under construction. The Wear Valley would penetrate Weardale as far as Frosterley, whence the Extension line was intended to continue right up the dale as far as the Beaumont smelter at Killhope, then pass through a tunnel two miles long to reach Nenthead. It would then have run down Nentdale to Alston and followed the South Tyne as far as Lambley, before heading across country to a junction with the N&C at Milton (Brampton Junction). With running powers over the N&C, this would effectively have extended the S&D main line to Carlisle, while a branch was also planned to serve Allendale. Leaving the main line two miles east of Killhope tunnel, this required a pair of inclines, worked by a stationary engine, to get over the watershed to Allenheads, then proceeding as a locomotive route down to Allendale Town.[2]

The WVE scheme had the potential to rob the N&C of much of its lead traffic, so the company responded by giving notice of its intention to promote branch lines to serve Allenheads and Alston Moor.[3] Allenheads was a tough nut to crack, since the dale is walled off from the Tyne Valley by hills through which the River Allen is admitted by a quite narrow ravine, while however the railway was routed there would be quite a lot of height to gain in a short distance. So the N&C shelved Allendale, but formally deposited plans on 29 November 1845 for a line up the South Tyne to Alston and Nenthead, as part of its proposals for the Parliamentary session 1845-6.[4] The Darlington party also deposited plans for the WVE but - mindful of their finances - did not follow these up with a Bill, leaving the field to the N&C, whose scheme received the royal assent on 28 August 1846. The Earl of Carlisle's support for the N&C was ensured by including a short branch from Lambley to Halton-Lea-Gate, providing an eastern outlet for his colliery railway.

The N&C survey had been prepared in some haste, and the directors were in no hurry to proceed with construction, so they took the opportunity to make some revisions to the Alston Branch alignment, for which the landowners' consent was secured before incorporating them in the N&C Act of 13 July 1849.[5] Most of the changes involved minor deviations from the original route, but there were two very significant ones, indicated in Figure 10.1. One was a complete revision of the first mile of the route, so that it now swung east out of Haltwhistle station, rather than west; this gave better gradients and took the line away from Bellister Castle. The other was the abandonment of the line from Alston up to Nenthead. This had involved some steep gradients to get over the threshold of Nentdale, notably an initial mile at 1/39, and the Commons had inserted a clause in the 1846 Act forbidding the use of locomotives on this section without the consent of the Board of Trade.[6] By 1849 some construction work had taken place at the north end, but the new Act extended the original three-year time limit for completion for a further three years. The branch eventually opened, in three stages, during 1851-2.

Allendale was not forgotten. Thomas Sopwith had succeeded William and George Crawhall as the Beaumont lead agent for Allendale and Weardale in 1845 and was very much a new broom, one of his aims being to persuade the N&C to build a branch. On 6 July 1846 the directors took a train from Newcastle to Haydon Bridge, inspecting the railway *en route*, and then went with Sopwith by way of Staward and Cupola Bridge to examine a possible route from near the mouth of the Allen up to Allendale Town.[7] Three months later, on 5 October, the Managing committee - Wood and Johnson - inspected the route of a possible line between Nenthead and Allenheads, where they met up with other directors.[8] It would have been a fine, but costly enterprise, and any hope of it materialising vanished in the worsening economic climate of the late eighteen-forties. Allendale did get its railway eventually, in 1867-8, but only through its own efforts.

Building the Line

Within months of obtaining the Alston Branch Act, at the end of August 1846, the directors were considering changes in the route.[9] This gave them an excuse to delay starting construction, but Plummer reported to the March 1847 AGM that the 'alterations and improvements' could be carried into effect 'without further authority from Parliament', implying that at this stage they were not intending a significant departure from the authorised line. The first two contracts were let on 10 May 1847 and covered the first four miles from Haltwhistle to Shaft Hill (Coanwood), just short of Lambley Viaduct, which is the most prominent feature of the railway.[10] The viaduct across the South Tyne at Haltwhistle was entrusted to the late George Grahamsley's partner and successor, Edward Reid. The remainder was given to Cowen, Marshall & Ridley. The *Carlisle Journal* of 19 June reported that work had begun, but it cannot have continued for very long because Plummer and his colleagues now began to have further thoughts about the route, largely with a view to making economies. Indeed, a payment made to Reid in August 1847 looks suspiciously like compensation for work suspended.[11]

On 8 November 1847 the directors held a meeting at Haltwhistle and examined an alternative route.[12] There were divergent views but, after much discussion, a decision was taken to adopt the new route and apply to Parliament in the current session for the necessary powers. One change was presumably the complete revision of the first mile of the line at Haltwhistle, already referred to. This was likely, if anything, to make the line more acceptable to local landowners. A more significant, and reckless, innovation was the abandonment of the costly viaduct at Lambley, required to take the line across to the west side of the valley in order to link up with the Earl of Carlisle's Railway. Instead, they proposed continuing down the east side of the river to Alston. This would also have dispensed with the need for a Tyne bridge at Alston - it being important to finish on the east bank, so as to provide a railhead for the Nent Head lead traffic. However, Lord Carlisle was not pleased by the abandonment of the link to his railway.[13] His agent at Naworth, John Ramshay, was one of the Earl's three nominees on the N&C Board, and must have argued the issue strongly with his colleagues prior to their November decision. He followed up with a stern letter to Matthew Plummer, pointing out that 'Lord Carlisle can look upon this proceeding in no other light than as a direct attack upon his interests as a coalowner and as a most hostile proceeding'. After some further correspondence, the Board saw sense and reinstated something close to the original route between Shaft Hill and Alston but were obliged to defer their application to Parliament for a further year, having missed the time limit for depositing plans.

Although the N&C required a second Act to sanction the changes, they had no need to wait for this prior to starting construction, given the consent of the relevant landowners. On 19 February 1848, therefore, they entered a revised contract with Cowen and partners for the stretch from Haltwhistle to Shaft Hill.[14] Presumably a new contract was agreed with Edward Reid for the Tyne bridge at the same time, but this is not documented. By the end of the year about 200,000 cubic yards of earthworks had been carried out under Cowen's contract, along with the minor bridges, while Reid's Tyne bridge had progressed as far as the piers.[15] A new factor had entered the equation, however, to complicate matters. George Hudson had leased the N&C. In theory, the Alston branch works should have remained the responsibility of the N&C Board and shareholders. In practice, the work was brought under Hudson's engineer, Thomas Elliot Harrison, now designated Engineer in Chief to the N&C. Plummer and friends seem to have sat back and let Harrison and Hudson get on with it.

By the end of 1848, £43,761 had been expended on the branch, of which it is reasonable, knowing the final costs of land purchases and legal expenses, to suggest that at least £25,000 represented construction work.[16] By contrast, 1849 saw an expenditure of only £12,560. It seems therefore that, as soon as Hudson lost his grip on power in the spring of 1849, work was again halted on the branch. The Act for the deviations was obtained in July 1849, and in August Plummer and his colleagues resumed the initiative and asked Peter Tate to stake out the remainder of the route, between Shaft Hill and Alston.[17] In the straightened financial climate then prevailing, some shareholders would gladly have abandoned the scheme but the November SGM which agreed to terminate Hudson's lease also cleared the way for work to resume.

It is likely that work on the northern section, from Haltwhistle to Shaft Hill, resumed at the start of 1850, but the contracts for the continuation to Alston were not let until April.[18] The work was divided into three contracts - Nos. 3, 4, and 5 - all of which went to John Rush & Benjamin Lawton, who had recently completed the masonry work of Newcastle's High Level Bridge. No. 3 covered the first two miles from Shaft Hill together with the branch to the Earl of Carlisle's railway at Halton-Lea-Gate. It included Lambley Viaduct, but the start of work on this was deferred pending the completion of the northern section, so as to facilitate the supply of building stone.[19] In the event this seems to have delayed the start of the viaduct until March 1851, when Plummer reported that the northern section was 'now finished and already used for the carriage of minerals and goods'.[20] Passengers had to wait a bit longer. Captain Wynne inspected the northern section for the Board of Trade on 10 June 1851 but declined to allow its opening to the public until the company had sorted out such prominent defects as the lack of any platform or signal at the temporary terminus at Shaft Hill. He revisited the following month and passed the line.[21] Four years had elapsed since the start of construction, and only a third of the route had opened.

Things then progressed faster, and the first approximation to a through train along the entire branch came on 8 September 1851, when the directors made an inspection from end to end.[22] A special train took them to Shaft Hill, where they got out to examine Lambley Viaduct, which by that stage had its river piers above water level. They resumed their railway journey on the opposite bank, travelling, courtesy of Rush and Lawton, in horse-drawn wagons, specially decorated for the occasion. Four months later came the only formal opening ceremony recorded. This marked the opening of the line from Lambley to Alston, still divorced from the remainder of the branch by the gap at Lambley Viaduct but linked to the rest of the world via the Earl of Carlisle's Railway. On 5 January 1852, the Alston Town Band accompanied the first train from Lambley, comprising three carriages and a number of coal wagons, which arrived at Alston about 10.30 a.m. to 'deafening cheers, bells and roar of cannon'. In a more thoughtful celebration than most, seventy cartloads of coal were distributed to the poor, paid for by the proceeds of church collections.[23] Lambley Viaduct was eventually inspected and approved by Captain Douglas Galton of the Board of Trade on 27 November, but its opening was something of an anticlimax, and went unrecorded in the local press.[24]

Thanks to the 1851 census, we know a little more about the navvies building the Alston branch than those engaged on earlier N&C works. A Board of Trade return shows that on 26 June 1850 the contractors had 724 men working on the branch, while the railway were employing a resident engineer and three inspectors to supervise the work, plus a messenger.[25] This probably represents the peak of activity: midsummer with work proceeding north and south of Lambley. David Brooke's enquiries into the census conducted in March 1851 suggest that the workforce had fallen by then to about 400.[26]

Looked at individually, the census returns show that most of the navvies were living in Knarsdale parish in locations stretching from Eals to Slaggyford, between two and four miles south of Lambley viaduct.[27] Some lodged with local farmers, such as Edward Hudspith of Eals, who had ten Irish 'railway labourers' living on the premises. In some cases, married navvies had rented a house for their family and took in their fellows as lodgers. A lot, however, were housed in specially-built huts, provided by Rush & Lawton and run by a married navvy and his wife. The biggest concentration of these was near the hamlet of Knarsdale itself, and they typically housed about six to ten men in addition to the family in charge. The largest hut encountered is that run by Charles MacNab and his wife Sarah. They came from Ireland but had been living in the area for the past three years and housed thirteen navvies in addition to their three young sons and a relation, possibly Charles's sister, who was listed as 'house servant'.

A rare glimpse of the settlement is provided by the *Newcastle Journal* of 13 September 1851, describing the directors' trip along the railway. South of Burnstones, the line runs through a shallow cutting, half a mile long. 'Here a row of huts has been erected for the accommodation of labourers along the line, and designated New Slaggyford. A National School, built of stone, stands upon the brow of the hill, but the dominie and his pupils appeared to be too deeply engrossed in their studies to honour the party with their attention ... The female occupants of the cabins, however, mustered in strong force, and their clean and healthy appearance was the subject of general remark.'

During the building of the Lancaster & Carlisle Railway, just a few years before, there were press reports of riots, with Irish navvies being picked on by their English counterparts. Press reports of the Alston opening commented, by contrast, on the good behaviour of the navvies throughout the line's construction. Nonetheless, the Irish tended to live apart from the others. There were exceptions, however, and John Carter and his wife, both Scots, ran a small hut with four Irishmen and one Scot. The age range is interesting. In the case of the MacNab hut, it extended from 20 to 40, with an average of 27, and four of the lodgers were married men, with wives somewhere back home. The late twenties seems a fairly typical average age for the huts but farmer Hudspith's lodgers were in the main distinctly older: ranging in age from 18 to 53, with an average of 35.

Engineering the Line

The engineering history of the Alston Branch is complicated by the death of John Blackmore and the Hudson lease. Deprived of their engineer, Plummer and his colleagues turned to Nicholas Wood to advise them on the original route, while John Bourne (1811-74) was engaged to make the surveys for the first Bill.[28] Bourne had much experience in this field and went on to a very commendable engineering career with the Leeds Northern and North Eastern Railways. Had the N&C progressed with the line immediately on obtaining their Act it is quite likely that he would have ended up supervising the work. Instead, Peter Tate seems to have taken charge of the section between Haltwhistle and Shaft Hill, designing the smaller bridges, which are very much in the Giles/Blackmore tradition. However, the Tyne Viaduct, or Alston Arches, at Haltwhistle is a complete puzzle.

Edward Reid's original contract was for iron arches on stone piers, but just two months later, on 6 July 1847, the directors decided to substitute stone arches, following the failure of Robert Stephenson's cast-iron bridge over the River Dee at Chester.[29] They then, of course, changed the site. Throughout all this the N&C records and contemporary reports provide no clue as to who actually designed the Alston Arches. Nor does their appearance offer much help. It is very unlikely to have been Tate, and the probability is that the directors called in some unrecorded bridge specialist, such as John Green.

10.2. *Thomas Elliot Harrison in his late seventies, from the portrait painted by Walter William Ouless for the NER board room. He was born at North End, Fulham, on 4 April 1808, second son of the entrepreneur William Harrison and his wife Elizabeth Anna Maria Hall, daughter of a wealthy London attorney. They moved to Sunderland when Thomas was about five, and he grew up in the North East. He began his career as a pupil of William Chapman. During the eighteen-thirties he gained extensive experience of both the construction and operation of railways through his work on the Stanhope & Tyne and Durham Junction Railways, of which his father was a leading promoter. During the following decade he was Robert Stephenson's right-hand man in the building of the railways which became the York, Newcastle & Berwick. He succeeded Robert as YNB Engineer in Chief and also took over from Allport as general manager. Harrison was the originator of the merger which, in 1854, formed the North Eastern Railway and is best known as its Engineer, holding the post until his death on 21 March 1888. He also, however, built up a considerable private consultancy and, for example, became Consulting Engineer to the London & South Western Railway following the deaths of Joseph Locke in 1860 and John Errington in 1861.*

The Hudson lease brought T. E. Harrison on the scene, and he drafted in a younger brother, John Thornhill Harrison (1815-91) to deal with the branch. John had been articled to brother Tom until 1838, when he went to work for Brunel, first in Gloucestershire and then on the South Devon Railway.[30] This was completed in 1848, freeing him to come north probably in the late summer, since he carried out the survey for the deviations proposed in the second Alston Branch Bill, the plans for which were formally deposited at the end of November 1848.[31]

Some contractors' certificates survive, showing that John Harrison was supervising construction on the northern section by the end of 1848 and he may well have been doing so prior to that.[32] Then came the fallow period during 1849, but in December, with the N&C about to resume full control, Matthew Plummer arranged that John should continue as resident engineer, and he stayed on for a further year, leaving at the end of November 1850 to take up a new career, first in farming then as a Government Inspector.[33] He was succeeded by George Barclay Bruce (1821-1908), who had been resident engineer on Robert Stephenson's Royal Border Bridge at Berwick.[34] Bruce spent just a year on the line before heading off to India to supervise some railway construction.[35] He was followed by another engineer drawn from the works on the Newcastle & Berwick line: Francis Charlton (1816-81), a former pupil of T. E. Harrison.[36] Charlton saw the Alston branch through to completion and remained a little longer, to assist Peter Tate, before leaving in 1853 to oversee the building of the Marquess of Londonderry's railway from Seaham to Sunderland.

Because of various misconceptions which have sprung up over the years, it is necessary to point out that Bruce was not involved at the design stages. The design of the bridges north of Lambley viaduct predates even John Harrison, who was asked to produce the working drawings for the southern end, from Alston to Lambley, at the end of January 1850.[37] These, including the detailed drawings for Lambley Viaduct, are referred to in the contract specifications signed in April 1850 so it is clear that the design of Lambley had been completed long before Bruce arrived on the scene.[38] Because work on the viaduct was deferred until about March 1851, Bruce was responsible for overseeing the critical first eight months of the viaduct's construction, and he may have found it necessary to alter some details as work progressed. The final arbiter was no doubt T. E. Harrison.[39]

The design of Lambley Viaduct and the bridges south of it can be firmly attributed to the Harrisons. What remains unclear is the respective contributions of John and Thomas. When we come to look at the bridges it will be seen that the smaller ones fit closely into T. E. Harrison's canon of work and are derived from designs being used at that time by Robert Stephenson on the York, Newcastle & Berwick. The larger bridges, however, display an individuality and *joie de vivre* which it is tempting to suggest represent John doing his own thing after having spent so many years under the thumb of Brunel. Unfortunately, his departure for a farming life is not wholly consistent with this picture, and it was probably T.E.H., a man with an eye for appearances, who was enjoying the freedom to range through a variety of designs.

Engineering Features

The Alston Branch was thirteen miles long, leaving the main line at the east end of Haltwhistle station and almost immediately crossing the South Tyne on the Alston Arches. A steady climb took it to the temporary terminus at Shaft Hill (near the later Coanwood station) followed by the curves onto and off Lambley Viaduct. A variety of notable bridges and viaducts, such as Burnstones, Alston and Gilderdale, was crowded into the remainder of the line. Unlike Lambley, none of them is particularly large or high but all are handsome and interesting. With the exception of Lambley Viaduct, the line was built throughout as a double-track formation, although only one track was laid initially and that proved more than adequate.

Above and Right:
Viewed from the south west.

Left: East bastion pier, with its original arch infilled with a smaller one to strengthen the structure.

10.3. Lambley Viaduct
(Bill Fawcett)

Spandrel and parapet details. Note the very small facing stones compared with the large rock-faced blocks employed for the piers.

Lambley impresses one by its scale and setting: the great bridge and the fine scenery acting as perfect foils to one another. The actual design is quite simple and plain - a round-arched bridge very similar to both Stephenson's Royal Border Bridge and Thomas Harrison's early viaducts for the North Eastern Railway, such as Newton Cap and Durham. It differs from these, however, in the adoption of sandstone ashlar for the entire arches, rather than employing stone voussoirs to face a brick arch; the stone itself is reported to have come both from a quarry nearby and from Bardon Mill, on the N&C main line.[40] The contract actually specified stone from Prudham or Barcome Fell quarries 'or other stone to be approved of by the Engineer'.[41] The site of the bridge was chosen to coincide with a buried whinstone dyke, a foundation on this being obtained by piling up to thirty feet through the gravel riverbed. The Tyne at this point is a fairly modest river, save in flood, and it was temporarily diverted to allow construction of the river piers, rather than employing the customary cofferdams.

The rails were borne 113 feet above the riverbed on nine principal spans of 58 feet each. These are framed by bastion piers, followed by small arches of twenty feet span, with those on the east bank carrying the railway on quite a sharp curve. Deep courses of stone project from the inner faces of the piers (i.e. those under the arches) about three-quarters of the way up, and were presumably used to support the timber centering on which the arches were formed. The roadway itself is quite narrow, at twelve feet between parapets, but adequate for a single track. Its parapets are embellished with curious, chunky dentils which project well out from the bridge sides, raising the question whether there was originally an intention to provide a more elaborate machicolated parapet of the type found on the Royal Border Bridge. An interesting question is posed by the Parliamentary plan deposited in November 1848. This refers to a Lambley Viaduct of '24 arches of 20 feet span'. Clearly, this would not have been a masonry structure and the likelihood is that T. E. Harrison initially suggested a timber viaduct, on the lines of his highly successful designs for the Newcastle & Darlington Junction Railway, as a means of saving money and speeding construction.

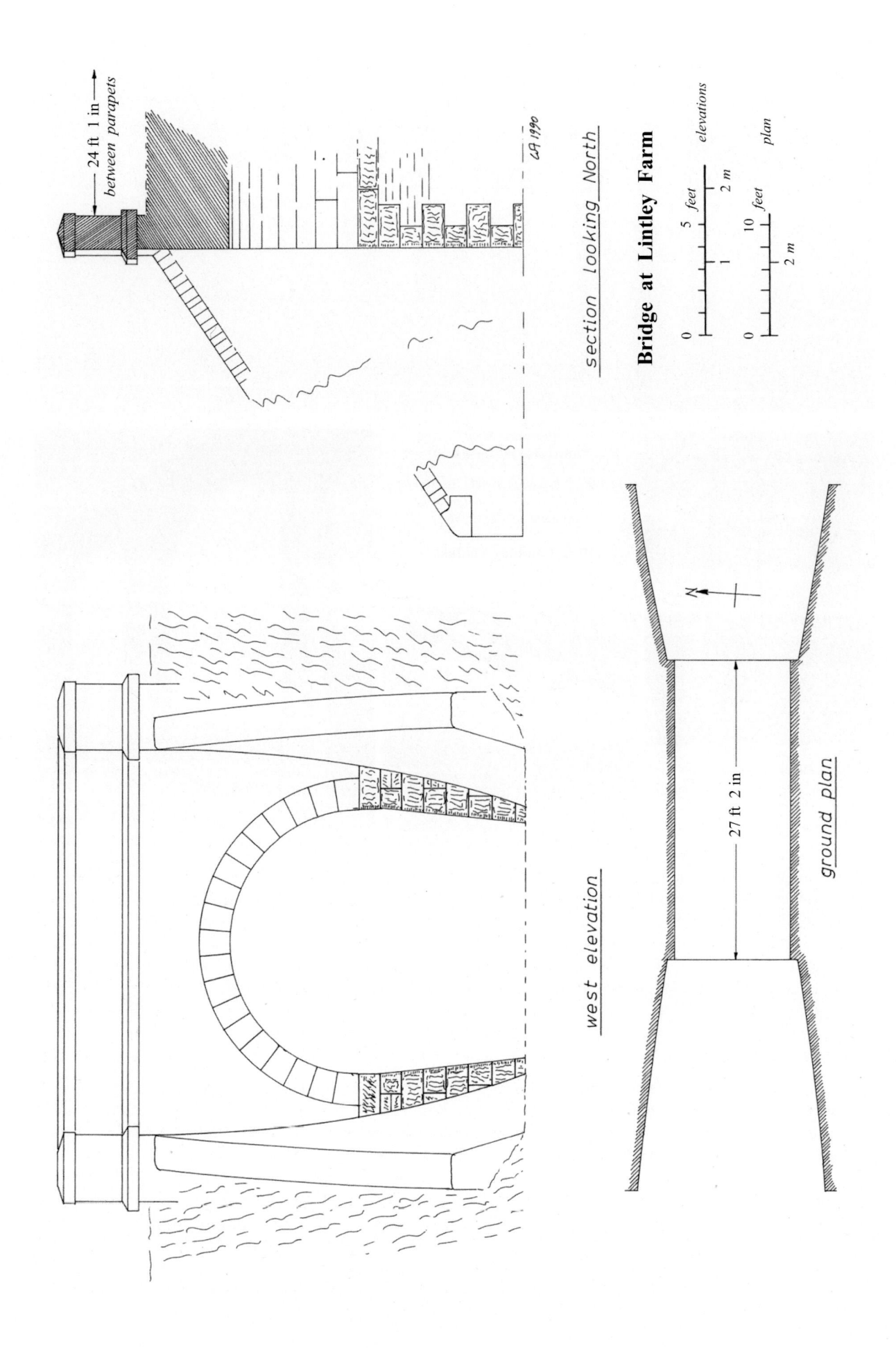

Bridge at Lintley Farm

section looking North

24 ft 1 in between parapets

west elevation

ground plan

27 ft 2 in

elevations: 0 — 5 feet / 0 — 1 — 2 m
plan: 0 — 10 feet / 0 — 2 m

South of Lambley, the overbridges, with their semi-elliptical arches, are very similar to those used by Stephenson between Darlington and Berwick and subsequently adopted by Harrison as a standard design for the North Eastern Railway. The small, round-arched underbridges also show a strong affinity with these other lines. The Lintley Farm bridge, illustrated here, typifies the underbridges generally in the use of large ashlar blocks for the arch. By contrast, the overbridges have arches formed from small, almost brick-like courses of masonry behind the bolder facing voussoirs. They, of course, were expected to carry much lighter loads.

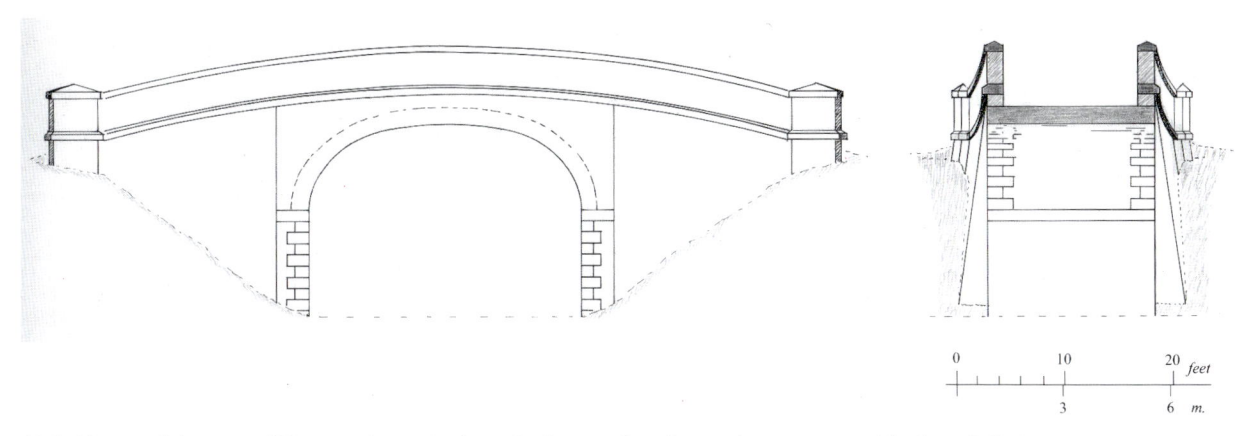

10.5. Measured drawing of Harrison's standard overbridge, used on the southern portion of the line. (Bill Fawcett)

10.6. Farm bridge near Slaggyford. (Bill Fawcett)

10.7. (left) A segmental arch was used for the skew bridge carrying the turnpike road near Lintley. (GR 684512) View looking south. (Bill Fawcett)

10.4. (left) Measured drawing of the bridge giving access to Lintley Farm. (GR 687511) (Bill Fawcett)

10.8. (right) Lintley Farm bridge. (Bill Fawcett)

Gilderdale Bridge

10.9. *West elevation of Gilderdale Bridge. (GR 783486) (Bill Fawcett)*

10.10. *(right) Detail of Gilderdale Bridge, brought back into use by the South Tynedale Railway. (Bill Fawcett)*

10.11. *(left) Viaduct over the Knar Burn. (GR 673528) (Bill Fawcett)*

The larger underbridges - notably Gilderdale, Burnstones Viaduct and the final Tyne crossing near Alston - display considerable individuality. Gilderdale is the most impressive in some ways, with a middle span of fifty feet flanked by side ones of thirty, almost like a triumphal arch. It is carefully detailed in the fine local sandstone, with prominent keystones to the arches and a roll-moulded coping. Knar Burn viaduct is a related design, with four round-arched spans of 30 feet.

10.12. *Details of the Knar Burn Viaduct. (Bill Fawcett)*

The Tyne bridge at Alston is a more squat, but attractively proportioned design, with a sequence of semi-elliptical arches rising from boldly rock-faced piers. Burnstones viaduct is also quite low, with a sequence of skew arches spanning the burn and its meadows, followed by a skew in the opposite direction to cross the turnpike from Alston to Brampton. The conflict between these two is resolved in a remarkable fashion, by introducing a somewhat narrower arch, which tapers in width and is walled off from view at its narrowest end. Thus the bridge reads as having one more span on the west side than on the east. It looks rather like a technical flourish on the part of Harrison since there is no absolute need to adopt skew arches over the burn and meadows, though they do ease the flow of water during floods.

130

10.13. *Burnstones Viaduct (GR 675543), from the west, with the arch over the road at the far end.   (Bill Fawcett).*

10.14. *(Below) The tapering arch, closed by a wall at the far (east) end. (Bill Fawcett)*

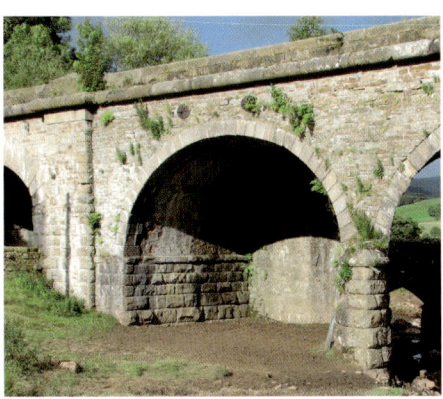

10.15. *The span over the roadway has very bold sandstone voussoirs, behind which it is actually a brick arch, The tapering arch immediately to the right is also built in brick, behind a stone facing, but the spans crossing the meadows and burn are crafted entirely in stone. (Bill Fawcett)*

10.16. *Often, railway engineers had to squeeze the line between existing features. The former Alston to Brampton turnpike road (A689) crosses the Thinhope Burn immediately downstream of the viaduct and then passes underneath it, producing this complex juxtaposition of arches. Note the ashlar winding courses of the railway's skew arches and the elegantly sharp cutwaters of Harrison's piers. This view was taken a few weeks after a severe flood which left the viaduct unscathed but damaged the rounded cutwater of the two-span road bridge, as seen here.
(Bill Fawcett)*

Alston Arches, Haltwhistle

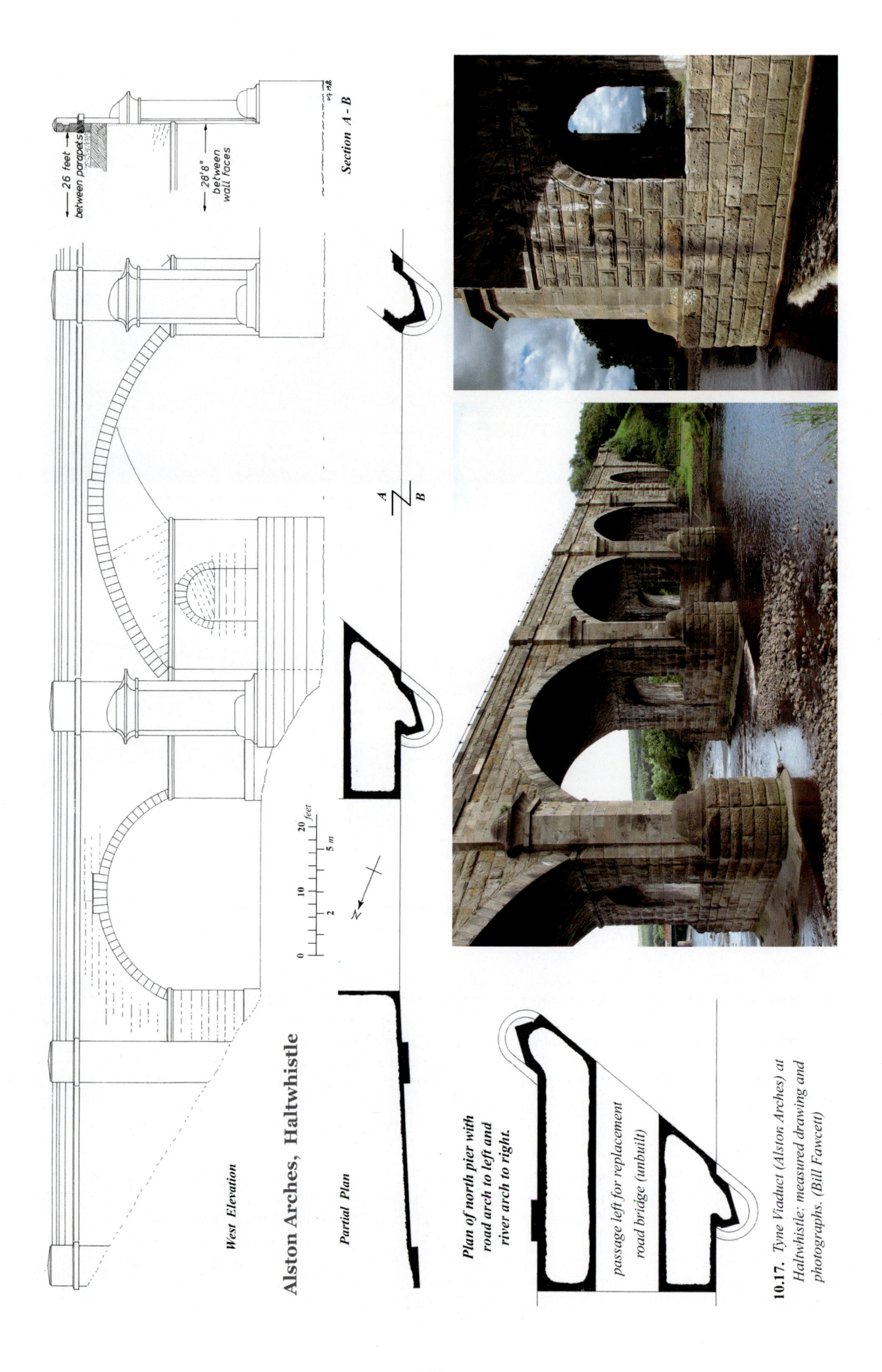

West Elevation

Section A - B

Partial Plan

26 feet between parapets

28'8" between wall faces

Plan of north pier with road arch to left and river arch to right.

passage left for replacement road bridge (unbuilt)

10.17. *Tyne Viaduct (Alston Arches) at Haltwhistle: measured drawing and photographs. (Bill Fawcett)*

10.18. *A typical Tate overbridge near Coanwood at GR 679600. Note the bold rock-faced masonry, not commonly found in earlier N&C bridges and contrasting with the treatment of the voussoirs and the inner faces of the parapets. (Bill Fawcett)*

10.19. *Measured drawing of the same bridge. (Bill Fawcett)*

North of Shaft Hill, the standard overbridges change to a very different design, which is clearly the work of Peter Tate. They are wider (to the railway) than those on the N&C main line, at 25 feet, but in other respects they are very similar to those of Giles and Blackmore, with the same shallow segmental arches and steep wing walls embracing the track. Tate also had the opportunity to design a 'tunnel', similar in appearance to that at Whitchester, though this one runs under the railway, taking the Park Burn through a substantial embankment (GR 685612). Oddly, though the embankment is very wide at the bottom, it tapers to just single track width at the top, though the rest of the route is double track width, except for Lambley Viaduct.

The Haltwhistle Viaduct comprises six segmental arches: four skew ones spanning the river, flanked by a pair of straight ones to accommodate roads. These are punctuated on the upstream side by angular buttresses rising from rounded cutwaters and ending in prominent, moulded caps. These give quite a bold effect but tend to make the arch rings look rather thin and unsatisfactory by comparison. The 1846 Act gave the company powers to build a roadway into the structure and charge tolls, and this was provided for by threading a sequence of arches through the river piers. The idea was to provide a replacement for the wooden bridge over the Tyne, designed by the architect John Dobson and built in 1826.[42] In the event the N&C chose not to proceed with the roadway, and a cast-iron road bridge, now reserved to cyclists and pedestrians, was provided at local expense in the eighteen-seventies.

The Alston Arches, as they are known locally, soon fell foul of the River Tyne, with a flood in late December 1852 which carried away part of the pier at the south end of the river spans. Viewed along the line, half the width of the pier had gone and half of the adjoining arch with it.[43] Amid fears that the rest might fall, Tate came to the rescue and by 7 February 1853 temporary repairs had been completed, enabling traffic to resume. He was assisted by Francis Charlton, the resident engineer, who was still in post. Tate's proposals for the permanent repairs were only approved in late April, the contract for these being given to the original builder, Edward Reid, on 2 May.[44] In recent years the structure has been adopted by the North Pennines Heritage Trust. They earlier took on Lambley Viaduct following extensive repairs by the British Rail Property Board in 1995-6, part funded by English Heritage and the Railway Heritage Trust.

Buildings

It is worth considering the Alston branch buildings separately from the rest of the N&C, since they form a race apart. By the time the line was completed station design had matured, and railways were expected to provide things which had been unthinkable in the early days of the N&C, such as platforms and waiting rooms. Possibly stemming from the involvement of Hudson and the Harrisons, the design of these buildings was entrusted to an architect, Benjamin Green (1813-58), the son of John Green, whom we have encountered several times as a bridge designer.[45] Naturally, they were among the last works to be started, with the building contract being advertised in August 1851.[46] By then the northern section had opened to passengers, so a wooden hut must have been provided initially at Featherstone, the one intermediate station, as well as the temporary terminus at Shaft Hill.

Benjamin Green had recently completed a sequence of very handsome 'Jacobethan' stations between Newcastle and Berwick for George Hudson.[47] Those were expensive and mildly ostentatious: the sort Hudson might have built on the Alston Branch had he remained in control but not calculated to win favour with the tighter purses of Plummer and friends. The outcome is a tribute to Green's talent and versatility. For the wayside stations at Featherstone Park, Lambley and Slaggyford (Coanwood was a later creation) he devised a simple but dignified building in the Tudor-Revival fashion - a two-storey house enlivened by a central gable on the platform frontage.

10.20. Slaggyford station at the present day. (Bill Fawcett)

10.21. Lambley station, looking north in NER days. The bracket signal controls the junction with the branch to the Earl of Carlisle's Railway, heading straight on, and the line to Haltwhistle curves sharply right onto the viaduct. In front of the original station building is a wooden booking office and waiting room range built by the NER. (Private collection)

For Alston he produced a modified version of his Newcastle & Berwick designs, in which the suave ashlar stonework of those manorial creations is replaced by a rough-textured, randomly-coursed masonry, more appropriate to this location. The station building was the most lavish on the entire N&C, except of course for Newcastle Central, and the agent was given a large sitting room and bedrooms upstairs, with a kitchen on the ground floor of one of the cross wings. The entrance frontage is quite formal: symmetrical, with large mullioned windows of a late Tudor character. The platform frontage is more relaxed: the style of the openings is early Tudor and they are disposed according to need without any worries about symmetry.

The vagaries of the Pennine weather were recognised by a trainshed spanning the single platform, running line and loop, which also provided overnight shelter for the timber-bodied coaching stock. This spanned between the main building and a small engine shed and workshop, forming a very picturesque ensemble. Though only 34½ feet in span, the trainshed was of some technical interest. Like his father, Benjamin was alert to technical innovations, and the curved roof at Alston was borne on a series of wrought-iron crescent trusses, miniature versions of those recently pioneered by the Dublin ironfounder, Richard Turner, at Liverpool's Lime Street station. In this respect Alston found itself ahead of London. When Lewis Cubitt's Kings Cross station opened in 1852, economy and speed dictated the use of laminated timber arch ribs, something the Greens had tried at North Shields station a dozen years earlier and moved on from.

However, the Alston trainshed was not without problems. About 1872-3 the NER lengthened it and took the opportunity to raise the roof by about a foot, retaining the crescent trusses but providing them with new cladding to a mansard profile. They had already replaced the ingenious but somewhat lightweight wrought-iron trusses of the engine shed with more substantial timber ones. In its later form the trainshed was a distinctive feature of the Northern railway scene until its demolition in the nineteen-sixties. The station building survives as does Green's handsome hip-roofed goods shed, with its prominent corner buttresses.[48]

10.22. *Alston station, carefully conserved by the South Tynedale Railway. At each end of the façade was an entrance flanked by a pair of windows. The one at the left-hand end served the agent's house; the one at the right, now converted into a window, was the public entrance until the NER extended the building, providing the new entrance seen at far right. Note the rather nice touch provided by the ball-finialled kneelers reaching out in the angles between the front and end gables. (Bill Fawcett)*

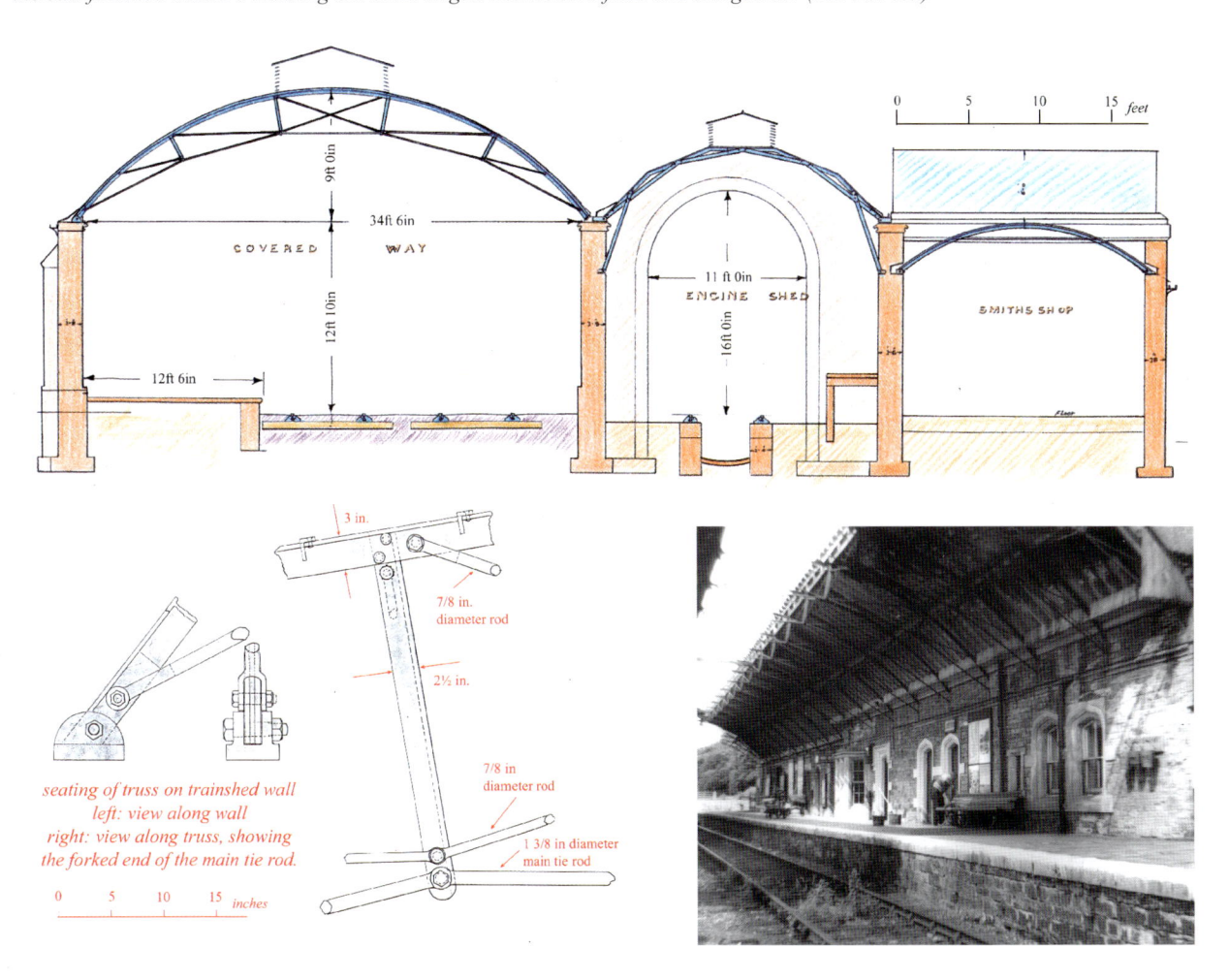

10.23. *1851 drawing, coloured up, giving a cross-section through Alston station just beyond the end of the station house. It shows the iron roofs of the trainshed or 'covered way', the engine shed, with its pit, and the workshop or smithy. Behind the latter is the wall of a store-room, with a water tank perched on top. The two detail drawings illustrate Green's trainshed roof truss. The left-hand one shows its seating on top of the trainshed wall. The other shows the portion just below the edge of the skylight/ventilator which runs down the middle of the roof.*

10.24. *(right) Trainshed interior showing the early Tudor style windows, which contrast with the formality of the façade. The horizontal moulding above these marks the original springing point of the roof trusses before the NER raised these and buried them in the wall above. They also raised the platform from its original height of about a foot. (E.E. Smith, Neville Stead coll.)*

10.25. *The branch train nestling in the Alston trainshed on 24 June 1952, behind its regular engine, No. 67315, one of the ubiquitous 0-4-4 tank engines designed by Wilson Worsdell as NER Class O. This one was built in 1900 and withdrawn from service at the end of 1958. The industrial premises on the left were built at the mouth of the Nent Force Level, past which the line would have continued to Nent Head under the original plan (A.G. Ellis)*

10.26. *The Alston ensemble, seen from the buffer stops in the late nineteen-fifties. On the right J39 0-6-0 No. 64812 had arrived on a special train, although it worked regular goods and passenger trains on the branch for some time. Hiding in the engine shed is one of the British Railways standard 2-6-0s latterly used, No. 77014. (E.E. Smith, Neville Stead coll.)*

Costs and Benefits

To allow for any items overlooked in the earlier accounts, the final figures for the cost of the Alston Branch have been taken from the capital account at the end of 1855.[49] By then a total of £205,862 had been spent on the line, broken down as follows (rounded to the nearest pound):

Land & Compensation	£18,363
Construction & Permanent Way	£163,334
Legal & Parliamentary Expenses & Engineering Fees	£12,146
Incidental Expenses	£281
Interest on Loans	£10,739

This compares with an original estimate of £210,000, which also included the four miles from Alston to Nenthead. The engineering works on that stretch would have been very much lighter than on the rest, though the other costs per mile would presumably have been similar. Assessing the Nenthead section at 80% of the construction and track costs (per mile) of the remainder, that gives a conservative figure of £53,291 for the cost of continuing to that terminus and a notional total therefore of £259,153 for comparison with the £210,000 forecast. This is a very respectable outcome, far different from the threefold discrepancy in the costs of the original main line. In part, this shows how much more mature and predictable the construction industry had become in the course of two decades.

The benefits to the people of Alston were considerable - even the initial service of just two trains a day, each way, represented a transformation from the situation in the pre-railway age, back in 1834, when a coach ground through the town three times a week on its way from Penrith to Newcastle. The lead business also benefited, but it did not prosper as a result. Foreign imports were already eating into the British market, and by the eighteen-seventies the industry was in terminal decline. The local coalfield developed under the stimulus of the railway, with two prominent N&C figures, Thomas Wilson and Isaac Crawhall, sinking a new colliery at Coanwood in 1860-3.[50] This was a very successful attempt to develop an alternative to Blenkinsopp, where their lease was about to expire, and they also established coke ovens. Writing in 1902, Daniel Polson remarked that Coanwood had produced between seventy and ninety thousand tons of coal annually until its temporary closure in 1894 due to flooding.

Despite the coal traffic, the benefits of the branch to the railway company were largely strategic. Having occupied the valley, no other railway was likely to obtain a foothold in the area. Matthew Plummer commented in November 1849 that the branch would not in itself be remunerative but would act as a feeder to the main line and 'greatly increase the receipts'.[50] The operation of the line will have been profitable in N&C and NER days, but it is unlikely that the increase in receipts ever represented an adequate return on the considerable capital expended.

10.27. *Alston goods shed. (NERA)*

10.28. *In the best Giles/Thompson tradition, the railway approaches Alston on this substantial river wall. (Bill Fawcett)*

Chapter 11: The Final Lap: 1852-70

Introduction

1849 had seen a general collapse in railway dividends and share prices. Comparing January 1847 and March 1850, ordinary shares in the London & North Western Railway had fallen from a premium of 92% to one of just 5, while the Great Western had gone from 27% premium to 44% discount.[1] Hudson's companies were naturally among the worst affected: the Midland went from 24% premium to 62% discount, the YNB from +58 to -30 and the York & North Midland slid from +84 to -67. Amid this gloom, Newcastle & Carlisle shares held up quite well, swinging from +15% to around 17% discount. By late September 1850 railway shares generally were picking up, but the N&C's eastern neighbour, the York, Newcastle & Berwick, took longer to recover and then found itself in a debilitating competition for traffic with the Leeds Northern Railway. This was resolved by the two companies merging with the York & North Midland to form a North Eastern Railway (NER). Since all three had been incorporated by Acts of Parliament, the consent of that body was required, but the companies worked as one for most practical purposes under an agreement of 31 March 1853. The Amalgamation Act received the royal assent on 31 July 1854, and the NER came into being the following day.

This was the third in a series of major mergers, which had produced the Midland Railway, in 1844, and London & North Western (LNWR), in 1846. The LNWR, forged from the London & Birmingham, Grand Junction and Manchester & Birmingham companies, owned much of the west-coast main line and in 1859 strengthened its hold by leasing the Lancaster & Carlisle Railway. The Newcastle & Carlisle found itself sandwiched between two of Britain's largest railways, and finally merged with the North Eastern in July 1862. For many years the 'Carlisle Section' of the NER continued to enjoy a distinct identity, and this story is therefore carried as far as 1870, to cover the transitional period.

A New Organisation

The slim new Board, put in place at the end of May 1852, was less distinctive than its predecessor. Gone were the engineer directors: Johnson had died and Nicholas Wood was busy building up his colliery holdings. The remaining directors were more like the businessmen and landowners to be found running any other railway, and they lost their liveliest colleague with the death, in April 1853, of Joseph Crawhall, who was succeeded by his youngest brother, Isaac. 1853 brought the resignation of James Losh, on becoming a judge, and the banker William Woods, last survivor of the 1829 Board, became chairman on 6 June. George Dixon remained his deputy but retired at the March 1856 AGM. This swapped one founding dynasty for another. Philip Henry Howard had been a director from 1835 to 1852; now he came back as deputy chairman and guardian of the Carlisle interest.

During the Hudson lease James Allport had involved one of his YNB staff, Henry Smiles (1818-98), in the line's management. Smiles was retained by the N&C, which felt the need of a manager with commercial experience, and on 5 December 1849 created the new post of General Manager and Commercial Secretary, to which he was appointed at a salary of £300.[2] This left John Adamson as the Company Secretary and Clerk to the Company, but he died on 27 September 1855, and his duties were then taken over by Smiles. Another break with the early days had come in 1851, with the retirement of the Chief Agent, John Challoner, in July.[3] He had been the company's first permanent employee, starting as their Clerk on 1 January 1830, and his career, along with that of Smiles, is explored further in chapter 16.

Improving Facilities

Having been conceived in the early days of railways, some aspects of the N&C looked rather old-fashioned by the eighteen-fifties. In evidence designed to demonstrate to Parliament the merits of the line's takeover by the NER, T. E. Harrison described it as 'perhaps the most old-fashioned company in existence, they run upon the wrong line [i.e. on the right rather than the left] as compared with every other line, except the West Hartlepool'. He admitted, however, that their dividends were greater than on the NER itself.[10] A popular view was expressed by the *Carlisle Journal*, remarking in 1851 that 'the Newcastle line loves the old system as much as railway directors love their old wine.'

In reality, the directors spent steadily, if cautiously, on improvements throughout the eighteen-fifties. The biggest call on their finances was for additional rolling stock to meet the rapidly growing coal and mineral traffic, but the fixed infrastructure also received attention. A programme was put in hand of providing platforms at their passenger stations, originally innocent of such luxuries, together with distinctive and handsome waiting sheds. There was considerable investment at Newcastle. Central Station had been their biggest such outlay, but its construction left vacant much of the large site west of Forth Banks once intended for the company's terminus. Part of that was used to provide a large and impressive goods station, designed by Peter Tate and built during 1852-3.

Carlisle was not so fortunate. The company's main passenger and goods station, at London Road, had been sited with the requirements of the Canal Branch, rather than the city, in mind and lay a mile from the city centre. The Maryport & Carlisle Railway lodged there until completing a temporary station of its own, at Crown Street, at the end of 1844, while the Lancaster & Carlisle was also a resident at London Road during 1846-7. The Lancaster company, however, only endured the privations of the N&C terminus because of delays in achieving its own ambition for a central station to serve all the city's railways.[11] Given the N&C directors' espousal of the same concept in Newcastle, they were surprisingly equivocal when it came to Carlisle, endorsing the principle but failing in practice.

John Adamson

John Adamson was born in Gateshead on 13 September 1787, and at the age of sixteen left school to learn a mercantile career from his elder brother, who had established himself as a merchant in Lisbon.[4] The prospect of a French invasion cut short his stay in Portugal but he retained a lifelong and scholarly interest in all things Portuguese. Returning to Newcastle, he took up a legal career instead but also developed a strong antiquarian interest, becoming a founder of Newcastle's Society of Antiquaries and one of its joint secretaries for the rest of his life. He was a great organiser, founding several other bodies, including the Newcastle Law Society, and applied these skills to the railway from 10 October 1833, when he was appointed Secretary in succession to Thomas Crawhall.[5] Interestingly, William Woods, the final N&C chairman, was a rival candidate for the post but will have opted out of the contest when it was decided that the Secretary could not also be a director.

Although it carried a salary of £200 initially (£400 by 1841) and required daily visits to the company's office, the post was not sufficiently arduous to interfere with Adamson's private business as a solicitor, nor did it involve legal work as such for the railway, that being the province of John Clayton. Instead, Adamson acted as the channel for formal communications to and from the company, fielded demands from the Board of Trade, serviced the directorial committees and also played a role in the recruitment of staff.

His services to Portuguese culture, including several literary translations, earned him honours from that country's government, and a writer in 1887 recalled with pleasure 'the annual meetings of the Newcastle & Carlisle Railway Literary Institute, where, with his foreign orders on his breast, the English biographer of [Luis de] Camoens, venerable in age, counselled the young men of his day to cultivate the graces and refinements of literature'.[6]

William Woods

William Woods was one of the most prominent and successful of the Newcastle bankers, though he was born at Bolton, in Lancashire, in 1787, the son of an iron merchant and landowner.[7] The war against Napoleon drew him from an intended mercantile career into a military one. At the close of the war he was quartered in Newcastle and 1815 found him marrying into the local banking firm of Anthony Hood & Company. His business interests rapidly expanded to embrace the 'Fire Office' (Newcastle Fire & Life Insurance Company) and a variety of private industrial enterprises. It is not surprising, therefore, that he recognised the potential of the N&C project, putting his name down for £2,000 in 1825. The eighteen-thirties saw him become the main proprietor of Benjamin Thompson's Brunton & Shields Railway and a director of the Blaydon, Gateshead & Hebburn and Durham Junction railways, seeing in the latter the prospect for a link between the Tyne and Tees.[8]

11.2. *Woods kept up his military interest as Adjutant to the Northumberland & Newcastle Yeomanry Cavalry.*

In commerce, his most public success came after the failure of the Newcastle Union Bank in 1847. He was appointed chairman of a committee to sort out the resulting claims, which he managed with great skill and ended up building the new banking firm of Woods & Company out of the ruins.[9] Fresh from this, the chairmanship of the N&C must have seemed a fairly straightforward task and one to which he brought the sort of financial acumen which had characterised Plummer's long reign. Lowry's diary indicates that Woods was quite approachable, like Plummer, but did not get involved to the same extent in the everyday detail of the railway. Nor did he need to, with a professional manager in post, in the form of Henry Smiles.

On 24 July 1845, terms for a joint station were agreed by representatives of the four companies involved: N&C, M&C, L&C and Caledonian.[12] The idea was to build a passenger station, with separate goods stations nearby for each company. London Road would be abandoned, and the N&C Board decided to raise the issue of offsetting past expenditure there against their share of the costs of the joint station. The other companies could see no justice in this, and the L&C's Colonel MacLean, of Lazonby Hall, who chaired the joint committee, seems to have become exasperated at times with the N&C. By November 1845 the Lancaster Board were expressing their unwillingness to give Plummer and his colleagues 'the trouble of further meetings'.[13] Another irritant was that the N&C Board felt that they knew far more about the business than their collaborators, overlooking the fact that the L&C and Caledonian were employing some of the most experienced engineers in the business, Locke & Errington, while the architect for the new station - (Sir) William Tite, was already making his mark in this field.

The Lancaster and Caledonian companies obtained an Act for the station and associated lines in July 1846, and, with the N&C still on board, construction went ahead. Targets were to open a partially complete Citadel Station on 1 July 1847 and finish it by October.[14] The Newcastle and Maryport companies, however, failed to come up with their contributions when asked, and in July 1847 the N&C were informed that they were no longer participants in the venture, but that room would be left for them in the station.[15]

During the Hudson lease the Railway King tried to bludgeon his way into Citadel on the cheap by threatening to build a rival station for the Maryport and Newcastle companies.[16] This got him nowhere, and the eighteen-fifties saw the N&C Board engaged in sporadic negotiations with Colonel MacLean and his committee. The Maryport company had entered Citadel in 1851, and in January 1854 MacLean and William Woods, by then N&C chairman, signed a draft agreement giving the N&C access for £500 a year rent plus £300 a year towards working expenses, to be reviewed after three years, when the second element would become a proportion of the actual costs.[17] The N&C delegation had, however, gone beyond the limits authorised by the full Board, which took fright at the unspecified future working costs; even as it stood the move would have added about 1% to the railway's total working expenses. The issue was eventually settled as part of the concessions offered to secure the passage of the NER/N&C Merger Bill.[18] Clause 43 embodied an agreement setting the rent at £1,000 a year plus working expenses and, an earlier stumbling block for the N&C, prevented the NER using any other passenger station within two miles.[19] NER trains entered Citadel Station at the start of 1863 and London Road was developed as their goods station. For the extra mile into Citadel, fares were raised by amounts ranging from a penny, third-class, to threepence, first-class.[20]

11.3. Sir William Tite's very handsome Citadel Station, looking at the south end of the portico. (Bill Fawcett)

Port Carlisle and Silloth

From the opening of the Maryport & Carlisle Railway, the Carlisle Canal became increasingly irrelevant to the city's transport needs and paid its last dividend in 1848. The previous year had brought a deputation of N&C directors to examine the canal, and they had concluded that it could readily be converted into a railway and that this would be highly desirable from an N&C viewpoint.[21] Carlisle's business leaders were keen to retain an independent route, free from control by other railways, so they took up the idea and in 1853 obtained an Act for the conversion. The canal closed on 1 August and reopened in 1854 as the Port Carlisle Dock & Railway, with locomotives and carriages provided initially by the N&C. At the same time, plans were underway for an extension to Silloth, strongly backed in Carlisle, but vigorously opposed by the Maryport company.[22] These received encouragement from the N&C, as a continuation of a through route from Newcastle, and both Henry Smiles and William Woods gave evidence for the scheme before Parliament, an Act being obtained, at the second attempt, in July 1855.[23] This was virtually the limit of N&C assistance. The Carlisle & Silloth Bay Railway & Dock Company opened a line from Drumburgh Junction, 2½ miles short of Port Carlisle, to a temporary jetty at Silloth in 1856, Marshall Dock being completed three years later.

Having begun so well, relations between the Silloth company and the N&C were soon blighted by a traffic agreement between the N&C and NER, of which more later. The finances of the Silloth venture were in any case hopelessly over-extended, and it and the Port Carlisle company sought refuge with the North British Railway. Money was raised by a sale and leaseback of their locomotives and rolling stock to the NB in August 1859, and the lines were leased to the Scottish company from 1862. At this time the North British was pursuing an aggressively expansionist policy under a chairman - Richard Hodgson, who was a brother of John Hodgson of Elswick. Central to Hodgson's policy was the promotion of an independent route from Edinburgh to Carlisle, serving the Border towns of Galashiels and Hawick and soon to become known as the Waverley route. The Port Carlisle line offered a foothold in the city, with the Waverley route joining it at the north end of the former canal basin, while the Silloth Dock also offered Hodgson a useful outlet. Running powers over the N&C's Canal branch were granted by an 1860 Act and used to facilitate North British goods traffic.[24]

The North Tyne Again

Although the North Tyne valley lost any prospect of a trunk line in the eighteen-forties, the desire for a railway only grew, and was addressed by the promotion of the Border Counties Railway. This originated with a prospectus for a line from Hexham to Hawick, tapping on its way a coalfield at Plashetts, on the North Tyne, which the landowner, the Duke of Northumberland, conceived as a mineral Eldorado.[25] This was something the N&C directors felt happy to encourage, knowing that it would provide feeder traffic without costing them anything.[26] The first Bill was only for the stretch up to the coalfield, and evidence in favour was given by an N&C director, George Clayton Atkinson. He was the managing partner of the Lemington ironworks, near Scotswood, and held out the prospect of ironmaking resuming at Hareshaw.

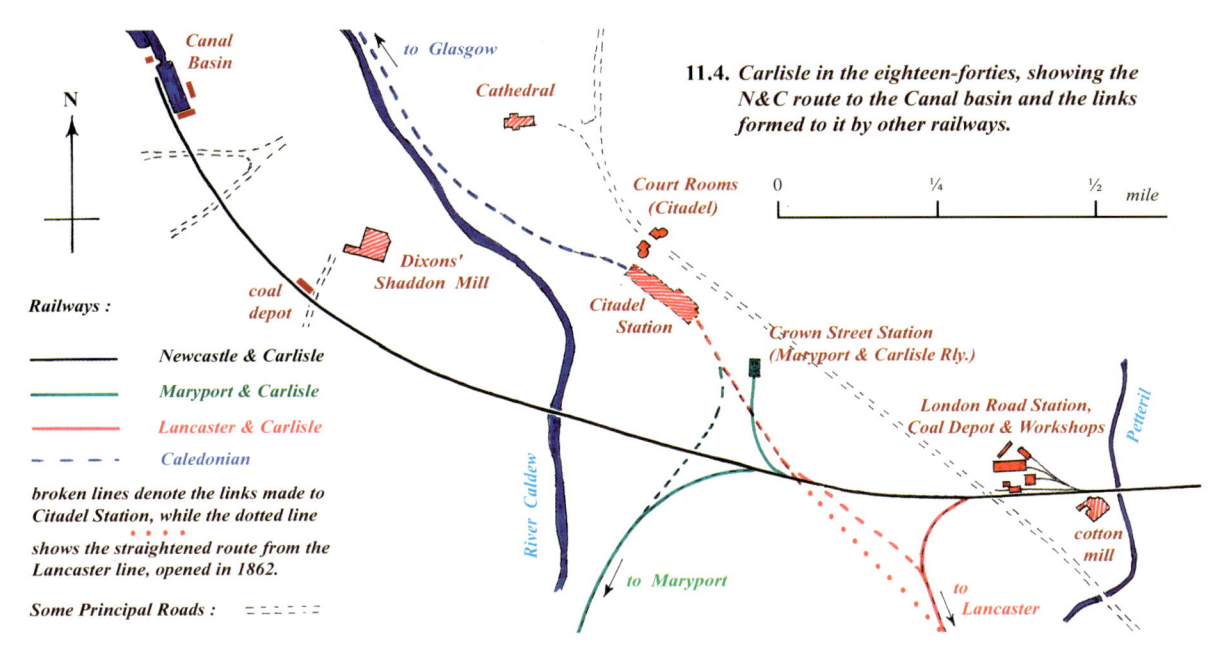

11.4. Carlisle in the eighteen-forties, showing the N&C route to the Canal basin and the links formed to it by other railways.

The Border Counties Act received the royal assent on 31 July 1854, authorising a line leaving the N&C a mile west of Hexham station and crossing the Tyne immediately before heading 25 miles up the valley to The Belling, an isolated house adjacent to the Plashetts coalfield.[27] A local laird, William Henry Charlton (1809-80) of Hesleyside, became chairman, and the first four miles, from Border Counties Junction on the N&C to Chollerford, opened on 5 April 1858, with assistance from the N&C. Woods and his Board loaned the BC directors an engine and carriage with which to inspect their line on the day of their AGM, 25 February 1858, and then provided a number of 'old engines' for the Board of Trade's test of the BC's Tyne Bridge.[28] They did not, however, take up the option, provided in the Border Counties Act, of subscribing N&C capital towards the venture. By a neat coincidence, the Border Counties chairman was the father of Francis Charlton, the last Alston branch engineer.

Progress with the rest of the route limped along, starved of capital. If completed as first conceived, it might have ended up being swallowed into the North Eastern Railway. Instead it fell into the hands of the North British, Hodgson seeing it as a potential feeder to the Waverley Route and a way into Newcastle, via the N&C. A second Act, of 1859, authorised an extension up to the Waverley Route at Lees Bog, later Riccarton Junction, and permitted generous financial assistance from the NB. A third Act, of 1860, permitted a North British takeover. The final stage of the Border Counties opened on 1 July 1862, timed to coincide with the formal opening of the last part of the Waverley Route itself.

The NB also gave generous funding to a locally-sponsored branch, the Wansbeck Railway, running from Redesmouth, on the Border Counties, to Morpeth. This progressed in stages from Morpeth, with the final stretch to Redesmouth opening on 1 May 1865. At the same time, a spur was opened to serve the iron ore workings, near Ridsdale, which Sir William Armstrong was opening up to supply his Elswick Works. This traffic was the only significant one the NB's Northumbrian network ever managed to acquire, and, sent out via Hexham, it proved a modest boon to the Carlisle section of the NER as well. That is more than can be said for the Plashetts coalfield. This proved to be a sore disappointment, and neither the Border Counties nor the 'Wanny' could be regarded as a commercial success.

11.5. Border Counties Junction, looking east towards Hexham in the nineteen-fifties. The Border Counties line curves sharply left onto the Tyne Bridge, whose handrail can just be seen. Lack of space led the NER to build the cantilever signalbox, with the lattice girder footbridge giving access to it across the tracks. The line closed to passengers in 1956, with the freight service being withdrawn in stages from 1958. The only evidence at this spot today is provided by the stumps of the Tyne bridge.
(C.J.B. Sanderson)

Iron Ore and its Consequences.

The eighteen-forties saw enormous growth in the North-East iron industry. The first big development was at Consett, but the opening up of the Cleveland ironstone saw several large works being established near the Tees. At the same time, technical developments had enhanced the utility of West Cumberland's haematite iron ore, and several of the North East ironworks, notably Consett, began employing a mixture of Cleveland and Cumbrian ore. Happily for the railways involved, there was a considerable call in Cumberland for the high-quality Durham coking coal as a raw material for blast furnace coke, while coke itself was shipped over the N&C to fuel the locomotives of some of the west coast railways. This meant substantial traffic flows in both directions, rather than the usual situation with mineral traffic: high volumes one way and very little the other.

The N&C was ideally placed to benefit from this, though as usual the directors proceeded carefully. Before taking on contracts to handle large volumes of ore they would have to invest in more wagons and wanted to be sure the traffic would not then vanish. Thus in November 1856 Smiles accompanied two directors on a visit to the principal users of haematite ore on Teesside, to find out the probable demand for ore from the Whitehaven area and whether this was likely to be affected by recent discoveries of ore nearer home, in Rosedale. [29] One customer, Mr. Hannay, was quoted a rate from Port Carlisle to Middlesbrough, implying that ore was being shipped round by sea from Whitehaven, although in fact most of the later traffic came over the Maryport & Carlisle.[30] He was told 'he might calculate on waggons at the rate of ten thousand tons per annum.' At 8s 3d a ton, this meant a possible revenue of over £4,000 from that customer, but it had to be split with two other railways: the North Eastern and S&D.

The N&C was wholly dependent on these neighbours in bidding for the Middlesbrough traffic in the first place, which meant in return that Woods and his colleagues had to be prepared to co-operate in the matter of traffic agreements. In particular, this meant the agreement with regard to traffic between Newcastle and Liverpool. Although the major companies were often in competition, they also saw the sense in agreeing to share traffic over some routes in order to maintain prices, a policy keenly espoused by the LNWR general manager, Mark Huish, whose thinking underlies the *Sextuple Agreement*, signed in 1851.[31] The YNB and LNWR were among the principal signatories, and one clause provided for all goods between the Liverpool/Manchester area and stations on the YNB and the Berwick to Edinburgh line (other than Edinburgh) to be routed via York.[32] Thus the Lancaster & Carlisle agreed to close its route to Liverpool traffic which would otherwise have continued via the N&C, although the latter still received some goods consigned by the somewhat cheaper steamers plying from Liverpool to Whitehaven and Maryport.

The NER was keen to freeze out the steamer route as well, in order to keep up prices, and the outcome was an agreement which took effect from the start of 1856. By this, the N&C and other railways involved in the Maryport and Whitehaven traffic agreed not to offer rates for goods for Liverpool. In return, the NER lowered its rates on haematite ore from the Whitehaven area and raised those on the competing ore from the Furness district, which was consigned via Leeds. This caused objections elsewhere, so the differential ore rates were abolished and from the end of March 1857 a new agreement came into place by which the N&C and other companies, including the steamers, were paid not to take the Liverpool traffic. Instead, the North Eastern paid them the profit which it was estimated they would have earned on their existing share of this traffic - about a third of the total.[33] In return the N&C had to pay the NER any receipts arising from goods which people insisted on consigning by their route. The NER used its new monopoly to raise slightly the rates on cotton but by 1859 its Liverpool rates were, on the whole, less than they had been when the agreement was signed. [34]

Such agreements were not well publicised. Caution is evident in the N&C directors' instruction of December 1855 that *verbal* notice be given to senders and consignees of Liverpool traffic of the ending of the 'through rate'.[35] The realisation that they were being frozen out of the through Liverpool traffic was ill received by the Port Carlisle and Silloth directors. Woods and his colleagues met with them in November 1856, holding out the prospect that the traffic agreement might not be renewed, as his directors held 'a strong feeling against all special arrangements'.[36] This may have been their feeling, but in reality the N&C had little choice but to fall in with the wishes of its powerful neighbours, and the Liverpool agreement persisted until August 1860. Through rates were, however, offered for passenger traffic via the western ports to Liverpool, as well as Belfast and Dublin. The Silloth company was entitled to a small share of the compensation money from the NER but its directors decided it was not worth compromising their principles by accepting it.[37]

Financial Performance

The iron ore and coke traffics brought a significant boost to N&C receipts, which had risen from £118,138 in 1851 to £175,288 in 1856, of which 40% was accounted for by coal and mineral traffic.[38] The company's revenues were broadly based, however, with other goods traffic contributing 26% and passengers and related business 29%; the remaining 5% comprised cattle traffic and 'miscellaneous receipts'. This made it less vulnerable to the cyclic booms and recessions of the industrial economy than a company like the Stockton & Darlington, which was hugely profitable in the good times but had gone through a very bad patch during the slump at the end of the eighteen-forties.[39]

The N&C's new investment of the eighteen-fifties was met in part from revenue, but heavy reliance was still placed on raising capital. In 1850, with the investment market weak, the company had been obliged to raise money by the issue of Preference Shares, with a guaranteed 4% dividend. By the start of 1854 the capital had reached £1,305,000 in shares plus borrowings (Debenture debt) of £465,000. Woods set about converting the debt into shares, obtaining an Act in July 1854 which allowed the company to create a 'Debenture Stock' which would have first claim on revenues; the cash raised by selling these shares would be used to pay off the debts.[40] The Act also provided for an increase in the ordinary share capital of £230,000 to cope with 'the expenditure necessitated by the increase in traffic'. As a result, the total share capital became two million pounds. The new shares were not released immediately onto the market, instead they were issued gradually, whenever market conditions were good, in order to secure premiums to the company.

Revenues saw a significant fall in 1858, due to a downturn in trade in the latter months of the year and a particularly sharp decline in coke traffic. Woods and his directors became quite concerned, but business soon picked up again, and revenues peaked at £195,900 during 1860. At the same time costs were kept under firm control, and the operating ratio was improved even further, from 40% in 1856 to 38% in 1860-1. This was a very impressive performance, with Britain's largest railway company, the LNWR, averaging 49% over the same period.[41] N&C dividends tell the story: reaching 5½ % for 1856-7, dropping very slightly for 1858, and keeping above 6 % for the remainder of the company's existence, with a peak of 7 % in 1860.

Pressures for Amalgamation: The Stainmore Route and the North British.

Given such a good performance, one might ask why did Woods and his directors not seek the continued independence of their railway. After all, the North Eastern only returned an equivalent average dividend of 4.2 % over the period 1856-61.[42] The answer is that they were realists, and recognised two important factors. One was that the NER had more potential for future traffic growth than the N&C; the other was that their lucrative monopoly of the West Cumberland traffic was about to be broken by the Stockton & Darlington.

The S&D plan was to extend its main line across the Pennines to Tebay, on the west-coast route, via a satellite company, the South Durham & Lancashire Union (SDLU), which obtained its Act in July 1857. This would facilitate access to the Furness area, thereby depriving the North Eastern of that traffic. The Eden Valley Railway got its Act the following year for a line branching from the SDLU at Kirkby Stephen and running to Penrith, where it would link up with another railway in which the S&D had a stake to provide access to Workington, enabling the S&D to compete with the N&C for the West Cumberland traffic.

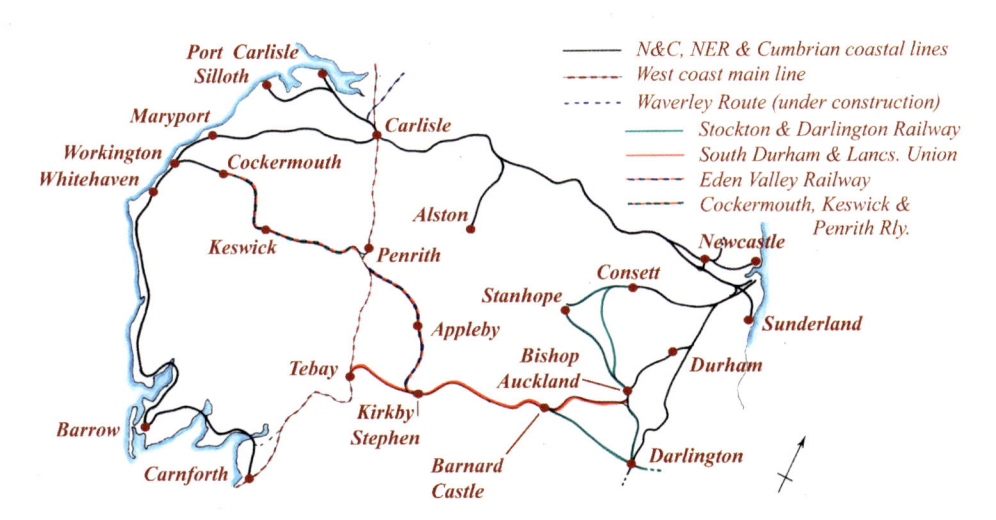

11.6. *Trans-Pennine Rivals. The S&D thrust west would give it a significant advantage in distance when it came to the South Durham traffic. Only a selection of NER routes is shown, but note how its main line bypassed Durham, served by the Bishop Auckland branch.*

Although these routes did not open until 1859-62, the N&C directors were in no doubt as to the threat they might pose to their company's prosperity. Their minds were also focused by the downturn in the latter months of 1858, which was accompanied by a drop in coke shipments as the west-coast railways began using coal as a locomotive fuel.[43] Discussions therefore began with the NER in November 1858 as to the possibility of a merger, although these are said to have started almost by accident. The North Eastern itself was becoming apprehensive about prospective North British incursions into Northumberland. During 1857 Richard Hodgson had made an approach to Woods about taking the N&C into the North British fold, but Woods had declined even to place the idea before his Board.[44] The NER was therefore receptive to the N&C overtures, with its chairman, Harry Meysey-Thompson, remarking that it was necessary for 'the old companies to choose their friends and make such alliances' as will secure them against all-comers.[45]

Woods entered the negotiations hoping that the NER could be persuaded to offer a guaranteed return of 6 or 7% on the N&C capital. Instead, Thompson and his Board insisted on making the past receipts of the two companies a basis for the division of future income. This was not only reasonable; in the end it gave the Carlisle shareholders a better return than the guarantee would have done. Final terms were agreed during January 1859 and a shareholders' meeting was called for 18 February.[46] At this point, the resentment caused by the Board's treatment of the Silloth company really began to make itself felt, both in letters to the newspapers and at the N&C shareholders' meetings. To a great extent the Silloth line was being used as a stalking horse by the North British, which would have liked to frustrate the merger. There is no doubt, however, that the Silloth chairman, Peter James Dixon, son of the former N&C director John Dixon, felt badly let down by Woods and company.

John Irving, a prosperous wholesale grocer and deputy chairman of the Silloth company, was their public spokesman, and in February 1859 he bought one share in the N&C to give himself a voice at their meetings, expanding his holding to ten in the vain hope of being elected to the Board.[47] He also managed to enlist the more prominent figure of Somerset Beaumont, of the lead dynasty. Much fuss was created at the 18 February meeting, and four days later a number of concerned investors met at Newcastle's *Queen's Head Hotel*, where they elected a committee, under Beaumont, to scrutinise the figures put forward by the Board. The *Railway Times* came out strongly against the directors, referring to traffic belonging to the N&C having been 'illegally purchased or improperly diverted' by the North Eastern, and taxed Woods with seeking the 'easy method of sinking into the lap of the North-Eastern, and so ending all the troubles and anxieties of a railway life lately become too burdensome for him'.[48]

Beaumont's scrutiny committee contained four other members, including Irving, and was given full co-operation by the Board. It confirmed the accounts and a majority of its members emerged convinced, even if reluctantly, of the necessity for the merger.[49] Irving, naturally, remained resolutely opposed as did Beaumont. The shareholders' decision came at a meeting on 15 March 1859 when votes representing £609,275 of shares were cast for the merger and £193,475 against.[50] Arrangements were then made for the North Eastern to take on the working of the line from 1 May, prior to going to Parliament for an Act to sanction the merger.[51] As part of a general tidying up of loose ends the N&C also got round to giving Greenwich Hospital the purchase money for the land which the railway had acquired almost thirty years before.[52]

Winning the Amalgamation

This was not the end of the story. The working arrangement with the North Eastern was challenged in a Chancery suit brought in June 1859 by Francis Charlton and Thomas Lowry Bonnell. Both were N&C shareholders, but not apparently of long standing, and they were acting in the interests of the NB chairman, Richard Hodgson, who had promised to meet any costs involved.[53] The NER and N&C were advised that their agreement, under which the latter had surrendered the operation of its own line, exceeded their powers. They therefore abandoned the May agreement, and entered a new one, on 5 July, by which the N&C resumed the management of its own traffic, but far-reaching arrangements were put in place to facilitate through traffic between the two railways.[54] Charlton's suit was finally heard in February 1860, but by then it was all somewhat academic as the issue was being placed in the hands of Parliament in the form of an Amalgamation Bill.[55]

The importance of securing the Carlisle line was brought home to the North Eastern by a new railway proposed for the Derwent Valley, stretching south from Blaydon towards Consett and its ironworks. Consett was served by both S&D and NER. It was one of the most important customers of both railways, but the NER's route was very unsatisfactory, entailing the use of the Pontop Branch, a stretch of the former Stanhope & Tyne Railway, well endowed with stationary inclines. A direct route could be built down the Derwent Valley to the N&C, but this was probably unattractive to the North Eastern because its potential to tap local coal traffic had been partially pre-empted by long-established waggonways. To fill the void, along came the promoters of a Newcastle & Derwent Valley line, connecting at one end with the N&C and at the other with the S&D. The Darlington company thought this an excellent idea, while the LNWR backed it as part of a direct route from Liverpool to Newcastle, via the South Durham & Lancashire Union. The LNWR and North British contributed towards the Parliamentary expenses, and the Bill provided for both companies to subscribe to the venture. The Hodgson brothers were at the heart of the mischief, with John Hodgson Hinde (formerly encountered as John Hodgson of Elswick) as chairman, strongly encouraged by Richard.

The North Eastern fought back with plans for their own Derwent Valley line, and the spring of 1860 saw Parliament discussing the two rival schemes as well as the N&C/NER Merger Bill, which was strongly opposed by other railways.[56] In the event all three bills failed, the Newcastle & Derwent scheme having been undermined by the defection of the S&D, which was moving into a closer relationship with the NER. John Irving made a strong showing against the NER, with his account of the Liverpool Traffic Agreement, and this was clearly a factor in the Parliamentary committee's decision that the NER had not proved the preamble of (i.e. made out the basic case for) their merger Bill. Woods and his colleagues took the hint, and repudiated the Liverpool Agreement shortly after.[57]

1861 brought a repeat contest, with the rival Derwent Valley scheme much expanded in scope as a Newcastle, Derwent & Weardale Railway (NDW). For almost four weeks, from the end of May, a Commons committee heard evidence on the rival merits of this and the NER's Blaydon & Consett Bill.[58] Charles Attwood's Weardale Iron Company strongly supported the NDW but Consett Iron Company, indebted to both the NER and S&D, argued for the NER. Nicholas Wood turned up to argue for the NDW, largely in the interests of his own Marley Hill colliery, but the N&C naturally gave evidence against, their counsel pointing out that the line stemmed merely from 'the itch of the North Western [LNWR] to fish in waters which belonged to others.' Interestingly, although the current LNWR general manager, William Cawkwell, spoke for the NDW, his redoubtable predecessor, Captain Mark Huish, turned up to argue for the NER instead. The Commons threw out the NER's Blaydon & Consett Bill but passed the NDW, however a further battle in the Lords managed to get that rejected as well. Recognising the degree of hostility around, the NER found it prudent to withdraw the N&C merger Bill.[59]

The merger proposals seem to have been widely unpopular in Newcastle, where there were fears about extending the NER monopoly, and the North Eastern was slow to address these. However, a variety of concessions was eventually made, which brought Parliamentary success in 1862. The support of Newcastle Corporation was won with agreements to extend opportunities for third-class travel, to build a railway down to the Quayside, and to construct the great portico to Newcastle Central Station, abandoned during the crisis of 1849 but not forgotten.[60] The North British was conciliated by the offer of running powers between Border Counties Junction and Newcastle, in return for which the NER won the right to work East-Coast expresses north of Berwick. Carlisle was appeased by a promise to run trains into Citadel Station, but the attempt to secure compulsory running powers for this antagonised the LNWR and Caley, with whom an agreement, on their terms, was eventually hammered out while the Bill was before the Parliamentary committee.[61] The N&C directors were strangely passive throughout the Parliamentary proceedings, leaving the NER to make most of the running, backed up by various customers and the general manager of the Maryport & Carlisle. This time, Nicholas Wood gave evidence in support. The Amalgamation Act received the royal assent on 17 July 1862, while the NER's Blaydon & Consett (Derwent Valley) Bill also passed at this third attempt. Meanwhile, the S&D had been heading into the NER fold; the two companies entered a traffic agreement at the start of 1861, and their merger was authorised by an Act of July 1863.

Implementing the Merger.

While these Parliamentary contests took place, life continued as normal on the N&C. The directors generally met weekly, apparently alternating between a full Board and working committee, while twice a year, normally in March and August, they made a formal inspection of the line. On these occasions a special train bore the directors from Newcastle, accompanied by Peter Tate and stopping *en route* to examine works in progress and proposed; the day finished up with a Board meeting at Carlisle. New investment was sustained at quite a high level, with large quantities of new wagons being ordered, further station improvements, permanent-way renewals and replacement of some of Blackmore's timber bridges. Scotswood Bridge forced its way into the renewals agenda by burning down in 1860, while the River Team bridge was replaced by a Peter Tate iron structure without any such drama.[62]

So far as the N&C Board were concerned, all this ended in July 1862. The N&C shares became the 'Carlisle' shares of the NER, which meant there were now five groups of NER stock: Carlisle, Berwick (YNB), York (YNM), Leeds (Leeds Northern), and Malton (Malton & Driffield Railway). The basis of the merger was the same as that which had governed the formation of the NER in 1854, namely that the nett receipts of the united company be divided up so as to reflect the performance of the two separate companies over a three-year period.[63] Because the negotiations began in 1858, the reference period was 1855-7, and, as can be seen from Table 11.1, this was a good choice from an N&C viewpoint, since the NER's relative performance was improving. On a strict calculation, the Carlisle shareholders were entitled to 9.66% of total revenue, but the inclusion of reserve and contingency funds raised this to 9¾, and the NER Board finally conceded 10%, less an annual charge of £1,450.

Table 11.1. Receipts of the N&C and NER: 1855-1861

	Gross Receipts (£)			Operating Ratio (%)	
	N&C	NER	N&C/NER (%)	N&C	NER
1855	167,041	1,688,395	9.89	40.87	48.27
1856	175,288	1,751,702	10.01	40.09	46.15
1857	179,465	1,883,737	9.53	39.95	44.50
1858	163,532	1,796,618	9.10	38.51	45.14
1859	(177,805) *	1,968,000	(9.03)	39.26	43.15
1860	195,899	2,027,486	9.66	38.46	43.06
1861	190,676	2,056,486	9.27	38.49	44.52

* because the NER operated the N&C for part of the first half of 1859, only the nett income is available for the first half year, so the operating ratio for the second half of the year has been used to predict the first half's contribution to gross revenue. The N&C operating ratios take account of all working expenses but do not include passenger duty and taxes, which generally amounted to about £4,000 p.a. in this period.

The NER's financial performance during the eighteen-sixties was extremely good, and the Carlisle shareholders had no reason to regret the merger, receiving dividends on the ordinary shares of 8.625% in 1869. The following year the North Eastern consolidated its stock, doing away with the old divisions and allocating the new stock in the ratios 1.33 for one Carlisle section £100 share, 1.36 for the Darlington section (former S&D), 1.0 for Berwick, 0.98 for York, 0.65 for Leeds, and 0.1 for Malton.[64] The first annual dividend on the new consols was 7.875%, which meant that for 1870 the former Carlisle shareholders were earning the equivalent of almost 10½ % in terms of their old shares.

The 1862 Act provided for two Carlisle directors to join the NER Board, and the first pair was John Fogg Elliot and William Dunn, a Newcastle solicitor, both of whom had served from 1859 on a joint committee responsible for sorting out through traffic with the NER. Elliot remained on the Board until his death in February 1881, but Dunn was only a brief presence, dying in September 1862. William Woods was drafted back into harness, becoming an NER director in February 1863, but he died on 12 June 1864, ending the formal involvement of the original N&C promoters in the direction of their line.

Among the people who actually ran and operated the railway, there was little immediate change. Henry Smiles continued as Manager of the Carlisle Section, responsible directly to the NER general manager, William O'Brien, and the section retained its own (Traffic) Superintendent in the form of Joseph Parker, formally designated 'outdoor assistant' to Smiles.[65] Peter Tate, though he was almost seventy at the time of the merger, carried on for a further decade as Engineer, responsible to the NER Northern Division Engineer, John Bourne, and ultimately to T. E. Harrison as Engineer in Chief, as in the days of the Hudson lease. One person for whom the future was less rosy was Anthony Hall, who had been Locomotive Superintendent since 1835. He continued as Locomotive Foreman of the Carlisle Section but his scope was much curtailed, with the N&C workshops gradually being run down and their activities transferred across the Tyne to the NER's Gateshead Works.

For the travelling public, the most obvious change was to the direction of running. In September 1862, Bourne and Tate were asked to report on the cost of altering the line to enable trains to run on the left-hand track, and the changeover was approved at a cost of £4,000, to be carried out during the summer of 1863.[66] It evidently took longer than anticipated and was made in stages, with Newcastle to Milton (Brampton Junction) switching on 7 March 1864. No doubt there was a period during which passengers continued to turn up on the wrong platform. They will also have noticed a gradual change in the liveries of engines and coaching stock, as they came up for overhaul, together with increasingly frequent appearances by locomotives from the stable of Edward Fletcher, the NER Locomotive Superintendent. However, N&C engines lingered on for a long time on goods and mineral trains, with the last only disappearing in 1886. By then, most of the senior figures inherited from the old company had long gone.

> **NORTH EASTERN RAILWAY.**
>
> **CHANGING OF LINES**
>
> **NEWCASTLE AND CARLISLE**
>
> **SECTION.**
>
> **TAKE NOTICE,**
>
> That on and after MONDAY the 7th day of March, 1864, the Trains on this Section are to run according to the following arrangement, viz.---
>
> Trains from NEWCASTLE to MILTON are to run on the SOUTH LINE.
>
> Trains from MILTON to NEWCASTLE are to run on the NORTH LINE.
>
> BY ORDER.
> Dated this Third day of March, 1864.

The relative independence of the Carlisle Section lasted until 1870, when two things combined to bring it to an end. One was a drive to integrate more fully the sometimes disparate elements of the NER 'federation'; this is exemplified by the consolidation of the share capital in 1870 and the equalisation of goods rates between different sections of the railway in 1871. The other factor was a loss of confidence in the existing management of the Carlisle Section brought about by the St. Nicholas accident of July 1870, in which an NER Canal Branch train, driven by an inebriated fireman, ran straight into a West-Coast express. The subsequent enquiry revealed a very slack state of affairs at Carlisle - Lowry commented on the interim report that 'everyone at Carlisle appears to do whatever he pleases' - and the directors asked O'Brien to report further on the management of the Carlisle line.[67] In due course, Smiles was asked to resign as manager, and did so from 8 February 1871, when the section was brought under Robert Pauling, the divisional goods manager.[68] Joseph Parker, the Superintendent, also resigned and left the company, whereas Smiles was found another post within the NER.[69]

A third departure in February 1871 was that of Captain O'Brien, who was evidently not an entirely well man and left on the 25th. His place was taken by Henry Tennant, the NER Accountant and architect of the consolidated stock scheme, who was to manage the company for the next twenty years.

Allendale, at last.

The eighteen-sixties brought two new branches to feed the Carlisle line. One was the NER's Derwent Valley line from Blackhill (Consett) to Blaydon, which was completed in 1867, opening to freight in June and passengers on 2 December. Two junctions were provided at Blaydon, one facing west to handle the Cumbrian traffic, and the other bridging over the Redheugh Branch to gain access to the south end of Scotswood bridge; this enabled passenger trains to run directly into Central Station.

The other branch was provided by the independent Hexham & Allendale Railway. Thomas Sopwith had continued to press the case for a railway into the dale with both the N&C and his employers. T. W. Beaumont had died at the end of 1848, aged 56, and his eldest son, Wentworth Blackett Beaumont (1829-1907) succeeded to the estates. W. B. was a steadier character than his father and made an energetic attempt to encourage the lead industry by improving facilities.[70] Faced with rising imports of cheap foreign lead, the new railway was seen as a way of cutting costs and remaining competitive. The NER and Greenwich Hospital, which still owned the Langley smelter, each subscribed ten thousand pounds towards the scheme, which received the royal assent on 19 June 1865, and each nominated one director. William Rutherford Hunter represented the NER, Sopwith was, naturally, a director and Beaumont was an active chairman,.[71] The engineer was Thomas John Bewick, engineer to the Beaumont lead mines.[72] Construction got underway briskly and was placed in the hands of William Ritson, his last contract before retiring, just thirty years after helping cousin Jacob to build the N&C itself.

11.8. *Bewick was born in Northumberland and in 1837 became a pupil of Thomas Sopwith. He is said to have been involved in laying out railways during the 'Mania' years of 1844-6 but, as he was still working for Sopwith in autumn 1844, it may be that he was assisting the latter with railway surveys. In 1845 Sopwith became Chief Agent to the Beaumont lead mines and, soon after, Bewick was appointed engineer to the enterprise. At the end of 1865 he gave up this post to supervise the construction of the Allendale line, while he also began to develop an extensive consultancy practice in mining engineering. He invested in mining as well, taking a lease from Greenwich Hospital in 1868 of the mineral rights in Langley barony and establishing Bewick & Partners to work the lead. He lived latterly in London, where he died on 29 August 1897.*

The Act provided for two phases of line: from Border Counties Junction, on the N&C, up to Allendale Town - thirteen miles, and from there up to Allenheads - a further seven.[73] Both entailed savage gradients, with long stretches at 1/50, including the first three miles climbing from the junction; that these were now deemed practical is a tribute to the advance in the steam locomotive since the inception of the Carlisle line. The scheme ran into chronic funding problems, and the second phase was never begun, while the first ran out of steam a mile short of Allendale Town at Catton Road, where the company established its passenger and goods facilities, though a siding continued half a mile further to serve Beaumont's Allen Smelt Mill. This truncated route opened in stages, goods traffic reaching Langley in August 1867 and Catton Road in January 1868. The start of passenger services was delayed until 1 March 1869, largely because of problems in complying with the Board of Trade's requirements at the junction.

The Hexham & Allendale had little future as an independent company, and, under an Act of July 1876, it was sold to the North Eastern at a discount of 40% on the capital actually invested. Its receipts for the first half of that year were similar to earlier ones: £1,148 from goods and only £290 from mineral traffic. By then the local lead industry was in terminal decline. The Allenheads smelter closed in 1870, while Coalcleugh, one of the most productive mines in the area, was given up ten years later. The Allenheads mine and the Allen Smelt Mill closed in 1896, marking the end of the Beaumont lead business.[74] Thus perished, by degrees, the industry which had contributed so much towards the original formation of the 'Newcastle & Carlisle Rail Road'.

11.9. *The Allendale line traffic was a factor in forcing the NER to remodel Hexham station, seen here c1902. Improvements made in 1870-1 include the present platform roofs, while the bay on the right was provided for the Allendale trains The platform and roof disappearing off the picture to the left were added in 1901 for the local service to Newcastle. They have been removed.*
(NERA collection)

Chapter 12: Train Services and Traffic

Road Transport on the Eve of the Railway

Prior to the coming of railways, most people's travelling was very limited, with the vast majority of it being conducted on foot. In rural areas there were some coach services, priced way beyond the reach of ordinary folk, and there were carriers, whose carts and wagons gradually superseded the pack-horses which had long been the mainstay of goods transport. The carriers also conveyed some passengers, and, by the end of 1790, a service of 'stage waggons' was being advertised between Carlisle and London.[1] This took ten days, running via Appleby and York, which was a lot slower than the coaches.

The first third of the nineteenth century brought considerable advances in road services. In 1801 there was just one coach running through between Newcastle and Carlisle, taking all day to complete the journey.[2] On Mondays, Wednesdays and Fridays it set off from Newcastle at 5 a.m. and was forecast to reach Carlisle about 10 in the evening. The following day - Tuesday, Thursday and Saturday - it made the return journey. It will have run via Corbridge to Hexham, while another coach operated a service between Newcastle and Hexham along the south bank of the Tyne, through Ryton. This *Hexham Post* ran from Newcastle on Mondays, Thursdays and Saturdays, filling in the gaps left by the Carlisle service. Its departure was timed to connect with the arrival of the Mail Coach from London - after a two day journey which looks impressively fast compared with the Carlisle route. By 1811 the Carlisle route had acquired a mail coach as well, presumably offering the first daily service.

In 1801 three carriers appear to have operated right through between Newcastle and Carlisle, continuing further west to Whitehaven, Cockermouth and Dumfries. They left Newcastle on Tuesdays and Thursdays, the Tuesday service arriving in Carlisle on Friday evening, while the Thursday service was more speedy - getting there on Saturday. In addition one carrier operated on the more demanding route from Newcastle to Alston, serving Corbridge and Hexham on the way. This was a weekly service, leaving Newcastle each Monday and getting back on Friday. The Alston Moor road improvements sponsored by Greenwich Hospital enabled a coach to be introduced on this route in 1828, running between Hexham and Penrith. This was evidently a success, and the following year saw the introduction of a brand-new four-horse coach, *Balloon*, and an extension of the service through to Newcastle.[3]

Vignette by Thomas Bewick

The London, York & Newcastle coach outside Newcastle's Turf Hotel

Roads and road services generally improved a lot during the first third of the nineteenth century, and by 1834 the coach services in the Tyne Valley had reached the position shown in Table 12.1, with two running through between Newcastle and Carlisle and a further three serving the stretch east of Hexham.

Table 12.1. Coach services between Newcastle and Carlisle in 1834

	Westbound					Eastbound				
	M	**TB**	**B**	**BQ**	**DS**	**DS**	**BQ**	**M**	**TB**	**B**
Newcastle	07.00	08.00	09.00	16.00	16.00	10.30	10.30	13.30	16.30	19.00
Ryton		09.00			17.00	09.30			15.30	
Corbridge	09.00		11.30	18.00			08.30	11.30		16.30
Hexham	09.30	10.45	12.00	18.30	19.00	07.30	08.00	10.45	13.30	16.00
Haydon Bridge	10.30	12.00	13.00					10.00	12.00	15.00
Alston			16.00							12.00
Penrith			19.00							09.00
Haltwhistle	11.30	13.15						09.30	11.30	
Brampton	13.30	15.00						07.00	09.00	
Carlisle	14.30	16.00						06.00	08.00	

M - *Royal Mail*   Every Day. *Queen's Head*, Newcastle; *White Hart*, Hexham; *Red Lion*, Haltwhistle; *Howard Arms*, Brampton.
TB - *True Briton*   Mon. to Sat. *Turf*, Newcastle; *Black Bull*, Hexham; *Sun*, Haltwhistle; *Scotch Arms*, Brampton.
B - *Balloon.*   Westbound: Mon., Wed., Fri. Eastbound: Tue., Thur., Sat. *Half Moon*, Newcastle.
BQ - *British Queen*   Mon. to Sat. *Half Moon*, Newcastle.
DS - *Dr. Syntax*   Mon. to Sat. *White Hart*, Newcastle.

These are departure times, and the hour and a quarter allowed for the *True Briton* between Hexham and Haydon Bridge hints at the refreshment stops which were included in some of these schedules. It and the *Royal Mail* differed from the other operators in requiring two coaches each to provide their daily service.

148

Railway Traffic and Train Services: 1834-5

As we observed in chapter 6, traffic on the railway began in 1834, but was limited to Beaumont and Crawhall lead, conveyed under the private arrangement made during August. Joseph Ritson was engaged to carry it at ¾d per ton-mile, finding his own horses and probably employing the company's spoil wagons. It is unclear whether the lead began to trickle through on schedule from the end of August, but 491½ tons had been conveyed from Hexham by the end of the year as well as 115½ tons from Stocksfield, railhead for Beaumont's Dukesfield smelter, which was then being run down prior to closure.[4] In November the Board discussed an application by the owners of the *Dr. Syntax* coach, who wished to have their vehicle conveyed along the line, but the Managing directors discouraged this idea because of the danger posed by stretches of temporary way. The first goods were conveyed on the line on Christmas Eve 1834 for Mr. Stobart, a Hexham tanner, reported in the *Newcastle Chronicle* of 3 January.

Public services began on 10 March 1835, the day after the formal opening between Hexham and Blaydon. The company had only just acquired its first two locomotives, *Comet* and *Rapid*, and one was based at either end of the line. Each ran two return trips per day on the scheduled trains, which left Blaydon and Hexham simultaneously, at 8 and 11 a.m. and 2 and 5 p.m.[5] Arrival times were not published at first, but the seventeen-mile journey was allowed an hour and a half, the trains being mixed - in that they conveyed both passengers and goods. The goods wagons were marshalled between the engine and the passenger carriages, so that they could easily be attached or detached, if required, at the intermediate stations. Connections between Blaydon and Newcastle were provided by coaches operated by Joseph Hindhaugh, in an arrangement with the company, while there was also a steamer service, but the sailing times of the one boat varied according to the tides.

A passenger setting out for the first train from Blaydon would have caught the coach from St. Nicholas Square, Newcastle, at 7.15 a.m. and arrived at Hexham by about 9.30, which is barely an improvement on the timing of the *Royal Mail* coach, which continued to run. However, the railway offered far more accommodation than the coaches and a much wider choice of travel times. It was not, however, all that cheap. For its first decade the N&C only offered first and second-class carriages, plus the option of travelling 'outside' in the old stage-coach fashion. Thus in March 1835 the railway fares for a single journey from Blaydon to Hexham were 2s first class and 1s 6d second class or outside, with Mr. Hindhaugh's coach adding a further 8d inside or 6d outside. To put this in context, an agricultural labourer was earning about two shillings a day.[6]

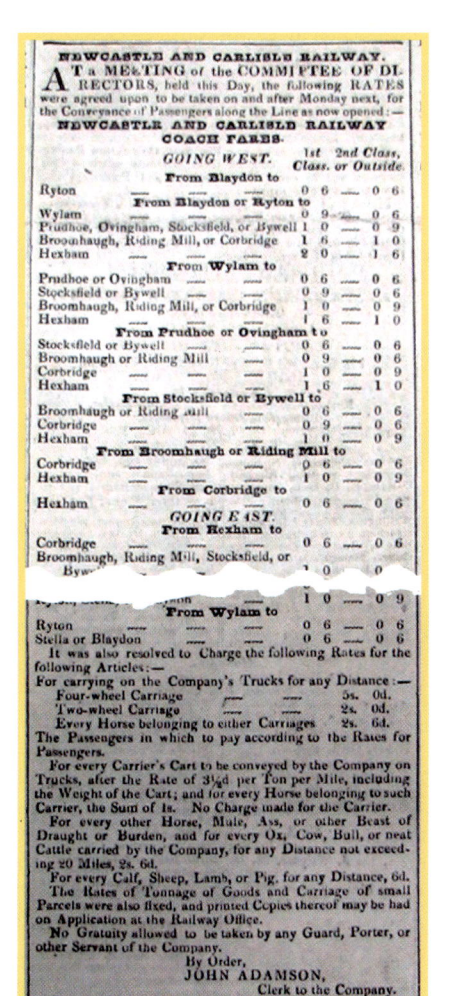

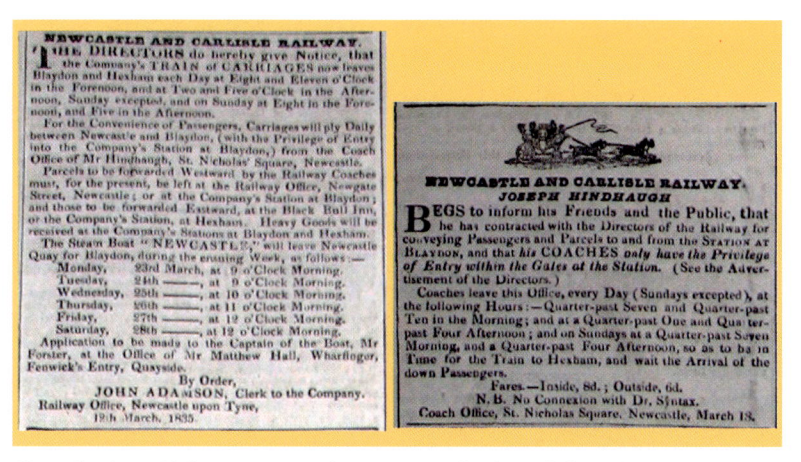

12.1. *The first N&C newspaper advertisements for fares (left) and services.*

The railway also conveyed private carriages, which would be roped down on a low flat wagon, then commonly known as a 'truck'. The charge for this was five shillings (two shillings if it was a small, two-wheeler) plus the usual passenger fares. Mr. Radford, proprietor of the *True Briton* coach, took up this option and was granted favourable terms in that the railway waived the carriage fee and just charged him the passenger fares. The directors also offered these terms to the GPO in September 1835 for the conveyance of the mail coach.[7] Despite an accident in October 1835, when the *True Briton* overturned while travelling on the railway, the coach continued in business like this until shortly after the opening of the west end of the line in July 1836.[8]

The traffic receipts from the beginning of the lead traffic through to the end of 1835 tell their own story. The company earned gross revenues of £4,503 from passengers, £2,997 from lead, and £1,737 from goods and parcels.[9] This was a very creditable start, given that the coal traffic would not become substantial until further stretches of line had opened.

Train Services: 1836-9

June 1836 brought the extension of services to Haydon Bridge, which became the railhead for Allendale and Alston lead traffic and a locomotive stabling point. The following month saw the opening between Blenkinsopp and Carlisle, with public trains operating from Greenhead and a road coach filling in the gap between there and Haydon Bridge. The west end completion also brought significant amounts of coal traffic onto the railway at last, principally from the Earl of Carlisle's collieries. The benefits of this can be seen in the gross revenue for 1836, which was £23,688. The coal trains heading down from Milton (Brampton Junction) to Carlisle must have been an awesome sight to people accustomed to horses and carts. In May 1837 the *Carlisle Journal* reported one of 73 wagons, drawn by the *Goliah* engine and weighing 330 tons gross. Two months later they reported *Atlas* taking a hundred wagons of coal in a train a quarter mile long and weighing some 450 tons. Most of this journey was down a gradient of 1/107 so the engine had little work to do but there was very little braking power available other than the wagon brakes themselves.

At this stage, operating practices on the line were still somewhat primitive, as recorded at the time by Richard Lowry, who began his railway career as a clerk at the Carlisle station on the day it opened. Each train was accompanied by a guard, some of whom worked right through from Newcastle on train and coach. On several occasions Lowry found himself standing in for a guard who had been ordered elsewhere, usually on the first train of the day - the 7 o'clock from Carlisle to Greenhead. This evidently made a pleasant change from London Road, but one day he got slightly more than he bargained for. When he got to Greenhead he found that no guard had come through from Newcastle, and he was therefore obliged to accompany the passengers on their onward journey.[10] He ended up acting as guard most of the way to Newcastle, on a stretch of line he had never before travelled, on which he 'was ignorant when to make the signals'. Fortunately from Hexham, George Bates, the agent, went on the train with him 'until we met the regular guard'. The outcome was a night in Newcastle and a leisurely stroll next morning round the town where Lowry was later to become agent. He also gives us an idea just what a mixed train might have entailed in the early days, referring to one in August 1836 which comprised '48 wagons'. This was evidently a mineral train with additional vehicles, not one of the timetabled mixed passenger trains, and he referred to 34 being coal wagons, 8 or 9 were full of passengers and there were some with carriages and horses.

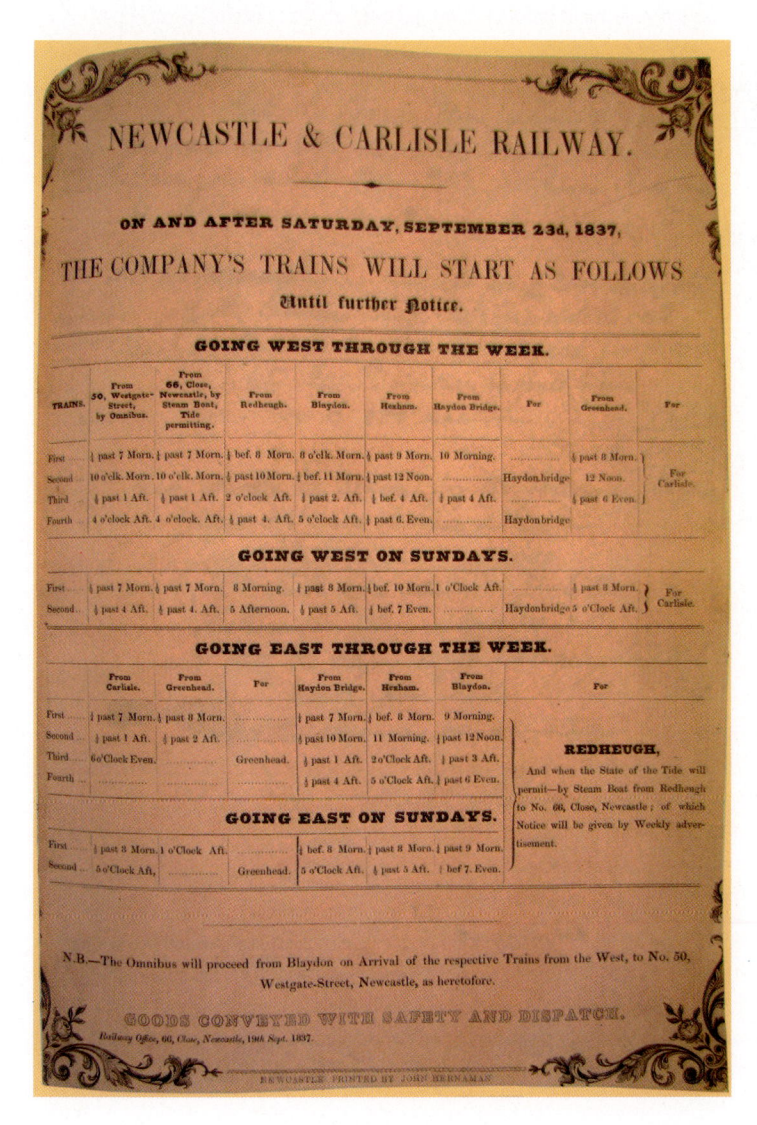

March 1837 saw the public opening of the extension to Redheugh, and the N&C began to offer a through service for goods, which entailed transhipment at Haydon Bridge and Greenhead. Lowry noted that this began with no warehousing facilities at Carlisle and without even weighing machines to check the weights stated by their customers.[11] A lot of grain was soon shipped west and at the end of March the company received a bill for 178 stones (1.11 tonnes) of wheat which had allegedly gone astray.[12] It transpired that it had been rebagged to facilitate carriage and none had been lost, though in the absence of recorded weights this was hard to prove.

The directors' negligence in this matter is hard to credit since the Stockton & Darlington had employed weighing apparatus from the outset. Machines were soon purchased for Redheugh and Carlisle, the latter one coming into use on 22 May, when Lowry observed how the railway had been exploited by some customers. One consignment, nominally 2 tons 15 cwt, weighed in at 3 tons and another, said to be 1 ton 10 cwt, came in at 1 ton 18 cwt. Correcting these two alone meant an extra revenue of 4s 2d for the journey from Carlisle to Greenhead.

The Redheugh opening brought a new look to passenger services. The company provided a steam boat across the Tyne from Redheugh to a Newcastle riverside 'station' at 66, The Close, but the upper town was still served by an omnibus running between Blaydon and an office at 50, Westgate Road. The winter timetable, starting 23 September, is reproduced here and shows still four trains each way - all mixed traffic - running over the east end as far as Haydon Bridge.[13]

150

Two of these trains continued as coach services from Haydon Bridge to Greenhead, whence there were three trains daily to Carlisle. A traveller could now leave Redheugh at 7.45 a.m., transferring to a 10 a.m. coach from Haydon Bridge. Then came the slowest part of the journey, two hours being allowed for transfers and the twelve mile stretch to Greenhead; from there the noon departure brought an arrival in Carlisle soon after one o-clock.

June 1838 brought the completion of the central section, and through running at last. One consequence was the introduction of express trains, conveying only passengers and calling at only seven of the intermediate stations (a third of the total), which did the sixty mile trip in exactly three hours. The station stops were Blaydon, Stocksfield, Hexham, Haydon Bridge, Haltwhistle, Rose Hill (Gilsland) and Milton. These must have taken up about half an hour, implying an average speed of 24 mph. Something close to three hours remained the best time between Newcastle and Carlisle for the next two decades. There were four through trains each way: two ran as expresses and the other two continued as mixed trains, conveying both passengers and goods, and taking four hours. Speed came at a cost, with passengers paying a shilling more to travel the full length of the line on the 'quick' trains; this made the first and second class express fares from Newcastle to Carlisle 11s and 8s 6d (single). As well as the through service there was a mixed train in the evening from Redheugh to Haydon Bridge, whose stock presumably returned on the morning stopping train from Carlisle. There was also, for a few months, a comparable evening train from Carlisle to Haltwhistle, but this had been dropped before the introduction of the 1839 summer timetable, reproduced here. A feature of this era was the survival of local time, Carlisle being twelve minutes behind Greenwich until the adoption of 'London time' in December 1841. Trains kept Newcastle time, and some timetable sheets bore a notice to this effect.

The completion of the route is reflected in the growth of passenger traffic from just over three million passenger miles in 1838 to a little over four million the following year. This made the N&C the largest passenger carrier in the North East, though if you divide these figures by the route mileage to obtain an index, its performance was not very different from that of the Leeds & Selby Railway, opened in 1834 and a line which also enjoyed a broad range of traffic.

12.2. *(opposite)*
The timetable starting in September 1837, with coach services filling in the gap in the middle. Note that the steam boat from Redheugh to The Close could only operate at reasonably high tides, because of the sand banks in the river, so a weekly timetable for this was advertised in the newspapers.

12.3. *(right)*
The Summer 1839 Timetable. The train vignette at the head is the printer's standard one but does convey something of the atmosphere of early travel on the N&C, with a 'close' first-class carriage followed by an open-sided second.

151

Making Connections: 1839-49

October 1839 brought the long-awaited opening of the railway to Newcastle, with the temporary station at Railway Street being linked to the town centre, barely a mile distant, by omnibus. Despite this, the company's first Newcastle 'station', the old riverside mansion at No. 66, The Close, served by boat from Redheugh, remained in use for goods until the end of 1841, closing then as an economy. Its site is now occupied by the west end of the former fishmarket. 1839 also saw an end to the railway's isolation, with the opening of the Brandling Junction and Newcastle & North Shields Railways, though the N&C had no physical link to the latter. Goods and mineral traffic could now be exchanged with the Brandling company. Since passenger trains now served both banks of the Tyne, the through trains to and from Carlisle were combined and split at Blaydon. The actual pattern of services was little altered.

The timetabled service was augmented by a variety of special trains, such as the one laid on in March 1842 to convey the assize judge and barristers from Newcastle to Carlisle. Security was ensured by the presence of Lowry, Blackmore, John Chantler, the Traffic Superintendent, and Anthony Hall, the Locomotive Superintendent, who all enjoyed their day out. Hall took the opportunity to show what his engines could do on a light train by completing the journey in only 2¼ hours.[14]

1844 brought the main line from London to Tyneside, though little of it by the familiar route. Passengers started from Euston station, travelling via Rugby and Derby to York; they left the present route again at Ferryhill and entered Gateshead over the tracks now used by the Sunderland trains. At Gateshead, George Hudson provided an elegant passenger terminus, designed by his friend George Townsend Andrews, and this became a connecting point between his trains and those of the Carlisle company. The main line from the south was formally opened on 18 June, with regular services beginning the following day, when the N&C introduced a new timetable, giving Gateshead as its south bank terminus. This, for the first time, entailed the haulage of N&C passenger trains by stationary engine - as Benjamin Thompson had originally wished - in order to travel up and down the Redheugh Incline. Perhaps to avoid the incline, some trains now ran only to and from Newcastle.

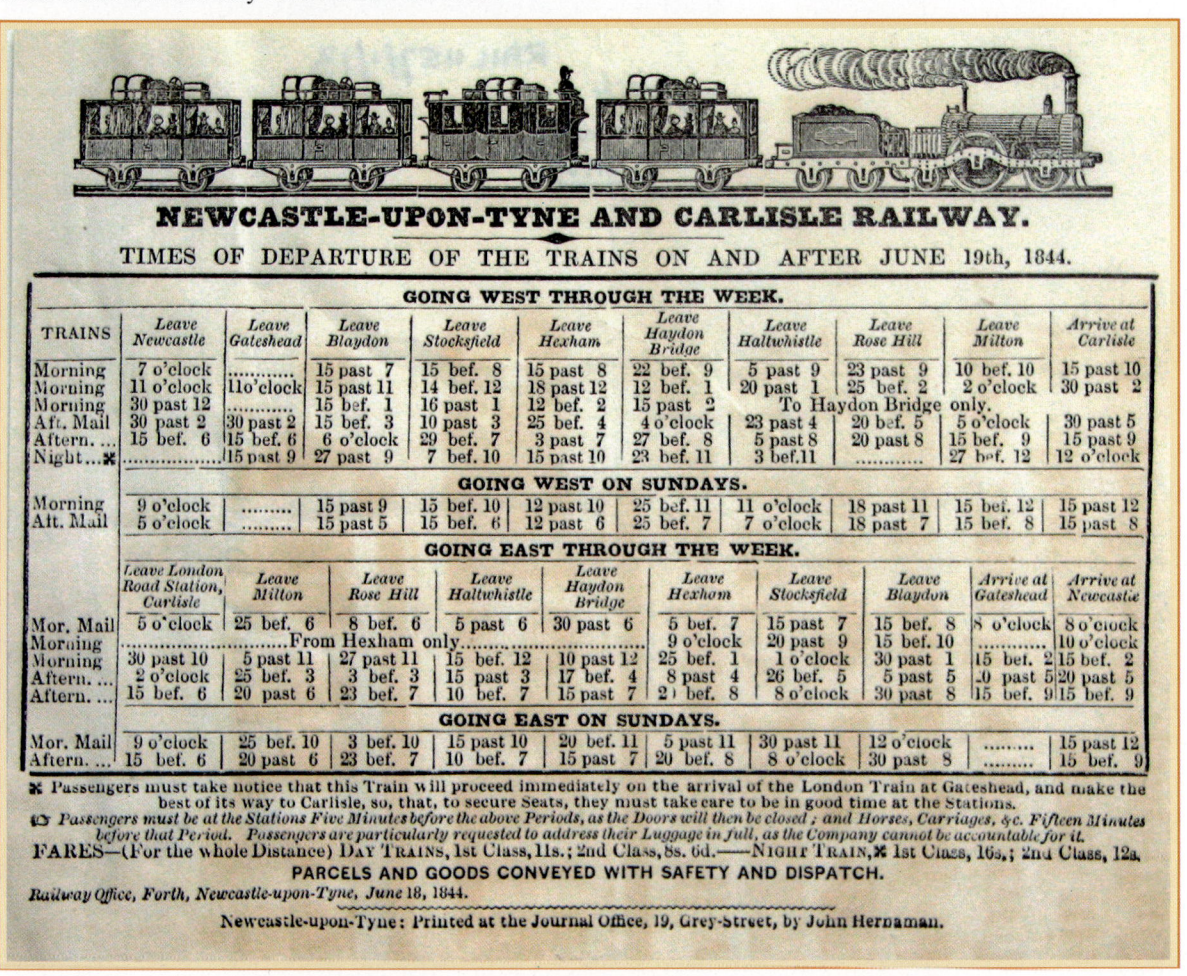

The London connection entailed a recasting of the N&C timetable. One of the few trains not to be altered was the express *Afternoon Mail*, which still left Newcastle and Gateshead at 2.30. A major innovation was an evening express, connecting with the London train and requiring hefty surcharges of 5s, first class, and 3s 6d, second. This left Gateshead nominally at 9.15 p.m. and was scheduled to reach Carlisle at midnight. Waiting for the London train probably entailed more than a few late departures and it probably had difficulty keeping time. Bradshaw's 1845 timetable shows it retimed and allowed the usual three hours.

12.5. *The Carlisle end of Gateshead Greenesfield station, with the replacement Redheugh incline engine house, also completed in 1844, on the left. (Bill Fawcett)*

12.4. *(opposite) The new timetable of 19 June 1844. The 'single-driver' engine shown in the vignette is a type of express locomotive unknown on the N&C.*

Connections at Carlisle were a different matter. It is easy to visualise the railway ending in splendid isolation until the arrival of the Maryport company in May 1843 and the Lancaster & Carlisle in December 1846. This is very misleading, however, since it linked up with a variety of steamer services, principally those to Liverpool, Dublin, Belfast and Glasgow. Passenger trains only ran as far as London Road, with connecting omnibuses to the Canal Basin. The arrival of other railways at Carlisle seems to have had little effect on N&C passenger schedules, and the main feature of the later eighteen-forties is an increase in the number of through services. 1844 had seen the introduction of five each way and a speeding up of the stopping trains, implying that the practice of mixed trains had probably been abandoned, a change which John Blackmore had advocated for several years.[15] 1847 saw six through trains, but the Hudson lease and the depressed financial climate of 1849 saw this drop back to five.

Third-class accommodation was introduced from 13 April 1846, initially by attaching a converted second-class carriage to two trains in each direction: the 6 a.m. and 4 p.m. from Newcastle and the 5.45 a.m. and 4.15 p.m. from Carlisle.[16] This was something the N&C had resisted at first, because of a fear, common to most Victorian railways, that they would lose second-class traffic as a result. Plummer told the March AGM that the directors' aim was 'to offer the humbler classes a cheap conveyance.' In reality, their minds had been concentrated by Gladstone's Regulation of Railways Act, passed in August 1844. Clause 6 of this stipulated that new railways should provide daily trains, stopping at all stations and providing covered third-class accommodation at a rate of no more than one penny a mile. The N&C was not obliged to provide such 'Parliamentary' trains but the Act extended these provisions to existing railways once they sought extended powers. Thus the company's Alston Branch Bill, before Parliament in the spring of 1846, would have brought them within the scope of Gladstone's Act anyway. However, in providing third-class carriages on two trains they were going beyond the bare minimum.

Passenger timetables give no idea of the actual number of trains using the line. Collieries were developing at both ends, although much of their traffic will initially have involved fairly short hauls. The west end, for example, had coal traffic heading into Carlisle from the South Tyne colliery at Haltwhistle, as well as Blenkinsopp and those of the Earl of Carlisle. It was to get a lot busier with the traffic in iron ore and Durham coal and coke, which built up during the following decade.

Train Services: 1850 - 1870

Given the financial problems facing almost all British railways at the start of the eighteen-fifties, it is not surprising to find the passenger service further cut back, so that only four trains ran right through, with another simply operating between Newcastle and Hexham. On 29 August 1850 Queen Victoria and Prince Albert opened Newcastle Central Station, and the following day saw it come into use for the traffic of the York, Newcastle & Berwick Railway, whereupon Gateshead Greenesfield station was closed. This left the N&C without a south bank home, other than Redheugh, and the daily passenger service on the Redheugh branch was subsequently abandoned. Central Station was, however, incomplete and the N&C did not transfer their trains into it until 1 January 1851. This only entailed a short hop, since the company's temporary Forth terminus, in use since 1 March 1847, lay only yards from the west end of Central.

The 1854 timetable provides an interesting snapshot of services. Of the four through trains two did the journey in three hours, the others in three and a quarter; unlike the expresses of 1838, however, they all stopped at all twenty intermediate stations. At Haltwhistle, connections were made with the two trains operating each way on the Alston Branch, worked by an engine based overnight at the terminus. East of Blaydon, there were no fewer than nine Saturday market trains running each way to Newcastle, three of which worked to and from Derwenthaugh to provide the only passenger service on the Redheugh branch. Once a day connecting coach services ran from Hexham to Bellingham and Haydon Bridge to Allenheads.

No-one would pretend that the Newcastle & Carlisle was a swift railway, but nor was it outrageously slow. A York & North Midland Railway stopping train on the 32 mile route from York to Leeds (then operating via Castleford) took at best 1½ hours, while stopping trains on the 90 mile Carlisle - Preston route were allowed four hours. Nonetheless, the N&C enjoyed a dubious reputation. William Woods referred to this when addressing a shareholders' meeting on the subject of amalgamation, in February 1859. 'They were called a slow coach. (hear! hear!) But perhaps they were not aware that when their carriages and engines were in motion they moved at the rate of thirty miles an hour ... the trains were compelled to stop ... at about 20 places regularly, and others where they were obliged to stop if there was a signal shown for the purpose. [the private 'flag' stopping places for Naworth Castle, Blenkinsopp Hall, Ridley Hall and Dilston] It was impossible to transact all the business ... at these places without occupying a full hour...'

Despite Woods' claims, there was room for improvement. Merger with the NER was followed by the move into Carlisle Citadel station, from 1 January 1863, while limited-stop expresses were re-introduced. The 1865 timetable shows two westbound mails doing the journey in 2 hours 40 minutes; the eastbound time was ten minutes longer, while the stopping trains had also been speeded a little. The Alston Branch had gone up to three trains, still worked by the one engine, and also acquired a Sunday service of two trains, timed to allow a full day there for visitors or away for residents. Sunday trains were, however, not to everyone's liking.

Sunday Trains and Excursions

In England, concerns about Sunday observance were largely a fruit of the Evangelical movement. Thus a majority of railway directors, while usually practising Christians, saw nothing incompatible about running trains on Sundays, so long as they paid their way. The N&C ran regular Sunday trains from the outset, although a determined effort was made by opponents to secure a clause banning these in the 1835 Act which enabled the use of locomotives. Petitions were raised for and against Sunday travel, with many more names being enlisted for than against, but the bishops fought hard for the ban, which was defeated in the Lords by only a single vote. Sunday also became a popular day on which to run excursions, since for most people this was the only day of the week free from work.

Although railway fares were very expensive at this time, companies were quick to latch on to the potential of excursion traffic, indeed the Liverpool & Manchester ran its first excursions in 1830. The N&C also developed a considerable excursion traffic. Two examples from 1840 illustrate the use of excursion tickets, on regular trains, and special excursion trains. During May the company offered excursion fares for people wishing to attend the Polytechnic Exhibition in Newcastle.[17] The following month brought a special Sunday train from Newcastle to Carlisle, run for employees of the Tyneside engine building firm of R & W. Hawthorn and their friends. This ran on 14 June, and attracted 320 passengers, paying half fare. This was good business, and also a very popular enterprise.

Richard Lowry moved to Newcastle in April 1841 as Agent in charge of goods and passenger traffic at the Railway Street station, and he soon became a keen advocate of excursion trains, finding a ready response from Matthew Plummer. Some were arranged to serve sporting fixtures such as the races or social institutions like Stagshaw Bank Fair, near Corbridge. The special train Lowry organised from Newcastle to Carlisle on 16 May 1842 displayed his ingenuity to the full.[18] Through the efforts of John Scott, agent at Blaydon, they got the services of the well-known Winlaton Band for nothing (the bandsmen welcomed the outing) and they played at Blaydon and along the way. Passenger numbers were a respectable 150 by the time they reached Haydon Bridge and about forty of these got out at Rose Hill, for Gilsland. A special stop was made on the Eden Viaduct, so that passengers could admire the scenery, again serenaded by the band. This made for a slow outward journey: leaving Newcastle at half past seven and reaching Carlisle at noon. The return was much swifter, leaving the Border City about five and reaching Newcastle at eight. The fare was 7s 6d and Lowry noted that the depressed state of the economy meant there were 'very few workmen' on the train.

Sunday excursions were a contentious issue. One to Carlisle in August 1841 led to the well-known poster denouncing it as a trip to Hell - a diatribe mounted by a Scottish clergyman, Burns, who happened to be in Newcastle at the time. The following year Lowry eased the directors into the idea of running Sunday trips from Newcastle to Gilsland and Carlisle as a regular summer feature. He began with one of 14 August, which carried 244 passengers, about 150 of whom got out for Gilsland, producing a clear profit of about £50, enough to pay Lowry's salary for six months.[19] However, the directors were unwilling to sanction Sunday trips from Carlisle because of the opposition of the Board's 'Sunday Saints', notably Peter Dixon. He took up the cudgels against all Sunday trains, and excursions in particular, at a directors' meeting in May 1843, but found little support. Indeed, John Brandling made the point that 'Sunday was made for the poor man to enjoy recreation and were he a poor man he should enjoy it to the fullest extent'.[20] Perhaps this cleared the air, since on 9 September the *Carlisle Journal* was to be found advertising an excursion to Newcastle on Sunday the 17th, leaving at 6.30 in the morning with the options of returning that day or on Monday morning.

The 1847 AGM brought a two-pronged attack on Sunday travel by a west-end landowner, Thomas Graham of Edmonds Castle, and Christopher Bird, Vicar of Warden.[21] Graham presented memorials on behalf of Lord's Day observance societies in Carlisle and Newcastle, while Bird produced one signed by forty clergymen - almost all those whose parishes lay along the railway. In the discussion that followed it emerged that the directors had reduced the number of regular Sunday trains, while they received support from a distinguished cleric, John Collinson, who argued that Sunday trains were a 'proper and suitable accommodation for the public.' The motion against Sunday travel was overwhelmingly lost, but one was readily passed asking the Board to consider regulations which would prevent the trains from 'interfering

Carlisle Market: Tickets available by the ordinary trains. Similar facilities were provided for the Hexham market on Tuesdays.

Naworth Castle was gutted by fire on 18 May 1844, despite the efforts of the railway, which bore the Carlisle fire engine to the scene. A valuable collection of paintings and books was destroyed, but at least the ruins provided popular entertainment and traffic for the railway, which ran several excursion trains. These also served the more traditional venue of Gilsland Spa.

Special trains were run for the races and other sporting events, such as wrestling and boat races on the Tyne.

12.6. Special Fares and Special Trains

with the hours of divine service.' The outcome was an own goal. Trains were halted at Haydon Bridge and Haltwhistle to let passengers attend church, but instead most went to public houses (unrestricted in opening hours) and 'were in danger of losing their lives from the drink they had taken, besides being a source of great trouble and anxiety to those in charge of the train'.[22] So the trains ran straight through, as before, excursionists being allowed half-fare on the regular Sunday services.

The Sunday trains vote became a regular feature of each AGM, with only a handful of shareholders supporting the motion. It achieved nothing, but it let off steam and was generally conducted with courtesy. Meanwhile the excursions themselves grew in scope. 1845 brought one from Newcastle to Dublin and the Isle of Man in conjunction with the steamer *Royal Victoria*, for 30s (to Dublin) 'first class and cabin' and 15s 'second class and deck'.[23] Leaving Newcastle at 5 in the morning of 19 August, passengers were due to reach Dublin early the following day and leave it at 2 p.m. on the 21st. Subsequently, the arrival of the Caledonian Railway saw excursions extended into Scotland.

155

12.7. *An early view of Scotby station, with the engine of an eastbound train standing in front of the coal and lime depot. This was roofed to protect the lime, which was a very important commodity for both construction and agriculture. The east gable and chimneys of the station house can just be glimpsed on the left, while the factory was Sutton's leather works. The locomotive was evidently designed in the artist's imagination. The revolving disk signal, on the pole to the right, may be a genuine feature as it also appears in another engraving of this spot. The vignette was engraved by MacMillan, of Carlisle, for Sutton's billhead. (courtesy of Carlisle Library)*

Traffic

We have seen that, at the outset, the revenue of the company was split almost equally between passengers and freight. This gives a somewhat misleading picture, in that the coal traffic had not then developed. By 1839, for example, though passenger traffic was growing rapidly it formed only 38% of gross revenue. If we look at the last full year of the company's existence, 1861, gross revenue was £190,676, to which passengers contributed a quarter. Goods traffic accounted for a third, and coal and minerals 35%. The cattle trade contributed all of £5,714 - just 3%, respectable but not quite the important feature which the early promoters had in mind when talking of the Belfast cattle trade.

Coal, coke and iron ore were the most important single elements in the freight sector, and, despite the opening of the competing route across Stainmore at the beginning of the eighteen-sixties, the N&C continued to handle a considerable traffic in these. In one sense, of course, the Stainmore route ceased to be a competitor in 1863, with the merger of the S&D into the NER. In reality, there was enough business around for both, and the Carlisle route retained a major share, though its traffic now displayed a more local catchment, with all the South Durham business going via Stainmore.

Coke shipments to the West Cumberland ironworks make the point.[24] The volume handled by the Carlisle line rose from 123,982 tons in 1865 to 238,086 in 1870, but it tended to come from collieries readily served by the route. The figures for September 1867 illustrate this, with 31% being consigned by the Mickley Coal Company at Prudhoe, which had developed because of its location on the N&C. Marley Hill, which shipped 24%, was served by the Tanfield Branch, which fed into the Redheugh line. The iron ore tells a similar story. 88,819 tons were shipped over the N&C route from Cumberland in 1865, but Consett accounted for 76% of this and generated £27,086 of revenue, although just under a third of this had to be handed over to the Cumbrian railways.

Traffic with Ireland had been one of the prospects held out in the early days, and the N&C did develop a considerable export traffic in coal, shipped out via Maryport and Silloth. Nicholas Wood made the point in respect of Marley Hill colliery when giving evidence on the 1862 NER/N&C merger Bill.[25] 'We [Marley Hill] had a good many coke ovens in Ireland and sent the coal up the line to Maryport and then sent it to Ireland for the locomotives - I believe we did at one time supply almost all Ireland with coke.' He spoke in the past tense because of the changeover to burning coal in locomotives, but the railway was still handling a considerable 'export' coal traffic in the eighteen-sixties. In 1864 Maryport took 32,598 tons and Silloth 24,430. The Silloth trade was dominated by the Earl of Carlisle's collieries - contributing 96%. By contrast they formed only 19% of the Maryport business, with the Mickley Coal Company having the largest share, at 53%. There was also a considerable traffic to the landsale coal depots in Carlisle, which were taking just over fifty thousand tons a year in the eighteen-sixties, supplied largely by the Earl of Carlisle and Coanwood colliery, opened up by the Blenkinsopp proprietors on the Alston branch.

The Irish goods traffic was encouraged by combining with the steamer companies to offer through rates from Belfast and Dublin, but proved useful rather than important. The main business was in farm exports, particularly bacon and live cattle. The bacon had formerly found its chief market in London, but the railway opened up a profitable market on Tyneside, to the benefit of producers and consumers alike. In addition, the company found itself part of another sea link in the late thirties and early forties, with Irish provisions being forwarded from the Tyne by boat to Hull.[26]

12.9. *(opposite) A rare photograph of a train in Newcastle & Carlisle days, apparently taken in the late eighteen-fifties. The setting is Blaydon station and we are looking east from a front window of the agent's house. (stationmaster in later parlance) The station layout at this time is shown in figure 6.9. The station building is on the right, with a hipped trainshed sheltering the single platform and its track which loops off the running lines In front of the station building is a chaldron wagon, standing on the coal depot, which is at right angles to the running lines, and reached by a turnplate. The coal train waiting to head west appears to be hauled by a recent product of Robert Hawthorn, while the train behind looks to have one of the earlier locomotives. To the right of the leading engine is a locomotive water crane possibly supplied by the Carlisle cranemakers, Cowans Sheldon. Note the revolving disk signal atop a tall white pole in front of the trainshed.*

(supplied by Stafford Linsley)

12.8. *The operation of a coal depot is evident from this view of Hexham, taken about 1970, with the station house, original but much extended, in the background. Bottom-door hopper wagons, successors to the original chaldron wagons, run onto tracks laid on timber waybeams. These are supported on a series of stone cross-walls, forming a sequence of cells into which the wagons can discharge. Originally, a number of different tenants might have leased cells at a depot. Under the North Eastern Railway, this 'landsale' coal business became a perquisite of the stationmaster, sometimes a very valuable one. Hexham coalyard continued in use long after coal had ceased to arrive there by rail, but it is now the station car park.* (Bill Fawcett)

Mails

Railways were under a legal obligation to carry the Mails when requested to do so by the Post Master General, and the railway began conveying them between Newcastle and Carlisle on 24 July 1838. Francis Whishaw, visiting the line the following year, recorded the well-designed mail carriages provided by the company. (see chapter 13) At the end of July 1854, the N&C made the last of successive agreements with the Post Office for the mail traffic on the main line, and this is worth closer examination.[27]

It provided for the N&C to receive a thousand pounds a year, in quarterly payments, in return for conveying 'Mails and Post Letter Bags' between Carlisle and Newcastle and Gateshead. Mail carriages were 'to be provided as hitherto at the sole cost and charge' of the railway, 'which shall take up and deliver mail' at the intermediate stations. The mails were to be placed in the charge of the N&C's passenger guards. The agreement included a schedule setting out a timetable for those trains regularly conveying the mails, while the Post Office retained the right to require their conveyance also on other trains when necessary. The Alston Branch did not feature in this agreement, and was the subject of a separate one, of 7 November 1859, which made no reference to any previous arrangement. Thus the conveyance of mails by train between Haltwhistle and Alston appears to have begun at the start of December 1859, in return for an annual fee of £50.

Through Rates and Through Traffic

In evidence on the unsuccessful 1860 NER/N&C merger Bill, T. E. Harrison made much of the N&C's reluctance to develop through traffic onto other railways.[28] This was a somewhat ingenuous argument. It is true that Woods and his colleagues took a rather parochial view, aimed at producing a good revenue with minimum investment, yet they had developed the Cumbrian ore and coke traffic and they had also offered through rates for Liverpool traffic until dissuaded from doing so by the NER itself. Through traffic posed two significant problems: one was to ensure an adequate return from goods and minerals which might be travelling only a short distance along one's line; the other was how to avoid an expensive investment in additional rolling stock.

To take the latter issue first. The N&C had a wagon stock which was entirely adequate for the traffic running between Newcastle and Carlisle; if it were to run through any significant distance on other lines, either the company would require extra stock or arrangements would have to be put in hand for the common running of its wagons with those of other companies. Such arrangements did develop, but a stumbling block here was Harrison himself, who had no wish to see unsprung N&C chaldron wagons, in particular, working significant distances over NER rails at a time when he was trying to abolish this type of stock on the NER in order to reduce permanent-way maintenance costs.[29] He was also seeking to introduce larger wagons, in order to reduce working costs.

Thus a bizarre situation developed with respect to the Cumbrian ore traffic. In the eighteen-fifties this was worked from the Whitehaven area, over the Whitehaven & Furness Junction and Maryport & Carlisle Railways, in wagons provided by the N&C but these only ran through to Blaydon.[30] There the ore was transhipped into lighters, owned by the railway, and taken down river for delivery onto the NER. The exact arrangements are unclear, but it is likely that Consett ore was shipped to the NER's Gateshead (Hillgate) Quay, to be despatched via Washington over the Pontop Branch.[31]

The short distance issue should have been easier to resolve. Because goods and minerals incurred handling costs at either end of their journey which were independent of journey length, railways charged higher rates for short distances. The N&C charged all traffic consigned for less than six miles at the rate applicable to a six mile journey. This meant that, in the absence of a through rate, people would pay through the nose for goods travelling a short distance over the N&C as part of a much longer railway journey. The problem is exemplified by the case of Sir William Armstrong, who had the potential to become a valuable customer of the railway.[32]

William George Armstrong (1810-1900), later Baron Armstrong of Cragside, was one of the major figures of nineteenth-century industry. He first developed the neglected science of hydraulic power, then established a modern ordnance industry, and went on to build warships as well. Elswick was the locus of Armstrong's activity. Here, in 1847, he established his factory on a site sandwiched between two valuable transport links: the Carlisle Railway and the River Tyne. It developed into an integrated plant, with its own blast furnaces, taking in raw materials and churning out finished products, initially hydraulic cranes for railways and docks. Armstrong and the railway were good neighbours; the directors allowed him to build his workshops partly on top of the retaining wall forming the southern boundary of the line, yet the traffic which developed for the N&C during the eighteen-fifties was comparatively small. The reason for this was that most of Armstrong's traffic was heading to and from the east, with little more than a mile to travel over the Carlisle line.

Two traffic flows exemplify this: the supply of coal and despatch of ordnance. At this time Armstrong obtained his coal from collieries north-east of Newcastle, served by the Blyth & Tyne Railway (B&T). To haul it throughout by train would have entailed running over the NER's Tynemouth Branch and then the N&C. The Carlisle directors were apparently reluctant to grant a through rate, and there was no arrangement in hand for the NER to run over that part of their line - an obvious alternative. The coal therefore came via the B&T to Northumberland Dock, and was then shipped up river to Elswick. Ordnance was despatched to Woolwich Arsenal, and one would have thought there was a case for sending it by coastal steamer. Armstrong preferred, however, to send it by train - possibly for security. All the guns went this way and the bulk of the ammunition. They began their journey, however, by being shipped across the Tyne from Elswick to the NER's quay at Gateshead (the former Brandling Junction quay), where they were craned into railway wagons.

12.10 *Elswick Works in 1889. (Newcastle Monthly Chronicle)*

The second working agreement between the NER and N&C, made in July 1859, made provision for through traffic and through rates, with a committee of directors from both companies being set up to sort these out. One consequence was that the two companies' locomotives and rolling stock began to work routinely over each other's lines to convey through trains, and Armstrong was soon consigning the bulk of his goods by rail throughout. His coal supply patterns also changed, and in the 12 months ending September 1867 Elswick Works took 6,450 tons of coal and 7,181 tons of coke from Towneley Main colliery, near Blaydon; the distance over the railway was only three miles but the NER had presumably conceded rather more favourable terms than the normal short distance rate.[33] The ore traffic also benefited from the through working, although the greatest boon to this was the opening in 1867 of the NER's Derwent Valley line from Blaydon to Consett, which offered a much shorter and simpler route to and from the Carlisle line.

12.11. *The North Eastern Railway briskly disposed of the N&C's passenger locomotives and put the through trains between Newcastle and Carlisle in the charge of 2-4-0 engines designed by the NER Locomotive Superintendent, Edward Fletcher. A late example of these is No. 367, built at the NER's Gateshead Works in 1880 and seen here outside the east end of the workshop building at London Road. (J.M. Fleming collection)*

Table 13.1. Locomotives Supplied to the Newcastle & Carlisle Railway

Dimensions given are: Coupled Wheel Diameter; Boiler Diameter and Length; Cylinder Diameter and Piston Stroke. Cylinder dimensions are in inches; the others in feet and inches. The notional pressure is given in pounds-force per square inch, with the corresponding theoretical horsepower at a speed of 20 mph. Dimensions are those of the locomotives as originally supplied.
* denotes date of despatch by manufacturer, otherwise dates are those of arrival at the railway

#	Name	Wheels		Boiler	Cylinders	Pressure	Horsepower	Delivery Date	Builder
1	Rapid	0-4-0	4ft 0in	3ft 0in x 7ft 4in	12 x 16	50	-	1835 - 3 March *	Stephenson
2	Comet			3ft 0in x 7ft 6in	12 x 16	60	103	1835 - February	Hawthorn
3	Meteor			3ft 0in a 7ft 6in	12 x 16	55	90	1835 - 7 September	Bury
4	Hercules	0-4-2	4ft 6in	3ft 6in x 8ft 6in	14 x 18	-	-	1836 - 5 January *	Stephenson
5	Samson					75	199	1836 - 25 May	Hawthorn
6	Goliath	0-6-0	4ft 0in	3ft 6in x 8ft 6in	14 x 18	70	195	1836 - 18 July	Hawthorn
7	Atlas					-	-	1836 - 19 August *	Stephenson
8	Tyne	0-4-0	4ft 6in	3ft 6in x 8ft 0in	14 x 15	60	75	1836 - 13 October	Hawthorn
9	Eden					80	199	1836 - 10 Nov. *	Stephenson
10	Lightning		*'Hawks' denotes Hawks & Thompson, of Gateshead*			65	126	1837 - 21 January	Hawks
12	Carlisle					-	-	1837 - 9 June	Hawks
11	Newcastle	0-6-0	4ft 0in	3ft 6in x 8ft 6in	14 x 18	65	184	1837 - 6 May	Hawthorn
13	Victoria	2-4-0	5ft 0in	3ft 6in x 8ft 6in	14 x 18	80	198	1838 - 9 June	Hawks
14	Wellington					80	198	1838 - 24 May	Hawthorn
15	Nelson					80	198	1838 - 12 June	Hawthorn
16	Northumberland					80	198	1838 - 17 October	Hawthorn
17	Cumberland					80	198	1838 - 26 October	Hawthorn
18	Durham	0-6-0	4ft 0in	3ft 6in x 8ft 6in	14 x 18	90	279	1839 - 11 July	Hawthorn
19	Matthew Plummer					60	164	1839 - 15 Nov.	Thompsons
20	Adelaide					60	164	1840 - 30 April	Thompsons
23	Mars		*'Thompsons' denotes Thompson Brothers, of Wylam*			80	243	1840 - 12 Sept.	Thompsons
26	Saturn	*Saturn differed from the rest of this group in having 4ft 6in wheels*				80	216	1841 - 5 April	Thompsons
21	Sun	0-4-2	4ft 9in	3ft 6in x 8ft 6in	14 x 18	80	204	1839 - 12 Nov.	Hawthorn
22	Star			3ft 6in x 8ft 6in		75	188	1839 - 14 Nov.	Hawthorn
24	Jupiter			3ft 6in x **9ft 0in**		90	235	1840 - 30 Nov.	Thompsons
25	Venus			3ft 6in x 8ft 6in		70	171	1841 - 18 Jany.	Thompsons
27	Globe	0-6-0	4ft 3in	3ft 6in x 10ft 0in	15 x 24	90	406	1846 - 26 Oct.	Hawthorn
28	Planet					90	406	1846 - 28 Dec.	Hawthorn
29	Albert	0-4-2	5ft 0in	3ft 10in x 10ft 1in	15 x 21	90	302	1847 - 2 April	Hawthorn
30	Swift	2-4-0 or 0-4-2	5ft 6in			90	275	1847 - 20 Dec.	Hawthorn
31	Collingwood	0-6-0	4ft 6in	3ft 10in x 10ft 0in	16 x 24	85	430	1848 - 15 Sept.	Hawthorn
32	Allen					85	430	1848 - 30 Oct.	Hawthorn

All locomotives subsequently supplied to the railway by outside builders were 0-6-0s with 15 x 22 inch cylinders, The pressure was 110 psi, except for Alston and Hexham, which were 90. Most had 4ft 6in wheels, the exceptions being Nos. 38, 40, 41 & 43, which were 2 inches larger. Hawthorn engines had boilers 3ft 10in x 10ft. Stephenson boilers were 2 inches longer, with the exception of the replacement Nos. 7 & 9. The table below records suppliers and date. * denotes a new engine taking the name and number of an old one withdrawn.

Hawthorn Locomotives:

35 Prudhoe 31/12/52; 36 Naworth 31/1/53; 39 Dilston 20/3/55; 40 Langley 25/5/55; 4 * Hercules 19/4/57
43 Featherstonehaugh 30/4/57; 11 * Newcastle 25/6/60; 12 * Carlisle 13/8/60; 8 * Tyne 27/12/61.

Stephenson Locomotives:

33 Alston 17/6/50; 34 Hexham 17/9/50; 37 Blenkinsopp 30/11/53; 38 Bywell 24/12/53
41 Thirlwall 23/6/55; 42 Lanercost 2/7/55; 7 * Atlas 24/6/61; 9 * Eden 29/6/61.

Chapter 13: Locomotives and Rolling Stock

Introduction

It is helpful to begin by looking at the situation towards the end of the Newcastle & Carlisle Railway's independent existence, since that gives us an idea of the stock required to work the traffic of the mature railway and its costs. At the end of 1861, the last full year of independent life, the company owned 39 locomotives, the operation and maintenance of which consumed £21,559 during the year, 29% of the total working expenses of £73,386.[1] The capital account had been increased by £4,180 in respect of two new engines supplied during the year. A list of N&C engines and their provenance is given in Table 13.1, opposite.[2] Rolling stock at the end of 1861 comprised 3,726 vehicles, 85 of which were passenger carriages, but the vast majority, 2,621, were chaldron wagons; the actual breakdown being given in Table 13.2. During the year, repairs to this stock had cost £13,383, representing 18% of total working expenses. This may seem quite a lot, but the coal and mineral wagons will have had a pretty rough life and required frequent attention. The year had also seen 298 new coal wagons and a guard's van being added to stock at a capital cost of £11,853. The maintenance and running of this stock were the responsibility of Anthony Hall, appointed Locomotive Superintendent in 1835.

Table 13.2 Rolling Stock at 31 December 1861

W denotes stock in working order. **R** is stock under repair. **B** is stock being rebuilt. **A** is stock awaiting rebuilding.

Type	W	R	B	A	Type	W	R	B	A
Carriages, First Class	9	1	1	0	Goods Trucks, 5 ton	182	7	0	0
Carriages, Composite	6	0	0	0	Goods Trucks, 3 ton	102	9	0	25
Carriages, Second Class	22	1	0	1	Corn Trucks	95	7	0	0
Carriages, Third Class	40	3	0	1	Cattle Trucks	73	4	0	0
Passenger Train Vans *	8	0	0	0	Coke Trucks	180	6	0	0
Horse Boxes	13	0	0	0	Stone Wagons	82	3	0	0
Carriage Trucks	7	2	0	0	Coal Wagons, 6 ton	188	11	0	0
Goods Train Vans *	15	1	0	0	Chaldron Wagons	2,582	39	0	0

(* These are Guard's Vans)

One thing stands out from the coaching stock figures, and that is the extent to which third-class traffic had developed in the fifteen years since its introduction in 1846, with third-class carriages now accounting for over half the total. Among the wagon stock, it is notable that there is nothing specifically assigned to the very considerable iron-ore traffic. The company's minutes refer to some 'large wagons' being purchased for this but the assumption must be that a significant amount was carried in chaldron wagons, even though the original return, on which this table is based, refers to them as 'chaldron coal wagons'.

To see how the N&C got to this position we must go back to 1834, when the decisions were taken that the company should act as sole carrier and employ steam traction instead of horses.

Locomotive Policy and its Development from 1834

The procurement of locomotives and rolling stock was left to the Managing directors: Nicholas Wood and his colleagues, George Johnson and Benjamin Thompson. They met with representatives of the two great Tyneside locomotive builders, Robert Stephenson and Robert Hawthorn, on 14 October 1834, and agreed a specification for an 0-4-0, paying particular attention to such details as boiler and cylinder dimensions and the number and size of the boiler firetubes.[3] A week later, the Board made its formal decision in favour of steam and asked the managing committee to contract with 'Messrs. Berry of Liverpool' (Bury, Curtis & Kennedy) or any other manufacturer for the supply of 'locomotive engines.' Wood and his colleagues went on to order one from each of the three firms, to a standard specification and at a uniform price of £940 for each locomotive plus £140 for the tender.[4] In the case of Stephenson and Hawthorn delivery was requested by February 1835, but this was a busy time for engine builders so that could not be guaranteed.

In the event, Hawthorn's *Comet* arrived in February, and may have been engaged in hauling lead trains, which the company took over from the contractor, Ritson.[5] Stephenson's *Rapid* just got there in time for the 9 March opening, being despatched only six days beforehand.[6] Both engines probably made their way to Blaydon by boat, up the Tyne. Despite repeated promises, Bury fell well behind and on 22 July John Challoner wrote cancelling the order. The engine was needed, however, and the directors relented, so Bury's *Meteor* was delivered to Hexham in September. Its journey from Liverpool is a reminder of travel in what was still virtually the canal and coach era. Thus it came by ship to Port Carlisle, by barge along the canal to the city, and thence on a horse-drawn wagon.

13.1. *Hawthorn's* Comet *was typical of contemporary practice, with cylinders set low and their piston rods passing below the front axle. The steam-collecting dome was placed just behind the chimney to minimise steam pipe length and to lessen the risk of priming, the water surface being less turbulent away from the firebox The tall brass column housed a safety valve. Along with* **Rapid** *and* **Meteor** *it had cylinders of 12 inch diameter and 16 inch stroke, and 4 feet diameter wheels. The boiler was 7 feet long and 3 feet in diameter, with 66 firetubes of 2-inch outside diameter, giving a heating area, including firebox, of almost 300 square feet. Used latterly as a pilot engine, it was sold back to Hawthorns in September 1858 for a respectable £275. They used it to drive a circular saw until 1877, when it was scrapped. (engraving from F.W. Simms'* Public Works of Great Britain, *1838)*

The three engines were typical of the period. *Rapid* was a version of Stephenson's highly-successful *Planet* type of locomotive, and its appearance can be inferred from drawings of a later Stephenson 0-4-0: *Eden*, supplied in 1836. *Comet* (above) was similar in appearance but with inside frames only. *Rapid* had outside frames, which became the N&C norm for the next decade. *Meteor* will have looked somewhat different, having Bury's characteristic high firebox, rising well above the boiler, and bar frames. *Comet* had a higher boiler pressure - 60 psi (pounds per square inch), compared with 50 for *Rapid* and 55 for *Meteor*, giving it a theoretical capability of 103 horsepower when travelling at 20 mph. Bury built no further engines for the company, and Stephenson and Hawthorn became their major suppliers, although nine were also provided by ventures involving Benjamin Thompson and his sons.

The three 0-4-0s worked satisfactorily, but greater hauling capacity would be required in future, and this was provided by the next pair of engines: *Hercules*, supplied by Stephenson in January 1836, and *Samson*, which arrived from Hawthorn in May. The specification for these was again set out in detail by the Managing directors, after discussions with both builders, and is summarised in Table 13.3.[7] Compared with the earlier engines, these ones had much larger boilers and fireboxes, increased in length by about a quarter and in diameter by one sixth, while the boiler pressure and coupled wheel diameter were also raised. A further change was in the boiler firetubes, doubled in number to 130 but reduced in outside diameter from 2 inches to 1.625, which should have improved their steam-raising. The additional weight and length were catered for by providing a pair of smaller carrying wheels at the rear, making the wheel arrangement 0-4-2. This gave more stable running, although the company was to revert to 0-4-0s for four of its future engines. The boiler pressure was not actually specified by the directors, though Wood no doubt had an understanding about this, and once again Hawthorn went for a slightly higher pressure, 75 psi compared with 70 for the Stephenson locomotive. This gave *Samson* a notional rating of almost 200 hp at 20 mph. Both were ordered with 600 gallon tenders. The boiler and cylinder dimensions of these two engines were adopted as standard for the majority of further orders until a pause in procurement in 1841.

Table 13.3 Specification agreed by Managing Committee on 14 July 1835 for ***Hercules & Samson***.

Weight: about 10 tons. Cylinders: 14 in diameter by 18 in stroke. Tender: 600 gallons.
Wheels: Four of 4 ft 6 in diameter and two of 3 ft 6 in diameter.
Boiler: 8 ft 6 in long by 3 ft 6 in diameter. Copper firebox 2 ft 11½ in by 3 ft 6 in 'outside measurement of inner case, 3 in water round sides and front and 4 in round the back of the firebox.' 130 copper firetubes 8 ft 11 in long and 1.625 in outside diameter. (a later specification, for Tyne and Eden, requires brass tubes of 14 wire gauge metal thickness)

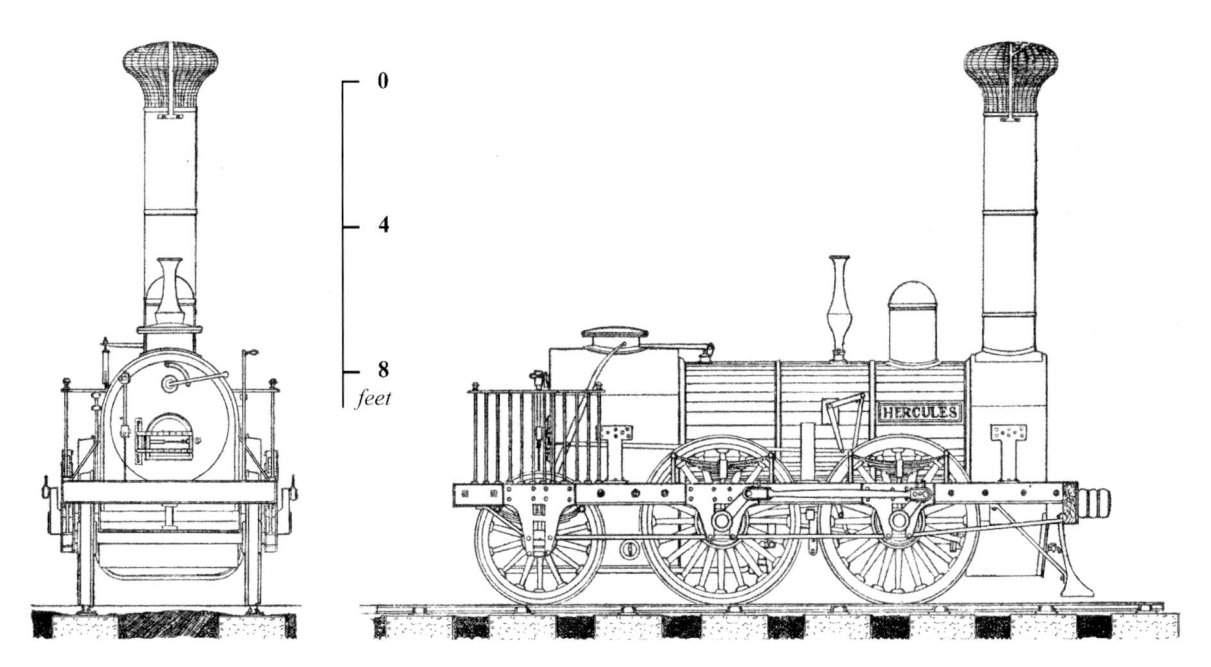

13.2. *Stephenson's* Hercules *is shown with a spark-arresting cage attached to the chimney top, but the splashers and footplate steps have been omitted, though both would have been provided. It entered service in January 1836 and cost £1,120 plus £150 for the tender. After two decades it was scrapped and its name taken by an 0-6-0 delivered in April 1857. (J.S. MacLean)*

The west end opening, in 1836, made that a busy year for locomotive orders. It also brought the prospect of a big increase in coal and mineral traffic, and on 9 February 1836 the Managing directors had a meeting with Robert Hawthorn and William Hutchinson, representing Stephensons, regarding engines for these slow, heavy trains.[8] The outcome was a pair of 0-6-0s, with smaller wheels than their predecessors: reduced in diameter by 6 inches to 4 feet. In other respects they were very similar to *Samson* and *Hercules*. *Goliah (Goliath)* was supplied by Hawthorn in July, and *Atlas* came from Stephenson in August. An earlier *Atlas*, designed by Robert Stephenson for the Leicester & Swannington Railway and built in 1834, has been described as the prototype for the six-coupled goods engine which became the 'maid-of-all-work' of Britain's railways. Future N&C mineral engines were all 0-6-0s and came to form the majority of their locomotive stock.

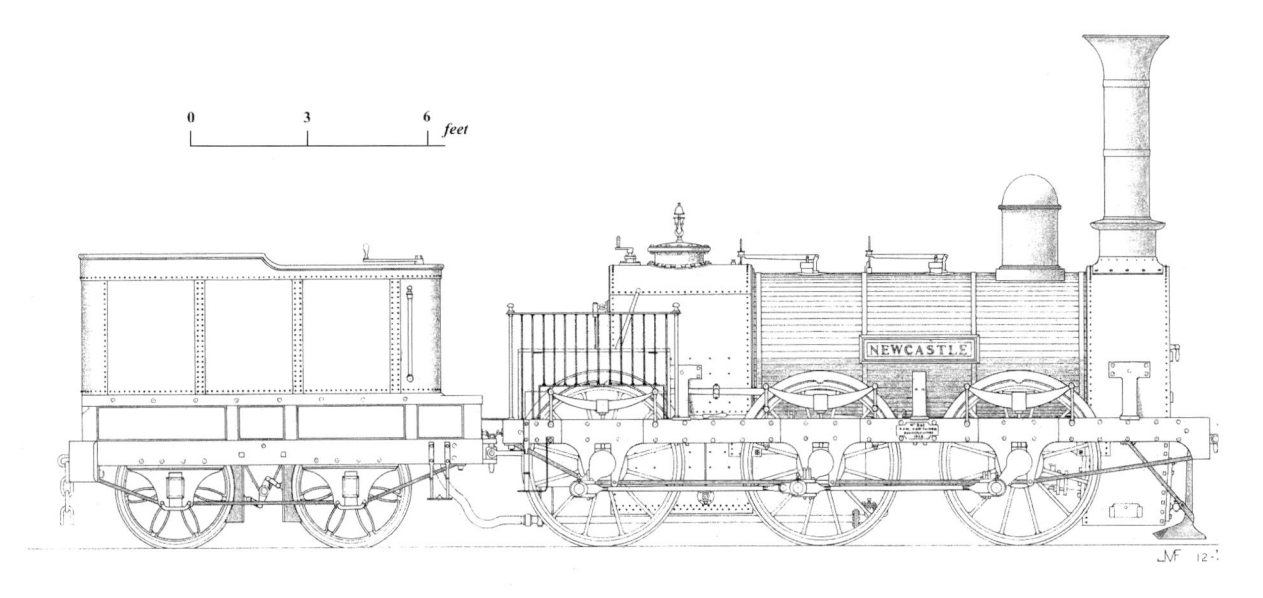

13.3. *The early 0-6-0s are typified by* Newcastle, *which was the third to be purchased, arriving from Hawthorns in May 1837 (see next page). It cost £1,320 plus £170 for the tender. The 700 gallon tender was introduced with* Goliah *and* Atlas *and remained standard as far as No.12,* Carlisle, *after which a 750 gallon version was adopted for new orders. The boiler and cylinders of* Newcastle *have the same dimensions as* Hercules, *above, and, like all the other early engines, the boiler is clad with timber planking. Within a few years this would be superseded by the use of sheet-iron cladding on top of the boiler lagging. Note that the regulator handle, seen on the face of the firebox in the case of* Hercules, *is here mounted on top, which became the standard position on N&C locomotives. After twenty years service,* Newcastle *was put up for sale in February 1858 and sold in September for £185 to John Anderson of Middlesbrough.   (J.M. Fleming, December 1942)*

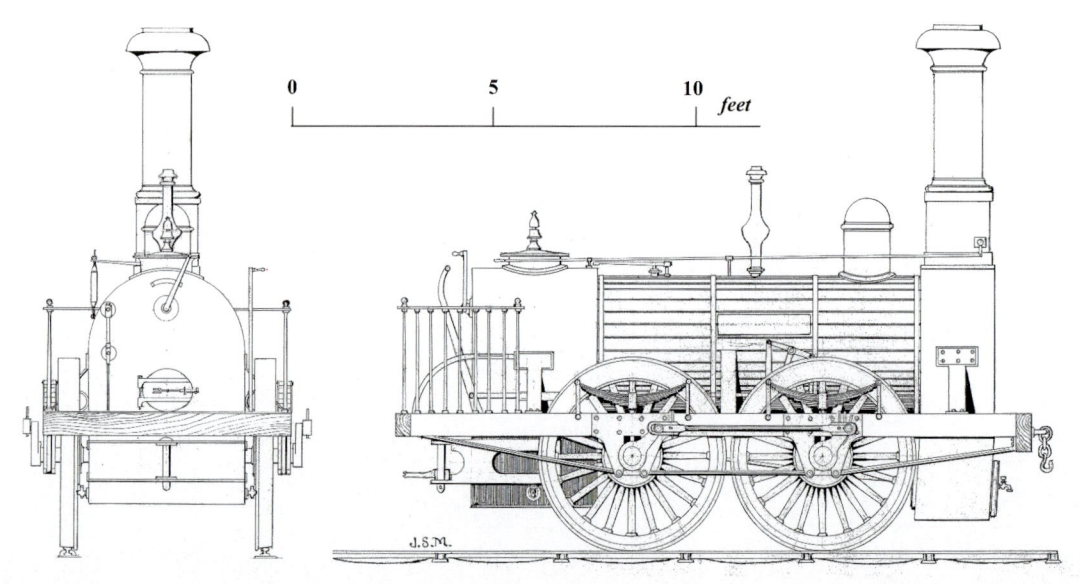

13.4. Stephenson's Eden *entered service on 10 November 1836 and was very similar in appearance to* Rapid *and* Hercules, *despite the latter's extra pair of carrying wheels.* Eden *itself seems to have emerged as an 0-4-2 from some expensive 'repairs' carried out by Stephensons in the latter part of 1841. Anthony Hall probably carried out further improvements, for the engine commanded a respectable £750 when sold to a contractor, Mr. Shrimpton, in 1860.   (J.S. MacLean)*

Four-coupled engines, with larger driving wheels, remained the policy for passenger and mixed trains, and two more of these were procured following a meeting with representatives of Stephenson and Hawthorn on 26 April 1836.[9] The usual detailed specification was agreed, and the firms offered a price of £1,350 for each engine and £180 for a 700 gallon tender; four days later the directors managed to get the prices down to £1,260 and £170, paid in cash. The engines materialised as Hawthorn's *Tyne*, delivered in October, and Stephenson's *Eden*, which came in November, both 0-4-0s.

A further pair of engines was sought in September 1836, one an 0-4-0, the other an 0-6-0, but again with identical boilers and cylinders. This time the company invited sealed tenders from three suppliers: the usual pair and Hawks & Company, of Gateshead. Stephensons were very busy, and said they could not supply the engines in less than twelve months, so the order was split between Hawthorn, who got the 0-6-0 *Newcastle*, and Hawks.[10] This was an interesting development. Hawks's foundry was a considerable enterprise, the largest employer in Gateshead during the first half of the nineteenth century. It included stationary steam engines among its products, but locomotives were a novelty, entered on with enthusiasm by Sir Robert Hawks in partnership with Benjamin Thompson's eldest son, George Annesley Thompson (c1808-1881). The N&C engine was their first, ordered on 27 September for delivery in January 1837, and the 0-4-0 *Lightning* duly appeared on January 21, followed in June by an 0-6-0 *Carlisle*. These look very similar to the Stephenson engines. (Sir) Daniel Gooch was engaged to develop Hawks's business and set up a new locomotive factory, but the venture was abandoned because of disagreements among the family.[11]

13.5. Hawks & Thompson's Lightning, *drawn by John Fleming in December 1942 and later coloured by him to indicate the N&C livery. This was basically maroon accompanied by a lot of polished brass. The lettering of the name on the tender seems to have taken both seriphed form and the sans-seriph seen here.* Lightning *underwent the usual conversion to an 0-4-2 and remained in stock until the NER merger, when it was promptly withdrawn.*

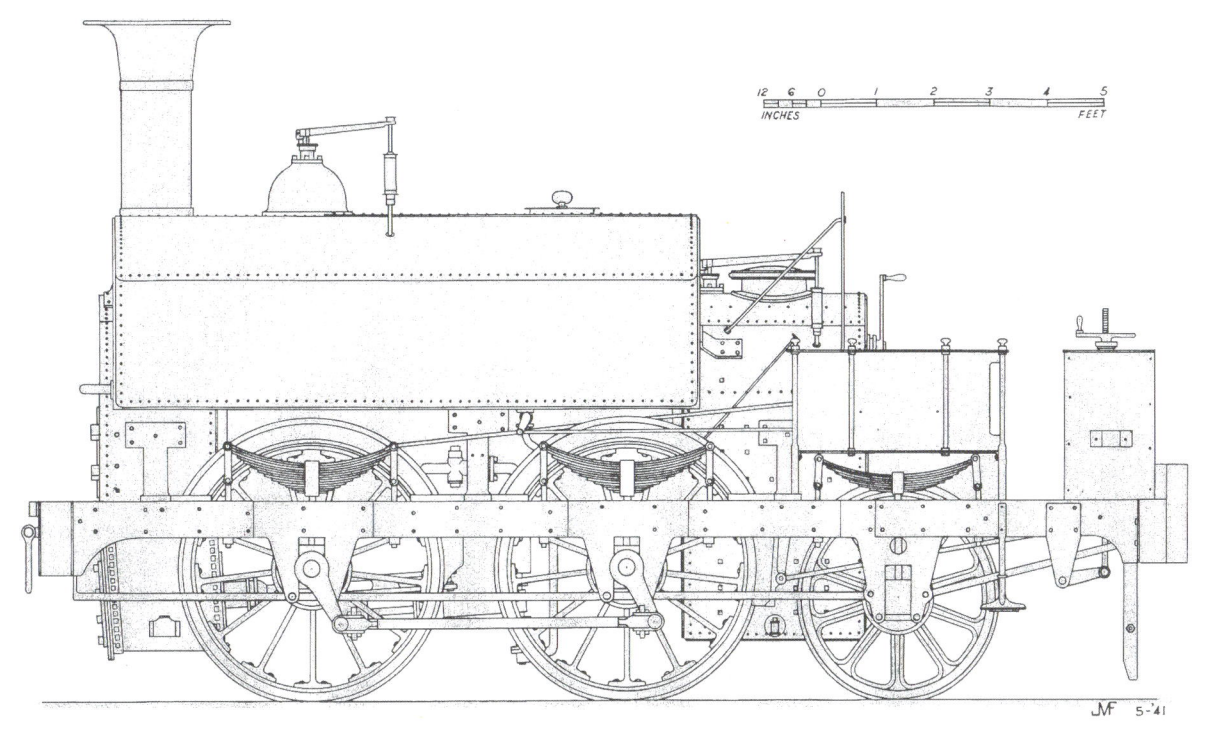

13.6. *Hawthorn's counterpart to* Eden *was* Tyne *seen above in its final incarnation as an 0-4-2 saddle tank, and below in its original form.   (J.M. Fleming May 1941 and February 1935)*

Hawthorns were very proud of the 'improved arrangement of hand gearing for working the slide valves' and invited visitors to a demonstration of Tyne *at their works on 12 October 1836. Over 90 'ladies and gentlemen' attended, including 'architects and engineers', and saw the 'ease and rapidity with which the motion of the engine was reversed.' Next day, it was despatched to Blaydon and made its trial run to Hexham at speeds up to 60mph, albeit with just a single carriage but against a strong headwind. (Tyne Mercury). *Tyne *soon acquired the distinction of an 8-pipe steam organ in place of the usual whistle. The idea for this is credited to the musical vicar of Ovingham, James Birkett, its implementation to Anthony Hall. In the eighteen-forties* Tyne *was given additional carrying wheels, seen below, making it an 0-4-2. It was later converted into a saddle tank but this seems to have involved no change to the original boiler other than resiting the safety valve to the top of the dome. However, since engines at this period only had brakes on the tender wheels, brakes were then fitted to its coupled wheels instead.*

By 1857 Tyne *had outlived its usefulness and was put up for sale. Eventually, on 6 August 1860, it was sold to Christopher Tarn for £550, for use in railway construction in the Colchester area. The N&C turned a deaf ear to subsequent complaints about the condition of the engine.*

13.7. Tyne *finished up in the Great Eastern Railway scrapyard at Stratford, where it was photographed. It stood there for some years, while the GER sought in vain for its owner, and was broken up in the Spring of 1869.*
(J.M. Fleming collection)

165

During August 1837, the Managing directors agreed a specification with Hawks and Hawthorn for a fast 2-4-0 with larger coupled wheels: five feet in diameter.[12] This was designed to haul the express trains which would be introduced following the completion of the central section of the line between Haydon Bridge and Greenhead the following summer. Hawthorns supplied four of these locomotives, while *Victoria* came from Hawks in June 1838. This was the last engine to be built by Hawks, and MacLean notes that it was rebuilt in 1842 with 6 feet wheels, which should have made it a real racer.

Nicholas Wood must have relished the opportunities for experiment which the railway afforded. One such was sanding. In later years it became customary to fit steam locomotives with apparatus which sanded the rail in front of the coupled wheels in order to improve adhesion under slippery conditions. The first trial of such a system appears to be that recorded on the N&C in June 1838 by the *Newcastle Journal*.

Another experiment was Robert Hawthorn's venture into the 'steam dryer', an early form of superheater, in which some of the exhaust gases passed through tubes in a steam chest. In November 1839 he supplied two 0-4-2s, *Sun* and *Star*, of identical dimensions except that *Sun* had a domeless boiler equipped with a steam dryer. During the following January comparative tests were carried out on eighteen scheduled trains, in which *Sun* returned an average coke consumption 15½% lower than *Star*.[13] As a result, when *Samson* fell due for heavy boiler repairs it was returned to Hawthorns and the boiler was rebuilt with a steam dryer and return fire tubes. It returned to service in May 1841, causing some surprise since the return tubes meant that the chimney was at the footplate end.[14] No further experiments of this sort are recorded on the line, and it is likely that maintenance problems offset the saving in fuel.

After the abandonment of the Hawks & Thompson locomotive building venture, the mantle was taken up by George Annesley Thompson and his brother Benjamin James (c1815-1900). In 1836 they and their father had set up an ironworks at Wylam, just across the Tyne from the railway. Father took up residence at Wylam Hall and his sons, trading as Thompson Brothers, built six locomotives - 4 mineral 0-6-0s and 2 passenger 0-4-2s - for the N&C, starting in 1839. Nothing is known of other engines manufactured by Thompson Brothers, except for two supplied to Benjamin's own Brunton & Shields Railway, one for Seaton Delaval Coal Company and perhaps one for Netherton colliery.[15] No engines are recorded after 1841 and the enterprise folded the following year, with the bankruptcies of Benjamin and his sons.

The railway's 1841-2 economy drive was reflected in locomotive orders. Thompsons delivered their last engine, the 0-6-0 *Saturn*, in April 1841. After that the N&C placed no new orders until 1846. With *Saturn*, they now had 26 engines on their books, and even if a third were under repair at any one time that left quite enough to meet their needs. Indeed the locomotive department seems to have outgrown the company's immediate needs, due to the dispersed establishment which arose with the piecemeal opening of the line. Thus they had 25 drivers, which the Committee of Economy reduced to 19, a number more in balance with the locomotive stock. The Managing directors seem to have contemplated even more drastic savings, producing a locomotive roster in January 1842 which purported to show that only 14 engines were required in regular service.[16] Even with the beginnings of a recovery in traffic during 1843, there was still surplus locomotive power, and in July the directors agreed to lease *Hercules* for use in one of the Earl of Durham's collieries. The terms, £40 plus £5 per week, included the services of its driver and fireman and they appear to have been away until the following March.

Locomotive orders resumed in 1846, and six engines were delivered during the next two years, all supplied by Hawthorns, four of them mineral 0-6-0s and two four-coupled passenger engines: *Albert* and *Swift*. These were very much standard products, *Albert* being replicated in engines supplied to the East Lancashire, Edinburgh Northern, Aberdeen, and Blackburn Darwen & Bolton Railways, as noted on the works' drawing. The last arrival was the 0-6-0 *Allen* in October 1848, and another pause in orders ensued, no new locomotives being purchased during the Hudson lease.

Deliveries began again in 1850, with the arrival of two Stephenson engines, in June and July, but purchases were now confined to the 0-6-0s, any further passenger needs being met by rebuilding existing locomotives in the N&C workshops, which had moved to new premises in 1844. 'Rebuilding' sometimes meant an almost totally new machine; for example, when *Samson* re-emerged from the shops in November 1852 as a passenger 2-4-0, it probably retained little more than the nameplates from the original engine. The last locomotive to be purchased was a Hawthorn 0-6-0, supplied in December 1861, which inherited the mantle of *Tyne*, sold four years earlier.

13.8. *The newly-rebuilt* Samson, *from a banner said to have been created for the opening of the final stage of the Alston branch in November 1852. The banner used to be at Newcastle's Museum of Science & Industry.*

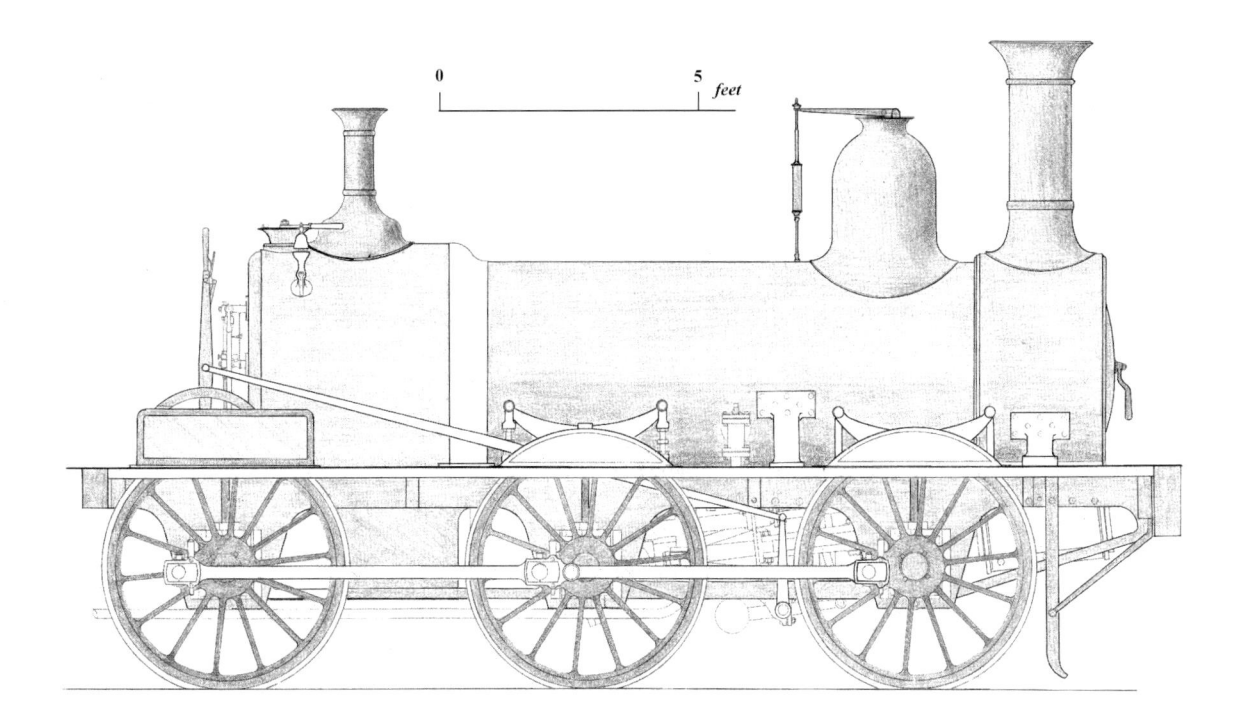

13.9. *The first locomotive to appear after the Hudson lease was* Alston, *arriving from Stephensons in June 1850. This illustration is based on a works drawing, and omits features such as buffers, footplate steps and side sheets; the latter shown in the detail view on the left.* Alston *was a typical modern mineral engine and put in two decades service before being rebuilt with a new boiler and cylinders at Gateshead in 1869. As NER No. 481 it was replaced in 1880. During the 1840's Stephenson and Hawthorn had moved to placing cylinders in the higher position seen here, with the piston rod passing above the leading axle. Stephenson continued to place the dome well forward, as here, with an integral safety valve controlled by the spring balance behind. Hawthorn moved the dome to the middle of the boiler, giving a quick means of distinguishing between the two builders. The regulator handle is still on the firebox top but another N&C feature, the 'plough' seen in the Samson picture, has been discarded in favour of simple guard irons in front of the leading wheels. The position of the reversing lever indicates that the driver stood on the right-hand side of the footplate.*

13.10. *Another Stephenson 0-6-0 was* Blenkinsopp, *which arrived on the N&C at the end of November 1853. It is seen as NER No. 485, after being reboilered in 1871 at Gateshead. The engine looks much as it did before, but has a Fletcher stovepipe chimney while the dome has moved to the middle of the boiler. A cab has been improvised by walling in between the weatherboard and sidesheets, while the engine has also been equipped with brakes. (J.M. Fleming collection/Loco. Publishing Co.)*

167

The N&C finished up with 39 locomotives, and a snapshot at the end of 1861 reveals that 30 of these were then in service, three were awaiting minor repairs, three were in the shops undergoing heavy repairs, two were being rebuilt, and another was waiting to be rebuilt.[17] The stock was divided between 10 passenger engines (i.e. four-coupled ones), 26 goods and mineral engines, and three 'pilot' engines - presumably older ones confined to light duties. All these passed to the North Eastern Railway and came under the control of its locomotive superintendent Edward Fletcher, who eventually dispensed with their names and meantime numbered them 453 to 491 in the NER list.

The NER quickly disposed of the passenger engines, including, it seems, most of those rebuilt or recreated by Anthony Hall. The mineral 0-6-0s were a different matter, and about half of these remained in service into the eighteen-eighties, with the last ones evidently being scrapped in 1886. This makes it a little difficult to interpret a remark made by T.E. Harrison in 1865, when he stated that the N&C engines 'were useless for the purposes of the present traffic' and were being 'absolutely and entirely remodelled'.[18] This would be fair comment for the passenger stock, which is perhaps what he intended, but the bulk of the mineral engines were modern products from two of the world's leading manufacturers, and the only distinction between them and those supplied to the NER over the same period is that the N&C boiler dimensions and heating area seem to have been a little smaller. In practice, what seems to have happened is the provision of new boilers when renewal became desirable, as in the case of *Blenkinsopp*, supplied in 1853 and reboilered in 1871. *Blenkinsopp* (fig. 13.10) was typical of the late engines, with 4ft 6in wheels, a boiler pressure of 110 psi and a theoretical capability of 450hp at 20 mph.

Locomotive Running and Liveries

As we have seen, N&C passenger trains did not involve high-speed running. The expresses called for, at best, average speeds of 30 mph between stops, while the stopping trains required something like 24 mph. Francis Whishaw published twelve runs made by passenger trains in the Autumn of 1839, recording average speeds generally in the range 22-24 mph, with maximum speeds up to 43 mph.[19] Something which emerges from these figures and the tests conducted by Hawthorns the following January is the susceptibility of the early trains to strong headwinds. Generally the men managed to keep time under such conditions, but only by working the engines hard, with a much-increased coke consumption.

High speeds were not favoured by the directors, because of the consequences for the track, but the men must occasionally have had a fling, to see just what their engines could do. A newspaper report in the Spring of 1837 claimed that Stephenson's *Eden* had travelled at 72 mph. Officially, the directors were not amused, and Blackmore was told to find out if it were true and warn the drivers against any repeat performance.[20] Yet this relatively mild response hints at a well-concealed pride in the prowess of their locomotives. In fact, the report seems to have been much exaggerated and the *Carlisle Journal* said *Eden* had done no more than manage a 31 mph average between Greenhead and Carlisle.

At times the mineral trains will have required double-heading, while banking was sometimes called for as well on the almost four-mile climb at 1/107 east from Corby, the most testing gradient on the main line. A return made in 1844 shows that one of the mineral 0-6-0s was capable of sustaining 15 mph up this bank with a gross load of 65 tons, made up of 13 wagons each loaded with 3 tons of goods.[21] Originally the heavy trains were heading down the bank towards Carlisle, laden with coal and coke, but the growth of ore traffic in the eighteen-fifties meant that there were increasingly heavy eastbound loads struggling up as well.

A distinctive feature of N&C engines is seen in a photograph of the Thompson passenger engine *Venus*, taken about 1863. This shows a pair of small iron ploughs, located in front of the leading wheels and intended to clear obstacles from the rails, just like the guard irons found in a similar position on many engines. The railway was fenced or walled throughout but fence rails were sometimes stolen and gates left open, so trains encountered stray livestock from time to time. The light engines could cope with sheep but not cattle, and there were quite a few derailments as a result of running into these. A particularly tragic one occurred near Ryton in December 1844, when Thomas Graham, driver of the Hawthorn 0-6-0 *Newcastle*, was fatally crushed by his engine rolling over on its side.[22] It was a dark morning and the crew knew nothing of the beast until they were almost upon it. The driver finished up beneath the tender but his fireman, Potts Graham, escaped with slight bruises.

13.13. Venus *was supplied by Thompson Brothers in January 1841, at a cost of £1,650, and appears to have undergone no significant external alterations prior to being sold by the NER very soon after the merger. It is seen here, still in N&C livery, working for the contractors John Watson and James Overend on the construction of the Mid Wales Railway, near Builth Wells. The line opened in July 1864, becoming part of the Cambrian Railways, and the engine may then have been disposed of. This is probably the best photograph of an N&C locomotive in its original state, the only obvious changes being the provision of a little extra protection for the enginemen, in the form of a weatherboard, on which the driver and fireman are leaning, and the insertion of side sheets behind the footplate railings. Note the additional pair of dumb buffers, placed between the normal sprung buffers, in order to cope with the narrow chaldron wagons which formed the bulk of N&C rolling stock. The tender will be a 750 gallon one, and the springs would originally have been concealed behind panels, as in the illustration of* Lightning *(Fig. 13.5).* Venus *was one of the principal 'express' locomotives in its early days and probably continued in passenger service for most of its career. (J.M. Fleming collection)*

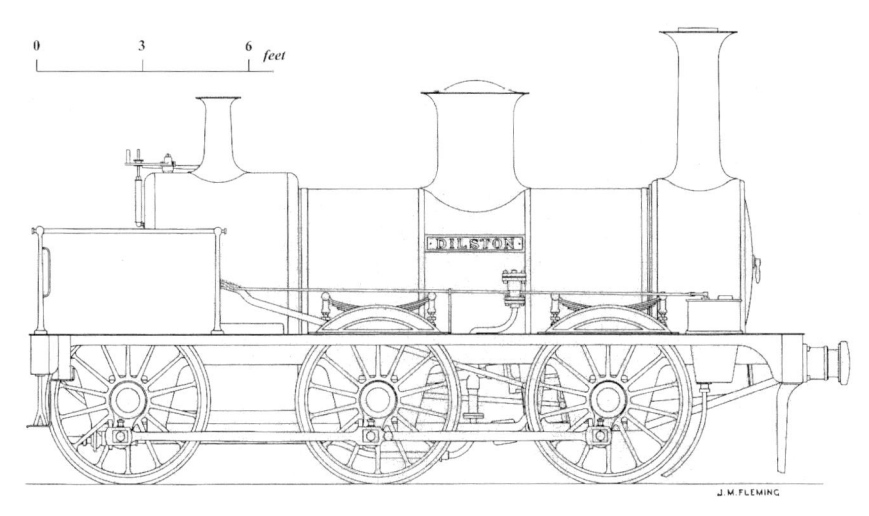

13.11. *A Hawthorn 0-6-0, Dilston, supplied in March 1855 at a cost of £2,250. Note the typically ponderous dome placed in the middle of the boiler. As NER No. 487, it apparently remained in service until 1882. (J.M. Fleming)*

13.12. *Hawthorn 0-6-0 Langley, supplied in May 1855, after receiving the Fletcher treatment as NER No. 488. The tender looks contemporary with the engine, though it may have belonged with another originally. No. 488 was scrapped in 1883. (J.M. Fleming coll./Loco. Publishing Co.)*

There was almost no protection for enginemen in those days; waist-high rails were provided at the sides of the footplate, later accompanied by side sheets and a low weatherboard in front. Anthony Hall, the N&C Locomotive Superintendent, had a go at introducing cabs in 1859, but the directors were not convinced by the result and told him not to proceed with any more 'canopies ... at the present time', though in April 1860 they agreed to a further experiment.[23] Hall's 'canopy' evidently comprised a full cab, with side windows and a wooden roof, as depicted in John Fleming's drawing of *Samson*.[24] In this respect Hall was something of a pioneer. The S&D's well-known experiment with cabs also dates from this period, but the NER's Edward Fletcher saw no need for such luxuries on his engines until about 1870. Some of the N&C 0-6-0s acquired improvised cabs during the NER era, as seen in the photographs of *Blenkinsopp* and *Langley*, and the difference in quality between these two suggests that they were built by the individual engine crews.

13.14. *Anthony Hall's* Samson, *equipped with a cab. Note the brake fitted to the front carrying wheel and, just behind, the sandbox for the coupled wheels. The N&C was a pioneer of sanding rails to improve adhesion. (drawing by J.M. Fleming, April 1935, coloured up to indicate livery)*

The *Venus* photograph is of particular interest, since it shows the engine still in N&C livery. Not only does it still bear its brass nameplates on the boiler, but one can make out the name painted on the tender side, and there seems to be no trace of its allotted NER number: 473. The N&C livery is well documented, thanks to the survival of some contemporary paintings and the patient researches of J. S. MacLean and John Fleming. It was also remarked on by George Watson, who had been a booking clerk at Newcastle Central in the eighteen-fifties. In a letter to MacLean he wrote that N&C engines were '… painted a bright scarlet and looked very smart with all the bright brass facings, the guards wearing scarlet gold-laced coats.' The predominant colour was maroon, applied to boiler and firebox, dome, footplate sides and wheels. Black was used for the smokebox and chimney, cylinders and the lower portion of the firebox, below the footplate. In addition there was a lot of polished brass; on *Venus*, for instance, one can see a prominent brass ring between the boiler and firebox. One engine even sported the extravagance of a brass chimney; this was *Matthew Plummer* - what better choice of name, which was the first engine to be supplied by Thompson Brothers from their Wylam ironworks, arriving in November 1839.[25]

All engines were named, and although they also had numbers, these were not in popular use. To begin with names emphasised desirable attributes, as with *Rapid* and *Hercules*. Then came local topography, interspersed with the patriotic *Victoria*, *Albert*, *Nelson* and *Collingwood* - very much a local hero. A few make subtle references to prominent shareholders, such as *Blenkinsopp* and *Bywell*, the seats of Colonel Coulson and T. W. Beaumont. The impact the early engines made on bystanders appears to be reflected in the naming of one Newcastle public house *The Victoria & Comet*, while an inn at Gilsland still has a painting of *Samson* as its sign.

Locomotives were a particular novelty in the west. Lowry recorded two arriving at Carlisle on 16 July 1836, only 3 days before the formal opening, noting that they went 'at the rate of a mile a minute' on some portions of the route; no doubt their road journey from the railhead at Haydon Bridge to Greenhead was very much slower.[26] One was *Hercules*, which he described as an 'amazing structure.' Carlisle went on to pay tribute with two public houses: the *Goliah* in Crown Street and London Road's own *Samson*, which ironically became a garage in later years.

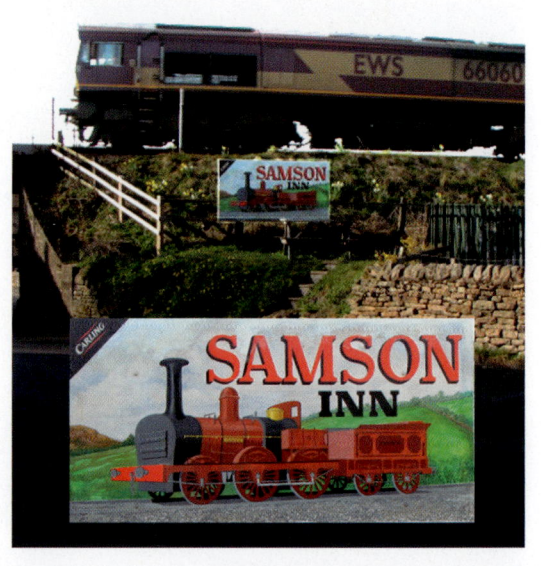

13.15. *A modern locomotive heads an empty coal train past its forerunner at Gilsland. (Bill Fawcett, 2007)*

170

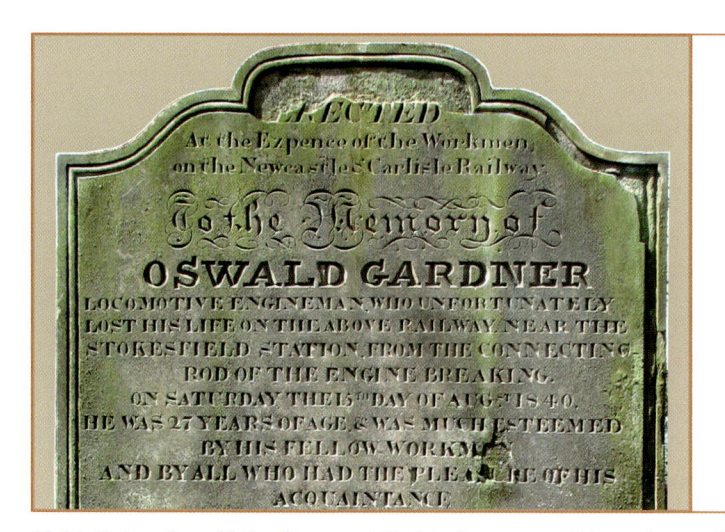

> *My engine now is cold and still*
> *No water does my boiler fill*
> *My coke affords its flame no more*
> *My days of usefulness are o'er*
> *My wheels deny their noted speed*
> *No more my guiding hand they heed*
> *My whistle too has lost its tone*
> *Its shrill and thrilling sounds are gone*
> *My valves are now thrown open wide*
> *My flanges all refuse to guide ...*
> *No more I feel each urging breath*
> *My steam is now condens'd in death*
> *Life's railway's o'er, each station's past*
> *In death I'm stopp'd and rest at last ...*

13.16. *Driver Oswald Gardner was killed in the course of his work near Stocksfield in August 1840. (see page 225) His workmates erected this memorial in Whickham churchyard, bearing a quaintly lugubrious verse 'composed by an unknowing friend ... and left at the Blaydon Station', the bulk of which is reproduced here. The same verse was employed, with only a couple of minor amendments, on a stone erected in 1842 in Bromsgrove churchyard to commemorate driver Thomas Scaife of the Birmingham & Gloucester Railway, who was killed by a boiler explosion in November 1840.* (Bill Fawcett)

Coaching Stock

Contemporary curiosity, and the writings of Nicholas Wood, mean that we know quite a lot about the early N&C coaching stock, which was typical of best practice on other railways of the time. Wood and his colleagues, Johnson and Thompson, finalised their plans for the first public service at a meeting on 27 February 1835, deciding that each train should comprise one 'close' carriage, one 'canopied' carriage, an open carriage and ten goods wagons, of four tons capacity.[27] The carriages translate as a closed vehicle, with roof and sides; an open-sided vehicle, with a roof; and one completely open. The closed carriage was for first-class passengers, the others for second-class. The vehicles themselves had been under construction for some months at the Newcastle workshops of Cuthbert Burnup, whose background was that of a joiner rather than an established coachbuilder.[28] Burnup was a man of high standards, whose work ranged from building timber bridges for the railway's Redheugh branch to constructing a celebrated Gothic sideboard for the refurbishment of Glamis Castle.

Newcastle & Carlisle Railway Second Class 'Canopied' Carriage
colours denote materials: brown - timber; blue-iron

Wood illustrated the early carriages in the 1838 edition of his *Practical Treatise on Railroads*, and a modified version of his drawings is given here. The original open-sided second-class carriages were divided into three sections, seating four a side on bench seats. Braking was provided by a simple arrangement of lever and push rod. The drawing of the second-class vehicle, which is a rather odd composite of elevation and section, shows the solebar, or side member of the carriage frame, set quite low in order to ease access to the vehicle. As a result, the springs were placed above it and secured to cast-iron boxes attached to the top of the frame.

side elevation

cross section *end elevation*

scale of elevations 0 — 3 feet

Newcastle & Carlisle Railway First Class Carriage
colours denote materials:
brown: timber
blue: ironwork

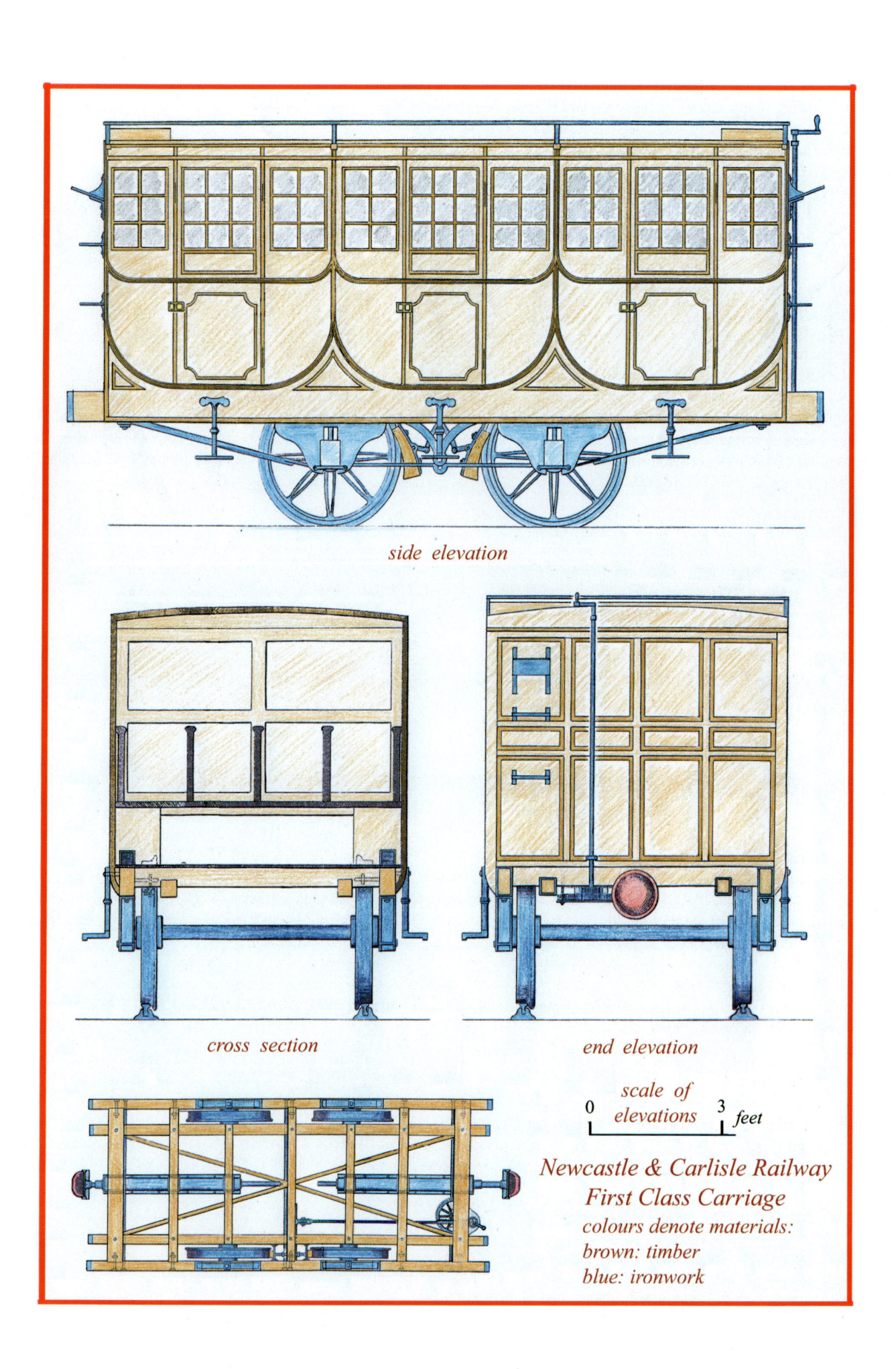

The original first-class carriage was also a three-compartment vehicle, seating 24 passengers, four a side, and owing much of its body design to traditional road coach practice. In coaching fashion, luggage could be carried on the roof, presumably strapped down to the low guard rail which surrounded it. At either end of the roof were low seating platforms, one of which could be occupied by the guard. He was expected to keep a lookout along the train from this lofty vantage point, and was provided with a hand brake. This took the form of a hand-wheel operating through a reduction gear train onto a rack and push rod, which transferred the movement to a rocker shaft located between the pair of brakes. N&C stations had no platforms prior to the eighteen-fifties, so individual steps were originally provided for each compartment door, though Whishaw noted in 1842 that the company had introduced 'perforated' iron footboards extending the full length of each carriage. Steps were provided at either end to give access to the roof, with the topmost one angled to provide a footrest for the guard.

Each carriage had no fewer than three sets of buffers. Two were 'dumb' buffers, formed by projecting the underframe beyond the ends of the vehicle. Of these, the outer set was designed to buffer up to other carriages and ordinary goods wagons; the inner set was provided for coupling up to chaldron wagons, which had a much narrower underframe. The third buffer was a combined central buffer and coupling, devised by John Blackmore. The idea had already been pioneered by Thomas Bergin on the Dublin and Kingstown Railway, which opened in December 1834, but Bergin's was a complicated design, which sought to compensate for the differences in height between laden and unladen vehicles.[29] Blackmore's chief objective was to minimise jerky movements when starting up and braking and so he opted for a simple, robust arrangement of sprung buffers held in contact by coupling rings. The long, powerful coil springs were housed in cast-iron tubes bolted to the underframe. The N&C soon discarded the Blackmore buffer in favour of the sprung side buffers and central hook and chain coupling which became standard on Britain's railways.

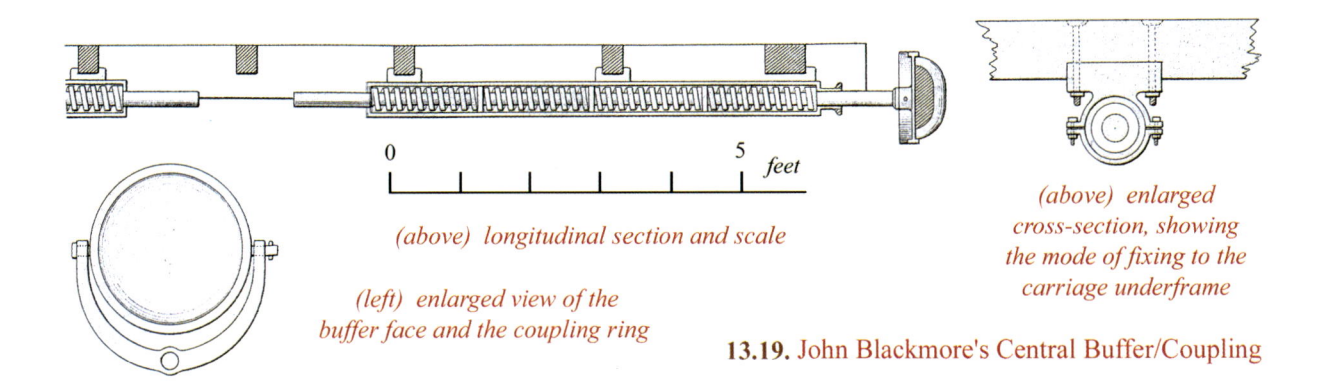

(above) longitudinal section and scale

(left) enlarged view of the buffer face and the coupling ring

(above) enlarged cross-section, showing the mode of fixing to the carriage underframe

13.19. John Blackmore's Central Buffer/Coupling

Within a short time, an improved first-class carriage had come into service, seating three a side (18 in total) on sprung seats with stuffed backs and individual mahogany arm rests. This helped to keep the first-class amenities ahead of the second class, when those passengers acquired fully closed-in carriages. In addition there were a number of composite vehicles, with a six-seater first-class compartment flanked by eight-seater second-class ones. Whishaw records the stock in the Autumn of 1839 as comprising twelve firsts, twelve seconds and six composites. This was presumably enough to cope with the regular services, but he noted that 'on thronged days, movable seats are set in the goods trucks, so that almost any number of passengers may be accommodated.' Assuming the first-class were by then all six-seat compartments, this gives a total coaching-stock capacity of only 252 first-class seats and 416 second. To put this in context, by the Summer of 1842 Lowry was recording a number of trains in connection with races and fairs with passenger numbers in excess of 250.

As well as passenger carriages, there were some luggage vans, with lockable compartments to convey passengers' luggage.[30] These had seats perched on top, available at a lower fare than the normal second class. Similar vehicles had previously been built by the Stockton & Darlington, but they can be seen as a legacy from the 'outside' seats of the road coaches, and some early travellers relished them for the view. However, railways posed hazards not commonly found on roads, as witness the death on 3 September 1846 of George Turnbull, a blacksmith, who was travelling with friends from Newcastle to Ryton, seated on top of a luggage van. His hat flew off and he stood up to shout to some lineside workmen to look after it, not realising the train was about to pass under a bridge.[31] The directors thereupon gave instructions that such seating should be dispensed with.

More affluent passengers often travelled in their private road carriages, so as to be able to continue the journey by road. Closed horseboxes were provided for their 'motive power' and the carriages were borne on flat wagons. In good weather, at the speeds customary on the N&C, it was attractive to sit outside on one's carriage as Lowry records the Marquess of Londonderry doing in September 1837.[32]

April 1846 saw the introduction of third-class accommodation on some trains, initially using adapted second-class stock. These were presumably the early open-sided carriages with boarding added to convert them into closed ones. At this time railways paid duty on their passenger receipts but Gladstone's 1844 Act provided that they should be exempted from this in respect of third-class passengers, carried at no more than a penny a mile, so long as the coaching stock provided had seats and was protected from the weather in a manner acceptable to the Board of Trade. The N&C therefore set about having some carriages built specially for third class but they had to make sure these were sufficiently unattractive to discourage defections by their existing second-class passengers.

The outcome was a design which satisfied the Board of Trade but cannot have been much fun to occupy for any length of time.[33] A carriage, 18 feet 6 inches long, seated 32 travellers on eight benches, facing one another with about a two feet gap in between; adjacent benches were separated by a back rail. The four doors on either side were provided with shuttered openings, for light and ventilation, in addition to which there were small windows and an oil lamp for use at night. This seems quite similar in layout to earlier third-class carriages built for the S&D. The new stock received the Board of Trade's approval in August 1847, with a certificate of exemption from duty back-dated to 24 May.

Early carriages were distinguished by names, such as *Expedition*, *Despatch*, and *Transit*, while their liveries made a bold distinction between first-class, with yellow bodies picked out in black, and second-class, in green and white.[34] Green was adopted for the luggage carriages and horseboxes. The firsts were also embellished with a rather splendid armorial device, contrived from the arms of Newcastle and Carlisle and illustrated on page 2. The bold early liveries were a legacy from the coaching age, with the Liverpool & Manchester also employing yellow and black for its original firsts. Decorum then took over, and in 1843 the N&C ordered a batch of firsts and seconds which were both painted claret, the distinctions of class being made in details of the livery.[35] This will have toned somewhat better with the red engines and may have been adopted as standard thereafter. The 1843 vehicles were supplied by the established Newcastle coachbuilders, Atkinson & Philipson, suppliers to other railways, who seem to have been the favoured choice thereafter.

Whishaw commented favourably on the mail vans supplied by the N&C, which he observed in 1839. These had a guard's compartment at one end, entered by a glazed sliding door, the remainder being a mailbag compartment, four feet high, with sliding doors along one side.

One thing which rightly concerned Nicholas Wood and his colleagues was the risk of wheel fractures. Their fellow director, William Losh, had invented a composite wheel, with cast-iron nave but wrought-iron spokes and rim, designed to minimise this possibility, and he made his 1830 patent available to the company free of charge.[36] As a result, it was standard practice from the outset for the N&C to order wheelsets for its rolling stock - carriages and wagons - separately and then supply them to the vehicle builders. In many cases these were obtained from the Walker foundry of Losh, Wilson & Bell.[37] Despite this care the N&C was not immune from trouble, and wheel fractures became a particular concern in the late eighteen-fifties. To combat this, Losh Wilson & Bell agreed to use tyres supplied by the Bowling and Low Moor ironworks in Yorkshire, both noted for the outstanding quality of their iron.[38]

13.20. Examples of Losh composite wheels from Nicholas Wood's 'Practical Treatise'.

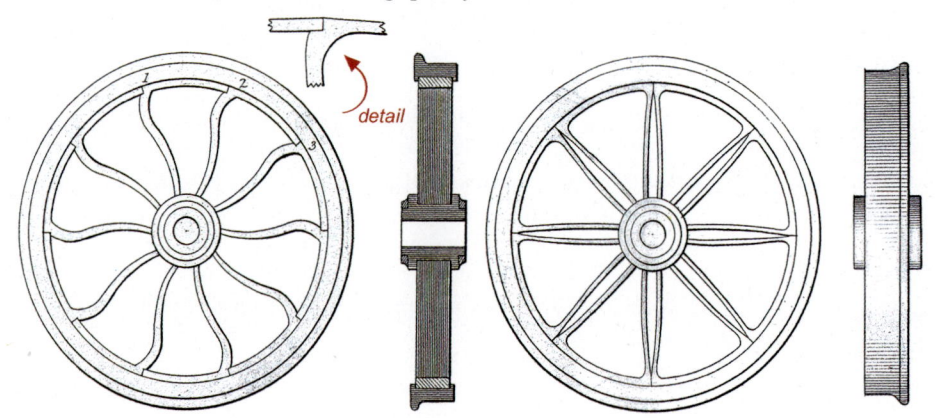

The main line of the N&C is well known for its curves, although they are often used to join up long sections of straight line. In the custom of the day they were made without transitions but were notable for their sometimes tight radius, as small as 15 chains (300 metres), which even Whishaw thought somewhat sharp. Wood described an experiment made in an attempt to reduce friction when traversing these: one wheel was left to run freely on each axle, rather than being rigidly attached. However, the workshop techniques of the day meant that the axle and wheel could not be matched with sufficient accuracy; the free wheels were found to vibrate badly and in some cases came off the rails, so the trial was abandoned.

Little is known of the details of the later N&C carriages. In appearance they will have been similar to other 'four-wheelers' of the period, but T.E. Harrison remarked that in general the N&C stock was somewhat lightly built and, while perfectly adequate for use on the Carlisle line, was unsuitable for use at the higher speeds prevailing on other parts of the NER system.[39] Most of the early carriages appear to have been still in service at the merger, no doubt substantially altered, and the NER seems to have carried out a fairly swift and thorough renewal programme.

Wagons

The company's requirement for wagons began early in the line's construction because of the decision to supply contractors with wagons and temporary way. In 1830 the directors advertised for designs for these 'ballast waggons', offering premiums of £5 and £2 , and the first prize went to Robert Wilson, engine builder, of Forth Street, Newcastle. A fortnight later, towards the end of November, the company invited tenders for their construction and Wilson went on to win the contract at a price of £13 each, only slightly less than the cost of the chaldron (coal) wagons which were to form the mainstay of the company's operational wagon fleet.[40] Wilson continued to supply ballast wagons over the next few years, though they obviously had a hard life at the hands of contractors, so in February 1832 the directors agreed to up the price by a pound in order to secure 'the best possible materials and craftsmanship'.[41] The bodies were built from oak while, after some problems with wheel failures, a number of wheelsets were ordered from Benjamin Thompson, who at that time had an ironworks near Birtley.[42] Carmichael sketched one of the ballast wagons, from which we can see that these had tipping bodies, to facilitate the discharge of spoil when forming embankments.

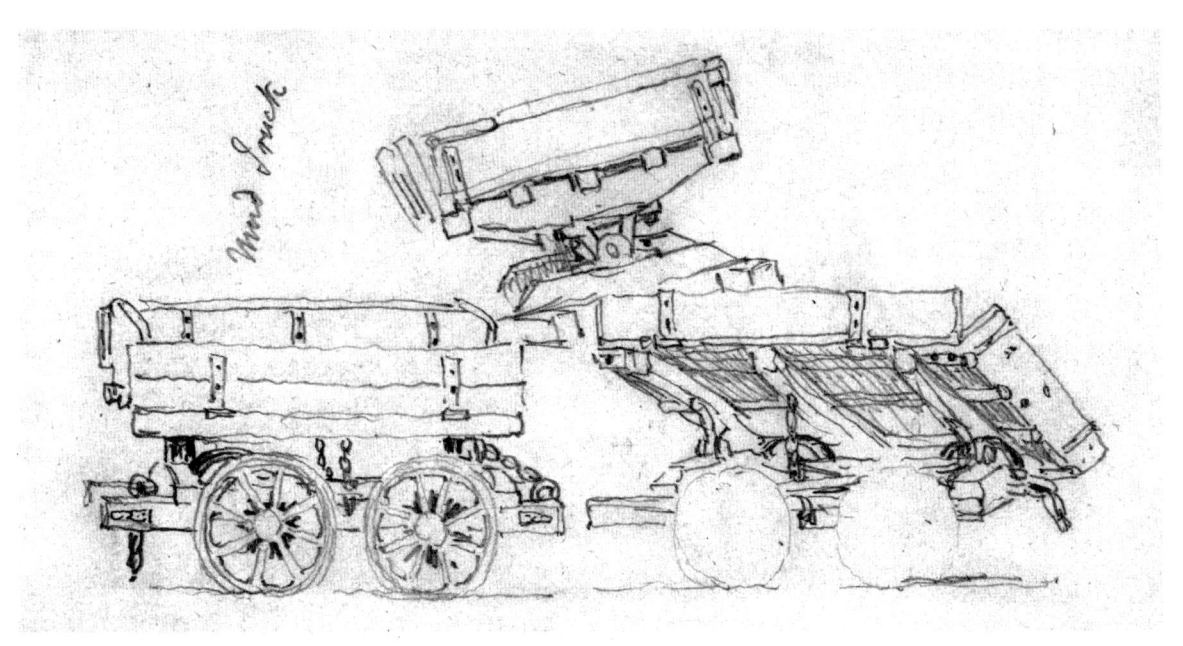

13.21. *John Wilson Carmichael's sketch of a ballast wagon or 'mud truck' in use during the construction of the N&C. (Laing Art Gallery, Newcastle, courtesy of Tyne & Wear Museums)*

Once the company had decided to act as sole carrier on its line, it clearly had to provide wagons for the goods and livestock traffic. Coal was a different matter. The Liverpool & Manchester Railway encouraged coal-owners to provide their own wagons, and this would have been an option for the N&C, with provision under their Act for the company to exclude any rolling stock which they deemed unsuitable or unfit. In practice the N&C coal traffic was largely conveyed in the railway's own rolling stock, though 'private owner' wagons were also to be found.[43] The railway rented wagons out to the collieries and differing practices seem to have built up under the Carlisle and Newcastle committees. Thus in April 1841 the Board decided that all wagons used at the east end of the line should be charged at ¼d per ton mile, and not let by the year as was the practice at the west end.[44] One problem with providing wagons was the risk that customers would hang on to them longer than was strictly necessary, and by the eighteen-fifties the company was making a demurrage charge of one shilling per chaldron wagon or two shillings per goods wagon for goods not unloaded within 24 hours of their arrival being notified.[45]

The mainstay of the company's rolling stock was the chaldron wagon, the standard coal wagon of the North East waggonways and railways. The chaldron was a traditional coal measure, whose exact capacity varied from one area to another but the 'imperial' standard was 53 hundredweight (2.65 tons), though Wood reckoned the Newcastle chaldron at 55 hundredweight, which could be pushed to nearly three tons by 'heaping a little.'[46] The chaldron wagon was distinguished by a hopper shape, with sides sloping in towards the bottom, which was hinged for discharging. The company advertised at the end of January 1835 for five hundred, to be mounted on 'Losh's patent malleable wheels which the Railway will supply.'[47]. The stock had only risen to 570 when Whishaw visited the railway in 1839, but then the coal business took off and numbers had grown almost five-fold by 1861, with large purchases from manufacturers like Mr. Hopper of Fencehouses, who supplied two hundred during 1856-7. These were ordered at a price of £16 each, plus the wheelsets, which the N&C consigned to Fencehouses station, but the railway obtained a discount of 4% by paying in cash.[48] The original deal had been for them to pay on receipt of the wagons by bills payable at six months, a common mode of business, so that if Hopper wanted his money immediately he would have had to cash these in at a discount, then standing at 8%.

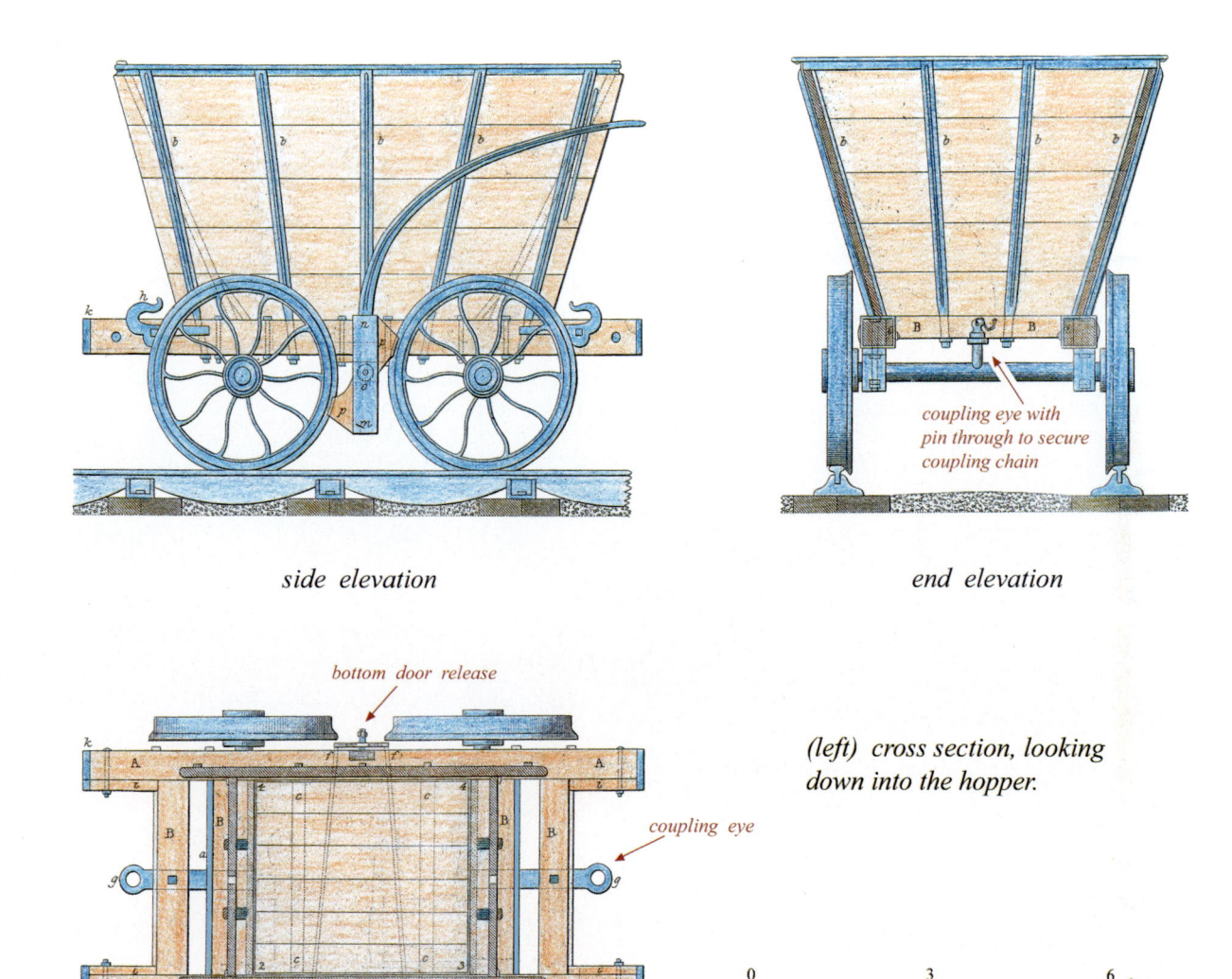

13.22. *N&C chaldron wagon, with Losh composite wheels, running on the original fish-bellied rail. (edited version of the illustration in Nicholas Wood's Practical Treatise)*

The chaldron wagons were unsprung, which will have hastened the deterioration of the early permanent way. The carriage of general goods required sprung vehicles, which Wood (and the railway) referred to as trucks. These had more elaborate underframes, broadly similar in construction to those of the passenger carriages, with the springs mounted above the solebars. The ends of the springs were secured into cast-iron housings, which also had sockets for the cross beams bearing the deck of the truck. The deck was formed of timber planking and slightly dished, to help locate the goods. Heavy commodities, like lead, could simply be stacked on the truck, but others would need roping down. Failure to do this properly was responsible for an embarrassing derailment in 1841, described in chapter 17.

The eighteen-fifties saw the company starting to increase the capacity of its wagons, and their final stock included a number of 6 ton coal wagons, no doubt sprung and probably similar to the North Eastern's 'double chaldrons'. As noted previously, a considerable amount of the iron ore traffic must have been handled in chaldrons, although towards the end of 1855 the directors decided to purchase fifty 'large' wagons for this and other traffic.[49] They followed this up by deciding to replace all their 3 ton goods wagons by 5 ton ones, as they came up for repair; six years later they were down to 102 three-tonners and had 182 five-tonners.

Whishaw commented on some of the specialised stock, of which we need only note the livestock wagons. In 1839 there were 36 cattle trucks and nine 'double sheep trucks', presumably double-decker ones like those running on the Liverpool & Manchester. The cattle trucks were open vehicles with railed sides, four feet high, and the ends were boarded flaps, which let down for loading. Low value horses would have travelled as 'cattle', but many equine travellers were expensive and nervous creatures which required better conditions: conveyed by passenger train, in what were evidently closed horseboxes, each housing up to two animals.

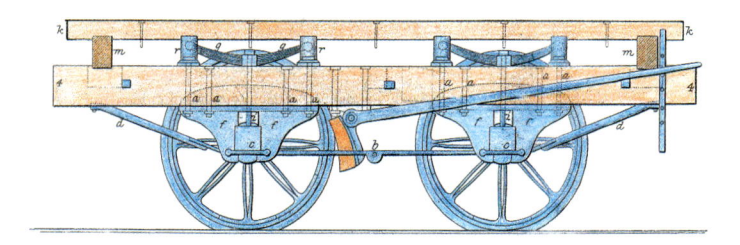

side elevation

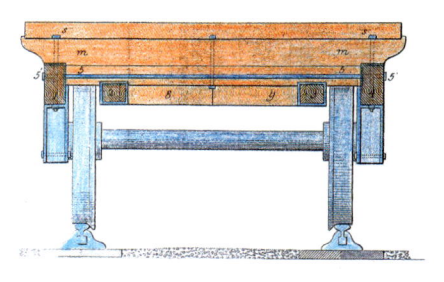

end elevation

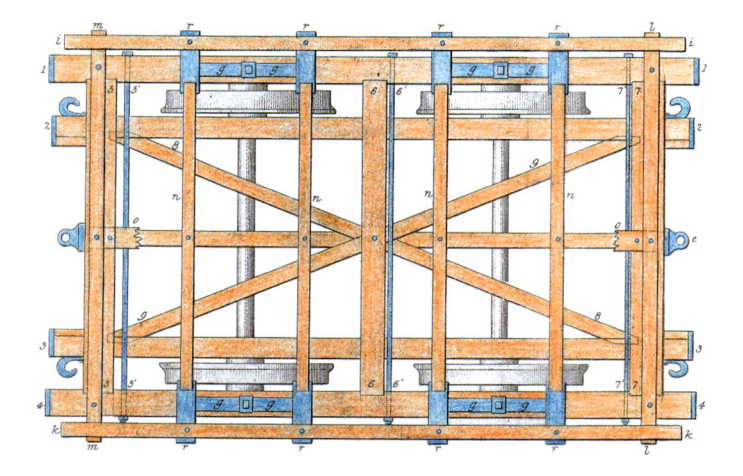

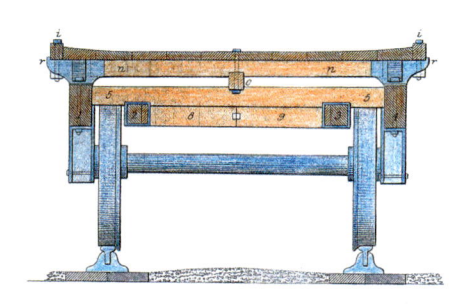

cross section

view from the top, with the deck planking removed, except for the side beams i-i

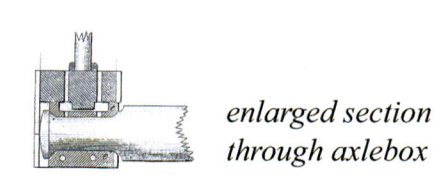

enlarged section through axlebox

13.23. *N&C flat wagon or truck. The solebars (1-1 & 4-4) were extended to form dumb buffers for mating with other flat wagons and coaching stock. The secondary beams (2-2 & 3-3) performed the same function in respect of chaldron wagons and were also provided with hooks for coupling by means of side chains. (edited version of illustration in Wood's 'Practical Treatise')*

Anthony Hall and the Locomotive Department

The company appointed its first enginemen in February 1835, placing them temporarily under the supervision of Blackmore and the Managing committee.[50] However, they needed someone to take charge of the running and maintenance of the locomotives and rolling stock, and advertised the post immediately after the March opening.[51] The job went to Anthony Hall, who remained Locomotive Superintendent throughout the company's operational existence.

Anthony Hall appears to be the son born in Newcastle on 18 August 1803 to Thomas Hall, millwright, and his wife, Dorothy Johnson.[52] Little is known of Anthony's early life, but he was presumably apprenticed as either a millwright or enginewright and worked in one of the Tyneside foundries or engine works. He may have worked on locomotive building, but was not involved with railways as such prior to obtaining a job with the Stockton & Darlington Railway about 1831.[53] In 1828 he had married Dorothy Lonsdale, in Newcastle, and their first child, Thomas, who also went on to join the N&C, was born there in March 1830. The S&D post took the family to Shildon, where Hall presumably worked under Timothy Hackworth in the S&D workshops, as a foreman. This will have provided an excellent practical background for his new job on the N&C.

Hall came to a railway which had two engines, one based at each end of the line along with its driver and fireman, together with a blacksmith and his apprentice to deal with minor repairs. There was one engine shed, a temporary affair, at Blaydon, but the Hexham engine presumably stood overnight in the station.[54] Hall based himself at Blaydon, which remained the operational hub of the railway for several years, though there is little evidence for the actual facilities which he built up there. The buildings may well have been makeshift in nature, pending the completion of the east-end route.

The staged completion of the railway brought a need in 1836 for further stabling facilities for locomotives at Haydon Bridge, Greenhead and Carlisle. The Haydon Bridge shed was purely temporary, but was accompanied by a low stone building, the workshop, which has been transformed into the local library. Greenhead has a more remarkable survival - the world's oldest engine shed, now used to stable lorries and considered further in chapter 15. Since the west end of the line was isolated from the rest for two years, until 1838, Greenhead developed as a repair centre, though with limited facilities, and then acquired a role as a place to change engines on the slow trains, while continuing to service the Blenkinsopp coal trains. Engines ran through between Newcastle and Carlisle on the fast trains, though Whishaw, writing in 1841, felt that this was a bit tough and they ought to be changed as well.

The staff audit of 1841 reveals the rapid growth of the locomotive department.[55] On the running side Anthony Hall had charge of 25 drivers and 25 firemen plus two engine cleaners, whose tasks included lighting up the engines each day. 16 drivers were allocated to the east end of the line and 9 to the west. Each pair of men was assigned to a particular engine, but obviously had to work others when their own was under repair. With only 26 engines in stock, and several of those under repair at any one time, the department was overmanned. Drivers had a standard wage of 4s 8d per day, and the company calculated their annual income on the basis of a six day week for 52 weeks - tough work but totalling £72-16-0, which was quite a respectable wage for the time. Firemen's wages varied according to experience, with most lying in the range 2s 8d to 3s. The notional working day for footplate crews was probably still the twelve hours specified when the first enginemen were appointed.

The Blaydon workshops were evidently confined to locomotive repairs, and a major feature was the blacksmiths' shop, with 19 smiths, plus a boilersmith and foreman. There were 19 enginewrights, plus foreman, 3 painters and a brazier. The foremen were on the same wage as a driver. Carlisle was the other major workshop centre, and this had facilities for handling both engines and rolling stock. The Carlisle locomotives came under Joseph Forster, 'Foreman of Mechanics', on 5s a day. He had 2 enginewrights, 6 smiths, 3 joiners and 2 painters. The bulk of the Carlisle workforce, however, came under Peter Tate, and seem to have included the company's main rolling stock workshop. Under his care came a pattern-maker, 3 fitters, 4 smiths, a 'truck maker', 2 joiners, 2 coach repairers, a coach painter, and a sawmill employing a further 3 people. This establishment was presumably responsible also for carpentry repairs to civil engineering works, such as timber bridges.

As well as these two centres, repair facilities were provided at strategic points throughout the railway so that things like wagons could be dealt with on the spot. Milton (Brampton Junction) had just two smiths, but Haydon Bridge, railhead for the lead traffic, was home to four plus two joiners and a painter. Greenhead had four smiths and a joiner. Redheugh had two smiths and a joiner, while the biggest outstation was the Newcastle terminus, at Railway Street, with six smiths, three men engaged on carriage and wagon repairs, and two cleaners.

Hall presided over this widely-dispersed empire with a salary of £200, only £50 less than that of the Chief Agent, John Challoner. If you discount John Blackmore and John Adamson, who are special cases, Hall and Challoner were the highest-paid officers, and justifiably so. The 1841-2 economy drive bore particularly heavily on Hall's department, with about 17 men being discharged during the first wave of cuts in December 1841, and more later on.[56] Most of those retained experienced wage cuts, of the order of 2d a day. Drivers were reduced in number from 25 to 19, with two being demoted to firemen and four discharged; it is unlikely they had much trouble finding jobs elsewhere in the burgeoning railway industry. There was a comparable reduction in firemen and a weeding out of the workshops. Blaydon lost three smiths and five wrights and Haydon Bridge two of its four smiths, though Greenhead was unscathed. The biggest savings were contemplated at Carlisle, with the Managing directors recommending a concentration of the main workshops at the east end of the line and a reduction of the Carlisle establishment to 'at most three fires for blacksmiths, two joiners and two men for fitting up the repairs of engines.'[57] The Blaydon site was too restricted to permit expansion there, so a decision was taken to build new workshops on part of the huge site owned by the N&C close to its temporary Newcastle terminus.[58]

Nicholas Wood and George Johnson made the point strongly in their report to the March 1842 AGM, realising that some shareholders might not welcome the expenditure. 'The most efficient and most economical system can only be established by a concentration of all the workshops, storehouses and workmen at Newcastle ... your Committee are, with the assistance of your engineer [Blackmore] now having prepared the requisite plans ... and they strongly urge upon you the necessity of proceeding ... without delay.' The financial climate of 1842 persuaded the directors to limit that year's work to building the storehouse, but the Carlisle workforce was drastically reduced during the course of the Summer.[59] In the Spring of 1843 Peter Tate was despatched to study workshops on other railways, and in June our old friends Grahamsley & Reid were given the contract for the new Forth engine shed and shops.[60] These were probably finished by the end of the year, and Blaydon will have been abandoned during the course of 1844.

The initial facilities at the Forth were far from lavish but they were expanded over the years and the final layout, determined from early maps, is shown in Figure 13.1. The shops were built at the start of the climb up to Central Station, and included a three-road engine shed, 200 feet long and able to accommodate about eighteen

Newcastle & Carlisle Railway   Forth Workshops

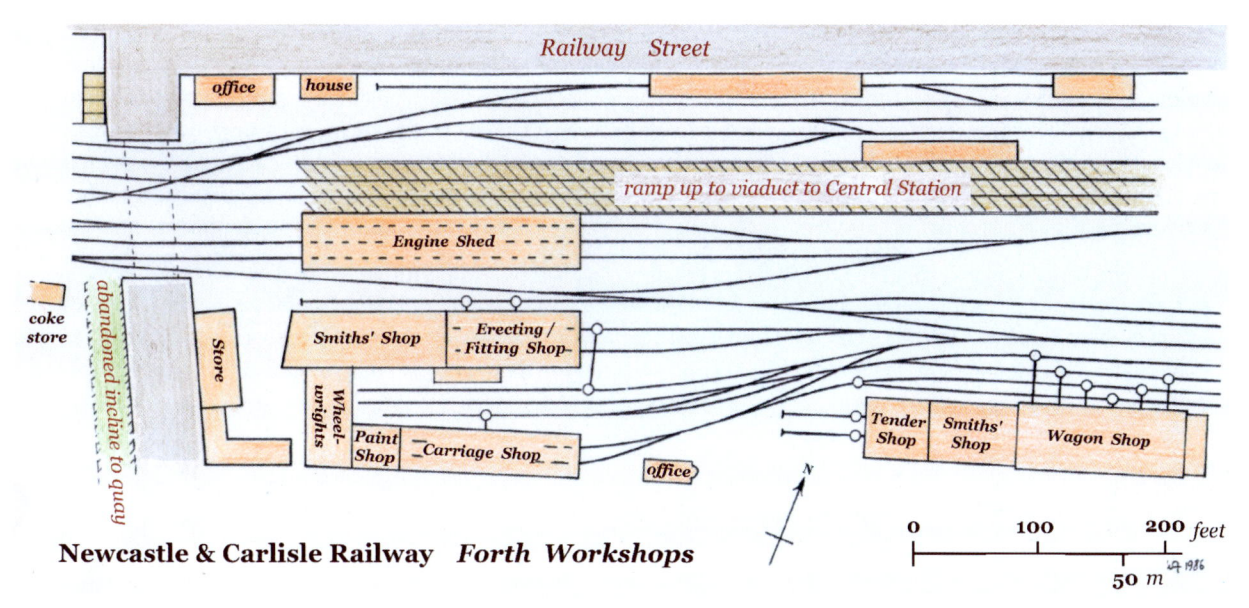

13.24. The Forth Workshops at their full extent, in the late eighteen-fifties. The main site is bounded on the left by Tyneside Terrace, bridged by the railway. West of that, the landsale coal depot occupied the north side of the line as far as Dunn Street, with the locomotive coke store, where engines were fuelled, on the south. Some of the tracks leading past the wagon shop at right centre continued over Shot Factory Lane to give access to the Forth Goods Station. (Bill Fawcett)

locomotives, almost half the company's total stock. Parallel to this ran a two-road erecting shop, a hundred feet long and capable, therefore, of handling about six engines at once. Boilers will have been built and repaired in the smiths' shop at the west end of this building. The adjoining carriage shop will have been used almost entirely for repairs, with new coaching stock continuing to be ordered from outside builders.

Wagon repairs continued to be dispersed to a number of localities, but the wagon shop at the Forth was the main centre for this activity. It was also, not surprisingly, the largest of the shops: about fifty feet wide, with six tracks entering transversely via wagon turntables. Each line could probably accommodate three wagons, enabling eighteen to be under repair indoors at any one time. At times of pressure, repairs will have been carried out in the open air as well. Nothing has been found to indicate the presence of a sawmill and joiners' shop, though these would have been required in connection with the rolling stock repairs.

Little is known of the works' equipment, but the most sophisticated of its machine tools will have been the locomotive crank-axle lathe ordered late in 1857.[61] This entailed some expensive stone foundations in order to provide a bed sufficiently immune from vibration to achieve the tolerances needed in machining. Like most locomotives of the period, those of the N&C had inside cylinders, hence the need for crank axles, which were a perennial source of weakness at this time. October 1858 was a particularly unfortunate month, with axles failing on *Saturn*, *Albert* and *Planet* in the space of a fortnight.[62]

With these facilities Hall and his men managed to do an excellent job. The 1861 figures for locomotive and rolling stock availability are testimony to this.[63] Expressed as the ratio of stock available for service to total stock, including that under or awaiting repair and rebuilding, the figures are:

Locomotives	77%
Carriages	91%
Wagons and other rolling stock	97%

This is an impressive performance by any standard, and an experienced critic, T. E. Harrison, pointed out the high standards of maintenance when reporting on the company prior to the merger. In addition, the move to the new workshops gave Hall more scope for rebuilding the old locomotives to his own ideas. With the relinquishing of Hudson's lease at the end of 1849 Hall entered on a new phase in his career, free from the oversight of the Managing directors, and any new passenger engines required were obtained by 'rebuilding' old stock, though the 0-6-0 mineral engines continued to be bought in.

In the pursuit of economy, Hall also found himself in charge of coke ovens. Before ways were found of improving the efficiency with which coal could be burned in locomotives, they were fuelled by coke; landowners insisted on this to avoid the nasty black smoke and the company's 1835 Act included a clause to that effect, as did those of many other railways. Coke was relatively expensive, and the Managing directors advised that it would be more economical for the company to make its own.

The company built a first bank of coke ovens at Derwenthaugh in 1839.[64] These were sandwiched between the railway and the Tyne, allowing coal to be brought in by either means, and had coal cellars accessible to the river keels. Two further sets of ovens were added during the eighteen-fifties. The supply of coal was generally let by tender half-yearly, so as to obtain a competitive price.[65] Initially the company employed its own coke burners, for whom cottages were built nearby, but as an economy the operation was later let out to tender, with the railway employing a superintendent to oversee the standard of work. 1857 brought another innovation in the interests of economy: enginemen were offered premiums for those who 'exercised the greatest care in the consumption of coke.' First prize was £3 - just over a week's wage for an engine crew.[66]

The Hudson lease probably had little impact on the Locomotive Department, other than the halt in new orders. The NER merger was a different matter, and Hall's department was brought under the control of the NER Locomotive Superintendent, Edward Fletcher. Hall stayed on as 'Locomotive Foreman' of the Carlisle Section, but the passing of the old era was marked in September 1862 by a formal presentation to him in the Forth wagon shop, suitably decorated with flowers and banners for the occasion.[67] Hall's workmen and many of his friends subscribed to a testimonial and were present to see it handed over by the last chairman, William Woods, in the form of a silver tea service, a gold watch and chain, and a purse of gold.

By then the Forth establishment was already under threat. Given the existence of the NER's main locomotive works and engine sheds just across the Tyne in Gateshead, it was obvious to T. E. Harrison that two benefits would accrue from moving the work across the river: economies in operation and the freeing up of a very useful site at the Forth. The first move came in September and October 1862 with the transfer of most of the Carlisle Section stores to Gateshead, and Woods was moved to write to the NER directors following the September presentation requesting that the former N&C locomotive and carriage shops 'be kept open as formerly' and the men 'not removed to Gateshead or York', York being home to the NER's main carriage works.[68] In reality Gateshead, as it then stood, did not have space to accommodate the Carlisle Section work. However, the Gateshead site was re-arranged, and in 1869-70 the workshops there were extended and a new roundhouse built specifically to accommodate the Carlisle engines.[69] The Forth Works then closed and its workforce and equipment were transferred across the river. The buildings were demolished to make way for the approach tracks to a huge new goods station then being built on the site of the N&C's Forth Goods. Anthony Hall probably did not live to see this; he seems to have died in 1867.[70] His son Thomas had been a draughtsman in the Forth establishment, where he may have played a significant part in the design of the later engines rebuilt by the N&C, and continued in service with the NER, becoming one of Fletcher's locomotive inspectors.[71]

13.25. *The Carlisle shed at Gateshead Works, designed by the NER Architect Thomas Prosser, and home to Carlisle Section locomotives from 1870. It had 20 tracks, giving a capacity of 19 engines, much the same as the former shed at the Forth. It lay in the south-east corner of the Gateshead site, separated from the main workshops and shed by the running lines from the High Level Bridge to the Team Valley. By 1896 the roundhouse had been converted into a paint shop for the Works. It began life as a regular polygon, but the three gables on the right were cut back, as seen here, to make more space for the running lines.*

(J.M. Fleming, April 1962)

Chapter 14: Permanent Way and Signalling

Permanent Way

Permanent way is literally the foundation of a successful railway, yet it has always been quite a costly one, as the figures given in Table 14.1 indicate.[1] It accounted for almost a fifth of the original capital expenditure up to the end of 1839, and its maintenance and renewal continued to be heavy burdens in later years, amounting in a typical year, 1856, to 16% of total working expenses.

Table 14.1a.   Capital Expenditure on Permanent Way to the end of 1839.

Iron rails and chairs	£99,966-6-8
Stone sleepers	£20,031-16-6
'Coating' of way (including materials) and laying track	£37,949-15-0
Total	**£157,947-18-2**

Table 14.1b.   Recurrent Expenditure on Permanent Way during 1856.

Platelayers' wages	£5,652-14-1
Superintendent's & Inspectors' wages	£625-4-0
Repairs of side drains	£55-12-4
Cleaning & ballasting station yards	£42-9-4
Blacksmiths' work, repairs of switches etc.	£373-5-3
Rails, chairs, sleepers, keys & pins	£4,240-1-0
Total	**£10,989-5-12**

In addition, £484 was spent on maintaining lineside fences and gates, while routine road and bridge repairs were predictably modest at £213.

The early directors were fortunate to have in their midst not only people like Benjamin Thompson and Nicholas Wood, with wide experience of waggonways, but also William Losh, holder of two patents in respect of rail design. The first rails provided by the company were those purchased for temporary use by the contractors, comprising plain bar iron on larch sleepers. The issue of permanent way was addressed in 1832. Cast-iron rails had been under consideration for the line as originally envisaged, but the influence of Wood and Losh can be seen in a decision of February that year to adopt 'malleable', i.e. wrought iron.[2] This was followed by a trip to study practice on other lines.

For months the directors had been contemplating a mass visit to the Liverpool & Manchester Railway, but this was repeatedly put off because of unrest in the north-east collieries; they wanted to be near home to deal with this. Eventually, on 21 and 22 August 1832 Benjamin Thompson led a party of eight other directors, including Losh, Wood and James Thompson of Kirkhouse, plus Francis Giles, to look at practice on the Stockton & Darlington, Clarence and Seaham Railways.[3] Their observations were discussed at the Board on 3 August, where a decision was taken in principle to adopt rail of 50 pounds per yard weight, made from No. 3 iron. A Rail Committee was set up under Benjamin Thompson, comprising Wood, Losh, James Thompson and William Woods. The latter seems the odd one out, being a banker, but he was a very active director and, of course, later chairman.

The directors were keen to let a contract for rails while the price of iron was going through one of its periodic troughs, and also had exaggerated expectations of how soon their line would be completed. They therefore advertised for six thousand tons of rail, enough to lay the entire line, in September 1832.[4] Meanwhile experiments were conducted at William Losh's Walker Iron Works to assess the relative merits of parallel and fish-bellied rails. These were fairly simplistic, observing the behaviour of different rails under static load, and, not surprisingly, led to the conclusion that a 42 pounds per yard fish-bellied rail was as effective as a 50 pounds parallel one. As rails were priced by weight this represented a significant saving. Unfortunately, the tests did not allow them to determine the effects of wear and side-cutting, so the 42 pound rails for which they opted soon proved inadequate. Both Giles and George Stephenson were present at the tests, though not simultaneously, and - not for the first time - drew contrary conclusions.[5] George was reinforced in his belief in fish-bellied rails on stone blocks, while Giles favoured parallel rails on transverse timber sleepers. Time was to prove Giles correct.

William Losh allowed the company free use of his 1830 patent, but did not supply the rails. The contract for these was let in November 1832 to two South Wales firms: Guest, Lewis & Co. and Harford Davis & Co. at a price of £8 per ton, though this appears to have been modified later to £8-15-0 per ton.[6] The N&C were to appoint an inspector, to attend the factory and ensure quality, while deliveries were to be made monthly, starting May 1833, by sea to Newcastle Quay and the Carlisle Canal Basin.

The contract was predominantly for fish-bellied rails, with the N&C supplying a pattern to show their exact requirement, but some 50 pound parallel rails were also purchased. These were needed for switch and crossing work, and evidently gave trouble since in February 1835 Harford Davis were informed that the quality of iron in them was inferior to the fish-bellied ones.[7] By then some of the rails would have been in use for the best part of a year conveying the contractors' traffic over completed stretches of the Blaydon-Hexham line. The 'coating' of the formation and laying of the rails had been let by contract in March 1834, and in July Plummer observed that nine miles of permanent way had been laid by the contractor for the Hexham to Prudhoe section, John Taylor, 'an active, clever man.'[8]

Fish-bellied rails were still the norm at this time. Indeed Robert Stephenson laid some miles of fifty pound ones at the south end of the London & Birmingham before moving over to parallel rails, following a report by Peter Barlow who pioneered a scientific study of strength of materials. Those on the N&C conformed to Losh's patent and were secured by wrought-iron keys (tapered wedges) in cast-iron chairs fastened to stone sleeper blocks by pairs of oak pins. In February 1834 the company advertised for a hundred thousand of these pins, specifying that they 'be made from old Ship Timber'. Figure 14.1 shows the track, based on illustrations in the final, 1838 edition of Nicholas Wood's *Practical Treatise on Rail-Roads*. The formation was prepared by 'coating' it with gravel or broken stone, which gave a well-drained foundation.[9] The blocks were then packed in with what later acquired the name 'ballast' and should have comprised smaller stones, gravel or cinders. Whishaw also records the use of fine waste coal, then common practice in the North-East, and 'loam', which seems entirely unsuitable.[10] Neither he nor Wood is explicit about the steps normally taken to maintain the gauge, though he does mention the use on some Redheugh branch curves of iron ties at ten feet intervals - lengths of iron bent up at the ends and clipped over the bottom of the rails.

The two distinctive features of Losh's 1830 patent relate to the fixing of the rail in the chairs. One is his use of a key tapered on two axes, rather than the customary single axis, which Wood reported as being much more effective in holding the rail down into the chair. The other was provision to allow the sleeper block to tilt, as they often did, without distorting the rail. So the chair bed was formed with a curved recess corresponding to a knuckle on the bottom of the rail, while the lower rim of its cheek had a similar curve. The idea was that these features should allow the chair some freedom to pivot with respect to the rail. An innovation on the N&C track was the employment of two keys per chair, one on either face of the rail.

Rails were supplied in fifteen feet lengths, and supported at three feet centres. The stone blocks were readily obtained from local sandstone, so that they were distinctively red at the west end. The original specification called for them to be between 18 inches and two feet square and a foot thick, while Whishaw records them as being two feet square and nine inches thick.[11] This accords with Wood's illustration, showing them laid diagonally and forming a continuous line. However, significant numbers survive, recycled into protecting riverside stretches of the formation from scour, and they reveal a different story. Those examined average about two feet square and a foot thick, and all have been laid square to the rail. On some embankments, where the formation had not yet consolidated, wooden sleepers were employed instead. On timber bridges the chairs were fastened to timber waybeams, running lengthwise.

The early track was not easy to maintain. The sheer weight of the stone blocks was not enough to deter movement under the increasingly heavy locomotives, while the keys were forever working loose and being clouted back in. Richard Lowry, that inveterate diarist, noted the jolting motion in passenger trains travelling over the stone sleepers, contrasting it with a much smoother ride over transverse timber sleepers. The N&C maintained its track in as good an order as was practical, and instituted twice-daily inspections. Up to the end of the company's existence, lengthmen walked their stretch of line checking for blockages and defects prior to the passage of the first goods train; they then walked it again before the first passenger train.[12]

By 1838 fish-bellied rails had fallen out of favour, and Wood reported that about four miles were laid with parallel rail.[13] This will have been 50 or 52 pounds per yard, which remained the standard for the company for several years. Stone blocks were still being used for new construction by many railways but by 1839 the N&C seemed about to give these up in favour of timber, since the Newcastle extension was laid with parallel rails on timber sleepers.[14] That was an improvement, but Blackmore chose to bolt the chairs directly to the girders of his cast-iron bridges on that section – a shortsighted move in view of the vibration to which they were subject. His successor, Peter Tate, reported that this led to 'such a jiggling and shaking to pieces' and he put in wooden sleepers to 'take the jar'.[15] In the event, stone blocks continued to be used for the new track laid under the line doubling programme, and as late as March 1844 the *Carlisle Journal* carried an advertisement for 20,000 blocks for the final stage of this work, between Stocksfield and Hexham. This would have been enough to furnish three-quarters of the eight route miles; tenders were also invited for 2,000 larch sleepers. The rail specification had, however, been upgraded to 60 pounds per yard.

The Hudson lease brought the permanent way under the scrutiny of T. E. Harrison, who had high standards and was not impressed with what he found. This was probably little changed from the situation reported in November 1845, when there were 48 route miles laid with mixed weights of rail on stone blocks.[16] Harrison began a programme of relaying almost the entire line with 82 pound rails on timber sleepers. This started in 1849 and continued after the old management resumed control. The need for it was shown by an accident which happened about 3½ miles east of Haltwhistle on 3 August 1851. The 5 p.m. passenger train from Carlisle was running fast to make up lost time when a rail joint gave way under the engine, which began 'oscillating violently, bending the rails at every rebound'. Despite the driver's best efforts, the tender and carriages derailed, with three carriages running down the embankment. The passengers escaped with, at worst, slight bruises.

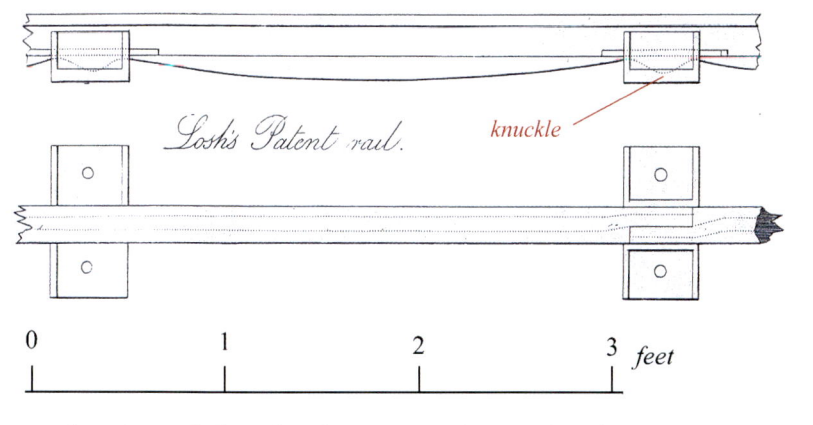

elevation and plan of Losh's patent rail, as used on the N&C

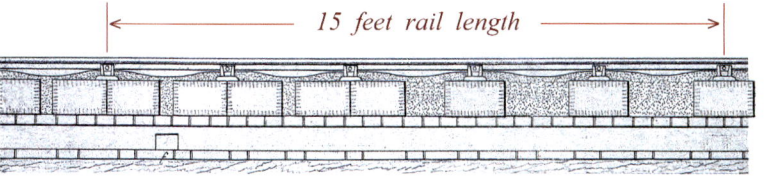

section along track, with blocks laid diagonally (left) and square (right)

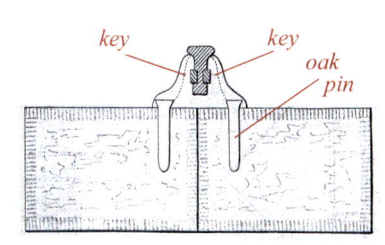

Sections through the double-keyed chairs used on the N&C. The lower shows the chair secured by oak pins to a stone block laid diagonally, with a corner facing the viewer.

14.1. *N&C track from Wood's 'Practical Treatise', modified to shows blocks laid on the square as well as diagonally.*

14,2. *Stone sleeper blocks recycled into river defences. They are typically 23 to 27 inches square and about 13 inches deep. The flat seating cut in for the chair measures 2.5 by 5.75 inches. (Bill Fawcett)*

The Board of Trade sent Captain Laffan to investigate, and he found that the accident had happened on a stretch still laid with 52 pound rails, of which about thirty single-track miles still remained; in addition fishbellied rails were still to be found on 3½ miles of the up line at the Carlisle end.[17] Laffan felt that the timetables called for excessive speed, particularly in the event of delays, over these old stretches of track, and pointed out that, in normal use, their rails were 'bent and distorted [so] that the principal work of the platelayers consists in straightening them.' He was also critical of the signal and platform arrangements at stations and demanded a relaxation of the timetables until all this had been sorted. After some prevarication, the N&C Board amended the timings a little and pressed ahead with the relaying.

The work took until 1853 and its considerable cost was charged to capital as being an expense attributable to the increase in traffic. By March 1853 the rails comprised, in single track miles:[18]

45½ miles at	84 pounds/yard	56½ miles at	76½ pounds
14½ miles at	63 pounds	2½ miles at	60 pounds

This was a major investment, but a few years later, the accountants who did the annual audit of the company's books pointed out that renewals would be a significant recurring cost, which should in future be charged against revenue.[19] They recommended setting up a separate 'Renewals Account', financed by annual investments from revenue. This was something T. E. Harrison had already pioneered on the York, Newcastle & Berwick Railway. The N&C directors therefore set aside £6,300 a year to build up their permanent way renewals fund.

The 1841 staff audit gives an idea of the workforce involved in routine track maintenance. There were eleven 'Quick' cleaners, responsible for lineside growth and drainage and probably also fence and wall repairs. In addition there was one person specialising in drain repairs, with an assistant. The track was the responsibility of 43 platelayers, assisted by 104 labourers. The platelayers were organised into five groups, each under a foreman and timekeeper, not included in the previous total. That does not mean that they were based in just five locations though. The company had about 65 route miles of line, and this suggests that about 1½ miles would have been under the daily supervision of a particular platelayer or lengthman, in later terminology. Wages ranged from 2s 6d a day for labourers to 3s 4d for all platelayers and either 4s or 5s for foremen.

On some lines, such as George Hudson's original York & North Midland route, built in the late eighteen-thirties, housing was specifically provided for platelayers in rural areas. The N&C seems to have offered none. Its early housing was largely confined to station agents. Even gatekeepers' cottages date, in the main, from the eighteen-forties. Platelayers and their labourers evidently found accommodation in the villages, from which most of them were, no doubt, recruited.

Signalling

We are so used to railways equipped with a plethora of fixed lineside signals that it can come as a surprise to realise that it was not always so. The early railways relied, like most present-day roads, not on some external control but on the common-sense of drivers and some operating rules. To appreciate how this worked on the N&C we first have to consider the mix of double and single track route which existed during the first decade of operation.

The original intention was to build a double-track formation but open as a single-track line with three 'sidings' - passing loops - per mile.[20] With a view to coal traffic from the Prudhoe area, the Managing directors recommended in 1833 that the stretch from Blaydon to The Hagg, at the west end of the Wylam river wall, be laid as double track. Despite the objections of the Carlisle directors, who felt this might draw resources away from their end of the line, this was done. At the same time some economies were made in the earthworks, including the construction of Farnley tunnel as single track. The various stages of the line duly originated in the following form: Carlisle to Milton (Brampton Junction): double; Milton to Haltwhistle: single; Haltwhistle to Haydon Bridge: double; Haydon Bridge to The Hagg: single; The Hagg to Redheugh and Newcastle: double.[21] This meant that there were 31 miles of single-track route. The rapid growth in traffic made this a bottleneck, and a doubling programme got underway in 1839. By March 1840 double track had been extended from The Hagg to Stocksfield and was in progress elsewhere. A year later it had been completed between Hexham and Haydon Bridge (entailing the Warden Bridge widening) and Haltwhistle to Gilsland. The remaining stretches were delayed by the 1841-2 economy drive, but Gilsland to Milton was finished in 1843 and the last part of the route, between Hexham and Stocksfield, was finished with the completion of the Farnley tunnel widening in 1845.

The 1835 Blaydon to Hexham opening was therefore of a mix of double track - 5 miles - and single - 11½ miles. The number of passing loops on the single track section had been reduced to one per mile, but in the early days there will have been little routine need for most of these.[22] The line was worked by two engines, based at opposite ends and doing two return trips each per day. They set off at the same time from either end and must have passed at a station on the single-track section, probably Stocksfield, where there was a small goods yard and siding at which the mixed train will have picked up and set down wagons from time to time. Problems arose if one train broke down or was significantly late, and there will have been a protocol as to how long the first train would wait before proceeding cautiously on its way. The despatch of trains was the responsibility of the station agent and there was a convention of hand signals, flags by day and lamps by night, for communication between him and the guard and driver.

The system relied on drivers having some visibility ahead, though in the early days this was not helped by the absence of tail lights, something which Sir Frederic Smith, the Board of Trade's first Inspector of Railways, noted in September 1841.[23] The company subsequently adopted red tail lights and white lights at the head of each train. The single-track Farnley Tunnel posed a particular problem, anticipated by the directors in August 1834, when they noted that it would require a watchman, with lamps and a [mechanical] telegraph or signal posts.[24] The actual arrangement adopted, prior to its doubling, is unknown.

Most double-track railways were operated on the 'time-interval' system until the eighteen-seventies, the station agent (later stationmaster) observing a fixed interval after the departure of one train before permitting the despatch of another. The 1853 N&C rule book specified that five minutes should elapse before permitting a following train to depart, and that for a further five minutes the driver should be instructed to proceed with caution.[25] On the N&C, with stations at three-mile intervals, this would only have allowed a slow mineral train, doing about 12 mph, to reach the next station a minute before an express, leaving ten minutes later and doing 30. Prior to the adoption of Cooke & Wheatstone's electric telegraph, there was no means of remote, instantaneous communication between stations, and the implications of this are shown by an incident recorded by Richard Lowry in 1836. On 23 August *Hercules* broke down at Milton, due to an axle failure, and sat there overnight blocking the westbound track of the double-track section. Next morning Lowry went as guard on the first eastbound train from Carlisle, and just after leaving Scotby, the first station, they encountered a horseman galloping down the line. He had been sent from Milton to tell them to cross to the opposite track at Wetheral and wait there for the westbound train, hauled by *Samson*, which would be travelling on the wrong track to get past *Hercules*. They waited an hour and a half for *Samson* to appear, as it had been waiting an hour at Milton expecting them to come through first.

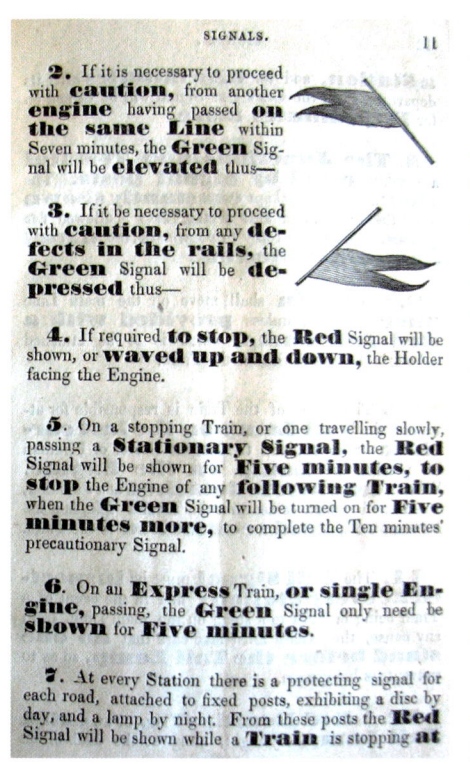

14.3. Page from the 1853 Rule Book.

This problem was eased by the electric telegraph, installed during the Autumn and Winter of 1852-3, though its purpose was initially more commercial than operational. [26] The N&C signed an agreement in May 1852 with the British Electric Telegraph Company, which used railway linesides to provide a solum for its wires. The N&C paid an annual rent of £120 and in return got priority use of the system and five instruments, paying extra for any further ones. BET had establishments in Newcastle and Carlisle, while station clerks were to send and receive public messages on their behalf at intermediate points. In January 1853 the N&C directors decided to have their instruments set up at Carlisle, Milton, Haltwhistle, Alston, Haydon Bridge, Hexham, Mickley, Blaydon, Redheugh and Newcastle.[27] This left more than half the stations unconnected. Mickley is an interesting case - included on account of the Mickley Coal Company and the need to communicate about their traffic. The telegraph obviously could be used to pass information about breakdowns and suchlike, but routine train operation was still based on the old methods. The telegraph was eventually nationalised, becoming part of the GPO, with whom the railway already had a relationship, not simply through the conveyance of the mails, but because a number of stationmasters also became sub-postmasters, with the directors' blessing.

The first fixed signals are said to have been introduced on the line about 1841, and they were eventually provided at all stations and junctions. The signals comprised revolving disks mounted on top of posts, accompanied by lamps for use by night.

The disk had red and green faces, and its indication corresponded to the manual flag and lamp signals. Thus no signal - with the disk turned parallel to the track - meant that it was safe to proceed. Red meant stop and green signified proceed with caution. Captain Laffan observed in 1851 that most intermediate stations had just one signal, serving both tracks. More stringent rules applied at junctions, where the normal indication was red, and engine drivers were required to whistle on their approach in order to have the signal cleared, observing as they did so a speed limit of 10 mph. At the two places of greatest danger, the level crossings of the Maryport & Carlisle and Lancaster & Carlisle Railways, on the Canal Branch, the limit was reduced to 4 mph and drivers were eventually required to stop before whistling for a signal.

The 1841 staff list confirms that the railway then had no policemen, the term being used in those days for someone who both helped to keep order and regulated the trains by operating signals. At most stations there were labourers, who also looked after the points, but a number of locations had 'point keepers'. These were fifteen in all, among the lowest-paid of the company's employees on 2s or 2s 6d per day. Most were situated at the junctions with colliery lines and therefore had a signalling function. Locations include Wylam, presumably for the track leading across the river to Thompson Brothers ironworks; Mickley; Allerwash Lime Kilns; Blenkinsopp Colliery; Milton, for the junctions with the Earl of Carlisle's railway; and Broadwath, where there was a lime and coal depot. Even at the two main stations, Newcastle and Carlisle, operating the switches initially involved scurrying round the tracks to individual points.

Road level crossings have always been a potential problem, and the visiting directors in May 1835 suggested providing train guards with bells to be rung on the approach to crossings and minor stations. [28] The introduction of the steam whistle, early in the line's history, was obviously of more benefit. Under its 1829 Act the company was obliged to provide gates at public road crossings and to have these closed normally against the railway; in practice they were normally closed to road traffic. The 1835 Act, which permitted the railway to introduce steam locomotives, stipulated that the turnpike road crossings should be replaced by bridges, but no action was taken on that until Parliament insisted as a condition of the 1846 Alston Branch Act.[29] Meantime, gatekeepers were employed, but they were not given housing on the spot, unlike later railway practice. Wooden huts were provided, from which they were supposed to watch over the traffic, but there must have been a strong temptation to forsake these for other pastimes during the quiet spells between trains. The Carlisle committee of directors raised this point in connection with the deaths of two horses at Broadwath crossing in December 1843.[30]

Under the Turnpike Act of 1839, railways were required to construct their crossing gates so that these closed fully across the roads when open for the railway, however almost none of those on the N&C did so, tempting pedestrians to cross the line in the path of oncoming trains, which resulted in a number of deaths. The Board of Trade's Sir Frederic Smith pointed this out following a journey over the line in September 1841, and Adamson replied that the company were looking at the provision of new gates, and in some cases bridges, but that 22 crossings would be affected and it would all take time.[31] Indeed it did. The second Regulation of Railways Act, passed in July 1842, gave the Board of Trade power to make railways alter their existing gates, and these were eventually invoked following a visit by the Board's General Pasley in April 1844.

Pasley was brought in by the Scotswood Bridge Company at the urging of that inveterate mischief-maker, George Thomas Dunn. At issue was a level crossing at the east end of Blaydon station, where the road to the chain bridge crossed the Redheugh Branch at a very oblique angle.[32] Pasley vindicated the railway company, recognising that it was impractical to provide gates which closed across the road, since they would have been immensely long and wholly unmanageable. Yet the visit opened up the whole issue of compliance with the Act, and in June 1844 the directors gave orders for new gates to be fitted at manned crossings as soon as possible.[33] Blaydon remained as it was, but a year later they condescended to provide the man there with a flag 'to show road users when trains are coming.'[34]

The death of an old lady at Tyne Green crossing, near Hexham, in August 1845 led to an edict from the Board of Trade that the company should provide a policeman there and at Blaydon. Hitherto, the company had employed no policemen, but it advertised the two posts in October 1845.[35] In a later development the directors agreed to build a house at Tyne Green so that the policeman's wife could man the crossing, while he presumably looked after shunting and other operations at Hexham station.[36] 1856 saw the provision of two more policemen, at Carlisle and Newcastle stations, though Plummer undertook to see if this could be achieved by redeploying other staff rather than recruiting more.[37] By 1858 the railway had eleven 'policemen and watchmen' on its payroll.[38]

Signalling on the N&C can look very primitive to modern eyes, yet the trains were not fast and its directors were able to demit office in 1862 with the proud boast that they had never actually killed a passenger.

14.4. *Another vignette of Scotby station (cf figure 12.7). This seems to depict a revolving disk signal mounted on the post adjacent to the bridge parapet in the left foreground. Ahead are the covered coal and lime cells and the gable end of the station house. Like the other view, this was engraved for Sutton's leatherworks, which provides the backdrop.*
(per Mr. Clarke of Scotby)

14.5. *A striking contrast is provided by this array of signals at the west end of Newcastle Central, seen c1893, during work to extend the station. When the N&C platforms opened, at the start of 1851, one signal was deemed sufficient to control all their traffic. The station was fully signalled when extra platforms were added in 1871-2. The early 70's also saw the NER introduce block signalling throughout the system, and the Carlisle line acquired a profusion of signals and cabins. In this view, the typical NER gantry is flanked on the left by Forth Banks Junction signal cabin, opened c1880, and its replacement, No. 3 box, brought into use during 1894.*
(NERA collection)

Chapter 15: Buildings

Introduction

In 1841 Dr. Augustus Granville published a guidebook: *The Spas of England*.[1] His researches took him to Gilsland Spa, a genteely popular resort on the Newcastle & Carlisle Railway, whose stations he described as 'perfect specimens of taste and style in architecture.' They were, indeed, attractive and picturesque essays in the fashionable Tudor-Revival style, and most survive with their original character intact, despite having all been extended. In their original form, they were the sort of dwellings which any ambitious landowner might choose to employ as a gate lodge

Plans for the early N&C buildings were prepared by John Blackmore, who supervised their construction. There is no evidence for the engagement of an architect, though that does not preclude the provision of some basic designs by one. It is more than likely, however, that the inspiration for these buildings was culled from pattern books, possibly in Henry Howard's well-stocked library. Blackmore certainly went on to re-use one of the railway designs, little altered, for his toll-house at Norham Bridge and to display his neo-Tudor skills at Aspatria, on the Maryport & Carlisle.

15.1. *Norham Bridge toll house is a smaller version of Stocksfield, one of the earliest N&C station designs, lacking Stocksfield's attic bedrooms. Over the years both have lost the central mullions of their Tudor-revival windows to accommodate larger sashes, while the tall stone chimneys have in this case been replaced by stumpy brick ones. (Bill Fawcett)*

The 'house architect', quite literally, to many of the leading directors was John Dobson, who designed Holme Eden for Peter Dixon and Benwell Tower for Thomas Crawhall, as well as doing work at James Losh's Jesmond villa and Matthew Plummer's Sheriff Hill Hall; he also designed the 1847-8 Ouseburn Flax Mill for Plummer and his son Robert. Dobson is not recorded on the N&C scene, however, until he was engaged in connection with the Newcastle station and bridge in the eighteen-forties, culminating in his appointment at Central Station. He was probably, however, the architect of an 1839 'plan of elevation' for an unbuilt terminus.[2]

Benjamin Green was engaged to design the Alston Branch stations (described in chapter 10), but that appears to be in some way a consequence of the Hudson lease, and was evidently a 'one-off'. The directors, always conscious of the pennies, were not keen to be paying architects' fees if they could possibly avoid it. Following Blackmore's death in 1844, building design and supervision was taken over by Peter Tate, who appears to have relished the task, continuing the tradition of impeccably-built neo-Tudor for station extensions and offices but making his own mark with the elegant waiting sheds of the eighteen-fifties and proudly signing his name to the water tower at Haltwhistle.

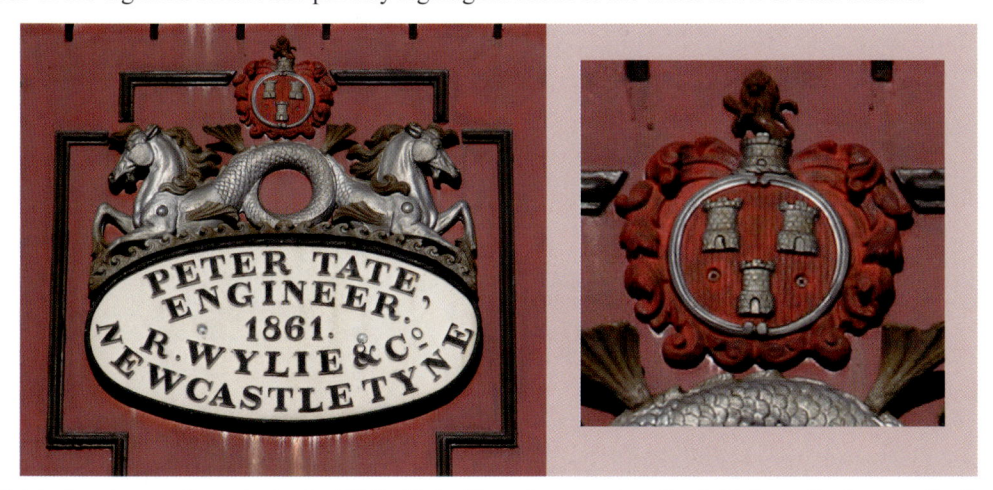

15.2. *Peter Tate's signature on the water tank at Haltwhistle. The enlargement on the right shows the three castles from the coat of arms of Newcastle, while the sea-horses are also based on its supporters. (Bill Fawcett)*

187

Stocksfield Station

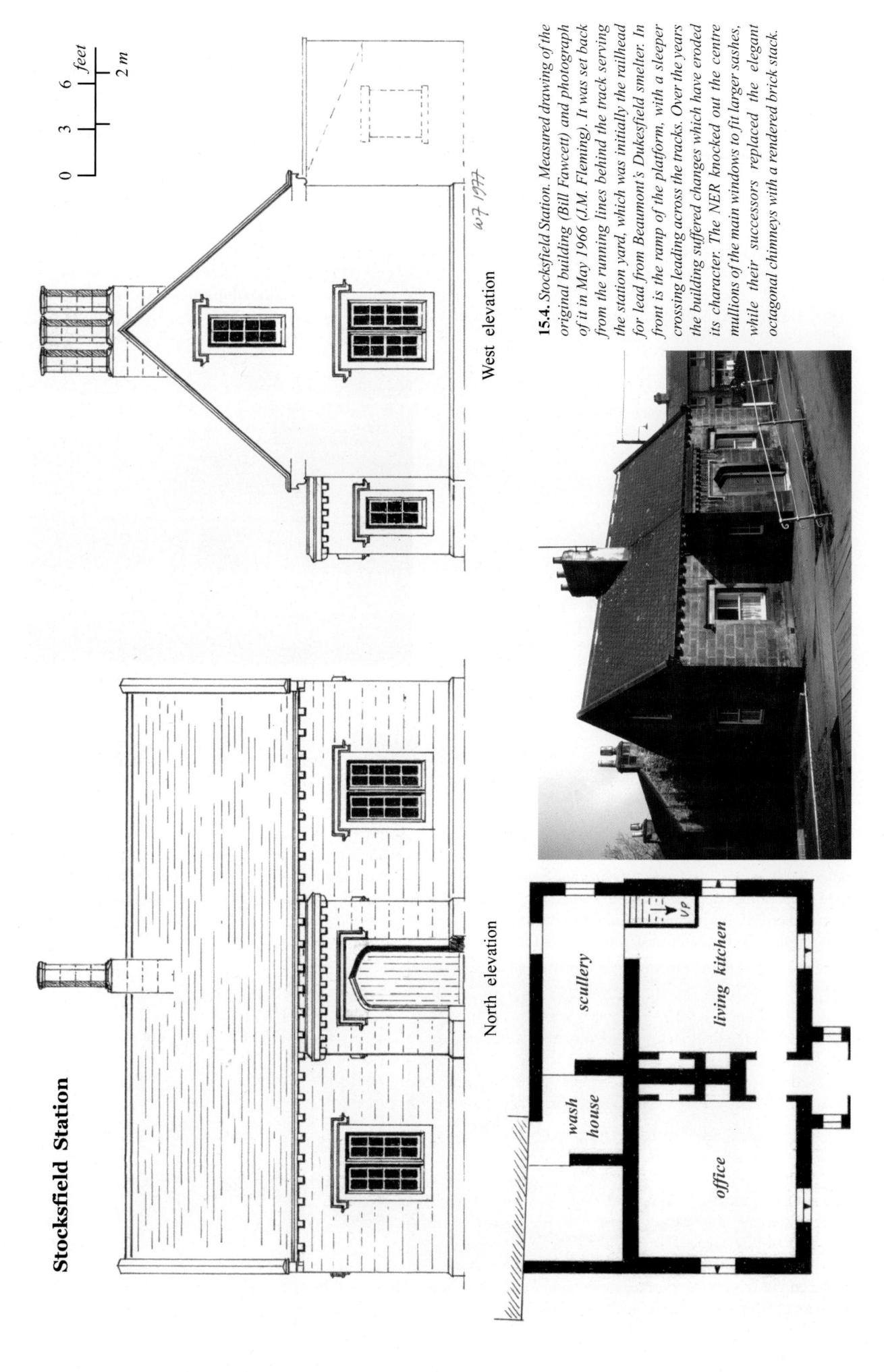

West elevation

North elevation

15.4. *Stocksfield Station. Measured drawing of the original building (Bill Fawcett) and photograph of it in May 1966 (J.M. Fleming). It was set back from the running lines behind the track serving the station yard, which was initially the railhead for lead from Beaumont's Dukesfield smelter. In front is the ramp of the platform, with a sleeper crossing leading across the tracks. Over the years the building suffered changes which have eroded its character. The NER knocked out the centre mullions of the main windows to fit larger sashes, while their successors replaced the elegant octagonal chimneys with a rendered brick stack.*

wash house

scullery

office

living kitchen

188

Station designs: 1835-9

There were few railway prototypes for the directors to draw on, so to put the stations in context, one might consider the toll-houses provided on the turnpike road through Hexham and Haltwhistle. Some survive, and we can see that they were quaint and humble, with few stylistic embellishments. They were polygonal in plan, following the turnpike tradition of presenting a splayed front to the road, to provide a good view of approaching traffic. By comparison, the early N&C stations seem almost generous.

15.3. *Toll house on the former Shibdon Bar to Greenhead turnpike road, forerunner of the present A69, at Whitchester, not far from the east portal of the railway tunnel. (GR 726638)*

(Bill Fawcett)

At the outset an N&C station amounted to no more than a house and some paving, not a raised platform, at the side of the running lines. It was usually accompanied by a siding and coal depot but there will have been no storage facilities for goods and little or nothing in the way of waiting facilities for passengers. The directors were reluctant at first to build any houses for their employees, and the station house was provided so that the agent might be available on the spot, seven days a week, to keep an eye on the company's property and deal with its business. When the first stretch of line opened in March 1835, few of these buildings had even been started, but most were completed in the course of a year.[3]

The question of where to site the stations and what their accommodation should be was examined in detail during a line inspection on 14 August 1834 by Matthew Plummer, William Losh and Joseph Crawhall, accompanied by George Johnson, John Clayton, John Adamson, John Blackmore and John Challoner, their Head Clerk and future Chief Agent.[4] At Blaydon they agreed to use the western yard of Beaumont's lead refinery as their depot site, and the company went on to adapt one of its buildings for an office and waiting room.[5] At Wylam they looked at a cottage and stable built on their land by George Grahamsley, the contractor, for his own use, and decided to buy these to meet the immediate station needs. At Prudhoe they recommended a depot for goods and passengers and 'a proper person to attend it', while at Stocksfield they specified a station with a cottage for the person in charge. Riding Mill 'will be a station of importance' and required a 'proper person ... for whom a house and office will be required.' 'Tinkler Bank Foot' (Corbridge) was to receive a station house 'and other erections, also a weighing machine.' Dilston was to get a gatehouse on the turnpike road from Corbridge, which actually took a decade to materialise. Finally, Hexham would need warehouses, staiths for lime and coal and a lead depot; buildings for passengers; dwelling house and offices for clerks; stables; engine house (i.e. engine shed); and a spacious yard. This sounds quite impressive, but Plummer and companions went on to recommend that temporary sheds be provided in the first instance, so that they could judge, from experience, the best layout for the permanent buildings.

On that basis, the line opened with the pair of temporary sheds, sixty feet long, ten feet wide and 'high enough for the engines to pass underneath', ordered for Hexham on 20 January 1835, along with 'temporary watch or shelter houses' at places like Stocksfield and Riding Mill.[6] In the first instance, passenger bookings were only taken at the terminal stations and some locations in Newcastle, including the company's first office in Newgate Street, along with Hexham's *Black Bull Inn*. Passengers joining at intermediate points paid their fares to the guard.[7]

What of the permanent station houses? A good starting point is Stocksfield, one of the earliest to be built. This is a one-storey and attic building, with two bedrooms on the upper floor, originally lit just by a small window in each gable. The ground floor was also divided into two rooms, each with independent access through a substantial, enclosed porch. One of these served as the living room and kitchen, with a scullery projecting at the rear and a corner taken out to accommodate the bedroom stairs. The other front room probably doubled as an office and an occasional waiting room for Mr. Beaumont and his friends. A similar design was probably employed for the first station at Corbridge, to judge from early maps, but no illustration appears to have survived. It lay south west of the present road bridge, which replaced the original level crossing in 1847. A new station was built on the opposite side of the road which forms the nucleus of the existing building.

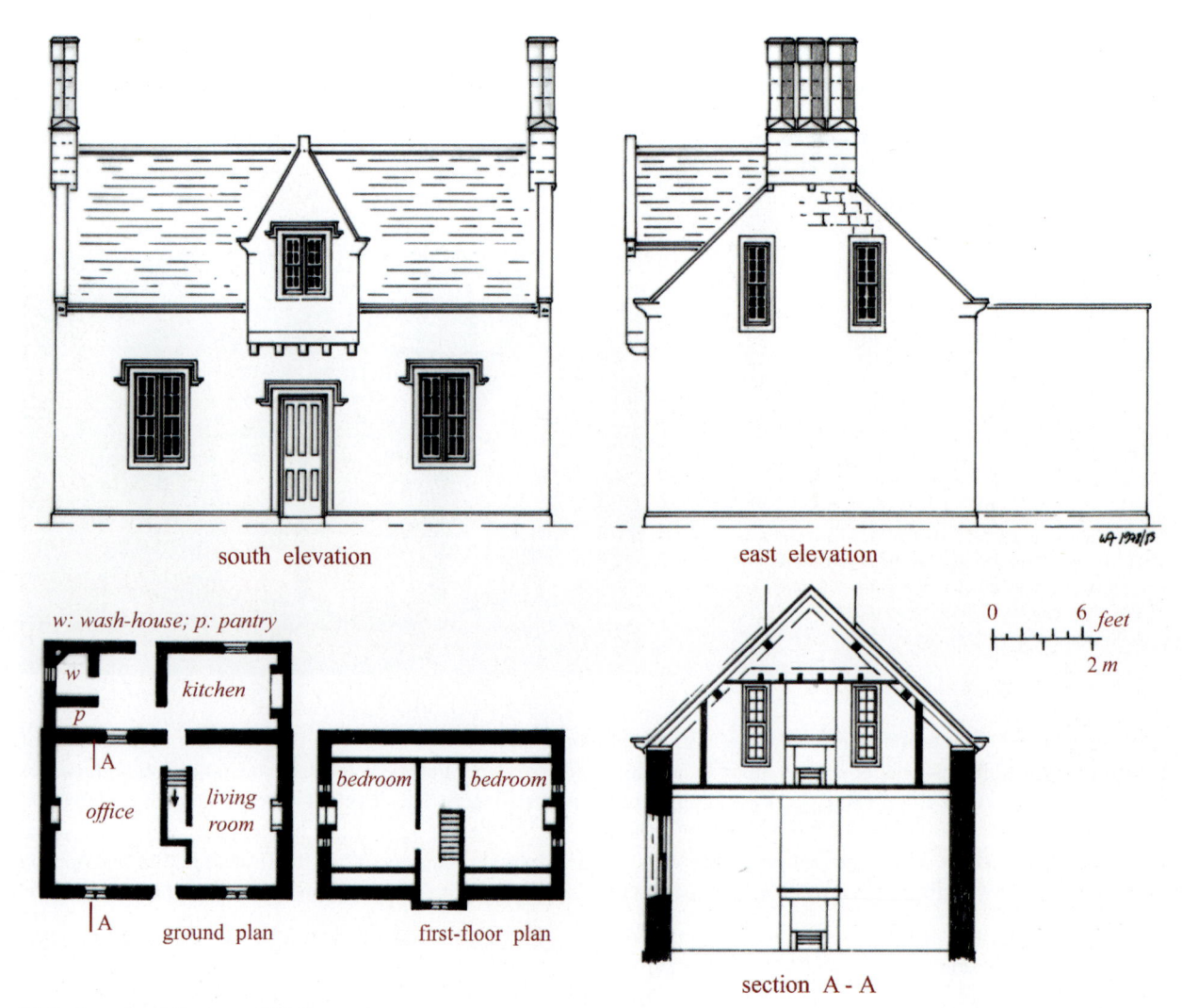

15.5. *Greenhead Station. (Bill Fawcett)*

The design which is most characteristic of the railway originated at Riding Mill and Wylam, where Mr. Grahamsley's cottage was relegated to other purposes. It is almost six feet shorter than Stocksfield and has the chimneys moved to the end walls and the stairs moved to the middle of the building, where their half-landing is lit by the corbelled-out dormer window which is such a distinctive feature. The bedrooms are lit by pairs of slit windows in each gable. A particularly subtle touch in the front elevation is the way the dormer gable ends in a slender panel reaching up – much more delicate and effective than any finial would be. The drawing here is of Greenhead, the design having been adopted for the original stations between there and Carlisle, except for Wetheral, which was given special treatment.

The Managing committee observed on 16 May 1836, two months before opening, that the Greenhead station building had not been started but the stones were ready, so evidently the contractor got the carefully-dressed ashlar masonry ready in advance. The directors fondly anticipated completion in six weeks from then, but it was a wet summer, and the building was still incomplete in October. At Gilsland (initially known as Rose Hill station) the dimensions were scaled up to give a taller and more extensive building than usual, though still of the same floor plan. This provided a much larger office/waiting room, almost twenty feet square, and was clearly directed towards Dr. Granville and other visitors to the two long-established springs. Gilsland flourished under the influence of the railway, which was obliged to extend the station as we shall see later. How Mill and Low Row did not receive their stations until 1839 but the latter is still the dormer-gabled type.[8]

The domestic accommodation provided in these dwellings was somewhat limited, particularly by the standards of North Eastern Railway stationmasters, and a variety of extensions appeared from the eighteen-seventies onwards, often carried out with careful regard for the original. At Riding Mill a second range was built in 1871 onto the rear of the house, leaving its original appearance otherwise largely unimpaired. This includes the wooden corbels and bressumer of the dormer gable, which were faithfully renewed during renovation in 1983. Wylam was the subject of a sensitive but more radical enlargement in 1897. Under William Bell, then NER Architect, the bedroom floor was raised to a full storey but the dormer gable was retained and the new windows of the upper floor conform with the original ones beneath.

15.6. *(left) Greenhead in 1990. Despite some changes from the original windows, the overall character is kept. The 'magpie' behind was the Co-op store, mentioned later.* (Bill Fawcett)

15.7. *(above) Riding Mill: west gable, showing how the NER extension has been grafted on.*
(Bill Fawcett, 1970)

15.8. *Gilsland in 1966. The column in the foreground was a survivor from the hideously clumsy platform shed built by the NER in 1902. To the left is the additional waiting-room block designed by Peter Tate. The NER inserted the booking window seen just left of the original station doorway, with a classic back rest standing in front.* (Bill Fawcett)

15.9. *Wylam station in May 1966. The waiting shed stretching left from the original house was added in 1860.* (J.M. Fleming)

191

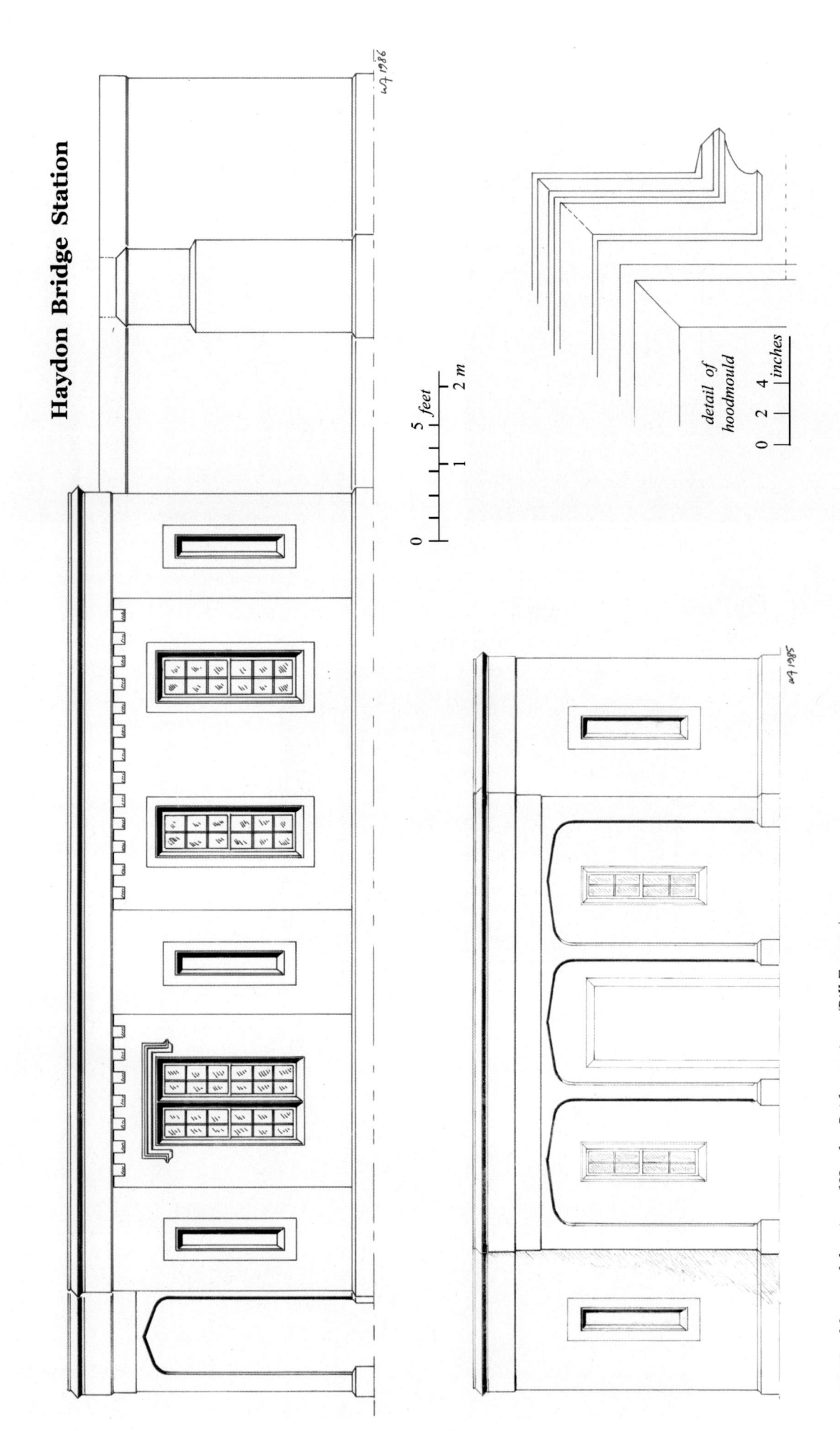

15.10. *Measured drawing of Haydon Bridge station. (Bill Fawcett)*

1836 saw the arrival of another, and more formal, design in the repertoire.[9] The beneficiaries were Haydon Bridge, railhead for Allendale, and Wetheral, the station for Corby Castle. The two magnates whom the directors wished to please were no doubt T. W. Beaumont (with the Crawhall brothers also in mind, perhaps) and Henry Howard, and the buildings were put in hand more speedily than those on the first section. Thus Haydon Bridge was being roofed by April 1836 and may have been usable by the opening on 28 June. In this design a parapet is carried around the building, partially concealing a hipped roof, and the front wall breaks forward into a neat portico of three shallow Gothic arches. A first-class waiting room and office probably occupied the front portion of the building and each was marked out on the side elevation by a hoodmoulded window. Wetheral has suffered from the removal of its portico in 1861 to accommodate a rather charming N&C verandah, but Haydon Bridge remains largely in its original state, having been superseded by a new station building and house in 1876. In both cases, however, the roof has been reconstructed so that it sweeps down onto the top of the parapet wall, thereby giving it undue visual prominence but doing away with the maintenance problems posed by a concealed gutter.

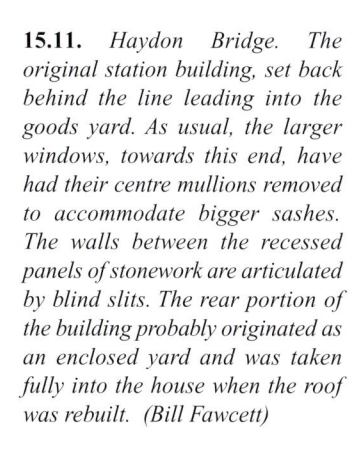

15.11. *Haydon Bridge. The original station building, set back behind the line leading into the goods yard. As usual, the larger windows, towards this end, have had their centre mullions removed to accommodate bigger sashes. The walls between the recessed panels of stonework are articulated by blind slits. The rear portion of the building probably originated as an enclosed yard and was taken fully into the house when the roof was rebuilt. (Bill Fawcett)*

A design which departs from the Tudor-Revival idiom of the others is found at Fourstones, a somewhat late station, whose catchment area was originally served by temporary stations at Quality Corner, near Warden, and Allerwash. Fourstones lies halfway between them, conveniently close to the village of Newbrough, and was confirmed as the new location in November 1836.[10] There was some delay in building the station, it being noted at the end of 1837 that Mr. Thorburn, the 'collector' - another synonym for agent or station keeper - was without a house, and he was given five pounds a year in lieu.[11] The building was eventually erected in 1839 and began life as one of the smallest of all N&C stations: just three rooms arranged in a T-plan, the stem of which has a bowed end and is emphasised by rusticated (channelled) masonry.[12] This suave little building could be an acknowledgement of either Greenwich Hospital, who owned the area, or John Clayton, whose country seat lay only two miles away, at Chesters. It was extended in two phases: first by adding a sitting room to the right-hand (east) end, then by building an extra wing out to the west, housing a general waiting room and ladies' waiting room, with toilet. Despite this, its original character and sense of modest scale survives.

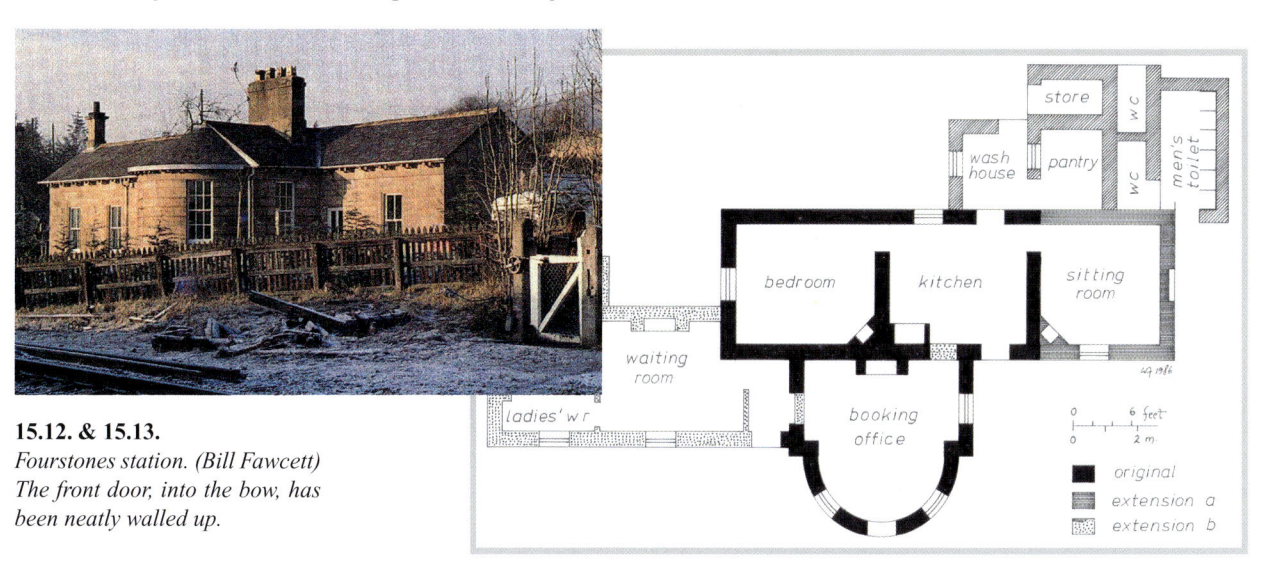

15.12. & 15.13.
Fourstones station. (Bill Fawcett) The front door, into the bow, has been neatly walled up.

193

north elevation (facing tracks)

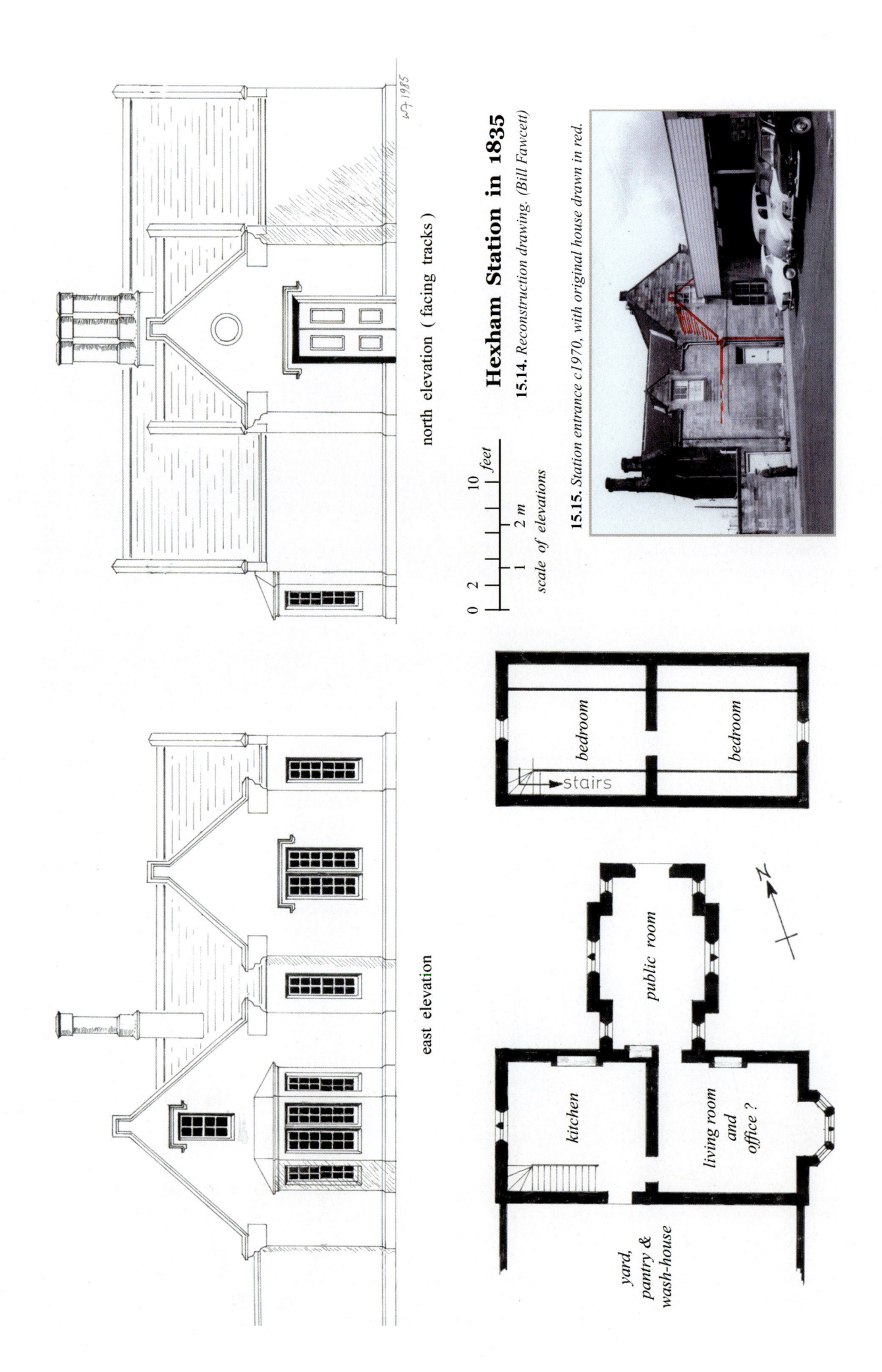

east elevation

Hexham Station in 1835

15.14. *Reconstruction drawing. (Bill Fawcett)*

15.15. *Station entrance c1970, with original house drawn in red.*

scale of elevations

bedroom

bedroom

stairs

kitchen

public room

living room and office ?

yard, pantry & wash-house

In some ways, Hexham station, with its prominent gables and canted bay window, anticipates the larger buildings erected at Carlisle and Haltwhistle. Yet it is essentially the Stocksfield house, augmented by a boldly projecting public room, gabled on its three visible sides. Despite reading on plan rather like a vestibule, this had a fireplace and presumably functioned as the first-class (and only) waiting room. It communicated directly with one of the two ground-floor rooms of the house, which was given a large bay window and will have served chiefly as the agent's office. William Greene, the first agent, received a surprisingly small house, slightly smaller on plan than Stocksfield.

Minor alterations to the house culminated in an extensive remodelling in 1881, resulting in a very much larger dwelling. In the first phase the kitchen was transferred to an extension in what had been the yard, while the former kitchen was remodelled as the main living room and given the bay window originally situated on the east gable. In the second phase the house was raised to a full two storeys. However, the original building survives within this, as noted in figure 15.15, though it may not be immediately apparent. From the tracks, one's first impression is of the fine platform roofs provided by the NER in 1871, but again the original entrance can still be seen in the midst of the waiting rooms and offices added by the N&C itself, from the eighteen-fifties onwards, and the NER.[13]

15.16. *Beneath Thomas Prosser's handsome platform roof of 1871, we see the entrance to the original station, under the 'waiting room' sign. The N&C extended the offices along the platform. This meant removing the main east and west windows from the public room but they were re-used; one can be seen just to the right of the near column.*
(Bill Fawcett)

15.17. *(right) Looking the opposite way, with resited west window on the right. (Bill Fawcett)*

15.18. *The much-enlarged house from the south west, complete with the bay window moved over from the east gable. A car park has taken the place of the coal yard and tiny garden seen in figure 12.8, and this is the taxi turning area.   (Bill Fawcett, 2007)*

Carlisle London Road Station

15.19. *This carefully-posed photograph, with Carr's biscuit boxes in the foreground, is thought to have been taken shortly before the N&C buildings were demolished to make way for the new goods station, begun in 1881. The 1836 station building is on the right, with the running lines out of sight behind it. The wooden goods shed lies straight ahead, with the locomotive yard of the engine shed and workshops on the left.*

15.20. *A detail from the sketch of London Road station made by J.W. Carmichael. Comparing this with the photograph above, it is striking how little the station building had changed in some 45 years. (Tullie House Museum & Art Gallery, Carlisle)*

The Carlisle depot was given a large site on the east side of London Road, with the running lines through to the Canal Basin bypassing it on the south side and gradually dropping below the level of the station yard. The station building was much larger than any the company had built hitherto, so the directors had clearly recognised the need for explicit office and waiting room accommodation. As usual, the buildings were the last things to be started, as the line neared completion.[14] They were built by George Grahamsley, whose efforts were hampered by wet weather and a strike by the stonemasons, who clearly thought they had the contractor at their mercy.[15] Latterly he concentrated his efforts on having the engine and carriage sheds finished in time for the opening, which they were. The station was a different matter, as Richard Lowry related. On 29 June 1836 he remarked that 'the roof still wants to be on the station house'. 19 July saw the formal opening and the following day the start of normal traffic. It was still raining, and he noted that 'The office in which we are has no roof upon and we have been nearly perished today. I think if the weather does not take up soon, or we don't get into another office, a fresh supply of clerks will be in request.' Next day Blackmore gave orders for some temporary roofing and a stove, but the station house was not completely finished until the following February.[16] Meanwhile, William Greene, having transferred from Hexham to Carlisle as agent, had taken up residence elsewhere, relegating the station house to one of his subordinates.

From 1843 London Road played host to successively the Maryport and Lancaster & Carlisle railways but, pending the joint station, this did not involve any permanent additions to the premises. An idea of the limited facilities and of the railway's sometimes cavalier attitude is revealed by the *Carlisle Journal* of 14 January 1848, reporting that a first-class passenger making a connection with the Maryport line had to wait out in the cold because one of the directors was having breakfast in the first-class waiting room and no-one else could be admitted. The station house contained the offices for both passenger and goods traffic and simply continued as the goods office following the transfer of passengers to Citadel station in 1863. It was demolished to make way for the NER's 1881 goods station, now itself sadly derelict, but a hint of it lingers on in the substantial buildings erected at Haltwhistle and Bardon Mill on the central stretch of line, opened in 1838.

15.21. *Haltwhistle: 'Change for Alston & Carlisle', in the late nineteen-sixties. The detached one-storey block behind the nameboard was built in 1855, to the design of Peter Tate, to provide a pair of waiting rooms. The NER transferred the booking office into this range and enlarged it by thrusting a wing out to the rear.*
(Bill Fawcett)

15.22. *Haltwhistle in 2008. The scene has changed relatively little, though the Alston branch has gone and the gas lamps have been replaced by at least two generations of electric lighting. 'Pay trains' removed the need for the station offices, now occupied in part by the tourist information centre.* *(Bill Fawcett)*

15.23. *(below) Bardon Mill station in October 1964. This is a delightfully quirky, yet formal design, with a two-storey centrepiece rising from the low range behind. The NER provided a booking office and waiting rooms in the wooden building erected in 1889.*
(J.M. Fleming)

Housing

Plummer and his colleagues were reluctant to provide housing, except where it was desirable to have someone on hand to keep an eye on the company's property. So they provided no accommodation initially for platelayers and gatekeepers, the two groups usually catered for in rural areas by later railways. They did, however, provide watchmen's cottages at Scotswood and Warden bridges, on account of the fire risk.

About 1839-40 the company made a significant increase in the housing stock by building four terraces, each of six dwellings.[17] One was at Derwenthaugh, for coke burners at the ovens which the company was building to supply locomotive coke. Another was at Wylam. The surviving examples are at Haydon Bridge and Greenhead, and originated as one-storey cottages, with two rooms - a living-kitchen and bedroom, accompanied by a scullery.[18] The survivors have been raised to two storeys to provide upstairs bedrooms, with Haydon Bridge being done in a particularly careful manner so that the roof is now graced by a handsome line of dormer windows.

Gatehouses made a significant appearance on the scene in the mid eighteen-forties. The 1841 survey reveals that the company then employed nineteen gatekeepers, most of them on a wage of 2s 6d a day: at 7 days a week that gave them £45-10-0 per year. During their long working day they were provided with a wooden cabin, several of which blew down in a great storm in January 1839 and were left 'lying across the rails'. Given the temptation to go off and do other things in the intervals between trains, Blackmore evidently favoured the provision of houses at important crossings and was authorised to prepare plans for these in October 1836, and again three years later.[19] In neither case does anything seem to have happened.

The last chapter described how the Board of Trade focused the directors' minds on the issue of level crossings during 1844-5. At the same time they finally became persuaded of the merits of providing gatehouses, and a batch was ordered in August 1845.[20] They were similar in scale and accommodation to the earlier dwellings, so you ended up with a three bay frontage with a central door, often a central chimney, and a room either side. Perhaps the most elegant example was Sandy Lane, near Corby, which had handsome Tudor windows with prominent hoodmoulds. That, no doubt, reflected the proximity of Mr. Howard. Brampton Fell is more typical, with careful masonry and an elegant chimney but no specifically decorative features. These two were built in dressed stone but sometimes the masonry was rubble stonework, rendered over except for dressed-stone architraves and quoins, as seen at Tyne Green cottage, near Hexham, dating from 1847.

15.24. *Sandy Lane crossing. (GR 476549) Looking west, in the nineteen-seventies, with the tracks curving round onto Corby Glen viaduct. The diminutive house was extended by the NER, which also rebuilt the chimney; it would have had a pair of stone shafts originally. The crossing has been closed and the house demolished. (Bill Fawcett)*

15.25. *Brampton Fell crossing. (GR 539591) This house survives, complete with original chimney, and typifies the simple 2-room design. The roof would have oversailed the gable, as at Sandy Lane, but has been trimmed back to the wall. (Bill Fawcett, 2007)*

Haydon Bridge cottages

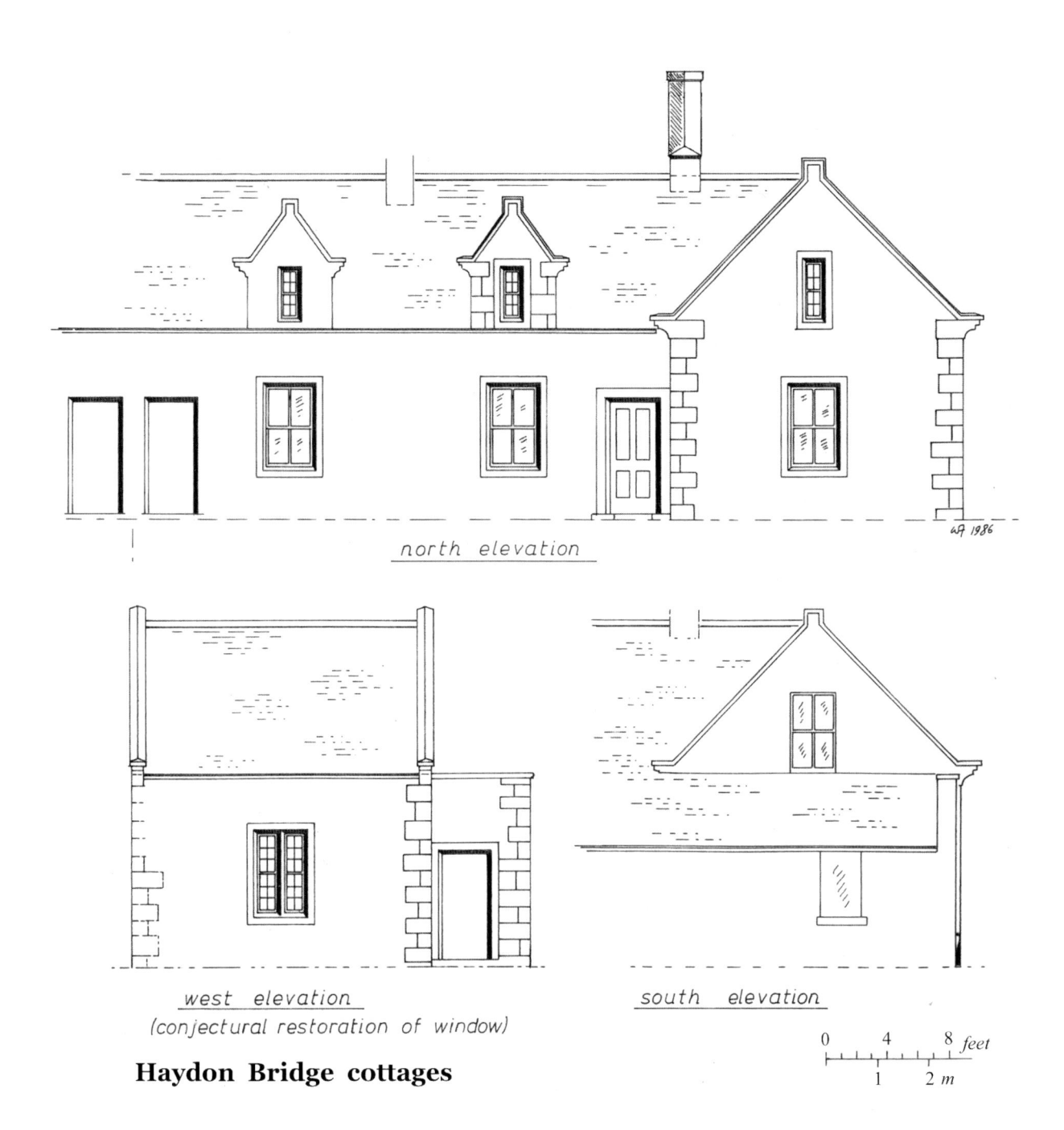

north elevation

west elevation
(conjectural restoration of window)

south elevation

15.26. *Measured drawing of the cottages at Haydon Bridge station.*
(Bill Fawcett)

15.27. *The Haydon Bridge cottages in the nineteen-seventies, at which time replacement windows were just beginning to destroy the unity of the design. The copings to the gable walls are not made of sandstone, as first appears, but moulded fireclay.*
(Bill Fawcett)

On the whole, platelayers were still left to fend for themselves, unless an arrangement could be come to whereby a man received a gate cottage rent free in return for his wife or family looking after the gates, as at Dilston Lane, near Corbridge. There were three crossings in this area: the Hexham turnpike at Dilston Gate, which received its gatehouse in 1845 [21]; Dilston Lane, about two hundred yards to the east; and the turnpike at Corbridge station, replaced by an overbridge in 1847. In 1853 the company built a semi-detached pair of cottages at Dilston Lane, letting one rent free plus a payment of 3s 6d a week to their tenant on condition he (and his family) looked after the gates in addition to his normal work.[22] At this time the directors voiced criticisms of Peter Tate's one-storey designs, not because they wished to provide more space for their employees as such, but because they thought having a spare bedroom would enable them to take in a lodger and help solve the housing problems of single men working for the company. This contrasts markedly with the Stockton & Darlington, whose policy was to have three bedrooms: one for the parents and separate ones for male and female children. On George Hudson's lines as well, housing provision was far more generous than on the N&C, leading to quite a disparity when they all ended up within the NER.

Nonetheless, the N&C's housing accommodation had expanded considerably in quantity, if not amenity, by 1855, when some 71 dwellings were recorded.[23] In addition there were the station houses, Richard Lowry's villa at the entrance to the Forth Goods and the 'three convenient dwellings' then under construction at the gates of the company's Forth workshops for 'trustworthy foremen, whose constant presence on the spot will afford increased protection to the general property'. [24]

Flag Stations

The N&C allowed a number of landowners to stop trains by request: the Earl of Carlisle at Naworth crossing; Colonel Coulson at the west lodge of Blenkinsopp Hall; John Davidson at Ridley Hall bridge; John Grey, the Greenwich Hospital Receiver, at Dilston crossing. The agreement with Davidson was probably typical. While negotiating land for the line the directors had offered to stop all trains there, but he waived his right to stop the fast trains. The mixed trains would stop on seeing a flag hoisted, but no (road) carriages were to be taken up or set down there, in order to avoid delays.[25] The company had agreed to build a lodge and gate there, but Davidson accepted a payment of £200 instead and no facilities were ever provided.

Only one of these private halts ever matured into a proper station. That was Naworth, a manned crossing where the Carlisle committee urged the provision of a gatekeeper's cottage as early as September 1840, but to no avail.[26] Three years later the Board agreed to provide a cottage and waiting room, but waited until 1844 before proceeding with what turned out to be the usual three-roomed cottage.[27] It was a stylish example of the type, however, with careful Tudor-revival detail and must have been prepared before Blackmore's illness since it is virtually the same as his Norham toll cottage (fig. 15.1). It survives, though somewhat transformed by the NER, which lengthened it in 1881 and subsequently added an upper floor.

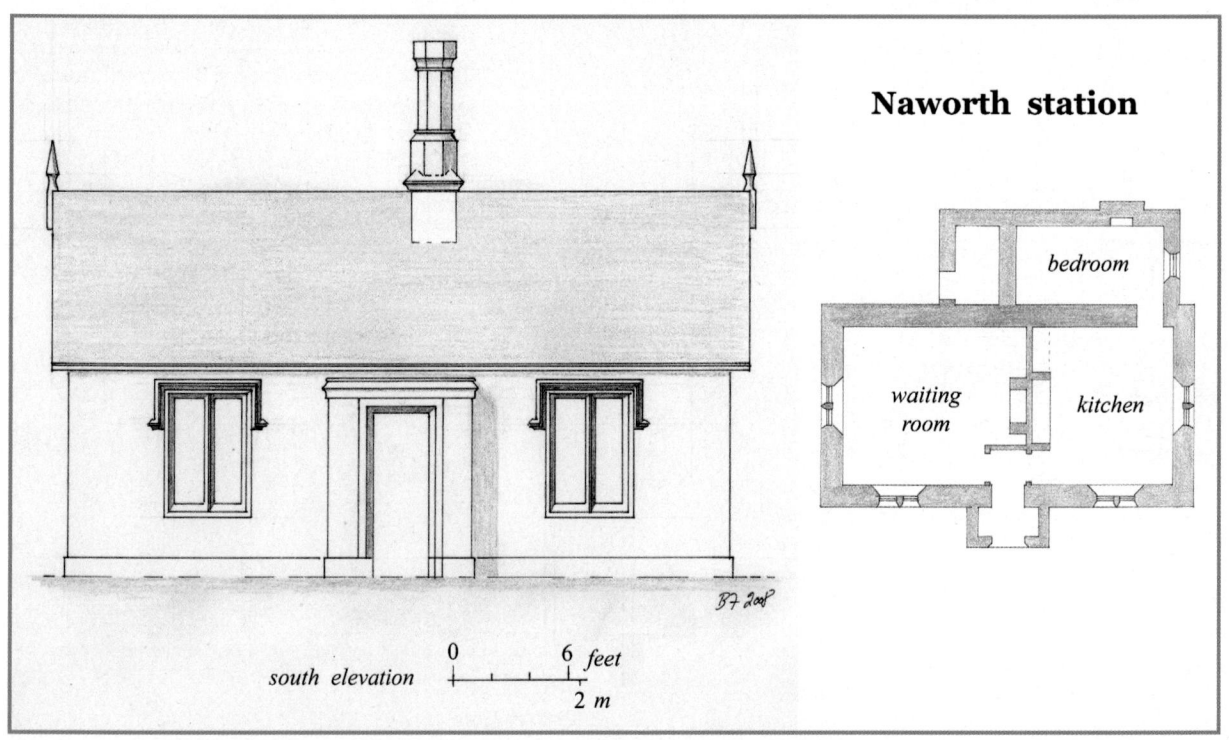

15.28. *Naworth station in its original condition. The sparse accommodation reflects the directors' requirement that it should cost no more than £100. The dimensions have been taken from an NER survey drawing made in 1881 and have not been checked on site. That year saw the extension of the building to the right to provide an extra bedroom, and the new work carefully matched the original. The upper floor, probably added in 1910, has much simpler detailing.* (Bill Fawcett)

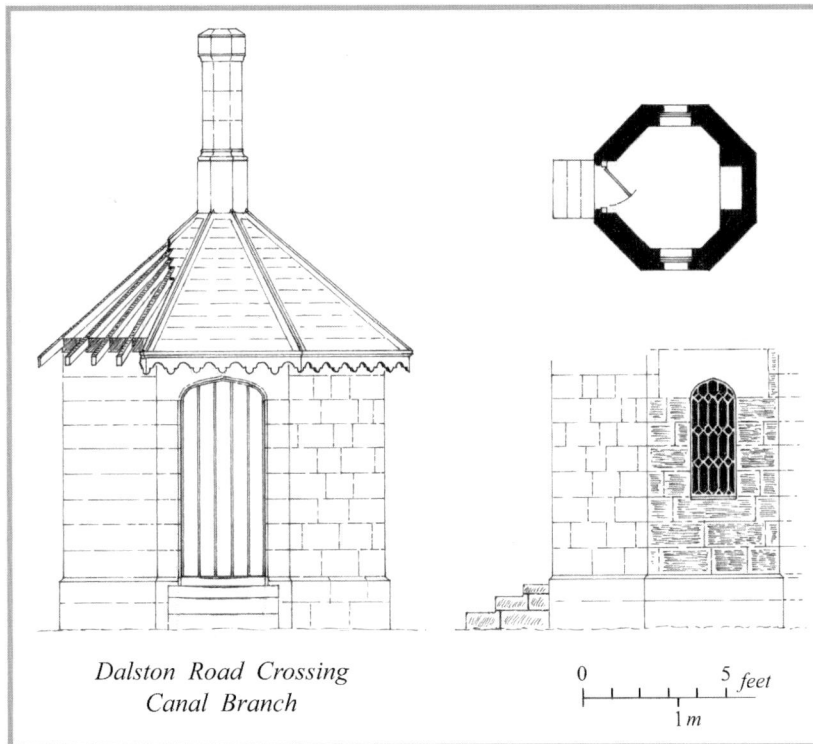

15.29. *A handsome, and apparently unique, crossing-keeper's hut on the Canal Branch. After the branch closure, it was dismantled and re-erected elsewhere. Measured drawing reconstructing the original chimney. (Bill Fawcett, 1972) Photograph by John Fleming, showing the replacement chimney and latterly felted roof. (May 1971).*

Dalston Road Crossing
Canal Branch

Keeping the rain off, and other station improvements

Richard Lowry was not alone in suffering the elements when attending the N&C in its early days. The handsome stations provided few facilities and little shelter for most passengers. Some rapidly acquired trainsheds of a design peculiar to the company, the best known being Hexham and Carlisle, which were sketched, but sheds also appeared at Blaydon, Haydon Bridge and Greenhead - all serving for a time as railheads for road coaches.[28] Most comprised transverse ridge-and-furrow roofs, timber-framed and borne on slender cast-iron columns. The Carlisle roof had fifteen feet spans, viewed from the side, supported on two lines of columns thirty feet apart. The winds no doubt howled through at times, but the rain will have been kept partly at bay while passengers retrieved their belongings from the luggage vans.

15.30. *Another detail from Carmichael's sketch of London Road station, showing a train waiting to depart beneath the trainshed. This was, no doubt, designed by Blackmore and is a rather more thoughtful building than the simple sheds generally associated with early railways. The coach on the left may have provided the connecting service from the Canal Basin.*
(Tullie House Museum & Art Gallery, Carlisle)

15.31. *Hexham station, apparently in the eighteen-fifties. The station is depicted with rather more accuracy than the train. Thus the artist shows the ridge and furrow trainshed, as at Carlisle, and the extensions made to the station offices in the early fifties – notably the hip-roofed block in the foreground. Just visible at far left is a corner of the goods shed.*
(courtesy of Hilary Kristensen)

Blaydon's trainshed was wrecked in a gale at the beginning of 1839, when it was presumably rebuilt in the form seen in figure 12.9: a hipped roof borne on tall columns with some timber cladding along the side.[29] Hexham's lasted until 1870, when, having become rather decrepit, it was replaced by the present platform roofs. The NER also replaced Hexham's platform, which barely warranted the name, being six inches high and barely three feet wide, squeezed into the gap between the running lines.[30] In N&C days it would probably have functioned like some Continental stations do today, with the staff ensuring that only one train at a time stood in the station.

The lack of platforms at intermediate stations, and their inadequacy where provided, was one of several features roundly criticised by the Board of Trade's Captain Laffan in 1851.[31] The BoT then had no powers to insist on action but the directors responded briskly, putting some platforms in hand later that year, and all but Low Row and Wetheral had received them by October 1855.[32] In practice these platforms could be quite humble affairs, judging by the one completed at Haydon Bridge by January 1852.[33] It was built between the tracks, using 'old planking from the Wylam Bridge'. At the same time, Peter Tate was called on to provide waiting sheds. These are very substantial and follow the conventions of the period in being open-fronted sheds, with a roof sloping up from rear to front. They are, however, among the most attractive examples of the genre. The walls are built in lightly-tooled sandstone, with elegant, shaped corbels where the valanced timber canopy thrusts forward.

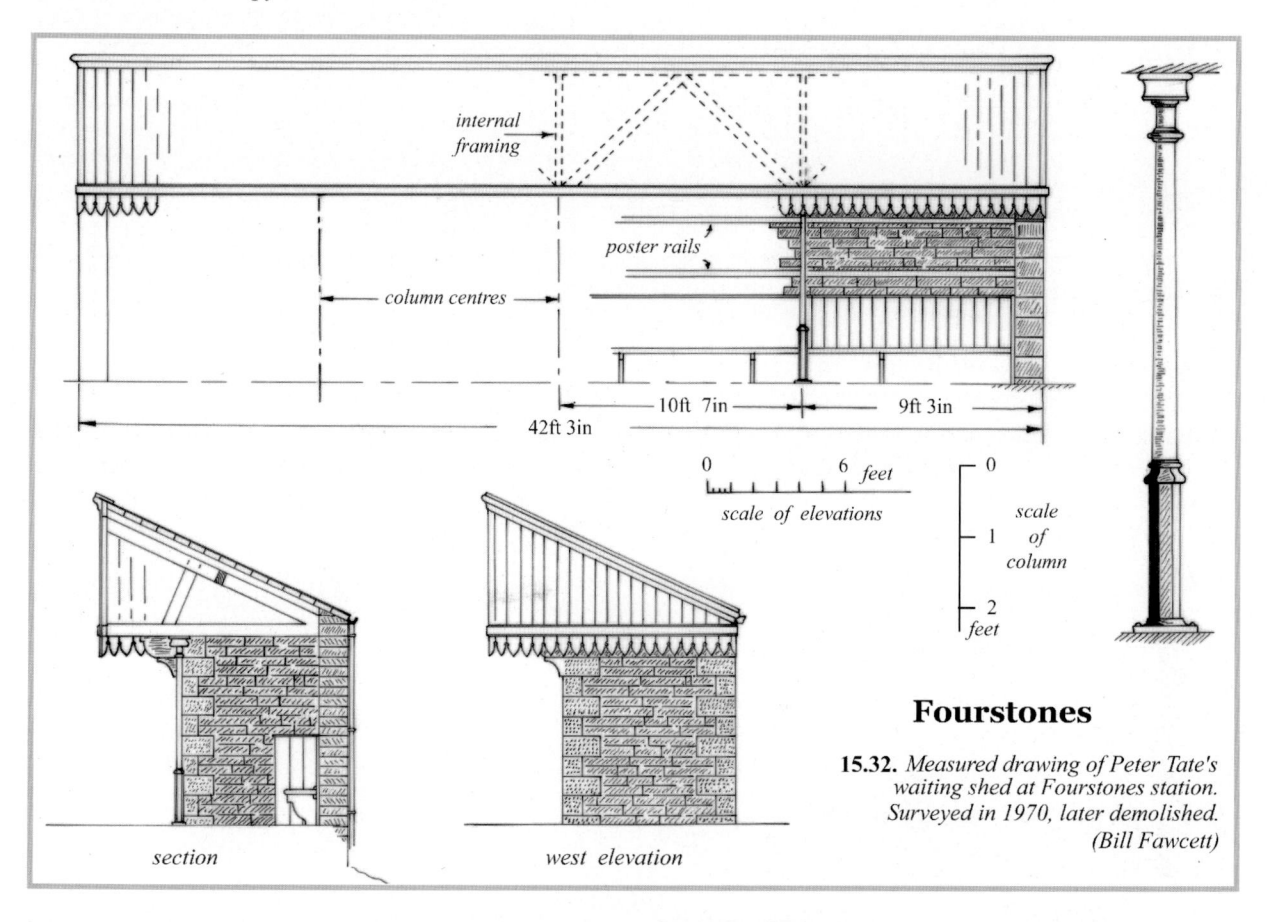

Fourstones

15.32. *Measured drawing of Peter Tate's waiting shed at Fourstones station. Surveyed in 1970, later demolished. (Bill Fawcett)*

Hexham station was enlarged in stages to provide more waiting rooms and offices, and a few other places also acquired waiting rooms, the most conspicuous examples being the free-standing blocks built at Haltwhistle, Gilsland and Wetheral. The case of Haltwhistle shows how improvements came about. The need for extra facilities was raised by the Reverend Octavius Jones at the company's March 1855 AGM, and Tate was asked to plan a waiting room. The scheme had expanded a little when the Board paid a site visit during a line inspection, work being authorised in October.[34] Haltwhistle and Gilsland follow a common design: a two-roomed, detached block replicating the detail of the station building in terms of mullioned windows and hoodmoulds.

Wetheral was tackled in 1860-1, and was probably the last station on the line to receive platforms.[35] Philip Henry Howard had long succeeded his father as laird of Corby and was also the railway's deputy chairman, so he acquired a first-class waiting room linked by a neat, glazed cast-iron verandah to the original building. Unfortunately this entailed doing away with the portico. Such verandahs were very unusual on the N&C, but Gilsland, in its role of genteel resort, was also given one, complete with some frilly iron cresting. A much more economical but still pleasant example of platform roofing was provided in 1860 at Wylam (fig. 15.9), in the form of a hip-roofed extension to the original house: part waiting shed, part waiting room and office.[36]

south elevation with verandah omitted

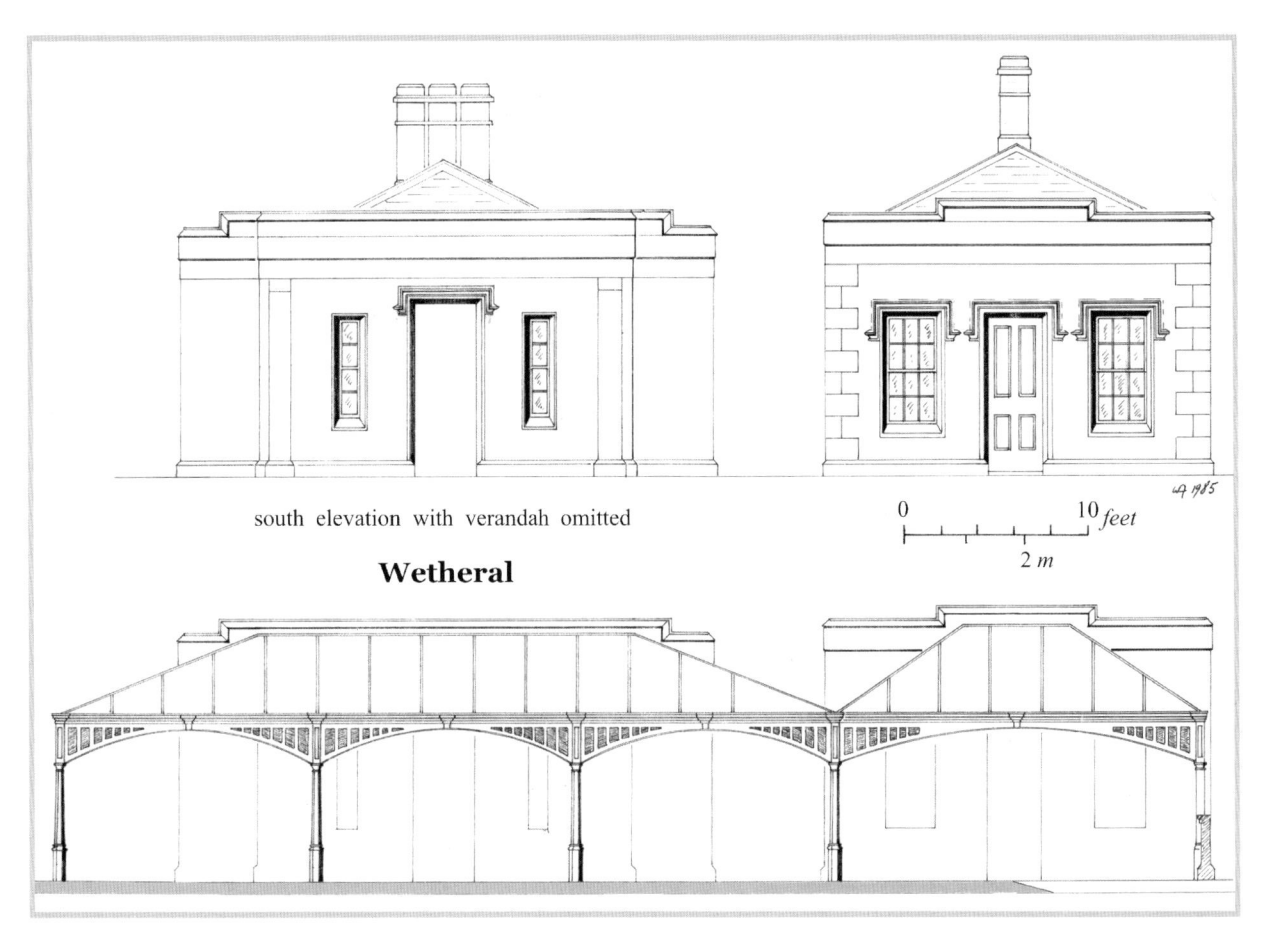

Wetheral

0　　　　10 *feet*
2 *m*

15.33. *Measured drawing of Wetheral station, showing the verandah added in 1860-61 and the low N&C platform. (based on site measurements, aided by an original drawing; Bill Fawcett) By the nineteen-sixties only the left-most bay of the verandah remained. It had been kept to provide a sheltered area in front of the external booking windows provided in the wooden extension seen in the photograph below. This remains today, but the first-class waiting room, which is the detached block on the right, has been demolished.*

15.34. *Fourstones station, looking west. On the right can be seen part of the NER's new station building of 1879-80. The photograph was taken c1970, the station having closed in January 1967. The buildings were demolished not long after. (Bill Fawcett)*

15.35. *Wetheral station c1970. (Bill Fawcett) The first-class waiting room was perched on the brink of the ravine. The viaduct parapet can be glimpsed on the right.*

Building for the Locomotive Department

Relatively little survives of the buildings erected for Anthony Hall's department. Haydon Bridge retains most of the small workshop/smithy built in 1836, which has been truncated and restored to provide a branch library. It is a neat, but fairly nondescript sandstone building, with no obvious evidence of its original function. That portion of the London Road workshop which lasted into modern times was fairly similar. Carlisle was quite a large establishment originally, with the low workshop range accompanied by a pair of sheds, eighty feet long, one for carriages and the other for locomotives.[37]

Greenhead had a similar pair of sheds, and is remarkable in that most of its 1836 buildings still remain, including what must be the world's oldest surviving engine shed. This is a two-road building, which presumably began life with a louvred ridge ventilator, while each track had a pit, infilled in modern times. Stepping up at its east end is an elegant stable built by the company for Colonel Coulson, to replace one rendered useless by the raising of the Brampton road to bridge the railway. Adjoining ranges housed the smithy and workshop, and one of these underwent a curious afterlife, when the NER had no further operational need for it. The building became the home of the Greenhead Industrial Co-operative Society, founded in 1874, which added an upper floor and built a shop on the side furthest away from the railway. With the demise of the local Co-op, it has been remodelled again to form housing but the ground floor, next to the railway, still wears its earlier face.[38]

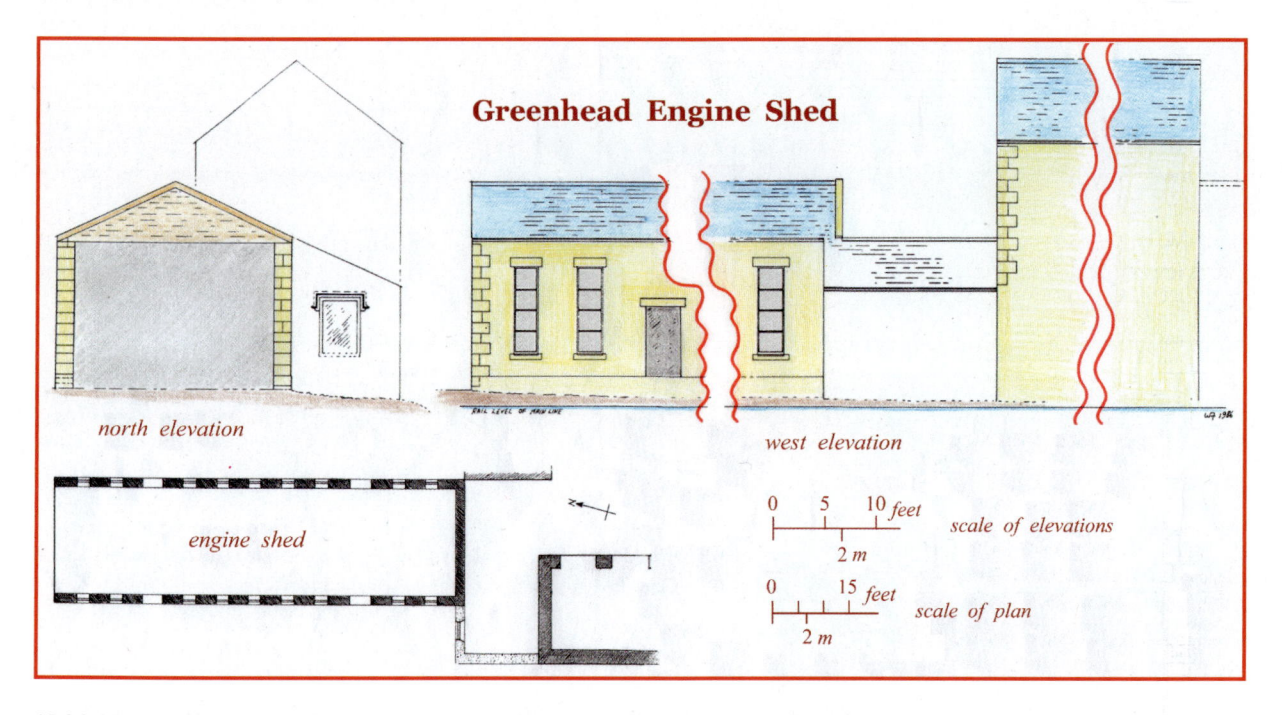

15.36. *Measured drawing of the former engine shed at Greenhead. The tracks serving it will have run between the main running lines and the station house, adding to the fun for prospective passengers. (Bill Fawcett)*

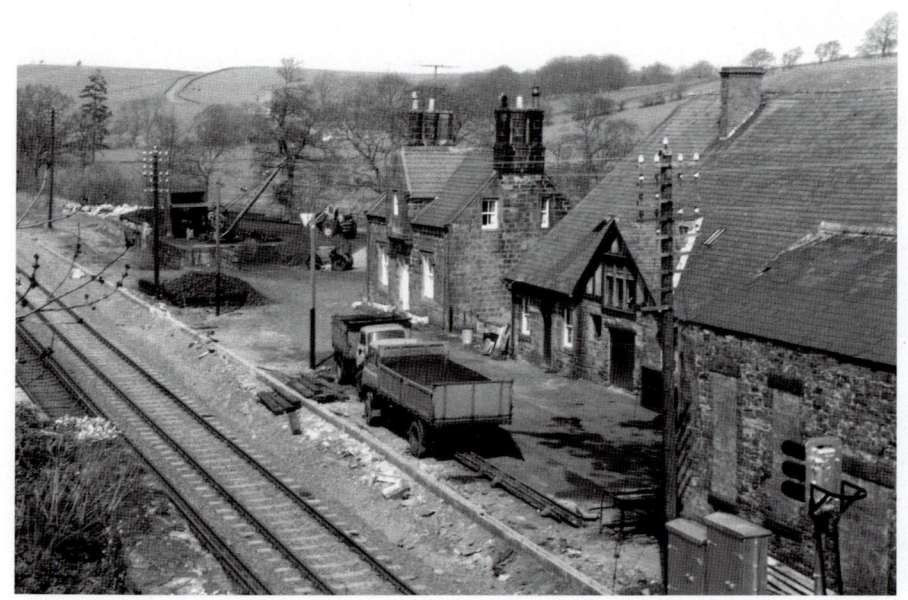

15.37. *Greenhead station in May 1971, looking north. The station closed in January 1967, and the platforms and NER wooden office range had recently been demolished, opening up this view of the station house, the former Co-op store and the engine shed, extreme right. The Co-op incorporated part of the original workshop buildings. (J.M. Fleming)*

The layout of the Forth workshops has been described in chapter 13, but nothing is known of their appearance. They may have been of some interest, since the contract for the first building, the storehouse, refers to a cast-iron roof. Elegance, however, entered the locomotive department through its water towers, of which two remain: Hexham and Haltwhistle. The company employed the tanks customary at that time, bolted together from flanged cast-iron panels, and in the early days these were set on a simple brick or stone base or borne on cast-iron beams, as at London Road. A contemporary illustration shows one of these, with the locomotive water crane built in.

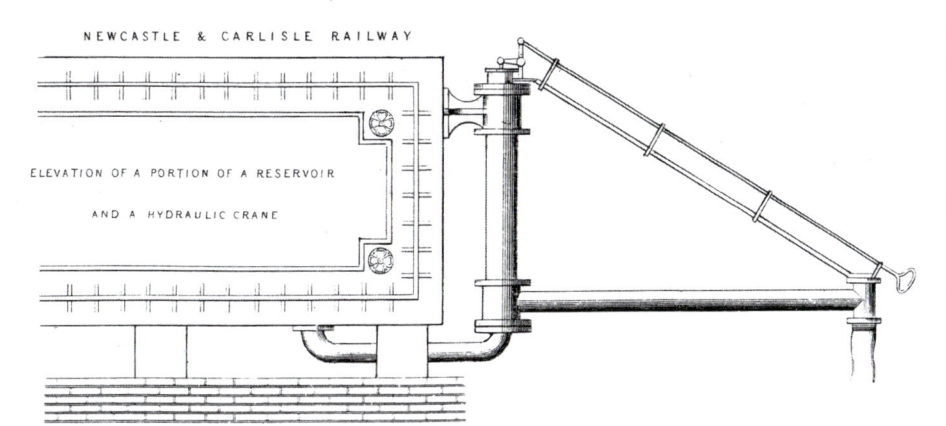

15.38. *An early N&C water tank and crane, from Brees' 'Railway Practice' of 1837. It appears to be the one at Milton (Brampton Junction) described by Whishaw as standing on brick arches. The middle arch housed a boiler from which steam was piped through the tank in cold weather to prevent the water from freezing. His dimensions imply a capacity of 2,500 gallons.*

Hall and Blackmore soon recognised the need for larger tanks, to provide a secure supply, and a particularly handsome water tower was provided at Haydon Bridge, drawing water from the adjacent river by means of an engine and pump housed in the base. This was evidently designed by Blackmore, since it is very similar to his water tower at Curthwaite, on the Maryport & Carlisle, and must therefore have been built by 1843. The arcaded base provided an economical way of providing a sturdy support for the considerable weight of water, and proved popular with a number of early railways. The beams bearing the tank were also supported midway by cast-iron columns.

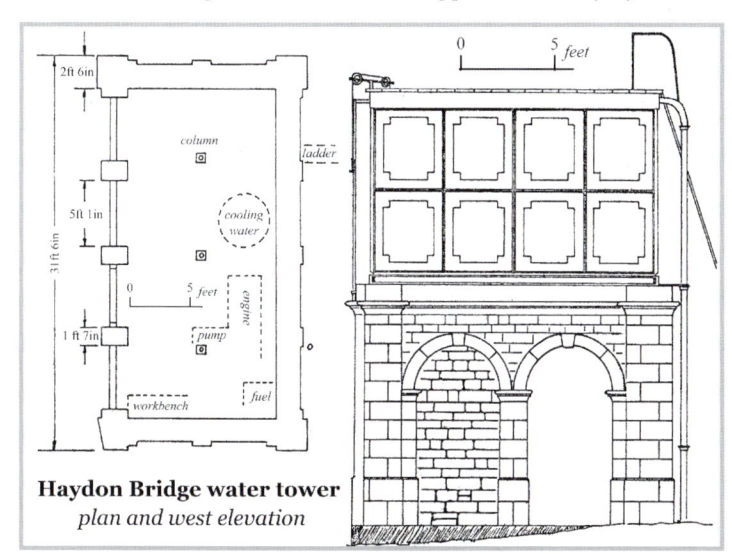

15.39. *Haydon Bridge water tower: measured drawing. The face of the north-west pier was angled to allow clearance for the line serving the goods yard. When surveyed, in 1969, the pump was driven by a single-cylinder Crossley engine but the installation was out of use. The building was demolished in the 1970's. (Bill Fawcett)*

15.40. *(bottom left) Haydon Bridge water tower from the north west. (Bill Fawcett, 1969)*

15.41. *Curthwaite water tower. (GR 325493) The ironwork was supplied by the Hareshaw ironworks, of Bellingham, and cast at their Hexham foundry. (Bill Fawcett)*

205

15.42. *Peter Tate's elegant Haltwhistle water tower has been carefully conserved. Built in 1861, probably almost two decades after Haydon Bridge, it is very similar but Tate has altered a number of the details, introducing for example a slender moulding which outlines the extrados of the arches. Less happy, perhaps, is his use of a chunky, square cornice in place of the roll moulding of the earlier building. (Bill Fawcett, 2007)*

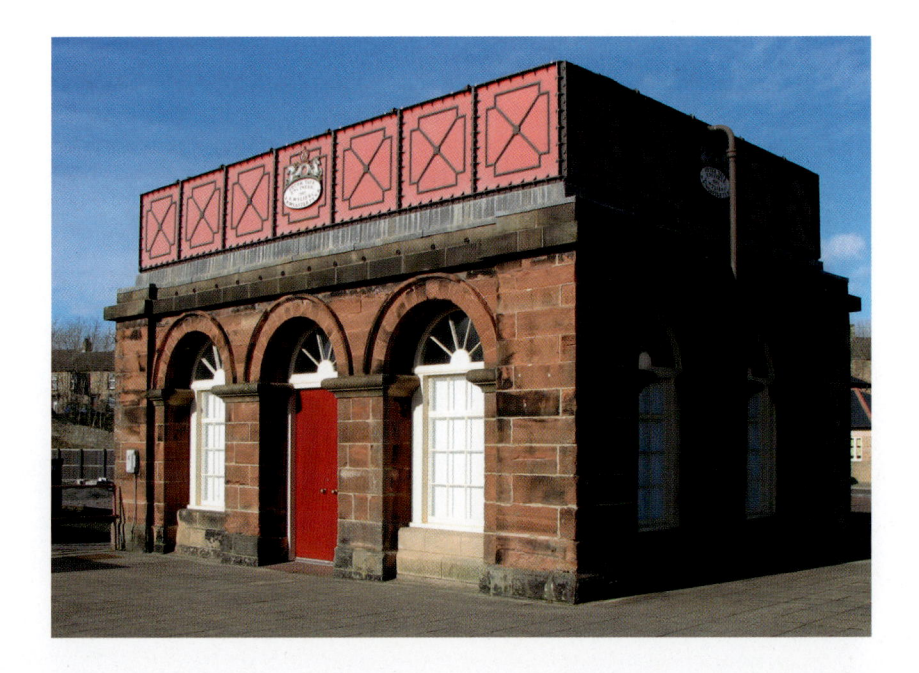

The Goods Department

As we saw earlier, the directors realised the need for specialised buildings for the goods department, noting in August 1834 the requirement for warehousing and coal and lime staiths at Hexham. Nothing was done immediately about the warehouse, but the staiths were a priority, and from the outset they took the form noted in figure 12.8, of a track running over the top of a series of masonry cross walls which delineate a set of depots or cells into which coal would be discharged by the bottom-door chaldron wagons. For their larger depots the N&C preferred to arrange a line of cells down each side of a yard. This was the arrangement at London Road, where the Managing directors noted in May 1836 that a line of 21 cells was under construction, each ten feet by eight 'with an eight foot drop. The far side will be appropriated to an equal number when they may be required'.[39] The far side was in use by the time Whishaw visited the railway, in 1839, and he noted that the cells were roofed throughout. The remains of the depot can still be seen along the north flank of the 1881 goods warehouse.

The Carlisle arrangement was replicated on a small scale at Broadwath, about a mile east of Corby, where much of the depot survives, colonised to form a number of sheds, along with the cottage at its entrance. Henry Howard insisted that the depot be sited there, though the Earl of Carlisle also built coal cells adjoining Corby crossing.[40] The 1839 Railway Street coal and lime depot in Newcastle had an ingenious variation on this layout. The site was a relatively narrow strip, sandwiched between the road and the running lines, and this was divided into five yards separated by back-to-back blocks of coal cells projecting at right angles from the railway and reached via wagon turntables or turnplates. The NER eventually rebuilt it with a conventional layout of three lines of coal cells running the length of the site.

15.43. *Railway Street coal and lime depot, Newcastle, based on the 1/500 OS of 1857-8 and an NER plan of 1866. The block adjoining Dunn Street was evidently a small house, whose occupants could keep an eye on things at night. Some of the yard walls and entrances of the depot are still to be seen.*

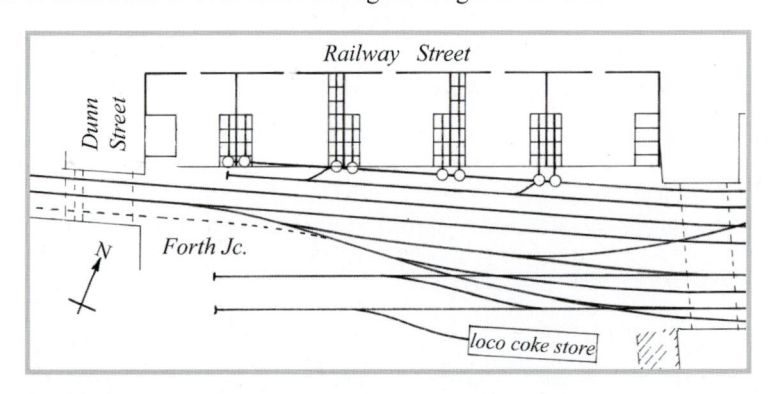

Warehouses took longer to arrive and, even at Carlisle and Hexham, were very modest compared with those the Leeds & Selby Railway (opened 1834) had provided at its termini. Those which appeared at the busier wayside stations, such as Stocksfield, were simple, hip-roofed stone sheds: unsophisticated buildings, with no internal access for railway vehicles but a loading platform alongside. Stocksfield has been demolished but a comparable building survives at Fourstones, now in the grounds of a modern house.[41] Hexham's first goods shed was ordered by the Board in March 1835, though Carmichael does not show it on a sketch he made in December 1835.[42] It is a very unusual building and a very fortunate survival. It comprises a roof of narrow ridge-and-furrow spans, not unlike the early passenger sheds but supported originally on a forest of wooden posts and, on one side, a sturdy stone wall. The other sides were either open or timber clad. Rail access was provided by a siding branching off one of the running lines at right angles via a turnplate. The original concept, as in the nearby passenger trainshed, seems to have been that of an umbrella rather than a building.

north elevation

east elevation (to former road)

west elevation

Hexham Goods Warehouse

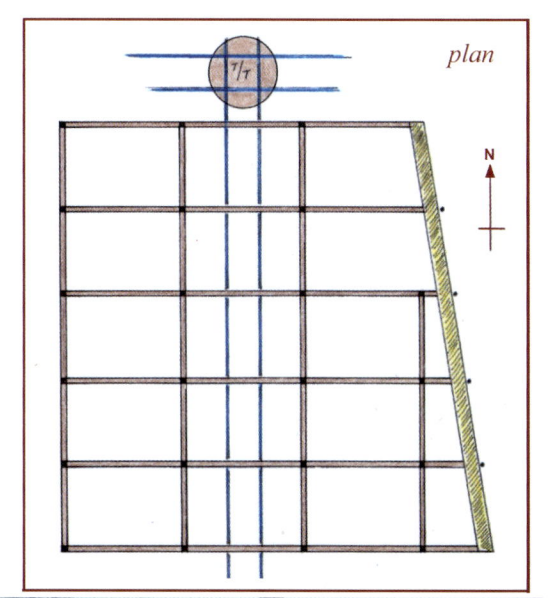

plan

15.44. *Measured drawing of the original Hexham goods shed. Cast-iron seatings and junction pieces (shown in blue) enabled its framework to be assembled from simple timber joists without sophisticated joints. It was apparently intended as a sheltered loading area rather than a secure warehouse, however it was later equipped with some timber cladding and brick walls infilled between the columns. (Bill Fawcett)*

15.45. *Coal stocks at Stocksfield station in the winter of 1966. The goods shed is in the centre of the picture with the yard crane to the left and station house far right. The green poster was an all-too-common sight in those days, announcing a proposal for the 'withdrawal of railway passenger services'. In this case, the victims were probably the stations west of Hexham, which were drastically thinned out from January 1967. (Bill Fawcett)*

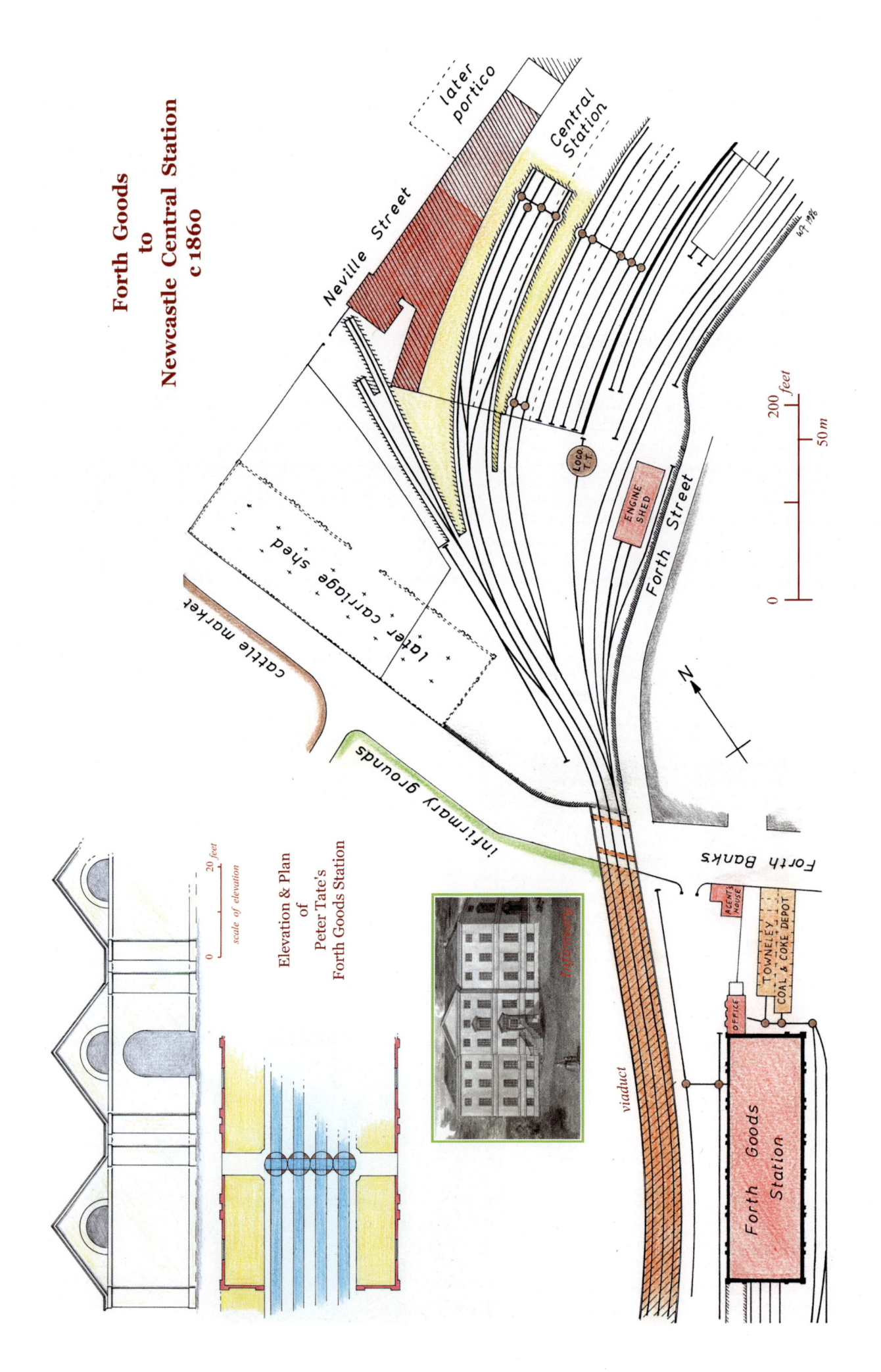

Forth Goods to Newcastle Central Station c1860

later portico

Central Station

Neville Street

later carriage shed

cattle market

LOCO T.T.

ENGINE SHED

Forth Street

infirmary grounds

200 feet / 50 m

N

viaduct

Infirmary

Forth Banks

AGENT'S HOUSE

OFFICE

TOWNELEY COAL & COKE DEPOT

Forth Goods Station

Elevation & Plan of Peter Tate's Forth Goods Station

scale of elevation 0 — 20 feet

Hexham goods shed was very close to the passenger station, served from a line which ran between the station building and the main running lines, posing a further hazard to passengers. The NER's reconstruction of the station in 1871 meant removing this track to make space for the down platform, and as a consequence Hexham got a new goods shed, though not until two years later, in 1873. Both it and the original one survive, providing an interesting contrast. Carlisle retained its N&C wooden building for almost a decade more, until a fine new goods warehouse was built at London Road in 1881. Its predecessor, seen in figure 15.19, looks like another design from the ingenious Blackmore, with wooden posts supporting a roof in two spans running east-west, intersected by cross-spans running north-south.

Newcastle also had to make do with wooden sheds at Railway Street, in the first place, but a permanent building was erected at Forth Banks during 1852-3.[43] Ironically, it survived for not quite twenty years before being replaced by something bigger. Occupying a small part of the site originally destined for the N&C's Newcastle terminus, it was a substantial and well-planned building, designed by Peter Tate in consultation with Richard Lowry, who by then had put in a decade as Agent at Newcastle.

In its overall appearance Tate's design seems to owe quite a lot to John Dobson's Trafalgar Goods Station in Newcastle, then recently completed for the YNB, although the Forth was a lot smaller. Both had ridge-and-furrow roofs running across the building and ending in a sequence of gables treated as neo-classical pediments enclosing bold Diocletian windows. Coincidentally, although the work was let by competitive tender, the contract for the Forth went to Richard Cail, who had built Trafalgar Goods. The work was let in October 1852, and the new building opened on 2 January 1854.[44] Lowry celebrated the transfer from Railway Street by giving all the men a glass of gin. A few months later he moved into a spacious company house adjoining the road entrance from Forth Banks.[45]

This Forth goods station was approximately 260 feet long and 80 feet broad, with an office range projecting from the east end. The roof spans were framed by king-post timber trusses resting on iron beams which spanned between the side walls with intermediate support from a pair of cast-iron columns. A conjectural reconstruction of the elevation and plan is given in figure 15.[46]; it is certain that there was a platform along the north side of the building and it is presumed that there was one on the opposite side as well.[46] It would have been normal to segregate them, with one dealing with received goods and the other with outward traffic. Four tracks were provided, so that wagons could be run to and from intermediate points along the platforms by means of turnplates and cross tracks.

Much of the work of the goods department was done outdoors in the yard and Lowry recorded a curious encounter with Joseph Crawhall when the directors were finalising the plans for the Forth. On 2 August 1852, he was summoned to meet the Board at Central Station, where he found them assembled outside the west end 'furiously discussing ... the site for the goods station'.[47] The plans had already been approved and tenders invited but Crawhall was arguing the case for building on the restricted site formerly occupied by the temporary passenger station at the west end of Central. Lowry pointed out, among the other advantages of the Forth site, the need for yard space, while Peter Tate said bluntly that Crawhall's argument was 'all moonshine and the thing was totally impossible'. Crawhall's was a lone voice but, to assuage him, his dissent was recorded in the minutes and a final decision was put off until the next meeting, when they went ahead as planned.

Tate's Forth Goods was perfectly adequate for its purpose, and designed to permit expansion, but lasted less than twenty years. Trafalgar was the NER's main Newcastle goods station, but traffic growth rapidly made this inadequate and there was little scope to expand the building. The Forth Goods, on the other hand, was well situated on a decidedly underused site. T. E. Harrison therefore persuaded his directors to build a huge new goods station at the Forth.[48] Tate's building stood in the middle of the site and had to be removed, but Harrison's original intention was to re-erect it elsewhere at the Forth as 'warehouse number 2'. This did not happen. Instead, on completion of the first phase of the new station, in 1871, Tate's building was dismantled and removed to the very site advocated by Joseph Crawhall, where it began a new career as a carriage shed.

Some modifications were made during the transplant, notably an enlargement of the building. A second metamorphosis occurred in 1883, when the walls were raised and offices built above the carriage sidings for the NER Accountant, who was based in Newcastle rather than the company headquarters at York. The new roof ran lengthwise in three spans and a light well was left under the middle one for the carriage shed, flanked by lines of offices terminating in the handsome entrance building now known as No. 1, Neville Street. All this remains, albeit in quite different use. Tate's N&C goods offices survived the rebuilding of the Forth Goods, and remained for a further three decades before being demolished to make way for the approach to the NER's King Edward Bridge.

15.47. *Central Station west end in the 1970s. St. Mary's spire climbs above the former carriage shed and offices. The gabled block to the right (dem) was a railway house. Far right, the retaining wall dates from extensions in 1906. Far left is the derelict site of the Infirmary.*
(Bill Fawcett)

Newcastle Central Station

Newcastle Central Station ranks on the world stage as one of the great monuments of the Railway Age, conceived in the civic pride of Newcastle at a time when Tyneside was a world leader in industrial innovation and Richard Grainger had recently provided its capital with a new and eminently worthy heart. That the station was built on a sufficiently grand scale to cope with huge increases in traffic, without a major enlargement until the eighteen-nineties, is thanks to the liberal purse of George Hudson. That it was built at all is thanks to the directors of the Newcastle & Carlisle Railway.

As we saw in chapter 9, Central Station was the price which an initially unwilling Railway King had to pay for the N&C's endorsement of his Newcastle & Berwick Railway (N&B). He agreed to their demands in January 1845, the N&B Act was passed by Parliament at the end of August and work was soon underway on various stretches of the railway, although the High Level Bridge contracts were not let until the following year. By then it will have been evident that the Carlisle line would be extended through to the site of the station some time in 1847, and the Carlisle directors approved John Dobson's design for the building on 1 June 1846, no doubt expecting construction to start within a few months. Indeed, he was asked to consult with the Managing committee, Wood and Johnson, about the requirements for the N&C head office so that working drawings could be prepared 'without delay'.[49] Dobson then went round to Hudson and his colleagues and got their approval on 18 August.[50] Meanwhile T.E. Harrison had been working on the platform layout in consultation with Peter Tate, and the outcome was a classic Robert Stephenson one-sided plan with a single through platform and bays at each end.

Hudson was in no hurry, however. Tenders were eventually invited for February 1847 but they were held in abeyance, with the main contract only being let on 7 August.[51] This covered everything except the trainshed ironwork and the interior plastering of the station offices, which were reserved for specialist contracts to be let later. Standard practice was for the ironfounders to tender for the supply and erection of their portion, the main contractors having built the shed walls and the foundations for the roof columns. McKay & Blackstock got the main contract for the sum of £92,000 and within six weeks site clearance was underway, entailing the loss of such well-known landmarks as the old grammar school and the barber-surgeons' guild hall. In March 1848 *Herapath's Railway Journal* reported a start being made on the foundations of the office range and by August the first purchases were being made of ashlar masonry for the visible walls.[52] This came from the Prudham quarries near Fourstones and so provided useful income for the railway, though by then this was in Hudson's hands under the lease.[53] The building progressed slowly for the remainder of 1848, something for which McKay & Blackstock took the blame, but by April 1849 Hudson and his colleagues felt able to proceed with advertising the trainshed ironwork. On 16 April they approved Dobson's revised design for this, in which he managed to reduce the cost from £12,000 to £10,000.[54] Shortly after, Hudson resigned the chair.

Hudson himself had recognised a need for economy in the worsening financial climate and the YNB shareholders' committee were even more conscious of this as they watched their share price plummet. As a result the most ostentatious feature of Dobson's design was dropped. This was a continuous portico or arcade stretching the entire length of the station frontage. In its place Dobson substituted a simpler facade, breaking out in the centre into a huge carriage portico. The Carlisle directors were keen to proceed with this, and John Clayton did his best to sell it to the YNB, putting forward a suggestion that Newcastle Corporation might contribute £2,000 towards the estimated £10,000 cost of the portico as being a civic improvement.[55] This was impractical, however, given the YNB shareholders' loss of confidence, and the portico remained in abeyance until 1863, when it was built to a modified design, still by Dobson, as part of the price of Newcastle's support for the NER merger with the N&C.

Central Station was formally opened by Queen Victoria and Prince Albert on 29 August 1850 and YNB passengers began using it the following day. The offices were still a building site, however, and the N&C continued to use their temporary premises at the west end. They moved their trains into Central on 1 January 1851 and took possession of their new head office some months later but work was still continuing in areas like the YNB refreshment rooms, and the scaffolding did not vanish from the front of the station until the beginning of September.[56]

Having discussed the details of the building and its stylistic and structural origins in two other books, it seems appropriate here to concentrate simply on those aspects directly relevant to the N&C.[57] The trainshed comprises three arched spans, with wrought-iron ribs resting apparently on a very slender cast-iron arcade, though in fact much of the load is taken by a timber truss running along the top of this and concealed behind the panelling below the raised middle span. Almost half the area of the shed was occupied by carriage sidings, which gave plenty of scope for future expansion. Most of the routine YNB traffic was dealt with at the bay platforms at the east end, and the reversal this entailed for Anglo-Scottish expresses was no hardship since the trains had to change engines and the passengers needed a break for the refreshment rooms and toilets.

15.50. *The original layout of Central Station, based on the 1/500 Ordnance Survey of 1857-8, early NER drawings and the plan accompanying Dobson's specification, published in T.L. Donaldson, 'Handbook of Specifications', vol. 2. The isolated turnplate shown on the second of the four N&C tracks may have been linked to the turnplate on track 3. (Bill Fawcett)*

15.48. *Curves upon curves: a reconstruction of the trainshed roof screens at the Carlisle end of Central Station. It is likely that the original intention was to leave the area open beneath the lower arches. However, those on the right were glazed in to protect YNB coaching stock standing in the carriage sidings, while the central arch probably received its rather lumpish lower screen to mitigate the winds blowing through the station. The right-hand arches were opened up after the merger, and an island platform was opened in that part of the trainshed in 1871. Twenty years later work began on extending the trainshed to the south and building a much larger island platform; in the course of this the original end screens were replaced by new ones with a straight soffit in place of Dobson's elliptical arches.* (Bill Fawcett)

15.49. *Perspective by John Dobson, with figures and other detail by J.W. Carmichael, looking along the Carlisle platforms (only eighteen inches high) with the station entrance towards the left. Note the provision of two tracks between the platform lines, with turnplates and cross tracks to facilitate stock movements.* (Laing Art Gallery, Newcastle, courtesy of Tyne & Wear Museums)

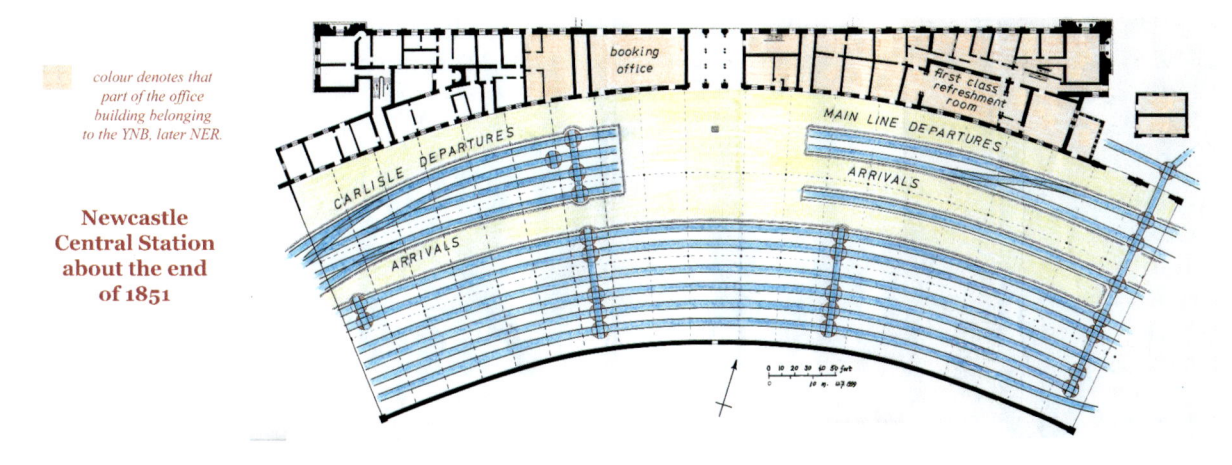

Newcastle Central Station about the end of 1851

colour denotes that part of the office building belonging to the YNB, later NER.

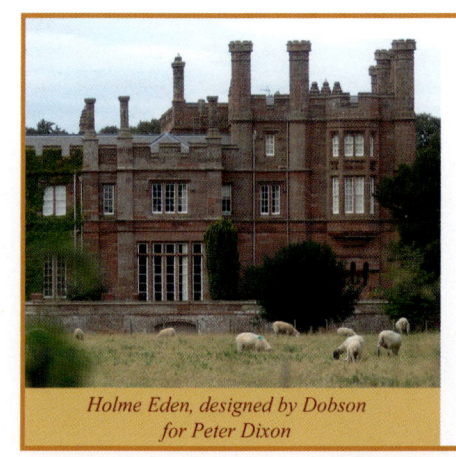

> ***John Dobson*** *(1787-1865) was born at Chirton, near North Shields. By 1830 he was the acknowledged leader of the architectural profession in the North East. He worked for prominent N&C figures, such as James Losh, Thomas Crawhall, Colonel Coulson, Matthew Plummer and Peter Dixon. In the 1830's he was a promoter of a coastal railway from Newcastle to Berwick. As well as preparing Tyne bridge proposals for the N&C he also drew up plans for a terminus near the Infirmary. He was therefore a natural choice as architect for Central Station. He seems to have got on well with Hudson, and in 1849 supplanted George Townsend Andrews as architect to Hudson's Whitby West Cliff development. A Dobson drawing in the collection of the Royal Institute of British Architects depicts a terminus in the style of Holme Eden, entitled 'Carlisle Railway Station'. This could refer either to Carlisle or the Carlisle Railway. If the former, it might represent Hudson's braggart attempt to pressurise the Citadel Station owners by threatening to build his own city centre terminus. We are unlikely ever to find out.*

Holme Eden, designed by Dobson for Peter Dixon

15.52.
Newcastle Central Station
N&C offices on ground floor

tel. telegraph office
w.r. waiting room
Supt. Superintendent's office and house.

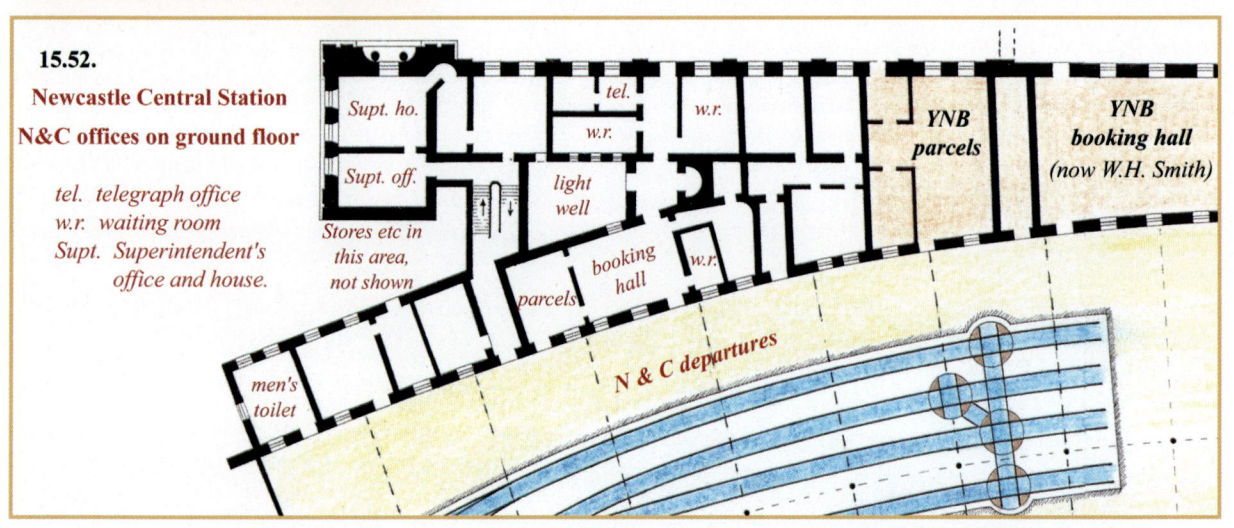

Central really comprised two terminal stations laid out back to back, with each railway providing its own self-contained suite of booking office, waiting rooms etc. The YNB passenger facilities were laid out in an orderly line along their platform frontage, with the company's head office on the floor above.[58] The N&C was confined to about a quarter of the station frontage and chose to make the access to its waiting rooms from an internal lobby reached by way of the booking hall. The only other public rooms opening off their platform were the parcels office and men's toilet, separated by 'backstage' activities, such as the lamp room. No refreshment facilities were offered; passengers used the YNB ones at the far end of the station. Because the platform curves away from the street, the N&C office building splits into two diverging ranges, separated by a light well and then linked again by the main staircase. The latter gives access to the main rooms of the head office, on the first floor, notably the boardroom. This occupies the west pavilion, which provides a rather flamboyant termination to the street façade and also houses the directors' toilet and a vaulted muniment room or 'safe'. Ranged along the main frontage from there are three sizeable offices, each lit by one of the arched windows or 'lunettes' on the façade. All these rooms survive, little altered, at the present day.

Downstairs, a surprising amount of space was given over to the 'Superintendent's' office and dwelling, having originally been earmarked entirely for offices. This suggests that the N&C was not pressed for space. Indeed, William Woods remarked to the 1857 AGM that 'they had double the room they required as regarded offices'. He went on to imply that the N&C's quarter share of the capital cost of Central Station had been about £30,000, and compared the equivalent annual charge, of £1,500 computed at 5% interest, very favourably with the £800 a year then being asked as the price of admission to Citadel Station, with working expenses to go on top.[59] Indeed, Newcastle Central seems to have been a good long-term investment for all involved.

The merger with the NER allowed some rationalisation of passenger facilities, with the booking and parcels functions eventually being transferred to the NER offices, though some west-end waiting rooms were retained. Upstairs, the N&C boardroom became the venue for Newcastle meetings of the NER Board, having previously served for the general meetings of N&C shareholders, formerly held in Newcastle's Assembly Rooms, as well as its directorial function. The N&C even enjoyed the luxury of an engine shed at Central Station, though quite why is not obvious, since the Forth Works and shed lay only half a mile away. After the merger it was eventually rented out to the North British Railway, who had acquired running powers from Border Counties Junction to Newcastle.

15.53. *Newcastle Central, from the west. The N&C premises occupied most of this end of the building.* (Bill Fawcett)

15.54. *NER drawing, for adding the portico. The main façade (right) is juxtaposed with that behind the portico (left) giving an idea of the station's curious appearance in the early years.*

15.55. *(right). The Carlisle platforms in 1993, during the last years of British Rail.* (Bill Fawcett)

15.56. *(left) View north over the roof of the Carlisle platforms.*
(Bill Fawcett)

15.57. *A North British Railway visitor waiting to head back along the Carlisle line at the end of the nineteenth century. The view was taken after the opening of the southern extension to the station, in 1894, but before work started in 1904 on the remodelling of the west end. Thus the roof has its new end screens but the platforms have yet to be extended and equipped with verandahs.*
(Tony Cormack collection)

213

Chapter 16: Organisation and People

Organisation

When the Committee of Economy came to make its staff audit in the latter part of 1841 it discovered that the railway had about 574 employees.[1] The net was widely drawn, to include the three managing directors as well as the two part-time Secretaries - the lawyers John Adamson and William Nanson, Secretary to the Carlisle Committee.

The largest single group in the workforce was the 174 men engaged in maintaining the permanent way, including drains and fences. Next came the locomotive department and workshops, with 164 men. On the operating side there were 16 guards - 8 passenger and 8 goods, 21 gate keepers, 2 bridge keepers (watchmen), and 19 point keepers. The various stations accounted for a manual workforce of 126 and a clerical one, including agents, of 37. Head office activities accounted for a mere 12.

We have seen something of the engineering organisation, under Blackmore and Hall, in earlier chapters. The remainder came under a Chief Agent, to whom the various stations were responsible. The term station master had not yet come into currency, and 'agent' was the official title, with 'station keeper' and 'collector' sometimes being used instead. The Chief Agent in 1841 was John Challoner, who enjoys the distinction of having been the railway's first full-time employee. He was probably born in Morpeth about 1786, but his background before coming to the railway remains unclear. He was appointed Clerk to the Railway on 5 February 1830, but had evidently been working for them already, since the appointment, at a salary of £150, was backdated to 1 January.[2] It is likely that he was previously employed by or well known to some of the directors.

Initially Challoner's main task was to keep the accounts relating to shares and construction and see to payments and receipts. Correspondence with outside bodies was largely in the hands of John Adamson, as Secretary. With the opening of the line, the individual station agents took on responsibility to encourage traffic, run their stations and keep accounts, which were then forwarded to head office, where Challoner took charge. Though public traffic began in March 1835, the directors wanted to see how he made out in this role, and deferred giving him a pay rise until March 1836, when his salary was raised to £200, backdated to 9 March 1835.[3] With the completion of the line he got a further £50 from March 1839 plus a gratuity of £50 for the previous year.[4]

Meanwhile, the directors needed someone to oversee the traffic. In many ways, train running remained the responsibility of Anthony Hall, as locomotive superintendent, but as traffic grew they realised the need for an 'Inspector of Traffic' or Superintendent. The post was advertised in February 1839, and in April the Board considered the rival claims of Benjamin Cail, the Haydon Bridge agent, and John Chantler.[5] It went to a vote, with Cail proposed by Colonel Coulson and Chantler by Joseph Crawhall. No doubt there had been lobbying behind the scenes; posts on the railway were much sought after. Chantler won. He was an outsider, born in Manchester about 1799 and with previous experience in the carrying business.[6] His role was twofold: to develop traffic as well as seeing that it was handled efficiently.

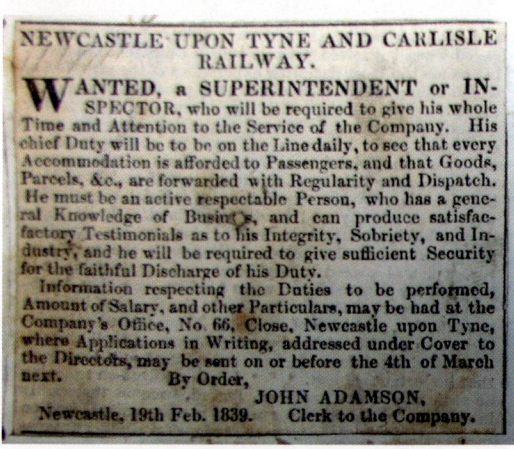

> NEWCASTLE UPON TYNE AND CARLISLE RAILWAY.
>
> WANTED, a SUPERINTENDENT or INSPECTOR, who will be required to give his whole Time and Attention to the Service of the Company. His chief Duty will be to be on the Line daily, to see that every Accommodation is afforded to Passengers, and that Goods, Parcels, &c., are forwarded with Regularity and Dispatch. He must be an active respectable Person, who has a general Knowledge of Business, and can produce satisfactory Testimonials as to his Integrity, Sobriety, and Industry, and he will be required to give sufficient Security for the faithful Discharge of his Duty.
>
> Information respecting the Duties to be performed, Amount of Salary, and other Particulars, may be had at the Company's Office, No. 66, Close, Newcastle upon Tyne, where Applications in Writing, addressed under Cover to the Directors, may be sent on or before the 4th of March next.
>
> By Order,
> JOHN ADAMSON,
> Newcastle, 19th Feb. 1839.   Clerk to the Company.

He travelled to places as far afield as Dundee to seek new business, and also advised Challoner and the Board on pricing policy. The latter frequently brought him into conflict with Richard Lowry, once the energetic Cumbrian had become agent at Newcastle. Chantler was a keen advocate of reducing prices to encourage goods traffic, while Lowry generally felt, often with justification, that this would have little impact on traffic volumes and merely reduce the railway's income. Chantler was an odd character, whose personal finances left a lot to be desired. He borrowed money from the agents and in April 1843 was even bailed out by a loan from the directors, though his problems may have been partly of their creation.[7] Agents were only paid quarterly, while even the workmen had to put up for a time with a monthly pay, later fortunately eased to a fortnightly one.

The 1842 Cuts and After

Chapter 9 has outlined the wage and staff cuts introduced during 1842 and 1843. In part, these represented the rationalisation of a workforce which had evolved in an *ad hoc* fashion. Hence the dismissal of four of the six boatmen at Blaydon and the winding down of the workshop establishment at Carlisle in favour of concentration at the east end. The only group to make a collective protest were the engine drivers, who tended to be more independent, feeling that they were a scarce and skilled resource. Their wage cuts were modest, 2d in a daily wage of 4s 8d, but were accompanied by unspecified changes in working practices. In a formal response they stated 'their inability to account for the safety of passengers under the new regulations', but left it at that.[8]

The cuts were effective in reducing costs, with the wage bill for 1843 down by 31% on that for 1841. From 1845 traffic was building up rapidly and the workforce had to increase again, while pay levels were gradually restored. By May 1847 the company had 612 employees, not counting the two managing directors and including the novelty of four 'policemen'.[9] The next upheaval came as a consequence of George Hudson's lease of the railway from July 1848 to December 1849.

This brought the railway under James Allport, the YNB general manager, who proceeded to make a number of staff economies, including the replacement of some senior agents by men on lower salaries. Meanwhile, the others got to grips with the bureaucratic ways of the new regime and the complexities of its accounting procedures.[10] Challoner remained in post throughout, even though his role must have been much reduced. For example, the goods traffic and its accounts were placed directly under Charles Henry Smith, the YNB Goods Manager. Chantler lasted until the summer of 1849, when Allport dispensed with his services.[11]

Despite integrating the Carlisle line into some of the operational practices of the YNB, Allport kept separate accounts of its costs and receipts, and at some point introduced one of his staff, Henry Smiles, into its management. On regaining control of their railway, Matthew Plummer and his colleagues did not simply return to their old ways. Instead, they sought someone with commercial experience to act as manager, and on 5 December 1849 appointed Smiles as General Manager and Commercial Clerk at a salary of £300, to which he added the post of Secretary following Adamson's death in 1855. John Challoner was left in a somewhat anomalous situation, partially deputising for Smiles during the latter's frequent absences on company business,[12] and chose to retire in 1851, aged 65. He left on 2 July, accompanied by the best wishes of the directors and a gratuity of £100.[13] He went on to participate in the business of his son, John Sadler Challoner, a Newcastle sharebroker.[14]

> **Henry Smiles** was born in Newcastle in 1818, son of Edward Smiles, a surgeon, and his wife Mary.[15] Edward had been elected an honorary surgeon to the Newcastle Infirmary in 1804 and held that post until his death in February 1832. After that Mary took Henry and his sisters to Westoe, near South Shields, which was her home town. Henry joined the Stanhope & Tyne Railway, presumably working in its South Shields office from soon after the 1834 opening. Through Hudson's purchase of the line he eventually found himself working for the Newcastle & Darlington Junction Railway, and hence the YNB, at Gateshead station.
>
> Smiles seems to have run the N&C in a capable and professional manner, but as one of a team rather than in any sense a leader or innovator. Under the NER he continued as manager of the Carlisle Section, answerable directly to William O'Brien, the general manager. The sloppy working practices revealed by the St. Nicholas accident in 1870 led the NER to integrate the section more fully into its management structure, and Smiles was obliged to resign his post from 8 February 1871. The NER found him another job as an 'agent' but this was no doubt something of a comedown. By then his mother and sisters had moved to Kensington, and Henry, after working a bit longer for the NER, eventually moved south also, dying at Tonbridge in 1898.

The slimmer Board put in place in May 1852 seems to have adopted a more detached approach to the running of the railway, placing greater reliance on professional management than Plummer and his colleagues had done. This is reflected in the decision taken in July of that year to recruit a 'person of energy and general business experience to undertake the outdoor management of the traffic department', though to some extent this revived the post formerly held by Chantler.[16] No fewer than 76 applications were received, and on 8 August 1852 the directors appointed John Relton, a 42-year-old Scot, who was then manager of the Caledonian Railway's goods station in Carlisle.[17] Relton was given a salary of £150 plus a £50 bonus, conditional on his exertions in developing traffic. These were evidently successful, since he got his bonus and the company's traffic flourished.

Relton left in March 1857 and the post was then split between a Superintendent of Goods Traffic and a Superintendent of Mineral Traffic.[18] The latter went to Joseph Vartey and the goods to Joseph Parker, both of whom carried on after the NER merger as 'outdoor assistants' to Henry Smiles. In contrast to the early days, the N&C was now able to recruit people with railway experience, as shown by the career of Arthur Tranah, who was the only N&C officer to progress high up the NER hierarchy. Born at Rochester (Kent) in 1825, Tranah joined the Railway Clearing House at the age of 23 and was recruited from there in February 1854 to head the N&C accounts office.[19] By 1859 he was being referred to as Chief Agent but the amalgamation did away with his post and gave him a better one instead as Collector of Mineral Dues for the NER's Northern Division. In 1893, at the age of 68, he became NER Treasurer and held the post for thirteen years, retiring in 1906.

The considerable traffic growth in the eighteen-fifties was accompanied by tight control over costs, particularly the size of the workforce. Having reached 612 in 1847 and then fallen as a result of the Hudson economies, it only got to 693 by 1858.[20] This worked out at 8.86 men per route mile compared with 10.58 on the North Eastern, which had a total workforce of 7,623. It is instructive to look closer at some of these people, and see how the N&C recruited them and what sort of a career it offered.

Early Agents

The earliest appointments of agents were made in February 1835, the two most important being those of Benjamin Cail at Blaydon and William Greene at Hexham.[21] Greene went on to a long and creditable career, ended only by the Hudson lease; Cail's career was quite short and can be dealt with first. He made a good job of the Blaydon post, assisted by his clerk, John Scott, and was sent to Haydon Bridge on a salary of £100 when the line was extended in 1836. Haydon Bridge was an important station at that time, both as the main railhead for lead and as the interchange point with the coaches to the west. Lowry found Cail a rather haughty person and commented sourly that he 'dressed like a Lord and not as a Clerk to the Railway'.[22] Cail seems to have misjudged the tolerance of the directors by absenting himself from the station without leave, and their displeasure was indicated in the 1842 pay cuts, when his salary was slashed to £60, a far more drastic cut than any other agent. In part this reflected the reduced importance of Haydon Bridge once the line had been completed throughout, but he took the hint and resigned in May.[23]

Cail's successor at Blaydon was his assistant John Scott, a resourceful character who had lost the use of his legs as a boy and got around on a donkey.[24] Scott had worked for the Beaumont lead business, whose Chief Agent, Benjamin Johnson, felt it would be mutually beneficial to transfer one of his men to the railway. The same thing happened three years later with Thomas Dixon, who has been the subject of a recent study by Stafford Linsley.

Dixon was born in 1805 at Dukesfield, a hamlet south of Hexham in the valley of the Devil's Water.[25] He began his career working alongside his father at Beaumont's Dukesfield lead smelter, but that began to be run down in the autumn of 1834, in anticipation of a shift in production to Blagill smelter at Langley, in Allendale, which would be more accessible to the new railway. Thomas therefore moved in May 1835 to a clerical post at the Blaydon lead refinery, initially retaining his home at Dukesfield but lodging at Blaydon during the week and using the new trains to help him get home on a Saturday evening and return early on Monday.

The Blaydon refinery was next door to the N&C terminus, and in September 1838 Dixon joined the railway as a clerk there under John Scott. This seems to have been done entirely on the initiative of Benjamin Johnson, but Thomas was happy with the change and proved good at his job, receiving a pay rise to £60 in 1839. He stayed at Blaydon for four years and in June 1842 was promoted to Haydon Bridge as agent, on the same salary but with the rent-free station house as well.[26] His final move was to Hexham, where he succeeded George Bates as agent at the end of June 1843.[27] Dixon held this post for two decades, before retiring. He became a respected figure in the local community and in 1864, in his retirement, joined the Hexham Board of Guardians. He died in February 1871.

'Little Scott', as Lowry characterised John Scott, was less fortunate. Hudson closed the Maryport & Carlisle Railway booking office in Carlisle in October 1848, transferring its business to London Road and its chief clerk, John Palmer Dalton, to Blaydon as agent, where he evidently remained until 1861. Scott, having served at Blaydon for almost fifteen years, fourteen as agent, was simply turfed out, but found himself new employment back in the lead business.[28] The old directors, on regaining control, seem to have done little for the people Allport dispossessed, but they granted Scott free second-class travel between Haydon Bridge and Newcastle for six months from March 1850.[29] Another Hudson casualty was William Greene, who was first agent at Hexham then at Carlisle.

Greene was born on 28 July 1788, the son of a Newcastle merchant, also William, and his wife Isabella.[30] He was presumably well known to Plummer or some of the other directors and may indeed have been working for one of them when he was appointed to Hexham in February 1835, at a salary of £100. In his late-forties by this time, Greene was evidently a reliable man with plenty of experience of business and book-keeping. This is backed up by the picture we get from Lowry of a rather cautious individual who was courteous and careful in his handling of other people, including his own staff. In May 1836 Greene was appointed to take charge of the Carlisle station at a salary of £150, which reflected his greatly increased responsibilities.[31] He was succeeded at Hexham by George Bates.

Greene's position at Carlisle was very different from that of any other agent, particularly once the Canal branch opened, and the 1841 staff audit referred to him as 'Collector and General Superintendent of the London Road and Canal Station'. He reported to each meeting of the Carlisle Committee of directors and had an extensive managerial role, though this did not extend to the engineering staff. After a small cut during the economy drive, his salary rose to £200 in December 1846, as against £120 for Lowry, his counterpart at Newcastle. For a time he also received an allowance for rent. The London Road station house had been far from ready when he arrived, so Greene arranged his own accommodation and Joseph Forster, Carlisle's 'superintendent of engines', took on this 'commodious' house instead.[32]

James Allport did not place the same value on Greene's services and gave him notice to quit in September 1848.[33] Lowry hints that Greene was thinking of leaving anyway, but not that quickly, and he may indeed have been allowed to stay until the end of the year. Greene planned to retire to Lancaster but his sister's illness brought him back to Newcastle, where he died in May 1861.[34] An obituary noted that he had been 'an artist of considerable ability.' He evidently had an ingenious turn of mind, since he devised an alternative to the small 'ploughs' fitted by Blackmore in front of locomotive wheels. The managing directors took Greene's *Remover* seriously enough to give it a trial in March 1838 but it was not a robust design and the disrespectful Lowry watched gleefully as 'bits flew off'.[35]

Richard Lowry

Richard Lowry's diaries have provided numerous insights into the workings of the railway, and his own career fleshes out our picture of the enterprise a little further. He was born on 29 December 1811, the youngest child of John Lowry, yeoman, and his wife Sarah. The family had long been established at Cargo, four miles down the Eden from Carlisle.[36] After a brief flirtation with teaching, Richard became a clerk in the office of William Nanson, and soon found himself routinely handling the minutes and accounts of the Carlisle Committee of the railway.

Lowry was an ambitious person and saw the railway opening up new job prospects. At first his hopes centred on the Blenkinsopp Coal Company, and he was mortified to learn that another clerk had secured the post as their Carlisle agent.[37] He then turned his attention to the railway itself, and began to sound out his employer. Nanson encouraged him, though the post which Lowry next coveted, that of assistant to William Greene, went, not surprisingly, to someone with experience of working in a coaching office: George Thompson.[38] John Adamson wrote a kindly letter, suggesting that the post of agent at Milton was still open, but in the end Lowry was recruited as junior clerk at London Road, starting work on the opening day in July 1836.[39]

Nominally Lowry was involved with the goods and mineral traffic, but you had to be an all-rounder in the early days, and we have already noted him taking a turn as train guard when the regular man was unavailable. He also got the job of making the monthly pay to the workmen at the west end of the line, principally platelayers and their labourers. This entailed getting a cheque from Nanson and drawing out sums of the order of £350 in coins small enough to be of use to men whose weekly wage was well under a pound. With a bulging satchel he set out on the first train of the day, accompanied by one colleague for security, and proceeded to pay the men as far as Greenhead.

One of Lowry's earliest pay days was 4 October 1836, when he caught the 7 a.m. train as far as Wetheral. Having dealt with the men in that area, he took the 9.30 train to Milton (Brampton Junction) to conduct another pay. 'We had to wait at this barren cold place nearly three hours before the one o'clock train came up. We went to a public house in Milton about half an hour and had a quart of ale. We rode right on to Greenhead by the one o'clock train and had dinner [midday meal] previously to our coming to pay the men there.' Business over, they got the next train on to Rose Hill and took a walk up to Gilsland Spa. This was Lowry's first visit and the scenery impressed him very much. This became a routine and to expedite the business, and gain more time at Gilsland, Lowry got lifts on mineral trains, which gave him opportunities for riding on the engine and some brisk runs when there were few wagons in tow.

Lowry gives us an insight into the working day, when shift working, as now understood, barely existed outside factories and mills. In summer, London Road could be handling departures as early as 5 in the morning and arrivals up to 8 in the evening. This did not mean that staff were expected to work 14 or 15 continuous hours. Lowry lodged nearby and would rise early to despatch the first train, probably getting breakfast afterwards and taking time off during the day in the long intervals between trains or while colleagues attended to some of them. On 16 February 1837, for instance, he worked at the station in the morning until nearly eleven, then walked to Harraby to attend the sale of the farm and domestic possessions of William Smith Denton, the bankrupt builder of the Eden Viaduct. This was being handled by William Nanson, and Lowry enjoyed himself helping out some of his old colleagues. He went back to the station to start the 3 p.m. train and then returned to Harraby to see the auction through to the end.

Lowry rarely worked Sundays, but on 9 July 1837 he did so, standing in as the other two clerks were away. He and Greene worked at the office until noon, then Lowry got a meal and walked to Cargo. This gave him half an hour with his parents before walking back to Carlisle to assist Greene with despatching the last train, after which they had tea and then worked on the weekly accounts until 8.30.

Lowry found the goods business far more interesting than passenger traffic and proved adept at handling the Carlisle manufacturers and traders. Urged by Nanson to stay put when colleagues were being tempted away by much higher wages on the Manchester & Leeds Railway, he got his reward in 1841 when he was appointed Agent and Collector at Newcastle in succession to John Kent Pow, whose accounts had gradually degenerated into chaos.[40] Lowry took up the new post on 27 May, initially at the same salary, £75, as he had latterly enjoyed at Carlisle. Given that William Greene was then on £180 a year, Lowry had cause to feel disgruntled and his case was argued with the directors by John Challoner. At the end of June they both went to see Matthew Plummer, who showed his usual charm: 'Oh Mr. Lowry, it was fully intended by the directors when you left Carlisle that your salary should be advanced', but he would not say how much. However, next day Challoner gave Lowry £20 on account and a few weeks later his salary was fixed at £100.[41]

Lowry soon had the station sorted, but, despite his hard work and evident ability in fostering business, the directors were never particularly generous with him. One senses that they knew their man and realised there was little likelihood of his ever leaving on this account. The only serious temptation to go seems to have been in September 1846, when he visited the Maryport & Carlisle Railway and spoke with several of its officers, including the hapless Secretary, William Mitchell. Although Mitchell was not evicted until 1847, moves were already being made against him and a Mr. Fletcher of Maryport wrote to Lowry encouraging him to apply for the Secretary's post, with its £350 salary.[42] After some soul-searching he decided not to, put off by the acrimony within the M&C Board.

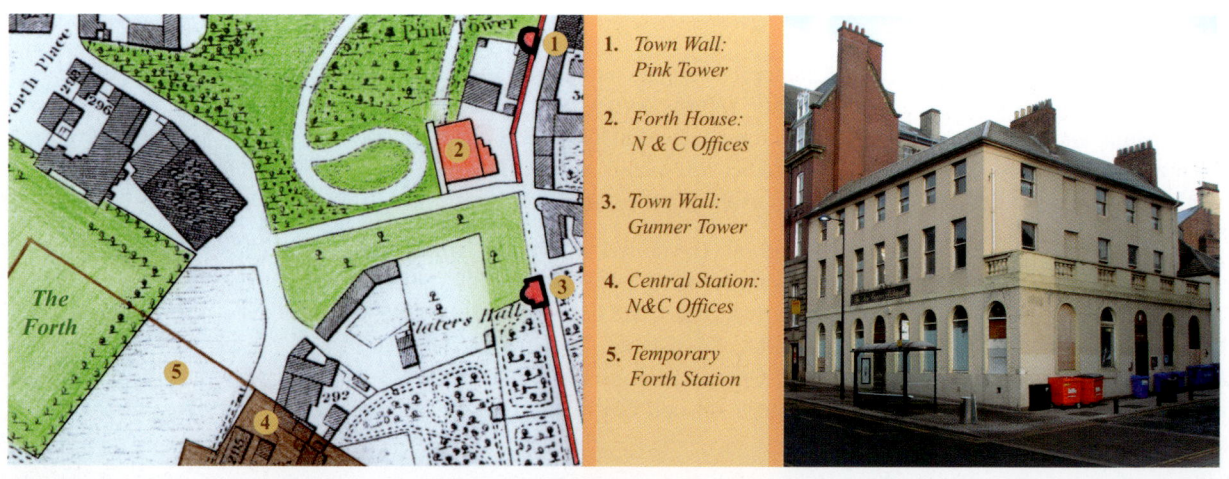

1. Town Wall: Pink Tower
2. Forth House: N & C Offices
3. Town Wall: Gunner Tower
4. Central Station: N&C Offices
5. Temporary Forth Station

16.2. The Newcastle & Carlisle Railway Head Office at Forth House, on Thomas Oliver's 1830 plan of Newcastle and at the present day. The company offices were formerly situated in their 'station' at 66, The Close but on 19 January 1841 the Board agreed to take 'Mr. Rankine's house' for their head office. This survives as Forth House, though in a very different setting from the gardens shown on Oliver's map. The offices only occupied a part of the building and the remainder was let out by the company as staff accommodation. George Robson, the senior passenger clerk at Newcastle, was their principal tenant and his wife was paid to look after the premises, including the rooms let out to other employees. Richard Lowry was a lodger at Forth House when he first went to Newcastle. By that time the open areas depicted on Oliver's map were fast disappearing. Clayton Street had recently been driven through nearby and work was about to start on the construction of St. Mary's cathedral, almost opposite, though Forth House still retained a small garden. The N&C transferred their offices into Central Station in about May 1851.

At Newcastle, Lowry frequently found himself at odds with Chantler over goods rates and was not backward in putting his case, not simply to Challoner as Chief Agent, but also to the chairman, showing little reluctance about bearding Plummer in his den on the Quayside. He also found a sympathetic ear in George Johnson, the managing director, who was a frequent visitor to the station. With the railway's extension to the Forth in 1847, Lowry became increasingly detached from the passenger business, now physically separate from the goods station, but retained overall responsibility and resented any attempt to diminish his formal role. However, the Hudson lease brought a final division between passenger and freight activities and Lowry can thereafter be regarded as goods manager.

A high point in his career came in 1854 with the move into the Forth goods station and his new house at its entrance. In its early months the directors made a number of visits, and Lowry found himself fending off carping remarks about cost and, in particular, the marble fireplace and chandelier in his own office: 'Tate, as usual, threw the blame from his own back onto mine ... Indeed, such is the case as the whole station was planned by me although he takes all the credit to himself, especially those parts which they approve of'.[43]

Lowry ploughed his savings back into railway shares and was doubly apprehensive of the likely consequences of the merger with the NER. In June 1861 William Woods, the chairman, called round to tell him of the failure of the merger Bill and Lowry did not trouble to hide his glee, remarking that there was a strong public feeling against both the amalgamation and the NER itself.[44] In the end, the merger went smoothly and had no immediate impact on work at the Forth. Change was in store, however, with T.E. Harrison's ambitions to build a new goods station there to serve most of the NER's Newcastle traffic. Robert Pauling, the NER Northern Division Goods Manager, based at Newcastle, had the task of tactfully sidelining Lowry, whom he thought too set in his ways to take on its management. He achieved this by getting the directors to approve a new post of District Inspector for the Carlisle Section and appoint Lowry to it. The first portion of the new Forth Goods opened in March 1871 and on 10 April Richard began his new duties, operating from an office just above his old one.[45] A sore point was the loss of his house, which went to the new man, Robert Dove, and Lowry ended up building himself *Lea Villa*, at Riding Mill.

An affront to Lowry's dignity was his Carlisle Section pass, 'a shabby second class', which he used to rove around the line reporting, as required, on the need for station improvements, extra sidings and the like.[46] Lowry was only sixty when he made the change, which in those days could mean working for another ten or twenty years if one lasted out. The new job was viewed on both sides as a partial retirement, yet it lasted for two decades and it took some diplomacy for the NER to finally persuade Lowry to retire in 1892. Tactfully, they allowed him to depart on the anniversary of his start at London Road, 56 years earlier, and he lived on, still keeping up his diary, until the summer of 1898.

16.3. *This N&C house stood at the Railway Street depot, in Newcastle, and was probably Lowry's residence, as agent, prior to his move to Forth Banks in 1854. It was on the road to ruin when photographed in July 1966 and was demolished not long after. (J.M. Fleming)*

Richard's energetic longevity was matched by that of his elder brother William, born in 1788, who was appointed the first agent at How Mill in September 1836, though he had to wait three years for the station house to be built.[47] How Mill was a quiet spot, reflected in William's £50 salary, reduced to £40 at the 1842 cuts. The opening of the Alston branch took him as agent to Featherstone, also an uneventful place, where he served until his death on 30 April 1876, aged 87. Finding berths for one's family was a feature of railway employment and one that could be beneficial to the company as they had some insight into the people they were recruiting while the new men had advance knowledge of the practice and ethos of the work. Thus several Lowry's appeared on the N&C. Most convenient for William was his grandson, who was stationmaster at Lambley under the NER.[48]

The Mechanics' Institute

In the early nineteenth century Mechanics Institutes became recognised as a valuable medium of self-improvement for working men, and both James Losh (the elder) and Thomas Crawhall had been strong supporters of the one founded in Newcastle in the eighteen-twenties. Richard Lowry joined the committee of one in Carlisle and subsequently became active in another set up by N&C employees in Newcastle, chiefly men from Anthony Hall's workshops. Lowry and Hall acted as intermediaries with the directors, who were keen to support the movement, and the move of the goods department from Railway Street to the Forth enabled them to provide more spacious premises for lectures and meetings.[49] The old goods station 'had been out of repair for some time', implying that it had become quite run down prior to closure. Urged on by John Adamson, the directors arranged for the roof to be repaired, gas lighting introduced and a floor laid. The inauguration came on 20 June 1854 with the annual *soirée* of the railway institute.[50] At 4.30 'seven hundred ladies and gentlemen sat down to tea', all members of the institute and their friends. At six Adamson took the chair, attended by William Woods, Anthony Hall and Peter Tate, and a performance of *Rule Britannia* by a band of railwaymen was followed by a lecture on the merits of mechanics' institutions by one of Hall's staff. Further music and addresses concluded with Richard Lowry giving a vote of thanks to the directors, to which Woods responded. Then the real pleasure began, the dancing, and 'till a late hour upwards of 200 couples prolonged the evening's festivities.'

In later years the institute obtained a home in part of the goods offices at Forth Banks, and, as the British Railways Staff Association, found itself occupying part of the former carriage shed at Central Station. Thus it ended up making use of two successive N&C goods stations once their original role was over.

Thomas Edmondson and N&C Ticketing

Thomas Edmondson, inventor of the once-familiar card ticket and date-stamping machine, had a very different background from many of the early agents. He was born on 30 June 1792 in Lancaster, where he trained as a cabinet-maker. By the mid eighteen-twenties he had his own business in Carlisle in partnership with Mr. Brockbank, but this failed and, after working for an upholsterer, he set up as a grocer in November 1835.[51] A brighter future opened up on 3 June 1836 with his appointment as agent at the station about to open at Milton (Brampton Junction) on a salary of £75.[52] Despite his former business problems Edmondson evidently had no trouble arranging the £200 surety required by the directors for all agents. Milton was a responsible position, given the coal traffic coming off the Earl of Carlisle's Railway, but Thomas found enough quiet intervals to ponder on the business of ticket issue and work out how to simplify and expedite it.

219

When the N&C first opened between Blaydon and Hexham, tickets were only issued at the terminal stations and certain designated places in Newcastle and Hexham. Passengers joining at intermediate stations paid their fares to the guard, who entered them on a waybill, coaching fashion. By 1836, however, as a check against fraud, the company was providing books of tickets for all its agents, with counterfoils which were retained in the book. The tickets were printed with the stations between which the journey was being made, but the clerk had to fill in a ticket number as well as the date and time of the train. Tickets were collected at the end of the journey, while the guard still entered the passenger details in his waybill, so there were various checks built into the system. It was tightened up further at the end of 1837, with a requirement that the agents at the 'minor stations' send a waybill with each train and a duplicate by the following train, the second one being placed in a locked box 'the key of which is to be kept at the terminus'.[53] Tickets were to be collected by the guards and compared with the waybill to see 'if any are wanting.'

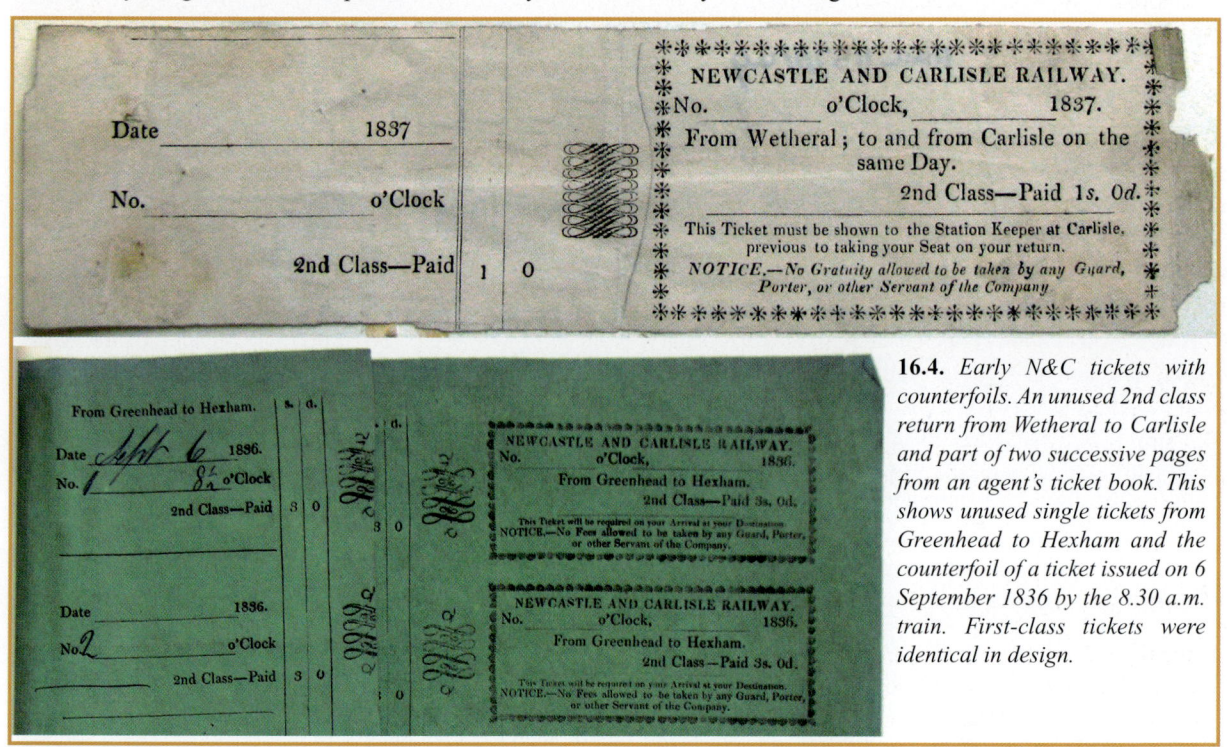

16.4. Early N&C tickets with counterfoils. An unused 2nd class return from Wetheral to Carlisle and part of two successive pages from an agent's ticket book. This shows unused single tickets from Greenhead to Hexham and the counterfoil of a ticket issued on 6 September 1836 by the 8.30 a.m. train. First-class tickets were identical in design.

Edmondson introduced two innovations while he was at Milton. The first was a small, square pasteboard ticket, pre-numbered and stacked in spring-loaded tubes, one for each ticket type and destination. The clerk took the tickets in numbered sequence from the top of the tube. They still had to be dated, however, and for this Edmondson devised a dating press, into which the clerk could rapidly insert the ticket and have it stamped. Lowry remarked on Edmondson's activities on a pay visit to Milton in April 1837: 'Mr. Edmondson prints all the tickets himself. He is the most systematic man I ever saw'.[54] On 1 September Edmondson 'showed me a small machine he has invented for dating the tickets. His plan of delivering the tickets was objected to on account of their having no date upon them, so to remedy this the present machine has been invented ... I think it might be adopted with advantage upon all railways. He can date the tickets twice as fast as with the pen.'

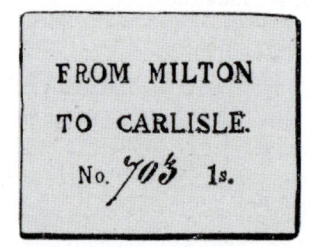

16.5. An early, hand-printed Edmondson card ticket.

The prototype dating press was made under Edmondson's direction by Ralph Cairns, a Brampton watchmaker, while a Carlisle watchmaker, John Blaylock, eventually took on its commercial manufacture. Edmondson went on to invent a ticket printing machine which produced batches of tickets with sequential numbering. Both this and the dating press became standard equipment for railways. The N&C directors adopted Edmondson's system generally in the course of 1838 and installed a ticket printing machine in their offices at The Close, but there was little they could offer him in the way of career opportunities. Captain Lawes, manager of the Manchester & Leeds Railway, encountered Edmondson's system while visiting Tyneside, and in March 1839 offered the inventor a post at their Manchester station at a salary of £200 with a bonus of £50 should he fit up the tickets to their satisfaction.[55] Edmondson left Milton about the end of April and two years later left railway employment altogether to pursue his own very successful business. He died in 1851. Another migrant to the M&L was George Thompson, the senior clerk under Greene at Carlisle, who was offered a job at the same time as Edmondson on a wage of £150, which he could never have hoped for with the Carlisle company.[56]

Later Recruits: the Parker Brothers

The Parker brothers, of Carlisle, furnish our last example of N&C recruitment, this time in the eighteen-forties. John and Joseph Parker were evidently twins, born into a farming family in the parish of Addingham in Cumberland, about eight miles NNE of Penrith.[57] They were christened in September 1827 and their early employment by the railway has not been traced.[58] However, John joined about 1843 and made rapid progress through the ranks. In January 1851 he became Head Agent and Superintendent at Carlisle, succeeding Mr. Carr, who was the second of two short-term successors to William Greene.[59] John then spent the remainder of his career as chief officer at Carlisle, remaining goods manager at London Road when the passenger traffic was transferred to Citadel Station. He retired in October 1895 and lived finally in a handsome Victorian villa at Wetheral.[60]

Joseph appears to have started in 1844 and followed initially in his brother's footsteps, taking on John's former post when the latter became Carlisle Agent. Joseph then moved to a position in Newcastle, as Smiles's 'corresponding clerk', and in March 1857 was appointed Superintendent of Goods Traffic for the whole line as part of the reorganisation following the departure of John Relton.

16.6. A studio photograph of John Parker, apparently taken about the time of his retirement.

Under the NER Joseph's role was little changed at first, being designated 'Outdoor Goods Assistant' to Henry Smiles, though he was later described as Goods and Passenger Superintendent.[61] The St. Nicholas accident changed things a lot more, and at the end of 1870 he confided to Richard Lowry his intention of leaving within a few months.[62] The NER directors accepted his resignation on 14 February 1871, and in May there was a formal presentation from his colleagues at Central Station.[63] Joseph Parker moved back to Carlisle, where he established a successful business as a coal merchant.

Conditions of Service

At the time we are considering, and for long after, the normal working week was six days. The N&C operated passenger trains on Sundays, so a proportion of staff will have been required on the seventh day as well, but it is unclear how this was organised. In the case of station agents there was no problem, since they normally lived on the job in order to provide full-time surveillance of the company's property and deal with any problems which might arise. Gatekeepers, once they received company housing, could also be held to a seven day week, relying on other family members to do the job when necessary.

Wage rates were reasonable by the standards of the time. Engine drivers were particularly prized - the directors did not want them being poached by other railways - and in 1841 they were receiving 4s 8d a day, equivalent to £72 16s a year. This compares with a salary of £84 for John Scott as agent at Blaydon. Near the bottom of the pecking order were the platelayers' labourers on 15s 9d a week (£40-19s a year). This was still better than the agricultural labourer's wage of typically 2s a day but the farmworker could usually expect a tied cottage as well.[64] The labourers' wages were cut to 15s as a result of the 1842 economies, and remained there, but the Board gave a favourable response to an approach by Peter Tate in December 1855, when he recommended that 'if provisions [i.e. food prices] continued high' they should have an increase of a shilling in March 'when the days lengthen'.[65]

Whatever the wage might be while in work, there was no formal provision for cases of sickness or eventual retirement. In most employment there never had been, the expectation being that the family would provide. The N&C directors approached this matter in an *ad hoc* fashion. Thus we find a case in December 1854 where a porter at Hexham, Mr. Leslie, had been off work through illness for some time.[66] During this period he had received no wage and on learning this, and that he was not likely to be back at work in a hurry, the Board made him an allowance of 7s a week. Retirement was something for which people were expected to make their own provision, but for the lowest-paid staff this really meant relying on the family. A gesture was made by the Board in April 1860, when they tackled the issue that some of the gatekeepers were now too old to do the job reliably or safely.[67] They therefore decided to pension them off with an annual allowance of £10.

This is more generous than the assistance given when staff were killed or injured at work, even when they were in no way to blame. An example is provided by Thomas Graham, a driver killed when his locomotive overturned after hitting a cow. His young widow received, as a one-off payment, a meagre £10, less than two months pay, and the directors evidently relied on his workmates to whip round and help out.[68] Fortunately the men usually did. When Thomas Topham, the first agent at Wetheral, died in January 1837 during an outbreak of scarlet fever, the other agents organised a testimonial for his widow.

Richard Lowry was rather grumpy about the Topham testimonial but he was not slow to step in and help when necessary. Thus in 1843 he and Anthony Hall took on the case of a boy who had lost a leg through one of their trains, arranged a free school for him and raised enough money among the men to pay his mother four shillings a week for the best part of a year.[69]

When it came to discipline, the directors were firm but not vindictive, as shown by the case of Blaydon station in January 1838. John Scott was faced with a strike by his porters and labourers, demanding extra pay for overtime and Sunday working.[70] To keep the trains running he was obliged to concede their request, though they must have realised that this was not in his gift. The Board responded predictably by sending Adamson and Blackmore to tell the men that they had been dismissed, and this rapidly had the desired effect. The porters were reinstated on paying a fine of ten shillings and submitting a written apology, which was sent to each of the larger stations, where the agent read it to his men.

16.7. Keeping the carriers in order. A notice of 1836.

The enginemen tended to be a race apart, and posed their own problems. In June 1837 two mineral trains were abandoned near the Gelt Bridge one day while the men got a quick drink at a pub. The directors' reponse was measured, with fines of 20s each for the drivers, 15s for the firemen and 12s 6d for the brakesmen, backed up by the sanction of dismissal if they did not pay or, no doubt, if the offence was repeated. This, however, induced the Carlisle committee to consider retaining a part of every engineman's wage in future as a security of good behaviour. This was already done with gate and point keepers but it is unclear whether the idea was ever followed through.[71]

As the railway system expanded, drivers were liable to be poached by other companies. This may lie behind a raising of drivers' wages to 5s 6d a day at the end of June 1858, while six months later John Parker was telling a meeting of the N&C Carlisle Mechanics Institute that membership was down by fourteen, 'some enginemen having gone to Egypt and India', where British enterprise was hard at work.[72] They did not remain there long, and in December 1860 the directors gave leave for the re-engagement of any enginemen lately returned from Egypt who had formerly been with the company. Evidently this did not suit those who had stayed, and just a week later, after considering their letters, the Board instructed Hall to give the Egyptian returnees a fortnight's notice.[73]

16.8. As well as losing drivers to Egypt, the N&C played host to this remarkable train built by Robert Stephenson & Co. for the country's Khedive. It was tested on the line in October 1858, prior to being finally fitted out in the sumptuous fashion seen here by the leading London decorator John Crace.
(Postcard by Raphael Tuck & Sons)

Hall was an effective manager, and saw to it that his men, particularly those in the workshops, benefited from the works outings which were a creation of the Railway Age. He therefore got the directors to provide an annual outing from Newcastle to Carlisle. July 1852 provides a typical example, with a special train, free to the company's men and their families, and charged at the bargain rate of 2s 6d to any friends and half price to children under twelve.[74] It is to be noted that at this time railwaymen did not generally enjoy free or concessionary travel.

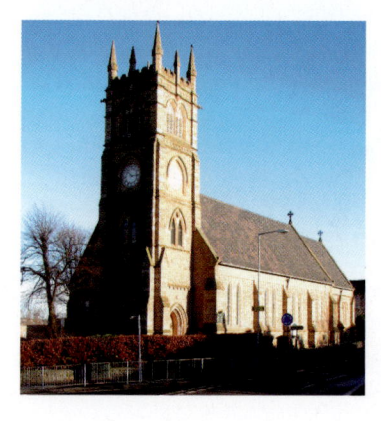

The company was always under pressure to contribute to worthy causes in its area but this was not its purpose. Unusually, it subscribed towards a new church built at Blaydon in 1844-5 and towards its enlargement in 1860. That was an isolated case, recognising the part which the railway had played in swelling the population of what had been a small village.[75] However, at the March 1857 AGM Christopher Bird, Vicar of Warden, requested a subscription of £2 a year towards each of the three schools in the township of Warden and Newbrough, noting that railway children formed a significant part of their inmates. The directors could not equitably single out one part of the line for special attention, but shortly after they agreed to subscribe a total of £100 annually to the various schools throughout their district.[76]

16.9. St. Cuthbert's church, Blaydon. The first building campaign provided the nave and the second the chancel. The tower was added in 1869. (Bill Fawcett)

222

The NER and the 1867 Strike

At the merger, the outgoing directors secured a formal assurance from Harry Meysey-Thompson and his Board that this would not prejudice the interests of any N&C employees and that they would be treated on equal terms with existing NER staff. This provided a useful reassurance for the staff, but in any case the NER was an essentially decent employer, though sometimes remarkably thoughtless, as in the excessive hours worked by some signalmen.

Inevitably, old practices tended to linger on in the Carlisle Section even when they were at variance with those of the NER, an example being provided by an accident which occurred at Haltwhistle on 2 February 1870. Three platelayers' bogies had been attached to a passenger train but came to grief when a wheel broke and they were derailed. The bogies were meant to be hand-propelled; they were not designed to travel at speed and offered no protection to the men, three of whom were killed. The practice was forbidden by NER regulations but it transpired that it had been customary under the old company and the district permanent-way inspector, William Rutherford, had continued to condone it in order to expedite the work.

Strikes were not unknown on Tyneside, notably among colliers and keelmen, but the N&C had been noticeably free from such things, discounting the one-day wonder at Blaydon. Just five years after the merger came a strike by enginemen which paralysed services on much of the NER and led to much grief for the men involved. In January 1867 NER drivers and firemen presented the Board with a list of demands referring to wages, overtime and working hours.[77] After applying a little pressure, the men secured one of their main objectives, a ten hour day, and the dispute seemed to have been resolved. However, there was a misunderstanding over one issue and, claiming a breach of faith, the men struck without notice at 3 a.m. on 11 April. The management responded by calling out other staff to try and maintain the service and by quickly recruiting new men, there being no dearth of applicants.

The Carlisle Section coped particularly well, with almost no diminution in services as Lowry proudly recorded. Called from bed at 4 a.m. he went to the Forth shed, where only two enginemen had turned up 'but we contrived to collect together engine drivers that had been discharged, firemen, cleaners and even guards. This enabled us to run every train today ... the traffic was stopped at Trafalgar, so the old N&C has done better than the NER has been able to.' The next day he noted that 'we have received numbers of applications for the situation of engine drivers and firemen and have filled all the vacancies up in our section. We send a man on the engine that is acquainted with the road to direct the men and make them acquainted with the signals and road.'

The strike was soon over, but in most cases the men did not have jobs to return to, assurances having been given to the new recruits that their places were permanent. This must have been heartbreaking for old railway 'servants', many of whom were probably forced into the strike against their better judgement. Anthony Hall was no longer around to intercede and Edward Fletcher, the locomotive superintendent, probably felt let down and in no mood for compassion. Lowry was a hardliner and betrayed no sympathy. On 20 April he noted that the drivers 'are applying to be taken back on any terms. Some will be. D. Dunn [Daniel Dunn, driver of *Northumbrian* in 1841], one of the oldest or rather the oldest, has suffered severely for his folly - he has been over to Mr. Fletcher several times begging to be taken back and when refused he sheds tears ... I believe it has been agreed to take him on under certain conditions. All of those who come back have to sign an undertaking that they are not connected with any Union - they are fairly conquered.'

On 22 April a few of the 'old enginemen' started work but a month later some were still 'begging for employment at any wages they can get'. Some were engaged as guards but only where a vacancy happened to occur, and Tomlinson records how, across the NER as a whole, many ended up emigrating to America, with assistance from trades unions. One feels this would not have happened on the old N&C, not because the directors were kinder or more considerate - even the liberal James Losh (the elder) had no compunction about turning his miners out of their tied houses if they struck.[78] In the smaller company though, with Hall gauging the feelings of his men, the issue would not have been allowed to boil up and get out of hand.

Chapter 17: Accidents and Incidents

Introduction

To our eyes travel on the Newcastle & Carlisle Railway during the eighteen-thirties and forties can appear somewhat hazardous, with trains derailing, axles breaking and the occasional firebox failure. Contemporaries, however, would have found it a lot safer than coach travel, where bolting horses, wheels falling off and carriages overturning were the regular stuff of newspaper reports. Indeed, the N&C directors were able to boast that they never actually killed a passenger, though there were quite a few deaths among their own workforce, as well as unlucky pedestrians and horsemen.

The N&C was no more accident prone than other railways at the time, and during the eighteen-fifties the accident rate seems to have declined, despite a considerable increase in traffic. Among the factors contributing to this improvement will be the modern permanent way, instituted by T. E. Harrison, and a generally more careful and organised approach to the operation of the railway, symbolised by the new and comprehensive rule book which came out in 1853.

Derailments

Derailments were quite common during the first decade and a half of operation, and were rarely attended by serious consequences.[1] One cause was a failure to reset switches after shunting operations and this led to a serious accident at Corby in December 1836.[2] *Samson* was heading a westbound train, with several goods wagons and 26 passengers, across Corby Beck viaduct when driver William Simpson realised that the points were set for the coal depot adjoining Corby crossing. Fortunately, the train was already slowing down to stop at Wetheral and, having thrown the engine into reverse, he and his fireman jumped off and escaped unscathed. The train ran into some wagons standing in the depot, whose walls then collapsed beneath the engine. The passenger carriages, being in the rear, came to a halt before reaching the depot and the passenger injuries were minimal. However, an unfortunate man who had been standing on the depot was killed as were two boys who had stolen a lift under the tarpaulin of a grain wagon.

Corby depot had been built by the Earl of Carlisle and the points were operated by his man, John Rowlandson, who had failed to reset them after shunting wagons onto the coal cells. The Newcastle directors were somewhat resentful of the Earl's right to link depots to their line wherever he chose, and had therefore made no provision for supervising their operation. Despite this, the coroner's jury let the railway off lightly, with a lecture and a deodand of £15, but the directors learned their lesson and afterwards took steps to bring such private connections under their own control.

Two years later, a careless N&C pointsman caused a derailment near Fourstones on 17 November 1838.[3] The train was carrying Irish butter and beef to Newcastle, and the engine shot down the bank taking the wagons with it; 'the goods flew in all directions.' The driver had the presence of mind to jump but the fireman was on the engine when it hit the ground, fortunately he experienced no worse than a good shaking. More serious was a derailment on 23 December 1840, when *Comet* was bringing a passenger train from Redheugh past Derwenthaugh. Again, the entire train came off, and, though no passengers were injured, *Comet* was 'thrown over a wall' causing some injury to the driver. In his report to the directors, Anthony Hall stressed that the delinquent point keeper was 'a very sober and discreet man'. These were the dramatic cases. Most derailments occurred within station limits, at low speeds and without serious results. The light locomotives and rolling stock of the period could be re-railed with relative ease and the workforce got quite slick at doing this. Thus on 15 August 1842 *Nelson* was derailed at Haydon Bridge station, but was only held up for twenty minutes, and had made up most of the lost time on reaching Newcastle. The point keeper was fined, the usual response.

Cattle could be a problem. George Stephenson's famous dictum about an encounter between a train and a cow, implying that the train would get off scot free, was utter blarney. The N&C was fenced or walled throughout, but there were occasions when gates were left open or fence rails stolen and cattle got on the line. At night, the first the enginemen knew of this was when they were almost upon the beast and the rudimentary braking provision of the day meant there was little they could do except jump off. We noted the death of driver Thomas Graham following one such encounter in December 1844. Two months before there had been a more typical affray, where cattle got on the line at a crossing and derailed the engine. No-one was hurt but the passengers had to wait more than three hours for another engine to arrive and take them on their way. November 1845 brought another encounter, in which *Rapid* was derailed near Haltwhistle and the driver and fireman, John Gallon and his son, were thrown off but they were unhurt and the engine was little damaged.

Speed is not something we associate with the N&C, but enginemen did their best to make up lost time, and this resulted in a derailment on the Redheugh branch on 31 October 1844. The 11 a.m. train from Gateshead Greenesfield station had been held up awaiting a connection from the south and, speeding along, came off the rails near Dunston. There were only six passengers, the guard and one of the company's workmen on board and no-one was significantly injured. Anthony Hall and John Chantler were soon on the spot, and the passengers were eventually forwarded by the 2 p.m. train, all but one man who was making his first journey on the line and decided to walk back to Gateshead and get his money back. The first-class carriage, with two passengers, ended bottom up but the worst injury was a badly bruised arm and shoulder for Andrew Carruthers, a cattle-dealer from Lockerbie. William Greene, at Carlisle, arranged for a local doctor to examine him at home, and John Challoner then trooped off to Carlisle to negotiate a payment of £25 in settlement of Carruthers' claims.

An embarrassing derailment near Stocksfield on 10 May 1841 involved Dr. Thomas Headlam, prominent both as a physician and as the Whig leader on Newcastle Corporation. He was travelling from Hexham to Newcastle in a private (road) carriage on one of the low carriage trucks, with a servant riding behind on one of the outside coach seats. It was a mixed train, with the goods wagons in front, as usual, just behind the engine, and a bale of goods, insecurely roped down, came loose from one of the wagons and fell on the track. The train was travelling at speed, and no doubt jolting quite a lot on the rough early track, and the bale proceeded to derail a 'Close Carriage' (probably first-class), a luggage van and Dr. Headlam's carriage truck. Headlam and his companion inside the carriage were not hurt, but the servant was thrown off, landing on his face and ending up 'much bruised.' The private 'chariot' was also much damaged and Adamson wrote promptly to express the directors' readiness to make compensation. He took the opportunity to point out that it was safer for people's servants to travel in one of the railway carriages rather than on an outside coach seat. Sir Frederic Smith, reporting on the affair for the Board of Trade, took his chance to point out that he preferred goods wagons to be marshalled behind passenger vehicles on mixed trains, but the N&C, true to form, stuck to their established practice.

Mechanical Failures

Given the fairly primitive workshop techniques of the day and the difficulty of ensuring consistent quality of materials, especially when it came to both cast and wrought iron, mechanical failures are not to be wondered at. Locomotive axles were a particular problem, notably the crank axles required for inside-cylinder engines. Usually the outcome was no more than a modest delay, though sometimes there were consequential problems, as on 26 April 1844 when *Samson* broke a tender axle on the approach to Corbridge. While it was being manoeuvred, *Jupiter* came up on another train and was derailed because no-one had alerted the driver to the points being changed.

Whickham churchyard contains a memorial (page 171) to Oswald Gardner, a 27-year old engine driver killed after a connecting rod broke on 15 August 1840. A fragment forced itself into the boiler and firebox, and as the 'stoker' was firing at the time there was a blow back of coke and hot water onto the footplate. Gardner jumped off and hit his head, dying next day from concussion. Matthew Hall, his fireman, was badly scalded but 'not dangerously' so, and recovered.

The most dramatic sort of engine failure was a boiler explosion but these were fortunately rare. However, two of the Thompson Brothers' engines experienced firebox failures in successive years. On 1 May 1844 *Adelaide's* firebox exploded while waiting at London Road with a coal train. The boiler had been thoroughly repaired only six days before, and it transpired that the enginemen had allowed the water level to sink dangerously low. The driver was William Simpson, whom we encountered at Corby, and this time his luck ran out. He was badly scalded in his lower body, but lingered on in 'great agony', from which he was relieved by death on 8 December. His fireman, Peter Short, made a brisk recovery.

On 25 January 1845 *Venus's* firebox exploded while standing on a goods train at How Mill, apparently through no fault of the enginemen. Driver John Gardner and fireman Michael Watton were thrown almost twenty yards into one of the coal cells yet escaped serious injury. Gardner was slightly scalded on one leg but the pain had gone by the following day and he was soon back at work. The engine also was, in other respects, 'little injured'.

Failures of boiler tubes were not uncommon in the early days, and the enginemen carried materials to make running repairs. Thus on the occasion of a tube bursting at Hexham in October 1844, the crew put out the fire, plugged the tube, and then got the engine going again with about three hours delay in total. The 1853 Rule Book gives some hint of what might be expected. The driver was required to carry, in addition to lamps, signal flags, oil cans and a water bucket:

1 complete set of screw keys.	1 large and 1 small monkey-wrench.	2 hammers.
1 crowbar.	2 short chains, with hooks.	3 cold chisels.
1 screw jack.	A quantity of flax, twine and yarn.	A tail rope.
2 pairs of scotches.	2 glass tubes (for the water gauge).	Plugs for tubes.
2 wooden chocks for the motion bars.	2 spare clacks (pipe valves).	

Wood packing for the axleguards and axleboxes.

'Routine' Accidents

Many accidents were of what might be termed a routine nature, where an individual was injured or killed due to their own momentary inattention or carelessness, something which is difficult to guard against. A particularly poignant example is the case of Thomas Oswald Blackett, who had surveyed the east end of the railway. On 11 December 1847 he was visiting friends in Prudhoe and chose, like many people, to take a short cut along the line. A train bound for Carlisle came on him and he was struck by the engine, receiving injuries from which he died the following day. Pedestrians were particularly vulnerable. Though they were not meant to walk along the line, there was probably a failure for some years to realise that trains took a long time to stop and could not take any sort of avoiding action.

Trouble usually arose at level crossings, and a group west of Hexham station, bordering Kingshaw Green and Tyne Green, acquired a bad reputation. Rebecca Robson was killed at one of these in August 1841, despite her companions having warned her that a train was coming. August 1845 saw the death of Mary Anne Scott, 'an old woman which had been laying out some clothes to dry and was returning home'. In response, the Board of Trade required the company to provide a gatekeeper at Tyne Green. A year later, a pedlar - Abraham Waller - 'somewhat taken to drink', was run over near Kingshaw Green, the eventual upshot being the construction of an underbridge there.

17.1. *Peter Tate's cast-iron skew bridge at Kingshaw Green.*
(GR 915657)
Built to replace the deadly level crossings, it is seen here c1984. At that time, the rails were borne on timber waybeams resting in trough girders. These were not original but its outward appearance remained unaltered. A clumsy reconstruction has since destroyed its character.
(Bill Fawcett)

The most vulnerable people were the company's own employees, particularly those engaged in shunting and similar activities. Death and loss of limbs were all too common, and the generally slow speeds seem to have encouraged men to clamber between vehicles while in motion, at the risk of losing their footing due to the jolting on the rough early track. The directors took no responsibility but, in some instances at least, found new employment for men injured at work.

A sad case is that of John Scott, not the Blaydon agent, but a younger man appointed agent at Bardon Mill on 3 December 1844. His predecessor, Mr. Hubbuck, had been discharged for absenting himself from his work and being somewhat taken to liquor. Drink was to be Scott's downfall, but not in the same way. The evening of 27 December 1844 was dark and misty and he had to cope with an intoxicated passenger who wished to catch an approaching train. Scott, probably distracted, failed to show the usual red light to signal the train to stop; instead he went out with a lantern. Seeing this the engine slackened speed and the guard put on his brake but Scott then found that the passenger had come out on the track behind him. In his effort to save the passenger from danger Scott was run over and killed. In the circumstances the directors' response seems niggardly in the extreme. They granted his widow just £10, probably about two months' salary.[4]

St. Nicholas Crossing: 10 July 1870

Only one major accident ever occurred on the Carlisle line, and that - curiously - happened eight years into NER ownership, just at the end of the period under consideration, and on the stretch of line best protected by fixed signals. A few hundred yards west of London Road, the Canal Branch was crossed on the level by the Lancaster & Carlisle main line at St. Nicholas Crossing. The dangers were obvious and so it was well protected. Drivers were instructed to approach at a speed of no more than 4 miles per hour, and the crossing was controlled by a signal cabin. The signals on both routes were normally held at danger, and drivers were ordered to whistle on approach, when the signals would be cleared if there was a clear path available. In addition, the Canal Branch was equipped with stop boards, thirty yards in advance of the signals, at which drivers were instructed to halt until the signals were clear.[5]

On the evening of Saturday 9 July 1870 a NER goods engine (apparently the former N&C 0-6-0 *Naworth*) was due to work a return trip from London Road to Canal. It was employed as a 'pilot' engine at London Road yard, where driver Pattinson and fireman Rowell came on duty at 7 p.m. There wasn't much shunting to do, and at nine they adjourned to a nearby public house, resuming work a couple of hours later. The train eventually left about midnight, Pattinson having been left behind and Rowell taking charge, with his guard, Shields, accompanying him on the footplate.[6] All this was quite common practice at Carlisle, regardless of what the rules might say.

The journey to Canal was made without problems, and Rowell set off on his return trip about 12.40 on the Sunday morning, alone on the footplate as Shields was now riding on the last wagon, the train having no brakevan. The lamp of the distant signal at St. Nicholas Crossing was out, but Rowell was clearly not keeping a proper lookout and seems to have been totally oblivious to his actual position, since he passed the stop board and the crossing signal and ploughed straight into the side of an overnight express from Glasgow to Euston. Six passengers died and thirty were injured. Rowell was indicted for manslaughter but was eventually released because further investigations revealed a general laxity on the part of the NER authorities at Carlisle, who seem to have ignored the rulebook and treated these local workings to and from Canal yard as if they were merely shunting operations around the London Road yard. The NER directors responded by dismissing Pattinson, Rowell and Shields, along with night shunter Anderson, who had been working with them at London Road, and the locomotive foreman, Marshall.[7] The affair also, as we have seen, called into question the whole issue of the Carlisle Section management and may have precipitated the resignation of Joseph Parker as Superintendent.

17.2. *The classic view of St. Nicholas Crossing, taken in 1876 when work was far advanced on the new lines and bridges which would replace it. At far left, just beyond the junction of the Canal Branch with the line from Citadel Station, is the overbridge built by the NER in the late eighteen-sixties to replace a level crossing of the road to Upperby. This was about to be superseded by a new span just to the right, forming part of the lengthy structure which went on to span the LNWR main line – this was rebuilt as the present St. Nicholas viaduct in 1928 in the course of road widening. Hidden from view is the south-east loop from London Road to the LNWR, skirting the hill crowned by Harraby workhouse, whose site was adopted for the enginemen's hostel built by the London Midland & Scottish Railway when they rebuilt Upperby engine shed in 1948.   (J.M. Fleming collection)*

17.3. *View in 1877, with the new lines in place. At extreme right is the main line from Penrith into Citadel Station. The three bridges carry the line into the LNWR goods station at Crown Street. The Canal Branch has been displaced a little to the south, while the tracks curving right alongside it form part of the extensive network of goods lines put in place during the eighteen-seventies. These ones gave access from the LNWR main line to all the other companies.   (J.M. Fleming collection)*

Ordeal by Water

The most dramatic incidents on the railway were those in which the forces of Nature struck out at its civil engineering features. Flood damage has been mentioned, but it seems appropriate at this point to quote the account given by John Grey of the destruction of the Capons Cleugh and Allerwash bridges on 7 July 1852. Grey, the Greenwich Hospital Receiver, lived at Dilston Hall, only seven miles away, and was soon on the spot; this description was written the following day in a letter to his wife, Hannah. The problem arose not with the Tyne itself, but with a local downpour swelling its tributary streams in the vicinity of Fourstones and Haydon Bridge.[8]

'A messenger from Fourstones came for me early. I went, and found the colliery at Fourstones full of water run in at the mouth: nothing could resist it ... Capon's Cleugh bridge and road, which cost us £530 six years ago, all gone into the Tyne, where it has formed an island with trees washed down, and nearly obstructed the river; the roads broken up and impassable all the way to Haydon Bridge ... A workman was on the [railway] line near Allerwash bridge at our mill; saw the water coming like an avalanche, stepped back, and in a moment saw the [railway] bridge over Allerwash [Settlingstones] Burn carried bodily into the Tyne and swept away in fragments. A mile further west, the ruins of our Capons Cleugh bridge, etc, came in a deluge of water and stones and trees against the railway. The culvert for the passing of the small burn was stopped; the train [from Carlisle] came up; the engine and tender got over, but the line broke under the carriages. The guard fell through the bottom of his van, was swept in the flood of the burn across the Tyne, and landed unhurt in our plantation on the south side! How he escaped being crushed to death among the splinters and broken planks of the carriages I cannot conceive. It is a miraculous escape, and he can tell little about it, but that he thought he was to be drowned. It was the little red-faced man. No passengers were killed; seven were rather hurt. I saw three carriages in fragments hanging over the chasm, and about 100 men, directors and engineers besides, trying to get them out.'

Lowry went up with the directors on 8 July and found a gap 80 feet wide at the Allerwash Burn.[9] At Capons Cleugh the wreck of the guard's van was hanging over the gap, with the 'carriages behind dreadfully broken.' Tate was already there with his men and got a temporary bridge across one breach during the course of the day, dealing with the other the following day. Thus the line was back in business in just over two days. William Woods, who had only just become chairman, attended the scene both days.

... and Fire

Fire was another hazard, and the two great timber bridge fires - at Warden and Scotswood - warrant a closer look. Warden occurred on 27 July 1848, during the early weeks of the Hudson lease, and was probably started by a cinder from an engine. Four of the five spans were burned but Peter Tate worked his usual miracle and had a temporary way operational by the 30th. Goods, other than perishable traffic such as fish, were halted during this period but passengers were taken to either end and at first walked round via the West Boat suspension bridge, though an omnibus was soon laid on for them.[10]

The permanent replacement is something of a puzzle. Hudson did nothing about this, nor did the old directors until January 1851, when they decided to proceed 'immediately' with it. It is unclear whether the design was left solely to Peter Tate or advice was sought from T. E. Harrison, with whom the company would still have been in touch regarding the Alston Branch.[11] The outcome was a series of cast-iron arches borne on the original piers, one line having been replaced by the end of the year.[12] In January 1852 the directors described the work as a 'good sound job' which 'to all appearances will last a hundred years.' In fact it managed little more than half a century, partly because of a tight, twelve chain radius curve on the west approach. In 1906 the NER eliminated this by building a new bridge on a much better alignment, subsequently removing most of the old structure except for the lower courses of some piers.

17.4. *The 1851-2 Warden Bridge plays second fiddle in this view showing the present one under construction. We are looking east along the timber bridge used to convey materials. It has a pair of light rails laid on waybeams. The east abutment has been completed and the two pairs of tubes which form the river piers are above the water. (J.M. Fleming collection)*

17.6. *(opposite) Charles Augustus Harrison's sternly functional 1906-7 Warden Bridge, looking west. (Bill Fawcett)*

The demise of Scotswood bridge in 1860 was well recorded and widely welcomed. For years it had been an object of scorn. Keelmen thought it a hazard to river traffic, while timid passengers felt it rumbled and shook too much for comfort. The Board of Trade was called in and on 9 May Colonel Yolland conducted a series of tests, accompanied by Peter Tate and John Bourne.[13] Two mineral engines, *Atlas* and *Planet*, were run in various combinations, together with a rake of 44 coke wagons, and at the end Colonel Yolland indicated that he was satisfied with the safety of the bridge, though he made suggestions as to its strengthening. Fate evidently thought otherwise, and it appears that ash from the locomotives lodged in the bridge structure, unseen by the bridge keeper living in the cottage at the end. In the middle of the night he discovered that the bridge was on fire, and it was entirely burned down to the water line, despite the efforts of the N&C and NER which despatched their fire engines by train to the site. Adjoining the bridge on the north bank was the paper mill of Grace & Company, with over a hundred barrels of resin stacked on a riverside quay. These took fire, with dramatic effect, but the combined efforts of Grace's men and the *Newcastle* fire engine managed to prevent serious damage to the mill itself.

The close working relationship between the N&C and NER now bore fruit. Goods, minerals, private carriages and horses were handled via the Redheugh incline, while an omnibus service was laid on between Central Station and Blaydon, via Scotswood Road and the Chain Bridge, without any alteration in the scheduled train times.[14] Within hours of the fire, Tate was able to report that one span had been cleared of debris to permit the passage of river traffic. That just left the question of the temporary and permanent replacement bridges, on which the directors sought the advice of T. E. Harrison.

In the event, arguments with the Tyne Commissioners and the Admiralty regarding the temporary bridge were bypassed by building it on the structure surviving below the water-line, and in conformity with the 1829 Act. This was supervised by Tate, with the work being let to Benjamin Lawton in early June.[15] Tate's obituary claims that the temporary structure employed laminated timber beams and was completed in only three weeks. The permanent bridge took nearly a decade to sort out. The problem arose with the demands of the Tyne Commissioners, who had taken over the management of the river from Newcastle Corporation. They had embarked on a programme of dredging and other river improvements and were already planning the replacement of the Tyne Bridge by one with an opening span. They therefore attempted to persuade the N&C and NER to make the permanent Scotswood bridge with a swinging section but this was unrealistic, given that no assistance was being offered towards the extra cost.[16] In any case, it was most improbable that ships of any size would ever be seen that far upstream.

The Commissioners used the merger Bill as an opportunity to press for a start on the permanent bridge, while continuing to argue the case for an opening span. They failed in the latter endeavour, but work on the new bridge began in 1868, with a contract for ironwork being let towards the end of August.[17] It was a typical Harrison design of the period, with hog-backed wrought-iron girders carried on tubular piers. This approach maximised the clearance available to river traffic, while the individual spans, at 110 feet, were wide enough to meet all legitimate grievances. The first bridge had carried a water main for the Whittle Dean Water Company, and though that failed to quench the fire, the presence of a replacement main has ensured the survival of Harrison's bridge despite its closure to traffic in October 1982.

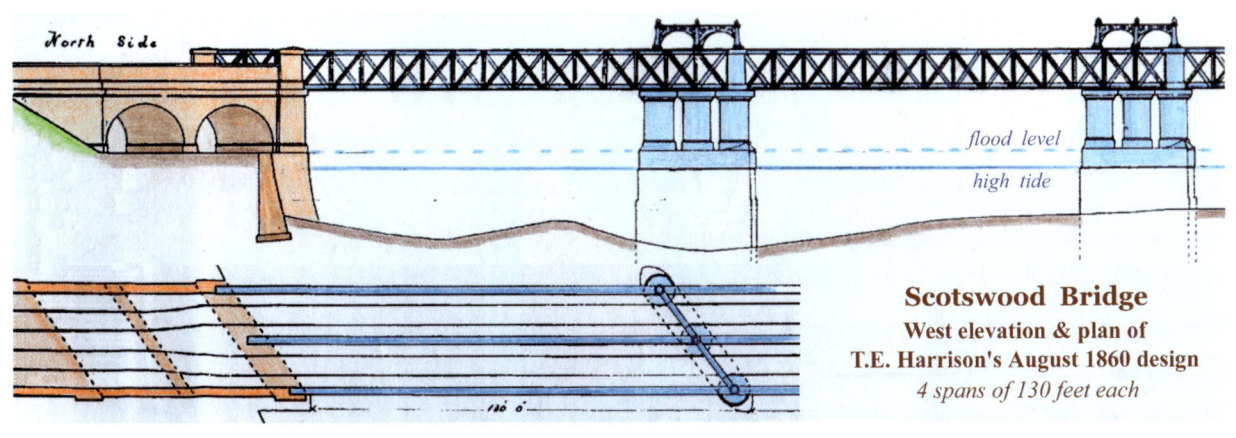

Scotswood Bridge
West elevation & plan of
T.E. Harrison's August 1860 design
4 spans of 130 feet each

*17.5. (above)
Harrison's first design for the new Scotswood bridge was this Warren truss, which was approved by the Admiralty but not by the Tyne Commissioners. By the time the bridge was ready to proceed, technology and Harrison had moved on to plate girders, for which he ended up adopting slightly shorter spans.*

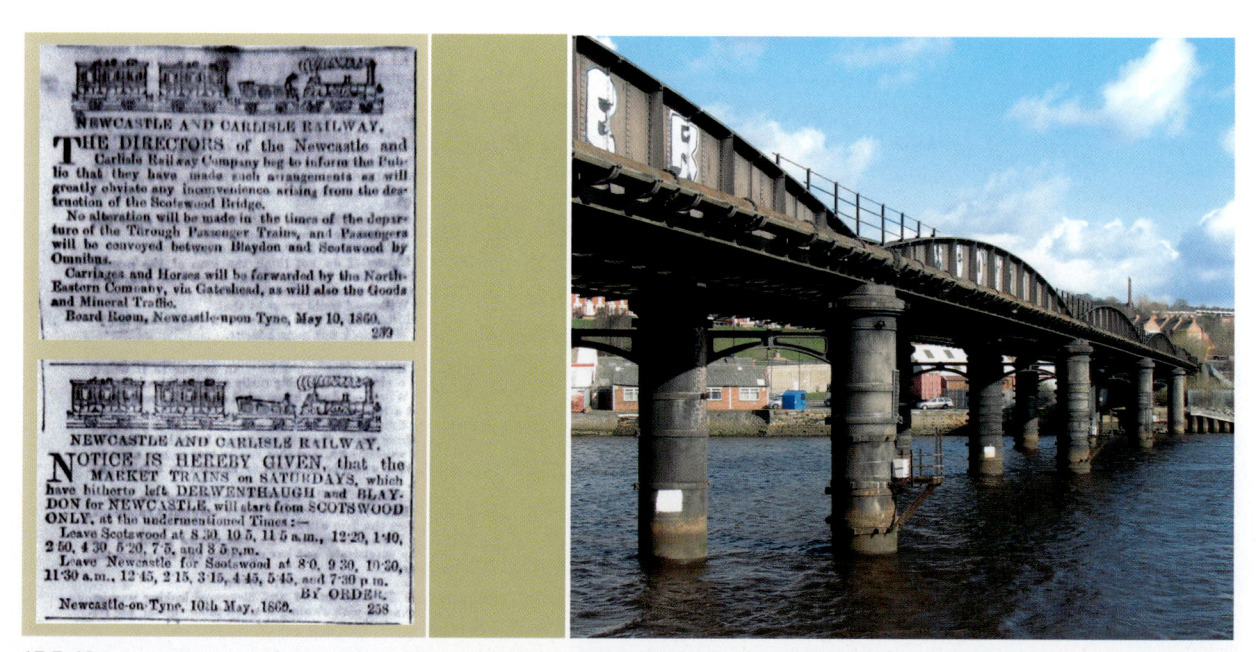

17.7. *Newspaper notices of temporary traffic arrangements following the Scotswood Bridge fire, and Harrison's replacement, seen from the south bank, together with the water main. It has 6 spans. The rails were fixed to timber waybeams borne on iron joists spanning between the main girders. These are carried by three lines of cast-iron columns six feet in diameter. These began to show problems in the nineteen-twenties, in response to which they have been bound with the hoops seen here.* (Bill Fawcett)

Another fire victim was the engine shed at London Road, which was destroyed during the late evening of 30 April 1864, despite the efforts of the Carlisle fire engines. The priority was to rescue the engines within, and a locomotive was sent from the Lancaster & Carlisle to drag them out, but four were damaged. The shed was rebuilt on a larger scale to accommodate ten locomotives but a new one, a typical NER 'square roundhouse', was begun alongside in 1881 and eight years later the 1864 shed was removed to make way for a second roundhouse.[18]

On two occasions the railway was used to transport Carlisle's city fire engine to rural outbreaks. We've already noted the fruitless attempt to help out at Naworth Castle in May 1844, and the other venue was *Shaw's Hotel* at Gilsland. The fire was discovered at 1.45 p.m. on 27 August 1859 and a horseman was despatched to Haltwhistle, the nearest station with a telegraph instrument, to call the Carlisle engine. His message was slow to get through but the engine and horses were put on the 4.25 train and got to the hotel about 5. By then, of course, the building was beyond hope. Its owner, the lawyer and one-time N&C director George Gill Mounsey, lost little time rebuilding it as the present large yellow-brick pile.

Human incidents, of course, pepper the history of the railway and it is impractical to delve into more than a few. We may wonder, though, about the 'madman' who was found wandering about Carlisle in May 1844 'nearly in a state of nudity'. The parish officers consigned him by train to Newcastle, for treatment at Dunston Lodge, binding his hands and feet and throwing a cloak over him. Somewhat amazingly, he was placed in a carriage with other passengers whom he then did his best to annoy.[19] At Milton he was transferred to a locked dog box, but soon managed to break out and the train had to set back some half mile to recover him. Milton was evidently an exciting place, for in 1853 the station clerk followed some men who had travelled from Rose Hill (Gilsland) without tickets. Keeping behind as they walked to Brampton, he overtook them at the start of the town, produced a pistol and marched them off to a local solicitor. They were summoned to Carlisle Petty Sessions but settled out of court.[20]

In January 1847 Richard Lowry and his staff 'took five prisoners' one night, for travelling without tickets, and had them up before the magistrates next day. Lowry pointed out to Matthew Plummer, that they were poor Irishmen and the charges ought not to be pressed. Plummer agreed, and the case was taken only to the point of securing publicity to deter others. This seems to have been common practice, with the company getting miscreants to pay costs and insert a public apology in the newspapers. On 17 July 1846 the *Cumberland Paquet* reported the case of one Brown, who had bought a ticket from Carlisle to Haltwhistle but went on to Newcastle. He was brought before the magistrate and could have been fined forty shillings with the alternative of 3 months imprisonment. However, the railway asked for a 'mitigated penalty', which turned out as 5s plus costs. The *Carlisle Journal* of 30 November 1844 bore an apology by Robert Robinson, having at 'London Road Station … attempted to pass to the train without first obtaining a ticket at the office, and having committed an unprovoked assault upon Isaac Scott, one of the servants of the Company … thank the Company for their lenity in forbearing to proceed against me upon condition of my making this Apology and paying the sum of ten shillings to the Carlisle Infirmary.' On 20 July 1846 the same paper carried Thomas Cairn's apology for attempting to defraud the railway by travelling beyond his booked station. Those with tickets must sometimes have felt short-changed though, as at Scotby three months later, when a westbound train over-ran the station and the driver could not be bothered to set back. A messenger was sent to Carlisle, demanding a train, which turned up in the form of an engine and no carriage. Adventurous souls might have relished a footplate trip but 'we all got amongst the coke and filth … and were annoyed all the way home by the steam and small particles of cinders being wafted in our faces'.[21]

Epilogue

It is now almost a hundred and forty years since the end of the period we are considering. Yet the Newcastle & Carlisle line is still very recognisably the railway created by Giles and Blackmore, Losh and Plummer, and it still fulfills a strategic role in the network, handling a substantial coal traffic, though no longer local in origin, as well as passengers. That does not mean there has been no change, far from it, but that change has not been intrusive. We shall briskly skip through the intervening years to glimpse what has happened.

The North Eastern continued for another half century beyond 1870, being grouped into the London & North Eastern Railway (LNER) at the start of 1923. The first big investment was in block signalling, introduced to most of the NER during the eighteen-seventies. This meant recruiting large numbers of signalmen and erecting numerous block cabins and signals. A feature of the North Eastern was its use of bridge cabins spanning the tracks in places where space was at a premium. Other railways used these to a limited extent but nowhere were they so prevalent as on the Carlisle Section, which still boasts two, Hexham and Wylam, as well as an elegant space-saving cantilever box at Haltwhistle.

E1. *Haltwhistle station, looking west in the late nineteen-sixties, still with gas lighting to the platforms. The tall signalbox, cantilevered out from a narrow brick base, dates from 1901 and was squeezed between the main line and the Alston branch track. Note the cantilever signal post, supplied to the NER by McKenzie & Holland of Worcester. (Bill Fawcett)*

E2. *Hexham East signal cabin (also 1901), in the late sixties, with a Carlisle train heading away under it towards the station. By then the West cabin, beyond the station, had been abolished. Tracks on the left served the goods yard, while the engine shed, closed in 1959, lay behind the telegraph pole. (Bill Fawcett)*

Traffic growth meant that the NER had to increase the line capacity, and this was done by the provision of refuge sidings where mineral trains could be sidelined to let the passengers pass. A duplicate route was also provided by an independent company, the Scotswood, Newburn & Wylam Railway, which opened in stages during 1875-6. Its trains were worked from the outset by the North Eastern, which took the line over in 1883. Engineered by William George Laws, the railway left the Carlisle line at West Wylam Junction, at the east end of Prudhoe Haughs, and immediately crossed the Tyne on an elegant wrought-iron bridge of 240 feet span, with the deck hung from a lattice girder arch. This drew on the principle of George Leather's bridge at Leeds, half a century before, and set the pattern for Newcastle's Tyne Bridge, half a century later. The line then followed the north bank, never far from the river, and rejoined the Carlisle line just east of Scotswood station. It served collieries, iron foundries and glassworks on the way, and was a realisation of the north-bank route advocated by Francis Giles back in 1829-30.

E4. *William Laws' West Wylam bridge, from the west. (Bill Fawcett)*

E3. *After the merger with the NER, Edward Fletcher's 2-4-0's soon took over passenger workings. Later on, various classes of Worsdell 4-4-0 found their place on the line. The finest of these were Class R, of which this is No.1258, a late one, built in 1907 and seen here on a westbound train twelve years later. (NERA collection)*

Carlisle saw change in the eighteen-seventies, with the construction of new links within the city and the opening of the Midland Railway's Settle & Carlisle route in May 1876. This came alongside the N&C at Durran Hill and then joined it at the east end of the Petteril Bridge. The following year brought the opening of the new lines and bridges which did away with the St. Nicholas crossing. These formed part of a larger scheme which provided a route for goods traffic avoiding Citadel Station and entailed minor changes to the alignment of the Canal branch.

E5. *In 1881 the NER replaced the London Road terminus with this spacious goods station. By 1985, when this view was taken, it was the only remaining Carlisle goods depot and had acquired this awkward canopy and overspill offices. The ending of wagonload freight brought closure and the building has been abandoned.*
(Bill Fawcett)

At the east end of the railway, the big development stemmed from the Tyne Commissioners' improvements to the river. The present swing bridge opened in 1876 and, coupled with extensive dredging, this enabled seagoing vessels to proceed upriver. The immediate beneficiary was Sir William Armstrong, at Elswick Works, but this opened up the possibility of building staiths upstream of Newcastle to ship directly into colliers. The NER opened Dunston staiths in 1893, together with connecting lines which also served to bypass the Redheugh incline. The operation of this had been eased in 1875 when Edward Fletcher built a pair of hefty-looking tank engines which could assist trains up the incline by banking them in the rear. This did away with the need for rope haulage but the incline remained a bottleneck. The new route left the Redheugh branch just east of the Derwent and provided links both south and north to the main line from Darlington. This relieved pressure on the Carlisle main line east of Blaydon, although the NER also increased its capacity by providing four tracks from Scotswood to Central Station. The remainder of the Redheugh branch became very much a back number, serving various local industries and in part diverted from its original riverside route to accommodate them. The new Dunston lines were a factor in the construction of a large engine shed at Blaydon, which opened in 1900.

While these developments were planned to facilitate freight traffic, passengers were not overlooked. The number of trains increased markedly under the NER and a particular feature was the growth of commuter traffic east of Hexham. The 1898 timetable shows a train from Carlisle leaving Hexham at 7.53 a.m. and making stops at Corbridge, Riding Mill and Stocksfield before heading non-stop to Blaydon and Elswick, reaching Central Station at 8.42. A connecting train started from Stocksfield at 8.17 to fill in some of the stations missed out. The fastest run from Carlisle to Newcastle was provided by the 10.10 express, which got to Central at noon, but this was far from typical. Elswick was one of several new stations provided by the NER; it principally catered for workers at Armstrong's factory and opened in 1887. It was provided with lavish, glazed platform roofs as was Blaydon, whose decrepit old station was replaced during 1911-12. 1912 also saw the NER take a lease of the Earl of Carlisle's Railway between Brampton Junction (the former Milton) and the town, where the North Eastern built a small station, opening formally to passengers on 31 July 1913.

E6. *In 1949 ten brand-new 2-6-0's of Class K1 were supplied to Blaydon shed, principally for work on the Carlisle line. No. 62024 is seen hauling an eastbound goods on the approach to West Wylam Junction. (GR109642) The line to West Wylam Colliery heads off left, with the N&C Hagg cottage just beyond. The cutting seen here takes the railway through Hagg Bank, where Benjamin Thompson originally intended to have a short tunnel. The Scotswood, Newburn & Wylam tracks start to diverge under the overbridge, which is just to the right of our viewpoint. (E.E. Smith, Neville Stead collection)*

E7. *Brampton Junction station, renamed from Milton in 1870. On the left is the official group at the formal opening of the NER Brampton Town service on 31 July 1913, with Sir Walter Plummer, Matthew's grandson, representing the NER directors. On the right is a view by the author c1966 looking west and showing how the original station became engulfed in later buildings. The place sees little traffic nowadays and the only building to survive is the timber waiting shed on the right.*

The Brampton Town service did not last long; it was withdrawn during World War I. This brought a considerable pressure of traffic and various works were carried out to expedite this including the development of Addison Sidings, near Stella. Only a few years into the peace came a severe decline in the region's most important industries, coal, steel and shipbuilding, which deepened with the onset of the Depression. The clouds had only just begun to lift when the Second World War came along. This meant that the LNER had little need and few resources to develop the infrastructure of the line, although they continued to invest in new locomotives and rolling stock and to upgrade the quality of service provided to passengers. In 1938 they introduced an express which did the full run in 77 minutes, but this was soon ended by the War and the present best is still slightly slower.

    Nationalised from the start of 1948, the line found itself part of British Railways' North Eastern Region, although the stretch west of Durran Hill was lumped in with the Settle & Carlisle and transferred to the London Midland. The age of electricity brought two new coal-fired generating stations to west Tyneside: Stella South was served by the N&C main line and Stella North lay on the other bank. Gradually, however, the coal industry was retreating towards the coast as the old western coalfield became worked out. Thus the line gradually lost the traffic from the pits it had fostered, such as those in the vicinity of Prudhoe and Mickley. Economies were called for. The Allendale Branch had lost its passenger service in 1930 and closed altogether in 1950. The Derwent Valley from Blaydon to Consett lost its passengers in February 1954 and through freight traffic to Consett had virtually ceased by 1960, with the line closing completely three years later. The Border Counties closed to passengers in October 1956 and was gradually cut back over the ensuing decade. At the same time BR were improving passenger services by introducing diesel multiple units. DMUs appeared on the Newcastle & Carlisle in 1957 and gradually supplanted steam. Passengers found them spacious and attractive, with good views thanks to the large windows and open saloon layout. Those travelling the length of the line also had the facility of a miniature buffet in one carriage. Timings improved a little, and by 1962 one express was doing the run in 83 minutes, but only by restricting its stops to Haltwhistle and Hexham; a more typical timing was an hour and three-quarters.

Contrasts at Riding Mill

E8. *Collecting the mail by train in the late nineteen-sixties. The letterbox was on the station platform. (Bill Fawcett)*

E9. *Eastbound train in the nineteen-fifties, hauled by Class B1 4-6-0 No. 61238, built in 1947. A number of these were based at Gateshead shed working Carlisle trains and put in over a decade on the service before being supplanted by diesel multiple units. This 7-coach train makes a striking contrast with the 2-car 'sprinters' of later years.* (E.E. Smith, Neville Stead collection)

Richard Beeching's 1963 report, *The Reshaping of British Railways*, foresaw a bright future for the Newcastle & Carlisle, shorn of the Alston Branch. Two years later, his trunk routes study cast the line in an even stronger light, as the principal route between Newcastle and Scotland, with the main line through Berwick relegated to a secondary role. This might have delighted the shades of Nicholas Wood and Matthew Plummer, giving their line the central role they had sought in the eighteen-thirties. In practical terms, however, it was nonsense though the report did manage to blight investment in the Newcastle-Edinburgh route for a time. The role of the Carlisle line in Anglo-Scottish traffic remains that of a diversionary route and the East Coast Route has since gone from strength to strength. The Beeching axe did hit the Carlisle line in various ways. One was the gradual retreat from freight business which began at that time. More immediate was the closure of most of the stations west of Hexham from 2 January 1967. This left only Brampton Junction, Haltwhistle, Bardon Mill and Haydon Bridge, though Wetheral has since reopened. The Scotswood Newburn & Wylam route went in 1968 but the Alston branch lingered on until the beginning of May 1976, while road improvements were carried out to provide 'all weather' access from Haltwhistle. The last casualty was the main line from Blaydon to Central Station, with Scotswood bridge closing from 4 October 1982. The line had by then outlived its usefulness and it made more sense to route passengers and freight via the Dunston route.

E10. *The Newburn line platforms at Scotswood, taken about the time of the station's closure in 1967. View east, with the N&C main line coming in behind the station nameboard on the right. Ahead is the tall signalbox at Scotswood Junction, with tracks heading off on the right to serve the Scotswood Works of Vickers Armstrong. Today, the railway has become a footpath but the factory has been renewed and lives on as BAe Systems. (Bill Fawcett)*

The introduction of *Sprinter* trains in the later years of British Rail provided much better acceleration than the early DMUs and timings improved, achieving 80 minutes with expresses stopping at Haltwhistle, Hexham and the Metro Centre - Tyneside's principal retail venue, conveniently located next to the railway. Trains now work through to Middlesbrough, Morpeth, Glasgow and Stranraer. Through workings are a relatively recent feature, except for the Stranraer trains, which began in the nineteenth century to link Tyneside with the Ulster ferries. The line has a flourishing air, but the service to places like Haydon Bridge is deplorably infrequent: oddly so, since most of the trains which whizz past take almost as long as those which stop. Coal trains trundle by but the last colliery near the line closed in 2004. Aptly enough it was Blenkinsopp, which enjoyed a stop-go existence during the twentieth century but just managed to make it into the 21st, having severed its connection with the railway long ago.

Endnotes

Abbreviations

HoCC   House of Commons Committee
NRO   Northumberland Record Office, Woodhorn
PRO   National Archives, Kew
TWA   Tyne & Wear Archives, Newcastle
Lit & Phil   Literary & Philosophical Society of Newcastle

Pages 7 - 24

Chapter 1

1. William Lawson, 'Construction of the Military Road in Cumberland', *Transactions of the Cumberland & Westmorland Antiquarian & Archaeological Society*, vol. 79 (1979). The Act and minutes of the Cumbrian Trust are in Cumbria Records Office, Carlisle Castle.
2. Article by James Clephan in [Newcastle] *Monthly Chronicle*, 1891, p. 347. Great Flood of 1771 swept away all the Tyne bridges, other than Corbridge.
3. Chapman's proposed Tyne-Solway canal summit was 445 feet.
4. For Chapman's career see R.W. Rennison, in *A Biographical Dictionary of Civil Engineers in Great Britain & Ireland*, Thomas Telford/ICE, 2002.
5. Addressed variously to the 'Northumberland Committee of Subscribers to the Survey' and the 'Gentlemen delegated from the Committees of Northumberland and Cumberland'. Copy in Lit & Phil Local Tracts vol. 200.
6. Ullswater branch would have gone up the east side of the Eden Valley and then swung west to pass through Eamont Bridge, serving Penrith with a short branch. Chapman never appears to have surveyed this route in any detail.
7. William Chapman, 5 January 1825 Report.
8. Ralph Dodd, 5 June 1795, published a detailed report, strongly critical of Chapman and advocating a canal from Newcastle to Hexham; another contemporary claimed that Dodd was simply plagiarising someone else's idea.
9. Sutcliffe appears briefly in *Biographical Dictionary*, op. cit. Sutcliffe's first report proposed a canal from Stella to Hexham, taking much higher alignment than the railway later did - for example passing south of Prudhoe Castle.
10. William Chapman, *Report on a Proposed Navigation between the East and West Seas*, Newcastle, 1795. Part 1 (26 June) dealt with Newcastle to Haydon Bridge; Part 2 (10 July) covered the rest to Maryport; Part 3 (10 August) looked at south-side route at east end, in response to Dodd, and said it was a bad idea. (Lit & Phil)
11. NRO QRUp 2.
12. Lit & Phil Tracts vol. 200 contains a printed booklet giving some details of the Parliamentary progress of the bill, and the opposition evidence - with footnotes refuting it.
13. Report dated 3 January 1797. (Lit & Phil Tracts)
14. From William Chapman, *Observations* etc, 1824, see note 16.
15. Carlisle Canal Act: 59 Geo III Session 1819, in Lit & Phil Local Acts. David Ramshaw, *The Carlisle Navigation Canal*, P3 Publications, 1997. Mannix & Whellan, *History, Gazetteer & Directory of Cumberland*, 1847. Sydney Towill, *Carlisle*, Phillimore, 1991.
16. James Losh Diaries: ed. Edward Hughes, *Surtees Society*, vols. 171 (1956) and 174 (1959).
17. *Observations on Canals & Railways*, printed by G. Angus in 1825, reprints Thomas's essay, said to have been read to the Lit & Phil, together with Barodall Robert Dodd's 1810 paper on the canal. No mention of Thomas's paper is to be found in the Lit & Phil Reports, but they did not form a systematic record at that time.
18. William Chapman, *Observations on the Most Advisable Measures to be adopted in Forming a Communication ... to and from Newcastle and Carlisle*, Newcastle, 10 May 1824 (also two later supplements).
19. Graham succeeded to Netherby Estate on the Esk, two miles upstream of Longtown. He did not invest in N&C but, e.g., assisted promoters with their successful application to the Exchequer Loan Commissioners - accompanying them to the commissioners when he was First Lord of the Admiralty.
20. William Chapman, *Additional Supplement*, 21 July 1824, to the open letter to James Graham. 'I yesterday examined ...'
21. James Losh Diary op. cit., 6 October 1824.
22. William Chapman, *Report on the Costs and Separate Advantages of a Ship Canal and of a Railway from Newcastle to Carlisle*.
23. *Tyne Mercury*, 6 November 1824.
24. Josias Jessop, *Report ... to the Committee of Enquiry into the most desirable mode of improving the communication between Newcastle and Carlisle*.

Chapter 2

1. A printed circular gives the names of the directors elected on 9 April 1825, headed by John George Lambton, later first Earl of Durham. John Clayton and John Adamson were named as joint solicitors and Clayton, Scott & Clayton as their London agents. Shares could be had from these and three Newcastle banks, Forsters in Carlisle, and Curtis, Robarts & Curtis in London.
2. PRO RAIL 509 series - Typed transcript of 25 May 1825 subscription list.
3. James Losh Diaries: January 1826 credit squeeze; 11 & 12 February 1826.
4. Printed lists of shareholders having ten or more shares were circulated in advance of the March AGM's. The first list came out in August 1829. The earlier MSS list referred to is bound into the author's copy of the printed 1829 Parliamentary evidence.
5. Information re Forsters Bank from Denis Perriam.
6. PRO (IR series) bankrupcy records and *London Gazette*, 2 December 1836. Forsters filed for bankruptcy on 19 November 1836 (date of docket), the day on which William Forster made his last appearance at the N&C Board. Denton filed on the 21st. Fiat in bankruptcy awarded 22 November against Denton and on the 23rd against Joseph, John & William Forster.
7. Mannix & Whellan, *History, Gazetteer & Directory of Cumberland*, 1847. The Dixon empire crashed in 1872.
8. NRO QRUp 64a. Deposited plan of November 1839 for N&C to deviate turnpike road at Greenhead. The Book of Reference lists the proprietors of the Blenkinsopp Coal & Lime Company as George Crawhall (who inherited Thomas's share under his will), William Crawhall, Thomas Wilson, John Dixon, Peter Dixon, John Studholme, and the assignees of John and William Forster. The Crawhall interest later passed to Isaac.
9. Blenkinsopp shipping, ex info. Denis Perriam. Two ships were offered for sale at Port Carlisle in 1854, on account presumably of closure of the canal.
10. Greenwich Hospital: minutes of Commissioners and Directors are in PRO ADM 67. ADM 76/73 contains various Northumbrian railway documents from the 1840's and turnpike road material, including MacAdam's 1823 report on 'Aldstone Moor'.
11 PRO ADM 67/74 Greenwich Directors 30 March 1825 accepted the Receivers' recommendation that the Newcastle & Carlisle Railway proposal was advantageous, but decided not to subscribe 'in the present state of their information'. ADM 67/17 Court of Commissioners 14 March 1829 sealed the Hospital's formal assent to the resubmitted N&C Bill. The land arrangement was agreed in 1830 on the recommendation of Wailes & Brandling, with the details as to valuation and rent sorted out by John Grey, who succeeded as Receiver at the start of 1833.
12. *London Gazette*, 29 July 1851: Order of Court of Chancery, in the case of Brandling v. Plummer, for sale of all Brandling estates on Tyneside and in Yorkshire. Ralph, last of Brandling brothers, died on 26 August 1853. Their pioneering Middleton Colliery Railway, at Leeds, assures the family an honourable place in railway history.
13. NRO 672/E/1E/7 Allendale MSS: Newcastle Lead Office Chief Agent's Letter Book 1832-4. Benjamin Johnson to John Hodgson 11 January 1834.
14. NRO 672/E/1E/6 Chief Agent's Letter Book 1809-28. Thomas Crawhall to T R Beaumont 13 November 1827. The cash books show that Thomas received the chief agent's salary from that date.
15. James Losh Diaries: 29 December 1831.
16. William began to suffer attacks of 'paralysis' from January 1845, and in May Thomas Sopwith was approached to succeed him. Sopwith formally took over from 1 July, but in practice from August 1845.
17. Details of Thomas's interests are taken largely from his will, made on 18 May 1833 in London and proved on 15 March 1834.
18. His collection of antiquities is in Newcastle University's Museum of Antiquities, its provenance described in J. D. Cowen, 'the Crawhall Collection' in Archaeologia Aeliana, series 4, vol. 43, 1965.
19. PRO RAIL 509/2 N&C Board 5 March 1830.
20. PRO RAIL 509/4 N&C Board 24 September & 10 October 1833.
21. Newcastle Central Library, Local Studies Collection Cr 298544A is Joseph's account book for 1822-7, a highly revealing document. Cr 298562A is his farming diary, beginning in 1849 when he took over brother William's retirement country house at Stagshaw Close, near Corbridge. He appears in biographies of his grandson: Charles S. Felver, *Joseph Crawhall*..., Frank Graham, 1972; Vivien Hamilton, *Joseph Crawhall*, John Murray & Glasgow Museums & Art Galleries. George is a hero and dedicatee of Jacob Ralph Featherston, *Weardale Men & Manners*, 1840.
22. See also Tony Barrow, *The Whaling Trade of North-East England*.
23. The new road linked existing turnpikes at Branch End and Cowshill. Thomas, George, William, Isaac, Joseph & Allenby (a son of John) were trustees, as were various Beaumonts, Robert Brandling, John Blenkinsopp Coulson, John & Nathaniel Clayton and many others.
24. James Losh Diaries.
25. William was also the managing partner in the alkali works for many years.
26. *Newcastle Courant*, 21 July 1848. Matthew Bell also chaired the Newcastle & North Shields Railway.
27. William Fordyce, *History & Antiquities of the County Palatine of Durham*, vol. 2, Fullerton & Co., Newcastle, 1857: p790.
28. James Losh Diaries: 17 April 1826 & 27 January 1827.
29. Matthew Plummer's business interests were continued by his sons Benjamin and Robert. Benjamin was the father of Walter.
30. Sources for Clayton include Welford, *Men of Mark twixt Tyne and Tweed*. Some diaries are in Tyne & Wear Archives, but reveal little more than when he was down in London on Parliamentary business for the N&C. The Losh diaries reveal something of Clayton's very active role in the N&C. He was not slow to express his opinion about routes or about getting on with construction at the Newcastle end, at the expense of the west end, when money ran short.

Chapter 3

1. HoCC 1829 N&C Bill. Questioned by the committee on 29 March 1829, Thompson said he acted gratuitously as engineer on behalf of the promoters and expected no remuneration. Company records reveal that all he received were some modest out-of-pocket expenses.

Pages 24 - 41

2. A summary of Thompson's career is given in *Biographical Dictionary of Civil Engineers*, op. cit.
3. PRO B/3/2150 & 2151 Bankruptcy papers for Harrison, Cooke & Co. They were declared bankrupt in July 1810 and managers were appointed to keep the mines operating. Thompson was presumably brought in to facilitate the sale and with a view to his purchasing them himself.
4. Benjamin Thompson, *Inventions, Improvements & Practice of Benjamin Thompson*, 1847. This is a late valedictory book, largely devoted to his work between 1810 and 1830. His Durham railway ventures feature in Colin Mountford's account of the private railways of County Durham. Mining Institute Johnson Reports contain a lot on his later Seaham Railway.
5. NRO Accession 1183: papers of William Woods re Brunton & Shields Railway, including MSS prospectus of December 1835 for joint stock company to take over line. Thompson and Harrison were obliged to call in Shakespeare Reed to partly fund the venture and he obtained a half interest in the railway. This share was sold in early 1836 to Woods, with some profiteering by Reed's solicitor, R.B. Cay, en route.
6. NRO QRUp 17.
7. James Losh diary 17 August 1826 refers to the error 'supposed to have been made by Fryer'.
8. Although the railway eventually adopted a route much higher up the riverside, the quay was still built by the company.
9. This account is indebted to Brian Webb & David Gordon, *Lord Carlisle's Railways*, Railway Correspondence & Travel Society, 1978. This explained the interaction between James Thompson and the N&C, using Carlisle family papers at Durham University, and describes the various iterations in more detail than is possible here; its only weakness is an uncritical acceptance of the strategic aims of James Thompson and the sixth Earl.
10. James Loch, MP, was the leading example of a barrister-auditor, serving as chief agent and adviser simultaneously to several great landed estates, including the Earl of Carlisle and the Duke of Sutherland. James Losh did this on a much smaller scale for the Beaumonts. Loch was also a Liverpool & Manchester Railway director as nominee of Marquess of Stafford.
11. Joseph Locke's evidence to the House of Commons committee on the 1829 N&C Bill. This recounts several of his surveys for Stephenson along the route but is naturally vague as to dates. Thus he spent 2 or 3 weeks 'when this railway was agitated before' surveying the line from Carlisle to Greenhead.
12. ibid.
13. ibid. Stephenson's alternative entailed an incline 1¾ miles long at 1 in 36 from Corbridge up to Thornbrough, reaching about 300 feet above sea level, then descending very gently to Barras Bridge (site of Newcastle Civic Centre at about 200 feet), before dropping down to Newcastle Quayside at 1 in 48.
14. Michael Longridge to Robert Stephenson, 27 February 1826.
15. Brian Webb, op. cit.
16. James Losh Diary 8 April 1828. 'This was an important railroad meeting as we finally determined upon the line and gave directions to commence the survey etc forthwith.'
17. PRO RAIL 509/1 Henry Howard's Railway Diary. This begins with minutes of the 17 April 1828 Carlisle meeting of promoters. He sent his first letters off to other landowners the same day.
18. ibid. Henry Howard to Thomas Crawhall 29 April 1828: 'Sir Hew has closed all former differences' and subscribed for one share. A copy of Ross's letter was despatched to the Earl of Lonsdale in the hope of persuading him.
19. ibid. Henry Howard to Robert & George Mounsey (Carlisle solicitors and agents for the Earl), 1 July 1828.
20. ibid. 17 & 19 August 1828.
21. NRO QRUp 21, deposited 28 November 1828.

Chapter 4

1. HoCC proceedings on 1829 N&C Bill, pub. William Boag, Newcastle. Evidence by Paul Nixson, p64, and Oswald Blackett, p67.
2. HoCC: Oswald Blackett pp214-224.
3. PRO RAIL 509/1 Henry Howard's Railway Diary - April 1828 et seq.
4. James Losh Diaries - letters to Grey printed at end of Edward Hughes, *Surtees Society*, op. cit.
5. HoCC pp202-14.
6. HoCC pp195-202.
7. HoCC John Green pp79-86, 98, 135-6.
8. Thompson himself admitted that a loaded keel had a height of about 9 feet 6 inches above the waterline.
9. HoCC pp224-5 Testimony by William Ord, of Whitfield, a member of the Commons committee.
10. HoCC Oswald Blackett pp214-24.
11. HoCC Benjamin Thompson p25.
12. HoCC John Green p79.
13. HoCC - Leather's report was written in April 1829, with knowledge of the committee proceedings, and published by Boag along with the evidence. Leather's assertions regarding Thompson's riverside route, for example at Allerwash, were proved quite wrong.
14. Hekekyan Bey, *Journal vol. 1*, British Library MSS 37448. Francis Giles, *Report on the Parliamentary Line of Railway from Newcastle to Carlisle*, signed Newcastle, 29 May 1829, printed T & J. Hodgson, Newcastle, 1830.
15. Francis Giles, *Second Report on the Line of Railway from Newcastle to Carlisle with Estimate of the Cost thereof*, 19 August 1829, printed by T & J. Hodgson, Union Street, Newcastle, 1830.
16. James Losh Diary 19 August 1829 - 'we contrived among us to take up the remaining shares *pro tem*'.
PRO RAIL 509/2 N&C Board 18 August 1829; 12 November - agreed to send deputation to Liverpool to seek extra subscriptions: Plummer, Woods, Thomas Crawhall, Peter Dixon & John Forster jun. (Dixon & Forster because of the Carlisle-Liverpool trading link); 27 November - progress reported in getting *bona fide* proprietors for shares signed for *pro forma* by directors.
17. James Losh Diary 16 October 1829; PRO RAIL 509/2 16 October 1829.
18. Letter from James Loch to George Gill Mounsey, 10 November 1829, in Tullie House Museum, Carlisle.
19. PRO RAIL 509/2 N&C Board and Newcastle Committee 27 November, 3 & 29 December 1829; 5 & 8 January 1830. The full list of candidates, which had risen from 8 to 9 by 5 January, was Brunel, Matthias Dunn (a very able colliery viewer), Hamilton Fulton, Giles, Hedley, Nicholson, Luke Pearson, Storey and one very low-priced and unknown T. Forster.
20. James Losh Diary 8 January 1830.
21. PRO RAIL 509/2 N&C Board 8 January 1830.
22. Any sketch of Francis Giles is heavily indebted to Mike Chrimes' biography of him in *A Biographical Dictionary of Civil Engineers in Great Britain & Ireland*, Thomas Telford, 2002. Some insight into Giles is given by letters of his pupil, William Lindley, in the Lindley Papers at the Yorkshire Archaeological Society in Leeds: Accession MD280.
23. Sir John Rennie, *Autobiography*, 1875.
24. Joyce Gordon, *History of Bedfordshire*, Bedfordshire County Council, 1969. M.C. Ewans, *A Brief History of the River Ivel Navigation*, booklet in Biggleswade Library extracted from a three-part article in *The Lock Gate*.
25. Edwin Course (ed.), *Minutes of the Reading, Guildford & Reigate Railway*, Surrey Record Society vol. xxxiii, 1988.
26. British Library MSS 37448. Hekekyan Journal vol. 1. The account of his May trip is accompanied by some fascinating sketches, including details of 2 vanished Tyne bridges: John Dobson's timber bridge at Haltwhistle and Sir Samuel Brown's suspension bridge at West Boat.

Chapter 5

1. PRO RAIL 509/2 N&C Board 19 March 1830. The share call was to be paid by 30 April.
2. PRO RAIL 509/4 N&C Minute Book of the N&C Newcastle Ctee. and also the N&C Board.
3. PRO RAIL 509/1 Henry Howard's railway notebook and 509/15 Minutes of N&C Carlisle Ctee. from 1829 to 5 February 1846.
4. Richard Lowry Diary is in TWA DF.Low/1, with one volume per year.
5. PRO RAIL 509/1 Carlisle Ctee. 24 March 1830
6. ibid. 7 & 22 April 1830.
7. ibid. 24 March 1830 Directors authorised Giles to quarry the stone - as a trial - and to dispose of it by building the first pier west of the river, but the abutment seems to have been undertaken instead. He was authorised to employ direct labour and given a generous cost ceiling of £1,000.
8. PRO RAIL 509/4 N&C Newcastle Ctee. 16 April 1830.
9. ibid. 25 August 1830.
10. ibid. 3 & 17 December 1830.
11. Francis Giles, *Report for Improvement in the Line of Railway between Scotswood and Ryton so as to pass it through Lemington and Newburn instead of through Blaydon*, 11 September 1829.
12. Francis Giles, *Report upon the Comparative Qualities of a Line between Scotswood and Crawcrook Mill by way of Blaydon and between these places by way of Lemington*, 22 June 1830.
13. PRO RAIL 509/4 N&C Board 24 June 1830 and Newcastle Ctee. 25 & 26 June 1830.
14. ibid. 4 & 10 August 1830.
15. ibid. 18 October 1830.
16. ibid. 18 December 1830 and 11 February 1831.
17. ibid. 24 February 1832. the recalcitrant landowner was the inaptly named Mr. Humble.
18. PRO RAIL 509/1 N&C Carlisle Ctee 14 April 1830 agreed Studholme's terms for surveying and valuing land, to be confirmed by Newcastle Ctee. He'd already got on with some of the work and was ready to proceed with some of the contracts for land purchase.
19. PRO RAIL 509/4 N&C Newcastle Ctee. 10 December 1830.
20. Francis Giles, *Second Report on The Line of Railway from Newcastle to Carlisle with Estimate of the Cost Thereof*, 19 August 1829.
21. PRO RAIL 509/4 N&C Newcastle Ctee/Board. They'd considered buying conventional rails but on 15 October 1830 ordered instead 150 tons of No. 2 iron bars from Bailey Bros. of Liverpool at £6-10-0 per ton. This removed the need for chairs and they were presumably spiked to the wooden sleepers ordered on 19 November for delivery to various contract sites. They held a competition in October for a wagon design, awarded prizes and then ordered something different from Robert Wilson of Newcastle on 18 December: 30 to be delivered to Newcastle at £12 each and 30 to Carlisle at £13 each.
22. R.H.G. Thomas, *The Liverpool & Manchester Railway Project*, Batsford, 1980.

Pages 42 - 52

23. The date of Dodd's appointment has not been found but he was in post prior to October 1831. The Carlisle Ctee. Cash Book (PRO RAIL 509/17) implies that he was paid up to the end of February 1836. On 8 March 1836 the Board noted Dodd had left his work at 'the west end' and it was reputed that he had gone to join Giles on the London & Southampton. Giles was to be asked whether he had 'induced' Dodd to go. The Minutes of the London & Southampton Railway Court (PRO RAIL 412/1) confirm that he went there.
24. N&C Board 12 October 1831 appointed Wylam Walker as clerk and as Inspector of Works at 30s per week, the 'same as now paid to Mr. Dodd.'
25. PRO RAIL 509/6 N&C Board 9 August 1838. 1851 census. The Journal of John Grey, the Greenwich Hospital Receiver, records Walker's activities as lessee of the Prudham Quarry at Fourstones.
26. Sunninghill Parish Registers: James Larmer (c1776–1844) married Frances Giles, sister of Francis, there on 31 August 1802; George was their third son, christened there on 22 April 1807.
27. PRO RAIL 509/1 N&C Carlisle Ctee. 28 December 1831. Also 509/17 Carlisle Ctee. Cash Book.
28. Howard's account was written on an elevation drawing of Corby Beck Viaduct presented to him by Larmer on 22 November 1833, shortly after completion of the bridge. A copy is reproduced here at a very much reduced scale, with Howard's notes retyped.
29. N&C Board 10 October 1834. Carlisle Ctee. Cash Book enables one to trace the period he spent off.
30. N&C Carlisle Ctee. 5 September 1836 approved his request to leave. 29 September Blackmore reported Tate's appointment 'to supervise the masonry and other works now in progress.'
31. Yorkshire Archaeological Society MD280 contains Lindley family papers including letters from William to his mother, which show that he left the L&S in late July but stayed with Giles until September in order to design the L&S bridges for him. He went on to a very distinguished career on the Continent.
32. Parish Registers of St. Paul's, Covent Garden, and directories.
33. Hekekyan Bey, Journal vol. 1, British Library MSS 37448.
34. *Carlisle Journal*, 29 February 1844, Biographical sketch on the occasion of Addison's retirement from the Maryport & Carlisle; John Marshall, *A Biographical Dictionary of Railway Engineers*, David & Charles, 1978.
35. Larmer established his first office at Castle Street, Carlisle, and *Carlisle Journal*, 27 May 1837 noted that Grahamsley & Co., the N&C's favourite contractors, had built Holme Head Bay on the Caldew under Larmer's superintendence, for Town Council. In November 1837 the paper published a letter of Larmer's regarding the railway route from Lancaster to Carlisle.
36. Third Report of the Smith-Barlow Committee on Railway Communication between London, Dublin, Edinburgh & Glasgow, presented to Parliament on 14 November 1840.
37. PRO RAIL 346/1 Lancaster & Carlisle Railway Board. Larmer also gave evidence on the L&C Bill for Carlisle Citadel station. His departure was recorded by the Board meeting on 8 June 1847; the Scottish railway is not identified but may have been the Scottish Midland Junction. Census reveals he was settled at Reigate by 1851, and had recently married Emma, who was almost 20 years younger. By 1871 he called himself architect and surveyor.
38. PRO RAIL 509/4 N&C Board 18 October 1830.
39. ibid. 22 April 1831.
40. Giles's annual report to shareholders at March 1832 AGM.
41. Parliamentary Archives. Private Bill Evidence (1834) vol. 6. London & Southampton Railway.
42. PRO PWLB 2/11 Public Works Loans Board 25 October 1832.
43. e.g. in Diaries of James Losh, pp169-70: letter from Losh to Lord Howick, 6 May 1832.
44. PRO PWLB 2/11 Public Works Loans Board 25 October 1832.
45. PRO RAIL 509/4 N&C Board 8 June 1832.
46. ibid. Account of 18 March 1834 AGM in pp266-9.
47. Robert E. Carlson, *The Liverpool & Manchester Railway Project 1821-31*, Augustus M. Kelley, 1969.
48. PRO RAIL 509/4 N&C Newcastle Ctee. 18 November 1831.
49. ibid. N&C Board 5 March 1832.
50. PRO PWLB 2/11 Public Works Loans Board 20 June, 6 September, 25 October & 15 November 1832; PRO RAIL 509/4 N&C Board 31 August 1832; PRO RAIL 509/29 Papers relating to PWLB loan.
51. PRO RAIL 509/4 N&C Board 28 September and 6 October 1832.
52. James Losh Diaries: 4, 7 & 9 May 1833.
53. PRO PWLB 2/12 Public Works Loans Board 9 May 1833.
54. ibid. Various meetings from 23 July 1833 to 28 June 1835.
55. PRO RAIL 509/5 N&C Board 20 March 1835.
56. PRO PWLB 2/12 Public Works Loans Board 8 October 1835.
57. ibid. 26 November 1835.
58. James Losh Diaries: 27 March 1833.
59. PRO RAIL 509/4 N&C Board 18 December 1830.
60. ibid. 14 February 1831.
61. PRO RAIL 509/1 N&C Carlisle Ctee. 14 September 1831.
62. Parliamentary Archives. Private Bill Evidence (1834) vol. 6. London & Southampton Railway.
63. The history of Giles's Eden bridge at Warwick Bridge has been unearthed by Denis Perriam. *Carlisle Journal*, 7 January 1832, reported that the county magistrates had been presented for non-repair, part of the foundation having given way. Discussions were held with Giles, and tenders invited in June but magistrates could not agree on proceeding. *CJ*, 6 April 1833, reported laying of foundation stone and 5 July 1834 quoted Giles's report to quarter sessions, explaining delays in progress; by then only the western arch had been closed. Progress evidently remained slow, but *CJ*, 10 January 1835, reported that the bridge was so far finished as to have been brought into use. Giles's obituarist, in Proc. Inst. C. E., considered Warwick Bridge his *chef d'oeuvre*.
64. R. A. Williams, *London & Southampton Railway*, David & Charles, 1968.
65. PRO RAIL 509/4 N&C Board and Newcastle Ctee. 21 December 1832 to 18 January 1833.
66. Buddle Reports are summarised in Board minutes of March & April 1833, while Giles's considered response is detailed in minutes of 27 March. Principal actions decided are in minutes of Hexham meeting of 16 April, while Blackmore's reports on actions taken are in minutes of 19 & 26 April.
67. Giles expressed strenuous opposition to the abandonment of the Eltringham Wall, arguing that the railway would be unsafe without it, and the Hexham meeting of 16 April agreed to proceed with its height reduced by between 5 and 8 feet, which Blackmore estimated would save £920.
68. PRO RAIL 509/29: Papers relating to the PWLB loan including memoranda of meetings of the directors in London; Giles was discussed on Saturday 10 May.
69. PRO RAIL 509/4 N&C Board 6 & 25 June 1833.
70. PRO RAIL 412/1 London & Southampton Railway Court of Directors 11 & 12 September 1834.
71. ibid. The events of Giles's departure were not minuted at the time but are chronicled in a detailed memorandum entered into minutes of 19 May 1837.
72. John Addyman, *Robert Stephenson: Railway Engineer*, NERA, 2005.

Chapter 6

1. PRO RAIL 509/13 contains the Visiting Committee minutes.
2. Managing committee minutes 30 June 1833 to 10 January 1842 are in one volume - PRO RAIL 509/14. Subsequent proceedings were written up in the Board minutes. RAIL 509/21 contains a neater version from 1833 to 19 May 1835, presented to York Railway Museum in June 1934 by NER and LNER engineer, Frances E. Harrison, who took a great interest in N&C history.
3. NRO 1183, Brunton & Shields Railway papers, formerly in the possession of William Woods. Benjamin Thompson to William Woods, 23 & 30 March, 11 April and 17 July 1841.
4. *London Gazette* bankruptcy notices. Newspaper report March 1843 AGM.
5. NRO 1183, op. cit. Thompson got Woods to back a bill (promissory note) for £500 which Woods ended up paying, while Thompson had also failed to get on top of the accounts due from the collieries to the Brunton & Shields, notably Fawdon, which defaulted on its bills and in which he had a part share.
6. R. W. Rennison, entry on Johnson in *Biographical Dictionary of Civil Engineers*, Institution of Civil Engineers & Thomas Telford, 2002.
7. PRO RAIL 507/1 Newcastle & North Shields Railway Board. See also Mining Institute vols. of Johnson's Reports. For Brandling see Newcastle Library Local Tracts vol. C45 No. 1: *A Brief History of the Brandling Junction Railway by a late shareholder*, 1845.
8. Bennett, Clavering & Rounding, *A Fighting Trade: Rail Transport in Tyne Coal: 1600-1800*, Portcullis Press, Gateshead, 1990.
9. PRO RAIL 509/41 Certificate of completion granted by 3 Northumberland JP's at quarter sessions in Alnwick on 17 October 1839, on evidence sworn by John Adamson. The same was done by Cumberland and Durham justices.
10. Directors' Annual Report to March 1839 AGM.
11. The east end contracts, excluding Farnley tunnel, are in PRO RAIL 509/4 N&C Board and Newcastle Committee: 28 September, 18 & 22 October, 16 to 18 December 1830; 18 January, 22 April, 15 & 28 & 29 July, and 12 August 1831. The contracts, summarised, are:

Section 1. Gibson Kyle & Thomas Davidson - 22 April 1831.
Section 2.
Earthworks: Robert Atkinson - 18 October 1830; Masonry - Robert Wilson, Greaves & Grahamsley of Newcastle - 18 January 1831.
Section 3. Robert Wilson, Greaves & Grahamsley - 18 October 1830.
Section 4. Earthworks: Mansfield Gibson - 18 October 1830. Contract abandoned April 1831, apparently relet to Thomas Hall and then on 12 August 1831 to Robert Wilson & partners.
Masonry bridges: Robert Wilson, Greaves & Grahamsley - 18 January 1831.
Eltringham River Wall: Wilson, Greaves & Grahamsley - 22 April 1831.
Section 5. Earthworks: W. Graham - 23 October 1830 (let out of committee). Contract abandoned July 1831 and relet as:
Shilford to Merry Shields - Thomas & James Nurston of Sheriff Hill - 12 August 1831; Shilford to Farnley (i.e. into section 6) - William Hutchinson of Crawcrook - 29 July 1831.
Masonry: Alex Davidson of Whiteside Gate - 17 December 1830.
Section 6.
Earthworks: William Irving & John Allen - 22 October 1830.
Masonry: Jacob Ritson, Stokoe & Robinson of Allendale Town - 17 December 1830.
Farnley Tunnel: Ritson & Perry - 16 December 1831.
Cutting at east approach to Farnley Tunnel: Ritson & Perry - 20 May 1834.
Section 7 Earthworks: James Whitehead, Thomas Irwin & -- Thompson of Hexham - 22 July 1831.
Masonry: Jospeh Lowes - 22 July 1831.

12. PRO RAIL 509/4 N&C Newcastle Ctee. 31 October 1831.

Pages 53 - 71

13. Jacob Ritson was christened at Allendale Town on 4 October 1795 and there married Isabella Rowell on 7 November 1832. See L. Popplewell, *Gazetteer of Railway Contractors & Engineers* for confirmation of some of Jacob & William's contracts.
14. William Ritson was born on 6 August 1811, the son of William Ritson of Calf Closehill. He was living at Newcastleton in 1861 while building Whitrope Tunnel. He married Jane Alexander on 7 December 1840 and retired to Woodley Field, Hexham, where he died on 19 November 1893. *Hexham Herald* has a thorough obituary.
15. PRO RAIL 509/4 N&C Board 10 August 1832. The Managing Ctee. had advocated taking the extra land for spoil on 4 May.
16. PRO RAIL 509/13 N&C Visiting Ctee. 23 October 1832.
17. PRO RAIL 509/21 N&C Managing Ctee. 19 August 1833.
18. ibid. 22 April 1834.
19. PRO RAIL 509/4 N&C Board 12 August 1834; Visiting Ctee. 30 January 1835.
20 PRO RAIL 509/21 N&C Managing Ctee 21 March 1834.
21. PRO RAIL 509/4 N&C Board 20 May 1834.
22. PRO RAIL 509/13 N&C Visiting Ctee. 22 July 1834.
23. ibid. 14 August 1834.
24. PRO RAIL 509/21 N&C Managing Ctee. 3 December 1834 indicates progress with track. The lengths of permanent way then remaining to be laid were ½m at Hexham, ¾m between Stella and Blaydon, and 1½m below Corbridge - including Farnley tunnel. The directors had referred the Dr. *Syntax* application to the committee.
25. Press accounts of the first opening include *Tyne Mercury*, 10 March 1835.
26. PRO RAIL 509/4 N&C Board 16 March 1835: Grey met the directors and insisted on the immediate disuse of the locomotives. After the failure of every argument against 'so unpopular a course' he told them he would apply for an injunction and they said that if he persisted they would halt the use of locomotives in 10 days. 17 March: Adamson (Secretary) was told to write to Beaumont and ask him to use his influence and write to Grey. 20 March: agreed suspension of services.
27. ibid. 5 & 29 May 1833. Latter records fixing of Company seal to agreement (dated 1 June) with Grey.
28. PRO RAIL 509/4 N&C Newcastle Ctee 25 April 1830 contains Giles's 19 April Report suggesting that the initial 'Corby Bridge' (Eden Viaduct) contract could be kept under £1,000 by restricting it to the west abutment and west pier; the directors were evidently keen to proceed with all the pier foundations but keep below £1,000. RAIL 509/1 N&C Carlisle Ctee. 22 July 1830 for the contract; 4 August for the change of mind and decision to cancell Robsons' contract if possible;
29. PRO RAIL 509/1 N&C Carlisle Ctee. 10 September 1830 for Robsons' new contract.
30. PRO RAIL 507/1 Newcastle & North Shields Railway Board 25 March 1837 let the bridge and other works to Robsons, but a fiat in bankruptcy was awarded on 31 July.
31. PRO RAIL 509/1 N&C Carlisle Ctee. 15 December 1830.
32. ibid. 26 May 1831.
33. PRO RAIL 509/4 N&C Newcastle Ctee. 18 May 1832. Giles reported that 4 piers were up to the arch springing and the abutments underway at the Eden Viaduct; at Corby Beck all piers of the seven 40 feet arches were up to the springing. RAIL 509/1 N&C Carlisle Ctee. 12 June 1832 records Giles's alteration to the dimensions of the arch rings.
34. PRO RAIL 509/1 N&C Carlisle Ctee. 12 November 1833 - Corby Beck bridge reported complete and Nixson & Denton ask if it can be passed for payment; RAIL 509/21 N&C Managing Ctee. end of December 1833 visit saw Corby Beck bridge complete and all the Eden Viaduct arches turned - the fourth had been completed in October, the fifth presumably in December. Henry Howard recorded the completion of Corby Beck bridge in October.
35. PRO RAIL 509/21 N&C Managing Ctee. 17 June 1834. On 30 June to 1 July they met in Carlisle and spoke with Denton, they also observed the activity at Warwick Bridge and wrote formally to Denton regarding the progress required, adding that 'you must not expect any relief in regard to your liability, under the agreement, to bear all other charges contingent on quarrying.' They decided to allow one month for completion. Grahamsley had excavated the western half of Wetheral cutting but could not begin the rest until the viaduct was open to him.
36. ibid. west end visit: 28 September to 1 October.
37. This account of Nixson and Denton owes much to Denis Perriam, who also contributed much of the material for the sketches of Paul and William in Howard Colvin, *A Biographical Dictionary of British Architects: 1600-1840*. Some of Nixson's works are mentioned in Mannix & Whellan, *History, Directory & Gazetteer of Cumberland*, 1847. See also Denis Perriam, 'The Carlisle Academy of Fine Art' in *The Connoisseur*, August 1975.
38. *Carlisle Journal*, 24 January 1824, reporting the wedding said that Denton was a partner.
39. Parliamentary Archives, Private Bill Evidence (1834) vol. 6. London & Southampton Railway 4 June 1834.
40. Forsters filed for bankruptcy on 19 November and Denton 2 days later, with a fiat awarded on the 22nd. Richard Lowry recorded an auction of Denton's moveable property on 16 February 1837.
41. Sketch of Studholme is indebted to Dennis Perriam; also draws on R. W. Rennison's account in *Biographical Dictionary of Civil Engineers*, op. cit.

42. House of Commons evidence by Studholme on the 1829 N&C Bill.
43. PRO RAIL 509/21 N&C Managing Ctee. 3 September 1833.
44. PRO RAIL 509/1 N&C Carlisle Ctee. 9 September 1830 & 12 June 1832. McKay's contract price was 6¼ d per cubic yard, subject to the Earl of Carlisle giving permission to quarry in his adjoining plantation, which he evidently did.
45. PRO RAIL 509/21 N&C Managing Ctee. 3 & 16 July 1833. The original contract price was £3,645-16-8. He would complete a partially timber single-line structure for £1,955-6-4 but required extra £1,217-18-8 for cancellation of original contract. This brought saving down to just £472, so sense prevailed.
46 Francis Giles, *Second Report* ..., of 19 August 1829; PRO RAIL 509/1 N&C Carlisle Ctee. 9 December 1831.
47. PRO RAIL 509/1 N&C Carlisle Ctee. 17 May 1832; RAIL 509/4 N&C Board 1 & 18 May 1832. Drift to be 5 feet high and 6 feet wide, extending 2 feet below bottom of the approach cutting so that bottom could form a drain.
48. PRO RAIL 509/4 N&C Board 15 & 29 June; 6 & 13 July 1832.
49. ibid. 10 August 1832 with report by Giles.
50. ibid. 17 August 1832.
51. ibid. 23 August 1832. Cutting was advertised for tender with closing date 11 September. 31 August 1832 meeting considered Graham's complaint and said Giles would see him to explain. 21 December 1832 agreed to pay Graham £900 for extra land. 26 March 1833 Final settlement of Robert Wilson's account for Cowran, totalling £508-12-9.
52. PRO RAIL 509/21 N&C Managing Ctee.
53. Parliamentary Archives. Private Bill Evidence (1834) vol. 6. London & Southampton Railway, 3 & 4 June 1834.
54. PRO RAIL 509/21 N&C Managing Ctee. 1 July 1834 let Canal Branch contract to Grahamsley in the course of a west-end visit.
55. *Carlisle Journal*, 27 August 1836, has Grahamsley advertising Newcastle grindstones for sale at Robert Street; 5 January 1839 advertised for sale wood, tools and a steam engine at Robert Street, so Grahamsley was packing up. The premises were next used by Thomas Nelson for his marble works.
56. Reports of N&C Managing Ctee to March 1839 and 1840 AGM's.
57. Laverick Hall was at GR315613.
58. *Carlisle Journal*, 3 October 1846.
59. PRO RAIL 509/4 N&C Board 16 April 1833. On 26 April Blackmore reported suspension of these works except for some fences and drains.
60. PRO RAIL 509/1 N&C Carlisle Ctee. 11 February 1834 sought approval for beginning the Caldew Bridge foundations in time for completion before the winter, otherwise 'a whole year would be lost.' See 9 May 1834 for Clayton and the PWLB threat - the Managing Ctee. were in favour of 'proceeding with vigour' with the Canal Branch. See also 27 May 1834.
61. Brian Webb, *Lord Carlisle's Railways*, op. cit. claims the mine was worked out. However Nicholas Wood did a report for Coulson 5 August 1831 (in Johnson Reports, Mining Institute) which suggests there should have been coal left to work, though Thompson had worked in a way designed to get as much out as quickly as possible. The new lessees drove a new drift, datestone 1842, which remained the access until final closure in 2004.
62 PRO RAIL 509/1 N&C Carlisle Ctee. 20 October & 3 November 1836.
63. ibid. This was last Forster appearance at N&C meeting. Fiat in bankruptcy awarded 23 November; first dividend, of 4s in the pound, paid 13 May 1837. Richard Lowry noted this brought 'an immense number of people to town.'
64. *Carlisle Journal*, 21 January 1837.
65. *Carlisle Journal*, 30 March 1844.
66. PRO RAIL 509/1 N&C Carlisle Ctee. 13 April 1835.
67. PRO RAIL 509/21 N&C Managing Ctee. 19 May 1835.
68 ibid. July 1835.
69. Richard Lowry diary 25 February & 9 March 1837.
70. ibid. 24 February 1837. Lowry noted the directors decision to advertise the conveyance of goods through by railway at 21s per ton, but felt that their facilities were not yet adequate for this.
71. PRO RAIL 509/14 N&C Managing Ctee. 12 August 1834 let masonry. It also let earthworks Tyne Green to Fourstones to Hutchinson but offered the western section to Grahamsley; he declined (having presumably sought whole stretch) and on 2 September it was reported this had been let to Hutchinson.
72. ibid. 19 May and 3 September 1835.
73. N&C Managing Ctee. Report to March 1836 AGM.
74. PRO RAIL 509/5 N&C Board 18 July & 15 November 1836; 24 January & 9 March 1837.
75. PRO RAIL 509/14 N&C Managing Ctee. 5 & 6 September 1836.
76. ibid. 21 February 1837.
77. Press reports of the coast-to-coast opening include *Tyne Mercury*, 19 June 1838, and *Gateshead Observer*, 23 June 1838.

Chapter 7

1. *Views on the Newcastle & Carlisle Railway*, 1836. Descriptive text by John Blackmore.
2. PRO RAIL 509/13 N&C Visiting Ctee. 22 September 1835.
3. Bridge details are taken from, and cross-checked between, a variety of sources, principally the following four: *Views on the Newcastle & Carlisle Railway*, op. cit. The North Eastern Railway's Line Diagram. Two returns made by the N&CR to the Board of Trade: 1. Listing all bridges (with span dimensions and materials) and level crossings in response to a BoT letter of 11 May 1844; 2. A return of July 1847 listing cast-iron bridges of about 15 feet or more span, and giving details of girder dimensions.
4. PRO RAIL 509/1 Henry Howard's Railway Diary.

Pages 72 - 98

5. Giles had originally recommended Newbiggin stone in his first report of May 1829, making this remark, probably advised by Paul Nixson. N&C later considered leasing a quarry on Blaize Fell. Francis Whishaw, *Railways of Great Britain & Ireland*, John Weale, 1842, confirms the use of Newbiggin stone facing.
6. Francis Giles, *Second Report*, August 1829 proposed making the level of the rails on the bridge about an inch below the surface of the road so that 'country carriages may cross it without inconvenience'.
7. *Newcastle Chronicle*, 29 October & 19 November 1836.
8. *Carlisle Journal* 5 January 1833. PRO RAIL 527/39 NER Way & Works Ctee. Min. 5136 approving the scheme for widening the bridge indicates that there was already a timber extension; 17 October 1889 Min. 5158 let the widening to Beaty Bros. of Carlisle at £2,662-13-7.
9. *Carlisle Journal* 4 April & 1 August 1846.
10. NER Locomotive Ctee. 2 August 1867 Min. 8951 let contract for bridge girders; 31 January 1868 Min. 9242 reported completion.
11. Whishaw, op. cit. and *ex info* John Addyman.
12. Drawings at Network Rail Record Centre, York.
13. PRO RAIL 509/7 N&C Board 6 April 1844 asked Tate to report on doubling the tunnel.
14. ibid. 23 July 1844.
15. *Tyne Mercury* 1 January 1845 described the technique of enlargement while reporting on the 28 December 1844 incident.
16. PRO RAIL 527/29 NER Locomotive Ctee. 6 May 1870 Min. 10413 authorised repairs to both Farnley and Whitchester tunnels at £500 and £200 respectively. On 28 July 1871 Min. 11282 Alfred Harrison, Northern Division Engineer, reported on the Farnley repairs; excess expenditure of £500 was allowed retrospectively.
17. PRO AN 117/7 BR North Eastern Region Board.
18. PRO RAIL 509/13 N&C Visiting Ctee. 4 May 1832. It had sunk 2 inches at the crown with some cracking of stones but no 'ultimate danger'. Thompson & Wood visiting, accompanied by Giles & Blackmore.
19. Reconstruction drawing in Network Rail York Record Centre.
20. PRO RAIL 509/13 N&C Visiting Ctee. 12 December 1834. (Plummer, Losh & John Brandling on this occasion)
21. PRO RAIL 509/21 N&C Managing Ctee. 31 March 1835.
22. PRO RAIL 509/13 N&C Visiting Ctee. 13 August 1839 reported that the (widened) piers were all in and abutments in progrss, with Blackmore expecting completion in about 3 weeks.
23. *Carlisle Journal* 20 February 1847.
24. Balteschwiler is described in W. Blasere *Schweizer Holzbruecken*, Basel, 1982; information and drawing re Baden from a display at the bridge itself; Schaffhausen is taken from *Encyclopaedia Britannica*, 11th edition, 1910-11.
25. PRO RAIL 527/28 NER Locomotive Ctee. 11 May 1866 Min. 8253 let the Ridley Hall bridge reconstruction to Lishman & Co. of Stockton at £3,041. The other two, over the Allen and over the South Tyne at Lipwood had been dealt with just before this.
26. PRO RAIL 527/47 NER Way & Works Ctee. 2 June 1904 let the Warden contract to H. M. Nowell of Newcastle at £18,312-5-0.
27. Drawings in Network Rail York Record Centre.
28. Recorded in the 1844 return. PRO RAIL 509/5 N&C Board 9 July 1836 noted the magistrates complaints and referred them to the Carlisle Ctee. noting that the bridge would probably have to be rebuilt. There are numerous references to it in 509/15 Carlisle Ctee. during 1836.
29. Noted in 1844 return.
30. The ironwork for the Haltwhistle bridge was supplied by Porter & Co., ironfounders, of Carlisle.
31. Directors' Report to the March 1853 AGM reported the damage and reinstatement. PRO RAIL 509/9 N&C Board 2 August 1852 approved Peter Tate's plans for restoring the bridges; 8 August let contract to E. B. Reed.
32. ADM 80/29 John Grey's Journal 16 December 1844 – met Peter Tate at Haydon Bridge to show him work is needed to protect the Hospital's land from the damage done by the railway's 'weirs' put into the Tyne; concerns had also been raised in 1839.
33. Records of High Bridge (Presbyterian) Meeting House, Newcastle; Obituary in *Sunderland Daily Echo*, 21 February 1879.
34. In 1851 John was a 'railway engineer' living at The Ropery, Dearham; his son's age and birthplace indicates he'd been there at least 6 years. Perhaps he was involved with the Maryport & Carlisle Railway; 1871 & 1881 reveal the 'waggon maker'.
35. PRO RAIL 509/15 N&C Carlisle Ctee. 29 September 1836.
36. NER Board 5 July 1872.
37. Lowry Diary 28 July 1861.
38. ex info. R.W. Rennison.

Chapter 8

1. Annual Report of N&C Directors to March 1839 AGM.
2. Francis Giles, *Second Report*, August 1829. He advocated an alternative line, but intended even this to be stationary engine worked.
3. PRO RAIL 509/4 N&C Board 7 September 1830.
4. A good summary of these schemes is provided by William Weaver Tomlinson, *The North Eastern Railway: Its Rise & Development*, pp207-10.
5. William Losh was particularly interested because of his activities at Walker, however none of the N&C worthies became directors of the eventual Newcastle & North Shields Railway except for Matthew Bell, who became its chairman, though Hodgson appears to have done most of the work.
6. PRO RAIL 509/4 N&C Newcastle Ctee. 20 May 1831 Hodgson was ready to grant permission to build river walls so long as jury set compensation. 10 June 1831 directors met Giles and Clayton at Elswick and appointed valuers.
7. PRO RAIL 55/1 contains minutes of the Blaydon Gateshead & Hebburn Railway Board and shareholders' meetings. Formal resolution to set up company was passed at a meeting on 7 February 1834, chaired by N&C deputy chairman Ralph Brandling. Those present included Clayton, John Adamson, Benjamin Thompson, William Losh, George Johnson & Nicholas Wood. By then the BGH Bill was already before Parliament.
8. ibid. BGH Meeting of Provisional Directors 20 February 1834. The capital was set at £60,000.
9. John Clayton's notebook - Tyne & Wear Archives 925/1 - covering 11 April 1834 to 21 May 1835 gives some details of his visit to London to help the progress of the BGH Bill and the N&C third Bill, together with negotiations with the PWLB over the terms of the latter. On 4 May 1834, back in Newcastle, he recorded a long attendance on Nicholas Wood regarding the details of a company to lead coals from Tanfield Moor and Tanfield Lea to the 'Blaydon & Hebburn Railway'. Tomlinson, op. cit., gives much credit to Clayton with regard to the setting up of the BGH.
10. Newcastle Lit & Phil: Local Acts. N&C clause is on pp 97-8 of BGH Act.
11. Dunn had ten shares in the N&C and increased this to 25.
12. PRO RAIL 55/1 BGH Board 25 July 1834. These managing directors had already been advising BGH as extension of their N&C role. First contract - Gateshead tunnel - was advertised in September with closing date of the 30th.
13. PRO RAIL 509/4 N&C Board 21 August 1834. At a meeting on 21 October Crawhall sought compensation.
14. 5 & 6 William IV cap 31. Deposited plans in NRO QRUp31. If a crossing were made downstream of Scotswood, the 1829 powers to take Hodgson's land west of that crossing were to lapse.
15. Newcastle Central Library *Local Tracts vol. D-29*: Robert William Brandling, *A short account of the formation of the Brandling Junction Railway*, probably late 1840. Prospectus for 'Brandling's Junction Railway', 1835. Prospectus for the Brandling Junction Railway, 1836.
16. PRO RAIL 55/1 BGH Board 22 August 1834. Robert W Brandling first attended to show his plans; he further attended on 3 October & 19 November. 26 November the Board noted their feeling that his scheme and theirs were not incompatible if he was prepared to start from a junction 2¾ miles east of their Gateshead tunnel. 2 December he attended and told them he was determined to make the whole of his line.
17. ibid. 16 & 20 May 1831. *Tyne Mercury* 15 & 21 May 1831
18. 5 & 6 William IV cap 83.
19. Page 15 of the Act (6 William IV) established the post of Managing Director and p20 specified RWB, who 'shall remain in and exercise the said office during his lifetime or until he shall resign or be removed in manner hereafter mentioned.'
20. PRO RAIL 55/1 BGH Board 13 November; 3, 19 & 29 December 1835; Shareholders' meeting 18 February 1836. PRO RAIL 509/4 N&C Newcastle Ctee 3 December 1835 contains the full terms of an agreement made by them with Hawks, Potter & Dunn of the BGH..
21. PRO RAIL 509/4 BGH Board 29 December 1835 contains 2 annexes:
1. Report of Matthew Plummer, Ralph Brandling & William Losh on a 19 December meeting with BGH representatives and then Board and subsequent contacts with Brandling Jc parties.
        2. Letter from Brandling Jc dated 17 December and giving the terms for an agreement with the N&C approved by a Brandling Jc shareholders' meeting of the 15th.
22. *Newcastle Journal*, 15 November 1851, summarises the affair. Details are in Proceedings of Newcastle Town Council: 6 May, 17 June & 7 October 1840; 18 February, 7 May & 10 September 1845; 9 September 1846. Dunn was instigator, though not the actual promoter, of a Chancery suit against the Corporation in respect of an exchange of land bought by the N&C at the Spital, and no longer required, and land south of the putative Neville Street. He also stirred up an action by the Scotswood Bridge Co. against the railway c1840-1. He lived at Bath House, Bath Street, Newcastle and owned the baths (vapour baths etc) there; he was also a shipowner.
23. N&C Directors' Annual Reports to the shareholders' meetings of March 1836 & 1837. Northumberland Archives QRUp 31 are the deposited plans for the route from Blaydon to the Spital.
24. York City Archives DP 2/5 Plan deposited 30 November 1836 to accompany second GNE Bill contains whole route from Newcastle to York.
25. PRO RAIL 232/2 GNE Board 19 August 1836 contains report of the Tyne Bridge deputation; the Board recorded their thanks to the N&C but postponed a final decision. 26 August read letters from Clayton pressing for a speedy decision and Brandling asking them to consider accommodating his interests.
26. Richard Grainger, *A Proposal for Concentrating the Termini of the Newcastle & Carlisle, Great North of England, and Proposed Edinburgh Railways*, 1836.
27. Grainger's road was to be 1,600 yards long, compared with a shortest route of 650 yds from the Spital to the Markets. The GNE also approached him about making a bridge across the Tyne - PRO RAIL 232/2 GNE Board 6 & 13 October 1836.

Pages 98 - 115

28. PRO RAIL 509/4   N&C Board 29 November 1836. A discussion took place in Newcastle Town Council on 9 November 1836, in which Joseph Crawhall took the Board line on a low-level bridge and John Brandling advocated a high-level one.
29. PRO RAIL 509/4 N&C Board 14 February 1837.
30. ibid. 12, 18 & 25 April 1837.
31. ibid. 25 May 1837. The advertisement is pasted in and dated 27 May with a closing date of 12 June.
32. ibid. 14 June 1836.
33. T. Fordyce, *Local Records*, Newcastle, 1867; John S. MacLean, *The Newcastle & Carlisle Railway*.
34. Folding bridge described in Francis Whishaw, *Railways of Great Britain & Ireland*, John Weale, 1842. Others from an 1844 return to Board of Trade.
35. BGH route details taken from their deposited plan: TWA 289/590.
36. Fordyce, op. cit.
37. N&C Managing Ctee. Report to March 1839 AGM.
38. PRO 509/14 N&C Managing committee 27 February 1838 accepted Grahamsley's tender for masonry & earthworks, Scotswood to Newcastle.
39. Tyne & Wear Archives 589/455 Newcastle Corporation River Committee visited Elswick Shore April 1838, recommended allowing N&C to build quay from west end of 'Clayton's Raft Yard' to Herd's House; principle had already been established. Grainger contract in PRO RAIL 509/6 N&C Board 14 July 1838. Contract had been let to Jacob Ritson but rescinded due to change of plan and readvertised - N&C Board 29 June & 13 July 1838.
40. Report of N&C Managing Ctee. to March 1839 AGM.
41. For Grainger's financial problems see Lyall Wilkes & Gordon Dodds, *Tyneside Classical*, John Murray, 1964, pp 103-122. N&C Board 27 October 1840 considered his offer to sell his rights in the new quay to the N&C.
42. N&C Managing Ctee Report to March 1841 AGM. Thomas Oliver's 1851 plan shows no tracks laid on incline or quay. An 1868 plan by Newcastle Corporation surveyor, John Fulton, was made in readiness for forming a new street - Skinnerburn Road - along the riverside. This shows no advance in the quay compared with 1841. It ended on the east side of a small inlet at the foot of the proposed inclined plane.
43. In 1854 the gasworks purchased the site of the Elswick reservoirs and pumping station used to draw part of Newcastle's water supply from the River Tyne. The N&C retained a solum running east from the foot of the incline but the NER will have sold this to Newcastle Corporation soon after 1871 to facilitate the making of Skinnerburn Road.
44. PRO RAIL 509/6 N&C Board 21 May 1839. PRO RAIL 509/41 Certificate of Completion signed 17 October 1839 by 3 justices at the autumn quarter sessions in Alnwick. This certified completion before 21 May 1839 of all the authorised N&C except for the riverside line to the Close and the Redheugh bridge. Similar ones signed by JP's for Durham and Cumberland.
45. N&C Board 28 June 1839 discussed progress, noting that only the west end of the large depot site would be completed by the autumn, so settling on a temporary terminus at its west end. Board 1 October 1839 authorised opening on the 21st. *Newcastle Courant*, 25 October 1839, reported the opening.
46. N&C Managing Ctee. Report to March 1840 AGM.
47. Tyne & Wear Archives.
48. NRO QRUp 50.
49. N&C Directors Report to March 1841 AGM.
50. HoCC evidence on 1829 N&C Bill. Examination of Paul Nixson and Thomas Oswald Blackett.
51. Francis Giles, *Second Report*, August 1829.
52. PRO RAIL 509/4 N&C Board 21 September 1832. Giles was asked to lay plans and estimates for bridge before that meeting; reason for advertising is not given. An advert pasted in gives a closing date of 31 October 1832.
53. ibid. 30 July 1833. PRO RAIL 509/21 N&C Managing Ctee. 30 July & 6 August 1833. Unhelpfully, the Managing Ctee. went on, 17 September, to recommend a crossing 500 yards downstream, just below the chain bridge, whose piers were felt to offer protection. Further bridge details in Benjamin Green, 'On the Arched Timber Viaducts of the Newcastle & North Shields Railway', *Proc. Institution of Civil Engineers*, 1846, vol. 5, p. 219.
54. Peter Lane & Bill Fawcett, 'The Wear Bridge at Willington', *North Eastern Express*, No. 119, August 1990.
55. Drawings of Blackmore bridges published by John Weale, 1855.
56. Good coverage of the later vices and supposed dilapidation of the Scotswood bridge is given in *Newcastle Courant*, 11 May 1860. Earlier vices are found in TWA 589/455 Newcastle Corporation River Ctee 29 December 1837; 9 & 23 February 1838; 6 March & 15 June 1838; 2 September 1842.
57. Proceedings of Newcastle Town Council, 21 February 1838.
58. *Newcastle Courant*, 11 May 1860.
59. Details of the original bridge girders are from a return of cast-iron bridges made by the N&C to the Board of Trade in July 1847.
60. N&C Managing Ctee. Report to March 1839 AGM.
61. NRO QRUp 67, plan deposited 29 November 1845.
62. PRO MT6 4/3.
63. Lowry Diary 26 January 1847.
64 ibid. 15 February 1847.
65. *Newcastle Journal*, 27 February 1847, gave notice of the opening and the new timetable.
66. Lowry Diary 5 November 1846; *Newcastle Journal*, 7 November 1846.
67. When MacLean wrote, the painting hung in offices at Central Station.

Were it not for the differences noted here, one might imagine it had been commissioned by the directors to show the Infirmary governors what their new neighbour would look like.

Chapter 9

1. Figures are based largely on accounts presented to the March 1840 AGM, modified to include the Greenwich Hospital purchase money, and the original estimates bound in with the author's copy of the evidence on the 1829 Bill.
2. Figures taken from a transcript of the 31 December 1839 conveyance, kindly supplied by Richard Bibby. See also PRO ADM 80/24 John Grey's journal for 1839.
3. Robert Carlson, *The Liverpool & Manchester Railway Project*, Augustus Kelley, 1969. Abstract of Expenditure reported by Henry Booth in May 1830 and reproduced on p. 228. A route length of 30 miles has been used to calculate the averages.
4. John Addyman, *Robert Stephenson: Railway Engineer*, North Eastern Railway Association, 2005.
5. Francis Whishaw, *Analysis of Railways*, John Weale, 1837. Sand can be easier and cheaper to work with than other materials.
6. Robert Carlson, op. cit.
7. Figures primarily taken from the N&C Accounts, presented along with the Annual Report to each March AGM of shareholders.
8. PRO ADM 80/24 John Grey's Journal 18 & 20 April 1839.
9. Mannix & Whellan, *History, Directory & Gazetteer of Cumberland*, 1847.
10. Plummer's Report to the March 1841 AGM.
11. PRO RAIL 509/6 N&C Board 16 February 1841. They agreed to set up the committee immediately after the March AGM.
12. PRO RAIL 509/6 N&C Newcastle Ctee. 7 September 1841.
13. Lowry Diary 28 September 1841.
14. ibid. 15 & 16 October 1841.
15. ibid. various entries during October - December 1841.
16. PRO RAIL 509/6 N&C Board 30 November 1841, 11 January & 15 February 1842; the last meeting confirmed the remainder of the economies proposed in the original survey, which had not been complete at 30 November. See also Richard Lowry Diary 7 December 1841.
17. PRO RAIL 509/58.
18. Lowry Diary 10 December 1841.
19. ibid. 14 January & 21 February 1842 and PRO RAIL 509/58 Staff Audit.
20. Lowry Diary 27 November 1841 & 5 January 1842.
21. ibid. 31 March 1843 and N&C Board.
22. From N&C Annual reports and Accounts.
23. This is explained in more detail in reports of the shareholders' SGM on 7 November 1846 and the March 1847 AGM.
24. Wood & Harrison's description of Northern Union Railway with map, in Sir Frederic Smith & Peter Barlow, *Commission on Railway Communications between London, Dublin, Edinburgh & Glasgow: Fourth Report*, 1841.
25. PRO RAIL 509/6 N&C Board 31 August and 7 September 1841. PRO RAIL 772/3 Newcastle & Darlington Junction Railway Board begins with a full record of the September meeting.
26. Accounts presented to the N&C AGM of March 1844.
27. A new timetable was published straight away, giving Gateshead as the south bank terminus, but operating problems are implied in a Board minute of 15 August 1844 referring to a meeting with T. E. Harrison regarding improvements to the junction at Redheugh.
28. Useful account of 'Battle for the Border' is given by C. J. A. Robertson, *The Origins of the Scottish Railway System:1722-1844*, John Donald, 1983.
29. *Grand Eastern Union Railway* prospectus, 4 July 1836, signed by Matthew Dunn & Robert Hawthorn, engineers, and John Dobson, architect, was advertised on front page of papers such as *Newcastle Journal* in August 1836. It appeared from 10 September as *Grand North Eastern Union Railway*. Joshua Richardson, a former assistant to George Stephenson, did a survey for the Reed camp and inserted an advert on 12 November, in the form of a letter replying to George's criticisms of the route under Carter Bar.
30. PRO RAIL 509/6 N&C Board 25 September 1838, meeting at Carlisle.
31. ibid. 18 December 1838. Blackmore's report nearly ready but, as route would pass through Duke of Northumberland's Kielder estate, Duke was to be consulted. 2 January 1839 'highly approved' the report and a 'full meeting' of directors on 11 January decided to put it to the east-coast promoters.
32. ibid. 16 April 1839 and Robertson, op. cit.
33. PRO RAIL 509/19 Wood & Johnson Report.
34. N&C Directors' Report to March 1844 AGM. N&C Board 5 December 1843 considered Plummer's report on a meeting he, Clayton, Wood and Johnson had with Hudson and the Stephensons on the Central Union route.
35. N&C Directors' Report to March 1844 AGM and Board 20 February 1844. The Liverpool meeting decided to refer the question of route to the Government, aiming for the 'greatest possible public convenience' and 'least possible outlay'.
36 *Carlisle Journal*, April 1847.
37. PRO RAIL 509/7 N&C Board 19 November 1843 met Dobson to consider his plans; 28 November asked him to finalise deposited plans; 16 January 1844 decided to proceed with Parliamentary application; in February they suspended the idea pending further talks with Hudson.
38. George Stephenson had made his views very clear in a letter of 1 November 1843, reproduced in PRO RAIL 772/3 Newcastle & Darlington Junction Railway Board 9 November 1843.

Pages 116 - 124

39. PRO RAIL 509/7 N&C Board 7 January 1845 has Plummer's report on a meeting of himself, Johnson, William Woods, Joseph Crawhall & Adamson with Hudson, T.E. Harrison & George Stephenson. Plummer & Co. expressed their pleasure that Hudson was prepared to bribe them with a central station in Neville Street but pointed out that he had previously refused, and the Northumberland Railway promoters had already offered this. They stressed they were not prepared to delay building their line to Neville Street. Hudson stopped blustering, asked the N&C to furnish him with a plan of the intended station and they got down to discussing site details and accommodation needs.
40. Railway scheme formally initiated at meeting in Maryport, 4 December 1835, which set up Carlisle, Wigton & Maryport Railway Committee.
41. PRO RAIL 509/15 N&C Carlisle Ctee. 29 October 1835 having learned of the proposed Maryport & Carlisle Railway resolved that it be opposed as a threat to N&C coal traffic.
42. PRO RAIL 472/2 Maryport & Carlisle Railway Board 12 & 31 October 1839. Stephenson resigned with effect from 27 November and recommended that his resident engineer, Mr. Brunton, be employed in his place.
43. ibid. 9 & 19 November 1839
44. ibid. 12 February 1841.
45. ibid. During August-October 1842 Blackmore had to contend with Mitchell's proposals for an alternative, more northerly, and cheaper route between Aspatria and Wigton. However, its curves and gradients were worse than on Blackmore's, which the Board confirmed on 29 October.
46. ibid. Blackmore's letter of resignation was received on 16 May 1843. Mitchell was appointed Engineer on May 27.
47. PRO RAIL 509/58 1841 Audit of employees. Lowry Diary 20 July 1841 refers to meeting Scott at Blackmore's office and his being 'his manager and sub-engineer to the company'. In entry for 28-30 October 1841 Lowry refers to Scott as sub-engineer to the Maryport line.
48. R. W. Rennison, *Water to Tyneside*, Newcastle & Gateshead Water Company, 1979.
49. The surviving masonry bore two laminated timber arches. *Newcastle Journal* 27 September 1851 reported these insecure and in need of replacement. They were presumably replaced or strengthened. The present 4 masonry arches date from rebuilding in 1885-7
50. Lowry Diary 12 December 1841.
51. ibid. 25 February 1843. Lowry records nothing subsequently of Blackmore's illness and death.
52. *Railway Chronicle*, 20 April 1844 extensive details in long piece on N&C.
53. *Newcastle (Weekly) Chronicle* 19 March 1844.
54. PRO RAIL 509/7 N&C Board 19 March 1844.
55. For the ventures there see I. D. Roberts, 'Ironmaking in Redesdale & North Tynedale in the Nineteenth Century', *Northern History*, vol. 36, September 2000. Batson's death is reported in Fordyce, *Local Records*.
56. Parliamentary Archives Private Bill Evidence 1846 vols. C71 & 72. Evidence on both the N&C Bill and its rival was taken in the same sitting of the committee. Thompson's evidence on 11 June 1846 describes Hareshaw.
57. ibid. Evidence of John & Benjamin Green. Also NRO QRUp 66. Plan deposited 29 November 1845 for the Newcastle, Edinburgh & Direct Glasgow Railway.
58. NRO QRUp 67. N&C Plan deposited 29 November 1845. The estimated cost and revenue are taken from Plummer's report to shareholders.
59. *House of Commons Journal*, 1846.
60. See also chapter 14. Directors' Report to the March 1847 AGM said that the bridges were underway at a cost approaching £10,000.
61. PRO RAIL 509/7 N&C Board 17 December 1844.
62. ibid. 2 January 1845.
63. ibid. 17 February 1846 for Dixon's attack; 10 March for Blenkinsopp about to resume production and seeking wagons; Newcastle Library Local Tracts No. 8 contains Dixon's pamphlet 2nd edition.
64. ibid. 19 May 1846 for Dixon's 2nd letter and hoardings.
65. PRO ADM 76/73 Greenwich Hospital Box of papers relating to railways, including the Grey letter.
66. Reported to the March 1847 AGM of Newcastle & Carlisle shareholders.
67. First Board knew of Hudson's interest was 3 April 1848 (note in minutes to this effect), when Clayton read a letter from Hudson. Board adjourned discussion, to allow negotiations, until 11 April, when Plummer produced letter from Hope-Johnstone, Caledonian chairman, offering specific terms. Hudson had not made a specific offer but got Clayton to say he was ready to confer about terms. Board instead asked for an offer to put to the shareholders alongside Caledonian one. On 25 April Board compared the two and decided that neither was good enough to recommend to shareholders but a SGM should be held to discuss them. On 8 May Board asked the bidders for their final offers by 10 a.m. on 16 May, the day appointed for the SGM.
68. *Newcastle Journal*, 19 May 1848. Report of SGM on 16 May.
69. PRO RAIL 509/8 N&C Board 31 May 1848.
70. *Carlisle Journal* 6 October 1848.
71. PRO RAIL 509/8 N&C Board 26 June 1848 Clayton produced a draft lease, which was modified and approved and sent off to Hudson; 7 July 1848 confirmed the agreement between Plummer & Hudson and 'this day' appointed Allport manager.
72. Bill included clauses for perpetual lease of or amalgamation with N&C. After Hudson left YNB, N&C shareholders voted to delete merger clauses but Bill failed in any case. It passed Commons and Lords but was sent back to the Commons with the Lords' amendments which opponents in the Commons, led by Cumbrian MP, Sir James Graham, then succeeded in having rejected.
73. In doing so they acted on the advice of the shareholders' Committee of Investigation, which was probing Hudson's management of the YNB.
74. PRO RAIL 509/8 N&C Board 1 August 1849 was advised by Clayton that Hudson could still maintain his personal lease; 15 August Clayton explained Hudson's intentions, with Allport to remain in charge of the N&C even though the YNB had thrown out Hudson's director cronies in favour of a new Board.
75. ibid. 7 November 1849 At meeting with N&C Finance Ctee. Hudson had offered either a longer lease by himself or to relinquish it at end of 1849. Clayton had to disclaim acting as Hudson's agent and went to Hudson's solicitor to obtain a formal statement of offer, while meeting continued. They decided to recommend to shareholders acceptance of Hudson's surrender of the lease, which shareholders unanimously approved at an SGM later that day.
76. PRO RAIL 772/1 YNB Ctee of Management 6 July 1848 recorded that Allport was to keep separate accounts. More emerges in Allport's evidence to the YNB Committee of Investigation. Some of the new YNB directors appear to have had a grievance against Allport, wholly without justification.
77. Lowry Diary - various entries.
78. PRO 772/3 YNB Board 31 December 1848. The figure was for shareholders' consumption.
79. William Cowan, LLD, of Killhow. *Newcastle Journal*, 10 November 1849, reporting the SGM on 7 November; also report of the March 1850 AGM. Unlike G.T. Dunn, Cowan was a thoughtful critic, ready to give the directors credit when he thought due, but also a keen exponent of economy.
80. *Newcastle Courant* 21 July 1848.
81. *Newcastle Journal*, 29 March 1851 reports N&C AGM with good-humoured exchanges on this subject, initiated by Cowan.
82. Before each AGM Adamson circulated shareholders with a list showing those who, by virtue of their shareholding were eligible to stand; on this the recently co-opted directors were shown as existing Board members. So when reports say that the retiring members were all elected, some of those retiring members had in fact been elected for the first time.
83. PRO RAIL 509/9 N&C Board. Minute of 3 May 1852 SGM and 31 May 1852 SGM. Dr. Cowan and Gustavus Coulson were on the committee. *Newcastle Chronicle*, 4 June 1852, reported the 31 May meeting; after the voting this was adjourned to 3 June to allow the votes to be counted as there was some confusion over the process of voting, for which no-one really seemed to be prepared.
84. The actual outcome was:

Committee's Top Nine	Votes on 31 May	
George Clayton Atkinson	280	elected
Gustavus Coulson, Capt. RN	129	
Dr. William Cowan	126	
George Dixon	305	elected
John Fogg Elliott	165	elected
Francis Dixon Johnson	141	
Henry Liddell	317	elected
James Losh	304	elected
William Woods	245	elected.
Committee's Bottom Three		
Matthew Anderson	184	elected
John B. Coulson, jun.	150	elected
Joseph Crawhall	166	elected

Chapter 10

1. Tom Bell, 'Railways Planned and Built - The North Pennines (Part 3)', *North Eastern Express*, No. 155, 1999, NERA. This contains a detailed description of WVE route, based on deposited plans. See also T.M. Bell & R.W. Rennison, 'The Alston Branch of the Newcastle & Carlisle Railway' in *Transactions of the Cumberland & Westmorland Antiquarian & Archaeological Society*, 3rd Series, No.1, 2001.
2. Tom Bell, op. cit., Part 2, *North Eastern Express*, No. 156, 1999.
3. PRO RAIL 509/7 N&C Board 30 September 1845 ordered a survey of the Tyne and Allen valleys for these lines.
4. NRO QRUp 67.
5. NRO QRUp 75: 1848 deposited plans for route changes. Plummer told March 1848 AGM they had consent of landowners but extent of deviations was such as to require Parliament's sanction. Act is 12 & 13 Victoria, cap 43.
6. *House of Commons Journal*, 1846. .
7. PRO RAIL 509/7 N&C Board 29 June and 6 July 1846.
8. ibid. 5 October 1846.
9. N&C Board 2 November 1846 had considered Mr. Hope-Wallace's objections to the line passing 'in front of' Featherstone Park', and ordered a survey to see if this could be avoided.
10. PRO RAIL 509/8 N&C Board 3 & 10 May 1847.
11. ibid. 2 August 1847. The payment, to 'Grahamsley & Reed', is not accompanied by any explanation. Plummer reported to March 1848 AGM that 'during the prevalence of the high prices of labour and materials it was not deemed expedient to press forward the work on the Alston Branch'.
12. ibid. Board placed £20 at disposal of Joseph Crawhall and Thomas Wilson to organise a section being taken over part of the new route.
13. See Brian Webb & David Gordon, *Lord Carlisle's Railways*, from which the Ramshay letter is quoted.

241

Pages 124 - 142

14. The revised contract is not referred to in the N&C minutes, but is stated on payment certificates for Cowen et al, dating from 1849. (PRO RAIL 509/47). There is no contract date on a contemporary certificate for Reed.
15. PRO RAIL 509/47.
16. N&C Directors' Reports & Accounts for the AGMs of March 1849 and March 1850.
17. PRO RAIL 509/8 N&C Board 15 August 1849. Tate was told to stake out enough land for 2 tracks though only 1 was to be laid.
18. PRO RAIL 509/8 N&C Board 8 April 1850. Printed specifications, signed by Rush & Lawton, filled in with their schedule of prices, are in RAIL 509/49.
19. *Newcastle Journal*, 13 September 1851, reporting a directorial inspection said that the viaduct was only commenced 'a few months ago' as the line had not previously been sufficiently advanced to allow access for materials.
20. Plummer's report to the March 1851 N&C AGM.
21. PRO MT29/10&11. Report of BoT Inspections of Railways, 1851.
22. *Newcastle Journal* 13 September 1851.
23. *Carlisle Journal* 9 January 1852.
24. PRO MT6/10/44.
25. PRO RAIL 509/59.
26. David Brooke, *The Railway Navvy*, David & Charles, 1983.
27. In the 1851 census for Knarsdale parish, the examples given are: Hudspith - record 1; Scott - 53; MacNab - 88.
28. R. W. Rennison, 'The Newcastle & Carlisle Railway and its Engineers', *Transactions of the Newcomen Society*, No. 72, 2001: Nicholas Wood is 'Engineer' to Alston Branch in *Herepath's Railway Journal*. Deposited plans of November 1845 give Bourne as *Acting Engineer*, i.e. subordinate role. Both gave evidence to Commons committee on engineering aspects of the Bill. In August 1846 Bourne was recruited as a resident engineer on the Leeds & Thirsk Railway. Some career details are in Bill Fawcett, *A History of North Eastern Railway Architecture*, vol. 1, NERA, 2001. A further account, by R.W. Rennison, will appear in volume 2 of the *Biographical Dictionary of Civil Engineers*, Institution of Civil Engineers, 2008.
29. PRO RAIL 509/8 N&C Board 6 July 1847. The contract was to be amended accordingly.
30. An account of John Thornhill Harrison, by R.W. Rennison, will appear in the *Dictionary*, op. cit., note 28.
31. 1848 deposited plans are unsigned but the N&C Board on 5 December 1849 recorded that he had been employed on the Alston Branch survey.
32. PRO RAIL 509/47 contains two sets of Alston Branch contractors' certificates, signed by 'John T. Harrison' and in some cases also by 'Thomas E. Harrison'. These are YNB printed forms modified to serve as Carlisle ones.
  i. There is one certificate for Edward Reed's work at Tyne Bridge, Haltwhistle, covering 31 December 1848 to 25 February 1849.
  ii. There are three for earthworks and bridges by Cowen, Marshall & Ridley under a contract dated 19 February 1848. They cover the first 2½ miles of the route. The first - 31 December 1848 to 28 January 1849 - is certified by both Harrisons. The second - 28 January to 25 February 1849 - is certified by JTH only. The third - 26 March to 19 April - is signed by both.
33. PRO RAIL 509/8 N&C Board 5 & 14 December 1849. Harrison was engaged to the end of 1850 for a sum of £350, to include all outstanding claims in respect of earlier work.
34. ibid. 18 & 27 November 1850. Bruce appointed at £300 p.a.
35. *Newcastle Journal* 29 November 1851 reported that Bruce was to go to India 'by the next overland mail'.
36. PRO RAIL 509/9 N&C Board 1 December 1851. Details of Charlton's career *ex info* R.W. Rennison, who has contributed an account to the *Dictionary*, op. cit. note 28. He was the third son of William John Charlton of Hesleyside, near Bellingham – promoter of the Border Counties Railway.
37. ibid. 29 January 1850. Harrison to proceed with working plans prior to contract. Advertise for tenders from Lambley to Alston, including branch to Halton Lea Gate (Link to Earl's railway).
38. PRO RAIL 509/49 Printed specification for contracts 3 to 6.
39. The succession of engineers from the YNB stable - Bruce and Charlton - suggests that T. E. Harrison continued to advise long after the Hudson lease.
40. *Newcastle Journal*, 13 September 1851.
41. PRO RAIL 509/49 Contract specification.
42. Fordyce, *Local Records*, 9 December 1826, records Dobson as architect, that bridge had span of 272 feet and was completed during that year at a cost of £700, raised by local subscription. *Newcastle Courant*, 29 April 1826, contains advertisement to carpenters 'for the labour of a timber bridge over the River Tyne at Halwhistle', plans etc from Mr. Dobson. The Journal of Hekekyan Bey (chapter 4) contains a sketch of part of Dobson's bridge.
43. PRO RAIL 509/9 N&C Board meeting on site at Haltwhistle on 27 December 1852. Tate had made a plan for temporary repairs, which Charlton had approved and was to carry out with Tate's assistance. See also 3 January 1853 and Tate's obituary in *Sunderland Daily Echo*, 21 February 1879.
44. ibid. 7 February; 24 April - Tate gave a report on the proposed permanent repair and was told to obtain tenders from Rush & Lawton, Cail, & Reed; 2 May let to Reed the repairs and piling.
45. Green's authorship is confirmed by a signed 1851 drawing for Alston; N&C minutes are predictably uninformative on the subject.
46. *Newcastle Journal*, 9 August 1851
47. Details of the Greens and their railway works are given in Bill Fawcett, *A History of North Eastern Railway Architecture, vol. 1*, NERA, 2001.
48. Further details of Alston terminus, with John Addyman's drawings, in Ken Hoole, *North Eastern Banch Line Termini*, Oxford Publishing Co., 1985.
49. Directors' Report & Accounts to the March 1857 N&C AGM. These give the cumulative expenditure total to the end of 1855 and the very small additional amount spent in 1856.
50. Daniel Polson, *South Tynedale*, published at Haltwhistle in 1902. Stanley Jenkins, *The Alston Branch*, Oakwood Press, 1991; gives an account of the later history of the branch and various aspects of the industries it served.
51. Speaking at an N&C shareholders' SGM, reported in the *Newcastle Journal* of 10 November 1849.

Chapter 11

1. Share movements calculated from prices in *Herepath's Railway Journal*.
2. PRO RAIL 509/8 N&C Board 5 December 1849 gives some details of Smiles's previous career & his appointment; PRO ADM 76/73 (Greenwich Hospital) contains a letter in which Matthew Plummer refers to Smiles's previous employment at Greenesfield Station. RAIL 509/10 N&C Board 8 October 1855 appointed Smiles Clerk to the Company, *pro tem*. March 1856 AGM confirmed, though some shareholders felt the posts did not go together. Smiles evidently began taking Board minutes from 24 September, when Adamson's increasingly illegible hand was replaced by a much neater one
3. Fordyce, *Local Records*.
4. Biographical details from Richard Welford, *Men of Mark twixt Tyne and Tweed*. See also *Archaeologia Aeliana* for an obituary.
5. PRO RAIL 509/4 N&C Board 17 & 24 September and 10 October 1833.
6. Welford, op.cit, note 4.
7. ibid.
8. See NRO 1183 for Woods' papers re Brunton & Shields Railway including letters from Thompson.
9. Maberly Phillips, *A History of Banks, Bankers & Banking in Northumberland, Durham & North Yorkshire*, London, 1894.
10. Parliamentary Archives. Private Bill Evidence vol. 48 of 1860. Harrison giving evidence on the first NER/N&C Amalgamation Bill in May 1860.
11. Good accounts of the evolution of Carlisle's Citadel Station are given by Peter Robinson in *Rail Centres: Carlisle*, Ian Allan, 1986, and Denis Perriam & David Ramshaw, *Carlisle Citadel Station*, P3 Publications, Carlisle, 1998.
12. PRO RAIL 509/7 N&C Board 5 August 1845; 18 May 1846 estimates being prepared for a shareholders' SGM included £23,000 for the line to link the N&C to the joint station.
13. PRO RAIL 346/1 Lancaster & Carlisle Railway Board.
14. ibid. 5 October 1846. Has report on Tite meeting railway representatives on 26 September, and Plummer & other N&C directors meeting Joint Station Ctee. on 28 September. 19 October 1846 Report that Plummer, Losh & the Managing directors were to represent the N&C on the Joint Station Ctee.
15. ibid. 19 July 1847.
16. Peter Robinson, op. cit. (note 11)
17. PRO RAIL 509/10 N&C Board 19 January 1854, meeting at Carlisle. Woods and MacLean signed a plan setting out the N&C accommodation at Citadel, agreed between Tate and the L&C Engineer, Waddington. 23 January 1854 Board wanted situation clarified, to establish that N&C's share of working expenses after 3 years would not exceed £400 p.a. Citadel Ctee. were repeatedly pressed for information about actual working expenses, which might have cleared the air, but refused to divulge anything.
18. PRO RAIL 509/11 N&C Board 9 May 1859: N&C had asked for a statement of working costs for 1858 and a list of staff; after more consultation the Citadel Ctee. refused to give these to either N&C or NER. 11 February 1861 received MacLean's final offer - rent £800 and expenses £250, subject to periodical revision; rent to rise to £1,000 if N&C merged with NER or any other large company.
19. Royal assent 17 July 1862.
20. NER Traffic Ctee. 29 August 1862 Min. 5067. 2nd class was 2d.
21. *Carlisle Journal* 19 June 1847 & 7 July 1848. Canal Co AGM on 4 July paid a dividend of 1½ % (their last) on the advice of Peter Dixon, Treasurer, and against the wishes of the chairman, who felt it was not justified.
22. For Silloth venture see J. K. Walton, 'Railway & Resort Development in Northern England: The Case of Silloth', *Northern History*, vol. 15, 1979.
23. Parliamentary Archives. Parliamentary Bill Evidence vol. 48 of 1860. John Irving's evidence against the NER/N&C Amalgamation Bill cited the evidence of Smiles and Woods on the Silloth Bills.
24. Port Carlisle & Silloth Railway Companies Act 1860. 23 & 24 Victoria cap 134, r.a. 3 July 1860 gave running powers between Port Carlisle Railway and London Road station and use of latter. It was to enable Port Carlisle Co. to fulfill its obligations to the NB under the Border Union (NB) Act of 1859.
25. G. M. W. Sewell, *The North British Railway in Northumberland*, Merlin, 1992, is a valuable source on the Border Counties, and is used here.
26. PRO RAIL 509/9 N&C Board 7 November 1853 gave its formal assent, in Parliamentary terms, to the Border Counties.
27. NRO QRUp 85 is the deposited plan for the first phase 'North Tyne' of the Border Counties, deposited 29 November 1853.
28. PRO RAIL 509/11 N&C Board 22 February & 22 March 1858. Later minutes suggest the N&C also supplied coaching stock for the regular train services of the Border Counties for much of that year.
29. PRO RAIL 509/10 N&C Board 17 November 1856. Smiles went with George Clayton Atkinson, of the Lemington Ironworks, and John Fogg Elliot.
30. ibid. 24 November 1856.

Pages 142 - 161

31. For Huish's policy, see T. R. Gourvish, *Mark Huish & the London & North Western Railway*, Leicester University Press, 1972. Sextuple Agreement was signed 17 April 1851 by LNWR, Lancaster & Carlisle, Caledonian, Midland, YNB & North British.
32. PRO RAIL 527/1482 NER Traffic Agreements pp 6-10 gives the history of the Liverpool Traffic Agreement.
33. ibid. NER gave the N&C 6s 1d per ton on one third of the traffic, which the N&C was then to share with the M&C and Sillloth.
34. ibid. The figures seem to have been put together in 1859 in readiness to ward off criticism of the agreement.
35. PRO RAIL 509/10 N&C Board 24 December 1855; 15 October 1855 had considered a NER letter re the Ore and Liverpool traffic and agreed 'to entertain the proposal', the N&C reserving the power to determine (i.e. end) it 'if the carrying out of the agreement does not prove satisfactory'. The terms of the agreement are nowhere recorded in the minutes.
36. ibid. 3 November 1856 Meeting at Carlisle and seeing directors of the Port Carlisle and Silloth Railways.
37. Parliamentary Archives. Private Bill Evidence vol. 48 of 1860. John Irving's evidence on Amalgamation Bill.
38. Figures taken from N&C Annual Reports and Accounts.
39. See Maurice Kirby, *The Origins of Railway Enterprise: The Stockton & Darlington Railway, 1821-63*, Cambridge University Press, 1993.
40. Act 17 Victoria cap 57, royal assent 2 June 1854.
41. M.C. Reed, *London & North Western Railway: A History*, Atlantic, 1991.
42. Prior to 1870 the NER allotted a share of nett total revenue to each of its shareholding divisions: Berwick, York etc. Dividends paid on each division's ordinary shares depended on the prior claims of various preference shares. W. W. Tomlinson, *North Eastern Railway*, p776, tabulates an equivalent average of ordinary share dividends (weighted according to the size of each capital group) for 1854-69, which I have averaged for the years 1859-61.
43. Newspaper reports of William Woods addressing the N&C shareholders' SGM 18 February 1859 and AGM of March 1859.
44. Woods speaking to the 18 February 1859 SGM.
45. PRO RAIL 509/69 File of letters from NER to the N&C on the subject of merger. Thompson is quoted from a letter of 16 November 1858 to Woods.
46. N&C Board approved Heads of Agreement 24 January 1859.
47. Newspaper report of 18 February 1859 SGM. Irving acknowledged he had only become a shareholder in the last ten days 'to open the eyes of the proprietors to the bad management of the concern.' This was rich, given the ineptitude with which money was being sunk into the Silloth venture.
48. *Railway Times*, 26 February 1859.
49. Report of 15 March 1859 AGM and SGM which immediately followed.
50. To allow for counting, declaration of vote was left to following day: 16th.
51. PRO RAIL 509/11 N&C Board 28 April 1859 approved the terms of the working arrangement, after seeing a group of NER directors; 2 May sealed the preliminary & interim contracts.
52. ibid. 23 May 1859 Clayton to arrange the payment with John Grey, Greenwich receiver; 6 June 1859 Money had been paid and deeds received.
53. Parliamentary Archives. Private Bill Evidence vol. 48 of 1860. NER/N&C Amalgamation Bill. J. J. Gutch's opening address as NER Solicitor recounted the history of the Chancery suit and the committee called up Charlton's examination in Chancery which was recorded in the Bill evidence. Charlton admitted that Hodgson suggested bringing the suit and guaranteed the costs.
54. PRO RAIL 509/11 N&C Board 9 July 1859.
55. A newspaper account of the Vice-Chancellor's judgment is posted into the N&C Board Minutes; see also note 45.
56. Quite extensively covered in Tomlinson, op. cit.
57. Detailed daily reports of the Commons Ctee. evidence were carried by the *Northern Daily Express* from 29 May to 24 June.
58. Parliamentary Archives Private Bill Evidence.
59. Withdrawn 24 June 1861, excuse being it was late in Session. Evidence on both Derwent Valley Bills partly duplicated that to be led re. merger.
60. PRO RAIL 527/724 NER Agreements Book records formal agreement of NER and Newcastle Corporation, sorted earlier but only signed on 6 June 1862, by which Corporation withdrew its opposition & got these concessions.
61. On 15 May 1862 Liddell, the leading NER counsel, told the Parliamentary Ctee. that he was now relieved of the opposition of the LNWR and the only outstanding issue was Citadel Station, which was sorted out later that day.
62. PRO RAIL 509/11 N&C Board 13 August 1860: Trip down line during which directors inspected the 3 wooden river bridges between Haydon Bridge and Bardon Mill, no doubt put on their mettle by the Scotswood episode; for Team Bridge replacement see 27 August, 3 & 17 September 1860.
63. PRO RAIL 509/69 includes a printed circular sent to shareholders in advance of the 18 February 1859 SGM detailing these provisions.
64. W. W. Tomlinson, op. cit., p. 641.
65. PRO RAIL 627/63 NER Traffic Ctee. 1 August 1862 Min. 5024 set out the new organisation for the Carlisle Section.
66. NER Locomotive Ctee. 12 September 1862 Min 5835 and 27 February 1863 Min. 6091. 6 May 1864 Bourne reported completion of work.
67. See chapter 17 for details of accident. PRO RAIL 527/29 NER Loco. Ctee. 12 August 1870. Lowry Diary 3 August 1870.
68. Lowry Diary 17 December 1870, 7 & 24 February 1871. Smiles was at first thought to have resigned voluntarily but it then emerged that he had been required to. The NER records are predictably silent.
69. ibid. 17 December 1870 and 17 February 1871. NER Traffic Ctee. 14 February 1871 for Parker's resignation. Retirement presentation made by his fellows at Newcastle Central 2 months later. (*Carlisle Journal* 5 May 1871)
70. See, e.g., J. C. Hodgson, *Northumberland County History*, vol. 3, 1896.
71. PRO RAIL 303/1 Hexham & Allendale Railway Minutes.
72. For Bewick see the obituary by his son in *Proceedings of the Institution of Mining Engineers*, vol. 15, 1897-8, p. 172.
73. NRO QRUp 114 Hexham & Allendale Railway deposited plan, 29 November 1864.
74. Raymond Fairbairn, *Allendale, Tynedale & Derwent Lead Mines*, Northern Mines Research Society Monograph 65, May 2000. Contemporary account of the closures appears in the County History, op. cit., note 70.

Chapter 12

1. L. A. Williams, *Road Transport in Cumberland in the Nineteenth Century*, George Allen & Unwin, 1975.
2. Details of coaches and carriers from contemporary directories.
3. Williams, op. cit., drawing on Thomas Sopwith, *An Account of the Mining Districts of Alston Moor, Weardale & Teesdale*, 1833.
4. Stafford Linsley, *The Life & Times of Thomas Dixon: 1805-71*, Wagtail Press, 2006. Dixon was clerk at Dukesfield, then at the Blaydon refinery, before joining the N&C, ending up as stationmaster at Hexham.
5. PRO RAIL 509/21 N&C Managing Ctee 24 February 1835 finalised the arrangements for train services and staffing.
6. Agricultural wage based on evidence by N&C contractor George Grahamsley to 1834 London & Southampton Railway Bill.
7. PRO RAIL 509/5 N&C Board 25 September 1835.
8. *Carlisle Journal* 3 October 1835 reported accident. Whishaw's 1837 *Analysis of Railways* states coach had been carried on the railway but implies this practice had ceased. *Cumberland Pacquet*, 23 July 1836, said the coach 'formerly loaded to excess' had lost almost every passenger to the railway.
9. Annual Report to N&C AGM, March 1836. Subsequent traffic figures are generally taken from these reports, though from 1836 to about 1850 they fail to break down the sources of revenue.
10. Lowry Diary, 26 July 1836.
11. ibid. 24 February 1837.
12. ibid. 30 & 31 March and 1 April 1837.
13. Timetables are generally taken from those published in the Newcastle newspapers and timetable sheets pasted into the N&C Board minutes.
14. Lowry Diary 4 March 1842.
15. ibid. 17 June 1842.
16. Correspondence between John Adamson and the Board of Trade about third-class carriages in PRO RAIL 509/68.
17. W. W. Tomlinson, op. cit., p. 372 gives details of excursions.
18. Lowry Diary 16 May 1842.
19. ibid. 27 & 29 July and 3 & 14 August 1842.
20. ibid. 16 May 1843.
21. Newspaper account of March 1847 AGM.
22. Newspaper account of March 1849 AGM, Plummer replying to Rev. Bird.
23. *Newcastle Journal*, 16 August 1845.
24. PRO RAIL 527/1090. 2 volumes re. Carlisle Section traffic: 1864-70.
25. Parly. Archives. Private Bill Evidence vol. 59 of 1862 (May 1862).
26. Lowry Diary 22 November 1841.
27. PRO RAIL 527/724 NER Printed Agreements volume 2. *Carlisle Journal* 28 July 1838 reported despatch of first mail by N&C on the 24th.
28. Parly. Archives. Private Bill Evidence vol. 48 of 1860 (May 1860).
29. ibid.
30. Parly. Archives. Private Bill Evidence vol. 59 of 1862. John Addison, Secretary & General Manager of the Maryport & Carlisle Railway, and Peter Fisher, Partner in the Parkside [ore] Mining Co. and a Director of the Whitehaven, Cleator & Egremont and Whitehaven & Furness Junction Railways, giving evidence in support of the NER/N&C Merger Bill.
31. Parliamentary evidence on the Newcastle & Derwent scheme shows that the ore went via Washington to the Pontop Branch. The question is whether it was transhipped downstream of Gateshead. Following the opening of the Lanchester Valley Branch from Durham to Consett in 1862, the Consett Iron Co. persuaded the NER to route the ore traffic that way instead.
32. Parliamentary Archives. Private Bill Evidence vol. 59 of 1862. Sir William Armstrong, in support of NER/N&C Merger Bill.
33. PRO RAIL 527/1090.

Chapter 13

1. Accounts presented to the March 1862 AGM
2. Starting point for locos is MacLean's N&C history and his table at p. 74, based on info. collated by NER Loco. Dept. Accountant from his records. On checking, delivery dates prove reliable but costs not always so, particularly for early engines; MacLean's may be book value after rebuilding. Any prices given by me are from N&C minutes, those for first 26 engines being tabulated in Managing ctee. minutes. Overall boiler and cylinder dimensions tally but MacLean gives details, not used here, which in some cases seem to represent rebuilt condition, not original. Additional information supplied by John Fleming & Geoff Horsman; remainder culled largely from N&C minutes (not available to MacLean) and notes by R.H. Innes. N&C locos were always referred to by name, not by number. Numbers given here are based on Managing committee list and differ as following from those normally quoted: *Matthew Plummer*: 19 (21); *Adelaide*: 20 (22); *Star*: 22 (20); *Sun*: 21 (19).

Pages 161 - 184

3. PRO RAIL 509/14 N&C Managing Ctee. 14 October 1834. Stephenson and Hawthorn were asked to send proposals by letter based on the specification agreed at the meeting. It was modified a little on 11 November, when the committee considered their offers.
4. ibid. 11 November 1834.
5. PRO RAIL 509/4 N&C Newcastle Ctee. 17 February 1835 agreed that, until a new agreement was made with Col. Beaumont's agent, the Company would convey lead from Hexham to Blaydon at 3d per ton mile, the same terms being provided for Joseph Crawhall (present). No reference made to mode of haulage, but would have provided an opportunity to test out *Comet*.
6. Robert Stephenson & Co. records give 3 March as the date of despatch.
7. PRO RAIL 509/14 N&C Managing Ctee 14 July 1835.
8. ibid. 9 February 1836.
9. ibid. 26 April 1836 contains the specification; the previous meeting to this set out the overall requirement for locomotives.
10 ibid. 27 September 1836.
11. Robert Burdett Wilson, *Sir Daniel Gooch, Memoirs & Diaries*, David & Charles, 1972. Gooch says he left on 15 March 1837, the venture being given up after the family split, but loco building clearly went on for a further year.
12. PRO RAIL 509/14 N&C Managing Ctee. 17 July & 26 August 1837.
13. The results are tabulated in MacLean, pp 83-5.
14. PRO RAIL 509/65 Letter from Anthony Hall to Directors, 11 May 1841.
15. NRO 3410 Brunton & Shields Railway papers. Les Charlton & Colin Mountford, *Industrial Locomotives of Northumberland*, Industrial Railway Society, 1983 reproduces an early painting of the Delaval engine - an 0-4-0.
16. PRO RAIL 509/14 N&C Managing Ctee. 10 January 1842.
17. Accounts accompanying Annual Report to March 1862 N&C AGM.
18. *Proc. Inst. Civ. Eng.*, vol. 24, 1865, p. 495. Remarks made by Harrison on a paper by Edward Fletcher on 'Maintenance of Railway Rolling Stock.'
19. Francis Whishaw, *The Railways of Great Britain & Ireland*, John Weale, 1842: Appendix.
20. PRO RAIL 509/4 N&C Board 2 May 1837. Blackmore was also told to establish a speed at which locos. should haul coal and lime trains.
21. The report forms part of a return to the Board of Trade.
22. *Newcastle Journal* 11 December 1844 reports the inquest.
23. PRO RAIL 509/11 N&C Board 22 August 1859 and 30 April 1860.
24. ex info. John Fleming.
25. W. W. Tomlinson, *North Eastern Railway*, op. cit.
26. Richard Lowry Diary: 18 July 1836.
27. PRO RAIL 509/14 N&C Managing Ctee. 27 February 1835.
28. PRO RAIL 509/14 N&C Managing Ctee. 3 December 1834 went to inspect the carriages being built by Mr. Burnup and found the following almost finished: 2 'close' carriages, 2 open carriages, 3 trucks and 4 'goods carriages'. They ordered more of the latter.
29. Both are described and illustrated in Wood's *Practical Treatise*. Wood is dubious about Bergin's design but a more favourable view is taken by K. A. Murray, *Ireland's First Railway*, Irish Railway Record Society, 1981.
30. PRO RAIL 509/13 N&C Visiting Ctee. 22 September 1835. Get Burnup, who is building 'luggage carriages' to divide these into [lockable] compartments for the different stations.
31. PRO RAIL 509/7 N&C Board 7 September 1846 noted the inquest. More details in PRO RAIL 509/65 N&C accident returns to Board of Trade.
32. Lowry diary 6 September 1837.
33. PRO RAIL 509/68 Correspondence between N&C and Board of Trade re third-class carriages, with letter from Hall to Adamson, detailing design.
34. Whishaw and Tomlinson, op. cit.
35. W. W. Tomlinson, op. cit. drawing on lost Atkinson & Philipson records.
36. Described in Wood, op. cit. pp. 198-200.
37. Orders for LWB wheelsets are found throughout N&C history. Early examples: Board/Newcastle Ctee. 27 January, 3 February and 10 March 1835.
38. PRO RAIL 509/11 N&C Board 2 & 9 November 1857 and 19 April 1858.
39. *Proc. Inst. Civ. Eng.*, vol. 24, 1865, p. 492; see also the tables giving the ages of NER stock.
40. PRO RAIL 509/4 N&C Board 8 December 1830, 8 & 11 February 1831.
41. ibid. 10 February 1832.
42. ibid. 18 May 1832 requested 50 wheelsets from Thompson, delivered at Blaydon, & contracted with Wilson for 50 more wagons of 'very best quality' at £12 each, using American or Baltic white oak in place of British oak.
43. R. H. G. Thomas, *The Liverpool & Manchester Railway*, Batsford, 1980.
44. PRO RAIL 509/6 N&C Board 13 April 1841.
45. PRO RAIL 509/70 John Parker's pocket reference book giving various details of goods traffic practice.
46. Wood, op. cit. pp. 207-9.
47. PRO RAIL 509/4 N&C Board 27 January 1835.
48. PRO RAIL 509/10 N&C Board 15 September, 1 & 15 December 1856; 12 January 1857.
49. ibid. 19 November & 3 December 1855.
50. PRO RAIL 509/14 N&C Managing Ctee. 27 February 1835.
51. Newspaper advertisement, date 10 March 1835, sought a person to 'superintend the locomotive engines, workshops and a portion of the railway.'
52. Registers of St. John's, Newcastle: Anthony born 18 August 1803, christened 18 September. He married at St. Nicholas, Newcastle on 30 September 1828. Thomas was christened there 24 March 1830.
53. Some details of his September 1862 presentation. (note 67)

54. The N&C only decided to build an engine shed at Hexham late in 1838.
55. PRO RAIL 509/58. Hall had more workers in his charge than those here.
56. Lowry diary 10 December 1841 and PRO RAIL 509/58.
57. N&C Managing Ctee. Report (to Board) of 10 May 1842.
58. Blackmore was asked to prepare 'rough plans' for the storehouse on 15 March 1842 (Board) and the Board considered various detailed proposals from the Managing Ctee. on 10 May.
59. Annual report to March 1843 AGM.
60. PRO RAIL 509/7 N&C Board 28 March & 6 & 20 June 1843. Annual Report to March 1844 AGM.
61. PRO RAIL 509/11 N&C Board 5 & 14 October 1857; 22 February 1858; 29 March 1858 contract for lathe foundations (est. cost £82).
62. PRO RAIL 509/11 N&C Board 18 October 1858.
63. From Accounts presented to March 1862 AGM.
64. Annual report to March 1840 AGM and Whishaw, op. cit.
65. For example, 22 December 1856 Board let coke contract for locos & smiths' shops to Towneley Colliery at 11s per chaldron. Screened coals for stations from Hexham eastwards: Mickley Colliery at 15s. Station west of Hexham, including Alston branch: Benson of Fourstones Colliery at 14s 6d.
66. PRO RAIL 509/11 N&C Board 24 August 1857.
67. Fordyce, *Local Records*, Held on 13 September 1862.
68. PRO RAIL 527/26 NER Loco. Ctee. 26 September 1862 Min. 5854. Min. 5899 of 24 October records that the 'principal part' of the Carlisle Section stores had been transferred to Gateshead.
69. Details of these developments at Gateshead are in Bill Fawcett, *History of North Eastern Railway Architecture, vol. 3*, NERA, 2005.
70. Last reference found to Anthony Hall in NER minutes is September 1864, when Loco. Ctee. refused his request for a pay rise. He may be the AH who died at/near South Shields in 1867; he is absent from the 1871 census.
71. 1861 & 1871 censuses. Thomas Hall's salary rose to £50 in October 1853, when he was 23, £100 in July 1858 and £110 in January 1860 (N&C Board). He married Phyllis Wilson, daughter of an N&C enginewright.

Chapter 14

1. Taken from N&C Annual Reports & Accounts.
2. PRO RAIL 509/4 N&C Board 24 February 1832.
3. ibid. 3 & 23 August 1832. The other directors were Woods, Thomas Crawhall, John Forster junior, and John Dixon.
4. ibid. 12 September 1832.
5. Parly. Archives. Private Bill Evidence vol. 7 of 1834. Evidence by Giles for and Stephenson against London & Southampton Railway Bill, June 1834.
6. ibid. 23 November 1832. Original order was for 50 pound rails with the option of substituting lighter ones at the same price per ton. On 21 November John Challoner was told to inform them that the rails would be 40-42 pounds.
7. ibid. 17 February 1835.
8. PRO RAIL 509/21 N&C Managing Ctee. 21 March 1834 let the 'laying of the road' in 2 contracts: Blaydon to Stanley Burn (site of Prudhoe station) - Powell & Whitfield; Prudhoe to Hexham - John Taylor. Taylor's rate was 1s 8½d per lineal yard. PRO RAIL 509/13 N&C Visiting Ctee. 22 July 1834.
9. ibid. 30 October 1832. Benjamin Thompson noted gravel had been taken from Tyne for coating and questioned its suitability because of sand content.
10. Francis Whishaw, *Railways of Great Britain & Ireland*, Weale, 1842.
11. Specified in an advertisement approved by Board on 28 September 1832.
12. NER Loco. Ctee. Nov. 1863 Min. 6521. On Bourne's advice got rid of first daily inspection. Line was thereafter walked prior to 1st passenger train.
13. Nicholas Wood, *Practical Treatise on Rail-Roads*, 1838 edition.
14. PRO MT6/4/3 Captain Coddington's 22 February 1847 report on the extension from Railway Street to the Forth said it had edge rails on cross sleepers 'of the same description in use on the remainder of the line', meaning in this case the rest of the Blaydon-Newcastle section.
15. PRO RAIL 509/85 N&C Directors' Visits: February 1852.
16. PRO RAIL 509/59 N&C Return of 28 November 1845 to Board of Trade.
17. BoT Return of Railway Accidents 1851, Appendix 36, has Laffan's report and correspondence with N&C. See also PRO RAIL MT6/9/157. Laffan's account of N&C evolution from single to double track is not reliable and based on folklore. Relaying is chronicled in N&C annual reports & accounts.
18. PRO RAIL 509/59 N&C Return 18 March 1853 to Board of Trade.
19. Report & Accounts for March 1858 AGM.
20. PRO RAIL 509/21 N&C Managing Ctee. 20 August 1833. In 1834 the Managing directors said that 4 sidings per mile would be needed for horses and one for locomotives.
21. The March 1838 Report suggests that the whole of the Haydon Bridge - Greenhead section was conceived as single track, however east of Haltwhistle it materialised as double. Annual Reports chronicle subsequent progress.
22. PRO RAIL 509/21 N&C Managing Ctee. March 1835 made a trial run with *Rapid* and *Comet* and decided to remove the 'superfluous' sidings provided for horse traffic.
23. Sir Frederic Smith reporting to Board of Trade on 23 September 1841.
24. PRO RAIL 509/13 N&C Visiting Ctee. 8 may 1835.
25. PRO RAIL 509/71 John Parker's copy of the 1853 N&C Rule Book. This remained in force until the merger.
26. PRO RAIL 527/724 NER Printed Agreements Book 2 contains 17 May 1852 agreement between BET and N&C. October 1852 N&C Board noted that BET was installing its poles too close to the rails. 25 April 1853 they noted the telegraph was promised to be ready between Blaydon and Redheugh 'by the end of next week', possibly marking the final stage to be completed.

Pages 185 - 214

27. PRO RAIL 509/9 N&C Board 24 January 1853.
28. PRO RAIL 509/13 N&C Visiting Ctee. 8 May 1835.
29. Clause 21 of the 1835 Act. John Clayton and other witnesses went into the history of the turnpike road crossings in evidence in the 1846 Bill: Parliamentary Archives Private Bill Evidence 1846 vols. C71 & 72.
30. PRO RAIL 527/15 N&C Carlisle Ctee. 4 January 1844.
31. John Adamson to Board of Trade 4 November 1841.
32. PRO MT6/2/25
33. PRO RAIL 509/7 N&C Board 14 June 1844.
34. PRO RAIL 509/7 N&C Board 4 March 1845
35. ibid. 7 & 21 October 1845: advertisements for policemen pasted in.
36. ibid. 17 March 1846 and 10 May 1847.
37. ibid. 7 September 1846.
38. PRO RAIL 1053/162 N&C staff return to Board of Trade 30 June 1858.

Chapter 15

1. Augustus Bozzi Granville (1783-1872). Italian physician who settled in England.
2. PRO RAIL 509/6 N&C Board 21 May 1839.
3. For example PRO RAIL 509/4 N&C Board 13 March 1835 gave orders to proceed immediately with station house at Stocksfield but a wet season held up completion. Managing Ctee. reported to Board 23 March 1836 on completion of Hexham, Corbridge and Stocksfield.
4. PRO RAIL 509/13 N&C Visiting Ctee 14 August 1834.
5. PRO RAIL 509/21 N&C Managing Ctee 20 January 1835.
6. ibid.
7. PRO RAIL 509/5 N&C Board 3 March 1835.
8. PRO RAIL 509/6 N&C Board 16 October 1838 agreed to build a station house at How Mill. Board 13 August 1839 on a line inspection inspected site for station house at Low Row. (Managing Ctee. in January 1836 had decided against building a station there) Managing Ctee. report to March 1840 AGM reported the building of How Mill station house.
9. PRO RAIL 509/13 N&C Visiting Ctee.22 September 1835 fixed site for Haydon Bridge station; it was being roofed in April 1836.
10. PRO RAIL 509/5 N&C Board 15 November & 3 December 1836.
11. ibid. 5 December 1837: Visit along line.
12. Managing Ctee. Report to March 1840 AGM.
13. Evolution of Hexham station has been described by the author in *North Eastern Express* (Journal of the NERA), No. 99, of 1985.
14. PRO RAIL 509/14 N&C Managing Ctee. January 1836 saw excavations for London Road depot. 22 March London Road station house was behind schedule, Gilsland about to be started & nothing done at Scotby. 16 May London Road station house in progress; blacksmiths and wheelwrights shop covered; engine and carriage houses ready for roof in about 10 days.
15. *Carlisle Journal* 25 June and 2 July 1836.
16. PRO RAIL 509/14 N&C Managing Ctee. October 1836 - London Road station house, not one room finished; February 1837, nearly completed and very commodious.
17. These have proved hard to pin down in minutes, however Managing Ctee. Report to March 1840 AGM refers specifically to Derwenthaugh cottages and adds that 'several cottages [have been built] for workmen at different places.'
18. Details of accommodation, and its occupants, are in two NER schedules: PRO RAIL 527/1145 of 1862, and 527/952 of 1875.
19. PRO RAIL 509/5 N&C Board 11 October 1836 and 13 August 1839.
20. PRO RAIL 509/7 N&C Board 19 August 1845. The March 1846 Annual Report confirmed that 'much has been done in erecting cottages for labourers and for watching the gates.'
21. ibid. 5 August 1845.
22. PRO RAIL 509/85 Directors' Visits 14 January 1852 and 509/9 N&C Board 16 May 1853 considered plans for these and Board 30 May 1853 let the contract to Thomas Bulmer. 2 November 1853 Board Visit inspected them and Board 17 April 1854 made the arrangement regarding the gates.
23. PRO RAIL 509/125 N&C Rent Book 1851-5.
24. Directors' Report to March 1856 AGM.
25. PRO RAIL 509/6 N&C Board 26 June 1838.
26. PRO RAIL 509/1 N&C Carlisle Ctee. 24 September 1840.
27. Naworth Gate: PRO RAIL 509/7 N&C Board 16 August 1843 agreed to build station house and waiting room at cost of no more than £100, Tate to meet Ramshay there to discuss it. 19 March 1844 ordered plans for a cottage. I have counted Naworth among the 71 dwellings recorded in 1855.
28. PRO RAIL 509/14 N&C Managing Ctee. 9 February 1836 agreed to purchase 94 cast-iron 'pillars' for three sheds similar to those at Blaydon and Hexham, viz: Haydon Bridge 24, Carlisle 40, Greenhead 30.
29. Lowry Diary 7 January 1839. Hard storm during the night 'has swept our sheds away at Blaydon and injured those at Hexham.'
30. PRO RAIL 527/1740. NER file of reports and letters re Hexham Station in the 1860s.
31. PRO MT6/9/154 & 157; BoT Return on Railways for 1851, Appendix 39.
32. PRO RAIL 509/9 N&C Board 6 December 1852 gave one of the first orders to build platforms, at Scotby. Progress with these and passenger sheds is recorded in the Annual Reports of March 1854-6, with more detail in 509/85 Reports of Directors' site visits. Board 8 October 1855 noted that only Wetheral and Low Row remained to be done.

33. PRO RAIL 509/85 N&C Directors' Site Visit 14 January 1852.
34. PRO RAIL 509/10 N&C Board 26 March, 2 & 23 April, 1 October 1855.
35. PRO RAIL 509/11 N&C Board 13 August & 12 November 1860; 2 March & 19 August 1861.
36. ibid. 13 August 1860 Line visit approved the Wylam plan on site; 26 March 1861 Line visit noted progress.
37. PRO RAIL 509/21 N&C Managing Ctee. West End View 16 May 1836. This details both Carlisle and Greenhead.
38. Keith Hood, *The Co-operative Societies of the North Pennines*, North Pennines Heritage Trust, 2001. It closed as a shop in 1953, having merged with the Haltwhistle Co-op in 1923.
39. PRO RAIL 509/21 N&C Managing Ctee. 16 May 1836.
40. PRO RAIL 509/1 Howard set out his proposal for Broadwath in a letter of 20 November 1828 to Thomas Crawhall.
41. PRO RAIL 509/6 N&C Board 2 October 1838 told Blackmore to erect shed to protect goods at Fourstones. Assumed to be the small hip-roofed shed.
42. PRO RAIL 509/4 N&C Board 17 March 1835 Proceed immediately with shed to protect goods waiting at Hexham. Carmichael may have omitted it to open up the view of the Abbey.
43. PRO RAIL 509/9 N&C Board 2 August 1852 opened tenders and looked at site, where Joseph Crawhall suggested alternative. Ctee 8 August 1852 agreed to discuss with Cail his tender, but minute implies some dissent. 11 October 1852 let the contract. Board 30 January 1854 viewed new station.
44. Lowry Diary, 2 January 1854.
45. ibid. 24 March 1854. House approaching completion.
46. Reconstruction based on 1/500 OS of 1857-7 and NER plan of 1866 showing proposed new goods station overlaid on the existing site. Latter shows platform outside building but no details inside. Elevation draws on TWA T186/4270, drawing submitted to Newcastle Town Improvement Ctee. in 1871 for the Neville Street carriage shed. Goods station also appears in Storey's panorama of Newcastle, but somewhat distorted.
47. Lowry Diary, 2 August 1852.
48. Bill Fawcett, *A History of North Eastern Railway Architecture, vol. 2*, NERA, 2003 details the history of the new Forth Goods station and the reborn Tate building at No. 1, Neville Street (Latter also in vol. 3, 2005).
49. PRO RAIL 509/7 N&C Board 1 June 1846. Dobson was formally appointed architect for the station by the Newcastle & Berwick Railway on 23 February 1846. (PRO RAIL 506/1)
50 PRO RAIL 772/3 18 August 1846 – Dobson to prepare working drawings.
51. *Newcastle Journal* 14 August 1847 reported the contract.
52. PRO holds several of Dobson's certificates for payments to McKay & Blackstock. No. 6 covers 30 July to 4 September 1848 and records the first purchases of walling stone.
53. PRO ADM 80/33 Greenwich Hospital – John Grey Journal 1848. John Wardle & George Walker, Grainger's former architects, had leased land at Prudham Quarry adjoining existing workings, operated formerly by N&C and latterly by Wylam Walker. Wardle & Walker opened up a new quarry and Grey noted 31 January 1848 they 'had contracted to supply a large quantity of stone' for the Newcastle station and wished to have their lease settled.
54. PRO RAIL 772/3 YNB Board 19 March 1849 asked Dobson to draft advert inviting tenders for trainshed roof; 10 April approved his advert for 'cast & malleable iron' but 16 April agreed revised design. Contractor: John Abbot, Park Foundry, Gateshead, who began erecting shed in September.
55. Newcastle Corporation reports contain no record of a debate on helping to fund portico, but Clayton must have sounded out people to be so confident.
56. *Newcastle Journal* 6 September 1851.
57. John Addyman & Bill Fawcett, *High Level Bridge & Newcastle Central Station*, NERA, 1999. Shorter treatment, with some additional detail, in Bill Fawcett, *History of North Eastern Railway Architecture*, vols. 1 (2001) & 3.
58 Internal layout from 1/500 OS; a revised plan accompanying Dobson's specification in T.L. Donaldson, *Handbook of Specifications*, vol. 2; and NER plans, though room functions had changed by the time latter were drawn.
59. Woods' remark puts total cost of Central Station at £120,000; about what one would expect from contracts, allowing some extras offset by an abatement of McKay & Blackstock's price. Dobson Carlisle drawing referred to top of page is British Architectural Library Drawings Collection G6/39.

Chapter 16

1. PRO RAIL 509/58.
2. PRO RAIL 509/2 N&C Ctee. 29 January 1830 and Board 5 February 1830.
3. Challoner requested pay rise in March 1834 but Board deferred until they had some part of the line in service. Board 24 March 1836 approved the rise.
4. PRO RAIL 509/6 N&C Board 19 March 1839.
5. ibid. 19 February & 12 April 1839.
6. Lowry Diary has various entries relating to Chantler having been a carrier and employed by Pickersgill.
7 PRO RAIL 509/7 N&C Board 18 April 1843 authorised Plummer to advance Chantler £100 with interest 'if this will release him from his present difficulties'. Lowry refers to his borrowing from agents, e.g. 16 February 1843 and 2 February 1849. Lowry lent Chantler £17 at one stage.
8. PRO RAIL 509/6 N&C Board 18 January 1842. No follow up found.
9. PRO RAIL 509/59 N&C Return to the Board of Trade.
10. Lowry Diary 24 July 1848 'Smith & Chantler have been up the line instructing the station agents in the new [book-keeping] system'. 29 July 'Hudson's system was brought into operation with us today. Some of the station keepers don't understand it at all and I believe they never will.' RL had little difficulty but found the proliferation of memoranda rather tiresome.

245

Pages 215 - 230

11. Lowry Diary 2 February and 20 August 1849.
12. PRO RAIL 509/5 N&C Board 7 October 1850. Challoner to sit in Smiles' office as that gentleman is frequently absent on the Company's business.
13. PRO RAIL 509/9 N&C Board 28 March 1851. Challoner's leaving celebration is chronicled in Fordyce: *Local Records*.
14. Challoner had married Margaret Sadler at Morpeth on 14 August 1809 and their son was born on 17 July 1811.
15. Registers of St. Andrews parish, Newcastle; census; G.H. Hume, *History of Newcastle Infirmary*, Andrew Reid, 1906; PRO RAIL 509/8 N&C Board 5 December 1849. Smiles's final job within the NER is unclear.
16. PRO RAIL 509/9 N&C Board 12 July 1852.
17. ibid. 8 August 1852 and 19 September 1853 plus a Newcastle newspaper report of 16 September 1852..
18. PRO RAIL 509/10 N&C Board 2 March 1857.
19. ibid. 13 February 1854. Christened at St. Nicholas, Rochester on 31 July 1825, he died on 3 October 1911.
20. PRO RAIL 1053/162. Return of railway employment to Board of Trade at 30 June 1858. N&C route mileage was then 78m 21ch; the NER 720m 15ch.
21. PRO RAIL 509/4 N&C Board 20 February 1835 & Managing Ctee. 27 February 1835.
22. Lowry Diary 31 March 1837.
23. ibid. 21 February & 27 May 1852 and N&C Board 24 May 1842.
24. PRO RAIL 509/5 N&C Board 6 June 1836; 9 January & 17 July 1838.
25. Stafford M. Linsley, *The Life and Times of Thomas Dixon*, Wagtail Press, Hexham, 2006.
26. PRO RAIL 509/6 N&C Board 23 July 1839 & 21 June 1842.
27. PRO RAIL 509/7 N&C Board 20 June 1843. Bates was retiring.
28. Lowry Diary 20 January 1849.
29. PRO RAIL 509/8 N&C Board 14 March 1850.
30. St. Andrews parish registers, Newcastle.
31. PRO RAIL 509/5 N&C Board 2 May 1836. Recommended by Adamson.
32. PRO RAIL 509/15 N&C Carlisle Ctee. 10 November 1836.
33. Lowry Diary 7 & 8 October 1848 and 15 March 1849.
34. ibid. 19 May 1849. Obituary in *Carlisle Journal* 10 May 1861.
35. ibid. 16 & 18 October 1837 and 5 March 1848.
36. Norman McCord, 'Victorian Newcastle Observed: the Diary of Richard Lowry', *Northern History*, vol. 37, December 2000. This gives a biographical sketch of Lowry and entertaining extracts from his diaries. They are in TWA DF.LOW 1/1 to 66. Where I have quoted diary dates, no endnote is given.
37. Lowry Diary 4 February 1836.
38. ibid. 9 February, 20 & 21 April 1836.
39. ibid. 6, 12 & 23 May, 3 June & 19 July 1836.
40. ibid. 11 April 1839 for Nanson's advice. N&C Board 15 December 1840 noted Pow's resignation and resolved to appoint Lowry to Newcastle once Pow left. Pow had joined at Hexham under Greene (Board 17 March 1835) and then gone to the Close station in Newcastle as agent when it opened.
41. Lowry Diary and N&C Board 20 July 1841.
42. Lowry Diary various dates in second half of September. On 23rd he consulted George Johnson and decided not to apply.
43. ibid. 13 February 1854.
44. ibid. 22 June 1861. Lowry already knew of the Bill's failure.
45. ibid. 10 & 23 January, 8 & 24 February, 1 April, 9 & 10 May 1871.
46. ibid. 20 May 1871.
47. PRO RAIL 509/15 N&C Carlisle Ctee. 12 September 1836; *Carlisle Journal* 2 May 1876.
48. Lowry Diary 17, 21 & 22 February 1871.
49. PRO RAIL 509/10 N&C Board 10 April & 18 September 1854.
50. *Newcastle Chronicle* 23 June 1854.
51. I am much indebted to Denis Perriam for information about Edmondson.
52. PRO RAIL 509/15 N&C Carlisle Ctee. 3 June 1836.
53. PRO RAIL 509/5 N&C Board 5 December 1837.
54. Lowry Diary 18 April 1837.
55. ibid. 22 March 1839.
56. ibid. 6 April 1839.
57. Sons of Thomas & Elizabeth Parker.
58. Some early details are provided by newspaper accounts of their retirements, also PRO RAIL 509/73 a John Parker photograph and letter of 4 February 1898.
59. PRO RAIL 509/9 N&C Board 8 January 1851.
60. Barford House, The Plain, Wetheral. *Cumberland News* 30 July 1954 contains an article on John Parker.
61. PRO RAIL 527/63 NER Traffic Ctee. 1 August 1862 & 27 March 1868 Min. 7370.
62. Lowry Diary 17 December 1870.
63. ibid. 17 February & 13 March 1871; NER Traffic Ctee. 14 February 1871; *Carlisle Journal* 5 May 1871.
64. Agricultural wage cited by George Grahamsley, the N&C contractor, in evidence on the London & Southampton Railway Bill of 1834.
65. PRO RAIL 509/10 N&C Board 3 December 1855.
66. ibid. 28 December 1854.
67. PRO RAIL 509/11 N&C Board 16 April 1860.
68. PRO RAIL 509/7 N&C Board 17 December 1844.
69. Lowry Diary 16 March 1843.
70. PRO RAIL 509/6 N&C Board 9 & 16 January 1838.
71. PRO RAIL 509/15 N&C Carlisle Ctee. 22 June, 6 & 20 July 1837. Idea of retention met strong opposition from enginemen and was probably dropped.
72. Denis Perriam in *Cumberland News* 28 October 2005, p 10 & N&C Board 28 June 1858.
73. PRO RAIL 509/11 N&C Board3 & 10 December 1860.
74. PRO RAIL 509/9 N&C Board 26 July 1852.
75. Directors were perhaps under pressure from T.W. Beaumont, subscriber to church. N&C Board 26 March 1860 records £25 second contribution.
76. PRO RAIL 509/10 N&C Board 23 March 1857.
77. W.W. Tomlinson, *The North Eastern Railway*, op. cit. pp 629-30. Also Lowry Diary for this period. Lowry reckoned the newspaper reports of the strike's effects were inaccurate.
78. James Losh to Lord Howick 6 May 1832 re Tyne Main colliery, pub. in Surtees Society vols. 171 & 174. (1956 & 59)

Chapter 17

1. Accident details from PRO RAIL 509/65, accident returns to Board of Trade and correspondence, plus BoT returns to Parliament and newspapers.
2. *Carlisle Journal* 10 December 1836, et seq.
3. Lowry Diary 17 November 1838.
4. PRO RAIL 509/7 N&C Board 7 January 1845.
5. The signalling arrangements are detailed in supplements of 1862 pasted into the 1853 Rule Book: PRO RAIL 509/71.
6. Accident details taken from the report by Lieutenant-Colonel Hutchinson on 30 July 1870; note re manslaughter charge from Peter Robinson, *Rail Centres: Carlisle*, Ian Allan, 1986.
7. PRO RAIL 527/65 NER Traffic Ctee. 12 August 1870 Min. 8176.
8. Letter is in Josephine Butler, *Memoir of John Grey of Dilston*, Edmonston & Douglas, Edinburgh, 1869. John Grey (1785-1868) was her father.
9. Lowry Diary 7 to 9 July 1852.
10. Lowry Diary 27 & 29 July 1848. Because of the Hudson lease there is no record of the fire in any minutes.
11. PRO RAIL 509/9 N&C Board 8 January 1851. Tate's obituary makes no claim for the iron bridge but the Forth Banks example shows that he was perfectly capable of designing it.
12. PRO RAIL 509/85 Directors' Visit 14 January 1852.
13. Details from newspaper cutting, probably *Newcastle Journal*, 10 May 1860. Colonel Yolland reported to the Board of Trade that he did not think the fire was caused by ash from the locomotive tests.
14. PRO RAIL 509/10 N&C Board 10 May 1860 and newspaper advertisements of that date.
15. ibid. 28 May & 4 June 1860.
16. ibid. 18 June 1860.
17. PRO RAIL 527/28 NER Loco. Ctee. 28 August 1868 Min. 9543.
18. Cumbria Record Office, Carlisle Castle: CA/E4/268 & 900 are plans submitted to Carlisle Council re rebuilding the shed after the fire and a further alteration. They provide useful detail of the shed/workshop/coal depot area.
19. *Carlisle Journal* 25 May & 8 June 1844.
20. ibid. 16 December 1853.
21. ibid. 7 November 1846.

The Stephenson Locomotive Society paying farewell to the Alston Branch. (J.M. Fleming)

INDEX

Promoters & Directors
George Clayton Atkinson 140
Thomas R. Batson 21, 27, 38, 47, 54, 117
Thomas Richard Beaumont 20
Thomas Wentworth Beaumont 20, 40, 147
Wentworth B. Beaumont 147
John Brandling 20, 95, 154
Ralph Henry Brandling 20, 148
John Clayton 23, 33, 39, 40, 46, 62, 95, 114, 120, 210
John Blenkinsopp Coulson 14, 18, 38, 118
John Blenkinsopp Coulson (II) 18, 121
Isaac Crawhall 20, 137, 138
Joseph Crawhall 20, 39, 47, 50, 53, 95, 112, 118, 121, 138, 208
Thomas Crawhall 20, 38, 39, 46, 50, 95, 219
George Dixon 17, 121
John Dixon 16, 17, 18, 38, 43, 47, 118
Peter Dixon 16, 17, 18, 38, 47, 112, 118, 154
John Forster (II) 16, 17, 38
John Forster (III) 17, 18, 38, 47, 58, 62
William Forster 17, 58, 62
Alfred Hall 22, 38, 39
Henry Howard 29, 30, 38, 47, 56
Philip Henry Howard 56
George Johnson 48, 50, 51, 95, 115, 161, 178
James Losh 14, 15, 22, 30, 39, 45, 53, 95, 219
James Losh (junior) 23, 121, 138
William Losh 22, 38, 96, 181
George Gill Mounsey 38, 230
William Nanson 38, 113, 217
Matthew Plummer 21, 22, 27, 47, 48, 50, 54, 111, 118, 121, 230
John Ramshay 124
James Thompson 27, 28, 48, 62, 112, 118
Benjamin Thompson 24, 30, 48, 50, 85, 95, 117, 161, 166
Thomas Wilson 27, 137
Nicholas Wood 48, 50, 95, 113, 115, 125, 145, 156, 161, 171, 178
William Woods 23, 38, 47, 50, 112, 119, 121, 138, 139, 146, 180
Table of Directors 19
Reorganisation of Board 121
Directors' Fees 21, 49, 50, 121
Carlisle Committee 38, 50
Managing Committee 49, 50, 112
Newcastle Committee 38, 50

Engineers, Surveyors & Architects
Thomas John Bewick 147
Thomas Oswald Blackett 30, 38, 47, 225
John Blackmore 35, 38, 43, 49, 85, 93, 95, 103, 112, 113, 114, 116, 173
John Bourne 93, 106, 117, 125, 146
(Sir) George Barclay Bruce 126
Isambard K. Brunel 35
William Chapman 8, 12, 24, 26, 30, 74
Francis Charlton 126, 141, 144
John Dobson 115, 187, 210, 212
Thomas Dodd 42
William Fryer 26, 28, 30
Benjamin Green 117, 134, 187
John Green 32, 103, 117
Francis Giles 34, 35, 40, 47, 48, 59, 181, 231
John Thornhill Harrison 126
Thomas Elliot Harrison 93, 113, 124, 126, 138, 180, 182, 229
Josias Jessop 15
William Jessop 9
George Larmer 42
Joseph Locke 27, 28, 30, 34, 43
Benjamin Scott 92
Thomas Sopwith 20, 95, 123, 147
George Stephenson 27, 28, 35, 36, 40, 114, 181
Robert Stephenson 30, 52, 94, 113
Thomas Storey 35, 97
John Studholme 18, 26, 30, 40, 47, 58
Peter Tate 43, 83, 92, 93, 106, 113, 116, 133, 146, 178, 187, 200, 202, 208, 229
Wylam Walker 43, 71

Civil Engineering Contractors
Cowen, Marshall & Ridley 124
William Denton 17, 43, 47, 56, 58, 82
George Grahamsley 44, 52, 56, 60, 61, 63, 79, 83, 196
William Hutchinson 63, 65
Gibson Kyle 54, 93
McKay & Blackstock 210
John McKay 59
Edward Reid (Reed) 61, 124
Jacob Ritson 52, 53, 63, 65, 117
Joseph Ritson 54
William Ritson 53, 147
Robson Brothers 56
Rush & Lawton 124
Robert Wilson 44, 52, 59

Other Contractors/Suppliers
Cuthbert Burnup 171
Robert Hawthorn & Sons 161 et seq.
Robert Stephenson & Co. 161 et seq.
Hawks & Thompson 164
Thompson Brothers 166

Officers & Agents
John Adamson 21, 107, 112, 113, 138, 219
George Bates 216
Benjamin Cail 113, 214, 216
John Challoner 120, 138, 214, 215
John Chantler 214, 224
Thomas Dixon 216
Thomas Edmondson 219
William Greene 196, 216
Richard Lowry 38, 107, 150, 154, 196, 208, 214, 217, 230
William Lowry 113, 219
John Parker 221
Joseph Parker 146, 221
John Kent Pow 217
John Scott 154, 216
John Scott (2) 226
Henry Smiles 138, 146, 215
Thomas Topham 221
Arthur Tranah 215

Locomotive Dept.
Joseph Forster 178, 216
Daniel Dunn 223
John Gallon 224
Oswald Gardner 171, 225
Thomas Graham 168, 221
Anthony Hall 107, 170, 177, 180, 219, 222, 224
Thomas Hall 177, 180
William Simpson 224
1867 Strike 223

Workforce
Mechanics Institute 219
Wages 112, 113, 178, 184
Redundancies 112, 214
Size 111, 215

Other Personalities
James Allport 120, 138, 215
Sir William Armstrong 117, 141, 158
Charles Bacon 28, 31
Charles Bacon Grey 31, 40, 55, 56
Robert William Brandling 18, 96, 97
John Buddle 39, 48
Earls of Carlisle 18, 27, 30, 124, 224
George Thomas Dunn 95, 96, 101, 105, 117, 185
Sir James Graham 14, 46
Richard Grainger 98, 101
John Grey 110, 111, 119, 228
Thomas Emerson Headlam 225
John Hodgson 28, 32, 94, 140, 144
Richard Hodgson 140, 143, 144
George Hudson 113, 115, 119, 140, 210
John Irving 144
Benjamin Johnson 20, 54
James Loch 27, 35
Dukes of Northumberland 38, 40
William O'Brien 146
Harry S. Meysey Thompson 143
Benjamin James Thompson 25, 166
George Annesley Thompson 25, 166

Other Railways
Blaydon, Gateshead & Hebburn 95
Brandling Junction 96, 98, 100
Border Counties 140
Caledonian 115, 119, 138
Carlisle & Silloth Bay 140, 142
Carlisle Canal 12, 38, 67, 140
Central Union 115
Earl of Carlisle's 27, 62, 69, 123
Great North of England 51, 97, 113
Hexham & Allendale 147
Lancaster & Carlisle 43, 114, 138
London & North Western 36, 47, 49, 144
London & Southampton 36, 49
Maryport & Carlisle 43, 77, 79, 116, 119, 138, 205, 217
Newcastle & Berwick 115
Newcastle & Darlington Jc. 100, 113
N'castle Edinburgh & Dir. Glasgow 117
Newcastle & North Shields 57, 94
North British 115, 140, 143
North Eastern 138, 143
Reading, Guildford & Reigate 36
Scotswood, Newburn & Wylam 231
Stanhope & Tyne 95
Stockton & Darlington 143
York, Newcastle & Berwick 113, 120

247

Other Corporate Bodies
Greenwich Hospital 18, 40, 63, 111, 144
Newcastle Corporation 23, 101, 145
Tyne Commissioners 229

Roads
Military Road 7, 189
Norham Bridge 117, 187
Scotswood Road & Bridge 32, 95, 97
Tyne Valley Turnpikes 8
Warwick Bridge 47, 56
Coach Services 148

N&C Financial
Capital 111, 118, 143
Cash Flow 44
Costs: Construction 110, 137
Costs: Operating 113, 121, 143, 145, 215
Dividends 94, 113, 121, 143, 146
Public Works Loan 45, 52, 62, 94, 111
Revenue 111, 112, 121, 142, 143, 145, 149, 150, 156
Share Calls & Forfeits 45
Share Prices 113, 138
Subscriptions 16, 34

N&C General
Acts 34, 45, 56, 96, 111, 117, 140, 143, 145
Allendale Proposal 123
Alston Branch 117, 122, 234, 246
Canal Branch 62, 63, 66, 140
Direction of Running 146
Economy Drive 112, 178, 214
Electric Telegraph 185, 230
Express Trains 151
Fares 149
Head Office 120, 212, 218
Hudson Lease 119
Land Purchase 40, 111
Level Crossings 40, 52, 118, 185, 225
Line Openings 51, 55, 62, 63, 65, 98, 103, 107, 109
Liverpool Traffic Agreement 142, 144
Merger with NER 143, 145
Mixed Trains 62, 61, 149, 153, 225
Navvies 44, 111, 125
North Tyne proposals 117, 140
Policemen 186
Redheugh Branch 96, 98, 100, 153
Routes to Scotland 114
Rule Book 185
Single & Double Line 184
Signals 185, 231
Sunday Trains 154
Swalwell Branch 98
Third-Class Travel 153, 174
Tickets 220
Traffic: Prior to Opening 54, 55
    Coke 156
    Excursion 154
    Irish 156
    Iron Ore 142, 143
    Lead 54, 147, 149
    Mails 158, 174
    Through 158
Tyne Quay Access 26, 101, 145
Use of Locomotives 56
Weighing Machines 150

Bridges
Standard Overbridge 77
Standard Underbridge 82
Alston Branch Overbridges 93, 126, 129, 133
Alston Branch Underbridges 128
Iron Bridges 91, 104, 108, 226, 228
Timber bridges 85, 98, 103
Allen 88
Alston Arches (Haltwhistle) 125, 132
Blenkinsopp Hall Drive 88
Burnstones Viaduct 131
Caldew 41, 63, 76
Corby Beck Viaduct 42, 56, 72
Eden Viaduct 38, 56, 70
Forth Banks 107
Gelt 41, 59, 74
Gilderdale 130
Kingshaw Green 226
Knar Burn Viaduct 130
Lambley Viaduct 126
Lipwood (Tyne) 88
Petteril (Mains) 76
Poltross Burn 84
Ridley Hall (road) 91
Ridley Hall (Tyne) 86
Scarrow Hill 59, 80
Scotswood (Tyne) 32, 39, 93, 98, 101, 103, 109, 229
Tippalt 88
Warden 85, 93, 228

River Walls
Capons Cleugh 64, 92, 228
Eltringham 52
Stella 54
Wylam 25, 44, 52

Cowran Cutting 56, 59

Tunnels
Farnley 52, 83
Whitchester 65, 81

Buildings: General
Alston Branch 134
Coal Depots 157, 206
Crossing Cottages 198, 200
Flag Stations 200
Goods Sheds 206
Housing 198, 200
Stations 189
Station Improvements 202
Water Towers 205

Engine Sheds & Workshops
Blaydon 112, 177, 178
Brampton Jc. (Milton) 178
Carlisle 112, 159, 178, 230
Forth 178, 180
Greenhead 178, 204
Haydon Bridge 178, 204
Coke Ovens 179

Locations
Alston 134
Bardon Mill 197
Blaydon 69, 157, 189, 202
Brampton Fell Crossing 198
Brampton Jc. (Milton) 66, 205, 230, 233
Carlisle Citadel Sta. 139, 140, 145, 212
Carlisle London Road 67, 138, 196, 201, 206, 232
Corbridge 189
Dalston Road Crossing 201
Dilston Crossings 200
Fourstones 193, 202
Gateshead 100, 114
Gilsland (Rose Hill) 69, 191, 202
Greenhead 190
Haltwhistle 187, 192, 197, 199, 202, 206, 231
Haydon Bridge 192, 199, 202, 205
Hexham 55, 157, 189, 194, 201, 202, 206, 209
Lambley 134
Naworth 200
Newcastle Central 109, 152, 210
Newcastle Close Station 150, 152
Newcastle Forth Goods 208
Newcastle Forth Station 109, 153
Newcastle Railway St. Depot 103, 219
Riding Mill 189, 190, 234
Sandy Lane Crossing 198
Scotby 156
Scotswood Station 105, 234
Stocksfield 188, 206
Wetheral 202
Wylam 189, 190

Locomotives
Cabs 170
Livery 170
Steam Dryers 166
Adelaide 225
Alston 167
Atlas 150, 163
Blenkinsopp 167
Comet 161, 224
Dilston 169
Eden 164, 168
Goliah 150, 163
Hercules 161, 166, 171
Langley 169
Lightning 164
Meteor 161
Newcastle 163
Rapid 161, 224
Samson 161, 166, 170, 224
Tyne 164
Venus 169, 225
Victoria 166

Rolling Stock
Early Carriages 171
Ballast Wagons 175
Wagons 175
Blackmore's Buffer 173
Composite Wheels 22, 174

Other
Blenkinsopp Colliery 18, 62, 118, 137
Consett Ironworks 142, 144
Floods 92, 133, 228
Hareshaw Ironworks 117, 205
Prudham Stone 71, 210
Ridsdale Ironworks 117
George Turnbull Accident 173

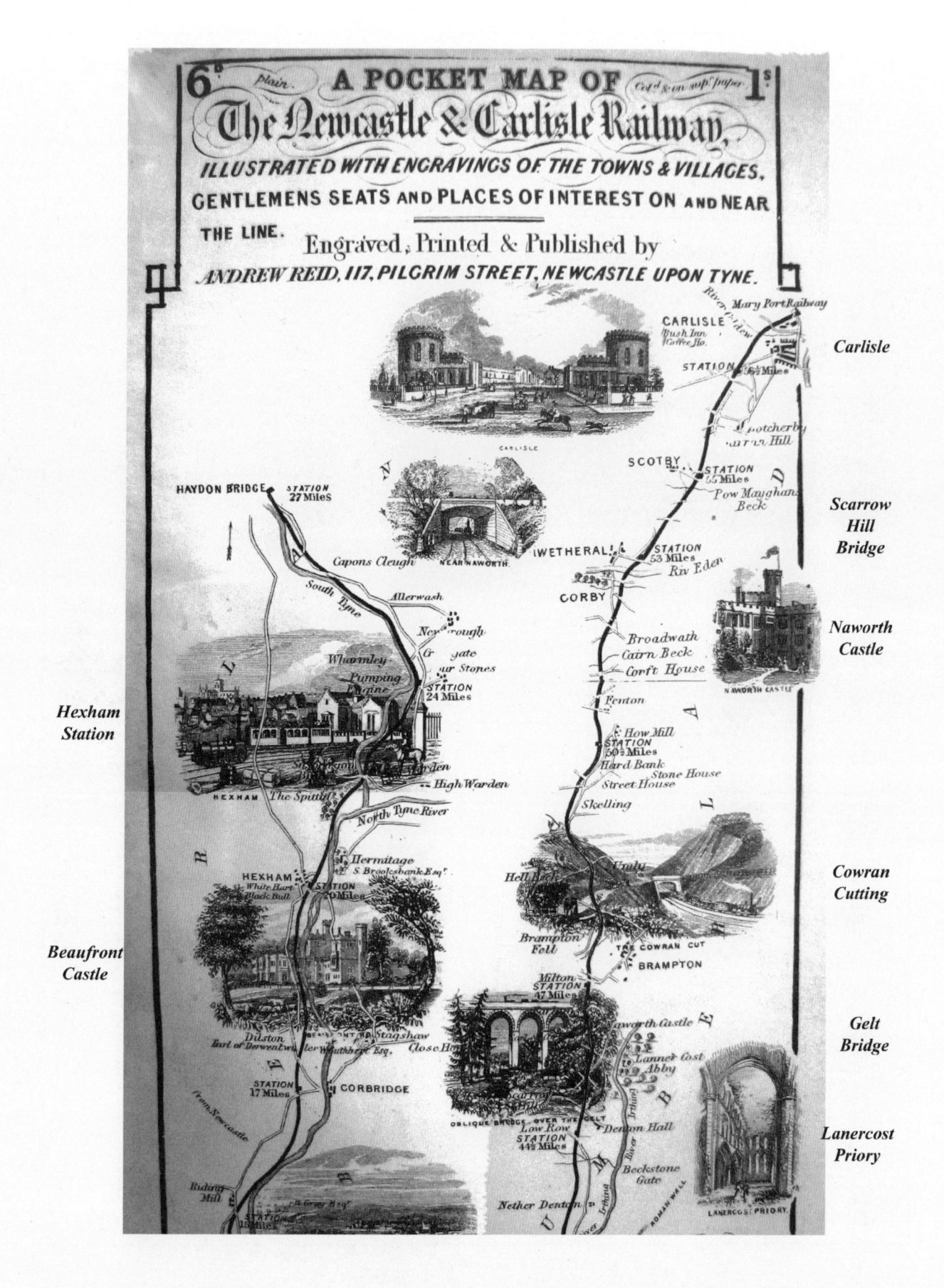

Part of the Pocket Map of the Newcastle & Carlisle Railway published by Andrew Reid of Newcastle. Reid's went on to publish Tomlinson's monumental history of the North Eastern Railway. At sixpence plain or a shilling coloured, the map was not cheap; a shilling was almost a half-day's wages for many railway employees. The illustrations of the railway are based on Carmichael's engravings, rather crudely redrawn.